THE ARMOR OF GOD

The Armor of God

AN ARMOR OFFICER'S FAITH, GROWTH AND PROTECTION IN COMBAT

Lieutenant Colonel Matthew Sacra

The Second Mission Foundation

Contents

DISCLAIMER	1
Dedications	2
Author's Note	3

I
Storm Troopers — 5

1	October	6
2	November	32
3	December	89
4	January, Part 1	175

II
Nomad — **197**

5	January, Part 2	198
6	February	250
7	March	321
8	April	380

III
Fobbit in the "Four" Shop 467

9	May	468
10	June	486
11	July	522
12	August	545
13	September	559
14	Epilogue	563
15	Author's Biography	564
Acronyms and Terms		566
Reference Map		568

DISCLAIMER

The views expressed herein are those of the author and do not reflect the position of the United States Military Academy, the Department of the Army, or the Department of Defense. This is not an official publication of the United States Military Academy, the Department of the Army, or the Department of Defense

Dedications

To: My LORD God, and my Savior Jesus Christ, for loving me, knowing me, blessing with me strength, love, wisdom, patience, and life every day

My amazing wife Rebecca and our daughter Katelyn who supported me and my fellow service members

Friends and family who prayed for us

The Storm Troopers, Nomad, and my other brothers in arms who served

Captain Jacobsen, Staff Sergeants Johnson and Vankomen, SPC Gertson and other fallen comrades, who gave all,

And their families, who survived them,

And those serving now, and will serve in the years to come…

Author's Note

This book is a historical collection of journal entries I wrote while deployed to Iraq in support of Operation Iraqi Freedom II and III between October 2004 and October 2005. I wrote most of these journal entries the day each event occurred, although a few I recorded within two days of an event. Most events are what I experienced in person, although some were based upon reports received within twenty-four hours. I did not add to my recollections any events or facts learned after the deployment.

My original intent was to record entries of missions only for historical purposes. But as I wrote my first one on October 21, 2004, I felt that God convicted me of a greater purpose – to share His protection and my growth, so others might be encouraged and come to know God, and His Son, Jesus Christ. Without their help, I would not have written journal entries night after night, nor could I have done so on such little sleep at times. I attained permission of several individuals to use their names in the book yet have shortened or changed most. Entries convey my observations, opinions, or feelings each day, not necessarily what I feel now. I hold no one in judgment – that is for God and His Messiah. I owe a great debt to my parents, and my friend Paul Nickerson for their careful patient editing of this book. I've reduced it by over 100 pages to a manageable size for many to read, eliminating as many acronyms, redundancies, jargon, and bad grammar as possible for civilian readers. Although some of my views regarding war and my faith have changed since writing these journals, I've left much of the text "as is" (with only 22 asterisks [*] and footnotes) to reflect my thoughts *now* versus my beliefs at the time (during this 2004-2005 deployment).

While this is a story about my experiences, it is also the story of the men and women I served alongside, who called themselves Storm Troopers and Nomads. This is a story about all of us. I pray it brings honor and glory to God, who loves us, and gave His Son for us.

I

Storm Troopers

1

October

October 14 to 20, 2004

I did not record journal entries for these dates because it was mostly travel to Forward Operating Base (FOB or base) Sykes from home at Fort Lewis, Washington. Our trip included four travel days, and three of receiving equipment, unpacking, unloading boxes and gear that continued to arrive, as we oriented ourselves to Sykes. We also attended the C/5-20 IN (Charlie Company, 5th Battalion, 20th Infantry Regiment) briefings in the evenings to understand major events in Tal Afar, and what type of missions we would execute. I had no idea what was in store for us in the months to come, yet we all tried to mentally prepare ourselves and face the fact that we would be here in combat for a year or more.

Significant things before the 21st: Kuwait was very hot (hotter than where I was in Iraq), and the C130 plane ride to FOB Sykes was the first C130 I've landed in (since I jumped out of the ones I rode in at Airborne School). The landing was horrible, and although I felt the need to vomit several times, God spared me.

October 21, 2004

We finally arrived at FOB Sykes – a small Forward Operating Base of concrete bunkers, metal living containers, and an airstrip all out in the middle of the desert just south of Tal Afar, a city located in northwest Iraq. We received a mission last night, and I wrote my first real combat Operations Order. It was short and to the point and felt good to roll out of there with a plan. My platoon sergeant SFC E (whom I'll call Heath) was in bad spirits about something, though I didn't know what. It put a damper on things, but the Lord didn't let it steal my joy. Our mission was to patrol the flight path behind our airstrip, which involved searching local farmers, stopping vehicles, scanning, and maneuvering to deter possible terrorists from attempting to shoot down planes as they flew out with 1st Squadron, 14th Cavalry Regiment troops to take them home. If we found anyone trying to shoot them down, we were to kill him immediately, and if we found any weapons, we were to detain the suspect and his weapons as well. Fortunately, it was easy because no one had weapons.

The first suspicious vehicle we had to stop was a pick-up truck with several men in it. I ordered one of my vehicles to pull in front of it while two others took up flanking positions. We dismounted personnel to search people and vehicles but found nothing. It made me uncomfortable how the visiting soldiers (from C/5-20IN) acted. (This is awkward. Consider: The behavior of the visiting soldiers from C/5-20IN made me uncomfortable. They were showing us how to do the mission, but they manhandled the Iraqi farmers. We rolled up on a couple tents of farmers, their families, and sheep. After searching their tents, we continued, scanned a bit, then stopped another car. When the Iraqis got out, one of them didn't comply with a 5-20th Infantry soldier. The soldier flipped the civilian to the ground, hands behind the back, and frisked him. I understood we needed to show some aggression so they wouldn't walk all over us, but it seemed wrong to take some farmer/tradesman who was just moving along, pull him from his car and knock him to the ground for resisting being searched.

After that experience, I decided to back off for a while, and just scan the area for weapons from our optics on the vehicles, not wanting to annoy any more Iraqis. As we did so, a giant sandstorm (easily 500 square miles) crept up on us. We sat in the vehicles for almost two hours, hatches closed, with no ventilation in the heat – not fun. The last part of those two hours we drove back in the storm, creeping along at 10 mph; what should have been a 15-minute trip back to the base took 50 minutes. We could only see only 10 meters in front of us most of the time, and sometimes we had as little as two meters visibility. We finally got back around 8p.m. only to find out that we had a route interdiction mission (stopping and searching along a route) starting at 7 a.m. tomorrow. I was sure we'd have contact with enemy, and some type of shooting.

October 22, 2004

Well, I was right. We had enemy contact, *and* some shooting. My three vehicles, plus two Mortar Carrier Vehicles (MCVs or mortar Strykers) rolled out on time. One of the MCVs carried the 'doc' (medic) and each of my vehicles carried a sniper in the loader's hatch. It felt cool rolling with such power. Heath felt better from his sickness (a bad smallpox shot reaction). We drove through the northern border of the city of Tal Afar for the first time. It was also the first time driving in a city – a bit scary, but God kept me strong through the whole thing, which made it feel kind of fun. I kept having the feeling someone was going to shoot at us, or something would explode against us, and we'd have to react. It felt so real – like an adrenaline rush and fear at the same time. Some people waved, some stared, and some just went about their business. The ING (Iraqi National Guard) held up traffic for us at the main intersections (which was nice), and a lot of citizens had to just sit and wait in traffic or pull over to the side of the road. I felt bad for them, as it must be a pain being forced to wait twenty minutes while a U.S. Stryker convoy rolls by.

I noticed how dilapidated their homes and shops were. I wondered how a family could live in such little huts of rock and stone as flimsy as the tents we saw yesterday. It was just farmers in a field of dirt and rock, with no crop, only some sheep and some donkeys – a bit sad.

We pulled off the road for a little while at about the middle of the northern section of the city to conduct our route interdiction. We pulled onto some smooth rolling hills where I ordered my three vehicles and one mortar Stryker to face the main section of the city, while the other faced away to the north covering our rear, all of us scanning. At about 8 a.m. I ordered our unit to the main road, and we went east near Fort Tal Afar, an ING encampment. We waited there for the cargo trucks and supply vehicles to arrive. Once all twenty vehicles had arrived, I placed three of our vehicles at the front to lead, then the twenty trucks, then our last two vehicles. It was frustrating moving back as the trucks could only go 20 mph so I felt like a sitting duck as we rolled back through the city to the base.

I also couldn't help but think about how blessed we are to live in the U.S. Our poor have it better than the middle class in Iraq. Most of them in Tal Afar lived in houses the size of an American kitchen, with windows which looked like our size windows except with no glass. Some didn't even have doors.

As we reached the middle of the city, a truck moved toward Heath's vehicle and didn't slow down. Heath told the vehicle to stop verbally and with hand signals, but it didn't. He shouted again, pointing his weapon, but it crept forward, so he told SPC Youn/Jo (his loader) to fire a couple rounds at the ground in front of it. The vehicle came to a screeching halt. Heath reported the details to me, and about seven minutes later we took fire from across a soccer field to our right (south inside the city). Children immediately started running, and we saw out of the corner of our eyes a white truck driving away. It went down a side street, and the kids were still in the way, so no one fired back. It was only three to five AK47 rounds from beyond the soccer field, fired at my vehicle and two others. I reported the location to the battalion TOC as we continued to move and scan. We made it back to base without further incident, but it was exciting that we had had our first contact.

Intelligence folks debriefed me, advising me to shoot at the hood of the car next time instead of the ground. We had one more interdiction between 8 and 10 p.m. It was 11 p.m. and I was finally back, two hours later than expected, and it was incredible! I recall that as we rolled out the gate, we discovered that we had no communication with the 5-20th Battalion TOC (Tactical Operations Center). At 7 p.m., we still sat at the FOB gate waiting to leave. I finally discovered the TOC wasn't using our former frequency on which we had our radios set until someone had left the base. They used a different frequency while inside the FOB.

We left after getting that fixed, and not five minutes down the road, Heath's vehicle was going 10 mph, and running off the road. He had serious issues with his driver, SPC Gumfi ('G'). I was furious and could only imagine how mad Heath was. It wasn't the first time, and I had the feeling it was intentional because 'G' didn't want to be in the Army. We were outside the FOB in a dangerous combat zone and he kept driving off the road, or going 10 mph. He could not shoot well, and in the past he'd said things to imply he wouldn't shoot a human being. He claimed to be a strong Christian, but his actions that night seriously endangered the lives of his companions SFC E (Heath), SGT Boss/Frank, SPC Youn/Jo, and our C/5-20 visitor, putting the entire platoon at risk of an ambush from the enemy.

After the mission was over, Heath said G told him he had motion sickness. I told the men on my vehicle right as this was happening that G was going to get somebody killed, and this behavior was completely insane. I also said that if I had my way, G would not go on any more combat missions with us, because he couldn't drive, couldn't shoot (or wouldn't shoot).

Heath finally got things going straight with G, and then we turned right at the intersection of FOB road and Hwy-47. Battalion then radioed that the ING at Checkpoint 201 received fire (later two wounded), so I determined we'd proceed to them instead of scanning at another checkpoint. We turned around and headed to the north hills to position for scanning.

Shortly after getting in position, the Iraqi National Guard (ING) nearby radioed our Battalion liaison officer claiming someone in a Stryker at their checkpoint shot at them. I double checked with Heath, then told them we had not fired a shot. We were about 500 meters north of Checkpoint 201 and had eyes on them, so I said we had not fired a shot that evening. The ING there then said they received mortar fire, which was not us. SGT B/Frank said he'd heard mortars fire, but none of us saw any explosions, and the ING were calm, not running or hiding frantically from mortar fire. At this point I concluded they must have been confused.

Our mission scheduled end time approached (9 p.m.), so I requested permission by radio for us to return to base. Due to the confusion about the friendly and indirect fire, they denied my request. It irritated all of us because we couldn't help the ING (we had no interpreter), and we were ready to come in, as our mission was essentially over. I also sent a message on our digital FBCB2 (Force Battlefield Command Brigade and Below) to the TOC (Tactical Operation Center) to inform them of our situation to the best of my knowledge.

Finally, they ordered us to come in, so I moved my platoon back to base. We entered the FOB, and the Intel officer ordered Heath and me to report to the TOC. We reported to Major O that we did not fire on the ING and I quickly added we did not fire a shot the entire night. He even asked us both thrice, "so you didn't fire a shot?" We answered, "no sir, none...no shots were fired by us tonight." I then told him that when we heard the report a Stryker had fired on the ING we were observing 201 and it couldn't have been us.

He said okay, and we walked back to our rooms, discussing the removal of SPC G from the platoon. Heath and I then talked to the commander, Captain Jacobsen, whereupon he asked us about contact. I told him we hadn't fired a shot. He asked about earlier that day, and we told him about that morning's report, but no shots fired that night. The captain again asked both of us individually about that night and I said, "no shots fired, sir."

But then Heath said, "no shots...well. okay, no sir, I'm sorry sir [to me], my vehicle did fire some rounds at a car." Wow! I was completely shocked he'd never told me, and then had lied to the Major up at the TOC. He said he was sorry he didn't tell me, but I had answered the major so quickly, he didn't want to correct me or the situation, so he just went along with what I said, and told the major 'no.' He explained to CPT J and me that in between two checkpoints, SPC Y had fired four rounds and SGT B had fired two rounds from their M-4's on our way to conduct the mission. He'd asked the visiting 5/20th Infantry platoon sergeant if they typically radioed every time they fired a weapon, and got the answer: 'no.' Heath had decided at that point to just call it up later, but he never did (until then).

Apparently, a car had sped around a slower car on its way to route Hwy-47, and SPC Y yelled stop very loudly several times, and when they failed to comply he fired into the engine grill of the car. I guess it was an ING car trying to get in front of traffic to stop it for our safe passage, and because we did not know, we shot at them. I felt horrible about it. Heath apologized profusely in front of the commander, called himself a "[expletive]-head", and said he would take full repercussions for whatever came down the chain of command. He also said he would talk to the major to apologize and set things straight. After the commander (CPT J) told us we'd sort it out and talk it over in the morning, Heath and I went to his room and talked.

He apologized more and said he couldn't believe he lied, and it entirely his fault. I told him we would just always report contact from then on, so I could report to higher. If shot at, I would radio "Contact" to higher, and report nothing further until we resolved the firefight. I said he should do the same, and he concurred. He said he hadn't lied in so long, and he wasn't okay with it (after I said it was okay). I said, "Don't beat yourself up over it, it's done, it'll be all right." I told him we have a wonderful Savior who forgives us. I wanted to say more about the love of Jesus, but that was all we had time for as we needed sleep.

23-24 OCTOBER 2004

That day never seemed to end. I oversaw a convoy of sixteen vehicles, including eight Strykers and eight unarmored vehicles of various types - Flatbeds, Humvees (High Mobility Multi-Wheeled Vehicle or Humvee), etc. We were to travel from FOB Sykes near Tal Afar to FOB Marez, in Mosul. Over one hundred miles, the trip would take three to four hours. I cranked out a plan for the order of my vehicles, a timeline, and then briefed my platoon on the details Heath and the rest of the platoon prepared more details while I talked to the commander. We organized the convoy on the road left of the dining facility (or chow hall) at about 2 p.m. and were there organizing and making refinements to the plan until about 4 p.m., when we conducted a company level rock drill – a rehearsal done on a terrain model kit or sand table, only this one was done with battalion support. During the painstakingly long briefing and rehearsal, we were promised graphics (for our maps in support of the mission) and told that we would leave at 3 a.m., which changed to 1 a.m., and then we all did radio checks on our vehicles.

After confirming each vehicle had a communication link with headquarters, it was 6 p.m. We ate some chow, cleared our rooms, and with seven hours remaining before our departure, Heath and I went to apologize to the ING for accidentally shooting at them and causing a shrapnel wound. The ING weren't there, so Heath apologized to the major we'd talked to the night prior. CPT J and I finally found the ING and apologized. They said to forget about it, because the guy with the shrapnel wound was given leave and paid forty dollars, which made him happy. The Iraqis said they all joked about the whole incident later, and no apology was necessary. My lungs soon got tight after drinking the Arabic tea because they all lit up cigarettes in their bunker headquarters room. Another captain noticed my discomfort and got CPT J and me out of there.

I did some last-minute preparations for our convoy mission, prayed, read the Bible, and we all went to sleep in our Strykers at about 10 p.m. I woke up an hour later from the cold, shutting my vehicle commander hatch as my men cranked the heater on. I went back to sleep, and woke up at midnight, whereupon we all hopped out of the vehicle to do our convoy briefing. Everyone in the convoy met me at the front of the vehicles, and I briefed the convoy on all our contingencies. As I closed, I told them all that I would be praying for our safety and success immediately following this brief, and then went to prep and pray. One soldier, PFC Bivens from supply, prayed with me. The Lord truly protected us during the entire mission because we were unharmed. In fact, there was only one incident. My abridged sworn statement given for my 15-6 (Commander's Inquiry) Investigation follows:

On October 24, 2004 between [before 4 a.m.], the front vehicle of my convoy reported contact while crossing [our route] (east) to Hwy-1 (north). They reported a semi had clipped their front 'slat' armor. Before they finished talking, another vehicle reported they needed a Stryker to block traffic because the semis were not stopping for the convoy. I ordered my driver to pull forward across traffic. There were three straight lanes running south, and one lane that ran southwest down [our route], which I assessed to be a turn lane [see attached diagram exhibit]. As I approached the turn lane, my gunner and I held up our hands, shouting "stop, stop" at the truck in the turn lane. SGT M pointed his M-4 at the semi-truck, I kept shouting while raising my hand at the tanker truck in the lane closest to me, which was the right southbound lane. I pointed my 240-machine gun at the front bumper of the tanker truck (which had green Arabic writing on its right side). The truck continued movement at about 10 mph. I was moving approximately 5 mph forward. The driver of the tanker truck saw me, but continued forward, so I fired a 2-3 round burst of aimed 7.62mm at the ground in front of the truck which it stopped.

The semi truck to the left side of the tanker truck (middle lane southbound Hwy-1), was fully stopped, but about 2 meters farther forward (south) of the tanker truck. I observed this semi to be an AAFES truck due to the stenciling in the top left corner of the windshield. Some of my rounds may have ricocheted and hit the bottom right tire or front corner of it. In the farthest lane away (southbound left lane) was another semi truck speeding up at about 20 mph, which I saw as it moved past the AAFES truck. I shouted with my hand raised and weapon pointed at the front bumper of this silver sided cargo-looking semi. My gunner did the same, and I fired another 2-3 round burst aimed at the front bumper. I was stationary across one lane of traffic at the time, as the driver of this silver sided cargo-looking semi pressed forward at 20 mph. All of this occurred in seconds, and as I fired, my rounds impacted the right side of this semi, and the third round impacted behind the right front tire of the right side of the semi. The semi still accelerated south, and I let it go. At that time, the driver of the AAFES truck got out of the cab, looking at the right side of his truck, and waving his arms, seemingly upset. I radioed my report to CPT Jacobsen, and waved my convoy across the highway, as all traffic was stopped. As the last Strykers from 1st platoon crossed the highway, so did I, heading north. As I rolled north, I noted that some of the vehicles among semi's in the middle southbound lane were US military. I did not shoot anymore. Other observers were SPC W, SGT M, and SGT L (on a Hummvee in the vicinity.) [End of statement]

Later that day (the 24th), Sergeant L came up and thanked me for saving his life. He was in the vehicle right behind me and said if I had not shot at that semi, it would have rolled right through him. I wasn't sure which of the three semis he referred to, since two of them were stopped when I had fired. The only thing I didn't include in my report was the fact that the driver of the silver cargo carrying semi looked at me as he sped up, even though I was shouting for him to stop while pointing my weapon at him. Other than this incident, the convoy was fine until I had an accidental discharge of my M240 machine gun as I cleared it upon my entry to FOB Marez upon our arrival to Mosul. My sworn statement for that 15-6 Investigation follows:

On 24 October 2004, [around 5 a.m.] my convoy entered FOB Marez. As we passed through the gate we cleared [emptied] weapons. I elevated my 240B machine gun and performed proper clearing procedures. I first confirmed the weapon was on safe still and opened the feed tray cover and feed tray sweeping the excess ammunition from the weapon. It was dawn and quite dark out, and the entire convoy still used white lights as ordered by the convoy commander, CPT Jacobsen. Therefore, I didn't use my night vision goggles. I squinted at the bolt carrier assembly, and noticed it was mostly ridden forward, but not all the way forward. I couldn't tell if there was a round in the chamber, as it was still dark, but my instincts told me there could be, and it could be a jam. I double checked that the weapon was still on safe, and with the feed tray cover still up, and weapon still max elevated, I pulled back on the charging handle with a careful firm grip.

As I pulled back with my right hand, I heard a pop, and a round fired into the air at an 80 to 85-degree angle. With the bolt forward and the weapon on safe still at this point, I closed the feed tray cover, and attempted to place the weapon on fire to see if it was possible, and the safe selector switch was completely jammed up. It would not budge, even when I slammed my right palm against it numerous times. I removed the M240, and informed my commander, Captain Jacobsen as soon as I parked my vehicle. My M240B has had malfunctions since Fort Lewis, at the Battalion zero and qualification ranges run by A Company. I informed my commander and the executive officer, LT Dale K that same day my weapon was a runaway gun and had several jams. He said it would not get fixed prior to deployment to Iraq, due to Army department of logistics delays. My platoon sergeant, SFC E, a master gunner, switched out the trigger assembly with his weapon, to troubleshoot the problem. He also carefully inspected, disassembled and reassembled the feed tray cover. My M240 still occasionally ran away and jammed that day, so SFC E switched the trigger assembly back to his weapon, and I qualified on a different weapon that day, as an armorer and several other M240 gunners looked at my weapon, attempting to figure out its malfunction.

My weapon was deployed 'as is', and the company XO and Commander both said we'd fix it when we arrived in Iraq. The day after our arrival at FOB Sykes, CPT Jacobsen ordered me to fire it on the range at FOB Sykes to confirm it was still a runaway gun. I confirmed this with the range sergeant. I informed the XO, who told me to [do maintenance on] the weapon with a 2404 form, and he would pick it up the next day. I also informed the commander, so he was aware. PFC B performed the [maintenance], and delivered the weapon to the armorer that day, explaining its problem. The armorer who looked at it, whom I do not know, told PFC B the trigger assembly needed fixing, and they'd place an order for the part, but did not need to take my M240. I asked the commander and XO if it would be possible for me to transfer my M240 to C/5-20 in for one of theirs, since we'd previously done so with others.

My commander and XO both said the likelihood of a transfer was low, but they'd see. The next time I mentioned the malfunction was a few days later when I received my first mission. I told the commander I didn't have an M240B to use effectively during that mission, and he said I had two others in the platoon, and I was to work through the problem. I felt I'd done all I could to resolve the issue, and had my company chain of command in the present situation so I continued missions aware I'd have to break the belt if the weapon became a runaway gun. It was better to have an M240 than none on my vehicle for two missions in Mosul, the Interdiction missions in Tal Afar, and my convoy from FOB Sykes to FOB Marez. At the point I left FOB Sykes, the new trigger parts were still not in for my M240B, and I elected to keep it on my vehicle for security of my platoon, and convoy. [End of Statement]

That was it. After arriving at the new FOB, we parked the vehicles and I reported to the commander. Lieutenant Colonel Eric Krella (LTC K) and Captain Jacobsen (CPT J) were talking about the accidental discharge incident later, after which LTC K called me over to him. He was upset with me, inquiring why I went out with a malfunctioning weapon, and I shrugged my shoulders and said my weapon was just messed up. He didn't seem to want to hear any more from me at that time, so I moved on. A lieutenant (LT) investigated me for the accidental discharge, and a captain (CPT) investigated me for the contact at Hwy-1. The Forward Operating Base (FOB) received some mortars, so I prayed with a couple of people as well as by myself later that evening for God to have His way in the investigations. I went to church that night and had a good time. The chaplain (Tim Welon) had already heard and was praying for me; we also prayed together that evening. I had faith God would see me through.

As I went to bed that night, our base fired four illumination rounds over Mosul, and I could hear several helicopter machine guns and .50 cals being shot in the city. Mortars exploded somewhere on our base. It was odd walking around this base, never knowing if a mortar would land near you and that's it, you're dead. A mortar round landed on the bed of a Lieutenant R from C Company Mobile Gun System Platoon; I took a picture of the damage. Thank God he was out on a mission when it happened. It peeled the ceiling inside, and left debris everywhere. His laptop and many belongings were toasted. I think it happened the day before I arrived – not a comforting feeling. I had much more to say, but we were going on a recon of our sector of the city – I had to wake up at 4:30 a.m., in four hours.

October 26, 2004

At FOB Marez I awoke feeling groggy and got ready for my mission. Our mounted (in vehicles) recon of the sector wasn't too bad. We left late though. We were supposed to go before 6 a.m. but didn't leave until 6 a.m. That was okay, I wasn't in charge, just along for the ride. The commander needed one of my vehicles to accompany 1st platoon (who was short one squad/vehicle due to tasks dictated from higher headquarters). I decided to ride in Staff Sergeant (SSG) Randy Ps vehicle. Heath and I rode, but I left Randy still in charge of his vehicle, to take orders from LT Raub N. Private (PVT) Jason G came too, with Private First Class (PFC) Darrell B as driver. We patrolled a good chunk of the city, crossing the Tigris River twice, scanning rooftops, cars, buildings, and people on foot. We were aware that any second we could be shot at, which was simultaneously exciting and scary.

Mosul is about 2.5 million people, and I didn't know how that compared to any US city, but it was big. It reminded me of Acapulco, Mexico, or maybe the slums of Los Angeles, California. Most houses and buildings are rock and sand colors, and the streets looked like exploded hampers – dirty rags, trash, clothing and such covering many blocks. It is sad people live like this. I felt no hatred for them, just pity. They deserve better, like all of God's children. It is a shame these terrorists are hindering the support and help the United States and its allies are trying to give the people. We verified six Voter Registration Centers in our sector, and the legislative election was due to occur the next January. I was excited to see people vote here. I hoped democracy would give them a better world to live in, but then again, it hasn't worked too well for the filth and slums in Mexico, so we'll see. The best blocks of Mosul seemed like the worst slums of L.A. - so sad.

I was thankful we had no enemy contact; God answered my prayers for nothing worse than a scratch on a person, and a dent on a vehicle. We got that dent when a first platoon vehicle smacked a concrete barrier upon re-entry to the base. A lesson learned by them I suppose. Oh, I received new mission orders after I was in bed. CPT J sent a runner to come get me, who said Battalion needed us to conduct Counter-Mortar patrols from 1-4 p.m., after first verifying we knew how to get to the CSH (Combat Support Hospital). I was given instructions to move to some northwestern quadrants of Mosul and fire a Tube-launched Optically-tracked Wire-guided (TOW) missile, or any other weapon, to destroy any enemy setting up 82mm mortars or 107mm rockets (which have been shelling our base every day). I was excited, looking forward to this key essential mission, briefed my platoon, and went to bed.

I refined my plan in the morning before we went out on this sector recon, and after grabbing breakfast on the way back in, I continued to refine my plan. I gave my men the timeline and went to my Stryker to build graphics for the platoon on the FBCB2 battle computer. I sent them out and went to Battalion Intelligence to get an update on the route I'd planned and find out if they had any better maps. Upon entry, a CPT told me I had another mission change, and I'd now be doing Counter-Manpad missions south of the airfield, so our C130's would not get shot down. I was still a crucial mission, but I was a bit disappointed. The hours were supposed to be roughly from 5 p.m. to midnight, but it was probably not going to be as exciting. I went back and briefed Randy and Heath, who both seemed quite irritated. I revised the timeline after receiving some intel from SFC E about the airfield and moved our start time to 4:30 p.m. We'd need night vision devices that night, which changed what equipment we inspected and brought with us.

Nothing spectacular took place during this mission. It was good to once again get out and see some of the city. I picked up some toys from the civil affairs people for us to throw out to the children as we drove through the town to the south of the base and Mosul airfield. At first, we saw a slow-moving car with two guys walking next to it in the middle of the desert hills. It looked suspicious, as did the guys, so we searched them and their vehicle. We even sprayed the vapor trace stuff that can tell if they've been working with explosives. We found a wad of cash on them, but no evidence of terrorism, so we let them go. They still seemed rather fishy though. I kept adding new points on FBCB2 to SSG P, and he'd plot them in his navigation device then figure out how to get there. Once we went in, we'd set up at that spot and observe. We saw a couple Iraqi National Guard at a camp who were dropping their pants and peeing. We also scanned some people fighting in the city (like a five on two brawl). Then we saw some dogs playing and attempting to mate, but the female played hard to get. I thank God we all made it safely. We got back and finally got in bed at around 2 a.m. CPT J told us we had a counter-mortar mission at 2 p.m. tomorrow, so I had 12 hours to sleep, eat, plan, and prepare.

October 27, 2004

Praise God - we survived another mission! It was the first time for us to "run the gauntlet" of Highway 1 (Hwy-1 runs directly through the center of Mosul - known for frequent ambushes by the enemy). From 2-5 p.m., just 3 hours, we covered three large sectors of Mosul. After throwing toys to kids in southeast Mosul, we took Hwy-1 to the northeastern quadrant of the city next to the Tigris River. Some people seemed happy we were here, waving or smiling as we drove by. Others stared, ignored us, or glared. One kid (under age 10) waved, and the mother walked up very slowly, and smacked the kid hard in the head, as if she strongly disapproved of her kids waving. It was sad, and sometimes a father would do it, but usually mothers. I don't know if they didn't want the kids drawing attention, or if they just hate us and want their kids to also. One girl (about age five) shook her fist when we rolled by and tried to spit on us, but the wind made it go back in her face, down her lip, and against her neck.

As we rolled north on Hwy-1, cars moved out of our way, and if they didn't, Randy had Darrell honk at them, while the rest of the crew motioned the cars over. Sometimes he would tap or bump their bumpers, and then they would move. We often traveled in the left lane, and sometimes on the median or the opposite lane, if traffic got bad. On the way back on Hwy-1, it got so congested at a traffic circle that we just cut right across the circle to the other side, as traffic stopped or moved for us. It felt as if we owned the city, yet we were simultaneously at its mercy. We constantly scanned traffic, shops, sidewalks, people, alleyways, rooftops, second and third stories – all while trying to find our way in a new city. Randy did most of the navigating as lead vehicle since I just told him a route and destinations.

Where Hwy-1 exits Mosul to the northwest, we drove by open rolling hills and edges of some city blocks and saw about 25 spent mortar rounds. I recorded the location and briefed the Intelligence folks upon return to base. It was such an adrenaline rush, but also scary going down the streets. I asked my crew if they felt like they were doing what they were born to do. DeArthur said he didn't, and he was just doing this for another year or so. Jason said he was just doing all he knows how to do, what he'd been trained to do. I told them it felt like what I was born to do - lead in combat. Combat here in Iraq, and combat in life against sin and the devil. Fighting for country and family, and for God. I enjoyed every second of it.

When we got off the vehicles, Heath asked Randy and me into his room and then asked if we were scared. He was mad we didn't get close enough to the city when scanning, and noticed we'd stood with only our eyes and top of head showing from the hatch. We explained it was so we could see and shoot rooftops or second stories, and to avoid any shrapnel or blast from roadside bombs, or RPGs that could hit us. It also makes us safer in a rollover. We said we weren't scared, and we were just doing as we were told to do. He said maybe he just wanted to get shot or something, because he stood high enough to shoot someone on the ground next to the vehicles as we drove. I thought it was unwise - people next to the vehicle aren't the main threat. The enemy will shoot from alleyways, or side streets, rooftops, or buildings off to the side, not from the sidewalk next to the vehicle. I kept in mind he also switched with SPC Y (Jo), so Heath was in the gunner position, and Jo was on the M240 in the other hatch. His business if he wanted to be more exposed on his vehicle, but I wouldn't do it on mine.

I felt death comes from two things: God's will, and human choice. Just like our lives, He gives us free will, yet He also reigns, molding things and people to His will at times, in wisdom. I felt death is the same way. I knew He would protect me and keep me safe to come home to my lovely wife and child, but it didn't mean I was going to jump in front of a car or stand tall in my vehicle so I'd be an easy sniper or shrapnel target. I bunked my beds for protection, but any mortar could still land next to my bed, and I'd be dead from the side blast. I could have all the protection and cover in the world, but if it was my time to go, and God allowed it, it would only take one bullet or one mortar round to be in the right place at the right time.

Heath then asked why I kept calling Randy on the radio and leaving him out. He thought we were against him. I told him truthfully and with God's strength and wisdom: "It's two things. One, by the time I tell him to move and my vehicle starts moving, you are already ready to roll in behind us. The second thing is this, and if I'm wrong you can correct me, but this is just the impression, you seem bothered when I call you [on the radio]. It sounds to me like you may be thinking 'why does he even bothering me by asking'." I was thankful God led me to speak my mind. God had helped me be more honest lately, even when it was not the most peaceful solution.

Heath admitted he may have had that attitude after he was upset about Randy's vehicle getting stuck in some mud (when my vehicle pulled him out), and us not getting close enough to the enemy. He said generally he wasn't sarcastic unless it was completely obvious. I tried to remember that, but it really seemed like he was often sarcastic when I called him, as if he didn't need me to say a thing because he always knew what to do better than I, since he'd been in the Army longer, and a tanker longer. He was the platoon leader for two months before I got to the platoon over a year ago. He told us he was confident anyone in the company would follow him anywhere, because he wasn't scared, or something. Was he implying no one would follow Randy or me? I don't know - maybe he was just implying he was the best person, at least leading men and fighting combat. We'd all only been in combat for less than 14 days, so we were all experienced the same regarding that. Was I just analyzing this too much, feeling angry and upset about his anger and my impression that he didn't have any confidence in me? I did't know – I did need more confidence, so I kept going knowing God had me where He wanted me for now.

Heath had also fired his weapon that day, and our medic ('doc') thought it was a mortar round being fired. Heath didn't tell me about it until we got back and were in the room. He said he was bored, and just fired it into the dirt in front of him. This upset me because he let us think 'doc' saw mortars and didn't explain it until after we returned. I almost radioed the "mortar explosion" to higher headquarters. If this occured again, I would take serious action, as I could not tolerate that attitude. Our conversation ended with us joking and laughing again, and then Heath and I went to brief the commander on the area we saw that day. It was cool, and I stressed the need for him to issue us a digital camera for our scanning missions. Well, we had force protection mission the next day (just guarding the FOB), so I went to sleep.

October 28, 2004

No missions for me, but I heard *Time* magazine officially declared Mosul the "worst place to be in Iraq." Not comforting, but I expected it. That's why we were here, to kick some evil terrorist behind. Oh, and at about 10 p.m. we got mortared. First Sergeant (1SG) and I counted about eight mortar rounds, which sounded like they possibly hit the chow hall area. We'd get details in the morning since we would be staging from there.

October 29, 2004

That day we were part of a huge Battalion level mission, and we patrolled all areas to the immediate north and west of the FOB. Pretty exciting, working with the Iraqi National Guard and then having our company operate together for the first time. It felt cool to be part of something so big. It may have intimidated the enemy, because other than a couple shots fired, we had no serious incidents. What a blessing. I was so thankful God has been watching us so closely and protecting us with His angels. Oh, and last nights' mortars did not damage the chow hall or surrounding area. We heard reports from local kids today that people fire mortars from their area every night, but the citizens are too scared to warn us. The ING that went with us seriously need a lot of good training. They got lazy and bored after only two hours on the objective. I blocked (a military task that prevents movement) a couple routes with my platoon and did a lot of planning today. I took quite a few pictures on the objective today too. I also ran into SSG C (our old supply sergeant) who gave me a ride in a four-wheeler to eat dinner. I picked up some food for the 1SG, whom I couldn't stand. Though hard to do, it felt good to bless someone I didn't like at all but still loved him as God wanted.

I took some notes during the company After-Action Review (a reflection on a mission to improve the unit), and then conducted one with my platoon. No one had much to say, so it lasted 10 minutes. Later that night, my platoon received orders for two counter mortar patrols the next day from 1-3 p.m. and 5-10 p.m. Before I could brief my guys, Heath had sown seeds of disgust in them for seven hours of missions. I wasn't fond of the length either, but we just needed to deal with it, because it was combat. Besides, the day after, we had Force Protection (guarding the FOB), which was usually pretty easy and slow. Heath ranted about quitting for the 20th time since I've worked with him (over 15 months), then told me I could tell the commander his feelings. I did, and the commander (CPT J) said "Tell him that he is more than welcome to be the company commander for one whole day...and I'm certain that he will do an excellent job at it, but he can go to all the meetings, and make all the plans, and stuff." I thought it funny, and CPT Jacobsen said he would try to get an hour cut off from 9-10 p.m., since it was BN's call. I planned my timeline, scheme of maneuver, and before I could finish this very sentence, I was called back to CPT J's room to talk about a change involving half of our company supporting some southern observation post, and now I was to do counter mortar patrols from 1-4 .p.m. and counter Manpad patrols from 10-11:59 p.m.

Sometimes it was frustrating being a leader. Here I was, still awake because I was writing a plan, trying to have a timeline and scheme of maneuver for our missions tomorrow while my men were sleeping. They had been asleep for a few hours now since it was quarter 'til midnight. If they were still awake, it was because they were socializing or enjoying some free time. I was planning, all to answer the questions, "What are we doing tomorrow, when are we doing it, and how are we going to execute it?" Those were the basic questions my platoon of 12 (to include me) tankers needed answers to, as I provided them. Then it all changed. Now I didn't know if the Mortar section (two vehicles, nine soldiers) and Sniper team (two to three soldiers) were still coming with me, or what our timeline would look like. I didn't know one thing. There were 14 minutes left in this evening, and I was going to spend them with my Father and His Son our Savior Jesus Christ as I read through His Word!

October 30-31, 2004

We patrolled just north of Baghdad traffic circle and cruised up Hwy-1 to the northwestern most corner of Mosul. I got some good pictures of the little village up there, and it even rained on the way back down. We passed a cemetery. We weren't allowed to go in those (or mosques unless receiving fire from them), so we reconnoitered all around it to include the surrounding populated buildings. A sergeant from the Mortar section accidentally ran into a telephone pole at a bad turn on a narrowing road. A couple of the wires started snapping, and people ran, and I felt bad. I considered filling out paperwork for damages to give the people, but kids started throwing rocks at us, so I moved us out. I felt even worse because that sector seemed so friendly, not just kids, but several of the adults as well. I guessed we wouldn't go up that street again.

On our way out, 2nd Platoon (led by LT Scotty R) was at the large roundabout up in the north on Hwy-1 discretely escorting some civilian cars to a Voter Registration area (it had to look like they weren't escorting, so no terrorists in the area would target the civilian vehicles). He and CPT J radioed for me to recon a route for them around the damage on Hwy-1 because earlier in the day two car bombs blew up there killing Iraqi civilians. They were just truckers supplying our FOB with food, water, fuel, and sundry items, Iraqis trying to make Iraq a better place, but our enemies saw this as collaborating with "the enemy" (U.S. forces), so the terrorists blew them up. There were five destroyed trucks from the circle in the north on Hwy-1 to south of there. Oh, and earlier at that circle, Heath almost took a rock to the head, which he thought was a grenade at first. Good thing it wasn't. Anyway, 2nd Platoon needed another route, so I screened the surrounding areas and drew one up on the FBCB2 battle computer.

I felt bad afterwards, because I was so annoyed at the time CPT J and Scotty requested help, but all in all, I was glad we did. Scotty told me later at chow when he and LT Dave V and I had fellowship how much it helped him, and he really appreciated it. God has a funny way of making me realize if I've been impatient or selfish – convicting me by His spirit in kindness later. When we got back to base and I dismounted, I expected Heath to complain about something, but he didn't. He just said it was amazing we did all of that driving, and still no contact. I got about 50 intelligence pictures to help for the future. We found out at the company brief that we were going to conduct Voter Registration Ballot Confirmation missions, which was basically driving up to the Voting Registration Centers and staring to make sure the ballots for all of northern Iraq were not stolen, since the police security force lacked discipline. Yeah, stolen ballots could seriously hinder an election, I think. We would conduct these missions around midnight, and around six to seven in the morning. I got to call Becky (for the second time since arrival) and we talked for maybe two minutes, then I had to run to a meeting.

We went on our Counter Manpad mission, and all the city lights in our sector went out all of a sudden. In Tal Afar it meant an ambush, but here it was a regular brownout occurrence, which I didn't know at the time. I looked on the map and decided to take us to the east side of the town (south of the airfield) to check the traffic ability of what looked to be the main drag near the river. Heath warned me 3rd Platoon drove through there earlier and some of the streets got narrow. I took it under advisement, but figured I'd take the widest street I could find. He turned out to be right, and we had to turn around (which took five minutes, although it seemed much longer). We could have been ambushed there, which would have been bad, but it was all quiet. I was very thankful and admitted my mistake upon our return. Heath simply replied "Yeah, but mistakes cost lives in Iraq, sir." I spoke to God about it and I knew He'd help me move on and do better.

We went to the Voting Registration Center to check out the ballots with a bad route given to us by 2nd Platoon, but it got us close enough to get in the ballpark, and we eventually found it. I took Hwy-1 back, and after about three hours of sleep, we went again to verify, and that time we took a different route back. God blessed us with easy travel. I named the routes booger, snot, etc., because I couldn't think of anything else at the time. It made most of the guys laugh, so maybe it was okay. Next time I'd do wives names or perhaps a Biblical theme.

I thanked God we were back safe and sound, and we didn't have the tentative 1000-1200 counter mortar mission. I discussed my sniper ambush plan with CPT J, who was cautious about using snipers, and then with the sniper team Non-Commissioned Officer (NCO). I thought we had a good plan, but CPT J hadn't approved it yet. It was high visibility, since apparently LTC K (Battalion Commander) was aware of it (he spoke to me on my last Voting Registration mission over the radio, asking about it). Time for bed, we wouldn't be leave until 5 p.m., so I finally got some time to sleep now that it was 10 p.m. It turned out the enemy threw grenades at the Voters' Registration Center at 2 a.m. on 31 October at 3rd platoon – a private and sergeant. PFC C became the first casualty of our company - a shrapnel wound to his leg, but still scary. The sergeant had one land at his feet as he turned his back to it, and there was not a scratch on him. Nothing but God's protection right there.

Well, our counter-mortar plan was beautiful. CPT J finally approved it, and we had calmed his nerves about inserting his snipers (or the Lord calmed his nerves). Either way, SGT P (sniper NCO) and his team, SSG N (Mortar Section NCO) and his men, SSG D (the Fire Support NCO) and his vehicle, and myself with my platoon were all ready to execute this counter mortar ambush from 5-10 p.m. We had a great setup. We'd move in and recon the area at 5 p.m., insert the snipers after a false insertion, moving 12 men into a building, four of them the sniper team and rear security. The eight remaining men would come out, as the six vehicles including three ATGM (Anti Tank Guided Missile) Strykers, two Mortar Carrier Strykers, and one Fire Support Stryker would roll out of the sector with white lights on, and sneak in a back way with no lights at all far away to observe the snipers. If the snipers couldn't get a clean shot on the enemy mortars, three of my vehicles would move north with three to the southern exits of the sector. The enemy would be trapped like a rat.

We left at 5 p.m., only to receive word the mission was cancelled. Heath guessed we'd be doing counter Manpad missions instead, and SGT P guessed the sniper counter mortar ambush was given to the battalion snipers instead of our company ones. Both were right. I talked to CPT J, and he said LTC K was almost sold on my plan as he briefed the 'colonel', but LTC K decided at the last minute he needed us to do a Manpad mission, and that he might want the battalion snipers to perform the ambush. CPT J said jokingly "of course, he makes love to the battalion snipers at night, so they'll probably get it." Darn it. I wanted it so badly, but perhaps it was God's will. Only He knows. We went on our hour-long counter Manpad missions, then returned to the FOB. After we were in line for fuel, we observed mortar rounds being fired and then three towers on the west side of the base fired at targets to the east. We knew it was exactly where the snipers would have been, had we been allowed to conduct my plan. My crew and I discussed if perhaps it was God's will for us to be there, but the 'colonel' had man's free choice in the matter, and he chose against God. Who is to say? We can only guess and speculate. Maybe something would have gone wrong had we gone that night – I don't know.

I briefed the Intel officer, and LTC K was in the TOC, watching a football game. He asked me how I was, and I said, "frustrated, sir." He asked why, and I said we could have killed those enemy mortar men if we'd been there, but he just said, "Don't be frustrated" and continued watching the TV. I called Becky to update her and shared how amazing God is in all of this. An SA7 rocket hit a C130 plane the other day, lodging itself into the fuselage yet failing to detonate – thank God! He saved the life of probably 60 to 100 people on that plane. Simply amazing. Well, it was bedtime. We should have fun prepping the vehicles for Logistics Support Area (LSA) Anaconda the next day. I heard we might go there for up to two weeks. That would seriously stink since it was such a long drive, and we'd stay in temporary tenting.

2

November

November 1, 2004

On this day, a U.S. soldier was kidnapped. Not in our unit, but somewhere in Iraq. We heard no details, but we got 100% accountability of our people. We should go for just two days to LSA Anaconda for a supply run. LTC K slapped me on the back and said, "pretty exciting having three 15-6s [investigations] on you in a week huh?" (Obviously joking). CPT J and I gave a halfhearted laugh and LTC K said seriously "I don't find it funny at all." I guess we weren't supposed to laugh at his jokes? Later Heath and I talked for a good hour and a half about issues I had with him, he with me, and mostly issues he had with this company and battalion. I couldn't really solve any except for the bad tactical decision the other night. That was about it. A good talk, and we established he still hated officers. I was honest with him on some things, like how we both felt about the 15-6 investigations (I told him I got the impression that he was okay, and my shooting was screwed up). We agreed no one can determine if another feels threatened. We talked about NCOs, and their relationships to officers, and about SFC Steve S (my old platoon sergeant in 2-14 Cav). All in all, we saw each other's point of view a little better afterwards.

November 5, 2004

The two-day mission lasted four days. We stopped at FOB Summerall on the way after a couple of mechanical problems with Randy's vehicle. We got it fixed at Summerall, and the only other thing on the way down was a temporary halt while another unit cleared the route of a couple of 155mm rounds emplaced as an Improvised Explosive Device (IED - roadside bomb). We got to Anaconda safely without incident. Praise God.

We had to stop and empty our weapons at multiple clearing barrels upon entry to Camp Anaconda. We were also required to wear our body armor and combat helmet everywhere we went – odd as this place was much safer than FOB Marez. We ran into so many people who had been in Iraq for months and hadn't been outside the wire (off the base) but twice. We've been in Iraq for two weeks or so and have been out of the wire two dozen times. That is why some call these folks "Pogues" (people-other-than-grunts) I guess, because they assume a support role and don't fight. I think they were still important to the Army, and they were still away for a year, missing their families, but they weren't getting shot at like we were. That was the biggest difference.

Oh, on the way down, we passed by the cities of Bayji, Tikrit (Saddam's hometown), and Samarra. I thought we had also been to more FOBs and cities in Iraq than most people who had been there for many months. Anyway, we stayed until the military police and civilian trucks arrived two days later and left on the morning of the 4th. Many people down at Anaconda (25 miles north of Baghdad) came by to gawk at our Strykers since they'd never seen them before. I guessed our Stryker Brigade was famous, since there were only two in the US Army at that time, and we were the only one in Iraq right then.

I also found out some disturbing news while at Anaconda. Apparently, Randy had been telling people in another platoon and those soldiers on his crew that I was finished as a Platoon Leader. He told them my negligent discharge investigation was going to Baghdad, and my career was over. He told them I'd never make it past Captain. I got mad because it seemed like he just made it up to sound like he knew what he was talking about or perhaps because he was mad at me for some reason. Everyone I asked quoted him verbatim. I corrected them all, explaining our shooting of the ING in Tal Afar (by SPC Y and SGT B) was what went to Baghdad, and a 15-6 is simply a commander's inquiry to find out what happened in a questionable situation. I said only a general letter of reprimand could stop me from making it past Captain, and those aren't given lightly. I'd have to lie, cheat, steal, or kill someone to get one, and I've done no such things, so it wasn't going to happen. I told everyone the worst that would happen would be I'd be reassigned to another job/unit, and no longer be the platoon leader anymore, but that's it. I hadn't talked to Randy yet, but would now that we were back at FOB Marez. I couldn't have him spreading inaccurate rumors like this garbage.

On the way back north, I oversaw 17 vehicles, including 12 unarmored semi trucks, two gun-trucks, and my three ATGM or antitank Strykers. I finished my convoy brief and risk assessment and told everyone I was going to pray for the convoy and our safety, and they could join me if they wished. "If not," I said, "you can go back to your vehicles." Surprisingly, 15 people stayed as I led us in prayer. With a "let's roll" from me to the convoy, Randy began movement from the front, and we headed off on our 200-mile journey. As we approached Bayji and FOB Summerall heading north, we had to decide to go through the FOB or go through the outskirts of the city. CPT J's guidance for me was to avoid going in the FOB, so I tried to find the bypass on the outskirts of the city, and we made one too many wrong turns. Randy radioed that the semi's would not be able to make the next turn he'd taken, so we'd have to back up. There was no way.

The semi's had already taken down some wires, and done some heavy maneuvering to get down that street, so backing up could not have worked. I prayed for our safety and a way out of that mess, and the Lord answered.

A section (two) of US M1 Abrams tanks showed up, one at the front near Randy, and one in the middle near me. Mine backed up down a street, and we asked the fellow tanker if we could fit down the road he just came down. He said that he had to take down a wall to get there, but we could try it. He then told us we were in a bad section of town and needed to hurry up and get out of there. After deliberation about the right turn up ahead, and Randy's insistence on us not being able to make it with semi's, I finally decided we'd try to back out. At the rear, Heath had a little more room, and got two trucks turned around, just as I saw the semi's at the front of the convoy making the right turn. I radioed and he said they had to take out a wall to get us through, and we could make it through the town now. Heath took the already turned around vehicles back the way we came and met us on the main drag that led to the bypass (the tankers showed us the way). As we rolled out of the city, the commander of the tank unit handed out 20 dollar bills to the locals for the damages we'd caused. It made me feel a lot better for damaging their stuff. These people also looked like they were much wealthier than most in Mosul since their houses had windows and walls around most of them.

We made it out and continued north on Hwy-1 until we reached FOB Endurance (home of 2-8 field artillery), to drop off the convoy vehicles with us. SFC T's section of vehicles (2nd Platoon's platoon sergeant) didn't make it that night, because they broke down very close to Anaconda, so they went back there to get fixed. We waited for them that night at Endurance, so we spent the night and most of the next day at Endurance. I ran into my friend Greg at Endurance, who had just pinned Captain a few days prior. I congratulated him, and we caught up on life. It was good to see him and Todd (our old Fire Support Officer) and we had a good talk. After sleeping the night in the Stryker, we finally left the next evening for FOB Marez, and once again, had a safe trip. Everyone was in good spirits because we were finally going "home," so there were many jokes on the radio for the return trip.

November 7, 2004

At FOB Marez the next morning we had non-exciting (yet still important) Counter Manpad operations - looking for bad guys that shot down aircraft - from 9 a.m. to 11 a.m., and the assistant intelligence officer and the intel NCO joined us. They hadn't been outside the wire in Mosul yet, so now they had. The only exciting thing was that the Mortar Section (SSG Ns vehicle specifically) snapped a tie rod. It was so bad we had to call the Quick Reaction Force which was 2nd platoon (Scotty), to escort the wrecker to tow it back, since a Stryker self-recovery wouldn't work. They said it snapped on a hole, but Heath later said it wasn't even that. On our way back in, a car tried to stop but skidded 20 feet after slamming on the brakes. It did stop, but only after SSG Pord fired a two to three round burst at the ground in front of it. I was sure we'd have another 15-6 investigation for that - fine.

We went to lunch after returning and prepared for our afternoon Counter Manpad Operation. When we left the dining facility, all three of our M240 machine guns were missing. Some guards told us "the 1-24 Infantry Sergeant Major took them." Heath and I were livid. The Command Sergeant Major wanted to play stupid games in a combat zone because he had nothing better to do with his time. His logic must have been that they were unsecured, but so were the .50 caliber machine guns and Mark 19 grenade launchers on Infantry Strykers. We told the company First Sergeant (1SG V) and the Commanding Officer (CPT J) in the chow hall, and the 1SG just looked at CPT J and said "Sir, I'm about to get fired." Before we rolled down to the Tactical Operations Center, 1SG V came out with our M240s. We loudly vented our frustrations, then left for our mission nearly five minutes late.

Oh, on a good note, I talked to Randy before we went to lunch. He said he'd "heard" the rumor he was spreading, but he knew it was no big deal. I don't know if he was dishonestly trying to talk his way out of it or not, but I told him the truth about the 15-6 investigations and set him straight about what they mean, and how insignificant they were to my career. He seemed to understand, and then we talked business.

Our afternoon mission was rather boring except for some videos and pictures I took, and some kids that spoke English trying to get some food and toys from us. I threw almost all of the candy bars Becky had sent me because I felt for the kids. One of the kids told Heath and Frank that there were no more *"boondookeya's, koonbela's"* (bombs or explosives or weapons) in that town anymore. Kids seemed generally honest. SGT M of the Mortars learned to not throw kids food until we were on our way out of a location or town (rather than upon arrival). This was because they'd swarm the vehicle until you left. We tried to tell him so earlier, but I guess he had to see for himself. Also, Bravo Company got into a scuffle at the roundabout we often passed north of Hwy-1. They said the enemy numbered 10 to 12 Anti-Iraqi Forces (AIF), and they killed six, possibly wounding two or three more. They were attacked with Rocket Propelled Grenades (RPGs), rifles and some grenades. It sounded exciting but thank God no one was hurt. Tomorrow we would conduct reconnaissance of our A Company sector.

November 8, 2004

As I told my men that day, and CPT J who rode on my vehicle - either the enemy was completely scared of us, or people at home were praying we don't ever encounter the enemy. Perhaps both; and the fact we all fired our weapons as warnings and the enemy heard about our

15-6 investigations for all kinds of shootings (I'm joking, of course). I was very thankful we'd not been fired upon in Mosul yet, but at the same time, I was itching for some type of firefight like the rest of the Battalion seemed to have had, as were my men. An odd desire, but the best way I can explain it is I wanted to eradicate some evil. In layman's terms, kill bad people and break their toys.

Today's recon was cut short, I assumed due to the CPT J being so tired. He, the XO and 1SG all went to FOB Freedom (on the other side of the Tigris) yesterday and got back at six that morning. He was tired when I knocked on his door earlier, and was incoherently babbling, as I do when seriously lacking sleep. I laughed because he reminded me of myself, or my dad, when exhausted. It was interesting having him on my vehicle though, along with the lead sniper, but we missed our loader. CPT J was funny, cracking jokes the entire time, yet maintaining his composure and command. It was usually a burden to have the commander ride with your platoon, but it was nice having him in my vehicle that day. CPT J, Frank, and six others got out and walked up and down some of the streets on a dismounted patrol. After the commander dismounted, I sent a military police vehicle behind him so he would have better communications and some mounted support. There was no enemy, and then we moved to one more spot, to talk to the Iraqi Police at a station. I threw some kids some individually wrapped twizzlers as we left (and they were happy), and we rolled back in the east gate on the base.

The following interruption was exciting. Just after I finished writing the account above, I played a computer game when I heard lots of people knocking on doors telling us Bravo Company had heavy contact at Baghdad Traffic Circle and we needed to be ready immediately. I got my gear on and got some guidance from CPT J, and met my men on the vehicles. Everyone was running out to the vehicles. It felt like something from the movie *Starship Troopers* when they were going to war. Everyone in the company moved to their vehicles, and the Mobile Gun System (MGS) platoon and the Mortar Section were the first five vehicles ready in the company, so I told them to get in our usual order of march and line up ready to roll. We waited for more guidance from CPT J, who waited for Battalion to give the word. Once the rest of the company was ready, we all moved up to the dining facility to prepare to roll out the gate. Everyone was so excited and full of adrenaline. It turned out that the contact was at Yarmuk Traffic Circle (north on Hwy-1), which is the circle we always pass when going north on Hwy-1. Battalion said the enemy force was nearly platoon-sized, and we got even more excited. We were all disturbed when thirteen Strykers already fighting had one casualty (wounded) and Battalion fought on; those Strykers left after killing most of the enemy. Everyone came back to the motor pool, and we stood down, and I relaxed in my room for a bit.

Then one of those neat God-things happened – where He shows you how involved He is in our lives. I decided to throw my body armor vest and helmet on and go to chow, stopping at the command post on my way up to see if there was going to be a battle update brief that night. Our Training Room NCO said they had already had the meeting. I felt so bad, because I had been a minute or two late to the meeting the last night. I thought since the entire company ran off to almost do a mission it would be moved to another time, but I started to worry I had missed it. I was worried about looking bad to others for Christ. I always try to be without fault as God said in scripture, so I can be the best example of Christ these people see. I felt horrible walking the mile-long trip up to the dining facility, imagining what they would say, how everyone was there except for me, and how bad it looked, especially after being a minute late the night before. I first thought of a million excuses, then ways to explain that I hadn't received the message in my room, or someone could have notified me. I realized I would just have to face up to it and apologize. I felt God say, "I got it," so I tried not to worry, and to trust Him more.

Suddenly, a civilian contractor bus pulled up after I had walked one third of a mile and picked me up, so I got to the chow hall ten minutes earlier. I went in and ordered my Stir Fry, and saw where CPT J, the XO, and all the other LTs were sitting. I could just imagine Dale (the XO) cursing at me, and the commander disappointed in me, and the rest of the LTs showing their silent disapproval. I dreaded it and prayed for help to say the right things as I walked over. I sat down at the table and Dale said to me, "Hey Matt, thanks for bringing me lunch today." I said, "You're welcome," and asked if it was still warm when he ate it, and he said it was great. That made me feel good, but I felt suspicious that no one else said anything. As I started to eat, I felt 'how weird is this that they haven't said anything.' Finally, they all got up and said bye to me. CPT Jacobsen tapped on the back of my body armor as he walked by, and I thought 'this is it; this is where he says something.' What did he say? "Hey Matt, thanks for getting your platoon ready so quickly earlier today, that was great. Sorry we didn't get to go out and react to the contact, but I really appreciate you and your guys being ready that fast." I responded accordingly, and then asked if we were going to get any more updates on that day, and he said no. I then asked if there was a brief tonight. "No." He replied. So there had not even been one; I had worried for nothing. The entire weight was lifted off me, and I silently thanked the Lord.

After chow, I called Mom and Dad, and then tried my friend Shelton. I told Mom about Psalm 91, and how I heard an unscathed WWII unit supposedly prayed it daily. I pulled out my pocket camouflaged NIV Bible I'd taken just about everywhere since Airborne School in 1999 and opened it. I hadn't read the Psalms since coming to Iraq. Another funny God-thing happened, and I shined my light on the pages. I had opened the Bible exactly to the page containing Psalm 91. I praised God, since it is so neat that He shows Himself in little ways like that. It turned out what I had told Mom was correct, and I praised God on the way back. After watching and editing some pictures and videos I took that day, I slept.

November 9, 2004

Our mission was cancelled that morning and given to Second Platoon, so our platoon had the day off aside from maintenance – mostly. Like yesterday, mid-afternoon we got word the enemy was massing on Hwy-1, and Battalion needed all units ready. Everyone was here except for Heath and Randy, so Sergeant Bryce Q and I knocked on doors, yelling out "REDCON 1!!!" meaning ready condition one – get the vehicle ready to roll for combat. As we ran to the vehicles, we passed Heath and Randy, and told them the news. Again, our platoon and the mortar section were ready first in the company and had two snipers (Sergeant P and Specialist Gertson) with us. The mortar section was short two soldiers, but otherwise we lined up in our usual order of march and ready to go, but Captain Jacobsen had to organize the rest of the company, which took some time. Once ready, Company waited on Battalion headquarters to send us, but only Third Platoon (LT Dan K) got to go, since they were the liaison for the Iraqi forces, with fourteen Iraqis on two trucks. We finally went to chow, since they never called for us, and our base was rocketed and mortared about ten times that day it seemed, mostly during the night.

November 10, 2004

This was the day. I got pulled from Bible study last night to get a Warning Order about an escort mission I had the next day. We linked up with a medical Lieutenant Colonel and his eight Humvees in the Dining Facility gravel parking lot. I was to take him 10 kilometers outside of Mosul via Hwy-1. I was told not to take any of his vehicles on Hwy-1 within the city (although we could cross it), and that I would lead the convoy (not him). He briefed his men, who were mostly Navy Corpsmen (medics) and senior enlisted. Each Humvee had a fifty-caliber machine gun on it. I positioned the Humvees between our Anti-Tank and Mortar Strykers.

We left the base when we were ready, after I prayed with many of the men. We took the east gate and zigzagged on a route which I named route "Dawn" (named for Randy's wife). It turned out the route was too congested, so Randy had to take alternate routes around. At one point, our only option was to go down a one-way road in the wrong direction. I simply told him "make it our way then." He did, and we continued to roll. The Humvee guys seemed quite scared, shaking a lot. One even dropped his weapon in an intersection but was able to pick up the hand guards and the rest of his rifle without further trouble.

Fifty meters before crossing Hwy-1 where it turns west, one of our mortar Stryker's hit a truck on the right side of the road, pushing it into another truck, crushing it like tin foil. The occupants barely squeezed out safely, okay but angry. We had tried to avoid it by turning left, but the Stryker didn't have enough momentum to jump up on the curb. We had no time to fill out an accident report for the damaged truck, so I radioed a report to Battalion. Once out of Mosul on the northwest portion of Hwy-1, we stopped on the side of the road in the plains and let the eight Humvees go their way. The LTC radioed thanking us for "protecting us and getting us through this crazy city" and then left.

The mortar section sergeant noticed his right front tire had punctured from hitting a hole back inside the city. I asked him if he wanted to change it, or if he thought it'd be better to do so back at the base, and he recommended the base. I said okay, and we headed back. I got some good videos on the way back in, up until we had contact with hostile forces. When Randy fired a small burst at a vehicle that wouldn't stop, there followed about fifteen seconds of inactivity. Suddenly, he reported "Contact, 9 o'clock!" I was shouting "where, where!" to my gunner, sergeant M (Jay), and he pointed to the left. Then came small arms fire from junkyard piles, second and third story windows, and alleyways on the left from trucks and on the ground. We fired in every direction where the enemy was. Other than seeing two men running from a junk pile and firing at them, all my firing was at second story windows and above. I peppered every window I saw smoke coming from (most of the enemy shot by firing their weapons above their heads, so I didn't see bodies) with 7.62mm rounds from my M240B machine gun. We kept rolling, and Randy asked if I wanted to turn everyone around to resume action against them, and I said, "No, keep going."

Heath warned about watching out for an ambush since we were taking the same route back, but I told SSG Pord to turn right (south) on Hwy-1, rather than returning the way we came. It turned out to be the best tactical decision I'd made so far (thank God), because we hit the enemy on their flank (and we all believe they expected us to continue straight down our old route). We turned the corner and noticed Hwy-1 and our old route were completely empty. No cars, no people, nothing. We expected contact, and Randy radioed so, and after I had just called a contact report to BN, my vehicle went around the corner. Randy and a mortar sergeant shot at the enemy in the road, and down alleyways. My vehicle and the mortar section sergeant shot our M240 and .50cal at all the second story windows (which for four blocks had fire coming from them). Heath did the same. A mortar Stryker .50 apparently destroyed two enemy trucks with occupants who shot from our old route as we turned right on Hwy-1. I will never forget the smoke and muzzle flashes I saw from the windows shooting down at us from both sides. My M240 jammed, and I troubleshot it twice, with no luck, so I picked up my M-4 and emptied a magazine on the enemy. I was so full of energy and adrenaline that I didn't realize I had two more magazines on my body armor, so I yelled, "More magazines! I need more magazines!" while reaching everywhere for them. Finally, I felt in my mind, 'This 240 is going to work this time!' I manhandled the M240, and got it working again, and shot more windows the enemy was shooting from.

I have no idea how many (if any) enemies I killed, but I fired one 30-round magazine of 5.56mm, and about 90-rounds of 7.62mm. We continued down Hwy-1, receiving fire from both sides. Randy reported RPGs repeatedly, had been hit with three of them, as two more whizzed past their faces. A mortar Stryker then got hit with an RPG, and caught a wire. Randy's vehicle caught in the road, triggering a parked car bomb, which blew up next to the mortar Strkyer (which dragged the wire all the way back to base). Just afterwards, two huge explosions occurred as 60mm mortars landed in between our two front vehicles. At this point, Randy had killed five enemy and wounded another two. He had seen men popping out of alleyways shooting RPGs and noticed several enemies running through the street with rifles. After the first one in the middle of the street was killed, just about every Stryker then rolled over his dead body. Darrel, Randy's driver, panicked and kept saying "RPG, RPG!" When RPGs hit, his ears rang and he couldn't hear his crew, so he thought they were all dead, which really scared him. He was okay after he heard them once again, but continued to accelerate, as did all the drivers. We fought through the ambush and drove at about 55 mph through a huge puddle in the road, getting spattered with nasty water. I radioed a report to Battalion and noticed our mortar section sergeant's right front tire flapping all over the place, ripped to shreds. I asked for a damage assessment and casualties. Everyone was fine, but there were three blown tires.

We re-entered base, and vehicles in need of repair went to get fixed, while I debriefed the intelligence officer. My first report was only after hearing from Randy, so I said three confirmed enemy dead; a low estimate which proved higher after I talked to others. The intel officer said it would help if we could get a wounded or dead body, but there was no way to do so in our situation. After talking to everyone else, I discovered we had about 13 confirmed kills, and three enemy wounded. The rest were unconfirmed kills, but the whole thing was just staggering. I reported this update to BN, informing them that at a minimum a Squad-sized element (nine enemy) divided on both sides of our old route with ten to twelve enemy personnel on both sides of Hwy-1. After talking to everyone else, it seemed that ten to twelve enemy were all I saw shooting from the windows. It was more like a minimum of 20 personnel on both sides from the windows, and an additional three teams (three enemy each) on the ground and in alleyways firing small arms and RPGs. Heath's driver (SPC G) seemed to redeem himself. He drove outstandingly and was constantly calling out clock directions of the enemy to his crew. Anyway, this diagram I sketched reflects the whole contact well.

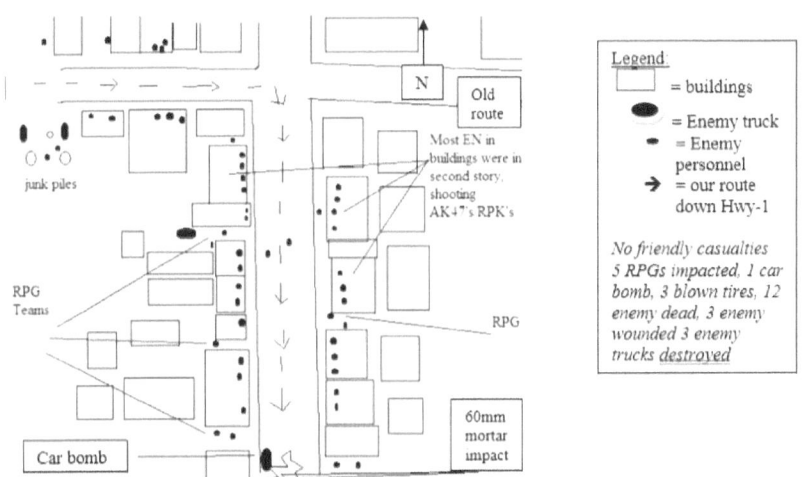

We would have a huge mission the next day. I prayed for safety as we planned to execute a Battalion attack in the afternoon; that God would continue to keep us all safe from mortars falling on our base as I wrote this.

November 11, 2004

Veterans day, and it was no joke - I was now a combat veteran. Our Battalion did a major operation that day. Alpha company (ours) was the main effort, attacking a large area of West Mosul. We were to clear every building in a certain sector west of Hwy-1, about two to three hundred meters north of where we had contact the day before. It looked like this sketch. The drawing locates me as "my specific vehicle" in the location where we were when chaos ensued. North of the sewage drain, and the small road were Second and Third Platoons, with First Platoon to my rear to the right of the objective (OBJ).

At first, I didn't even think we had made it to the objective yet, when we received heavy volumes of fire from both sides, although mostly on the right side. It was about 1p.m. when we entered the area, and the plan was for me to secure the right flank while two platoons went north, and one platoon cleared and searched the objective (which was empty). All of Hwy-1 was like a ghost town. Not a car or person on the street. We went across the median going north and about five seconds later, it was contact everywhere, from every side of us. The initial fighting lasted at least 45 minutes, because the next chance I had to look at my watch at a lull was nearly 2 p.m. Shortly before, we received several Rocket Propelled Grenades (RPGs) from our sides and front, and one of them flew between Private DeArthur P and Gary (an extra Lieutenant in my loaders hatch). DeArthur fell and Jay (SGT M, our gunner) yelled, "We have a casualty!!" I immediately radioed the casualty report up to company, and ducked down, turning to ask, "What's wrong; who's hit?" and saw DeArthur down inside his hatch looking up and pointing. Gary said he was okay, then the next thing I knew, both squeezed up right behind Jay and me at the front of the vehicle. They said the RPG flew between their heads and was stuck in the sandbags next to DeArthur. It was a dud, but they weren't getting near it. I looked at it to assess the situation, realizing if it fell, it would land at the most dangerous place possible, right inside the hatch. I radioed a request for Explosives Ordinance Disposal (EOD) to come and remove it. But Jay went over and carefully lifted the sandbag, flinging it off the vehicle with the RPG still embedded in it.

We kept receiving fire from the second story building on the right (at about my 2 o'clock), and we fired back with 240 and .50 caliber machine guns. The enemy delayed shooting for about one minute, then would shoot again from the same building. There must have been at least six enemy inside on the second story, and I have no idea how many on the first story. They waited another minute, and then fired again. My 240 jammed up about three times during this engagement, and I got frustrated. About the third time the enemy fired from that building, I shouted into my microphone, "THAT'S IT! [Randy's callsign] THIS IS [my callsign], FIRE A TOW [Tube-launched Optically-tracked Wire-guided missile] INTO THE SECOND STORY BUILDING ON THE RIGHT!" Randy answered, "You want me to fire a TOW?" I said "Yes, fire a TOW into the second story of that building on the right where we keep receiving fire." He asked if I was sure, and I said, "YES, LIGHT IT UP!" He answered, "roger," and fifteen seconds later said, "this is Two, firing a TOW," which I radioed on company channel.

Direct hit. The entire second story of that building was blown out and black, with only the sidewalls and roof remaining, most of the front wall destroyed, and most of the back wall destroyed. I was so excited and almost cussed I was so happy that he blew that building's occupants to kingdom come.* He asked if I wanted him to fire again, and I said yes for the next floor. He fired again and the huge explosion rocked the buildings around it as well, leveling everything on the first floor. Black smoke poured out from that building for one hour or more, and we received no further fire from it. Good. In fact, that was about it for about fifteen to twenty minutes for us.[1]

During that silence, I noticed Heath's vehicle's external fuel cans both leaked from bullet holes right through them. We moved back a little to better cover the company flank. Then mortars began to land around us. Several landed right between Randy and a mortar Stryker, and just to the left of me, about five meters away. I told everyone to close hatches and move forward a bit. As we moved forward, I had

Heath, Randy, and a mortar Stryker act on the location from where the mortars were fired. We then received RPG and SAF (small arms fire) from 12 o'clock, across from Yarmuk traffic circle. Randy identified the building from where it came and we peppered it with .50 cal and 7.62mm fire. He asked if I wanted to put a TOW in it, and I asked him if there was still an RPG team in it. He wasn't sure so I told him to keep scanning and fire when enemy engaged us from there again.

Sure enough, another RPG whizzed over all our heads, and he said it was from the same building. I ordered him to shoot it with a TOW, and he did (Bryce, his gunner fired). The TOW punctured the first wall, and exploded on the back wall, destroying most of the back of the building and the building behind it. He prepared to fire again, and the fourth TOW was a misfire (bad wiring) so it blew up fifty meters in front of his Stryker. That building was quiet for 10 minutes. We fired at targets that popped up on the right side behind some buildings and alleyways, and a mortar Stryker destroyed an RPG enemy with the .50 cal, exploding his body. I got up completely behind my 240, aiming my scope and spraying into the windows of the balcony we were receiving fire from about 300 meters back to my right.

The infantry platoons continued north until most of our block was cleared. The commander then called all platoon leaders to come, so I drove back to his location inside an abandoned schoolhouse, and we discussed plans further. He wanted our platoon to continue to watch the flank and north from there, so I mounted up and went back. Lieutenant Colonel Eric K was with our company at this point, behind me to my right. I had my vehicles on the sides and in the middle of the road. We then received more indirect fire, and three vehicles went up to the left junkyard (from where small arms fire had originated) and scanned for targets. At that point, an enemy with hip and elbow wounds came out to surrender. I told our team to make sure he had no bombs under his clothes as he approached the vehicles, so they could detain him as we took him to the medics. They complied with my order, and we returned to our position.

Just then we took more RPG fire from north of Yarmuk, and more mortar rounds. The XO (Dale) told me to move my vehicles out of the road, and up against the buildings. I told him that I had no field of view if I did so and I was in a good position to launch a TOW at the building north of Yarmuk (my vehicle was actually buttoned up and ready to fire, as soon as the enemy shot from that building again). He said, "Roger, but be advised that came from the colonel, so you might want to move." This irritated me, because I thought it was crazy to move up against the buildings, and it wouldn't have protected us any, just made us more vulnerable, but LTC K wanted it done. Everyone complained when he said that, and of course I preferred to maneuver my platoon myself. I ordered us to clear out a little, but no one up against any buildings. As I moved, an enemy in the north building fired an RPG again, and I got so mad, because we could have destroyed it, had we not moved.

We got word we'd leave near 3 p.m., and I passed it on. Infantry platoons continued into the buildings (which were all mostly empty), then began to rally back to their vehicles. Another frustrating thing during the entire battle here was the fact that my crew would ask a question, or tell me something, while I'd get a call on the platoon radio, and then company radio at the same time. We prepared to move, and our platoon was to lead the way. Instead of going south back down Hwy-1 to our base, LTC K told Captain Jacobsen to move us north to Yarmuk traffic circle and head east, eventually crossing the Tigris into Third Battalion Twenty-First Infantry's (3-21 IN) sector, then south, eventually crossing the Tigris River again, taking us near our base. It sounded odd, but we did it. We surprisingly made it past Yarmuk without contact.

About 200 meters down the road it came: small arms and RPG fire from the right, and some rifle fire from the left too. I fired at a truck to the right (south) and into some buildings. We passed a four story building where fire came out of every window at us (about seven windows, twelve shooters). They continued to fire even as we sprayed them with .50 cal and 240, but my 240 jammed again. I got so mad (and also scared at the sheer volume of gunfire and RPG's whizzing past us) that I popped my head down and max elevated the 240 to charge it repeatedly until the bolt locked to the rear, and it worked again. By the time it worked, I got a couple rounds off, and we had flown past that building safely. Just then, an RPG hit the road in front of us on the right side--possibly two or three RPG's. I saw two, Will (our driver) reported three, Jay saw one. Will swerved left and the RPG bounced and hit the median to the left, so he swerved right. After hitting the median, the RPG bounced again back to the right, finally exploding two feet away from our left front wheel, and Will drove on. He swerved so much the vehicle almost flipped. Others in the convoy thought he had been killed, and we were spinning out of control. He did an excellent job, especially since we (Jay and I) were shouting, "Left! Right! No! Left!! Straighten out! Come back on the road!" all within a couple of seconds.

As we drove, a mortar round landed about one foot in front of a mortar Stryker, and as they drove through the blast, they were spattered with debris. Had their driver been going two mph faster, the mortar round would have landed right on the sergeant's head. I also heard another mortar round go off to our right rear, barely missing us. We must have been going at least 45 mph at the time. A mortar round also exploded to our front left side, a couple of feet away. After talking to Randy, he and a mortar Stryker received rockets and a couple of roadside bombs that burst next to them. Our platoon had no further enemy contact today.

We returned safely after taking a wrong turn, then turned the convoy around, but no enemy was near at the time, so it was okay. The 3-21 Infantry Battalion had the bridges sealed off to civilian traffic, but they let us through. When we entered our base, we all shared war stories, discussed what happened, and it seemed we had about five confirmed enemy kills, and possibly up to 19 non-confirmed kills (based on the amount of fire that ceased from windows after we fired at them, and another six enemy dead from the building into which we fired TOW's). After watching a mortar soldier's video from his "combat camera," we noticed at least ten RPG's flying past our vehicles. Others in our platoon confirmed seeing RPG's hit some of our vehicles. I didn't even find out until later we had one RPG explode underneath my vehicle, blowing one of our tires. After getting back, Jay also noticed we had no antennae box to lower the antennae when firing a TOW. There was a good chance we would have blown them completely off if my vehicle had fired one, so I guess the Lord had His hand in that also. The unfortunate news is B Company had a casualty today; he was an infantryman in the loader hatch of an Anti-tank Stryker. I guess a sniper shot him in the head, and he died in the medical Stryker next to the chaplain.

November 12, 2004

It was 11:45 p.m., and the day was almost done. We had just had light machinegun fire come inside the base. They fired at a couple of our guard towers, two of our towers fired back, and I believe a tower from FOB Diamondback (where Mosul Airfield was) to our immediate east may have fired at our own towers, thinking they were enemy. The 25th Brigade Support Battalion was in the towers guarding us, and possibly on Diamondback. So much for my "in bed by midnight" rule I had tried to self-impose – thus far unsuccessful. It was 12:18 a.m., and we had a big mission the next day, so Iwent to bed. Oh, while talking with everyone earlier in our Mobile Gun System/Mortar Section we came up with a new name for ourselves: Storm Troopers. It sounded cool, and we planned to make our own markings and symbols for it. We would see.

November 13, 2004

I was listening to Jaci Velasquez' song "I Get On My Knees." It expressed my mood since I had returned from our mission that day. Getting down on my knees in prayer was also one of the first things I did soon after getting back to the base and my room safely that day. Praying, especially thanking God, should be the first thing I do in situations, so I felt guilty, although I did thank Him as soon as we were back inside the base, and for about 10 minutes afterwards. I was more scared than usual that morning as we rolled up to the chow hall to prepare for another battalion operation. C Company had primary responsibility for attacking both sides of Hwy-1 where my men and I had enemy contact on the tenth, just three days before. A Company (us), was to protect their right flank; both companies would advance north, clearing buildings as we went. I couldn't help thinking of our three-hour long mission on the eleventh though, with the intense 45-minute firefight, and how close we came to having many casualties. In prayer, I turned all my fear and doubt over to Jesus and as another song goes, he 'worked it out.' The chaplain came with us, and he prayed before we got on our vehicles. I prayed constantly while going over the route in my head and our role for the mission

We rolled up Hwy-1 and once the rest of the company was set, we circled a traffic roundabout intersection (much smaller than Yarmuk Traffic Circle) and covered our company rear. Beforehand, Heath came up to me and said, "Sir, it's your choice, since obviously you outrank me, so you can do whatever you want, but you really need to get out of that hatch and let SGT M [Jay] gun for you." I wrongly thought he was addressing my not being high enough out of my hatch again, but then my brain processed what he said. He continued "As good as you are, there's no way you can do twenty things at once, shooting the 240 [machine gun], talking to company, maneuvering the platoon, and talking to your crew at the same time. You may be good, but I don't care how good you are, no brain can keep track of all of that going on at once." Wow! I told him he was right, and I had given it much thought. He also stated "It's also your job to maneuver the platoon as the platoon leader, and you weren't really doing that very much yesterday. We were fine, and everything went okay, but I think I was doing more maneuvering of the platoon than you, and I think it's supposed to be the other way around, so you might want to switch to the gunner's seat. It's a lot easier to control things from there." He was so right. I agreed, "Yeah, I think the only time I maneuvered the platoon was when I sent you and SSG N up to get that detainee, and other than that, I didn't do any, so yeah, you're right."

The radio box to switch between company and platoon channels is easier to access in the gunner's hatch (on the left of the vehicle) behind the missile controls. There is also more room, and since I do pop down a lot to monitor the FBCB2 battle computer, my map, or other leader materials, it made sense that Jay would still be manning the M240 when I squatted down. I told him how happy Jay would be hearing that, since he had asked me just about every mission, "Sir, do you want me on the 240 today?" I always told him, "No, I'm fine, we'll keep it like it is for now. I'll let you know when we are going to switch." I realized something about myself when we had this conversation th day before. Sometimes I as an officer, and as a human being, had feelings of inadequacy, as if I wasn't doing enough work, or wasn't important enough. For some reason, I guess I felt like I was just providing a rough plan for an operation, and that was it. Since we usually fought the enemy and not the plan, I felt I needed to do more as a leader.

SGT Jay M and SFCE Heath were both right. I was trying to plan the mission, maneuver the platoon, fire the M240 while talking to company, and command my vehicle all at the same time. Jay had been telling me, and I was just brushing it off because of my feelings of inadequacy, to be completely honest. I should have listened to him sooner, but I guess I needed to be told by Heath as well, and then after praying about it, I felt it was God's will. NCOs are great for things like that (among their other good qualities) and as long as you are willing to listen as an officer, you can learn a great deal.

During a drill yesterday, Jay and I got a chance to swap out everything (he was incredibly happy), and I felt great about being in the gunner's hatch and he in the vehicle commander hatch. He still needed to teach me how to man and fire TOW missiles, but for the time being, if we really had to fire one, hatches would be shut, and we could quickly swap. Besides, Heath also suggested, "Why were you about to fire a TOW anyway, sir? That's what you have [Randy] and me for. You can maneuver us to take shots before you should need to go in and do that." Once again, he was so right! I had been trying to feel more adequate by having my vehicle fire a TOW. It wasn't enough the other day for me to have ordered Randy to fire his missiles into those buildings, I wanted to fire one from my vehicle, or so I had felt. I listened, changed, and learned a valuable lesson about my platoon and how to improve myself.

We also developed a hunter-killer team concept or technique. The Cavalry used this concept with Humvees and Tanks, or Bradleys and Tanks. The smaller more versatile vehicle finds the enemy and suppressed or marks it with smaller rounds, while the heavier hitting vehicle repositions or re-aims to destroy the target completely. We had done this the other day, though we were unaware of it as a tactic. I discussed with some mortar sergeants and Randy how we worked well together. CPT J said unless he ever stated otherwise, the term MGS always applies to MGS platoon and Mortar section together. A five Stryker, twenty-two personnel unit is a lethal hunter-killer platoon: The Storm Troopers. We look a bit like storm troopers with the Combat Vehicle Communications helmets we wear and our large goggles for eye protection. From then on we were organized in two sections, with myself coordinating the platoon, attaching my vehicle to whichever section needed me at the time. Randy's vehicle and a Mortar Stryker are "A" section, or hunter-killer-1, and Heath and SSG N were "B" section, or hunter-killer-2.

This arrangement had worked well two days ago, and we hadn't even planned it. Our anti-tank Stryker's would suppress or kill the enemy, marking them with 7.62mm fire, while the mortar Stryker's would destroy the enemy or his concrete walls, with .50 caliber armor-piercing rounds. I would remain in the middle of the platoon, maneuvering each section as needed, if we were to adjust to a different location. Also, if needed, we could reposition to fire a TOW into a building or target too menacing or numerous for the .50 caliber machine gun. If needed, a mortar Stryker could stop to set up 60mm or 120mm mortars and rain indirect fire from above on any enemy. Our platoon had the most firepower in the entire company in our five vehicles, and the Stryker was an outstanding vehicle. With God's protection and blessing, we could be unstoppable. Although we were so far away from our families (and I missed Becky and our unborn baby inside her), I felt this was part of what I was born to do, and to quote George C. Scott in the movie *Patton*, "I do love it so." The camaraderie the men and I shared improved daily.

Anyway, back to that day's mission. We either scared the enemy the other day, killed most of them, or they are regrouping. C Company had minimal enemy contact – a few enemies fired rifles and one or two RPG's in five hours in the objective area. Our platoon was last in order of march for a change (we usually are first every mission), and we didn't fire a shot that day. I think A Company (ours) probably had only five to nine enemy combatants in the entire sector who exposed themselves, and we covered a lot of area, going north all the way past Yarmuk. We received eight indirect fires, and they thankfully hit no one. It seemed just like training – when we sat too long in an area, while the enemy laid mortar targets and lobbed them in our direction.

At one point, an Iraqi National Guard Executive Officer was talking on a cell phone, and SSG Z and DeArthur on my vehicle (SSG Z was in my old platoon in A/2-14 Cavalry) told him to put away the phone. The interpreter said he couldn't tell him because he was the XO. Within one minute of this, we received indirect fire on our position. It may have been a coincidence, but my men and I thought not. We didn't trust half of these Iraqi soldiers. SSG Z was on one of the tactical human intelligence teams, gathering intelligence from the enemy and the locals to analyze it. It was good to work with him again.

CPT Jacobsen tasked me to find a route out of our area that headed west on Hwy-47, and south along the outskirts of the city to avoid as much of Hwy-1 as possible. I developed one and sent it to Randy, but ironically, he and I were both confused on what exact route I meant.

We pushed west on Hwy-47 and waited for the rest of the company to pull off its objectives, and I had my platoon and the Iraqi soldiers set up in a herringbone formation on Hwy-47. After sitting for thirty-five minutes, I told Randy to move forward about one hundred meters up the road. It wasn't a moment too soon, because as we moved, mortars landed to our rear – the enemy was targeting us again. No one was hurt, thankfully, and we moved up the road.

Randy led us down a route until he said he didn't quite understand where I wanted him to go. Heath suggested I take the lead in our platoon order of march since I knew where I wanted to go, and I took his suggestion. It is normally Randy's job, but since I couldn't paint an accurate picture for him of where we should go, it made better sense for me to take the lead position. I felt a great peace from above to do so, and I moved up and took the lead. I turned down routes, popping down and looking at the route screen, and back up scanning with my M-4 rifle, and praying for God to guide us, and He sure did. We had no further contact, and I found a route skirting the edge of the city, avoiding buildings as much as possible, eventually linking up with the last four hundred meters of Hwy-1. I led the entire company back that route, and the Lord guided us safely back to the base. Thankful to be alive, I was ready to do counter terrorist patrols the next day and go to FOB Sykes on a resupply escort the next night at 10 p.m. I loved the life I had, and just continued to pray that God would bring me home to my lovely wife and child, and the same for all the "Storm Troopers."

November 14, 2004 and November 15, 2004 together (you'll see why)

Before I went to bed the night before, CPT J came in and told me he had good news and bad news. I said, "We have new a mission tonight or in a couple hours, sir." He said "No, the good news is I just saved a bunch of money on my car insurance by switching to GEICO." I laughed, and he told me it was rumored some seventy-five phantom terrorists would attack the Mosul Airfield Gate to the base, and B Company would move to the airfield early in the morning for a few hours to defend from this phantom attack (which never occurred). The mission previously assigned to B Company was given to us – to link up at 5:30 a.m. at the Dining Facility to escort two trucks and one fueler to FOB Aggies. Neither the commander nor I knew where Aggies was, but it was supposedly an hour or less south of us.

I woke Jay and Frank to tell them we needed to be awake at 4:30 a.m. since originally, we had missions from 6:30-8:30 a.m. and 1:30-3:30 p.m. (now cancelled). CPT J said we'd then be escorting resupply at 10 p.m. (14 Nov) to FOB Sykes back at Tal Afar. We woke and escorted the vehicles, although it turned out to be one Palletized Loading System trailer truck, and one fueler. I briefed the men who rode the vehicles and prayed with them. We moved out of the gate, around Baghdad Traffic Circle, and headed south. I had gotten the graphics from the

Battalion Operations Officer earlier in the morning. The trip was uneventful (thank God) and we made it, only to discover what a dump the base was – just a building surrounded by dirt and concertina wire with some guard shacks, not more than a hundred by two hundred meters if that. I was thankful we weren't at that base.

An intel Lieutenant J traveled with us and we shared with him some intel we'd gathered the day before. I learned a lot from Randy and mortar sergeant talking about events from that day. They told him about how the same trucks would drive back and forth; empty one way, filled with people dressed in black the other way. We only saw weapons once (in the case of the silver station wagon the other day with an RPG), but C Company had Strykers on the other side of it, so it would have been unsafe to shoot. They mentioned the black flags on buildings in windows, and on cars, that usually meant it was a haven for terrorists. We also pointed out areas from which the enemy loved to fire mortars and where their resupply routes were. I went to brief the intel officer on all of this when I got a chance that day.

Upon return, I found out we were no longer going to FOB Sykes for a supply escort, but on Counter-Manpad missions from 1:30-3:30 p.m. We got out to just south of Mosul and sat in a screen for about thirty minutes. I was about to call everyone and let them know to get ready to move to our next location when Battalion Headquarters radioed for us to return immediately because the Quick Reaction Force (QRF) led by Lieutenant Raub with First Platoon had proceeded to 'Four West' police station, at the northernmost end of Hwy-1, right next to the Tigris river. I had joked about just such an event on the way out, saying to my crew, "Watch, we are joking around about another Counter-Manpad operation, and they'll call QRF somewhere, and then call us back to support the QRF or the colonel in contact." Boy did I call that one. It was exactly what happened, but it was 3-21 IN Battalion's Lieutenant Colonel Gible, who crossed the river with two infantry platoons and a Mobile Gun System platoon. They shot a TOW into one building, and

Kiowa helicopters put two Hellfire Missiles into another. First Platoon fired two Anti-Tank AT 4's, several 40mm rounds from the Mark 19 (MK19) Grenade Launcher, and a boatload of .50 cal into most of the buildings on the south side of Hwy-1 at that location.

I quickly arrived at the battalion Tactical Operations Center (TOC) and moved in to find out where they wanted me, and what exactly they wanted me to do. The Battalion Executive Officer was watching the Unmanned Aerial Vehicle and the FBCB2 battle computer screens, seeing where our troops and the enemy were. He was also talking on the radio to Brigade and 3-21 Infantry, and the QRF in contact with the enemy. He told me to watch the screen and familiarize myself with the situation, and he would let me know when to leave. Apparently, some Iraqi Commando's (better fighters than normal Iraqi soldiers) had gone there to occupy the police station and walked right into an enemy ambush. The enemy fired from every building south of Hwy-1 and had destroyed about four of the Dodge Rams they used for combat. There were about twenty dead of ninety Iraqi commandos, and apparently roughly forty enemy in the area. Once US Forces got there, the fight quickly ended, so it sounded like I would escort Medical Strykers back and forth, instead of engaging in battle. The enemy quickly retreated, dragging all their dead away, so we could not determine how many died.

The Operations Officer walked into the TOC and asked me if I was ready. I said I was, and he said, "Let's go, I'll fill you in on the specifics as we go." I ran out excited, surprisingly not scared, and briefed the Storm Troopers. We left with the Operations Officer's vehicles following, got a mile out, and the TOC radioed us to return. They didn't need us after all since the situation had died down. We turned around, got back, and I was released to my commander, who was readying the rest of my company. I told Captain Jacobsen we were ready to go at his word, and he gathered the platoon leaders together to brief us on the plan. Third Platoon (Lieutenant Dan Karney) led the company out to secure a section of Hwy-1, while First Platoon secured the Police Station. My job was to immediately turn around after crossing bridge five and protect the exit route, particularly the two hotels north and south of Hwy-1, on the river's edge. Enemy had fired heavily from those buildings, so my platoon would suppress it while the company left.

We arrived as planned – one section facing northeast watching the hotel north of Hwy-1, and the other southwest, watching the hotel south of Hwy-1. I sat in the middle, watching both. Once each section radioed it was set, I said from now on northern hotel would be "hotel two", and the southern "hotel one." We sat for hours until CPT J needed us to consolidate all food and water at his location. Once we did so, he said our platoon could leave because Third and First Platoons were going to stay the night. I felt bad for them, not knowing their fate or our own. Heath and SSG N collected our chow and water and dropped it off so the infantry platoons would be fed. The rest of the company failed to tell us there was concertina wire in the road, and it wrapped around the tires, slat armor and every possible axle of Heath's vehicle. Randy gave him a hand and more wire cutters, but my vehicle and a mortar Stryker stayed put to watch the hotels. After hours cutting wire it was almost 10 p.m. and Heath told me CPT J said something about leaving an anti-tank Stryker there with him. I prayed it wasn't so, but it was. The Lord wanted me to protect my brother at arms out there, so I chose my own vehicle to stay, and Heath, Randy, the mortar Strykers, and crews went back with the XO and medical Strykers.

Our vehicle got set in our new position on Hwy-1, watching down an alleyway until Captain Jacobsen climbed up on my Stryker to brief me on what the deal was. He told me they kept finding bodies of dead Iraqi Commandos, and the commando XO was petrified our company would leave. Our Battalion told us to stay, saying relief from B Company would arrive in the morning. I felt bad for the Iraqi Commandos because they sounded so brave earlier when they had helped our Special Forces troops defeat high value target enemy individuals weeks ago. When asked what they did, they said, "we drive up, we go in, and we kill people. Bad people." I had a high expectation of them, but I guess anyone can get badly caught in an ambush, crushing their spirits when almost out of ammunition after losing twenty men. I felt so sorry for them because here they were trying to take back control of their country, and the enemy just shoot at them as they did at us Americans. I suppose that's why they were called terrorists or AIF, since they were truly Anti-Iraqi Forces – against us and a free, democratic, peaceful Iraq.

Jay asked if I wanted to be included in the guard rotation for the evening, and I said of course (usually Platoon Leaders don't do shifts), since it was just five of us. One of us would always be awake to scan the alleyway from our ITAS (Independent Thermal Aiming System). Jay worked out the rotation and suggested Will (short for Williams, our driver) not do a shift since he'd have to climb up through the drivers' hole, and as the driver he needed the most sleep. I agreed and did the first shift, occasionally looking down at my Bible as I scanned, reading John to stay awake, then praying and reading Psalm 91. It was so true for our situation – God kept us safe, allowing no "disaster/scourge to come near our tent," as written. We didn't "fear the terror that comes by night," or the "arrow that flies by day." He protected us out there – when it felt unsafe to sleep in Mosul, outside the base, particularly on one of the worst spots in the city.

Except for engineers coming in with bomb disposal folks to blow up five unexploded 155mm howitzer rounds and some mortar and RPG rounds in the area, the night was quiet. None of us got good sleep doing guard shifts until 11 a.m. We woke when B Company was on its way to relieve us. It got hit with a car bomb near Yarmuk Traffic Circle. We don't know why they took that route instead of crossing the bridge from 3-21 Infantry's sector like we had – a safer route. Upon eye contact with the driver, he exploded his car – a 500 lb. explosion so powerful it knocked every sandbag into its adjacent hatch or shredded it. It blew the locked driver's hatch completely off the vehicle and blew out seven of eight Stryker tires. Rifle fire and RPGs preceded the bomb. B Company defeated remaining enemies and recovered the damaged vehicle and personnel. Originally casualties were reported as worse, but later it turned out to be some minor head trauma and damaged eardrums. I heard one guy with injured eardrums might have gone to Germany to get them reconstructed.

We then heard C Company would leave no earlier than 1 p.m. to relieve us. Before then, we received several rounds of indirect mortar fire. Will had just asked if he could smoke a cigarette out of his hatch. I said, "Sure, but only pop it a crack just to blow your smoke out." Five minutes later Jay said, "You know, we've been sitting here a long time; we're probably going to get mortared." Just then, BOOM! A mortar landed 20 meters in front of our vehicle, and Will quickly shut his hatch. We moved closer to buildings to avoid enemy line of sight (I felt in this case it was tactically wise to do so). A report came of a guy just south of the highway cloverleaf intersection of Hwy-1 and Hwy-47 looking through binoculars while talking on a cell phone. Our snipers couldn't shoot him since he was more than 800 meters away.

It was quiet, then we had contact to the north – an enemy popped out from behind a building and fired an RPG at First Platoon, then jumped into a truck. They shot the truck with Mark-19 grenades and .50 cal until it was a burning heap of metal, pluming with black smoke. The truck owner nearby stepped out with a hose to put out the fire on what was left of his truck. C Company arrived, and I linked up with a lieutenant to brief him on our corner of the area, and what had occurred the last twenty-two hours. In our vehicles we faced west, prepared to cross the river as soon as CPT Jacobsen finished briefing CPT Hossfeld of C Company on the situation. We received two more incoming enemy mortar and I moved even farther west. While we sat, scanning with hatches opened, we noticed we were right where Will dodged those RPG rounds and enemy mortars during our exit from our

11 November firefight. We could even identify the three-story building (formerly four-stories) where rifles fired at us from the windows. I took a video of it, and we finally moved back to the base, safe and sound.

After chow, a shower, and some sleep, I had a package. The hip holster my grandparents had sent me had finally arrived, and I set it up after a quick nap from 4-7 p.m. I ate again then went to our operations order mission planning session for a Brigade mission the next day. Things just kept ramping up there. The plan was as follows: our entire Brigade would clear Mosul with three Battalions and recapture every police station in the city. With the help of Iraqi National Guard and Commandos we would emplace new police officers (former police were either killed or ran away). My platoon had Counter-Manpad, a support role. Maybe we'll finally get some rest.

November 16, 2004

That day went as planned with Counter-Manpad missions from 8:30-10:30 a.m. and 2:30-4:30 p.m. We woke before 6 a.m. to do communications checks before chow. We went on our operation and returned. I thought we would fix the sandbags on all of the vehicles as soon as we returned to the motor pool, but after my debrief to the intel officer, I returned to the vehicles and no one was doing anything there. I headed to my room and talked to Frank and a couple of others for a bit. I overheard Frank say something about filling sandbags by 2 p.m., so I thought the plan was to do it before we left. As I passed Heath, I told him I was heading to lunch, "if anyone comes looking for me."

When I returned from chow, I had a quick conversation with Becky (less than 10 minutes) on the phone and made a quick internet check (neither of which I had done in about a week). I got to the vehicles at 1:40 p.m. and Frank said Heath was looking for me. I walked over to his vehicle and he asked me if I had eaten and I said I had. He said no one else in the platoon had eaten. I inquired as to why, and he said they were going to go up there as a platoon after filling sandbags and didn't want to leave without me. I felt horrible for putting my needs before those of my men, so I apologized. I think it was just bad communication between us. He hadn't remembered me mentioning I was going to chow, even though I remembered him responding at the time. It may have been an instance when someone talks to you, you see them talking, but afterwards don't remember what they've said, and aren't quite sure if they were talking to you or not. I apologized to a couple others in the platoon, and asked the Lord's forgiveness, but mostly felt bad that I had missed filling sandbags with the men and helping adjust them on the vehicles.[2]

I also found out from Bryce (SGT Q) that somehow his wife got word that Heath had to fix my M240 in the middle of a battle. I have no idea where that came from or who, but it sounded crazy. I asked Jay, who said he'd heard it, but not from Bryce. If somebody was starting the rumor game, I wasn't playing, so I dropped it right there. It was like the old game "telephone" where you tell somebody one thing, and it goes around the room, until it comes back to the person who said it, and the phrase is completely different.

The highlight of my day was a chapel Bible study which I invited several in the platoon to. All appreciated being invited, but none wanted to come. We discussed moral, civil, and ceremonial laws in the book of Exodus, and their application today. We also noted how they are a testimony of the truth of scripture, due to the sheer amount of details involved in each explanation of building the tabernacle. After the study ended, I hung around with SGT Kevin G (a brother and a medic) and a few others, just fellowshipping about denominations (which divide) in Christianity, and different versions of the Bible (King James, Revised Standard Version and New International Version). It was a great time, and I mentioned my violin had arrived that day, so I would be practicing to play with the worship team. I meditated on the fellowship and scripture when I got back to my room (as rain poured down outside) and thanked the Lord for protecting us from the mortars which landed very close to us in the chapel and sleeping areas during the Bible study. God is good.

November 17, 2004

That day we were scheduled for two patrols, but both missions were cancelled. As I reported to the TOC (Tactical Operations Center) as we were about to exit the base, they said "Stand down, your mission has been cancelled." I loved hearing those words. I radioed it to others, and everyone was happy as we returned to our rooms. I swung by the TOC, and they informed me the second mission was also cancelled – probably because of the bad weather, although it hasn't rained since last night. There was a huge thunderstorm last night as we slept, and I just marveled at how loud the thunderclaps were.

In all of this war, with our exploding manmade devices – mortars, rockets, hellfire and TOW missiles, Joint Direct Attack Munitions (JDAM) bombs from jets, and the like, nothing produces a boom quite like the power of God in the atmosphere. He is truly awesome. Most of today was spent napping and socializing around our rooms, with a few meals. I just got word from CPT Jacobsen that we must guard the south Mosul bridge at 8 p.m., probably until sometime the next day or even the next evening. I was glad we had gotten more rest because we'd need it. CPT J kept 'toying' with the idea of taking a mortar Stryker away from us so he could cruise the streets when he wanted to, in order to recon an area like the colonel did with the Battalion Scouts and Mortar Sectio from time to time. That wouldn't be good for the hunter-killer teams of the Storm Troopers, but maybe he'd decide not to do it.

LIEUTENANT COLONEL MATTHEW SACRA

November 18, 2004

We went to the bridge. We had a military police Humvee with us and had to drop off First Sergeant at provincial hal, where Second Platoon protected the governor and his palace. On our way to dropping him off we encountered a barricade of concertina wire that had not been reported to us by any observers and we had to move it before we could continue. This upset us since US obstacles by doctrine are supposed to be observed by US personnel. There was no observer, and it was right in our path. We quickly moved it – a dangerous job because we were surrounded by tall buildings from which any hidden enemy could have lobbed grenades at us. Thankfully, we had no enemy contact, and God got us to the bridge safely.

One section of the bride faced west, the other east. We talked with those we were replacing, and I spoke with their platoon leader. He and his men thanked us for the relief, said nothing interesting occurred and that a curfew was in effect from 10 p.m. to 6 a.m. so there shouldn't be any traffic. Only friendly traffic came through (Strykers and Semis), and it came at all hours. One convoy had two gun-trucks protecting it, and about 100 semi's with supplies, fuel, and the like – taking 15 minutes to cross the bridge. As they crossed, the whole bridge shook – not comforting for those positioned on it all night. At 10:30 p.m. I got word from the Operations Officer we didn't have to relieve 3-21 Infantry after all, and they were supposed to be still manning the bridge. I said I'd already done so and asked what they wanted us to do. Since we had already relieved them, we were to stay put. It would have been nice to know that two hours before we left. We divided the night into two-hour shifts: I was with DeArthur, so he and I scanned for two hours, and then woke Jay and our visiting sniper who scanned for two hours. Our sleep was often interrupted by radio traffic on the intercom, semi traffic on the bridge, or "nature's call" in our pee bottles. We sat on the bridge all night and into the next day, with little sleep, scanning.

A little after noon, Jay and I discussed how senseless our mission seemed. We weren't blocking traffic, but just sitting there allowing it to flow around us as we were told. There seemed to be no point in us being there – as I said this, Heath radioed that he was really just causing a traffic jam by waving traffic around him, and otherwise he didn't seem to have a purpose in being there. I agreed and said we'd been discussing the same thing. I radioed Battalion for clarification – they said our purpose was to monitor traffic. Define monitor, I asked. "Count the number of cars and denote the model and color they are." I answered there were three hundred cars passing every two minutes, there was no way to count them all, and it sounded like a ridiculous mission. They said to do the best we could, and 1SG V (our 1SG) radioed to them, "You've gotta be kidding me, right? Count *every car* that passed on that bridge? Who said to do that?" A battle captain on duty answered, "Stand by."

They finally told us to disregard. I again demanded a purpose for us being there, and they radioed we were to block traffic if an operation occurred requiring all bridge traffic to be stopped – this was almost as dumb as the first response. It came from Brigade and not Battalion, but essentially, we were a bridge standby force. Instead of staying on the base relaxing until called, we were in the city constantly alert, scanning and sitting on the bridge waiting for any enemy to randomly shoot at us, or drop mortars on us, or drive a car bomb into one of our Strykers. All so we could quickly block traffic, which could be done in ten minutes from the FOB if needed, since this bridge was only five minutes away from base. We did our job, and I moved each section farther from the middle of the bridge and closer to the ends in the city, so we could effectively block traffic if we received the order which never came.

We were out of our hatches all that day scanning, until it got dark enough to pop inside, shut hatches, and scan with thermal optics. We were finally relieved at 9 p.m, having been out there more than twenty-four hours. Two exciting things happened: one, a kid told us there were bad people with five guns in the house to our right; and two, we received one shot of enemy fire. It hit Randy's vehicle and whizzed overhead of a mortar Stryker. I reported to Battalion who sent word to 3-21 Infantry about the house with "bad people." We got back to base, refueled, and went to bed, just before receiving word we would have two Counter-Manpad missions the next day, the first from 8-10 a.m.

November 19, 2004

The missions went mostly as expected. I say mostly because 1-5 Infantry was out there with a company sized unit with several checkpoints running with a couple of vehicles and some concertina wire at two points in the town south of the airfield. They also had a platoon or more surrounding an area, sealing off all traffic, and knocking on doors looking for a bad guy or munitions. On our second mission from 1-3 p.m., we saw one of their checkpoints get hit from a mortar or rocket – hard to say what it was as they were so far away from us. We didn't hear of any casualties, but we were upset because we'd been to this friendly town area two dozen times or more and the people were always friendly and waving, never any trouble. Then 1-5 Infantry showed up and the area had enemy presence then. The kids and adults must have known our platoon's Strykers from others because they were still friendly to us, and on our way out, we got swarmed with kids as we watched the town's local soccer game at the soccer field.

Also, we didn't have our mortar Strykers with us today, so the Storm Troopers weren't complete. CPT J called us on our way out of the gate ordered me to give them up to escort him to a few places in Mosul to patrol the battlefield and check on the other platoons. I didn't like him taking the vehicles from my platoon of course, but it was his company to command, so I couldn't complain. So, we had nothing but Mobile Gun System Strykers today. We had a good laugh at the soccer field because as kids swarmed the back of Heath's vehicle, I radioed that his vehicle was like a kid magnet. He responded with, "The kids like Jackie Chan," – referring to SPC Youn (who is Korean), all in good fun. We all laughed. When we prepared to leave, I told him I would 'suppress' the children with some Jolly Rancher candies to 'cover' his move.

We arrived at base, and CPT Jacobsen had a quick company meeting to relay an order from above stating we can no longer drive Strykers to chow when we have missions near chow hours. Earlier at breakfast, the CSM had stopped me and said there was a temporary hold on my operation because he needed to see my platoon's sergeant and company first sergeant in his office. I couldn't believe he was worried about such things in a combat environment. He didn't even listen to Heath or let him state our case. It made us so mad, because it was about a half an hour walk both ways to the dining facility and we had missions at sporadic hours. It would give us zero time for maintenance and personal time during the day between missions. A sergeant major usually looks after the welfare and morale of the troops in combat. Ours seemed concerned about uniforms and driving Strykers to the chow hall – not good for morale or welfare. He seemed to pick on A Company Mobile Gun System Strykers too, because he had stolen our M240s on a previous occasion. Heath thought he must not have liked him, or must not have liked tankers, or both. CPT J said we could still go with his approval, but he would have to 'cut back' the times he approved chow before missions, making it the exception and not the rule.

At our meeting we also got our schedule for the next few days. We had no missions planned and had maintenance and services for the vehicles on a tentative agenda. We ate chow and were out using the phones and Internet when CPT J came knocking on all our living quarters' doors. I was in SPC Youn and PFC Bez's room talking with them, and CPT Jacobsen said I had to get everyone I could ready for a Special Forces mission. He asked if I had all my people, and I told him none of my NCOs were available. He said to gather all the MGS and Mortar Section together and consolidate people, getting as many vehicles ready as possible. As he left, he told me we would begin our mission from FOB Freedom at 9:30 p.m. – one hour from then. I didn't even know where Freedom was, except in northeast Mosul, somewhere on the other side of the river. There was no way to get everyone together and be ready to leave in one hour. Some of our men were on tower guard, so we were seriously undermanned.

We missed the deadline but finally rolled out with all anti-tank Stryker crews, two snipers included, and only three people per mortar Stryker (driver, gunner, and vehicle commander). We arrived at FOB Freedom, and I hopped on XOs Infantry Stryker, then to the Special Forces command center. It was odd there. Special Forces soldiers wore uniforms of whatever kind they wanted, some with full beards and mustaches, long hair, you name it. Most didn't even have nametags, just their blood type over one pocket, and a roster number on the other. Only CPT J was in the briefing at first, and we were allowed in later. Apparently, FOB Freedom was the base for Task Force Olympia, our northern Iraq command. I sent a message to inform our platoon what I knew after the briefing. Our target was Muhammed Khaluf Shakara, alias Abu Talha, the leader of the largest terrorist organization in Northern Iraq. If we could catch him, it would seriously hinder the enemy. We had his statistics, and sound interception equipment picking up cell phone conversations. Task Force had listened to his conversations for a few days and knew what few blocks of the city he was in, but not the exact building.

We left for the objective around midnight, and it was my job to block Hwy-47 to all civilian and vehicle traffic moving east and west. First platoon led the convoy, followed by Special Forces, Headquarters, and finally our Storm Troopers. We crossed the north Mosul bridge to Hwy-1 and passed the street where we'd slept in our vehicles almost a week ago with First Platoon. B Company was there now. Randy's vehicle broke a tie rod at that spot, so he pulled over with a mortar Stryker to work on the issue. I was glad B Company was there to make the area safer as well. The rest of the platoon went on, and we made it to our blocking position, where we sat for nearly two and a half hours. Special Forces moved from building to building, while we scanned, waiting for the enemy to rear its ugly head. It never did.

CPT Jacobsen radioed, "They got him." I responded immediately with, "Praise the Lord." This was the leader of the largest terrorist organization in Northern Iraq, and we were part of his capture. I felt honored to be there. God provided another miracle with my weapon infrared laser site. I usually kept the batteries in backwards because it was easy to accidentally turn it on at any time. With batteries in the wrong way, they don't run out. I was nearly certain I hadn't put them in the right way at the start of the mission, but sure enough, in the middle of our mission, I remembered to switch them out, which is a huge pain to perform. As I was about to fix them, I noticed that the laser bumped into active mode, and I realized the batteries were in correctly. I was so thankful, but the news of capturing the bad guy was even better – prayers answered!

We captured a few of Abu Talha's terrorist buddies too. We heard only a few shots fired in total. While preparing to withdraw, I tried to see if a maintenance wrecker would recover Randy's vehicle. We were told at first that no one was coming to help, and we'd have to return after the mission to escort a wrecker ourselves. We were unhappy to say the least, as it was 3 a.m. and we knew if the roles were reversed, one of our A Company platoons would have had to come out escorting a wrecker. Just then a B Company platoon radioed offering to escort a wrecker to us. It raised our morale, and CPT J thanked him for radioing on our own company channel, telling him how much he appreciated them looking after us.

Twenty minutes later, that platoon radioed to disregard – Battalion said we'd have to escort the wrecker ourselves. CPT J responded with,

"Okay, I take it all back." Funny, but still no wrecker for us. After a delay, we withdrew to FOB Freedom, preparing to move back to FOB Marez, when we heard the wrecker was on its way, escorted by B Company, for real this time. We got word to Randy and SSG N, who returned to FOB's Marez and Deuce, a couple of hours after us (we got back at 4:30 a.m.) FOB Deuce, by the way, is a "FOB inside a FOB" – a new strategy the colonel devised to keep 1-24 Infantry soldiers better protected from attempted attacks inside the FOB. We felt it just kept us prisoners by sealing us inside our sleeping area, making it harder, taking longer, to get to places outside our rooms. We came to sarcastically call it "Castle Krella." Around 5 a.m., I read some of the gospel of John, and called it a night, or 'morning.'

November 20, 2004

It was day again. I woke around noon, which was nice – seven hours of sleep, which may have been the most uninterrupted sleep I'd gotten since arriving in Iraq over a month ago. After quiet time with the Lord, I got dressed and went to the motor pool to get some things from the vehicle and straighten out my hatch area. I surprised Jay who said, "What are you doing here, sir?" I told him I just needed to straighten things out and grab one of my "apple juice" bottles (of urine) to throw away. Respectfully, he asked if I could hurry up and go away afterwards, so I did. It tends to be an insult to NCOs if you do any vehicle upkeep as an officer, since it is their responsibility.

On my way back to my room, I ran into Heath, who had talked to CPT J. The boss needed two vehicles from our platoon to escort him to the provincial palace. I decided to do it myself and told SSG N to give me one mortar Stryker to join me. Heath then mentioned his wife just had their baby Nathan today. I congratulated him and got things ready after I told Jay about our escort duty. We escorted CPT J at 3 p.m. and got back safely. DeArthur, Will, Jay and I traded wisecracks and joked with each other for about two hours while waiting for CPT J to finish so we could leave. It was a good bonding time.

I got an update on the guy we detained on Veterans Day. He tested positive for having messed with some explosive materials, and when he woke up in the hospital he blurted out in Arabic words to the effect of, "I want to kill Americans." He was a terrorist, and I was glad we captured him. I just couldn't understand the mentality of someone who just wakes up from being drugged and medicated and the first thing coming to his mind would be our deaths – crazy. That day and the next were supposed to be days of maintenance, but so far, we hadn't gotten a good chance to get the vehicles fixed up well like we wanted to. Maybe the next day.

November 21, 2004

We did maintenance, although when I say 'we' I mean my guys. Some of us got to go to the Post Exchange on FOB Diamondback, where I bought a rigger's belt to hold my pistol holster (and my pants) up better. It worked well. Higher finally lifted the requirement to wear our body armor and helmet to chow, and I was very very thankful – an answer to prayer. Not much else happened that day, except for a Battalion operation briefing at around 4 p.m., a Company operation briefing at 7 p.m., and church. I went to both services – Chaplain Barnett at 10 a.m., and Chaplain Welon at 8 p.m. Both were a blessing, but I felt more alive in the evening service. DeArthur and Darrel even came (DeArthur after a reminder of God's protection from that RPG).

Our operation the next day was in Old Town on the Tigris River, a section with half a million people and very tight living quarters. I didn't feel good about the blocking position the boss had me in, but someone had to do it, and I knew God would protect us. I already felt as if we would have some heavy contact, but only time would tell. I planned to brief my platoon at 10 a.m., and we would leave at 2 p.m. to execute the mission.

God works in amazing ways. I was just in the bathroom looking for my toothbrush (realizing I left it in there earlier) and I ran into Will, who asked about borrowing a movie. It was a funny "coincidence" as I was just thinking about it. (Will had said the other day he wanted to borrow it since sometimes Jay and I would talk about it). He'd stopped by when I was at church, so I told him to come by that night to get it. He did, and I asked if he was ready for the next day's mission. He shared a weird feeling he would get every time just before we went out on a mission, and how it was scary. I agreed, and the next thing you know, we talked about everything. I mentioned my journals (which I would eventually turn into a book) and he said he couldn't wait to read them, so I showed him the Veteran's Day contact pages. He said it seemed so vivid in his mind and we agreed we were blessed with God's protection and angels. He recalled seeing an RPG coming straight at our vehicle in the first forty-five minutes of battle, and he kept praying for it to swerve away, and not hit us, finally closing his eyes, and wondering where it went.

Apparently, others in our platoon saw it flying straight at us and then it dipped beneath our vehicle and exploded underneath or just behind us. He was sure it was an angel or 'ancestor' (he is both Native American and Catholic). We got into a big and interesting spiritual discussion, sharing miracle stories. I mentioned scripture from 2 Kings about Elisha praying for his servant to see God's army, adding my belief He has an army of angels out there with us, surrounding and protecting us. He agreed, and we compared his ancestors to angels. Jesus did say during the resurrection of the dead, people would neither be married nor given in marriage, but would be like angels in heaven (Matthew 22:30). Maybe our ancestors do become angels – I guess it could fit Biblically [see note].[3] It was cool to both learn more about each other, building our relationship. It was cool too, to be able to share with him about my relationship with Jesus, and how I came to know Him and love Him. It amazes me how God allowed things to happen just then – all from me looking for a toothbrush, so I could talk with 'Will.' God rocks!

November 22, 2004

I was blessed to talk to Becky for a while on the phone that day. I also answered a couple of emails briefly at the Internet center located near my living quarters (across the main boulevard on the base). FOB Deuce is enclosed with concertina wire, but there was a small crack in the barrier through which people my size could squeeze, making it easier to reach the phone and Internet centers and chow hall. The crack was by a power generator that made a loud, constant noise. Some of the guys showed it to me a week earlier; not everyone could fit, but I could barely squeeze through, so I used it. It was good to let Becky know how things were going and how much I missed her. I had taken some things for granted. I never realized quite how blessed I was, even on bad days, to wake up with her and go to bed with her every night. Even late nights and long days were so much better if I could share them with her, my love and best friend.

That day's mission, Operation Las Vegas, had A Company (us) as the main effort again with C Company covering our moves on our objectives. We had two objectives to the north, while they had one to our South. My job was to lead the company out, then establish two blocking positions. Heath and a Military Police Humvee with a .50cal manned the first, with my vehicle and Randy's on the second. We were almost immediately supplemented with two vehicles from First Platoon, and two vehicles from Third Platoon (who joined Heath). The route out was simply north on a jagged road, which I came to call the 'stealth bomber' of West Mosul. The way the road bent, it looked on a map like the wings and tail of a stealth bomber. Heath had the tail tip of the 'stealth bomber' with his section, and I had the right (or north) 'wingtip' of it.

I had a strong feeling we would have contact that day, but my instincts were wrong. Our platoon and most others didn't fire a shot (except infantry platoons using a shotgun to break open doors when searching buildings). It rained hard and continuously, which wasn't enjoyable while we just stood in our hatches scanning streets, rooftops, and first or second stories of buildings. A hiccup on the way out was our military police's .50 cal got stuck in the forward position and wouldn't rotate due to a strap. I reported it to CPT J since he kept asking why we had slowed down. He told me to just go ahead anyway, but I stalled until Heath said the problem was fixed, and he caught up with us. Once arriving on the objective, we set up our blocking positions, blocking all traffic at a five-way intersection. We put up a "Stop, deadly force authorized beyond this point" sign, but the wind and rain knocked it down after fifteen minutes. It fulfilled its purpose, since no traffic came our way again – maybe the six Strykers sitting in the intersection had something to do with that.

The streets slowly cleared out, as traffic saw it was futile to come down our street, and shops closed. Usually that's bad, since it means the enemy is preparing for a showdown with us. Today, it was because they weren't getting any business, and the pouring rain was freezing cold. It finally came time to return to the FOB, and the only thing of interest I heard was that one of the platoons or snipers (or some dismounted element) found some RPGs on a civilian's rooftop. They were confiscate, and I imagine those individuals were detained after the Tactical Human Intelligence Team questioned them, as ordered by the commander.

Around that time, one of Third Platoon's vehicle's engines completely died, and my vehicle attempted to jumpstart it. We got the slave cables out and hooked up, charging their battery. Jay dismounted with DeArthur, while the rest of the platoon scanned. The sergeant in charge of the disabled vehicle scanned with his M-4 since the Mark-19 weapon couldn't rotate without power to the Remote Weapon System. The rest of the company was leaving at this point, and we finally got the vehicle started. As soon as Jay got back on our vehicle, the other vehicle's engine died again. I reported this to the XO, who asked if we needed a wrecker or if we could self-recover it. I told him we needed a wrecker, since the disabled vehicle's tow bar was missing some essential pieces. Just after I reported that, the NCO said his vehicle also had a complete tow bar, with no parts missing. I radioed that change in status and said we would try to recover it with the disabled vehicle's tow bar.

The other Third platoon vehicle pulled around to position itself to hook up the tow bar, which was right about the time that the rest of my platoon (Heath's section) arrived. Heath got on the ground and took control of the situation, which made me glad, since he knew what he was doing, and I'm not mechanically inclined in the slightest bit. It took quite a while, because the disabled vehicle didn't have the tools to disengage the transfer case, and it took time to line a tow bar up to two vehicles. CPT J asked for situation reports every three to five minutes, but I really had nothing to tell him. Instead, I stupidly reported every detail about the disabled vehicle's lack of equipment, which made them look bad over the company radio. I didn't fully realize at the time how humiliating it must have sounded, so later I apologized to Third Platoon's leaders since it made them and their boys look bad.

After an hour, the vehicle was hooked up, and moving. Everyone was mad, Heath especially, because no one from our platoon was helping Third platoon out, when it was our duty to take care of their vehicles. Heath wanted Randy, Bryce, or Jay to dismount (since they are very mechanically inclined) to help our Third Platoon brethren. Understandably, he was also mad at how I reported on the radio. He and I had a good talk when we got back from our meeting with the first sergeant and the commander. He apologized for "calling me out" in front of SFC Burtl and LT Karney, and I apologized for sending up that garbage over the radio. He then said that it's always better to wait and send something that makes sense rather than just pushing the Combat Vehicle Communications microphone and, "Bukawwh!" We both had a good laugh and I accepted his good advice, then filled him in on what had happened up to the point when he arrived at the disabled vehicle. He talked with our NCOs after that, and we all called it a night (and a cold and wet one at that).

November 23, 2004

Nothing significant that day – it was cold, wet, and a nice blessing to have no missions.

November 24, 2004

On this day we had a Civil Affairs mission with a major and some of her Civil Affairs soldiers with handfuls of cash. We were just south of where C Company had been on 22 November. We stopped at three or four places (a hospital, clinic, and school) and gave them money for any damages to the community, while the interpreter translated our apologies and good wishes. It seemed to be successful, as most people didn't look angry with us, but you'd never know. One minute they could smile, and the next were hiding an RPG or weapons cache. It did feel good to be able to help the locals, because it was freezing out there that day, and so many people walked around in sandals. I didn't care if they were used to it, that had to hurt. We only took three vehicles out that day, had no contact, and basically just set up blocking positions. We laughed when cars quickly passed others speeding down a street, then the drivers saw us there (Jay behind the M240, and me behind my M-4), and they would come to a screeching halt and back up. It was as if the people thought, "Oh shoot, I don't think I should go down that road" or "I think I'll be leaving now." We came back safely once again with no incident, and I thanked the Lord.

November 25, 2004

Happy Thanksgiving – a happy one it was, with much to be thankful for. After sleeping past my watch alarm, I woke up and we took crew, platoon, and 'Storm Trooper' pictures. My only mission that day was to be at the chow hall at noon to serve food to enlisted soldiers. It had been a tradition since I arrived at Fort Lewis (my first duty station) and it continued in Iraq – officers and senior NCOs serving soldiers Thanksgiving dinner. It was nice, and I gave people their shrimp cocktails and bid them a blessed day.

After serving, I went to the back of the line, which was out the door (at least one hundred people long), and little did I know, God had me standing in that line for a reason. As it moved inside with fifty people left in it, I noticed Heath walking outside with his tray to finish his meal. I had gotten a ride with him and SFC B in an FMTV (a big army truck) and wondered how they could have finished already. He approached me and said they were done, and he would get my helmet for me since they were leaving. It would have been crazy for them to wait an hour for me to finish. I asked him how they got to eat so fast, and he said when they had finished serving, there were two plates waiting for them, so they moved to a table and feasted. I congratulated him, but the Lord let me know in my heart that even though I wished I had done likewise, He was teaching me a lesson on serving without reward, so it was good for me to wait. I also knew He was teaching me patience (something He does often) by waiting in this line, not to mention it was His will for me to be there. I could only imagine why, but He is full of surprises. As Alvin Darling sings in his song, God had "A blessing coming through, for me."

I grabbed my tray piled high with turkey, Cornish hens, roast beef, ham, corn, macaroni and cheese, cornbread, peas, and two sodas. I felt God telling me I'd have fellowship with someone at this meal but saw a crowded DFAC with no one I knew with whom to fellowship. I found an empty place at the end of a table and sat down, wondering why I had failed God once again (turning off my 6 a.m. watch alarm, made me miss the 7 o'clock prayer breakfast that morning).

Two minutes after sitting down, a warrant officer put his tray down two seats to my right and asked me where I had gotten the sodas. I told him and he got a soda and came back and sat down. The Lord was laying on my heart that this man was a brother in Christ, and I would have fellowship with him. He also had a glow about him from the Holy Spirit. The Lord was whispering to me to talk to Him. "What do I say?" I asked God in my head. "Ask him about the prayer breakfast to start the conversation," the Lord placed on my heart. I looked over, and after the man finished praying over his meal, I asked him, "Did you make it to the prayer breakfast this morning?" He said that he hadn't and hadn't known there was one. I told him there was, but I missed it because I slept in. The next thing I knew, we were talking about God's plan for us being there in Iraq, and how thankful we were that He blessed us with so many wonderful things, especially life in this combat zone.

I told him about Becky (whom I didn't get to call today) and our baby on the way, sharing the testimony of her getting pregnant, despite various complications. We then shared our many close calls, and the miracles God provided, along with His protection while we were down there. He said so long as God wanted us there, we should be doing His will. I concurred, and we shared some scripture back and forth to encourage each other and drive home our points. What a wonderful conversation! I asked him how he came to know the Lord, and funny enough, it was when he was seventeen that he accepted Christ, the same age as me. I finally noticed by the insignia on his collar that he was an Ordinance W-3 (Warrant Officer). I shared with him how blessed I am to still be a Platoon Leader after some twenty-five months, and I knew it was exactly where God wanted me. We must have talked for at least two hours, sharing, and giving God praise. It was so encouraging to both of us, and as we prepared to leave, we exchanged names and emails. His name is Jason Burns, and he was Contact Response Team Chief in the 25th Brigade Support Battalion. It was so nice, and it brought light to why God had me in line when He did, and why He had me sit where I did, which I shared with Jason. Our God is an awesome God!

November 26, 2004

Yet another blessed day in God's kingdom [see note].[4] The Iraqi source who was going to identify his terrorist neighbors was too scared to come with us on a mission, so we planned to try again the next night, after building up his trust on another mission. We had to be prepared to pick up Iraqi soldier and Iraqi commando bodies in the streets, but another company got tasked with that. At first, I wasn't sure whose bodies we would be picking up, enemy or friendly. When I heard it was friendly Iraqis, I was upset. These friendly Iraqis were all volunteers, trying to clean up Iraq by stopping Anti Iraqi Forces, terrorists, and freedom fighters. They were getting killed, mostly because they weren't trained very well, I suppose, but I was sure there was more to it than that. I knew we had God's protection when we went out there, and His protection was more effective than the best training in the world. But why wasn't He protecting them, too? Maybe He was blessing them, and they were blessed to have so few casualties compared to total annihilation. I just didn't know, but I included them in my prayers from then on, and I felt terrible that I hadn't prayed for them to this day. That changed immediately.

Walking to lunch that day, I saw LT Kyle K, who drove a green mini jeep. He used to be in A Company, First Platoon, but moved to operations shop staff. His job had been battle captain (monitoring and controlling the Tactical Operations Center when senior officers are not around). Now he is an Iraqi Company liaison, working under CPT McGrew (Headquarters Company Commander) who is the Iraqi Battalion liaison. A neat job I wouldn't have minded having if I got promoted to captain while here in Iraq, which was likely. It was probably neat to train them, and try to speak Arabic to them, molding them into better soldiers. In addition to wanting them to fight better, they were also our exit strategy. Once Iraqi soldiers and commandos could fight the enemy almost as well as we could (considering the equipment they are working with), then US and Coalition forces could begin to leave Iraq, so it was an important job. While I was still a first lieutenant, I hope to stay with my platoon and the 'Storm Troopers' here in A Company, 1-24 Infantry. It was nice to get a ride to chow for a change, and I thanked Kyle.

On the way back from chow, I tried to call Becky, but the phones were dead. Later that evening, I took my violin to the chapel, and played with others in the 'praise team worship.' We practiced "Lord I Lift Your Name On High", "Nothing But The Blood Of Jesus", "Sanctuary", and "We Fall Down." It felt great to have fellowship with others who praise the Lord and worship Him with instruments and voices. Kevin G, the medic and worship leader, SGT Patterson (A Company communications NCO), LT Liz C (Logistical Support Team platoon leader), our chaplain CPT Tim Welon, and a Christian Iraqi interpreter named Khalid, who was a choir leader at his church in Iraq were all there. Liz and SGT P played the guitar, I played the violin, and another NCO played the piano with us, but I didn't catch his name. We must have played for two hours, and it was so refreshing. I was amazed that even though I had never played these songs on the violin (although I had sung them many times), still God helped me to play them wonderfully to worship – with no music, just by ear and the Spirit. I talked to Liz afterwards, sharing how we met our spouses. It was nice to talk to someone about Becky, because I miss her so much, especially after reading her wonderful letter which I had opened that day. At my room after worship, I wrote the words, notes, and strings to two of the songs we had played. Even if it was God who guided me as I played the songs, someone else might benefit from them. I was Thankful to God for another day and night of life in the wilderness.

November 27, 2004

Our 9 a.m. mission happened on schedule. We arrived at a position where some bad guys had been seen and we were to nab them. My platoon (minus the mortars) had a task to block at an intersection, which we did well. It was scary at first, since any one of those vehicles could have been a car bomb smashing right into one of our Strykers. Our mortarmen transported the detainees we grabbed. We learned one detainee was the brother of a big terrorist leader we were looking for. We got a few other people, but some would likely be released later. I had another mission that afternoon (5:30 p.m.) to detain more terrorists.

All of us, including the ING soldiers (whom I prayed for as well) got back safely to base (God be praised) after capturing about seven bad guys on our afternoon mission. We'd see how many would be released and deemed "not bad" anymore, but that's how it was (a sorting process). We got back at 8 p.m., but Third Platoon was out there later (nearly 11 p.m.) because CPT J saw some pictures and determined our soldiers should have detained the civilians in one of the houses because pictures clearly showed electrical switches and bomb-making equipment. As far as internal "Storm Trooper" actions, some cars wouldn't stop advancing at Heath's position with the XO, so our soldiers fired warning shots at the cars which quickly turned around.

Before we left, CPT J said our target male had a limp, meaning we should detain anyone we saw limping near the objective. Sure enough, one hobbled down the road just south of my position. The road was below the off ramp, so I had no access to him, but as he headed east, Heath and SSG N were in a good position to detain him. I told them to grab him and check his identification while I radioed the XO or CPT J to inquire our target's name. It was Muhammed Ahmed, or something like that, but this guy had no ID, so we weren't sure. He had 25,000 denari in his pockets and we took him where our 'source' identified guys in his own neighborhood as enemy. Our hearts (Storm Troopers) jumped out of our body armor when one of our mortar NCOs fired a few .50 cal rounds at the road. He was startled by his water bottle hitting him on the head while scanning with his finger on the trigger. It scared the rest of us too, as we wondered what kind of firepower the enemy had for a second. A possible sniper shot one round from our south, but only once, so we didn't see which building it came from.

Upon return, I prepared a meal, then invited Kevin G (the brother in Christ from the chapel praise team) to my room to show him the song "We Fall Down." We had fellowship for over an hour. It was wonderful to share so many similar reactions to our relationships with Christ and our wives, as well as difficulties we've had, and our thoughts and feelings we endured during challenges. It was incredible to share with a brother who really understood my struggles. It was a wonderful end to another day of blessings in this place God had placed us. A missionary couple at my church in Washington shared this with us one night: "The safest place to be on earth is at the center of God's will." I agree. They had visited a violent Muslim-inhabited island in the Pacific Ocean, so theirs was a dangerous calling too. "The safest place to be on earth is where I am right now as I write, here at the center of His will. Thank you, Jesus."

November 28, 2004

Not much to report this day since it was a day of maintenance, and my NCOs and soldiers handled that (while I cleaned my M-4 in the morning). Once the vehicles were fixed (except Heath's, whose ramp still won't work right), everyone relaxed for the rest of the day. At 4 p.m. we had a "sensing session" at the chapel, for senior leaders (SFC and above). Battallion leaders told us areas we needed to fix inside the wire but made it clear what we had done outside the wire (in combat) had been outstanding. At 8 p.m. I played in the worship service – which was a blessing. I was nervous playing in front of everyone, but God had my back. My introduction solo to the song "Sanctuary" went well too. After the service, Liz, a soldier who had just accepted Christ* that week, and I called home from the Brigade Support Battalion phones.[5] When I got back and played the violin a bit more, I realized all the songs I played tonight were second violin parts, not first violin parts. I thought I sounded a bit off for the melody. I guess it was because I played second violin every year in high school, even senior year, when I was section leader of the second violins. I planned to rewrite the music and play the first violin version in the future. That was it for the night – no missions or mortar fire that day, which was truly something to be thankful for.

November 29, 2004

I woke at noon – the longest I had slept in this country. It was a day off for most in the battalion, to recover from all our missions. Heath's vehicle was still down, so it wasn't as nice for him and his crew, but they did shift rotations so they could go to the Post Exchange (PX). Company ferried soldiers over to FOB Diamondback to shop and eat all day. I didn't go because I talked to 'Storm Troopers' and spent time emailing friends and Becky. At 5 p.m. we had our company briefing for the next day's mission – we and First Platoon would reconnoiter an objective as we passed it on our way to the northern section of Old Town. While there, First would conduct a movement to contact from the northeast corner by the river, to the south. It was an area where a lot of Sudanese moved to that year, which could have been good or bad. Motivated terrorists were there in the same area with Christian refugees fleeing from Sudan.

I had a great talk with Heath in his room. It started about how I planned to write awards for our guys – ironic as this had been on my mind all day, and I had begun to write them. It drifted from awards to feelings of being there in Iraq and in combat, relationships with God, and with other officers and sergeants in the company and our Platoon Leader/Platoon Sergeant inter-relationship. It was an incredible unplanned conversation – one of the best and longest we'd had. I was thankful for my day off, but I missed Becky terribly. I guessed I could always dream about her.

November 30, 2004

November was over. I was still alive, and still thankful. Today our reconnaissance and "movement to contact" (basically driving around until the enemy attacks you) missions in Old Town were without serious incident. One of our mortarmen's cameras attached to the Remote Weapon System didn't turn on right away, so we couldn't record as we drove past the train station area we tried to recon. We sat in a blocking position and waited for First Platoon to move south through Old Town with the snipers and Iraqi soldiers. They moved quickly, and it happened that the road on the right flank was trafficable to Strykers, so we all moved down it as the dismounts moved forward. We even passed some Catholic churches – a rare sight. I first noticed one because it looked like a mosque, but was prettier, and there were crosses on top. The second one wasn't as pretty, but was closer to the area we were in. Most of the people were friendly in that area. It was nice, and the only hassle was that on our way out of Old Town the bridge we planned to exit on was one way and jam-packed. We ended up going south, through the rest of the city.

We returned, and I felt sick around dinnertime after the nightly briefing, so I napped. When I woke, I had twenty-five minutes to make it to Bible study. I needed to eat first, so I tried to heat water for soup, but my pot wouldn't work, and I realized my power converter had broken. I heated my water in Frank and Jay's room and ate my soup. I got to the chapel with soup in hand, but they were already praying, and I didn't want to rudely walk in late and eat soup during the study, so I turned around and went back to my room while asking God's forgiveness*. I'd have to get another power converter the next day.[6]

The next evening, we had a "deliver Iraqi soldiers chow" mission at Provincial Hall, the main Iraqi government building in Mosul. Others may have thought it was stupid, but I was glad to help foster good relations with them. I wanted to show them I was thankful they were doing their part for their country and show them Jesus' love.

---

[1] *I do not hold such sentiments about the death of others today – see Luke 9:56.

[2] I do not believe today such miscommunications are a sin against God.

[3] Today I understand the dead know nothing (Ecclesiastes 9:5), remaining dead or asleep (1 Corinthians 15:6, 20), until the resurrection (1 Thessalonians 4:13-16).

[4] Today I understand the kingdom to have been present in power in Jesus' day (Luke 11:20), and present now in a small spiritual sense (Romans 14:17, Ephesians 2:6), but *mostly* when he returns to establish it here on the Earth at the resurrection (Daniel 12:2, Luke 19:11, Acts 1:6-7, 14:22, 1 Corinthians 15:50).

[5] * I no longer use the phrase "accept Christ" but the Biblical term repentance (turn – a change of mind and ways).

[6] Today, I understand such a circumstance does not fit the scriptural definition of sin – which is a known lawless violation of God's moral law (Romans 4:15, James 4:17, 1 John 3:4).

3

December

December 1, 2004

The mission was cancelled at first. There were no soldiers at Provincial Hall for us to deliver chow to. When we finished the 5:30 p.m. brief, the mission was on again, but it only required two vehicles: one escort from Third Platoon and the other to deliver the chow to the Iraqi National Guard unit. I got ready, but Heath said, "We got it sir, we'll go" (speaking of him and Randy). I said okay and stayed behind to iron out issues for the next mission. Since our camera hadn't recorded the last recon of our target building (a coffee shop and taxi area across from a train station), we decided to get it done the next day. Enemy combatants worked at the coffee shop and checked identification. If they saw an Iraqi police or soldier ID, they'd kidnap him and anyone with him and cut off their heads. These people were just sick, and they were doing it to their own countrymen. I hoped we'd bring them to justice.

We promoted Specialist Joseph Youn to sergeant that day! He'd worked hard for it and his promotion was long overdue. At lunchtime, we heard that a squad from second platoon on route Hwy-47 at a gas station with the Battalion Commander was ambushed. It was supposed to be a meeting of 'officials,' but the enemy had set up an ambush. Rocket Propelled Grenades and rifle fire came from all directions, and a sergeant team leader was wounded in the leg. The bullet ricocheted from the ground, completely fracturing his tibia and fibula bones. By the time it hit the ground and penetrated both bones, it had lost so much force it didn't even go through the other side of his pant leg. The flattened round fell into his pant leg. He was rushed to the hospital and flown to Germany to get fixed up. He would undergo physical therapy in the months to come either there or back in the States. We thought we would not see him again for about four months. I admired the colonel's bravery, but he seemed to get into a lot of firefights. No force was large enough to oppose our Battalion of over 900 infantrymen, tankers, mortars, scouts, and engineers in our various infantry, anti-tank, mortar, reconnaissance, and engineer Strykers, respectively. With our snipers and other Battalion assets, the colonel practically owned half of the city. That night, I also got to talk to my friend Shelton online when sending emails – good stuff!

December 2, 2004

We had a slow day with one mission. CPT J said intelligence showed some 350 enemy combatants planned to "get their Jihad on" today. We saw none of that. We did our recon of that target objective and escorted a civil affairs major to Provincial Hall so she could talk to the governor of Mosul. All of it went safely. I got to webcam with Becky and had a good talk with Darrell and the newly promoted Sergeant Youn at chow. We reminisced about the past in our platoon and had some good laughs. Darrell came with me to "soldier led Bible study" tonight and we had a wonderful time. We were studying the mystery that Paul talks about in Ephesians 3, and all shared personal experiences with God with the rest of the group. To top off my night, I met Becky on the internet at 11 p.m. (noon her time in Washington state). We finally got webcam *and* voice chat working. It was wonderful to see her face and hear her voice at the same time. It took us about fifteen minutes to get things working. She started to cry and get emotional over the frustration of it, but God worked it all out. I didn't know how we finally got things working, but it just kind of came together. We talked for about two hours, and I went back to go to bed – another blessed day.

December 3, 2004

It seemed the intelligence was off by a day. Terrorists "got their Jihad on" on this day instead. We started with an 11 a.m. mission to block an intersection in the northern sector of Old Town. The infantry platoons were to grab every military age male in the entire vicinity of about two blocks by seven block and have our source identify them. The Iraqi commandos decided not to come so the mission was cancelled. We got new orders to conduct separate platoon missions, and ours was to recon a hospital up by the hotels at the north bridge on Hwy-1 where my platoon and I had blocked last month.

As I finished plotting on our battle computer map, some phase lines (reference lines used for command and control) which I named after my soldiers' kids, we got another change. I went to the company command post to be briefed with the other platoon leaders. We would conduct a movement-to-contact mission up Hwy-1 because the Battalion Operations Officer, Major Beaver, and some of his escorts were under heavy fire from approximately fifteen RPG teams and enemy rifle teams. C Company would move first up Hwy-1, and then A Company (us) would follow in support of them. I briefed my men of the change, and Heath also told them of some thirteen 155mm rounds the enemy had rigged to explode on us as we went by. I guessed they had already exploded when we got there, because we didn't see them at all.

When we left, we heard a huge amount of gunfire and explosions outside the base (some mortars even landed inside the wire), but we saw no enemy ourselves. Our Battalion even sent some 120mm mortar rounds out into the city on enemy targets – US forces rarely fire that size of indirect inside of a city. Apache helicopters circled the city almost the entire day. On our way out, we also heard that a section of First Platoon received rifle and mortar fire at Provincial Hall, which stopped mysteriously after they killed a man with a cell phone and binoculars. He was likely a spotter. There were enemy forces all over the city. Half of the police stations were mortared and shot at with rifle fire and an occasional RPG. I guessed the enemy tried to make a bunch of moves to destabilize the city once again. Fortunately, every Iraqi police station held its ground, and no one ran this time. C Company and our company moved up Hwy-1, clearing buildings and scanning for bad guys.

My platoon finally sat at an intersection on Hwy-1 purposefully blocking traffic to prevent enemy car bombs from coming onto Hwy-1. SSG N and Heath both observed a dump truck full of military age males dismounting and entering an alleyway and garage on a route, and they were all dressed in black. It seemed obvious they were enemy, but we couldn't engage them because they had no weapons. Randy asked for guidance when some military aged males crossed the western side of that route in a hurry, also peeking around corners. I could tell he wanted to engage but they had no weapons, so I told him we couldn't. I told the platoon if we received mortar fire, and they saw anyone on a cell phone with binoculars, they were to kill him, because he was most likely a spotter, and that was 'hostile intent.' It was not only hostile intent by my judgment, but also according to US Army ROE (Rules of Engagement).

We saw no one with a phone or binos, and received no mortar fire, so it didn't really apply for us. Heath and SSG N saw enemy movement from the dump truck into an alleyway, then into other cars which drove away. SSG N saw the same white station wagon going back and forth, so I told him if he saw it again, to disable the engine block of the vehicle, because it was an enemy re-supply vehicle. I radioed company for dismounted support to clear the garage building these "men in black" were in, but by the time help from Second platoon arrived, no one was there.

We continued to observe, and eventually patrolled Hwy-1 from Baghdad traffic circle, to Yarmuk traffic circle, while another section scanned a mosque and Hwy-1 looking south. After making several runs up and down Hwy-1 (it felt like we owned that route that day), I began to video tape it for intelligence later, and we finally got word to return to base. Praise God we made it, safe and sound. Battalion recon had casualties, I believe, but from what I heard, they were nothing close to critical wounds. A CPT Jeff Smith (a former LT acquaintance of mine) was shot in the shoulder, and there were two more minor casualties who shipped off to the Combat Support Hospital at FOB Diamondback across the street from our base.

December 4, 2004

We had a mission at 10 a.m. to conduct reconnaissance of an infirmary, a morgue, and a hospital in downtown Mosul. Before we left the motor pool, Battalion asked me for our route. I said Hwy-1, and they informed me that Brigade had closed Hwy-1, so we were not to take it. I revised our route, first to Provincial Hall to pick up the rest of Second Platoon, which was attached to us for this mission. Scotty (LT Riley) was coming with us with two of his vehicles. He knew the way to the infirmary, and I knew the way to the hospital. We stopped at the infirmary where he moved in with his dismounts (two squads) and the interpreter. After they determined the infirmary did not take people with gunshot wounds, we quickly moved on to the hospital, with Randy in the lead. We got to the hospital (near the north bridge) and my vehicles made a left turn to examine the routes in and around the hospital area. Scotty took his vehicles straight ahead (south) to the front of the hospital and radioed that the hospital was directly ahead, so he would go there.

My vehicles had already moved behind the hospital (Battalion radioed that was where the morgue was). At that point, Heath relayed to me what Scotty had said, as I had not heard all of Scotty's transmission because I was talking to my crew. We moved a section to the front of the hospital to cover the back of LT Riley's vehicles. Heath and SSG N stayed in the back at the morgue. Of the phase lines I had planned from the other day, we determined which ones were trafficable and which ones were not. Second Platoon dismounted and moved into the hospital, keeping me informed occasionally of their situation inside. Heath became frustrated and confused about his role, because it wasn't clear what his purpose was behind the hospital where nothing was happening. He and Frank dismounted to look for someone who could speak English. Someone finally answered him, saying the morgue was at the front of the hospital.

Meanwhile, a mortar sergeant asked someone else. Following his directions, we found the exact building civilians claimed was the morgue. I pulled my Stryker in front of it as Third Platoon from B Company arrived. I told their Platoon Leader the morgue and hospital locations since he also apparently had a mission to recon them. He and his men moved into the morgue, then came out reporting no one had been moved into it except a grandmother. Neither she nor anyone else had died of gunshot wounds. Then Scotty came out of the hospital reporting an individual with gunshot wounds, as well as two kids who had been caught in crossfire from a battle, possibly the day before. Otherwise, our mission seemed boring, because we obtained no leads on any wounded enemy who sought medical attention, which seemed to be the main purpose in checking the hospital.

We checked one more hospital in a location identified by a sign as the "medical city," but it turned out to be a different type of treatment hospital, so we prepared to roll out. While Second Platoon was in that hospital, Heath, Randy, and a mortar sergeant's vehicles moved to Four West Police Station a couple blocks northwest of our position to share the new communication security data upload for B Company's radios and satellite equipment. When Scotty returned, we were ready to go. A civilian had asked Scotty if we could help him by picking up a dead body at a bridge. I told him we could, but CPT Jacobsen had called telling us to return to base to for a communications changeover. I asked him if he needed support before we returned. He replied it didn't matter, but we could come if we wanted. There was no way I would allow just two vehicles to go anywhere by themselves, so we joined him. He followed directly behind the civilian, who led us to the body by the bridge.

The civilian then led us north of Hwy-1 opposite to a route leading to the bridge. We all quickly realized we weren't going in the right direction so everyone in my platoon suspected an ambush. I asked Scotty where this guy was taking us, and he said lackadaisically, "I don't know, we're just following him." I told him we needed to stop this guy and redirect him, because he was taking us down Hwy-1 past barriers our Brigade emplaced to stop vehicles from entering that route that day. Scotty didn't seem concerned about this at all, so I told him we weren't allowed on Hwy-1, since it had been closed off. He radioed "We have enough combat power here; we should be fine." I replied it wasn't an issue of combat power, and Battalion had said we are not to go on Hwy-1 – it was closed. He responded, "If he takes us to Yarmuk, we'll turn around." But by then it would be too late to turn. We made it halfway to Yarmuk traffic circle when we turned off the cloverleaf where Hwy-1 turns west. We were way out of our sector and shouldn't have been there at all. I was upset but said no more. We set up a tactical coil with the vehicles at the overpass of the cloverleaf. Scotty dismounted with his interpreter, only to find out deceased was a friend of the interpreter who enemy had killed for helping U.S. forces.

I only learned of this tragedy during a later conversation. I wish I had known at the time but got no update other than pictures being taken, which already took 10 minutes. We had sat there too long, so I bluntly radioed, "What, are they having a ceremony down there?" In hindsight, it was cold of me to say this since I didn't know what was happening. The interpreter had been crying beside the body of his dead friend. From there, we dropped the deceased off at the hospital with the civilian who led us there and returned to base.

Heath was 'furious.' Worse than the confusion we all experienced at the hospital, he belligerently asked me if Scotty and I could have our 'power struggle' somewhere other than on our platoon radio channel, as if I had a choice. I didn't think it was a 'power struggle.' I back-briefed the intelligence officer and CPT J, and also suggested to him that if two lieutenants ever conducted a mission together, it needed to be stated from the beginning which one was in charge, or CPT Jacobsen, himself, would have to come with us, to stop things like that from happening. I told him I assumed I was in charge since Second Platoon's vehicles were "attached" to me. I had five vehicles, an entire platoon, and Scotty had two vehicles, an infantry section. From the way Scotty had spoken, he assumed we were working together, each in charge of our own platoon, but he seemed to think we didn't have to work together. I hoped this would be a strong lesson in unity of command.

We ate lunch and prepared for our next unexpected mission. It was to go (without Second Platoon) to Provincial Hall and make sure the other section of Second Platoon had the new communications data 'fill' (as it is called) which the rest of the Company and Battalion received earlier. Our follow-on mission from there was the courthouse south of Old Town, to escort an EOD (Explosives Ordinance Disposal) team to take care of an unexploded mortar round on the courthouse roof.

I found coordinates to it as we prepared to move out, radioing EOD (who was already being escorted by the engineers) to meet us at the hall. Arriving at the courthouse, I dismounted with five of our Storm Troopers, the interpreter, and about six engineers and EOD personnel, who were led by a LT Miller. The gate personnel at the courthouse led us up to the roof where the unexploded ordinance was. We secured the roof, as the bomb experts examined where the mortars had hit.

Surprisingly, it felt good dismounting in the city. Other than the times CPT Jacobsen had called me to his vehicle for a meeting in the city, this was the first time I dismounted and moved somewhere. It was a nice change from just sitting in the vehicle eyeing buildings or scanning with our thermal sights. Our bomb experts couldn't blow up the round because it was too far embedded in the concrete, so they got tools to chip it loose from the weakened concrete. It turned out the round had already exploded upon impact, but the tail and fins stuck out of the concrete making it appear as if it hadn't exploded (usually tail and fins explode as shrapnel).

We took the tail and fins back with us, to show Battalion on our return. The intelligence officer didn't want it and told me to keep it as a 'war trophy.' I was sure it was against Brigade policy to keep it, which CPT J confirmed at the briefing tonight, so I just left it in his command post. I learned our colonel spoke to a source of his own on Hwy-1 today, inquiring why the people let the enemy set up ambushes the day before. The source explained how eight cars pulled up, each full of four or five enemy. They then pulled an innocent civilian out of a nearby vehicle, shot him in the head, and then told everyone to clear the streets while they set up explosives (on the north end of Hwy-1). The source asked the colonel, "What would you do?"

These enemies are sick, and obviously have no regard for Iraqi lives whatsoever. I am filled with anger at them at times, which may contradict my beliefs as a follower of Christ. Oddly, I didn't feel bad (or wasn't convicted by the Holy Spirit) [1]about such feelings, because I felt the eradication of such evil is God's will and is not a sin.* It is in fact the opposite of sin. I believe it is love – love for my brothers in arms, and for God's children in this country. I want them to be free from such evil, whether they choose Christ as their Savior or not.

December 5, 2004

The next morning was a neat example of God's faithfulness. The night before I prayed He would wake me up at 7:15 a.m., and at 7:13, two minutes early, He woke me up (no alarm). After some quiet time with the Lord, I moved out to the shooting range with the boys. It was the most relaxed and funny range I've ever been on. I'd call higher on the radio when we shot and ceased, and Heath just made sure he told people to stop firing when we were ready to go check out our 'targets' (pieces of notebook paper, soda cans, etc. we found to put on the target line). I fired well behind my rifle's aiming device, and hit my target several times while standing up, not firing at all in the prone position or kneeling. This is how we fired from our Strykers, and not from any other position. We fired rifle and machine gun rounds from the vehicles from about seventy-five meters or less. CPT Jacobsen fired from Heath's vehicle.

We got back from the range and went with all the Storm Troopers to recon a cell phone shop. We got a good video from the combat camera a mortar soldier set up in an ammo can attached to the Remote Weapon System of his vehicle. We copied and transferred it to CPT Jacobsen's computer, and he was impressed. After lunch, while my platoon conducted an inventory of all weapons and radio equipment, he pulled me into his room to talk. He and our interpreter spoke to an Iraqi soldier who claimed a former Baathist party member worked in the cell phone shop. He was labled as a valuable target. They discussed sending the soldier in civilian clothes to the shop. He would call up the intel officer to say whether the target was inside. We prepared to go as discussed, but it turned out the shop had already closed by then, so we decided we'd go the next day.

It was neat to see how quickly intelligence could be gathered for such an operation. Our current plan was for my platoon to block while First Platoon stormed in to grab everyone in the shop. The soldier would identify bad guys personally at the base, or by looking at digital camera pictures we took.

At 4 p.m. we had a "love-in" as the colonel called it – a Battalion brief on how things were going in Mosul lately. Sadly, two 3-21 Infantry soldiers were killed and four others from one Stryker were wounded. They were ambushed the day before on the other side of the river when enemy targeted all weapons on one Stryker. It was an effective tactic and an awful shame they were using it – scary too. We would have to be more careful. I prayed for comfort and faith for the families of the dead, and for the wounded to heal quickly. Intelligence reported the enemy was planning to destroy a Stryker with a car bomb. They were also planning to begin massive attacks on Iraqi Police and soldiers to punish them for being allied with Americans. I wished we could stop all these horrible people, but there were so many of them, and their number from all over the middle east (and maybe the world) continued to grow. It was like a free opportunity for them to come into the country to attack US troops. We could not search every vehicle in the country. I was blessed and thankful for this life God has given me to serve, love, and know Him better.

December 6, 2004

I woke at 5 a.m. and ran to the bathroom with pains in my lower abdomen. An hour and many liquids later, I was shaking uncontrollably and barely able to walk back to my room, where I embraced my trashcan, trying not to vomit. I crept next door, knocked on Joe's door, told him I wasn't going to make it, and could he please get the medic. When the medic-- 'doc' or sergeant M-- came I described my symptoms: dull intestinal pain, sometimes very sharp stomach pain, and constant liquids at the rear exit. He referred me to the aid station. I hobbled there in my physical training uniform and flip-flops and explained my symptoms. When they took my temperature and blood pressure, my right hand shriveled up due to loss of circulation. I couldn't even open it or move it for a minute after the medic took the blood pressure device off. He said it was due to a loss of potassium and sugars, which caused the blood to be slower at re-circulating. It happened two out of three times when he took my blood pressure (once standing up). After they gave me intravenous fluids, SGT Kevin G came up and laid hands on me, praying in Jesus' name that I'd be healed and protected. I had no pain for about four minutes, but then it came back.

I returned to my room and then went back to the aid station to see the physician's assistant at 9 a.m. Meanwhile, my platoon prepared for our cell phone store mission. By the time I got back to my room from the aid station, I had at least four more episodes of pain and diarrhea. Medicine didn't seem to help. LT Dave V acted as platoon leader. While I was in the aid station, CPT Smith came in to get his gunshot wound cleaned and packed. I talked to him, asking several questions, and looked at his arm and chest.

The 7.62mm round passed straight between his ulna and radius, through two full magazines of ammo attached to his body armor, penetrating the entire bulletproof plate inside his body armor. He showed me a huge welt or bruise on his chest where the bullet almost pierced the last layer of Kevlar of his vest. His arm was healing well, especially on the outside, but the exit wound still looked about the size of a half dollar. He recalled not even realizing the enemy hit him until he lost feeling in his fingers and had trouble moving them. The day he was hit, they just sped him to the hospital, and started fixing him up. He said the bulletproof plates work though, and I told him, "Yeah, so did your arm and two full magazines to slow down the bullet."

It was neat hearing another story of God's grace, and my problems seemed small in comparison. The physician's assistant gave me an antibiotic, advising me to take it easy for the day, only going on an evening mission if I felt a lot better. I went to my room and slept. Heath came by around 2 p.m., to tell me our earlier mission had been cancelled because the target Baathist wasn't in the store, so the platoon sat in the motor pool for two hours. Our afternoon police station assessment mission was cancelled, but we would leave for Provincial Hall in an hour. I told him I could maybe get a ride out there later that night, and he suggested I not bother, because they'd be back in the morning, and he would take LT W, who hadn't been a platoon leader yet, so it'd be good training. I'd just have to pray my guys did okay out there and stayed safe. It felt weird being here while they went out, but they were all capable, especially Heath.

December 7, 2004

This "day of infamy" I found out Becky and I are having a baby girl! Actually, I really found out that night on the internet computers while talking to my brother Chris, who heard it when he called Becky. I planned to call her the next day to talk more, but I was ecstatic about our healthy baby girl. The day started out with me waking up to silence. It was eerie, but in a peaceful sort of way. My platoon was on mission at Provincial Hall. I was ordered to take it easy while recuperating from my sickness, so I was the only person moving about in the entire Storm Trooper area (which the boys called 'Red Square'). After listening to music, I visited the Internet computers, and emailed Becky and my parents.

My guys came back in the afternoon and told me it wasn't so bad – they had it good out there. At the nightly briefing, we heard the Battalion scouts were near Yarmuk traffic circle, and the cloverleaf, when they cleared a building and found fifteen potential bombs. They confiscated several piles of Jihadist information and paperwork from the building. They also found a car wired to blow up, which they detonated themselves. CPT Jacobsen said the detainee's computer was full of Jihad info and had "tons of dirka dirka stuff on it." Everyone cracked up laughing, it was just so funny the way he said it, especially since saying "dirka dirka" is the way younger soldiers pretend to speak Arabic. 1-5 Infantry also detained thirty-five individuals in a city south of Mosul, and twenty-eight of them were on the Brigade bad guy wish list. Thank God we are capturing so many of the enemy and saving so many lives. I know there are still a lot of enemy combatants in the city, but I praise Him for allowing us to find those we have.

After the brief, I ate dinner with my guys, and went to Bible study. It was an awesome study, discussing who Jesus said he was in the book of John, and how God and Jesus would come and make their home in believers. Kevin G and a new believer and I discussed it after others left. Then Kevin and I set up the new drums for the praise team. From 8 p.m. to midnight it felt like I was among brothers back home, and not even in Iraq. All in all, it was a great night, especially because I found out about my baby girl, Katelyn.

December 8, 2004

I told everyone my news about our healthy daughter. I talked to Becky around 10 a.m., and she said our baby girl was healthy but was having trouble digesting her food in the womb. I just wanted my baby girl and wife to be healthy and I was thankful that the Lord had been blessing us so far.

Our 2 p.m. mission was to assess two damaged police stations to determine if they were still functioning and determine the extent of the damage. The first was south of Old Town, easily recognizable because it was about two-hundred meters west of Provincial Hall and had a burned out Toyota in front of it. We sat there for about an hour while our Fire Support Officer and our civilian contractor, Gerry, assessed the damage. They gathered many police helmets, bulletproof vests, identification cards, an AK 47 rifle and its magazines. The station was abandoned and as soon as we were gone civilians looted what was left. This station had five enemy drive by and attack, killing one of twenty-five Iraqi Police. The twenty-four remaining police ran out the back. I felt bad for them. I knew they had no self-confidence and little training compared to us. Kurdish sections of this country had little terrorist activity because the Kurds drove out the terrorists and stopped them from taking root. Others seemed to oppose the enemy as they lost family members and friends to the terrorists. Coalition forces with Iraqi police, commandos, and soldiers weren't enough. Individual citizens needed to support us and stop the enemy, or this war would continue until Jesus returns.

Our next station was about 100 meters north of the cell phone shop (which we still hadn't hit). Iraqi police there said they got mortared every day, and they needed more RPGs. We told them we would send a team to get rid of the unexploded ordinance mortar round in their station. We came back to base and met with CPT J about our assessments. We dropped the police gear off in our company container shed, and we all went to chow.

I watched *Pearl Harbor* the movie (a day late) and it all seemed so different. I wondered if every war movie I see in the future would be different from then on. I didn't even know if I could describe how it was different, but it just felt so much more sad, scary, and personal. It almost made me want to turn it off, or just hold Becky (which I obviously couldn't do then). It just felt vastly different. During the movie there was some heavy gunfire outside, but I was not sure why.

December 9, 2004

CPT J told me to link up with bomb disposal folks at Two West Police Station (the first one we assessed the day before) to blow up an unexploded mortar round. I was annoyed at first because it seemed like we just got every random escort, or "hey you" mission. Heath was angrier because we really should have blown the thing up at the time. I first tried to link up with bomb disposal folks to make sure we wouldn't wait out there for hours. CPT Jacobsen told me to call them when I got out there, but I could see where that was going, so I attempted to take some initiative and find out for myself what the process was.

After an unsuccessful attempt at contacting them from the Battalion radio, I went down to the 73rd Engineer motor pool and TOC. They told me Battalion must call Brigade who then would send a bomb disposal team out escorted by any engineer element. Brigade didn't like to send them without confirmation from a combat unit (that was us) that there was in fact still ordinance that needed to be exploded. Therefore, we would have to do it in the way CPT Jacobsen described, by going out and reconfirming the mortar round was still there, then call Battalion so they could call Brigade, who would send bomb disposal engineers. I could only imagine how long it would take. We got to Two West, and Battalion couldn't reach Brigade about the issue. Brigade eventually told Battalion the bomb disposal folks were on another mission and it would be at least an hour before they could come out to us. We sat and waited.

We blocked both sides of the road in the same spot as before, while the company Fires Support Officer and snipers, with two of our dismounts moved into the police building. An Iraqi civilian shop owner put out a metal sawhorse and an orange traffic cone ahead of our position, to stop cars from turning down that road. Normally, most cars would stop if they saw our Strykers sitting in both lanes on a road, but sometimes they kept coming a little, and after we'd put up our hands to stop them, we aimed an M240 or M-4 at their windshield or engine block. Usually at that point, they slammed on the brakes. This shop owner had put out the sawhorse and cone to stop traffic ahead of time, to help us out. I said a quick prayer for them and for all other Iraqis, because it'd sure be nice if the rest of them had that attitude towards us, and just their own country in general. This shop owner realized (I assume) that it would help his fellow citizens and our unit if he did that, and I really respected and appreciated it. I waved thanks to him and he waved back.

After an hour, I called Battalion again, and they said bomb folks were still on a mission, Brigade had no idea how long they would be. Forty-five minutes later Battalion radioed that our engineers were on the way. They showed up, grabbed the mortar round (since the firing pin was still in it, and it didn't need to be detonated), and we all moved out. We returned to base and ate chow. As I left the dining facility, I saw Brother Jason – the warrant officer I met Thanksgiving Day. We spoke again about how great God is and asked each other how things were going. We talked about this war, and ended the conversation at just the right time, because I had only twenty minutes to see Heath and Randy leave in the motor pool. CPT J only needed two of our vehicles to escort him to Blickenstaff, the Iraqi commando headquarters (named after a soldier from Third Brigade who was killed there).

As I arrived in the motor pool, I noticed all the Storm Troopers lined up (minus SSG N who was at a mortar firing point) and ready to leave. Heath stood with CPT J and the platoon leaders on the vehicle line in the motor pool. Second Platoon returned but had been ambushed half an hour ago at Yarmuk traffic circle, and we prepared to move out as a company to fight. I quickly grabbed my rifle and moved out. A section from Second Platoon moved out with the commander, and our platoon moved out behind the other section of Second Platoon.

We crept up Hwy-1 staying extra low in our hatches, since roadside bombs had gone off just south of Yarmuk traffic circle. Sadly, three Iraqi soldiers were killed, and two more were critically wounded. They were with Second Platoon when they were ambushed about an hour prior to our arrival. Both vehicles had been hit by roadside bombs, RPGs and rifle fire. It was sad we couldn't get them better vehicles. I knew we couldn't give them Strykers, but at least a semi-armored personnel carrier with no technical equipment, just armor and wheels. Anything is better than the 'Nissan Battlewagon's' – Nissan pickup trucks with five to seven men piled in the back. They needed protection when they rolled out of the gate to fight. They had no protection from the ankle to the head, and we owed them better than that. Maybe their ranks would have swelled if we had gotten them some vehicles with better protection.

Their trucks still burned as we got to Yarmuk and I got some video footage of it. We traversed Hwy-1 a few times until CPT J spoke to the Apache pilots, who spotted a large group of vehicles filled with a lot of people headed from Yarmuk to the west, probably fleeing enemy. Our whole company pursued. The pilots guided us to turn north, up near the northwestern section of Mosul (just south of the river). We followed their instructions, and finally cornered the people whom we were chasing. They fled in every direction, and some came toward Heath's vehicle.

As Randy and I watched from a hill (where we once spotted a camel), Heath almost fired on them. He had moved from safe to semi on his weapon, when Frank said on the intercom, "Is that a wedding?" Heath quickly realized it could be a wedding and put his rifle back to safe. After listening to their broken English, Heath realized they pointed to where "bad guys" had gone into a building on the northern hill. He asked for an interpreter up there, but it took ten minutes to locate one. CPT J went up and paid for any damage caused, after realizing there were no bad guys at all, and we had chased a wedding procession the whole time. Even though it was embarrassing, we were thankful no one was hurt. I was especially thankful; it would have been awful if we had killed innocent Iraqis trying to have a marriage ceremony.

The company soon pulled out and returned to base while my platoon escorted CPT J to Blickenstaff, where we sat for about two hours while he talked to an Iraqi commando colonel. We had a good time joking with each other in my vehicle and talking a bit with some of the commandos outside on our Strykers, but it took a while. Sadly, the commandos kept asking us for porn magazines. They would make symbols on their chest, and then a page-turning symbol with their hands, asking for them from us, but we shook our heads no. I certainly didn't have any on my vehicle, and I found it sad that somehow pornography has rubbed off on them from Americans. I supposed that is the way of this world sometimes – one I'd never know.

We returned to base, ate chow, got fuel, and went to Provincial Hall ('proverbial hall' as the guys have come to call it for some reason). It was not bad out there. It had carpeted rooms used as break areas and one dark main room with a smaller room attached where our M240 and its gunner faced out the window. The big room was where I set up my area. We inserted snipers into Two West at 4 a.m. They would wake me up before they left. CPT J radioed to tell me to make sure I was personally awake when they moved out. I laughed and answered, "Roger." He then told us to make sure we performed radio checks with the snipers after insertion every half an hour, on the half hour. He described, "That means 0400, 0430, 0500, 0530, etc." as if we didn't know what it meant, which was comical. Starving for comedy at this late hour, we found it hilarious, yet admirable he was up so late just checking on us. If the snipers were a minute late on a radio check after insertion, he said we must send a vehicle to extract them immediately (ready to start its engine and go). I informed him we had two vehicles ready. I asked three important questions: A) what time would the Iraqi soldiers arrive at Two West to help guard, B) how many should we expect, and C) would they all have ID cards on them? He answered: A) 9-10 a.m., B) three to five, and wasn't sure about C). It was kind of nice being out there in the city away from the base – not as scary as the last time I slept outside the FOB.

December 10, 2004

Various radio calls woke me between midnight and 2 a.m., as well as a firefight across the river at the mosque under construction. Jay woke me where I slept in the main guard room on the third floor of Provincial Hall at 3 a.m. The snipers prepared to move out to Two West, while I attempted to find an Iraqi soldier or police officer to tell them not to shoot at our guys who were walking down the street. I took Will with me as buddy, and we went downstairs and eventually to the roof, where I found a guy wrapped in a blanket in a guard tower. I used my broken Arabic to relay the message. He radioed his buddies at Provincial Hall, and I went back down to watch the snipers go. They reported insertion just after 4 a.m., and after their first radio check, I radioed Battalion (where CPT Jacobsen was located) to let him know. He then said he wanted to hear directly from the snipers every half hour on the half hour, and not from me. It made us all feel like he thought we couldn't handle things, but we complied.

I sat down again and tried to sleep at 5 a.m., but the Muslim call to prayer woke me up around 6 a.m. I fell asleep at 9 a.m. while our company was out doing patrols through the city in support of the Battalion and Brigade missions. They expected a lot of enemy activity, so we went out into the city in force. My platoon (minus Heath and crew) stayed at the hall all day. By 10 a.m. when no Iraqi police or soldiers had come to Two West, I went with DeArthur to talk to those there at the hall. The Iraqi officers said they didn't have enough men to move down to Two West but would call the City Police Management. The City Police were too scared to go, even after the officer said coalition forces would go with them. He told me when they came to collect salaries, the situation looked good, but other times they were too scared to show up to work at the police stations. If they had good training and banded together as a team, they could stop any enemies.

Despite warnings of enemy attacks, I did get in a nap and some guys played games and watched movies as we listened to random sporadic gunfire and mortars throughout the city. There was some more random gunfire around the hall from Iraqi soldiers in the evening and even a short firefight. We couldn't tell exactly where it came from, but when it happened, and all of us rushed to the windows and just then the Command and Conquer game Bryce was playing announced, "Our base is under attack." The coincidence of it was hilarious. Everyone started laughing, and soon the fire stopped.

When Heath and SSG N eventually arrived, Heath was furious about a (battle computer) message he'd sent (like an email) which no one responded to or passed up from the vehicles at Provincial Hall, to those of us on the third floor. I had nothing really to say, especially while he was yelling, so I just lay there in the dark, occasionally closing my eyes but hearing all the responses and other chatter. I had an amazing peace from the Lord that the chatter was inconsequential, and what mattered most was all of us getting home to see our families.

December 11, 2004

We got back to the base around 9 a.m., and CPT J said we had to go on a mission the afternoon with the company snipers to examine the tall buildings in the area to determine where good firing positions were. SGT P (the sniper team sergeant) and I didn't know what to look for, since the commander gave no context of potential objectives for said firing positions. CPT Jacobsen explained he simply wanted us to drive around our entire sector and take pictures of tall buildings, getting coordinates as well. After chow I went to the vehicle about three minutes after Jay did, which is something I planned do from then on. I'd stay out of his, Wills' and DeArthur's ways to let them get the vehicle ready (since it was their job), and just come down right before we needed to roll. It seemed smoother and the past few times I'd done it.

I briefed Randy on the route, and we left after getting fuel. I took about fifteen pictures, and we came back, as several routes were extremely backed up. Upon return, Heath said, "Next time we have a mission like that sir, I'm not going...that mission had zero point to it." Instead of what I wanted to say, I just smiled politely and nodded with an "okay." I went back to get some things from my vehicle, shaking my head as I walked away, and Randy asked me, "What?" I hesitated to tell him, but he asked again, and just quoted Heath's statement. Randy replied "Fine, he can stay back next time, that's okay; we don't need that yelling attitude anyway." I agreed, and we continued to talk as we walked back to the rooms. I didn't help that situation any.

Our meetings were cancelled because the colonel and his entourage got into a huge ambush and several other platoons went out to support. I went to train at the gym (which was rare for me). I practiced Aikido and Will joined me, since he'd asked me earlier in the tour about it. We focused on the basics, then walked to chow, ate stir-fry together, and talked the whole time. We even spoke about prayer and God, and how He has made this life all about relationships with Him, and with His people. We also talked about leadership, the platoon, and the Army in general. I then went to the chapel and saw Liz and Kevin G, so I told them the amazing news about my thus far healthy baby girl, and they were excited for me. Chaplain Tim W came and we all had fellowship. Liz seemed excited to get me caught up on the songs they would play for worship, so I practiced a bit. We all ended up having a good discussion on the frustration of being a slave to our feelings* and being free in Christ all at the same time.[2]

Our Battalion Commander, LTC Krella even came in, and joined in for a while. He then spoke of his firefight that day and other days. It was good to see him, know him better. He told us how proud he was of us, and what a tremendous job we were doing. We told him likewise. It was amazing that he is out there every day driving around, as well as leading back on the base, planning so many things. We'd complained about him at various times, but he was the best lieutenant colonel and battalion commander I had ever worked for. It's easy to find flaws in people when they are in the spotlight making so many decisions subject to everyone's criticism. It was the same to a smaller degree with CPT Jacobsen, and in an even smaller way for me as a Platoon Leader.

The colonel told us of the Stryker hit by a car bomb that, describing it as the biggest explosion he had ever seen in his life, to include bombs dropped by the Air Force. There were flames all over the Stryker, and its crew managed to put it out with eight fire extinguishers, then drove it back to base under its own power. Incredible – he mentioned how crushing it must have been to the enemy watching. They would always film it when they drove a vehicle into a Stryker because they wanted to blow up a Stryker completely, and show it to the world, especially to their fellow "Jihadists." The whole experience was a testament to how amazing God is in this place.

Others left, and Liz and I practiced, then ended up just talking about Christ, and leadership. I knew my decisions were seen, carried out, and subject to criticism by five vehicles and their crews: Twenty-two men, twenty-five if we have the snipers. But CPT Jacobsen's decisions affected and were subject to a total of twenty-one Strykers and over 180 men. The colonel had an even bigger responsibility: seventy Strykers and somewhere between 700 and 900 men. What an immense burden. It was a wonderful privilege to be a leader, but also lonely, and a very heavy weight to bear on one's shoulders. Liz and I shared platoon leader-platoon sergeant relationship stories, and other experiences. Before we knew it, it was past midnight. At the suggestion of my NCOs, I recommended CPT Jacobsen allow our platoon to do maintenance the next day, and he accepted. It would be a fun day, and as always, I was thankful to be blessed with life, safety, and a purpose. Every day that I built relationships with others, I knew I was fulfilling His will for me in Iraq. Praise God!

December 12, 2004

Jay didn't need me for maintenance, so I took off for worship at 9 a.m. and practiced a bit at the chapel, after tuning my violin. I played the one song I had practiced ("As the Deer") and didn't play the two I didn't know. The chaplain used a creative way of explaining how Israel was doing things their own way instead of God's way in the Book of Judges. I ate lunch with the platoon after cleaning my weapon, and stopped at the phones and MWR (Morale, Welfare, and Recreation) tent. I managed to call a few people and check emails. After a 4 p.m. battalion meeting, and our quick company brief, I made some noodles with beef jerky in my room and went to the chapel again to play for the evening service. Afterwards, Heath and I briefly discussed plans for tomorrow's interesting missions. I briefed CPT J of our plan when he and SFC H (First Platoon) returned at 8 p.m.

The plan was to move up to the train station, insert SFC H and one of his squads with the snipers, and leave with his two vehicles to Provincial Hall. From there, his two vehicles with my three anti-tank Strykers would move inside the hall area, where I would wait while his four vehicles (two are already at there) go back to get Iraqi soldiers and CPT J at the base. CPT J would insert the Iraqi soldiers at the train station, attempting to bait the enemy into coming out and fighting, thinking it was just Iraqis and one Stryker. Simultaneously, I would leave the hall to recon the Iraqi Provincial Authority, then link up with waste (poop) trucks at the base to escort them to Blikenstaff, where they will install bathrooms for the Iraqi commandos. This was estimated to take four hours, but we would be prepared to return to the train station if there was contact. If not, I was sure we'd get some reading done. After the waste trucks were done, we would escort them back to the base for the day.

This day seemed to have flown by. I didn't even have a mission yet felt so drained. Part of the reason was because I didn't spend enough time in prayer with the Lord, or enough time reading His word. I hated it when that happened, because I always noticed how much worse my day was when I neglect my quiet times with Him. Mistakes I intended to correct.

December 13, 2004

All went as planned, except First Platoon escorted the waste trucks to Blickenstaff, while our vehicles sat at Provincial Hall until it was time to leave. We visited the Iraqi police, then escorted the trucks back to base. Other than the enemy never showing up for the operation (how inconsiderate of them, haha), nothing really happened out there.

SGT P from the snipers passed his promotion board for Staff Sergeant that day. We learned the night before that SSG Nubear (our mortar section sergeant) made the Sergeant First Class promotion list. Someone congratulated him and he had no clue he was even being considered, so he checked online, and sure enough, he made it. I was so happy for him, because he was such an outstanding NCO, and deserved it. With seventeen years in the Army, he should have made it a long time ago, but as a mortar NCO, it was harder to get than in other fields.

He had thought he would retire in three years as an E-6, but now he would stay in longer.

Frank came into my room after chow and said he'd been at the chapel playing drums, and was interested in playing for the praise team. I had encouraged him to come down. He said he was a bit intimidated since he hadn't been to church in a while and had never really been very "religious." I told him no one would judge him – it is not about people being religious, but about making a joyful noise to the Lord. He said he wasn't particularly good, but I said none of us considered ourselves good and that we were all out of practice, do what we could, and just played for the Lord. He listened to a couple songs with me and said he would come to our next practice.

December 14, 2004

I had been here exactly two months and God willing, I would be home in 10 months, and at least this chapter of my life in Iraq would be over. From 10 a.m. to noon we patrolled our sector, and picked up CPT J. He wanted to examine a few areas. After our evening brief and chow, I joined Darrell and SPC Gumfi for Bible study. There was some theological controversy over branches being broken off and burned in John 15, but we didn't let it divide us.

On the way back Randy invited me in, and we talked for over an hour, mostly about God's will, and the difference between religion and a relationship with Jesus Christ. I got to understand his personal beliefs about God. I recommended a book to him which tackles some tough questions of skeptics. He sounded interested, so I arranged to have it sent out to him. His fear of walking into the chapel or a church service was wondering what he was doing there, like Frank's concerns the other night. He figured people would look at him thinking "he's not a church person, what is he doing here, he smokes, cusses, and isn't about this stuff."

I told him it was wrong for folks to think or judge that way, admitting I had felt such feelings in the past, and even though it is human nature, it is still sin, and it is wrong. It's a shame the biggest fear people seem to have in coming to church is that they will be judged and criticized for coming there because they are sinners.* It is the first place they should be welcomed and encouraged to come back, loved for who they are, but also for what they aren't-- perfect. If a person were perfect, there would be no need to come. The only perfect individual I've ever met is Jesus Christ, and even He is in church everyday. I must keep reminding myself that as a Christian, I'm not perfect, just forgiven. ** [see note][3]

December 15, 2004

This morning was foggy. We went to check out a possible car bomb making factory, and to assess the hospital we had already reconnoitered with Second Platoon over a week ago, this time with the physician's assistant, CPT W. Kurdish soldiers joined us in Nissan trucks. When we got in heavy traffic, they dismounted without firing a shot, yet looked forceful, moving traffic out of our way, so we could continue up to the hospital. At the hospital, a Kurdish soldier got in the prone position with his rifle on top of a parked car, looking down an alleyway. It was very motivating to see how hardworking and dedicated they were to fight for their country. I need to learn some Kurdish so I can tell them how much I respect them, and how brave they are. First Sergeant W, the physician's assistant, and dismounts moved into the hospital with the interpreter. They learned the hospital director had been murdered yesterday and the enemy used this hospital to treat their wounded. Now we knw where to go after a major firefight to set a trap for the terrorists who came for treatment.

We improved on our occupation of the hospital area – this time it was much less confusing for Heath, though confusing for me on the way back. 1SG V wanted to go a certain way back, so I humored him. Heath radioed, "Forget about Hwy-1, he wants us to just go back generally the same direction from which we came, but just using different roads." I was getting mad at this point because it wasn't his decision what way we went back, it was mine. I was about to get belligerent on the radio but decided to handle it more passively and kept quiet while Heath, and Randy discussed the route. Finally, Heath said to me, "It's your call...which route do you want to take?" I answered angrily, "Which way does [1SG] want to go?" I was quite angry at this point and gave Randy a route, planning to talk to CPT J when I got back, because I was not having this happen again. I jokingly said to Heath when we got back that I would just have the 1SG plan our platoon route for the next mission, and he responded "Don't even get me started sir, that was driving me nuts. I'm going to want to fight if we start talking about that."

I later talked to Captain Jacobsen, and after he finished clearing up the details of the next mission with me, I brought up my frustrations. He said I handled the situation much more tactfully than he would have and said I had done the right thing. He suggested something even better in the situation might have been to just say, "I'm jumping in the front, just follow me" and move to the front, leading the platoon from there. I agreed with him, and would do exactly that from then on, if that situation reoccurred. It probably wouldn't, but my tolerance level for such nonsense was nearly gone.

My brother and some folks I don't even know from Las Vegas sent packages which had arrived. I went to check email in the command post and ended up talking to a sergeant who reminded me of a conversation he and I had while at the Joint Readiness Training Center at Fort Polk, Louisiana. It was about his girlfriend and he was concerned they were not equally matched. He had wanted to be with someone who loves God. He had said to her, "What do you have to lose if you give your life to Christ?" She did so and was on fire for God and zealous for Jesus. It was great to hear, and I congratulated him on his engagement.

December 16, 2004

I now had served three years of active duty in the Army. We drove past the cell phone shop to determine if it was still open. We then drove up and down Hwy-1 for route interdiction, once up to Yarmuk traffic circle, and once back, then reconnoitered the possible sites for the alleged car bomb factory. Our afternoon mission was cancelled. The Tactical Operations Center summoned me, and the operations officer told me to get three vehicles ready as fast as possible, one of them being a medical Stryker. We were soon ready to go. It turned out CPT Jacobsen was out at Blikenstaff with Iraqi commandos when word got to him of the location of the second largest high value target in Mosul. He had moved out with commandos to the center of Old Town, joined by the battalian quick reaction force platoon. They had raided the wrong mosque due to bad intelligence. Commandos went in since US soldiers may only enter in an emergency. After searching two more mosques and detaining then releasing three people, the mission ended. CPT J said there were no more missions for the day.

I learned at the 5:30 p.m. brief that the Storm Troopers would be like a quick reaction force for the company the next day. Snipers would be at a police station with a squad from First Platoon from 6 a.m. to 1 p.m. We were to remain in our rooms or at the vehicles during those hours to react if the snipers got overwhelmed. At 2 p.m. CPT Jacobsen would go to Blikenstaff, with us.

As I walked out of the DFAC after chow, I joined Frank and Jo, then realized the whole platoon was there. Heath asked me to walk back with him, telling the platoon he would catch up with them later. During the mile walk back, taking the longest way possible, we talked, and even continued to talk in my room for another hour and a half. We hit just about every topic over the last five days and some which had bothered both of us. He started with the uniform issue, how he had told the men not to wear the black watch cap with the Desert Combat Uniform, even though it was authorized by brigade command. He also told them not to wear the physical fitness uniform to any meal but breakfast. Normally, I complied with the uniform standards he sets for the platoon, not violating them simply because I outranked Heath. I had worn the watch cap all day and wore my physical fitness uniform to chow that night, which he assumed I was doing out of spite. He said the men saw I was doing things he told them not to do, and they were curious as to why I could do it, and they weren't allowed. He said he had decided to allow them to wear those things. I was personally happy when battalion announced we could wear the black watch cap instead of our patrol caps, because I had to adjust mine all the time. It seemed 'spring-loaded' to quote Heath's term, and I didn't like the way it looked on me (like a top hat). I told him I was wearing it not to spite him, but because I thought it was ten times better than wearing the patrol cap.

We discussed the mission when the First Sergeant had tried to control things, and we agreed it should never happen again (I also said I had already discussed it with the commander). He then brought up that he could tell I was angry with him and that I had been acting differently lately around him. He was right that something was wrong and guessed at why, but I said the one thing I couldn't change in a person was his attitude. I told him his attitude had seriously frustrated me lately, and he inquired as to whether it was his attitude toward me, or his attitude to the men in the platoon. I started with his attitude with me, not ending there of course, and brought up some examples. I mentioned how he had brought up the platoon protocol of not going over the median while crossing a route, which I received as a shotgun blast of disagreement with me in front of the other NCOs. I affirmed I agreed with his reasons for the protocol, but completely disagreed with his attitude and tone at the time. I said, "The manner that you brought it up was just like 'raaaa, we are NOT going over that median, and the next one of us that does go over it, I'm going to skull crush them.'" He laughed at my blatant honesty and admitted that he went about it the wrong way, and said he would try to work on that.

I also brought up our December 11th 'pointless' mission where CPT J had us take pictures of tall buildings with the snipers, where I sort of "checked the block" and executed it quickly. I referenced his attitude at the time, and he admitted he was attempting to belittle me then and should have approached it differently. We discussed a few other incidents when he had an attitude and I chose not to talk to him at the time, because I told him I attempt to avoid conflicts with people, especially when they have an attitude I don't think I can fix. He said that he would try to stop himself in the future but asked me to please come discuss it with him afterward. I said I would give him some time to cool off after an incident, and at the very least, I would use the Biblical standard of "not letting the sun go down on [my] anger."

I told him I almost never do anything to intentionally cause a tear or even a small rip in any relationships, because I believe I have two purposes in life which are more important to me than anything else: my relationship with God, and my relationships with other people. I explained there may be one time out of ten when I might be immature, selfish, or spiteful, but most of the time, I try to improve relationships. He admitted some faults or character flaws and shared about how he gets mad when either: A) he is not listened to, B) he realizes he screwed something up, or C) we have radio problems. He said even when he screwed something up and got mad at himself, he exploded at others sometimes, and knew he needed to work on that.

We discussed the night of December 10th at Provincial Hall, and how he was furious about the message and radio communication issues. I told him I had listened to everything he said and everything happening since he'd walked in that night but decided to just relax and listen. He said my lying down when he came in that night irritated him, because Randy told him I had been in that position ninety percent of the time; as if to say I didn't have anything else to do.

This is the best conversation we'd had, because we both shared all our feelings, and gave each other the whole truth. He said if I were any other lieutenant, he wouldn't even be talking to me but would have given up. He knew how I was about relationships, respected me, and said he liked me, and it bothered him when the other LTs in the company (and First Sergeant) sppoke ill of me. He said it happened four times a week or so. I didn't know what they disliked about me, other than questions I asked during briefings (I had recently been going to CPT J privately after meetings to ask questions instead of asking before the whole group). He offered his opinion as to why other LTs didn't like me – they may have felt I lacked self-confidence – perhaps I didn't sound knowledgeable or confident at times, and they picked me apart for it. Heath and I recapped our conversation at the end and shared some personal life and Army experiences. He had tried to stop the conversation a couple times as we talked so I could make it to Bible study, but I told him this relationship and conversation was more important that night.

I was so thankful God gave me words to say, and the honesty and spirit of power, love, and self-discipline to say them, and the timing of it all. I needed to confront issues more often instead of letting them roll off my back, which was something God had been trying to teach me lately, although I'd been resistant to it. Confrontation does not necessarily mean seeking conflict, and if a relationship will improve as a result, it is always worth it. Any combination of three relationships may improve as a result. The person confronting another will have his relationship with God improve, the person confronted will improve his relationship with God, or the two people will improve their relationship with each other. All of this, of course, rests on both conducting themselves openly, honestly, maturely, and hopefully led by the Holy Spirit.

December 17, 2004

Both missions went as planned. I got to brush up on my Arabic with the Iraqi commandos at Blickenstaff, share candy, and be nice to them. When we got back, we had a briefing, and the next day we planned to escort the civil affairs major and her team to a couple of schools in our area to give them money and see what else they needed in the community. I told Heath I would brief the guys at 8 a.m., then studied the map on a special computer program to determine a plan. We would be executing it with Iraqi soldiers, so we planned to sandwich their vehicles between my mine and our 'B' section (Heath and SSG N).

I asked if Frank would join us for praise team practice. He did! He fit right in, practicing several songs. He then switched to the bass guitar because he was more comfortable on it. After an hour and a half, we packed up our instruments and headed for our bunks, as I asked him if he felt anyone judging him. He responded, "No, not at all." (I didn't think they would). We looked forward to playing on Sunday.

December 18, 2004

We went on the civil affairs mission and stopped at only one school and an oil plant after linking up with the major (Iraqi soldiers didn't show up – they went out with the engineers earlier and all three squads went, even though only one was supposed to go). It was okay though, because we managed with my five Strykers and a dismount team from the platoon combined with the civil affairs major and her troops. Regarding the oil plant, it turns out they had a contract for refined oil from Turkey, but the workers were on strike. They didn't want to supply Iraq with fuel because they kept getting blown up by the enemy. I didn't blame them for wanting more security. The kerosene and other refined oils shortages meant the school didn't have enough heat for the children. The terrorists sure didn't care who was hurt by their evil. We gave the kids a couple of bags of candy, which seemed to make their day.

CPT J invited me to go up to the dining facility with him in a Humvee, so I accepted his offer. He handed me the keys and asked me to bring it around – it was the first time I had ever driven a Humvee – not so different than a car, just a little more rudimentary. I didn't crash, which was a little blessing, and now I had driven a total of three military vehicles in my life: a Tank, a Stryker, and a Humvee. I didn't end up going to evening chow, because after doing some aikido in the gym, I took a shower, and felt like eating in my room. After dinner Frank, the others and I had a great practice at the chapel. Afterwards, SGT Patterson and I stopped at my room and I showed him a few songs and their lyrics. He shared some with me as well, and we briefly spoke of God's grace and scripture. Other than missing everyone at home, especially my wife and unborn daughter, the day was perfect, and I praised Him for it.

December 19, 2004

We had an amazing time of praise at the chapel. Frank, SGT Patterson, Liz, 'Guz', Dave V, and Kevin G and I all practiced for an hour then played during the service. God's Spirit moved, and it was simply amazing. Some mortarmen showed up, Darrell too (filming it), Specialist G and even Will were there. Chaplain W and everyone especially enjoyed our "ska" or "jazzy" version of "Joy to the World." God was pleased with our practice just as much as our praise and worship during the service. I was so thankful to play in the praise team – I had never been part of one and had felt called to be in one, but I didn't understand how. I neither had a great singing voice nor played typical praise team instruments. The calling was fulfilled at the chapel in Iraq I never thought a violin would fit on a praise team, but as Psalm 150 says, "Praise God in His sanctuary...with strings and pipe!"

I felt that God had called me to be an armor officer in the Army, and to be a history teacher some day. I also knew He had called me to participate in a peer Bible study, and also to lead a Bible study (not just in Iraq, but when I got back home). I felt called to be a loving husband and daddy, a faithful loving servant to Him, and to love others more daily, growing in all relationships, growing in scripture, and teaching others what it means to have a relationship with Him.

Our mission that day was to escort the First Sergeant to Gezlani police station just north of our base, which was difficult with no interpreter. Heath dropped off 1SG just inside our base afterwards, and we went back out to drive up Hwy-1 for route interdiction and a sector recon. While we were reconnoitering, battalion reported RPG and rifle fire at Yarmuk traffic circle on a unit of ours. I moved my Strykers closer to help, but they turned me down because battalion mortars were about to execute a 120mm fire mission near my location. So, we returned to base.

After fueling up, Heath and I went to a battalion meeting. The colonel and his staff shared their current assessment of Mosul, then he released everyone except for the officers to discuss "officer moves," which is where some officers in battalion will soon be transferred, and when. LTC K mentioned if a new armor lieutenant happened to come here to 1-24 IN, I would be replaced, since I was the senior MGS platoon leader in the battalion. I nodded, but I hoped it would not happen, unless it was the Lord's will. I asked the colonel where I would go if that happened, and he jokingly said, "Chaplain's Assistant!" Everyone laughed, and someone said something about "Ghandi," because when I took a personality test back in May for our Officer Agoge (four days of grueling training at Fort Lewis on little to no food and sleep), my personality type came up as the same as Ghandi. I was the only officer with that type, so 'Ghandi' became one of my nicknames among the officers of the battalion.

If there is one thing I could do here other than my current job it would be chaplain's assistant. Iraqi Company liaison would be nice too, but serving the Lord with more freedom and helping the chaplain would be phenomenal. It was nice the colonel and everyone else thought I'd be well suited to that job (all jokes aside), because serving Jesus Christ is truly my primary purpose in this life. After the meeting, our company brief and chow, I watched a movie which made me think about the life I am so anxious to have with my lovely Rebecca and baby Katelyn. I was so blessed. Praise God!

December 20, 2004

After falling asleep at 1 a.m. then waking up at 4:30 a.m., I prayed for energy as we met engineers (and their two dump trucks) in the motor pool for our mission. We escorted them to Blickenstaff to fill up a hole outside the entrance. They filled the hole, and we rolled back to the motor pool at 6:30 a.m. Before 9 a.m. we rolled up to the dining facility and met up with a CPT and his fifteen vehicles and forty personnel who needed a ride to Blickenstaff. He seemed paranoid about our route and was thankful to have our Strykers with him. It made me thankful to be in a Stryker Brigade seeing how much people admired and respected Strykers. (They also held up well against enemy assaults.) CPT Jacobsen came up with us and the other captain to make sure we linked up okay and told me to just hang out with the engineer CPT until his men finished their work, which would be a couple hours.

They had fifteen vehicles full of mattresses, blankets, food, water, pillows, and other things for the Iraqi commandos at Blickenstaff.

I was glad to help commandos get such nice things, and we talked with them when we got there. Several came up to our Strykers and climbed up to talk. I spoke the little Arabic I knew, and they got so excited every time I knew a word or phrase. While there, rifle and RPG fire broke out all around us, with enemy mortar explosions as they began to attack One-West police station, about 100 meters to our west. We heard it but couldn't see it from the high walls on the inside of the compound. LTC K moved to the location to take care of it, also calling LT Karney with Third Platoon to come as well. I let the colonel know I was right there, and could move out if he wanted, but he wanted to handle it. During the firefight, the engineer CPT came up to me, admitting his "national guard guys" were a little shaken by the firefight, and "their commander was too." I supposed I wouldn't be as bold if I hadn't been in combat before or I was in unarmored Humvees and flatbed trailer trucks. CPT Jacobsen eventually radioed we could drop off the fifteen vehicles at our FOB and return, so we did.

Our 8 p.m. mission was to flood Mosul with Strykers because when we filled the roads, bad guys called each other to talk. Satellites picked up on it and pinpointed where enemy leaders were, so we could grab them in their PJs at night. As we drove all over the streets of our sector, I gave Randy a heads up a couple turns in advance as to where I wanted us to go. It was freezing cold. I wore gloves with a hand warmer packet, but the wind still chilled right through to my bones. My microphone malfunctioned from the moisture of my breath, and so it sounded muffled. I radioed Randy and he answered in muffled mockery, "pahfffh mfffehm prhehrff mppppm." I laughed so hard I couldn't even answer back. He cracked me up a lot. CPT J radioed for us to return, and when we did I still had time to webcam Rebecca, which was exactly what I did for almost three hours. It was the first time in a couple weeks I had talked to her, and it really helped my morale.

December 21, 2004

This was a day I would never forget, for it was the worst day of my life, and the hardest day I had ever had to endure by far. The rest of this war and the rest of my life seemed small in comparison to that day. CPT Jacobsen woke me before 8 a.m., to meet him in his room and discuss plans for an operation the next two days. He told LT Raub N and me the plans since we were the only ones there. I then had a successful mounted combat patrol with the Storm Troopers in the morning from 10:30 to 11:30 a.m. All went smoothly, and we examined a few different routes. We returned to base, parked vehicles, and prepared to go to chow. I was about to walk up by myself through the crack in the wall leading to the straight road, but SGT Joseph Youn suggested we go the long way with everybody else, so I decided to go up with the platoon.

I'm thankful I did. SGT Youn and I joked and wrestled around for a minute or two, waiting for everyone to come out, as DeArthur tossed a football with Heath and the First Sergeant. We finally started walking up to the dining facility, as Frank and Jo and I joked at Heath and Private Jason G's fast pace asking, "What's the rush?" We arrived at the chow hall, and SPC Gumfi needed to use the bathroom. We contemplated waiting for him, deciding to wait. Frank and I joked as we threw pebbles at the porta pot Jo Youn went into. As we approached the concrete barriers on the outside of the DFAC, a close, huge explosion occurred, and I felt the blast in my chest. I looked up as I asked Jo and Frank, "Was that outgoing or incoming?" As they answered they didn't know, I noticed a lot of debris coming out of the DFAC, in the back corner where Iraqis usually sat. "It hit the DFAC," I said, as people erupted, running out from the concrete barriers. "People are running," said Frank. Jo added, "Why aren't we? Should we go in?" We all hesitated, as if waiting for a secondary mortar or explosion. I finally said, "Let's go!" We ran around the concrete barriers, and as we did, we saw SGT Patterson being carried out with a big wound in his leg, and blood on his face.

All seemed to move in slow motion after that, occasionally in fast motion. I saw a specialist held by someone, as she screamed, "My ears! It was so loud; I can't hear anything!" I rushed past the hand washing stations as fast as I could, ran inside and what I saw I'll never forget. The normally orderly dining facility was scattered into extreme chaos. I stared at the gaping hole in the DFAC tent roof where Iraqi soldiers usually sat. It was so big four pickup trucks could have easily fallen through the roof without touching the remaining tent edges. I saw no lighting anywhere; the power was off, and the air was filled with black and gray smoke. I breathed in its taste, coughing as I continued further into the DFAC. There were tables and chairs scattered everywhere.

I stepped in what looked like beef stew – but was a combination of food, human blood, internal organs, and who knows what else. There were bodies everywhere, several dead, many with gaping wounds, and several still alive, many of whom were already being given medical attention for their wounds. I moved to the first person I saw on the ground and flipped a table over, kicking chairs out of the way. SSG Nubear and I helped put a soldier on a tabletop. The soldier had a lot of blood on his legs, obviously couldn't walk, and had several cuts and shrapnel in his face, with blood running over his shaved head. SSG N and I carried him outside with the help of a couple of other people. People outside shouted to take casualties to the collection point by the fire engines in the parking lot. We carried him there and dropped him off, telling him he would be all right. I prayed for him as we carried him, asking God for strength. As soon as medics came to give him attention, I looked at SSG N and said, "Come on, let's go back in." He nodded almost before I got it out, and we ran inside to help more people.

When I came in the second time, I saw LT Karney shouting for people to quickly bring combat life saver bags. I kicked more chairs out of the path to the crater and helped carry another person outside.

When I came in a final time, I looked around for another person to carry. Everywhere I turned was a dead body, two or three soldiers bent over someone being treated, or people already carrying someone out. I caught my foot on something, and almost tripped. I recovered my balance and kept going though, until an Iraqi soldier stood in front of me pointing at the ground. I asked him "What's wrong? Are you okay, where are you hurt?" He started bending down to the ground. I thought he was about to lie down to show me he needed to be carried, but he grabbed a tablecloth from off my foot. As I wondered why, he put it back on the dead Iraqi soldier I had tripped over. I felt horrible, and apologized, watching as he covered up the soldier who was missing a large part of his head and chest.

I scanned for others needing help, and I saw another person lying face up on a table, obviously dead. His blue clothes were stained with blood, and he had a large piece of shrapnel in his chest, and several other pieces protruding from his head. I guessed he was a civilian contractor. I didn't even check his pulse because I could tell there was no life left in him. I stepped past more goo on the ground and found someone to help. He was already on a table, and two people were preparing to lift it up. I asked if they needed help, but they said they had it. I still stayed with them though, to guide their path out of the DFAC (to avoid chairs, as I kicked several chairs out of the way, pushed over a table, saying. "Make a hole!" and, "Coming through!"). Some people just stood in the way, doing nothing.

I spoke to the wounded man we were carrying. The name on his ID badge was Louis Thompkins. I asked if he could tell me his name, just to see if he could talk, and to keep his mind off the pain, treating him for shock. I attempted to keep his arm off the edge of the table so it wouldn't hit anything, and he grabbed my hand, not letting go. I cleared the way with my other hand, guiding the soldiers carrying him to the casualty collection point, where they put him down. I stayed with him, and he wouldn't let go of my hand. I asked him where the pain was, and he said he couldn't feel his legs, and his upper back was in "big pain." I told the other soldiers to get a medic, and one arrived as they ran back inside. The medic asked about his symptoms and I told him, so the medic and I cut open his shirt to feel Louis's back for blood. There was none, and the medic said it was spinal.

I asked God to heal his wounds, telling Louis he would be fine, and that God had already started his healing process. I thought he'd said yes when I asked if he was married, but when I asked if he had kids, he said, "No. I'm not married." He had a shrapnel cut across the top of his nose, bleeding into his eye, and a piece of shrapnel lodged in his cheek. The medic needed to move to a more urgent patient, so he gave me some gauze and said, "If anyone asks, this man [Louis] is priority" (one step below urgent). I unwrapped the bandage with my teeth and left hand since Louis still gripped my right. Another medic came by and I briefed him. I used the gauze to clean the pool of blood next to his eye, talking to him the whole time, explaining it was just a small cut, and he would be fine. The medic and another soldier tried to move him to his belly, but it put him in too much pain, so they stopped. They said he needed to get to the Combat Support Hospital (CSH), as our 1-24 Infantry medical platoon sergeant said they had one more spot for any priorities. I had someone pick Louis up, since he still gripped my hand, and we moved him into a medical Humvee.

With Louis loaded, I looked for others in need, since nearly all the wounded were out of the DFAC. I ran into LT Raub N, who spoke to LT Dave V about CPT Jacobsen. He was apparently litter urgent, and they rushed him in a Humvee to the CSH. I prayed again for CPT Jacobsen and so many others, as well as for strength for us all. I went back toward the DFAC to look for Heath to see if he and our platoon were all safe, and he said our boys were okay. He said everyone was headed back to our company area to get accountability of all personnel, so I walked back with him. He explained how they had 'revived' CPT J, but he didn't know how he was doing now. I didn't know what to say the whole way back, so I just thought about everything, and prayed a lot. When we got back to the Company area, Heath told me Randy had tried to stop the bleeding and save SGT Johnson, our company nuclear, biological, and chemical sergeant, but hadn't been able to. He suggested I talk to Randy. I went to his room but could tell he didn't want to talk, so I said, "You want to be alone right now?" He answered, "Yes sir," so I went to my room. I got on my knees and cried out to the Lord for CPT Jacobsen and others who were wounded, and for the families of the dead, asking why this had happened.

Later, I walked to the aid station, praying with PFC Bivens (from supply) on the way. Our snipers were there. SGT Pena was physically okay, but SPC Gertson had two holes in his back from shrapnel. SPC Pense sat on the other bed, with shrapnel wounds in his back and on the top of his head. Both were shaken up, and I talked to Pense first, since SGT P was with Gertson. I asked if he would mind if I prayed over him, and he said, "Not at all, Sir." I prayed for his body, mind, and heart to be healed from all of this. He said I should talk to Gertson too. SGT P and Gertson were in tears. I cried a bit too as I prayed over them.

I went back to the company area, and Heath and SGT P told me that the two of them had spoken to CPT Jacobsen as they carried him out, saying, "Stay with me, Sir, stay with me." Heath had held his head up as they carried him onto the Humvee, and Gertson and Pense had both ridden with him up the road. They described how his eyes would flutter, and they would try to focus him. Heath told Gertson to hold his head so CPT J wouldn't choke. SGT Pena had even given him mouth to mouth before they carried him out. They hadn't found a cut or any bleeding on him (it was all internal).

Heath said he had walked into the DFAC just as the explosion occurred, and it was the biggest fireball he had ever seen in his life, even in fourteen years of Army training with explosives. He said everyone ran out to the shelters waiting for a secondary blast, and when it didn't come, they ran in to treat people. The first guy he came to was dead, but Heath checked his pulse three times, thinking, "No, he has to have a pulse." SGT M (our company medic) came in, and Heath said "Doc, check this guy's pulse." SGT M checked it, looked at Heath, and without a word moved on to the next body in the chow hall.

As we discussed this, First Sergeant W came back from the CSH and said, "I wanna see all the platoon sergeants." I could tell in his eyes and in his voice, it wasn't good. We sat at the picnic table as he looked up and said, "Captain Jacobsen died." Several people started wailing, crying, or tearing up. He collected a list of wounded in the company, and we told him SGT Johnson had died. As I wrote this seven hours later, I was still in complete shock. I felt life would never be the same. The First Sergeant gathered the company together at the picnic table, so he could tell them as a group. Thoughts of Rikka Jacobsen (CPT J's wife) and his four children raced through my head. It wasn't fair. Why did they have to now face life without a daddy and her without a husband? I thought of how he and I had talked just that morning. He couldn't be dead – he was a great commander, a wonderful man and a good friend. Surely, he would brief us that night a 5:30 p.m. as usual. Such thoughts stirred in my mind, and I was barely able to fight back tears.

Dave and Raub walked up and heard the news for the first time. Dave dropped his bottle and Raub wailed aloud. I felt the pain of everyone standing there, and Dave just sat down on the wooden planks outside of his room, grabbing his face. So many cried, and I wanted to just let my tears fall, but couldn't. When the whole company was gathered, the First Sergeant began to cry as he said, "This Company lost two soldiers today...SGT Johnson, and CPT Jacobsen." I couldn't even watch their reactions because it was so heartbreaking. He cried for a quick couple seconds and then said, "It may sound heartless, but we have to focus on our mission here. We aren't just going to go home because of this." I prayed as he continued, "You need to pray for their families, and pray for each other. Talk to each other, and make sure you all are dealing with this." He was finished, and LT Dale C the XO (Executive Officer) said a quick word, along the same lines. The company went its separate ways, and I returned to my room.

I cried to God, thinking of how wonderful Captain Jacobsen was as a commander, and as a human being. I thought of his wife and family, and of SGT Johnson and his family. I prayed for them and for our company. I repeatedly asked why this had to happen, why He took CPT Jacobsen away from his wife and children. I could still barely type this, trying to collect my thoughts over this immense headache I have from crying so much. I felt guilty as I prayed, because CPT Jacobsen's death felt worse than SGT Johnson's; both of their deaths felt worse than the others I had heard of in the Brigade. I felt so horrible. I apologized to God but felt His whisper to my heart, "I am a God of relationships. These two were close to you. It's okay." That helped some, but I felt horrible anyway. It was hard to hear Him with all the chaos in my head, but I knew He was God, and was still in control, despite how helpless I felt.

I was torn between ensuring my soldiers were okay and taking my own time to grieve. I read Psalm 23 saying "my cup overflows"; I needed my cup to be filled before it could flow to others. I needed God to fill my cup because if I tried to encourage them without being filled with His Spirit or strength, I'd fail. I asked for strength, wisdom, patience, and love. I thanked Him for keeping my men and me safe, feeling selfish even for thanking Him for that. I felt there were no words or prayers I could pray because CPT Jacobsen was dead. I prayed Jesus would bring him back to life again, asking God, "Revive him Lord, please bring him back, he can't be dead." I prayed, "You raised others from the dead, including Your Son, please raise CPT Jacobsen."

I knew as I prayed that God wouldn't raise him; for some reason or another, it was his time to go. I began to contemplate if that was true. Was it really his time? Maybe it wasn't, and this evil act took him victim. I reminded myself that God doesn't allow evil to touch one He isn't ready to take home. I told myself there are no surprises for God, and He knew from the day CPT Jacobsen was born that he would die at that time.* I reminded myself that CPT J had already heard the words, "Well done, good and faithful servant," from his and my Lord and Savior Jesus Christ.** Bill Jacobsen was a Mormon, but more importantly, the love of Jesus shined from him. I knew that he was in heaven, and I must find peace in that, though I was devastated by his loss [see note].[4]

No one knew if it was a mortar or a bomb from inside the DFAC. I had heard both. The snipers and others inside said it was a giant fireball that exploded upward, yet the news and the Pentagon stated that it was a rocket attack. At 4:30 p.m. battalion held formation. One by one and in small groups I talked to about half of the platoon just beforehand, feeling more filled with strength. As we formed up, I noticed CPT WanTarp standing behind us, and I wondered if he would now be our Company Commander. I prayed for LTC Krella as he stood before us and began to speak. I never thought I'd see him cry, but I did that day. He said 1-24 Infantry had lost four soldiers: CPT Jacobsen and SGT Johnson from A Company, and two other names from 73rd Engineers (a unit attached to our battalion). He fought tears and choked up as he told us CPT Jacobsen was a great warrior and human being, and so was SGT Johnson.

He told us they still didn't know what the attack was (I assumed they would have a point of origin if it was a mortar or rocket attack). He said so far there were 22 dead, and 55 wounded from the Brigade. He then explained there would be a day to grieve, but we must now focus on the mission, as the enemy wanted nothing more than for us to stay inside the FOB and be scared because of this. He said we must fight this war and accomplish our mission, then told us to fall back into formation. After releasing the rest of the battalion, he told us CPT WanTarp would be our new Company Commander effective immediately, with no ceremony because we were in combat.

I was thankful to have CPT Wan, because I knew he also loved the Lord, and was a wonderful captain. I just wished it hadn't been because of losing CPT Jacobsen. We all went back to the company command post and had a quick brief with CPT Wan about that night's plans and the next operation. Heath pulled me aside afterward and said I needed to get myself together because it was all over my face that I wasn't handling this well and we couldn't afford to let the soldiers see me like that because it would kill morale. I wanted to slap him for expecting me to have a happy face just five hours after the death of my commander, friend, and brother in Christ – but he was right. I needed to show confidence and help the men know everything would be okay, or our platoon would be in serious trouble. He said I needed to make sure I had on a different face before I talked to our soldiers again. I prayed about it, then briefed the NCOs on the plans for the next day.

I forced a smile, sounding open and upbeat about the plans. After everyone's questions, I spoke to SSG N and Heath, then later just Heath in his room. I asked if I did better. He said he could still tell from my face, but, "Yes, you did look a lot better just talking to the guys." He reminded me of our talk the other night about confidence, adding if there was ever a time I needed more, it was then. He even said sometimes I should just tell him to shut up on the radio and say, "Roger! I GOT IT!" I laughed and said, "Okay." I felt cheap and worthless discussing leadership and confidence or feelings of being in the DFAC, compared to CPT Jacobsen's death. I supposed that was natural, but I did know God had me there for a reason, and it was not to flounder as a leader, so Heath was right once again. He said that day had really given him doubts about surviving this war. It was probably safe to say everyone in the company, maybe even everyone in the battalion, was having those doubts.

I heated up soup I had just received from my uncle Steve in the mail. He sent me every type of meal to cook, heat up, and prepare, along with oatmeal and snacks. Now that the chow hall would not be opened for a while, I would need them. Scary times, but I knew God would get us through them. I had a knock on my door as I listened to some praise music. It was LT Dale K, the XO, who said the brigade psychologist and the chaplain would be at the chapel talking to people on a case-by-case basis. He said Heath relayed that I had had trouble dealing with things, so I might want to go down there. Dale said, "I'm sure I'll have my day, I just don't think it has all hit me yet." I told him it hit me all at once and I had already had "my day." He reminded me to make sure my men didn't see it, and added he was available anytime I needed to talk. I told him I appreciated it – I didn't know if it was a personality conflict, or if he just had little respect for me as a peer, but I had always felt an intense disapproval from him, so his offer really meant a lot to me.

The new was on the chapel television, already reporting the incident. Some reporter had been in the dining facility taking pictures. SSG N said he kicked out the reporter while evacuating casualties and LT Raub N said he punched him after telling him to get out for the third time. They were reporting the incident as a rocket attack, and apparently a terrorist group was already claiming credit for it, calling it an attack on their 'occupiers' on 12/21/04. No one here believed it was a rocket and were convinced someone brought a bomb into the DFAC. Our battalion sent platoons throughout the base to search the post exchange and other shops, latrines, and even our rooms, to sweep for anything that looked like a bomb. We couldn't believe the news shared pictures of bodies, the hole in the DFAC, and soldiers evacuating people. It reported Forward Operating Base Marez in Mosul suffered a rocket attack that exploded at the chow hall around noon, at the height of lunchtime, with at least 22 dead and 55 wounded. We could only imagine what our families were thinking.

Our base Internet was shut down with a warning it would be a field grade article fifteen offense if any were caught near phone centers. We had no way to tell our families what happened, or even that we were okay. I had never more desperately wanted to go home or just to hold Becky tight and never let go, but it would still be at least another four months until that time came. Most of us in the company, if not the entire base, now felt anyone could go at any minute. There were no assurances or certainties of life at this point. I knew God would command angels to protect as in Psalm 91 and "no scourge shall come near [my] tent." I trusted He would deliver those who love him, and "with long life I will satisfy them" but I also knew CPT William Jacobsen loved God. Eternal life, God, and Jesus were not scary – it was the loved ones left behind to grieve and mourn if I died. My amazing wife and daughter could possibly grow old without their husband and daddy. I must trust God, knowing our lives were in His hands, and He would care for all of us and all our families, whether we lived or died. I knew if He had great plans for me on this earth, nothing could stop them.

At evening Bible study, Randy and the company snipers came to hang out at the back to listen and wait for their turns to talk to the chaplain and the brigade psychologist. We had a good talk about death, and whether we are immediately sharing eternity with Jesus when we die, or whether we "sleep in Jesus" until the resurrection at the end of mankind, to be awakened to live with Him then. We then shared stories of the day and explained why each of us thought God allowed evil to endure in the world. I left for a final meeting at the command post to discuss plans for the next day with CPT Wan and the other officers in the company. Our patrols would be from 10 p.m. to 6 a.m. the next day.

During our meeting, the entire command post shook, and we heard a loud boom outside. A car bomb exploded at an Iraqi checkpoint, just outside the base. It was so big we felt it almost a mile away. This day was simply the absolute hardest day I'd had to endure by far. I had lost family members growing up, mostly grandparents, and I had lost close friends, adults, and young adults I grew up with. I had lost two friends this past year, one of whom was my best friend for three years or more. Both committed suicide; one by a drug overdose and the other jumped off a balcony after he realized his ex-girlfriend would never be with him again. Both losses hurt tremendously, and I grieved their losses, but nothing seemed as bad as that day. CPT Jacobsen was more than my commander. He seemed a wonderful husband to his wife Rikka, and an amazing dad to his four kids. It still just didn't seem fair; I could do nothing about it. I knew this day would be burned into my mind for the rest of my life.

CPT Jacobsen's words echoed in my mind constantly. The words he spoke just that day, the day before, a week ago, and the two months we'd been there so far. I was still not sure if it was a bomb or a rocket, but if it was a bomb brought into the DFAC, a particular phrase would echo in my mind the rest of my life. Captain Jacobsen said it on numerous occasions, at least three times I could recall. When we first got pictures of FOB Sykes back at Fort Lewis and heard US troops allowed many Iraqis on bases to sell things, work in facilities, eat in the chow hall, and sleep, he said, "Yeah, we'll probably continue to let that happen until someone brings a bomb into the DFAC one day, and then everyone will learn to tighten up security. It isn't a good idea to let these people on our FOB." I heard him say it at Fort Lewis, and at FOB Sykes, before we moved to FOB Marez. If it was a bomb brought inside by some suicide bomber somehow, it would be the eeriest thing that ever echoed in my mind. It would almost seem he had a premonition, but perhaps it was just his logical thinking.

I missed him immensely, and the rest of this tour would be exceedingly difficult, as if it weren't bad enough already. I could only ask God for strength, wisdom, patience, and love to continue to fight this war against evil men and evil principalities, continuing to lead others to Him through His Son, Jesus. I prayed He would continue to protect us, our families, and that He would especially surround CPT Jacobsen's family, SGT Johnson's family, and all the other victims with His abounding love. It must hurt a hundred times worse for them. I didn't know how anyone could bear this without strength from the Lord. I prayed He would continue to help me lead my men with a spirit of power, love, and self-discipline, and that we could all learn from this event, to stop it from happening again if possible. I prayed for our new commander, CPT 'Van.' The burden of taking over his friends' company may be greater than I could imagine. This war was a terrible thing. The only reason I could think of to continue fighting in it was so these terrorists couldn't do things like this at home to our families and innocent civilians. That day was an up close and personal taste of what September 11, 2001 must have been like for victims and their friends and families. Life just seemed so confusing, but I found hope in Jesus.

December 22, 2004

After prayer and scripture, I went out and talked to the men. We shared our feelings about the bombing and what we saw and heard. SGT Cruver (a mortar NCO) was thankful he had decided not to go to the chow hall. He told me how his first concern was whether the Storm Troopers were okay, and when he heard the snipers were hit, he was devastated. He mentioned how they used to make fun of Pense for being short, and Pense used to wish he were taller, but after that awful day, he was thankful for his height. If he had been just a half an inch taller, the shrapnel that grazed the top of his scalp would have gone into his brain.

While SGT Cruver and I spoke, a huge boom came from the other side of the concrete barriers (blast walls) at the end of our platoon living area. An unconfirmed enemy mortar had just landed inside the FOB. I talked to SPC Gertson, and he told me one of the pieces of shrapnel in the chow hall had exited under his right arm. He described how he was sitting with CPT J, the XO, and SGT Pena talking about plans for the upcoming missions, when he saw a huge orange flash out of the corner of his eye and suddenly was struck by a tremendous heat wave. He immediately turned to check on CPT Jacobsen, who lay there beside him. The commander's last words were, "I'm okay, check on my men." He thinks CPT Jacobsen probably couldn't even feel his injury as he was lying there. He must have been bleeding internally without knowing it.

I wrote letters to everyone who sent me packages. It really improved my spirits to feel the love from friends and family who sent stuff. Randy came into my room later and we shared stories, asking each other if we were all right. He told me when he entered the chow hall, he saw a humungous fireball. He ran to the area where the plastic eating utensils were and began to treat someone bleeding out of his neck and jaw. He didn't even realize it was our chemical sergeant, SGT Johnson. He had help carrying him outside, and eventually laid him down to try CPR and a trachea pipe. After a few minutes, Randy and a medic realized there was nothing else they could do for him. He was dead, so Randy tried to get a body bag after covering SGT Johnson's face. Then he moved on to other wounded. We talked about SGT Johnson and CPT Jacobsen and how crazy everything was.

I really wanted to get out of the Army at that point, but God waned me in, so I had to stay. This hurt a lot though. As I wrote letters to friends and family thanking them for packages, support, and prayers, I explained the tragedy to them. Thisday was better than the day before, but my heart still ached with a pain only God could heal. I knew He would in time, yet part of me felt like this pain would be there my whole life. I didn't know how to explain it myself because it was so confusing. A sergeant said to me today, "It must have been his time." I agreed, but it still didn't make sense. Why when he had a wife and four young children who needed him? Nothing about it felt like it was his time to go; yet perhaps it was. I couldn't fathom how it all works –

what God allows. Perhaps many will come to know Jesus through this horrible incident, and perhaps others will grow in their faith. I don't know how to make sense of it, but I knew God did.

We would leave in one hour for our all-night missions. We planned to return at 6 a.m. I prayed the Lord would place His hedge of protection around us all, surrounding us with His angels. I prayed He would give us wisdom and strength to make and carry out good decisions and that no harm would come to us, not even a small scratch. I prayed He would confuse, slow and hinder the enemy, and that they would be extremely inaccurate. I prayed He would keep us fast, accurate, effective, and aware.

December 23, 2004

This day was rough, but I did it with God's strength. There was pain, hurt, and strife in our hearts, and even some platoon drama. I was so thankful we made it back safely from our patrols the night before. A huge blessing, and I was extremely grateful we made no contact.

We first went to Provincial Hall to pick up a section of third platoon and began to patrol every police station in our company area, and then had orders to escort two dump trucks to a bridge. Our waiting was in vain – after sitting just outside the FOB for nearly twenty minutes, we finally received word from Battalion that Brigade no longer needed us to escort the dump trucks, so we moved out to continue our patrols.

Being outside the wire for the first time since CPT Jacobsen and SGT Johnson died felt very strange. I was able to focus on the combat patrol, scanning houses, alleyways, cars, and rooftops, but I thought of them often, especially CPT J. It felt weird every time I radioed his call-sign, and CPT WanTarp answered instead of CPT Jacobsen. I kept hoping I would hear CPT Jacobsen's voice, but knew I would never hear it again. It saddened me so much, but still, I scanned and told Randy where to lead us. I still talked to my crew, acting slightly jovial, as if nothing were wrong, as if I hadn't just lost a friend, commander, and brother in Christ the other day to terrorism. I almost got mad at myself for it, but I knew these men needed to see dedication to them and this cause, not an upset and grieving platoon leader. So that was what I gave them.

The night air was bitterly cold, and my fingertips stung as we rolled down every street, at roughly fifteen miles an hour. There was little wind even, and I would alternate my hands from the trigger of my M-4 to the inside of my hatch, but still my fingers froze from the freezing cold night air. We went to Provincial Hall for a few breaks to grab an hour of sleep in our vehicles in the parking lot, but continued patrols until our last patrol from 4-6 a.m. It wasn't too bad except for the cold, and the boredom of dark and lifeless streets. After a while, I didn't even have to tell Randy where to go, because he was almost reading my mind and our movement was as smooth as glass. We passed by every police station in our area, moving up and down almost every street in our area, except the one block CPT J hadn't wanted us to go near without dismounted support.

I missed him so much. I knew the reason I missed him was the fact that I would never see him again this side of heaven. It was also because his wife and kids and other family and friends would live the rest of their lives without him here on earth with them. He was the best company commander I ever had. One of the best officers I've ever known was dead. I couldn't imagine how hard it must be for CPT WanTarp. He was close friends with CPT Jacobsen too, perhaps even closer than I, since they were peers. They worked on battalion staff together before CPT Jacobsen assumed command of A Company back in August. CPT Wan now commanded this company his friend and peer had – due to a quick and horrible death. He must deal with the sadness and confusion, picking up where CPT J had left off, filling his shoes, without completely knowing what was going on, and where those shoes had walked.

I still remember when CPT Jacobsen took command. He was so meticulous when signing for the company's equipment. We complained about how particular he was and how he seemed to want to work longer hours than the rest of us. I later came to respect and admire him for his attention to detail, his responsibility, and his work ethic. When I made it to his house for a BBQ about a month before we left the States, I got to know his wife and kids a little better. I saw his house, and the many pictures showing how much of a family man he was. He genuinely loved his wife and kids, and it showed all over him. From the day he took command of our company, he put his all into being the best leader he could be. He was training and family focused. If we completed our "five by five," he made sure we could go home early to be with our families.

"Five by five" was his concept of completing five training tasks by 5 p.m.: 1) Battle Drills, 2) Marksmanship Training, 3) Military Knowledge, 4) First Aid, and 5) Physical Training. We did them every day in some form or fashion, and I thought it was a brilliant training standard. He ran training meetings well, stuck to a timeline, and always accepted the input of other leaders in the company. He would sometimes meet with platoon leaders and sergeants (sometimes together, sometimes separately) to discuss how we had done a certain thing in the past, what worked, and what to change. He genuinely cared about every family, every soldier, and every mission. I even remembered him mentioning at our last meeting with all of the wives and families, "I'm a firm believer in the power of prayer, and I know that if you pray for us, that will make more of a difference than anything else you could do." My biggest regret was I never got to thank him or tell him what he meant to me. I tried to show it every day, but kind and encouraging words would have gone so much farther. I wished I could go back and tell him how wonderful it was to work with him, and what an impact he made on me. It was a huge responsibility to be a leader. Each decision affected so many who are critical of those decisions and might think they have a better idea. I knew the burden he faced at times, and it was such a sacrifice.

We returned to base from our night patrol and went to bed around 7 a.m. I woke and had to meet CPT Wan at the battalion TOC at 3 p.m. COL Brown, our brigade commander was talking to him. While I was waiting, I spoke to another lieutenant, who is the battalion mortar platoon leader. We asked each other how the other was doing, and then shared stories from the DFAC explosion. It turned out it wasn't a rocket attack at all. Explosives Ordinance Disposal experts and the FBI/CIA, after studying the chow hall and blast site/crater, determined by the evidence of all the ball bearings, grease, and C4 explosives, that it was in fact a suicide bomber. He said they even found a backpack with burned body parts still on it, that had some ball bearings still inside, although later I heard explosives were worn under the bomber's Iraqi Army jacket. It was a regular Iraqi Army soldier who walked in there with a backpack explosive during lunch and blew himself and twenty-two others in the DFAC to their deaths.

This LT I spoke with was 10 feet from the explosion, and only had a scratch on his foot. From where he was, he swore it was an 82mm mortar, but admitted he was wrong. He began treating people, one of whom was my old first sergeant from A Troop, 2-14 Cavalry Regiment, First Sergeant Shane Briel. His intestines were hanging out, and he had them, blood, and other things all over his face. LT Pry described how he had put what he could back in, and used gauze pads and other medical equipment to patch the 1SG up, while he was still conscious, inquiring, "What is wrong with my face?" And, "What about my head?" Pry answered, "First Sergeant, it looks beautiful, you're fine, hold still!" It turns out First Sergeant Briel was evacuated by air to a hospital either somewhere in Iraq, or most likely Germany. He was expected to be fine.

I shared with him CPT Jacobsen's words on the DFAC, "See, we are letting all these [Iraqis] in there, and all these other workers and stuff, and watch, one day, someone is going to bring a bomb in and blow up the DFAC, and then we'll finally learn and tighten up security." It would always give me chills. Pry said that he knew CPT J had no visible wounds, but blood had come out of his eyes, nose, and mouth, and he had surmised it must have been a traumatic brain injury. Who could say if it was due to the shock of the blast, or him hitting his head on the ground? It is just so sad.

Eventually, I went out to meet CPT WanTarp when he finished talking to COL Brown. He briefed me on my 6 p.m. mission to bring sandbags to the Gizlani Police Station, then route interdiction and escort missions until 8 p.m. I asked a few questions, got the answers, and went to brief the platoon. I told Heath that the sandbags were already filled and in the back of a truck in the motor pool, and we just needed to get them loaded on the mortar Strykers. We would load 225 of them. Heath said the NCOs and enlisted would load sandbags at at 5:15 p.m.

At 5:45 p.m., they were still loading sandbags. I walked up and asked if they would all fit, and Heath started asking me questions. "Why are we giving sandbags to some ungrateful people that won't even wear the Kevlar helmets and body armor that we gave them?" Just as quickly as I answered, "I don't know," the next one was out of his mouth, and he was shaking his head. "Do we even have an interpreter or a point of contact for this police station? How are we even supposed to get the sandbags up to the building when there are blast walls all around the entrance?" SGT Cruver and a couple others were looking strangely at us both, but there was a different unreadable look in their eyes when they stared at Heath and I wondered why he was doing this in front of them. It seemed he was suddenly furious at Iraqis, and with the mission as well.

He pointed away from everyone and requested to talk on the other side of the motor pool, and then it became completely obvious to me. He was losing it. He asked every question again and asked me if I even asked the commander any of those questions. I told him some of them I had, but not all of them, and he said, "I don't want to give any of those [expletive] anything after the other day! You can't answer me why we are giving them these sandbags?!? That's okay, I'm going to talk to the First Sergeant about this!" Again, I could feel his hurt, and had no answer for his question. He yelled, "They blew up OUR COMMANDER, sir, why are we helping them!" I realized he needed to hear what he had said to me the day CPT Jacobsen died. He needed to get himself together, because it was apparent to me, he was flipping out from the moment he bombarded me with questions in front of the others. I knew it would be one of those days where we would talk after the missions, keeping true to my word of telling him when there was a problem, and not letting the sun go down on my anger. I answered his question about the interpreter by saying I knew enough Arabic to say what was needed. As he vented to First Sergeant, I went to the TOC and discovered we had no point of contact at the police station.

Heath had been silent during our briefing from CPT Wan, but it was an appropriate time to ask his questions. In private with me afterward would have been fine too. But not in front of our men at the last minute before a planned mission. I was angry that he was doing exactly what he had accused me of just five hours after losing Captain Jacobsen: 'not having it together.' Was his anger better than my sorrow? It was not good for the soldiers to see either of those things right then. I knew he had really lost it when he said, "If we receive any tracer fire when we are out there, I'm shooting 360 degrees, and I don't care if those [expletive] are hit at the police station or not!" It sounded as if, in his mind, every single Iraqi was the enemy.

LTC Krella and CPT WanTarp both told all of us in the company that now was the time we must really watch our soldiers and be leaders, especially the officers and sergeants. When so many of us were angry after an attack was the greatest possibility of war crimes occurring. I spoke in confidence to someone about some issues which bugged me – he agreed completely, saying he had noticed angry discriminating talk against the Iraqis.

At the police station I asked in Arabic, "*minu almesul* (who is in charge)?" The Iraqi police and soldiers took me to their leader who was in a room filled with smoke. I found it hard to talk because I started choking and could barely breathe. I asked for his help, "*Sa id ne!*" and said, "*Ye-laa!* (Come on, hurry up!)". They walked outside and started carrying sandbags. I went in again and asked how many cans of fuel they needed, since CPT Wan needed to know, because we were responsible to supply them. "*Tehtaj benzene* (Do you need gasoline/kerosene)?" They answered 'yes,' so I asked, "*Ish ged* (How many)?" They answered "*Ithnayn* (two)", so I told them I would bring some tomorrow, "*In Sha'alla* (God willing)." After unloading the sandbags and moving back to base for our second trip, we did route interdiction, then returned for the day.

Before our 9 p.m. meeting, I went into Heath's room to talk, saying, "I'm here to keep my word and tell when there is a problem, and not let the sun go down on my anger." He answered, "Yeah, I thought you had a sore butt about some things. Lemme first just say, though, that if this is about my attitude towards those [expletive], you're wasting your time, because right now I couldn't care less about all of them, for what they did to our commander." I immediately responded, "Okay, I'll save that part for another day, but the main one that I wanted to talk to you about was this: When I briefed you on what we were doing tonight, and I briefed the platoon about the plan, that was the time to ask me the questions that you brought up. All good and valid questions, but when I said 'any questions' was the time to bring them up, and not ten minutes before we left. When you come up to me ten minutes prior and start yelling at me about all these issues, what am I supposed to do? I can't just pull them out of my butt. If you had asked me as soon as I finished briefing you and the rest of the NCOs, I could have run and caught CPT Wan before he left, but it did me no good to ask at the last minute."

He nodded his head the entire time, and saying, "Yes, I was wrong to bring them up then, and it probably wouldn't have helped even if you did have the answers to them, because I was so furious about these people we are supposed to be helping." He apologized, and then I brought up how he started to flip out in front of the soldiers, which immediately set him off. All I said was "Yeah, I was glad you started walking away to talk to me in private, because you were getting some looks when you started flipping out in front of the soldiers." He snapped and started saying he didn't flip out in front of them, and that I should go talk to someone about firing him if I thought that he flipped out in front of the soldiers. I said, "When we first started talking, you started to flip out, and then we walked away and finished the conversation." He looked at me as if I were crazy. He said it didn't happen that way and suggested perhaps he needed to see the chaplain and psychologist if I saw him flipping out, because he didn't remember that at all. "Are you serious?" I asked him. "Yeah, if you think that I flipped out in front of those soldiers back there, then I need to talk to somebody, and you need to talk to somebody about working with SSG Pord from now on, and getting me removed." I was in shock, so I said, "Obviously, our definitions of flipping out are different then, so never mind."

It also occurred to me at this point that I was getting into his attitude about the Iraqis, and dealing with the commander and everything, which I said we would talk about later. He told me he agreed he was wrong about the questions and he should have mentioned them earlier and I was right about that. He went on, "But that last thing you said, I don't agree with at all." I restated that we must just have different definitions on flipping out, so not to worry about it. I started to leave and said once more I was just keeping my word to tell him my issues with him. He affirmed it was good and that he'd do better to bring up the issues at a better time in the future.

At 9 p.m. CPT Wan briefed our next operation, deciding he would use three infantry platoons, while putting the Storm Troopers on Provincial Hall until whenever the operation ended. I couldn't help but wonder if CPT Wan would use our Mobile Gun System platoon like that in the future – by putting us in the hall during operations. Perhaps he wasn't sure how to use us. I decided I shouldn't assume such things after his operation order but could tell it was on Heath's face during the briefing. I knew my platoon sergeant well, I guess. When he and I briefed the NCOs, he told them not to expect us to ever play a big part in combat missions, because our new commander seemed to be reluctant to use us that way. I told them I knew Heath would say that, but I wasn't going to judge CPT Wans' command after one operations order. I said, "I'm keeping an open mind." Heath said, "Yeah, you need to keep an open mind, Sir, because mine is already closed." I just laughed.

Otherwise, Heath noted our need for a dismounted radio for the second story of Provincial Hall, and that first platoon needed to send one vehicle out with us so we wouldn't have to escort them back. Two vehicles were never allowed to travel anywhere without escort. Heath came by my room to remind me to ask with confidence, and not as though I was whining. He gave me an example, and I told him I would state it as he suggested. I did so, and CPT Wan denied both requests. He suggested for me to use a different radio and said it would be okay if I just left nine people at the hall while we left to escort the section of First Platoon. I made my request with complete confidence and was shot down by both the commander and the XO. Heath got mad and said, "Now it is my turn!" as he walked off to talk to them. He came back after 15 minutes, and I asked, "Any luck?" He told me he didn't even get a word in because they were discussing what buildings the infantry platoons would clear. Then he said, "You didn't know? You weren't even supposed to go to that back-brief, because they only cared what infantry were doing in this operation." I felt led to agree. He said it didn't matter in our company what issues tankers or mortarmen had. We shook our heads and moved out.

Between 2002 and 2004 when the Army equipped its first two "modular" Stryker brigades, it had needed a great breadth of experience from leaders and soldiers of all levels. Not only did they have new vehicles and equipment to work with, but they had to learn how to use them, fight with them, and integrate them with other variants. Whereas many leaders, especially commanders, had dealt with soldiers of other specialties, few had the experience of employing them simultaneously with new equipment, let alone in combat. Furthermore, each commander and leader had his own vision of "what right looks like" which could cause disillusionment amongst many of the soldiers.

December 24, 2004

This day had been nice. I had a good long conversation with SGT Bryce Q about CPT Jacobsen, and the bombing of the DFAC, and then we discussed the war and the Iraqi people on a larger scale. This duty wasn't such a bad gig even though we felt like outcasts sometimes. One operation that day was the clearing of just about every mechanic and car shop in northwestern Mosul, searching for the parts and supplies needed to make car bombs. I hoped they would be successful and would call us if they need a TOW missile fired. The phones and internet on the base have been turned on again, so I was able to check a couple emails, send one out to my parents to tell everyone that I was fine, and that CPT Jacobsen and SGT Johnson's families needed their prayers.

Most of that day I made sure I stayed awake, checking on the guys on guard at the time, talking to my men. I specifically made sure I didn't go back to sleep the entire day, until after midnight, so I wouldn't be accused of "sleeping the whole time." Little did I know that my mere presence was an offense to some people – perhaps my playing laptop video games at times with some of the men. It began to rain around midnight, which I guess was the best that Mosul, Iraq could come up with for a "white Christmas." At midnight, a lieutenant at the TOC said over the battalion radio, "Net call, Net call, Net call ...Merry Christmas." It was funny to hear, and even funnier when someone answered, "Roger, over." Battalion answered back, "Last calling station, this is [battalion callsign], Ho...Ho...Ho." The other call sign responded with a "Ho Ho Ho" and the TOC ended the conversation with a "Roger, over." It was hilarious, especially coming from something as serious as the Battalion Command radio net.

December 25, 2004

I woke up around 7 a.m. when Frank came in and told all the sleepyheads it was time to get up. While we waited for relief to come by 9 a.m., everyone just hung out, and I sat in a chair after packing my things, occasionally dozing off, until I finally stood up and walked around. I said jokingly to Heath (who had his hands in his pockets), "I see you have the same brand of Air Force gloves as me" (I also had my hands in my pockets...which we Army-folk typically refer to as "Air Force gloves" since it is against Army regulations to have your hands in your pockets, but there is no such regulation in the Air Force). He responded with, "That was almost funny, sir," and walked into the other room.

Our relief arrived and we drove back to the base. We were ordered to be with a buddy everywhere outside of "Castle Krella" and wearing body armor and a helmet on the rest of the base. We also always had to have our magazines always loaded. Part of this was because of the DFAC suicide bomber and part of it was because our intelligence reported that the enemy wanted to capture a US Soldier to behead on Christmas day on national television. Sickening.

I'd always felt bad that some people on this Earth would possibly spend eternity without God, in Hell. * Many people have asked me in the past, "How could a loving God send people to Hell?" My answer was always "First of all, He doesn't send people to Hell, they go by choice, and secondly, He doesn't want any to choose that path." I always felt I couldn't say "we deserve to go there," because I know all humans sin; I'm just as guilty as the next.** I've never known a case where I could say "Yeah, I'm 99 percent sure so and so is going to be in Hell," but that day I felt I could say it. I'm not God so I can't say for sure, but a suicide bomber like the one who killed and wounded so many people at the DFAC four days earlier...well, I found peace in the fact that he would suffer. I felt like a failure as a Christian for saying and even feeling so, but I knew he would be judged by God. It gave me great peace to know justice would be served when Jesus separated the sheep from the goats on judgment day [see note].[5]

I was thankful to be alive, and to have a wonderful, amazing family, unit, and friends who loved and cared about me. I found it hard to complain about anything, except negative attitudes. I really had no right to complain, because there were twenty-four people who lost their lives just four days before, and their families were having the worst Christmas of their lives. How could I even compare this Christmas in Iraq away from my family to that? It didn't come close, and I prayed so much for the families, especially CPT Jacobsen's and SGT Johnson's. I could only imagine a small fraction of the pain they were going through this holiday season. It was a pain I felt on December 21st, a pain I would feel the rest of my life, and for them, a much stronger, and more present, pain for the rest of their lives.

Heath came in to talk, suggesting that in the future, I stay behind when the platoon went to Provincial Hall, so they could get the flow of information for the next day from company and battalion. His tone changed as he said, "You really didn't do anything out there anyway except play the computer the whole time. A few people whose names I won't mention asked me why the LT was out there, and I told them because the platoon was out there, and platoon leaders don't pull guard shifts, it is an NCO thing." I explained that he hadn't seen me check on anyone while he slept, that I got up several times and talked to guys on guard rotations, specifically shutting my laptop and walking around to talk to our guys and check on them, offering them snacks, and watching with them on several occasions. We went back and forth like that, discussing the "Air Force Gloves" (hands in pockets thing), how some of us had fallen back asleep after Frank woke us up, and I explained my perspective on it all.

We digressed into discussing how he was without a platoon leader for the first several months in this platoon over two years ago followed by a PL who didn't care at all, then another period without a PL, then a temporary infantry lieutenant, another period with no PL, and then I arrived as platoon leader, and everyone could tell I wanted the job and really cared. His point was he had been so used to being the de facto platoon leader over time, perhaps he gave me 'the short end of the stick' when I arrived, and maybe he was guilty of still trying to be the PL. He suggested that I tell him, "I got this." I explained that my personality or leadership style was flexible. For instance, when someone is an excessive talker, I just let that person talk, only filling in the gaps as needed. In the opposite case, when I am with someone who talks little, I adapt and become an excessive talker.

I realized this after being the officer in charge of the Expert Field Medical Badge Land Navigation lane in December 2003. I worked with a sergeant who was very capable, but also quiet, so I did a great deal of talking, and gave a great number of orders. In contrast, Heath was more of a talker, so I didn't talk as much or give as many orders. Maybe that was the wrong approach for me to take with him, but it seemed to always provide balance in our relationship thus far. Maybe I would try a different approach in the future. In the end, our conversation was rather enlightening, and I learned a great deal indeed from it. I would of course pray that the Lord would strengthen our relationship further, and that He would give me the strength, wisdom, patience, and love, to seek His will for my leadership of this platoon.

I went to chow, which civilian contractors served in the gym, just two hundred meters from our sleeping pad area. The setup and music in the background warmed my heart. Most of the men complained about how terrible the food was, but I couldn't find it in my heart to complain. I was joyful and thankful. I ate what I could stomach, and we all moved back, as I thanked the workers on our way out. After chow Heath and I went over some evaluation reports, had a good laugh, and recapped on a couple things from our earlier discussion. I appreciated how easily we could resume a professional relationship again. There are many people in this world who hold a grudge, and that didn't seem to be the case with Heath. After he vented or discussed his concerns he picked up where he left off.

It's amazing how quickly a world can change. I just talked to CPT WanTarp at 4 p.m. and found out some specifics about the mission, but also learned that a new armor lieutenant arrived at the Battalion. "He will be replacing you," CPT Wan told me. "He will be riding around with the colonel for about five days, and then he'll come to the company. You are going back to 2-14 Cavalry." I was in shock. I didn't want to go back there, because I loved this unit, but if God wanted me there, then I would prayerfully follow His will. Heath and I talked about it, and SSG N heard as well, since he was near. I could tell they were both upset about it. Heath even said he thought the new armor LT should go to 2-14 Cav, so I would continue to be the Platoon Leader at least until March. I had served my first 10 months in 2-14 Cavalry as a reconnaissance platoon leader in 2002-2003. First Sergeant leaked the news to one of my sergeants, so I decided to tell the rest of the Storm Troopers after the mission.

Our mission didn't even take an hour. We noticed how many cars were at each gas station, parked and waiting overnight. We took note of how many people still had shops open in the marketplaces, and how many people were still on the streets walking around. Upon return, I briefed the boys of, "a new Armor LT [who] just arrived here, and he is replacing me within the next week or so. I've been a platoon leader for twenty-five months, and so it is time for me to move on and do something else. I don't know who the new LT is, but he is spending the next five days or so with the colonel, and then he'll come down and work with us." I let them know I wasn't sure how long the transition would be, but since Heath was going on leave for two weeks, it was safe to say he would have a new platoon leader upon return. I then briefed them on the missions for the next day and asked if there were any questions. Most of the questions were funny goofy ones, or about the new LT, or where exactly I was going in 2-14 Cavalry, the answers to which I didn't have.

At one point, I started to grieve for CPT J, wondering why he could no longer bring glory to God, losing his life at such a young age but I remembered our purpose and Jesus' purpose in life. He had the purpose of showing us God, of living for God, and of glorifying God with his life. Every follower of Christ has these purposes. The end state of Christ's life was to hang on a cross and die, with the sins of the world passing through Him.* We use the term "end state" in the military a lot – it is literally the conditions we desire to achieve at the end of any operation – the outcome. Christ's end state on Earth was to die, to be raised from the dead. His end state before being raised from the dead and returning to judge the world, was to die on a cross, and at a young age. How could I question if it was CPT Jacobsen's end state to die at such a young age after glorifying God with his life? How could I question if it is my end state to die at the young age of 25 while I was over here after showing others the way to God, living for Him, and glorifying Him? Who was I to question CPT J's death, and even my own possible death in Iraq, when the very God of the universe and all creation died around age 30?** I am nothing compared to him, and although my death would upset a great deal of people, it would not even come close to those saddened by Jesus' death. The good news is we will be raised again, just as my Lord and Savior was. He has power over death, and my heart longs for the anticipation of spending eternity with him [see note].[6]

December 26, 2004

I woke up with a sinus infection, got medication from the aid station, then napped before our 1 p.m. route interdiction and recon mission. Two mortar sergeants shared jokingly how we should secede from the battalion because they didn't want me to leave the unit. It was touching. Before our second mission at 6 p.m., I went to practice at chapel. While I was down there, I noticed soldiers getting into a formation, and after talking to LTC K, realized they were expecting a VIP. LTC Krella told me LTC Mavis (the 2-14 Cavalry Squadron Commander) sent him an Armor LT, and LTC Mavis decided the fate of Armor LTs. He said, "I know it is crushing, but you'll probably be going back to 2-14 Cav, and I don't know what job he has for you yet. LTC Mavis will be able to tell you." I asked him when my replacement would be effectively taking over. The colonel said LT Kim would stay with him a few days, then he would ride around with my commander (CPT Wan) and then he would transition with me. It sounded like that within a week I would be signing the platoon over to him.

I met LT Andrew Kim after talking to the colonel, because he stood off to the side of the formation at the TOC. As we talked, the Battalion Command Sergeant Major called everyone to attention, and 4-star General Schoomaker, Chief of Staff for the Army walked up. He gave out special coins and spoke, but I couldn't hear his quiet voice over the dull generator noise. I was standing only three feet away from him, but I had to concentrate just to make out his words. After he left, we went on our mission, and it was as smooth as glass. I told Randy to do that afternoon just what we did that morning, except backwards. He did, and our platoon radio was quiet. No one was mad at each other or anything, it was just smooth, and we all knew what to do. We checked out gas stations and found out the Iraqi Provisional Authority police station was now inaccessible due to a ditch blocking our way, which I reported when we got back. I also reported a hole Heath noticed in the fence to FOB Marez (our base). Upon return, I talked to Heath about the next day's plans, since we had a printout in our box regarding them. We were both upset about a couple of things on the printout, and I said I'd talk to CPT W about it later.

I went to chapel with Gumfi, and the chaplain related the Book of Ruth to the bombing at the DFAC. It was a good message, and the music was joyful. LT Kim was at the service, so I talked to him for a while, and then invited him to come back to my room. I showed him sites on the map, talked to him about Heath, the company, and the missions we did. I introduced him to Randy and Jay, and explained my role in the platoon to him, and how things worked. I invited him to come with us on our mission the next day at 8 a.m., so he could see what it was like. We had a recon of the marketplace in our sector, and I needed to determine the best time to visit in the future to catch the shop owners yet avoid a crowd. On our way out of my room, I introduced Andrew to Heath.

I went to talk to CPT W about our concerns. I told the boss my platoon hadn't had a recovery day yet. All other platoons had one or had it scheduled; we had neither. So, I suggested scheduling one and he agreed. We spoke of Provincial Hall and I explained what Heath and I discussed. Suddenly we heard huge explosions with small arms and machine gun fire in the background. It sounded like everything from

7.62mm and .50 cal, to hellfire missiles, AC 130 gun-ships and A-10's. It was basically a display of force, or as some said, "A live fire exercise demonstrating the capabilities and effectiveness of the massing of fires" for General Schoomaker. After it all died down, I gave SGT Bryce Q a book, since we'd discussed his purpose is in life way back when we were at Anaconda. I told him I hoped it would help him to find his purpose from God; he seemed grateful.

December 27, 2004

At 8 a.m. all the gas stations were jam packed, and the marketplace CPT WanTarp wanted me to video was crowded too. We had our overseas funeral for CPT Jacobsen and SGT Johnson at 11 a.m. at the recreation tent. I knew it would be sad, but I was trying to concentrate on the good. We were still alive, and the wounded were recovering. CPT Jacobsen had already heard the words from our Lord, "Well done, good and faithful servant" *[see note].[7] I wasn't sure about SGT Johnson, because I didn't really know him at all, but I guessed he was in the same boat as CPT J.

I hoped and prayed I would never have to repeat such a ceremony again in my life. I held back tears, but it was so sad I almost lost it. When they played the prelude, "Amazing Grace," on the bagpipes, it reminded me of when Capt James Kirk lost Spock at the end of *Star Trek II*. They played the same song at that funeral, and the loss of such a close friend hurt so deeply. SGT Kevin G sang the National Anthem, and Chaplain Welon did the invocation. LTC Krella got up and with much emotion in his voice, began his opening remarks about his heavy heart, the loss of these four soldiers, and their sacrifice. He then spoke specifically about the one loss that "tore at the very fiber of [his] soul," Captain Bill Jacobsen. He spoke of how amazing CPT Jacobsen was, and how he embodied everything a good soldier and leader should be, perfectly defining warrior ethos. He spoke of CPT 'J' always leading from the front, instilling confidence and direction in his men.

LT Dale K, our XO, spoke about CPT 'J' as well, and SSG Leopfe spoke about Staff Sergeant Robert Johnson. I don't know if they promoted SSG Johnson posthumously or if he just hadn't pinned on his rank yet, because he was a sergeant when he died. Both were posthumously awarded the Bronze Star Medal and Purple Heart, as were the other two killed from the 73rd Engineers, CPL Jonathan Castro, and SPC Lionel Ayro. CPT Golinghorst, their company commander, made remarks about Castro and Ayro, and a bit about CPT 'J'. He mentioned how the Lord has been his rock in this difficult time, and I felt a peace from the Holy Spirit move through that place. The 73rd Engineers First Sergeant also spoke, as did two enlisted men about their lost friends. When everyone was finished, Chaplain Welon gave his memorial message, quoting mostly from the book of Job.

At that time, First Sergeant Anderson (73rd Engineers) and First Sergeant Vright (A Company) did a roll call of a few names in the company. The individuals that were called answered with, "Here, First Sergeant!" Each first sergeant than called out the fallen soldiers' names, first with just rank and last name, then rank with first and last name, and then rank with full name. It was so sad and First Sergeant Vright choked up when he called out, "Captain William W. Jacobsen Jr." The silence was devastating. After the last roll call, a volley was fired for the men, and then taps played. Chaplain Welon gave the benediction, and they played a video showing each of the four soldiers' pictures in and out of uniform, with their families in some cases, and a pair of boots with a rifle and helmet at the top, dog tags in the corner. After the video, each row moved up as music continued to play to salute the four pairs of boots, four rifles, and four helmets with rank on them. After saluting, people would touch their hands to the helmets and cry, pray, or just be silent for a moment, before moving on. I said a prayer for their families and for us still there in combat and moved on after saluting and touching CPT Jacobsen's and SSG Johnson's helmets.

On the way back from the ceremony, we talked about how the latest count of wounded from the DFAC bombing had risen to 72. It was amazing how many of those could have been added to the 24 killed. I thanked God for His grace and healing for which I prayed. When we all returned from the ceremony, I talked to SSG D, who had just returned. He told me how blessed he was that he wasn't killed, because he was sitting right there, and saw the fireball. He still had a ball bearing in his knee, and the doctors weren't going to remove it because it could cause even more damage. He told me it would be constantly examined as he went through physical therapy. If it got infected, who knew what they would do then? I asked him if I could pray over his knee, and he welcomed the idea, saying how thankful he was the Lord had protected him. He referenced Psalm 91 and expressed the joy of God's blessings and Word.

CPT WanTarp told me the day's mission was cancelled. LTC Krella was granting us the rest of the day off to grieve. I gave more thought to the events surrounding the bombing, and then decided to go check my email, since I had sent out a long email to several friends and family members explaining my experiences during the bombing. Among several other emails, I received one from Rebecca. It made my heart ache to read of the pain she felt when she had thought I was dead. I held back tears welling in my eyes once again. She described her side of the events of December 21st and several days afterward, as well as her thoughts, feelings, and emotions. I imagined it is a fraction of what Captain Jacobsen's wife and children were feeling right then. Here are many things she said in her long email written December 21st after she arrived at my parents house in Maryland, having traveled from Washington State:

"Oh, my love, I found out about this tragedy at work today around 3 pm. People spoke of it by my desk. I asked for clarification, and they said, 'Haven't you heard a mess hall in Mosul was hit with an RPG? It is all over the news – several deaths and injuries.' I started to cry immediately and could not contain my tears. I told them you were in Mosul and composed myself so as not to disturb my patients. As soon as I left work, I called Dawn, who told me it WAS your dining facility, and no one had heard directly from anyone at the scene. I cannot explain or put into words the sense of impending dread I felt. 24-hours ago we had had a great amazing time on webcam and now I was going to be with family. I felt as if God was preparing me for your death. I could not stop crying uncontrollably. I called my mom who had heard (she was at Grandma's); even Grandma was crying. When I arrived home, Karrie greeted and held me while I fell apart in her arms. I told her, I just knew it was you, I knew you were dead, and knew God would take care of me. Before I ever called my mother, I was crying out to the Lord in a sob I have never cried before. I told Him it was okay; I had been blessed with so much from you and I understood. I told Him I trusted his will and then just sobbed to the Lord, telling Him my deepest feelings and pain. I knew only the Lord could understand. I don't know why I had such a horrible feeling. It wasn't worry; it was pain! I knew something was terribly wrong. After Karrie calmed me down, I waited and prepared for our flight.

When Mike got to the house the focus just shifted to getting the house ready to leave and getting the bags to the car. I had tons of messages from different people all wondering if you were ok. It was difficult for me, but I told them I didn't know and all we could do was pray, pray for you, your soldiers, and the families of the dead and injured. I told them as soon as I found out I would call to tell them if you were alive. That list got long. Among the people who called were Jacki and Paul, Tiffani and Brad, and many others. It surprised me I hadn't heard from some, but I figured they thought that if something were wrong, I would call them. Even Karen called countless times. I called Rikka and left a message not knowing that her husband had been killed.

As we went to the airport my cell phone just continued to ring. Nick and I got to the airport way too early. We thought due to the holiday there would be major lines. There were hardly any. We had three hours to wait for our plane. I thought CNN would be playing there but there were no TV's. I had no news; I just sat in the terminal crying. Nick tried to comfort me by telling me you were ok, and I tried to be strong for Katelyn and me especially. I couldn't stop thinking about good memories we had and special moments. I was terrified with the thought Katelyn would not have any memories of you. I was sure you were gone and not coming back. I just felt it in my heart. I was trying to just accept it. I was trying to make peace with why the Lord would allow something like this to occur.

Eventually our planes came. I tried to get some sleep on the first plane and didn't even bother on the second plane. I had brought magazines with me and I tried to keep my mind off how they would notify me. When we landed, your mom and my mom were waiting and I just ran up to them in tears. My mom took Nick. Your mom and I went to your house. I quickly went to unload the luggage and wrap the presents because when your dad came home from work we were supposed to leave for Grandma and Unkie's. For the first time my mind wasn't on you and sadness. Your dad came home, it was great to be hugged by him, it reminded me of you. Everything in their house reminded me of you. As I wrapped the pictures of you to give to mom and dad, gramdma and unkie, and my mom, I just sobbed. I was afraid this was the last picture they would have of you and how much it meant. Dad took me to lunch. It got me out of the house and got my mind onto other things, it also encouraged me to finally eat, which I hadn't really done since lunch the day prior. Back at the house I continued to wrap, and Dad called me down to put your ornaments on the tree. I just longed for you in every way. I just longed for you to hold me and never let me go. In my head I could hear you singing, "Everything's going to be okay." and, "Don't worry Beckybear, worrying is a sin". I remembered phrases of things we had talked about the day before and wonderful memories we had.

We spoke about Katelyn. I told them stories of all the adventures you had gotten me to go on: camping, climbing a tree, climbing a mountain, the glacier. All kinds of adventures and memories. Then we left and again I tried to sleep in the car. I couldn't. I decided to call Dawn and see how everyone was doing. Dawn informed me that everyone had been notified. I told her, that is strange, I hadn't been notified yet of that. I told her I would call Rikka and see. So, I called Rikka and left a cheerful message, telling her I had landed and was safe and just waiting to hear. I was trying to be cheerful so people wouldn't know how bad I was hurting or taking this. Then I called the colonel's wife. I thanked her and explained what I heard, and she confirmed it, she said someone was with Rikka and she went on to explain the injuries and all. I told her I did not have access to e-mail. I then asked her if she could tell me how many had died. She told me that two from Alpha had died. She then said Cpt. Jacobsen's name and I now was very confused. I said, "Are you saying that Capt. Jacobsen was killed?" and when she said yes, my heart jumped out of my body.

I know I turned white as a ghost and your father reached back and held my hand as I trembled and started to cry. I just sat there in shock. It was now making sense; that is why she told me someone was with Rikka. I immediately asked her if there was anything I could do for her or anyone. She said she appreciated it, but they had it under control. She told me she sent an e-mail out concerning that an hour before I called. I told her I would call my ladies personally. I got off the phone and explained to your parents what I learned, and we were all in shock. Just sitting there as if in a daze! I then started to call each *lady. I don't know how I did it, except the Lord gave me the strength. I wanted to be the one they heard it from, since you were close to him. Each lady was just as broken as I. We arrived at Grandma and Unkie's when I was on the last call. I collected myself and went inside because Grandma had fixed dinner, and everyone was waiting on me. I didn't feel like eating, or even being social. I just wanted to be there with you and hold you and comfort you during this time of loss.*

After dinner, I called people back to let them know you were alive and to pray for the Jacobsen's and Johnson's and everyone else who had had a death or injury. I told them all God was the only way to survive this and He was the one giving us both the strength to endure. I think the Lord really used this time to spread his Word. It was a witness to everyone. I finally went to bed around midnight. I hadn't felt Katelyn kick in the last 24-hours either, so it started to worry me. I didn't know if it was because we were on a different time schedule or because I didn't feel her move because my mind was preoccupied. I was praying for her as well. I didn't want to lose my husband and my baby in the same week. The next morning, I awoke early and had my quiet time; talking to the Lord about you and your men, asking for guidance and strength, and asking Him to heal your heart, mind, and soul. I made more calls and then we all ate breakfast, again I didn't feel much like eating but did for Katelyn. The night prior I gave Grandma and Unkie their picture of you and of us. I cried when they opened it, explaining how as I wrapped it, I was afraid you were dead. I will always remember that about those pictures.

We started on our way to Chris's house. I felt like I was in a dream. I felt so guilty for the relief I felt that you were alive and so torn and upset over the loss that Rikka was now experiencing. I felt so sad and alone. I cannot imagine how she feels with Christmas two days away and her best friend and husband and father of her children not ever coming back. I know it was a reality she (like all of us) never thought we would have to face. My heart just breaks for her. I feel bad that I have a husband coming home to me and she does not. I feel bad that her children will grow up without a daddy. I just feel so much pain for her. I am glad she has family and so much support with her church. I do not know how she will go on; I pray the Lord gives her and her children and their family strength.

We got your letter on Christmas and all gathered in the family room as I read it and we cried together. All morning my thoughts shifted to Rikka and how she was doing this alone without her love and without the daddy to her children. My heart just breaks for her. I hope you understand I knew how this was the worst day of your life; I think it was almost the worst day of my life as well. It was a day the war was brought deep into my heart, a day and a course of events I will never forget; a day that seemed to go in slow motion as if to engrave itself in my heart. Matt, I love you more than words can say. And these events made it a reality that you might not come back from this terrible war and you might not meet Katelyn or hold me ever again. It was all a nightmare and I wish over and over that it did not happen. However, I know the Lord had a plan and this is his will. I know the Lord will use you to the fullest. I know if He takes you that I WILL be okay! I know his will is the best plan for my future and for Katelyn's.

I know he hears and answers my prayers. I know our family loves us dearly and loves you as well. I am amazed at the friends and family who care for us both – even ones who have only met you or me a few times. I know the Lord is using this time to bring others to know Him. That is the only thing that gives me peace – The Lord. Please know I am okay because the Lord is in my heart and has and is giving me the strength to do all things! I love you more than words can say, I wish I could have shared all of this with you in person, but please know as I share this, you are in my heart and in every breath I breathe.

Also know Katelyn finally started to kick again. I think maybe in a way, she was grieving as well. I love you and I am going to start on all my other letters to you! Lots of hugs and kisses! You are strong and you are a warrior! Know that you are an LT in the Lord's ARMY sent out to bring others to Christ, HE GIVES YOU all strength and will get you and your men through this! Lots of hugs and kisses-- your true love—Rebecca"

I imagine this was only a fraction of what Rikka Jacobsen and her family had gone through on that terrible day and thereafter. It really brought even more perspective of the horrors of war people endure. I might even say it isn't the soldier who has life the hardest in war. It is his or her family. The families are left behind with uncertainty and loneliness should that unfortunate day come, in which their soldier is lost. It is families who must face the rest of their lives without that soldier, grieving his or her loss, and wondering why it had to happen in that way. It is the family that must cherish the pre-deployment memories as the last between them and their soldiers. Again, I thanked God my day had not come, and that my family and I continued to press on, fighting for freedom from terror in this world. I praised Him for my continued chance to bring glory to His name and asked for His strength for so many families and friends who were feeling the loss of loved ones from this terrible war.

This war, as terrible as it was, was necessary – it would have been worse if no one thought it was worth fighting; if no one thought freedom from terror and world peace were worth fighting for.* It would be sad if history recorded these heroes I've fought behind and alongside had died in vain, or if it ignored those who protected our country, its people and its citizen's rights to protest this war; a war which was started by terrorists claiming the lives of innocent civilians on September 11, 2001** [see note].[8]

After our 5:30 p.m. operation brief, Heath and I discussed plans for the next day, which would be the last day our whole platoon would be together, since he was going on leave and I'd be gone when he returned. He asked me if I would be doing my farewell speech when he wouldn't be around for it, and I hesitated. I told him it didn't feel right giving it when I still had a week left, but I could do it for him. He said never mind, but I know it is important to him, so I shall. I just prayed God would give me the words to say to leave a lasting impression for Jesus when I left. I spoke to the chaplain about my feelings of wanting to leave the Army and my confusion about following God's will. I couldn't stand hurting Becky by being gone and seeing what she went through that past week. He said I was going through a lot of emotions lately and advised me to continue to wait upon the Lord. That sounded like great advice, and God gave it in Isaiah 40:31 too, so I knew it was sound.

I love my God, and I love my chaplain. I talked to CPT Wan about it too, and he told me how important it was for the folks in the company to have someone to show them Jesus, and someone to take care of them. He shared with me how badly it hurt and still hurts having lost Captain Jacobsen. They worked together even before they both came to Fort Lewis, First Brigade, and 1-24th Infantry. He shared how he was crying to the Lord December 21st when LTC Krella knocked on his door, telling him he was taking command of A Company in three hours, so he needed to prepare himself. I really respected him for how well he had done so far, and for his faith in Christ. I wished I had more time to share with him before moving on to 2-14 Cavalry, but I knew our relationship could continue after we got back to Fort Lewis.

December 28, 2004

This was our recovery day. We all woke before 8 a.m. to have one final talk before Heath left. He shared expectations for while he was gone and joked with me about giving back all the expendable items issued to me that I never signed for. (Back before we left Fort Lewis during property accountability, CPT Jacobsen had wanted us to sign for everything, even expendable items usually just issued. Heath had given me a hard time about it then, as I told him I was just following orders.) He read off a list of all of the things he expected to get back from me, which was pretty funny, and he joked about the platoon not giving me a ride to FOB Sykes unless I handed them all back. I went to see him off, shaking hands as he got on the truck to ride to FOB Diamondback. I said I would pray for his flight and a safe trip and would continue to pray for him and the platoon after I left. God willing, I'd see him in ten months.

Most of that day I prayed to God, spoke to my men, practiced praise songs, emailed, cleaned my room, and attended a briefing before dinner and Bible study. CPT Wan wanted to be there when I briefed my men, so I was waiting for him. It felt weird, because I hadn't had to brief my guys with a captain around since we trained at Fort Polk, Louisiana's Joint Readiness Training Center where we had an "OC" or observer controller listen, to give us pointers and help us for when we deployed. It was odd to have him listen after 25 months as Platoon Leader when I was on my way out. I guessed that he just wanted to get an understanding of how we briefed our guys, which made sense.

Well, that was cool – the boss was thirty minutes late so I told the guys I would brief them and take a "butt chewing" if necessary, since they needed sleep. As I began to brief, CPT W walked up. The colonel had him tied up with stuff, so we understood. After I briefed the plan, CPT W talked to us about how to use our platoon. Ironically, we Storm Troopers had just discussed that subject and we were worried that he wasn't going to take our recommendation on how to employ us. SSG Nubear explained to CPT W how we operate, and how well the hunter-killer team concept worked. We shared past experiences and missions with him, explaining in detail how effective our concept was, our order of march, and even particulars of times we'd fired a TOW missile. We showed him the video of our Veteran's Day operation, and he was excited and impressed by the TOW shots. He said he would use us in the same way CPT Jacobsen had, and we were pleased, to say the least.

December 29, 2004

All went as planned. We got to Provincial Hall at 5 a.m. and 15-minutes later observed a bunch of tracers and heard an RPG explode. It was so sporadic we had no idea from where it came. We saw a couple cars drive by but couldn't positively identify any enemy. It was quiet for a few hours, and we left for Blickenstaff to link up with the Special Forces and Iraqi commandos. We took two Special Forces Hummvees, and eleven trucks with roughly 60 commandos. At our blocking position, there were over 100 cars backed up for gas, most abandoned, because people left their cars right where they were if they ran out of gas. It was amazing to me that they had such patience. The operation went okay, but we left early because there was a civilian casualty. He was found with several wire and bomb making materials, so we assumed he was bad. First Platoon shot him with three non-lethal rounds since he ran after they had told him to sit. He continued to run as he was shot with lethal rounds, and his guts flew out. While the mortar Strykers remained at Provincial Hall, we escorted the Medical Stryker carrying the wounded civilian to our hospital for treatment. By the time we moved back toward the company objective, the mission was over, so my platoon returned to Provincial Hall.

We cleared the third floor where we usually put the two M240s (7.62 mm Machine Gun), set up camp and a guard rotation schedule. LTC Krella stopped in the parking lot because he and his crew heard shots and wanted to figure out what it was, and where it came from. As the evening progressed, things got crazy. We heard radio traffic from the colonel, who was on Hwy-1. He was checking out a combat outpost we built on Hwy-1, to establish a better presence there. A car bomb crashed into its wall, leaving a ten-foot hole in it, and a parked car bomb exploded against the battalion scouts. The car bomb truck had vegetables in the back, leaning heavily on one side, which made the colonel suspicious when he noticed it. After these two explosions, they took heavy small arms fire from the north, and discovered three roadside bombs placed to the north and three placed to the south of Hwy-1. LTC Krella and the Operations Officer MAJ Beaver were trapped, so they called in someone to blow the bombs, while they resolved the contact.

As we continued to listen, we heard that one of the reconnaissance Strykers from the Battalion Scouts was a catastrophic kill, and the colonel began shouting over the radio to get some fire extinguishers on it, because the top of it was cooking off ammo. He also reported we had two casualties, one with lacerations on the head and chest, and the other with other lacerations. He called for C Company to evacuate them to the CSH, and we heard a later report that someone received CPR. The colonel called in air support, and a couple of US fighter attack planes came screaming in, ripping up the ground in the direction of the enemy. The gun run sounded like breaking wind, or as Frank said, "Like someone dragging a desk across a cement floor." The plane must have made about four or five passes, and we watched the whole thing. It is amazing what we could see from the third floor of the building. We saw the vegetable truck explode, and a giant ring of black smoke rose from the ground, forming first into a mushroom cloud, then morphing into the ring. Frank got a picture of it.

We continued to listen as the colonel called in some help from First Platoon. LT Raub N and his men evacuated all the US equipment and possible casualties from the outpost, and from the sound of things, he returned fire to the north as well. After everything was clear, and at LTC Krella's request, the Air Force dropped a JDAM bomb as they returned to the FOB. Things died down for a bit, and some Kurdish ING and Iraqi Police visited us. We talked to them for a while, and they told us how friendly and great the American Army was. It was nice to be able to talk to them about each other, and they were impressed with the Arabic Frank and I knew. We showed each other our weapons, letting them hold our M-4's, and we held their AK47's. It was nice soldiers from our two countries could bond like that. We are both fighting for the same thing – freedom – for this country, our country, and to rid the world of terror. They, just like us, were fighting for their families, not only to provide for them, but to protect them from harm and danger that would inevitably come if we did nothing.

December 30, 2004

The guys woke me at 8 a.m. because there was some gunfire outside. We could tell where it was coming from for a few seconds when tracer rounds were visible, but then it was too difficult to positively identify any enemy. After months of watching the disorganization of the friendly Iraqi forces, it was encouraging to watch them moving on the enemy with police. They moved out in a modified wedge formation, and slowly pushed forward. Some fired a couple of RPGs up at a building where they received enemy fire. The most frustrating thing was not being able to help them or pinpoint where the enemy was.

It got slow for a while, we played a card game, and suddenly there were shots fired repeatedly outside. A mini firefight ensued, and SGT Cruver said he saw two enemy on a building next to a mosque. He shot one, and the other ran (he said they were shooting at the mortar Stryker, and Iraqi soldiers also shot up at them.) We reported it on Battalion radio, and LTC Krella activated a quick reaction force - Dan Karney and Third Platoon. They moved out with a few Iraqi soldiers to enter the mosque and surrounding buildings. SSG Nubear shone a spotlight on the building where they were, and the enemy fired at him.

I told him to wait until LT Karney came by with his platoon to do it again, so we could tell Dan's men the location to attack. It took some time, but when they arrived after picking up Iraqi soldiers, they moved into the building and apparently found some wires rigged to a car with its doors pulled off. The car was being made into a car bomb but they disarmed it in time.

Iraqis and Kurds visited us at Provincial Hall again. They were impressed with us, and liked us a lot, which was nice to hear. One of them brought us a dinner of lamb kabobs. They were like tortillas with lamb and tomatoes in them-- delicious! I gave them some Army "MREs" (Meal-Ready-to-Eat) to take home to their families, and they left.

December 31, 2004

The fog was thick on the way back from Provincial Hall at 5 a.m. I took a nap after learning CPT Wan wanted us to be ready to roll to Destiny Range for target practice at 1 p.m. I briefed Randy on the plan and purpose and sent him the graphics via our battle computer. We went south on Hwy-1, until we turned west on a road to the range. Our platoon fired six TOW missiles (all TOW2As, which are non-bunker-buster missiles). Most of us missed. It was the first time I personally fired a TOW missile. Jay and Will (DeArthur couldn't see because he was loading) said I hit the junk pile I aimed at. I fired, and my TOW impacted, destroying the junk-pile. Bryce, Frank and Randy talked as though I missed, but to us it was the closest shot. There was an explosion where I aimed, but we each fired once more. My second shot missed, cutting the top of the pile, exploding a few hundred meters beyond.

Bryce scored a direct hit when he shot the last time. LTC Krella and CPT WanTarp both came out with us to shoot and lit up some targets with their .50 caliber machine guns. The Mortar crews had fun shooting white phosphorus, or "Willie P's" as they are called. They fired 120mm's, and 60mm's, and the Snipers fired a bunch of their different weapons too. A couple of Apache Helicopter pilots flew out and shot up some dirt with their machine guns and missiles.

Back at base, I briefed the sergeants on our out-of-sector mission for the next morning. Then Frank and I played in the praise team practice, learning four new songs. Liz stayed late with me to work out the notes and melodies. When I played the violin from third grade to my senior year of high school, I always thought I was bad at it, and just didn't have a gift. I had negative thoughts of my skills – I could only play a song if I practiced it like crazy. There, allowing the Holy Spirit to guide me with the gift the Lord has given me, I was able to play by ear almost every new song. I was still no star performer, but I praised God He allowed me to catch on so quickly and to minister to others through music.

---

[1] *Today, I see a fine line between the love of enemies Jesus commands for us in the new covenant in Matthew 5:44 and his and God's war to strike the nations in Revelation 19:11-15.

[2] I do not recall specifics of the conversation, but today I understand one cannot serve two masters, one is a slave to God by obedience and righteousness, or a slave to sin (Matthew 6:24, Romans 6:16-22).

[3] *This paragraph demonstrates several dangerously unscriptural views I held at the time. **First**, although some judgment is wrong (James 4:11-12), Jesus gave instructions for proper judgment to help others (Matthew 7:1-5) with an expectation for judging between right and wrong (Luke 12:57, John 7:24), as did Paul (1 Corinthians 2:15). **Second**, Biblically, any sinner must repent as Jesus preached repentance from sin some-96 times, beginning with Matthew 4:17 and Mark 1:15. Peter's first response to sinners questioning what they must do in Acts 2:38 started with "repent..." ****Third**, Jesus commanded us to

be perfect in Matthew 5:48 which is achievable, especially if scripture says Noah was "a just man, perfect in his generations" (Genesis 9:6), and God said Job was blameless or perfect (Job 1:8). Paul had the same expectation in Philippians 3:15 and Colossians 1:28.

[4]*Today, I still know God can protect anyone at anytime, but I do not believe Hebrews 9:27 indicates a predetermined day of death for each individual, especially since by wisdom and fear of God our days or years may be multiplied (Proverbs 9:11, 10:27), as King Hezekiah experienced in 2 Kings 20:1-6. **As stated in a previous footnote, today I know death is sleep, (Acts 7:60, 13:36), without awareness (Psalm 6:5, 13:3, 88:10-11), until the righteous awake to immortality as Jesus determines in his judgment (John 5:21-22, 26-29) upon his return to establish the kingdom of God. My peace today is in God and Jesus judging righteously on that future day.

[5] * Today I understand the wicked will ultimately be destroyed or "perish" as Jesus stated in Luke 13:3-5, as Paul and Peter declared in 2 Thessalonians 1:9 (a destruction that is eternal or forever), and 2 Peter 3:7, respectively. I do believe many will be punished to various degress prior to destruction, as Jesus implied in Matthew 10:15, 11:22-24, and Luke 12:47-48, but do not believe the destruction to be a forever-period of conscious torment. **Although I have sin in this life from my past making me guilty as Romans 3:23 and 1 John 1:8 show, I have been justified or made right or clear through faith, repentance (turning from all sin, cleansed), and walking in the light through obedience. Romans 3:24-25, Proverbs 28:13, and 1 John 1:7 make this clear. I also no longer believe all humans sin, as 1 John 3:6-9 makes clear for children of God, and of course Jesus never sinned as Hebrews 4:15 states. Scripture makes clear sinners (unless they repent) will be in the lake of fire – Revelation 21:8. Finally, I don't look forward to any suffering, but want all to repent, as God desires (2 Peter 3:9), even if some may not.

[6] *Although I still believe Jesus gave his life as "a ransom for many" (Matthew 20:28), I understand 1 Corinthians 5:21 "He made him who knew no sin to be sin for us" and 1 Peter 2:24 "who himself bore our sins in his own body on the tree" to bo examples of his love for God

and us. I also see them as metaphors or symbols like the Exodus 12:3-7 and Leviticus 16:15-22 animal offerings or sacrifices. I do not believe sin is a literal substance inside our body, but a known violation of God's law (James 4:17, 1 John 3:4). ** Today I agree with scripture such Isaiah 44:24, 45:18 and John 17:3 that Yahweh is the only true God who created the universe, not Jesus. Jesus is the Messiah and Son of the living God (Matthew 16:16). The God and Father of Jesus has now given Jesus all authority on heaven and earth (Matthew 28:18), but Jesus is not his Father, nor creator of the universe.

[7] Again, I do not believe any will hear this phrase until Jesus returns as the context of the parable implies in Matthew 25:21. The dead sleep as Jesus implied in John 11:11-14.

[8] * Today I believe many wars are not worth fighting, and the only necessary warfare is that mentioned in 2 Corinthians 10:3-6. We only gain true freedom from war or terror on this earth when Isaiah 2:4 and 65:17-**25** are fulfilled in God's kingdom. **I do not believe it to be in vain for those God uses as ministers (or agents) who bear the sword against those practicing evil (Romans 13:5, 1 Peter 2:14), even if followers of Christ in the new covenant are not called to take the sword (Matthew 26:52).

4

January, Part 1

January 1, 2005

We started with an alert to be ready at 6 a.m. CPT Wan went to FOB Diamondback to pick up "the source" who would identify the location of a weapons cache. It was an "out of sector" mission, meaning it wasn't in our company or battalion sector, but in 3-21 Infantry's sector. LTC Gibler (3-21 IN battalion commander) didn't want to support this operation directly but would keep a force on standby. The plan was interesting. During the briefing we heard there were horse stables in an area where sheep and goat herders had mud huts. Our plan was to link up at Blickenstaff before 8 a.m, drive with three Special Forces Humvees, 20 Chevy Trucks loaded with two hundred Iraqi commandos, all five of our Storm Trooper vehicles, and CPT WanTarp with crew. It looked like this (our initial position on the left, later position on the right – all dark buildings were where enemy shot at us except for the two far left):

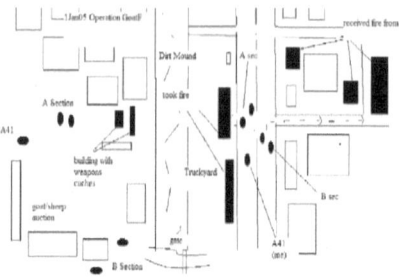

After turning north on the main road, we turned west on a little trail crossing a dirt mound. The trail had a gate in the front of it, and I told Randy to ram it, since CPT W told me we could. He was able to knock it over, and Special Forces in their Humvees pushed it off the road. We flowed in from the southeast corner of the objective with A Section in the north, B Section in the south, and me to the west. The boss moved his vehicle to the middle, and the 200 commandos began clearing the goat and sheep auction area, searching buildings and houses. Suddenly, CPT Wan told me to follow him north into more buildings. He told me "the source" had guided him to the weapons cache site. The source took a long time to look at the map, pop his head out, and tell CPT Wan where to take him in the mud and brick housing community.

Special Forces offered to take the source in their Humvees, to identify the house more easily, as we watched the sheep, goats, herders, and their dogs, which were running all over the place. The Iraqi Commandos seemed bothered by the dogs, and occasionally fired off a round or two. We listened to Special Forces talking on the company radio, and they didn't even use call signs for each other. They would say, "John this is Ron," or, "Alex this is John." It sounded so funny, so SGT B came on and said to SGT Q, "Bryce this is Frank, over." We started laughing, and then SSG Pord called him back and said, "Frank this is Randy, over." SGT boss answered, "Randy, this is Frank?" "Frank, this is Randy, how is your crew doing?" "Randy, this is Frank. Myself, Joseph and Owusu are all fine, over." SSG Pord then said, "This is Randy, roger, over."

I decided to play too, since we were all cracking up, and called up SSG Pord. "Randy, this is Matt." "Matt, this is Randy" he replied. "If I need you, Bryce and Jason to help out Alex and Ron, will you be able to?" He came back and said, "Matt, this is Randy. Myself, Bryce, Jason and Darrell will be ready to help Alex, Ron and John, over." "This is Matt, roger, over." SGT Minnock played too, calling SSG Pord, "Randy, this is Jay," but I can't remember what they said. We were all laughing so much by then it didn't matter what we said. SGT Cruver played too, calling SGT Boss three times, saying, "Frank, this is Shelby, over." Finally, SSG Pord cut in and said, "You are on company [radio], over!" We all lost it then, and I can't remember laughing so hard ever on a mission. It was just a very amusing time, and I was already missing my platoon, even though I hadn't left them yet.

Our source found the site and Randy helped CPT W and the Special Forces secure it. It was only about 50 meters from our spot, and we watched the Commandos and SF clear the room. I listened to the reports on the company radio and was amazed. It was the biggest stash or 'cache' of weapons I'd ever heard of being found in Mosul: 200 mortar (60mm) rounds, 100 artillery (105mm) rounds, two complete roadside bombs (all set up and ready to blow), six mortar firing tubes, a few RPGs, and a few home-made RPGs, blasting caps, detonation cord, TNT, Russian made rifles and light/heavy machine guns and various other weapons. Those were just the preliminary figures from their first count, and I was in shock. I felt so honored to be part of this mission, because its success meant our enemy would be seriously hurting for supplies.

CPT W called for a bomb disposal team from Brigade, who told him it would be a while, since they were getting rid of a car bomb just outside the gate of one of the bases in Mosul. While waiting, the commander wanted a few of my vehicles to move out to the east road, because Special Forces said something was going on over there. We drove back down through the destroyed gate, and as we did, B Section received indirect mortar fire. After a third round impacted all within one minute, we called them to move, even though the enemy was extremely inaccurate. The rounds impacted one hundred fifty to two hundred meters away from their location, on the road we were moving onto. As Randy, SGT Moorefield and I turned north on that road, we received small arms fire from our left in the truck yard. There were not only several mini-garages and shacks in there, but there were also several trucks and cars. We heard many shots, without seeing a single person or even smoke from a weapon, which was unusual.

The boss kept asking me to report, and I told him we were in contact from the left side in the truck yard but couldn't see any enemy. Due to the volume of fire, I estimated a squad-sized element (nine people) of enemy. He asked if we'd returned fire; we hadn't because we didn't positively identify anyone. Once B Section pulled up behind us on the right side of the road, we received small arms fire from the right side of the road. It appears our enemies made a futile attempt to stop us from taking their weapons cache. I noticed some gun smoke coming from the right two buildings north of our position, and pointed it out to Jay, who fired at the windows. SSG Nubear or SFC Nubear as of today, noticed people running out of the alleyway to our right. He asked to drive down with his section, and I told him to go ahead, and I would come behind him. We drove down the alleyway, and a couple of buildings at our 12 o'clock had shooters in them, and I pointed up to a third-story window about fifteen meters in front of me and fired my M-4 into it. Jay said, "Where?" and I tried to tell him as I shot it again.

I attempted to look through my laser scope with my helmet microphone in front of my mouth, and when I fired, the butt stock of my M-4 slammed into my upper lip, which was then punctured by my teeth. Jay said, "Oh!" as he aimed the M240 to begin firing at the window. Frank or Jo must have seen where I shot at the third story window or seen the smoke from the enemy's gun. Anyway, whoever was on the M240 began shooting at it, followed a half a second later by Jay's M240 and SGT Cruver's .50cal. Within a couple seconds, the window was full of smoke and debris, and its surrounding bricks crumbled. After two volleys from everyone, we stopped shooting, and no further fire came from that building.

A few other windows had fire coming from them, but Third Platoon (Dan Karney) arrived, and a section already dismounted behind us, while the other continued to escort the bomb disposal team. His boys cleared building after building, and I pulled back out to the main road, while B Section remained to support the infantry. We received more fire from the truck yard, so I drove down with the commander, letting Randy know, so they wouldn't shoot in our direction. As we moved, the enemy didn't fire a shot. We even sat immobile for a few minutes, but still no one fired on us. I recommended to CPT Wan that some dismounts clear the truck yard, but they were busy on the other side of the road. We continued to scan for enemy fire, but it seriously died down. I moved out of the truck yard with the boss, and he moved down the alleyway to dismount with Third Platoon.

Enemy fire started up from the left in the truck yard again as soon as we left it, and we concluded those enemies weren't even aiming anywhere near us. Occasionally a shot would sound close, whizzing by our Strykers, but they seemed desperate to avoid exposing themselves. I told Randy and his section to follow me, and I drove through the truck yard again. I decided for us to close our hatches and scan through our optic sites, so we could find where this fire was coming from. We set up in a coil formation with me facing north, Randy facing west and SGT Moorefield facing southeast into the truck yard, all from its northwestern corner. The fire again stopped, and we scanned while the infantry dismounts cleared the rest of the buildings and alleyways to the right of the main road. CPT W reported a civilian casualty, and I volunteered to escort him with my platoon back to the hospital, since it seemed like the enemy was done shooting. He had us escort him to the Mosul Medical Center just south of Hwy-1.

SFC Nubear and crew applied bandages to stop the bleeding. It was a big older gentleman with two wounds: a gunshot wound through his back and left side, and one through his arm. His arm bled profusely, but the crew managed to stop it, and give him an IV bag, which fell out in route. We got him to the hospital, while SGT Scott explained to him where he was hit, and that it would be okay. He was able to walk into the hospital with our help, and we moved off, squeezing through the southern gate of the Medical City. CPT Wan approved us to conduct our route interdiction right then, since we were outside the base already. As we patrolled, I told Randy to pass the gas stations in the area, and oddly all of them were closed.

We all spoke on the platoon radio about food, since it was past lunchtime and none of us had eaten anything all day. I told Randy I wanted one of those rotisserie chickens we always see roasting over a fire outside of shops. We went by one and stopped movement once my vehicle was right next to a chicken spot on what our platoon had called "Road 45" (since it is at a 45-degree angle). We were only a few shops away from a cell phone shop we had planned an operation against over a month ago. Everyone thought I was joking until we pulled up and stopped and I told everyone to give me a dismount or two from each vehicle. We had a dismount team of about seven people, including myself, and we ran up the sidewalk to a chicken roasting spot and asked the guy how much the chicken was. The guy sold us a couple chickens at five dollars, which included a few giant pieces of delicious pita bread, and vegetables. We ran back into the vehicles, raised our ramps, and took off. Operation "Chicken Run" was a success, and the looks on the faces of the people on the streets were so funny.

They were used to Strykers blocking traffic, dropping ramp, and detaining people, or searching buildings and such. They looked stunned when we ran up and asked to buy some of their chicken. I put the bagged chicken on the floor next to the heater and suggested Frank do the same. "Good call," he answered, and he did so. We retuned to base and heard an explosion from the other side of the Tigris River – bomb disposal folks had finally blown the remainder of the weapons they couldn't remove via trucks. We parked, eating, and sharing the chicken. It felt like the perfect day. We found the biggest weapon cache in Mosul, joked around together and had some laughs on the platoon radio, had contact for the first time in a month, and got some chicken on a "black op."

Jo reminded me of our 2003 National Training Center visit when we had done our last "black op." After 15 days straight in the desert, we had all run out of snacks and food. Heath and Frank were on a range detail then, and the rest of the platoon and I took a break from platoon training. We left our icons on the battle computer as stationary where we were training, rolling with our lights completely off. We got to the "dust bowl" inner base of Fort Irwin, California, as Bryce and I ran into the town to buy supplies for everyone from a 24-hour Convenience Store. It was filled with excitement and some risk, just like this day.

I told CPT Wan later though about us "attempting to bolster the Iraqi economy by purchasing some whole cooked chickens," and he just laughed, so I didn't get in trouble, not that I was too worried. After finishing the chickens and sharing them with the rest of the Storm Troopers, I cleaned up, and knocked on Kevin G's door and shared with him my wonderfully blessed day. The first words out of his mouth were, "You aren't moving!" "No," I answered, "still moving, sorry to get your hopes up! I just had a great day." I told him all about it, and then we talked about the last night's practice, our lovely wives, and so much more.

I then went to the chapel for a Battalion mission briefing, and LTC Krella briefed us all. There were many officers and senior NCOs of the 82nd Airborne ("All-American") Division. They were here to stay for a while to support us for the upcoming elections in Mosul. They brought an entire battalion, 3-25 Infantry, with another one (1-14 Infantry, "Gold Dragons") on the way. We would be able to flood the city of Mosul with enough troops to deny enemy freedom of movement in and around the city. It was exciting, and the colonel talked highly of them, offering them our support. I loved the camaraderie, and as I listened to the colonel and the other staff speak, I was amazed at how wonderful our Army can be at times. The plan was great and the organization and thought put into it were superb. I was happy we had the 82nd here to help, even though I would not be there long to enjoy it. I loved my battalion and my battalion commander, and I realized how much I would miss it when I moved back to 2-14 Cavalry. I ran into LT Kim after the briefing, and he asked me questions about the operation, my platoon (soon to be his), and our mission before we went to the company command post for our company briefing.

January 2, 2005

We rolled out to Provincial Hall at 7 a.m., escorted a two-vehicle section of First Platoon, back to the base, then went back to Provincial Hall. We parked in the parking lot and sent two people from each vehicle up to man the third floor, since we were only going to be there for about five hours. Randy went up, and I stayed on the vehicle with 'Will.' We talked about everything from our relationships with the rest of the members of the platoon and company, to favorite ice cream, food (my favorite – crabs), and crackers. I explained how people's priorities are all different from one another, and everyone needs validation in some way, shape, or form. When someone isn't getting validation from another person, or they have competing priorities, it causes conflict. He brought up some in the platoon, I agreed, and I also mentioned some at the company level. I explained how I'm not interested in sports or weightlifting, yet my fellow Lieutenants are, so we don't always connect. God and His people are my main personal priority – relationships. Regardless, I'll be gone by the end of the week. LT Kim takes over on Tuesday, the 4th of January, and my platoon will take me to FOB Sykes to join 2-14 Cavalry.

Second Platoon relieved us at 12:45 p.m., and I requested for us to knock out our route interdiction next, which CPT Wan approved. LT Kim rode with him today and asked if he could come with the Storm Troopers, and CPT W gave permission. Andrew hopped on my vehicle, and I hooked him up with a communications helmet, and we rolled out. I basically gave him a tour of our sector, to include the gas stations, train station, police stations, and other key places he would need to know about. We watched some civilians fighting at a five-way intersection, and after we stopped to watch, they resorted to simple pushing and shoving for gas hoses. We returned to the FOB, and while we were at the fueling point, battalion radioed to all units that bomb disposal folks would detonate a car bomb at the vicinity of the DFAC parking lot!

Shocked, I warned my platoon, and we all looked over there, since we could see it from the fuel point. Over a bunch of army trucks, I noticed a lone Toyota pickup truck sitting all by itself in the parking lot of the DFAC, just beyond the port-a-pots. I pointed it out to the platoon. Within a couple minutes, it exploded. I couldn't believe the enemy could possibly get a vehicle carried bomb into our base. I guess I shouldn't be too surprised though, since a suicide bomber walked into the DFAC and blew himself up along with several of my friends and comrades on 21 December, but it was still rather shocking. We finished watching and fueling, and we all rolled back to the motor pool. I showed LT Kim the video of our contact on Operation Indy, and we talked. I told him I wish I had a day to just sit around and talk to him all day, to help him soak up everything I had to say. I can't imagine the stress he has on him now. I explained to him how I need things broken down "Barney Style" or simply, so I would do so for him. He said it was perfect, because he needed the same thing, and it didn't offend him at all.

At 4 p.m. the colonel talked to many of us at the chapel about current and future situations and operations. He showed us the disturbing video of December 29th, where PFC Oscar Sanchez from C Company died. The video filmed three different angles, and terrorists performing their ritual before driving a dump truck full of 1,500 pounds of explosives into our Hwy-1 combat outpost that day. Sanchez died while firing at the vehicle out of the window. The explosion was huge. This dump truck drove up over the barriers and detonated, engulfing the entire street and much of the police building in a fireball the size of the Lincoln memorial in Washington D.C. standing up on its end. It was surreal, and I could barely believe my eyes. LTC Krella spoke plainly to us, not using his usual command voice, and we just listened as he asked, "How do you prepare for something like this?" It was a question he admitted he had no answer to, other than more barriers and sandbags. It had to crush enemy morale to see our outpost the next morning with fresh Strykers and an infantry section; most damages repaired, with additional barriers. Still, we sadly lost another fine soldier from this battalion. I didn't know Sanchez and I was on mission thatday during his memorial service, but he is the fifth soldier our battalion has lost, now totaling nearly eighty casualties including dead and wounded.

At 6 p.m. CPT Wan briefed us on our company role for our battalion (now task force with 82nd Airborne) mission tomorrow. The entire city of west Mosul will be flooded with boots on the ground, searching for enemy and their weapons caches. I briefed Randy and SFC Nubear on the plan for our platoon, then walked back to my room with Andrew to ensure he understood it too. He told me he was glad I was leading the platoon tomorrow because he was confused. I said I completely understood, and that it was natural. Hopefully, as I mentioned to him, I will be able to ride on my vehicle after I sign the platoon over to him on Tuesday, and be the voice in his head (literally by the communications helmet) from the back hatch, helping him with any advice if needed. I hope I can do so until I leave here in a few days for FOB Sykes. CPT W approved in front of LTC Krella for my platoon to take me to Sykes when that day comes. DeArthur brought me a plate of hot chow from the chow line outside of the gym while I was talking to LT Kim. I appreciated it, eating it all up, because I wouldn't have eaten dinner otherwise. I told Andrew if he had any question about any subject, or how to do anything as a platoon leader or as an MGS platoon leader, to come by my door anytime. I stressed even if it is early in the morning, I will talk to him about it, or answer any questions he has. I hope he takes me up on it, because I want to make sure he and the platoon are taken care of after I leave, and that I pass on to him everything I possibly can. I know I'll continue to pray for him and the rest of the platoon even after I leave, but I want to do as much as I can while I'm still here.

That night, Chaplain Welon spoke on 1 Samuel, and the condition of our ears, hearts, and strength. He related them all to Samuel, Eli, Saul, and David, explaining without being plugged into God with your ears and heart, you will have no strength. Powerful; I pray it ministered to those who aren't close with Jesus. The chaplain even prayed over Andrew and I. He thanked the Lord for my witness to others for Jesus Christ, and asked that the Lord would continue to comfort, strengthen, and bless me in the future, giving me a safe trip, and a wonderful time at my new job. He asked that LT Kim would be filled with wisdom beyond his years and experiences and continuing to set an example of Christ for others, leading my platoon safely. I was very humbled that he prayed with everyone for me and had me stand to be recognized. I'm going to miss everyone there, in my platoon and company, and the battalion.

After dropping off my violin at my room, I walked to the aid station, because MAJ Brown (our Battalion Surgeon) told me to drop by at the beginning of the service. After I answered the three questions about my ears, heart, and strength that Chaplain Welon told us to ask each other during the greeting, I had told him honestly my ears were open, but my heart hurt because I was leaving, and I also hadn't called my wife since December 20th, the day before the DFAC bombing. I also told him my strength was good, because I knew I was in the Lord's will.

MAJ Brown had said "Uh-oh, you are in the doghouse, we've got to get you out! Come by and use the satellite phone in the aid station after church." I thanked him and did so after the service. It was wonderful to hear Becky's voice again, and I talked to her for ten minutes. I thanked him on my way out and told him my heart was healed now. Becky and I will meet on webcam tonight, so I better read the gospel and go, since midnight approaches. So thankful the Lord has given me a joyful spirit for dwelling in His presence all day; He's so amazing!

January 3, 2005

This day's mission was my last mission as a platoon leader. The next mission that I go on, which is tomorrow afternoon; I will no longer be the PL. It was sad in a way, and I already started to miss my guys and my job today, but also exciting, because it is a new change in my life, and I'm sure God's will is involved. I included LT Kim in the planning process as much as possible; he was on my vehicle the entire mission, to learn as much as he could about maneuvering the platoon in combat. I briefly explained to the NCOs the general scheme of maneuver and handed each of them a mini map CPT WanTarp printed for me. CPT W shared his intent with the company at 10:30 a.m.; it reminded me of the briefs CPT Jacobsen used to do. I still miss him so much. CPT WanTarp prayed for all of us on the mission, and we loaded up onto the vehicles.

As we rolled out of the gate, some of us noticed the Abrams tanks driving on our base, in addition to the Bradley Fighting Vehicles. All of them were here for additional support in the upcoming election. What I wouldn't give to lead my platoon in four tanks for a day in combat here. The tanks apparently rolled up and down Hwy-1 all day, and the citizens and terrorists of Mosul peered out their windows and doorways in shock. It makes me feel proud to be in this army, and thankful, knowing the power and military presence in this area. The enemy would be completely insane to mess with us now. They have no chance of winning any type of firefight, as we saw today. Our whole battalion was out, while Abrams tanks and Bradley's patrolled the main supply routes, beefed up with 82nd Airborne platoons everywhere, flooding several sectors of the city. It was crucial to the success of the first general election in Iraq's history.

My platoon led the way for our company, with three Hummvees full of dismounts, ten additional dismounts, plus more in the XOs vehicle and a medical Stryker from C Company's Third Platoon of 3-25th Infantry. We moved to the northern end of our sector and blocked the main road to the west of the traffic circle, dropping dismounts from 3-25th Infantry. They began clearing when the rest of the company arrived. LT Riley and LT Karney's platoons cleared to the south of the 82nd Airborne guys toward the west. Once the company progressed a bit more westward, I led B Section up and down the railroad tracks, where CPT W wanted me to screen (scan) for enemy disruption of the main efforts. Randy screened on the main road on which we all had come, and after a couple hours of this, we all were bored. Like I told the men though, I will take boring over dangerous any day.

LTC Krella with his Strykers came to our area after LT Karney's platoon found a weapons cache in a flour-packaging store. Several RPGs and RPG launchers, and a stolen hotwired Turkish tanker truck – it was stripped down and prepared for explosives to be turned into a car bomb. Our bomb disposal team detonated the truck and garage. Black smoke poured out of the walls of the building for our remaining two hours on the objective, and it made me smile. Not only did we possibly save lives by destroying what would have been an enormously large car bomb, but we also showed the citizens what happens to your building or place of business if you house such things. There were no shots fired at the entire Task Force while we were out today, which was phenomenal. The enemy was likely scared and confused by all the infantry and especially the tanks (who will be here for at least a month, possibly 45 days). If the elections go smoothly, and the elected officials remain in office securely (not being weak or killed), our extra troops they will leave in a month. I feel like I'm here in a large part of history, which is neat for me, having a love of and degree in history.

After returning to base, I grabbed all my leadership items and personal stuff off the vehicle, leaving only body armor and helmet. I will ride out with the platoon tomorrow, but not as the PL (Platoon Leader). Will helped me carry my stuff, and when we got back to my room, I talked to LT Kim for a bit. I asked him how he thought the mission went, and if he had any questions. He said he just needed to learn the routes, but he was confident. We went to talk to CPT Wan about our plans for tomorrow. I said we planned to conduct our property inventory at 9 a.m., and I would prepare the hand receipts and other things tonight. He said my platoon would escort me to FOB Sykes on Wednesday, just two days from now. So that is it, I will sign everything over to Andrew tomorrow, he will execute his first mission as the new platoon leader, and I will pack my room up.

CPT WanTarp plans for us to have a "Hail and Farewell" tomorrow night, for myself and LT Vebb leaving the company (Dave got his platoon in C Co), and for LT Kim coming, as well as SGT Fees, our new supply sergeant (who seems to love the Lord). They are ordering pizzas and sodas for the company. Andrew came by to ask me some questions about the civil affairs mission with MAJ P tomorrow afternoon.

I gave details, and he completely understood. I really pray he does well, because he seems to have a good heart for the men, and for his job. After he left, SGT Patterson came by and asked if I wanted to come down to the chapel to "jam" with him and some other guys. I appreciated him wanting to play with me one last time before I go to FOB Sykes.

January 4, 2005

As of 10 a.m., I am no longer a platoon leader; I can't complain as I was blessed with 16 months with my men, and 26 months total, counting the ten months I led 1/A/2-14 Cav (First Platoon, A Troop, Second Squadron, Fourteenth Cavalry Regiment) as a Reconnaissance Platoon Leader. Other than in Special Forces and Ranger Battalions, the average Platoon Leader time is 12-18 months for most Army Lieutenants. I've known some who didn't even get twelve months, so I was grateful. In the motor pool at 9 a.m., Andrew signed for the platoon equipment: vehicles, optics, weapons, communications, and navigation devices, etc. Normally we'd lay out "BII" or "Basic Issue Items" as well; items such as the axe, wrenches, warning triangle lights, the first aid kit, bags, straps, etc. on each vehicle (this would have taken all morning). The XO said last night we didn't need to check those items since most we could order any missing en masse because we were in combat. I was thankful.

Afterwards, LT Kim talked to MAJ P and CPT Wan about our civil affairs mission that day. Andrew discussed his plan with me to see if it made sense (it did). I packed my room, and Andrew came back again to confirm I was going with him. I told him, 'Absolutely!' so in case he or the platoon needed me for anything, even just moral support, I was there. He sounded glad, and I met him and the rest of the platoon at the vehicles at 1:20 p.m. He introduced himself to the men, gave a quick brief, and I presented him on behalf of the platoon his 'cherry' communications helmet. The guys painted one of our helmets (normally army green in color) bright cherry red and wrote in black paint marker 'cherry' on the back. They also taped a strip of green tough army nylon cord to the top, simulating a stem. At first, he thought it was the bomb, but I explained he was a 'cherry' (new) LT before leading his first mission today as the A Company MGS Platoon Leader. He laughed, as did the rest of us, and we mounted the vehicles.

As we rolled near the gate, I advised him when to call Battalion, and what exactly to say. He called, and we left the base. Our mission was extremely quick. We went to a bridge just east of Old Town and dismounted. I dismounted from our vehicle with about six others, two of which were the civil affairs soldiers since Major P decided to send a sergeant and specialist instead of going herself. She was on another mission or had already been on two missions that day. We set up a blocking position and found the generator. I kept watch, and updated Jay on the small radio. The Civil Affairs sergeant said the generator powered the marketplace only, no houses, which was all the information he needed. We mounted up and drove back. Andrew did well for his first time. The platoon would be in good hands, and God would watch over and protect them.

I told LT Kim 'good job' when we returned and continued to pack my room. Andrew and I switched weapons, and he received the mission brief at 5:30 p.m. for MGS/Storm Troopers for the next several days. More friendly forces poured into the city today, to include Iraqi Intervention Forces, who were supposedly well disciplined, and very well-trained soldiers. They would secure all polling sites for this month's elections. After the brief, CPT Wan and First Sergeant gathered the company together and we had our hail and farewell. No pizza or soda as planned, because to quote CPT Wan, "It cost like a million dollars." It was funny the way he said it, and still a nice gesture or thought. He told everyone Dave Vebb would go to B Company, and I would go to 2-14 Cavalry Regiment, which he described to everyone as, "Hell on earth." He introduced Andrew as the new PL replacing me. Andrew shared where he was from, and that Iraq was his first duty station. I went next and said it was a pleasure getting to know and work with everyone, I'd never worked with a better group of guys, and I would miss them all, especially my platoon, the others in the company I got to know, and my brothers in Christ. I also said I would continue to pray for them from FOB Sykes. Dave said goodbyes too, and the First Sergeant nicely directed everyone to shake our hands.

The company brought us warm spaghetti and soda, and I called my parents on the new satellite phone to wish my dad a belated happy birthday. Andrew and I went to battalion to confirm our routes with the intelligence officer (I also got a copy of the Hwy-1 outpost car bomb explosion video). While there, the colonel spoke with his XO, MAJ Lawz, remarking how Brigade had twelve Battalions under its control. I was just about to shake his hand thanking him for the time I spent under his command, when he looked seriously at me, and said regarding my mustache, "What the 'F' is that on your lip?" He sounded angry, and it was so loud, so the entire Tactical Operations Center (TOC) heard it. I answered it was just a couple hairs (also surprised this was the first time he noticed it – most infantrymen hate mustaches). He then asked me when I was leaving, and I answered, "tomorrow morning sir." My intention to thank him suddenly left me after his comment, but maybe I'd get a chance before I left, since I did think he was the best Battalion Commander I had worked for.

Later Dave asked me how things were, so I went into his room and we talked of God's will for my life, 2-14 Cavalry, our company and battalion, CPT Jacobsen, being a PL, and just the Army in general. Before I left, we prayed for each other, hugged, and went to finish packing. This was a great day, and the next day I go to Sykes. I knew the Lord and His angels would go with us, and I was glad my platoon was taking me there. My bags should all fit in the back of a Mortar Stryker, and I'd ride in my loader's hatch one last time.

January 5, 2005

As we went to the vehicles the platoon helped me carry my stuff – three duffel bags, my rucksack, two boxes of food and stuff, a giant gym bag full of food and supplies, my stuffed assault pack and laptop case, camelback, folding chair, and my Basic Instructions Before Leaving Earth. I said goodbyes to Chaplain Welon and a few others and went to the TOC. LTC K wasn't there, so I knocked on his door as a sergeant suggested. He was either out cold, or on a mission - there was no answer. One day I'd see him again and thank him for everything he had done for the Battalion, including teaching, training, and leading me.

We dropped off a Third Platoon section at Provincial Hall and heard a huge explosion to the southeast. It was so powerful we noticed windows shaking in the buildings around us. We learned a car bomb blew up, destroying the cab of a tanker truck, and blowing the wheels off a couple Humvees possibly from 3-25 Infantry. As the Humvees turned back to the FOB, we noticed the smashed windshield of one of them, and the gunner wasn't out of the top scanning on his .50 cal. I was sure he was a casualty, but I prayed it was nothing too serious. I guessed he caught glass in his legs and groin from the shattering of the windshield. LT Kim reported it to battalion, and we continued west. We didn't render aid because they had medics with them, and they could have made it back to the hospital just as fast as we.

While passing Four West police station, the 3-25 Infantry Battalion radio had a guy reading a long signal intelligence report for over three minutes; no one could get a word in. There should be a separate information operations channel for such messages, so at my and Jay's suggestion, LT Kim radioed "Break Break Break." They responded, "You just interrupted an important transmission." He shared how we were passing through their sector, and they should know. They didn't seem to appreciate it, but he informed them – it was protocol to let an adjacent unit know when you passed through its operations area. As we left the city of Mosul on Hwy-47, it rained hard. Randy and the guys radioed jokes and complaints, so I answered them, "I'll talk to the Lord and see what I can do." He responded, "Yeah! Could you do that? That'd be great."

It reminded me of Yakima Training Center last June (in Washington State), when we complained about the heat, and I said I just wanted some wind. I told everyone I'd ask God for wind – as the day progressed, it was one of the strongest winds we'd ever been in, so strong we could barely stand up outside our Strykers. Heath and Randy told me my prayer had been answered thoroughly, and then some. Later the same trip in June, Randy reminded me of how I prayed for his dad when I first arrived in the platoon in September 2003, and his dad was healed of cancer. That June, he asked me to pray for his daughter for her surgery. He was uncomfortable praying, and I prayed with him, and thanked the Lord for Randy seeking Him during that scary time. I also thanked Him for using me as a tool to show how God answers prayers.

Sure enough, the rain stopped for the rest of the trip. At a checkpoint halfway to Tal Afar, we hit heavy traffic, so the platoon went around it, taking the northern exit of a traffic circle. It was hard for me to see from the back in the loaders hatch, but I had a feeling we were going the wrong way. I popped down and moved forward in the Stryker to see the FBCB2 battle computer map as the feeling kept prodding me. Sure enough, we were heading north from the Hwy-1 and Hwy-47 intersection and needed to head southwest. I mentioned to Andrew we should turn around, and he relayed to Randy. I was thankful I had that feeling (possibly from the Spirit). Who knows how far we would have gone before realizing we were going the wrong way? I wondered how close we came to Turkey or Syria. We adjusted, and as we approached Tal Afar, Andrew radioed to 2-14 Cavalry we were entering their sector with five Strykers, escorting LT Sacra. They responded, and we made it to FOB Sykes just as the rain returned and became stingingly painful. I radioed Randy and said, "at least God kept it off of us for most of the trip."

We entered the base, fueled, and parked outside of the DFAC and convenience store (or as some call it – Haji-mall). At the 2-14 TOC, Andrew and I saw my old (now current) Squadron Commander, LTC Mavis (Squadron is the Cavalry term for Battalion). He welcomed me but was unsure what job I'd have. I saw MAJ Rugrs, the S3 or Operations Officer sixteen months ago when I was in the Squadron last, but he was now the XO or Executive Officer. He welcomed me, said I needed to change my uniform armor insignia as he gave me crossed saber cavalry insignia, and said my wife should mail my Stetson hat and spurs, since they wore them each Friday. I met Andrew's friend Derek (a LT working in the TOC, while waiting for a platoon). He kindly showed me around the Squadron area and helped me get a room. For a minute, it seemed I might work in the TOC as a battle captain twelve hours a day, but we ran into MAJ Rugrs after lunch and he told me I would be CPT Bicks' XO for the Iraqi National Guard Battalion. I never thought I would be an XO. CPT Rob Bicks was the Personnel and Admin Officer when I arrived from Fort Knox back in October of 2002. When I left the Squadron ten months later, Rob took command of B Troop (a troop is the cavalry term for a company, as a squadron is the cavalry equivalent of a battalion). Now, he was the Headquarters Troop Commander.

I shook CPT Bicks' hand in shock, as I had just asked God to put me exactly where He wanted me. It sounded exciting and I might go outside the wire twice a week on cordon and search missions with Iraqis, kicking in doors, like the infantry platoons did in 1-24 Infantry. I got a temporary room behind LT Rich Durmsy, CPT Bicks' current XO. Rich and I were platoon leaders together in A Troop of of 2-14 Cavalry when I first got to Fort Lewis, Washington. He was on a mission at Sinjar, the next town over, southwest from Tal Afar. The boys helped me carry everything into my room – a room with one bed, no wall locker, no trashcans, and broken blinds. Andrew then brought the rest of the platoon over, and I said goodbye to them all, explaining what my job would be. I said how much I'd miss them, and how they were the best group of guys I had ever worked with. I said I learned a lot from them, hoped I had trained and led them well, and hoped I had glorified Jesus Christ in my time I spent with them.

They all shook my hand, and some gave hugs. It was an emotional moment, but none of us cried – we'd see each other again. They left, and I went to my room thanking God for getting me there safely, for this new job He'd prepare me for, and asked for continued protection of my men and me in this war. After praying, I talked to other 'Nomads' (our unit name and call sign), and scrounged around to get myself a wall locker, trashcan, and second bed (to put things on). I set things up in my room and went to the new command post. I got a ride to chow with SPC Sunburn and one of our interpreters. The chow hall checked identification upon entry, searching any non-US personnel with a metal detector wand. Inside, it had wooden booths with sandbag piles in between them. Such things could have saved CPT Jacobsen's life. As I discussed the improvements with SPC Sunburn, I learned that SGT Vankomen, the A Troop supply sergeant, died in the Mosul DFAC on December 21st. He was the supply sergeant when I was in A Troop. I couldn't believe it – of the horrible things in war for a soldier, the loss of loved ones, friends, comrades seem the worst tragedies. After chow, I showed SFC Aeris (the first sergeant) the Hwy-1 outpost car bomb video, and we talked for a bit. Rain began to pour again, and I returned to my room to organize and listen to praise music.

From left to right: The Storm Troopers; CPT Jacobsen (above a painting of the Armor insignia from our platoon office at Fort Lewis); My Stryker in Mosul the day of a big operation.

II

Nomad

5

January, Part 2

January 6, 2005

Praise the Lord; this day was amazing! I woke at 7 a.m., worked out, listened to praise music as I read scripture, and spoke to God. I joined SFC Walenz and an interpreter for breakfast. After chow, we went to check on a 9 a.m. Iraqi formation but they had already had it at 8 a.m. yet didn't let us know. SFC Walenz told them it was okay, since they oversaw their own unit, but they needed to let us know if they changed times, so we would know to meet them at whichever time they assembled. I learned so much talking to SFC Aeris, SFC Walenz, and SPC Sunburn. I followed SFC Aeris and SGT Edmundo ZT to the entry control point (front gate) of the base a few times, to sort issues with Iraqi soldiers coming and going on missions. They all taught me how our unit operates. Instead of being an Iraqi Company Command group, we were more like trainers and liaisons or coordinators for them, a bit like how Special Forces or Green Berets work with foreign military forces. They trained them, coordinated missions with them, managed and worked out any issues with them, and even fought with them in battle.

Our team was small (just as Green Berets units operate in small teams). There were eight of us, including Captain Bicks (the commander of our 'Nomad' unit, as well as of the Headquarters Troop for the Squadron). Headquarters Troop had an XO already, so I was just the XO for the Iraqi training detachment, or 'Nomad Five', as I was called. SFC 'Woody' Aeris was Nomad Seven, the equivalent of the 1SG (First Sergeant, non-commissioned officer in charge) of our unit. SFC Walenz was the training NCO for the Iraqis. I wasn't sure of SFC Puten's title. We had Sergeants ZT and Wadul who handled a lot, and Specialist Sunburn was our only enlisted solider who did a lot of work too. Lieutenant Rich Durmsy returned, and he said he'd been the Squadron Supply and Logistics Officer (or S4) for a couple of weeks already. After I returned from the Squadron Personnel and Administration office and headquarters troop to in-process, I ran into Rich Durmsy at the Nomad command post. He would keep his "double-wide" room, which was fine, because I had always had a singlewide room in Iraq, so it made no difference to me. He drove me to the Supply and Admin offices and gave me the keys to my Iraqi jeep – the official vehicle of 'Nomad Five.' It was cool that I got my own personal jeep. I was sure that CPT Bicks also had his own vehicle. We also had five cars with at least two seats to share between eight people. In addition, we had vehicles that had been confiscated from terrorists who had been arrested.

CPT Bicks flew to FOBs Freedom and Diamondback that day, and so I had to go to the Squadron 4:30 p.m. briefing. I was ten minutes late because we were out dealing with 70-some Iraqi soldiers returning from leave. After the briefing, MAJ Rugrs told me not to show up late for his or the SCOs (Squadron Commander's) meetings. I just said "Roger, sir," because he didn't seem to be concerned with a reason or an excuse. Afterwards, I met the Squadron Chaplain, CPT Ed Wells, and we spoke on the way into his office. He prayed with me, and seemed excited that I had brought my violin, and was willing to play on the praise team (which had not been started yet). I found out the times of all the Bible studies and events, and then found the chapel location. I returned to the Nomad command post, and SFC Aeris and SPC Sunburn invited me to go to the gym. I didn't really want to go, because I was just not the type of person that liked to go lift weights much, but I went to begin to build a relationship with these guys, since lifting was important to them. God taught me this with my peers in 1-24 Infantry (the unit I just left), but by the time it sank in, it was too late.

On our way to the gym, Sunburn said his 'faith' was in SFC Aeris, his battle buddy. He said he and God had an understanding: he wouldn't go into any churches, and God wouldn't blow up the church because he went in it. He almost seemed proud to say, "If there is a Heaven and a Hell, I'm probably going to the less nice of the two." I wondered where this anger and hurt towards God came from, and soon found out while lifting weights in the gym. His wife was three months pregnant with her second child when she had a miscarriage around December 20th. He seemed devastated, as I know Becky and I would be too. I told him I didn't like or agree with his view of faith or God, but understood it, and could relate, sharing with him the times I had been an atheist and several embraced other religions as a teenager.

After showering near our rooms, Sunburn and I got ready to go out to the recreation tent to use the internet. SFC Puten said he had noticed a sign outside of the chow hall about paying 200 dollars per soldier to hook up internet in rooms. As Nomad XO, it was my job to figure that out, so I read the rest of the details at the chow hall (just next door) and went to talk to the lieutenant who posted the sign. He gave me details (which I'd share with the team tomorrow), and I thanked him and returned to the morale tent. I spoke to my friend Shelton online, and then Becky with webcam. When Sunburn and I got to our rooms, I read the gospel. I was thankful I had such a busy day, and that God blessed me out here with an amazing job, neat people to work with, and outstanding living conditions.

January 7, 2005

CPT Bicks approved us getting the internet and found a way for us to pay for it in the budget, so I went early to meet that lieutenant again to let him know we would take the deal. I also fueled my jeep at the fuel station; it was so nice to fuel a vehicle without waiting in line, and without having to pay. I told CPT Bicks I reserved the internet contract and he and SFC 'Woody' Ayers were happy. CPT R hoped I could go to the Project Ordering Officer class on Diamondback the next day, so we began paperwork, including memoranda and signature cards. My other job title besides "Detachment XO" was "Project Ordering Officer," so I needed the class, and we tried to schedule it after we sent off my memoranda for the colonel's signature. I met some of the Iraqi National Guard soldiers and learned more while talking to the rest of the 'Nomads.'

During an Iraqi patrol, another soldier gave up his weapon and walked away from the checkpoint where he was posted, which made everyone mad. Iraqi soldiers got leave denied due to upcoming elections. There was a fear they may not come back, and there was a heightened sense of force protection on the base. From January 15 to February 15, only US soldiers or those Iraqi soldiers on missions would be allowed off base, with few exceptions. CPT Bicks returned from the brief with a change in internet plans – the Squadron XO and Commander wanted someone else to have the four-month hookup from that lieutenant, and wanted to fund us with an entire year's worth of internet at twice the price. It wasn't as reliable though, so most of us weren't interested. We'd rather have had the four months of reliable of internet, but it isn't really our call. SFC Puten, SFC Walenz, SGT Wadul and SPC Sunburn invited me to the gym again, and I decided to go, against my desires.

January 8, 2005

Praise God! This day was so awesome – I knew I was in God's will, and it felt great! The Iraqis had a formation in their area, but I didn't go, because CPT Bicks needed me to check on an email Rich Durmsy sent yesterday, in addition to getting $6,000 cash from him to pay the wounded Iraqi National Guard soldiers by 2 p.m. today. I said, "yes sir," and as I went to my jeep (which I learned is Russian made), he added for me to check on the flights while at the Squadron Tactical Operations Center. I drove to the TOC and spoke to everyone I needed to. I found out they needed mine and CPT Bicks' social security numbers, full name, rank, number and weight of bags, purpose of mission, and destination all on a piece of paper. I drove back to get CPT Rs info, submitted the paper, and got money from LT Rich D. It was the most cash I'd ever held, six thousand dollars. I went to the chapel to get the schedule printout for services and Bible studies, then took Derek to lunch and we caught up on things.

Becky wrote a long email, asking a lot of questions her friend Megan asked her about me: Have I killed anyone? Did I see their faces when they died? Was it hard? What did I do with the bodies afterwards? Becky said she wondered the same things, and even though the questions seemed a bit morbid at first, I was glad they asked. I explained mostly what I remembered of my biggest firefight (November 11th), and my frustrations at enemies who killed innocent people (Iraqi and US). I shared my hatred towards evil, and my desire for its eradication. I shared how in all three of my big firefights, I focused on stopping such evil, and saving the lives of my men by putting a stop to whomever was firing at us. I asked her if she considered my orders to my men to fire a TOW into a building with seven terrorists inside as killing someone. I said they may have continued to live and fire at us had I not ordered Randy to fire his missiles.

I admitted that I sprayed 7.62mm from my M240 machine gun into some back-of-the-house balconies, and I wondered if there were innocent civilians in there. "I asked for God's forgiveness if there were, but I don't think there were any in there," I wrote. Was it hard? Sure, it was hard to have the courage to stand up exposed behind my weapon and return fire when I was scared of being hit by an enemy bullet or RPG, but God gave me strength, as He did daily. I knew she meant 'hard' as in difficult to take a human life, so I elaborated it wasn't hard when I knew I was protecting my men and myself and stopping evil. I even mentioned how I cheered after the missiles hit, destroying the terrorists. I finally said I didn't usually see any bodies (although some of my men did), and we usually left the bodies in the streets so all of the enemy could see them and remind them of what would happen when they messed with us. It may have sounded gruesome, but it was the way I saw it and felt about it* [see note].[1]

After emailing, I ate lunch, and then ran into CPT Bicks. I let him know I had the money and everything was complete. Upon returning to the command post, I showed 'Woody' (SFC A) and Evan (one of our interpreters) the video of the November 11th firefight, and CPT Bicks watched too. They counted a few of the RPGs fired and enjoyed seeing the TOW missiles blast into the building from which we had received so much enemy fire. SGT Wadul and SFC Walenz asked who wanted to go to dinner after a while, and I volunteered, and the three of us went together while Woody went to pick up 70-some Iraqi soldiers at the gate. About 35 of them were brand new recruits, and the other 40 or so were returning from leave. SGT Wadul and SFC Walenz and I talked at dinner about chess mostly, and it felt good to get to know them better.

They said something about going to the gym again with Sunburn, and I told them I was going to Bible study at 8 p.m., so no gym tonight. Sunburn looked at Sergeant Wadul and said, "Yeah, you aren't the only Bible thumper anymore now!" We both gave him confused looks, and

I answered, "I'm not a Bible thumper, I just love the Lord." SGT Wadul said he went to the Latter-Day Saints services. SFC Puten came in asking for an update, since we were on the radio earlier when an Iraqi checkpoint in Tal Afar reported indirect fire and small arms fire. We didn't hear of any Iraqi soldier casualties, so Woody said it was nothing. SFC Puten stressed he just wanted to be informed of what was going on since everyone was leaving to the gym or elsewhere, so I filled him in. After almost everyone left, SFC Puten asked Omar (the other interpreter) and Evan to leave, as well as the other soldiers in there. He said, "I just want to talk to the LT for a while." He unexpectedly started with, "I'm sure you've probably heard some things about me, like that I am an [expletive]…"

He explained how important standards were and objected to being treated like he didn't need to know anything because he wasn't the sergeant who oversees our detachment. He was once the Platoon Sergeant for First Platoon of 'A' Troop but was relieved after an investigation. Ironically, that is the platoon I led as Scout Reconnaissance ("Recce") Platoon Leader when I was in 2-14 Cavalry the first time. SFC Puten took over from SFC Swafford (my first Platoon Sergeant) about eight months after I left my first platoon. He shared how he got yanked from his platoon before getting to Iraq because an investigation concluded he was too hard on his men. From his perspective, some sergeants and soldiers complained when he tried to get them to keep better track of their things and tried to train them better. There are two sides to every story, so I'd have to get the other side one day, but my instinct was to trust him – perhaps he was wronged.

We cut the conversation short for his 8 p.m. meeting, so I stayed in the command post to man the radio. The interpreter Omar came in and said an Iraqi soldier who was wounded a couple months ago and treated in a civilian hospital, now needed better surgery from a US military hospital. After listening to the Iraqi battalion's radio in Arabic, he said the guy had a bad gunshot wound in his side and needed better medical attention. For a few seconds I felt worried – my second or third day on the job, I didn't know much about how they work as a unit, and it was just Omar and I, while someone's health (possibly life) was in danger. As Omar talked on his radio, I prayed silently, asking God to help me represent Him well, and help me know exactly what to do to bring Him glory, be a good leader, and take care of this soldier. Immediately, my prayer was answered. I asked Omar if this man had already seen an American medic, and he asked them via radio.

They answered no, and I clarified to Omar to make sure I understood everything about this wounded Iraqi soldier, including the history of his wounds. As I repeated it back to Omar, Woody came in (another answer to prayer); every decision I made could then be either backed up by his concurrence, or by his correction, since I was so new. I got the soldier's name and rank, and his history. Corporal Gharib was wounded on the 25th of October by an enemy AK47 at a police station in Afghani, a town north of Tal Afar. He was taken to a civilian hospital in Sinjar, a town southwest of Tal Afar, and released to his home after an operation on some of his gunshot wounds. He had just entered the FOB today around 4 p.m. and was in pain. I called the medics and requested they dispatch medics to check him out, describing his condition, as I knew it.

Medics arrived, and I walked over to the Iraqi soldier barracks with Omar, to visit the wounded soldier and his sergeant. He was in a lot of pain and had a hole in the right side of his abdomen. I was saddened but knew God had me there for a reason, and I was determined to show this man and everyone else the love of Jesus through my care and leadership. The medics and I spoke to CPL Gharib through Omar, and I also filled them in on what I knew thus far. The medics tried to tell me he would be okay, and not to be too concerned with him, and I said I was asking them a lot of questions because I had just arrived at this unit as the XO and was wondering how the whole medical process worked. They immediately understood our situation and told me they would bring him to the Physician's Assistant to assess whether CPL Gharib needed to be shipped to the Mosul combat support hospital, or to Baghdad.

I returned to the command post to brief CPT R and Woody, then led the medics back to load CPL Gharib in their ambulance Humvee. SFC Puten arrived as they carried him. I told the Iraqi sergeant (CPL Gharib's boss) I would go with his soldier to the aid station this time, but next time he would go with his soldier. He said, "Thank you!" and seemed pleased. At the Squadron Aid Station, and the physician's assistant cleaned CPL Gharib, and gave him an IV bag. He struggled with the pain of the cleaning solution, as well as the needle. God led me to talk to Gharib through Omar, asking him about his wife (whose name was tattooed on his arm) and his children. I asked if his sons would be soldiers like him one day. He said his sons would join the Iraqi National Guard one day (his oldest is three), because they wanted to defend his country. I wanted to distract him from his pain and get to know him. As I asked questions about his wife and two sons and he told Omar to tell me that I was making him forget about the pain when I talked to him. I laughed and smiled, and said, "Good; that is what I'm trying to do."

SFC Puten and I spoke about the care Iraqi soldiers needed in general, and we drove back to Gharib's room. CPL Gharib will stay here for another day or so, because as it turned out, a surgical team was coming the next day to set up shop at our aid station. The team would examine him to determine his status and decide if he needed to be taken anywhere. I told Gharib, "*Alla ya adeek al aahfia,* and *Tisbah ala khair.*" (God give you health and good night). Omar briefed him on the deal with the surgeons, and we returned to the command post. On the short way back, SFC Puten said he has always caught flak for doing the right thing. He said he was not 'religious' but didn't smoke, drink, dip, or 'ooh and ahh' over women like other soldiers and was different than most guys in the Army. I told him I could relate, on a spiritual level, since I had a relationship with the Lord, which wasn't too popular in the Army either.

When I returned, I explained to Woody the new standard I wanted to put in place. I had earlier typed up a report on our Nomad computer with the time of report, the situation, actions taken, and follow up information on the major events for the day. CPL Gharib's incident was my first entry and the example. I said, "I'm all about playing games on the computer, but instead of doing that sometimes, we can put reports on here, so we have some type of running log of the events, and everyone will know what is going on. My format here doesn't have to be set in stone, and I'll take suggestions on any improvements, but it should look something like this." He agreed, and said it sounded like a great idea. I was also personally trying to learn two or three Arabic words or phrases per day. Evan taught me *"tisbah ala khair, maku akthar* and *ashed ghoul"* meaning "goodnight, no more, and "how do you say" respectively. I later praised God, feeling validated as His servant, as a leader in this unit, and as a soldier. It was wonderful to care for Gharib, and to help organize a standard here at the Nomad unit. I knew I was here for so many reasons, and I looked on them with anticipation and joy, knowing God's strength would carry me through them all.

January 9, 2005

CPT Bicks and I both checked on flights at the Tactical Operations Center before 6:30 a.m., but there were none going our direction. After 8 a.m., the TOC radioed for Nomad Six and Seven (CPT Bicks and SFC Aeris/Woody) to come up to the TOC. The front gate to FOB Sykes had just reported two Iraqi soldiers without badges and without pass papers trying to leave the FOB, and I told them to send the soldiers back to us. On his way out, Woody let me know we must pick up Iraqi soldiers from the gate whenever they were there, because we couldn't let them just wander around the base. These two soldiers were quitting because they thought the Iraqi National Guard would be different than they expected. Woody was especially mad because he briefed them all when they came in; if they were going to quit, that was the time to do so. We detained them, and eventually kicked them off the base.

I next decided to see about our internet situation, since we still weren't sure if we would get the cheaper four-month service or the full year service. CPT Bicks handed me the paper that mentioned the prices for everything on it, and he told me the questions I needed to ask when I called on one of the cell phones. He told me to grab 'Debusa,' the Squadron Commander's interpreter, and have him call, and help me to email the company as a backup. I walked into the Iraqi compound and found their TOC, where Debusa was located. He helped me call, but no one answered the phone calls. We decided to email the company in Arabic and English, but first, Major Sultan, the Iraqi National Guard Battalion XO, invited me in for Chai (Arabic Tea).

Upon entering his office, I was filled with images of the last time I had been there, almost three months ago. It was around October 23rd or 24th, that CPT Jacobsen and I walked into that same office, and apologized to Major Sultan for accidentally shooting one of his soldiers in the leg. I told MAJ Sultan (through Debusa) I had been in this room before, with my former commander, CPT Jacobsen. I asked if he remembered me, and described how tall CPT Jacobsen had been, and how we had apologized for the incident. He nodded, and seemed to remember, so I told him CPT Jacobsen was killed in the chow hall explosion in Mosul. He apologized, and said it was a shame, as we agreed he was a great commander, and a great man. After chatting about Arabic words and other small talk, Debusa and I drove to the internet café to email the internet company. I dropped Debusa off at the TOC on my way back to Nomad Base (our command post) since he had a mission to go on with LTC Mavis.

At Nomad Base, CPT Bicks showed me the importance of Checkpoint 201, also known as Avgani Checkpoint (it controls the intersection of Hwy-47 and the road running north and south leading to Avgani, about five miles north of Tal Afar). He explained how Iraqi soldiers kept getting mortared and fired upon at the checkpoint, and our Squadron was exploring how to defend it better with some type of fortifications. He briefed me on the different areas that were dangerous, the locations from where they received most fire, as well as the type of fire. I prayed silently as we began talking, that God's Spirit would help me use the gifts He gave me. I first confirmed the purpose of the checkpoint, and began to explain how to defend it better, using Hesco barriers (wire and wood filled with dirt) on either side of the road to offer some flank protection for the Iraqi soldiers when stopping vehicles. I also suggested a metal pole to be used as a gate, which would stop cars, and give fair warning if a car bomb were about to try and run the checkpoint or destroy it. I described fortifications which might help accomplish the task and purpose of the checkpoint and drew them out for him.

He was impressed, said it sounded great, and I asked if he would like me to sketch it on my computer to print so he could show the colonel. He said that would be great, so I did, then explained how to use the concrete bunkers (C-bunkers), stacking them to protect from indirect and small arms fire. They also would allow Iraqi soldiers to observe danger areas, mount floodlights for nighttime observation and defend from a safe static position, instead of running away from the checkpoint when shot at. I showed Woody, SFC Walenz (an infantryman), and Sunburn, who all liked the idea. Sunburn suggested adding a wall of sandbags on the ground level at the back of the bunker to offer better rear protection. It looked like this:

C-Bunker Fortifications

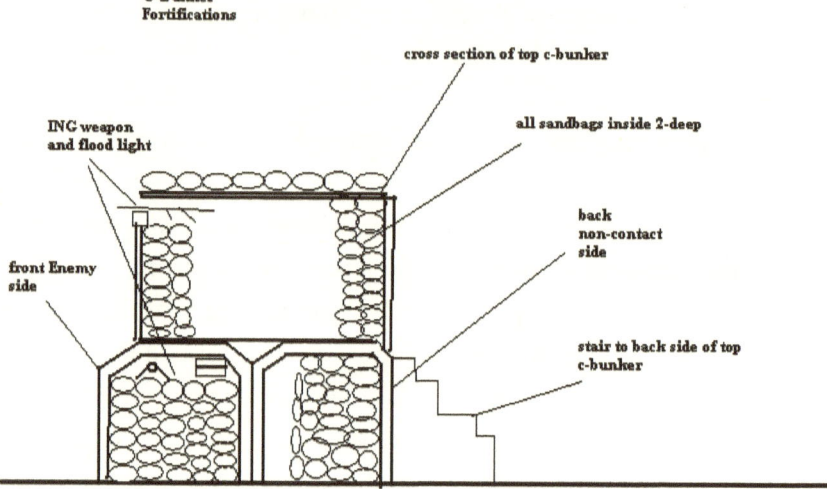

Overhead view of C-bunker fortification
All sandbags 2 deep at least

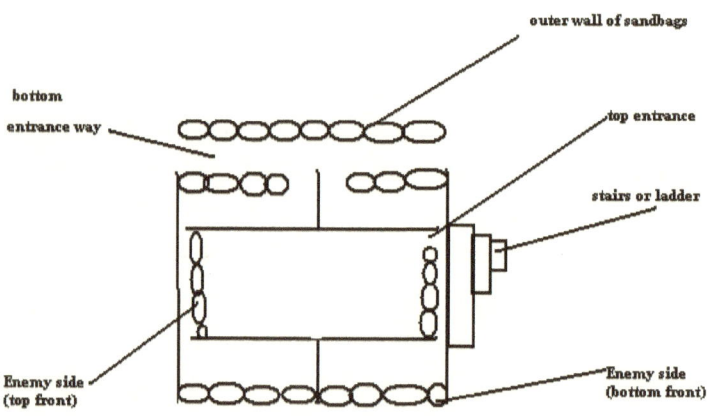

CPT Bicks later said the SCO (Squadron Commander) really liked the design, so assuming we could get the materials, we (or engineers) would build them at the checkpoint for the Iraqis. CPT Bicks mentioned sarcastically before leaving that we would call these fortifications a "Sacra," and we would put up "Sacra's" all over the checkpoint. We all were laughing, and when he got back, he said, "Yeah, not only did the SCO like them, but I told him how I came up with the idea, and that we were calling them 'Bicks's', and he told me it was a great job." As I was laughing, I answered, "Yeah, and then he promoted you to major on the spot, sir." He laughed and said, "Yes, that's right." The rest of the evening was Sunday school and Bible study, which were both nice, but I was so very tired from the lack of sleep, so it was difficult to stay awake.

Another significant thing that happened that day is MAJ Rugrs (the Squadron XO) called an NCO or above from every unit to the conference room regarding a missing piece of equipment. I represented Nomad, and when I got there, he threw a cut lock and chain on the table saying it had secured an ATV. Someone cut the lock and took it, and he wanted it back. He ordered for every all-terrain vehicle to be brought to the TOC parking lot from every unit on the base, to include civilians. If they weren't all there by morning, he said that he would make life very painful for everyone. His plan was to snatch anyone seen driving one after they were all consolidated at the TOC area, to catch the thief. We'd see how well it works.

January 10, 2005

After 8 a.m., CPT Bicks and and I flew to FOB Diamondback in Mosul for our budgeting class. The flight took exactly twenty minutes and it was nice to fly in a Blackhawk helicopter once again. I thanked the Lord we weren't shot at. We checked in at the Brigade Comptrollers office and discussed funds with him. CPT Halvorson, the Comptroller, told us that things didn't look promising, and he would see what could be done with the financial channels above him. CPT Halvorson was once B Troop Commander of 2-14 Cavalry when I was a Scout Reconnaissance Platoon Leader in A Troop a couple years ago, so it was good to see a familiar face. When he and CPT Bicks and another captain discussed the Mosul chow hall bombing, I shared details about CPT Jacobsen, and they were shocked – they thought he had died instantly. CPT Bicks and I then visited the Iraqi compound on FOB Diamondback to give the Iraqi soldiers some patches.

Specialist Grayson recognized me and filled me in on Mosul since I had left. Iraqi soldiers raided the Iraqi Islamic Party building the Storm Troopers and I always noted while driving north and south on a certain route. Whenever Ghizlani police station took fire, it was from there, so they raided it, finding a large stash of RPG launchers, RPGs and Russian made rifles and machine guns. He said A Company of 1-24 Infantry found an enormous stash of enemy weapons somewhere in their sector. There were tons of mortar rounds, RPGs, small arms weapons, and bomb making materials, and a truck already wired to be used as a car bomb. With all the additional units in Mosul, it is little wonder why intelligence reported many enemy freedom fighters and leaders there were heading back to Syria and other countries from whence they came. They were claiming they were losing too many people and weapons to the US.

As we left Grayson said he found his faith when two mortars landed just outside the Iraqi soldier gate where he worked. I congratulated him and suggested he talk to the chaplain. CPT Bicks and I returned to the comptroller officer after first stopping at the PX and food court to get some supplies and lunch (I bought a chess and checkers set for Nomad Base). CPT Halvorson gave me a five-minute class on my Project Ordering Officer duties, so I would be completely trained when the time came to change and verify the accounts. It turned out we would get no further funds for a month or so, so we shouldn't close the account in Rich Durmsy's name to re-open it in mine just yet. Our flights were late, but we were safely dropped off back at FOB Sykes.

We got to our command post, and a radio call came in from the gate of a roadside bomb exploding at Avgani checkpoint, wounding an Iraqi soldier who was now on the way to the aid station. He was hit through the cheeks and head with shrapnel and died of wounds just after arriving at the aid station. We all felt bad for him and the unit, but we could do nothing.

Sergeant Wadul and I both played a few games of chess with our interpreter Evan, who beat both of us three times apiece. After the "whipping," I took him to chow, and we had a good talk up and back. He said he really liked President Bush (who was on the TV in the chow hall), because he freed Iraq, was a good man, and because he just liked him. A woman named Elizabeth (another "Liz" as she preferred to be called) sat down and talked to me, asking if she saw me at the chapel last night. "That was me," I answered, and we began to talk about the DFAC in Mosul being bombed, but I changed the subject to how she came to know Jesus. Evan just kind of watched TV while "Liz" and I talked.

Back at the command post-- or Nomad Base, we spoke of missions forthe next two days. As everyone gradually cleared out to go to the gym and bed, I grabbed Omar, and he and I went to check on the previously wounded CPL Gharib, to see how he was – we'd heard the surgeons wouldn't operate on him because he was so small and skinny, and it could damage him badly. He had already been informed of this, but I decided to bring him snacks and food to eat in between large meals to fatten him up. Omar explained it to him, and he was pleased I gave him snacks, but told me it hurt him to eat. It was sad seeing him in such a serious condition and with a colostomy bag.

Upon return to our command post, Omar went over a lot of Arabic words and phrases with me, and even began to teach me to read and write it. As midnight approached, we received a knock on the door from Iraqi Major Waad. He was upset because one of his soldiers shot himself in the foot at a checkpoint. They brought him to the FOB just now for medical attention. I told them to put gauze on it while I called the medics to let them know. They replied they didn't have any gauze, which was inaccurate, so I quickly balled up some toilet paper, and ripped the cardboard toilet paper tube, explaining to them to place it over the wound, cardboard between the hand and paper, and apply firm pressure. The aid station answered me on the radio and said to bring the soldier to them as soon as possible. I took Omar with me, locked up Nomad Base and said *"Ilhagnee"* (follow me).

They followed me in their Nissan "battlewagon" as I led them to the aid station in my jeep. On my way out, I passed CPT Bicks, updated him, and he met me at the aid station. The wounded soldier was in a lot of pain, but we told him to calm down, and to shoot the enemy next time, instead of himself. He seemed more afraid of getting injected with a morphine needle than about the status of his foot. Through Omar, I explained the importance of keeping his weapon on safe when there is no enemy, and he understood. I even gave him a demonstration with my selector switch on my weapon, so he could visualize when to keep it on safe, and when to switch it to fire when *"al adu"* (the enemy) was nearby. They numbed his foot and wrapped it with a sterile dressing and sent him back with medication to take a few times a day. I took him back to his room and told him to be ready for a checkup after 9 a.m. the next day. I typed everything in the running computer log, told Omar goodnight and to enjoy his *"mujas"* (five days of leave or vacation).

January 11, 2005

At 9:30 a.m. I drove the Iraqi soldier Khalaf to the aid station – the bandage was soaked in blood, and he seemed in more pain. The medics rewrapped him after cleaning the wound and told me to bring him back after 1 p.m. to have him sent to Mosul. He seemed to panic when we said Mosul because he didn't want to go there. I explained to him through the Iraqi soldier who spoke broken English (both of our interpreters were on missions) that American military doctors would see him, and they would fix him up. He should be back in five or six days. After dropping him off, I exchanged my M-16 for an M-4, and then drove to the range on FOB Sykes to zero (set sight mechanism for accuracy) my new weapon. When finished, I took Khalaf to the aid station for his flight.

Later, SFC Puten and SFC Walenz invited me to tour the Iraqi National Guard compound to show me what they are trying to fix in it. They seemed to have faith I would fix some things around there and take care of the ING soldiers. I hoped I didn't disappoint them. SFC Puten corrected himself when he said the 'F' word, saying "freaking" instead, which I never asked him to do, but I appreciated it. I shared several ideas with them as we toured the whole compound, and was impressed by what they had already done, particularly with the obstacle course. I told them as soon as I figured out the budget and how the funds worked for our unit, I intended to do many of the projects we had discussed. One project was making plywood houses to train on room clearing techniques. Another was to put up tents over a cement floor for a training classroom, and yet another was fixing up the motor pool to have a combat general supply yard, and building a metal container into the outer dirt wall to store ammunition. It all needed to be mapped out and begun, but I knew in time we could do it. I couldn't wait to see what would come of it all.

When we returned to Nomad Base, CPT Bicks and Woody discussed officer moves in the Iraqi battalion. LTC Ahmed, the Battalion Commander, was presumed to be AWOL (Absent without Leave) at this point, so MAJ Sultan would likely take command. I took notes and started making a chart to understand the organization of their officers, their battalion, and their companies. I typed a spreadsheet of supplies we needed to order for Iraqi soldiers and went to chow with CPT Bicks. We discussed some of the things I wanted to do, and some of the items I wanted to order, and he approved most. He said some items would be difficult to obtain, but we could try. After chow he met with MAJ Sultan to discuss recent concerns each of them had. MAJ Rugrs and LTC Mavis radioed for CPT Bicks. I was manning the radio, so I went to get him. I arrived at the ING TOC to inform him, and he asked if I could take over with MAJ Sultan for him, so he filled me in on what they already discussed, and the information I needed to bring up to MAJ Sultan.

The two biggest issues were the names of the thirteen soldiers who left with LTC Ahmed, and the serial numbers of their weapons. I wrote down every name, and the number of weapons, but MAJ Sultan didn't have the serial numbers on hand. CPT Bicks returned and I finished getting all the information on each soldier's hometown. CPT Bicks told MAJ Sultan he would personally detain the officer in charge of the next patrol if he left a checkpoint abandoned. We left on a good note, thanking MAJ Sultan for his hard work and telling him goodnight. I learned a lot that day and thanked God for it all. I felt it was amazing that He brought me here to help make a difference in this unit and with the Iraqi soldiers.

January 12, 2005

In the morning I practiced reading Arabic with Evan, as Major Sultan came over to visit. He had some questions, and I did too, so we talked for a bit. I had him answer my questions about an officer and senior NCO organization chart I designed last night, so we could understand who oversaw which company, and who each officer was in each staff position. He gave me the serial numbers of the missing weapons which disappeared with LTC Ahmed, and said he needed to plan an Iraqi patrol with CPT Bicks to Baghdad. He also needed three trucks from Woody. I then had Evan write a word in Arabic on the white erase board for me to translate, and MAJ Sultan smiled – I thought it was important that he see I was trying to learn his language. Maybe by the time I left, I would be able to slowly read and write Arabic, and hold conversations.

Woody came in and wrote the word "LOYALTY" in all caps on the white board, and said he was about to have an enlisted meeting, so I ran some errands up at the communications office. Upon return I learned Woody had fired SFC Puten. Woody told him to pack his things, and to find himself a new place to work, because he wasn't going to have disloyalty in our unit. A third party had previously told Woody that SFC Puten complained to others in the Squadron about how SFC Walenz and himself were the only ones who got things done in Nomad, and Woody didn't do much but sit around all day. I was shocked, and SFC Puten talked to Woody about exactly what he had said to people and gave him complete honesty. After SFC Aeris (Woody) calmed down and had a heart to heart with SFC Puten, he changed his mind, and "rehired" SFC Puten.

SFC Puten was in a sour mood the rest of the day, because of how he felt he was treated, and because Command Sergeant Major Weldo (our most senior Squadron NCO) chewed him out a few times for his 'attitude.' SFC Puten was convinced he didn't have an attitude, always did the right thing, and gave people truth without sugar coating anything. That was the way he saw things, but others saw it differently. Reality could have been in the middle, but I hadn't been there long enough to form a sound opinion. I really started to notice how different the Infantry was from the Cavalry, or at least how different LTC Krella was from LTC Mavis.

At 5 p.m., about 70 new recruits showed up at the gate to join the Iraqi National Guard. They were escorted from the city of Da'hook (north of Mosul) by its Iraqi Police Battalion. We began the screening process for weapons or explosives, and our Tactical Human Intelligence Team began the slow screening process (many questions, taking over a half hour per individual). This process helped determine if they were joining merely to infiltrate our base, or some other wrong reason. After screening four recruits in two hours in the cold night air, we decided to move everyone back into the barracks (trailer rooms) and post a guard on them. They were Peschmerga, or Kurdish people who were told by the KDP (Kurdish Democratic Party) to come join the Iraqi National Guard. They told us 700 more would come to join. We were all in shock, but it was simply amazing they wanted to help the cause of freedom in their own country. We currently had 225 people and could hold over 800 to complete the battalion. If 700 came, we would be over strengthened, which was the opposite of our current situation. I didn't even know if we had enough supplies for them all.

Some of the leaders from Squadron didn't want them allowed into the FOB at first, and then wanted us to leave them in the holding area at the gate overnight in the cold instead of letting them into rooms. They were afraid anyone wanting to join was a terrorist attempting to infiltrate the base just before national elections. We posted a guard on them, and Sergeants ZT and Wadul supervised the guards all night long. After screening each one, we had a large job ahead of us, getting the new recruits their uniforms after in-processing all of them, especially if 700 more showed up.

January 13, 2005

This day flew by – fast and busy days were good in Iraq, but at the same time, I looked up at the date and thought, "It's only the 13th of January?" I needed to just focus on the day at hand, but the date seemed to say, "You miss your wife, and you have so long before you see her again." I inspected some Iraqi bunkers with SFC Walenz, fueled my 'whaz' (Russian version of a jeep), picked up supplies for Nomad and sat down with Rich Durmsy up at the Squadron logistics office to go over the budget information. He showed me all the documents involved with it, and how to fill out the receipts, including purchase request documents, memoranda, and receipts for everything – all official financially specific forms.

I inquired further about our internet installation and returned to Nomad Base. We should be able to install it on the fifteenth, in just two days. I filled everyone in when I got back and read over some of the Project Ordering Officer documents to summarize it and make sense of it all in my head. Then I studied some Arabic in the mini book the Army issued me. I remembered a lot but struggled with some new letters and symbols I hadn't seen before. Evan was over at the ING compound interpreting for most of the rest of our Nomad team, since we were still in-processing the new soldiers who arrived the day before. CPT Bicks attended the mission planning meeting and rehearsal, and then briefed us on the plan for our objective, which we would execute early the next morning.

We would operate in three teams, riding on a Stryker. SGT ZT and I would occupy the southernmost buildings of our sub-objective, while the other two teams occupy the northern buildings. I asked Woody how involved in the ordering around of ING I should be, and he at first said I should run the show. I then asked what Iraqi officers and sergeants did and he said, "I told someone else perfectly at lunch today: Picture the opening scene of *Star Wars*, where the Storm Troopers burst onto Princess Leia's ship and take over and then Darth Vader walks in. You are Darth Vader in that scenario." I laughed at how easily it put the picture into my head, and at the 'Storm Troopers' reference, as it'd been a week or so since I'd heard it. It was a good analogy, and a good laugh.

When I got maps with graphics printed, I ran into LTC Mavis, and he asked me "Matt, are you ready for tomorrow?" "Oh yes sir, I got it,"

I answered with a 'too easy' tone to my voice. He then asked me why I wasn't at the rehearsal, and I told him I wasn't aware I needed to be. He said to make sure I was from then on. When I told CPT Bicks after getting back, he said none of the other XOs in the Squadron came to the rehearsal – odd.

Some Iraqi soldiers took a long time to get onto the base from their patrol. Every time they went on a mission, they wrote down in Arabic the names of all the personnel for the mission, weapons and serial numbers, as well as the officer in charge of the patrol. They made two copies, keeping the original, and gave one copy to us and one copy to the front gate, so the soldiers at the gate could verify numbers and personnel upon entering and exiting base. That day's patrol lost the original and attempted to verbally verify Iraqi soldiers present against the copy of the patrol sheet the gate had. There were four names missing, so the gate wouldn't let them enter the FOB. Even after the Iraqi Sergeant Major (top ranking NCO of the Iraqi National Guard) went up there, they still weren't allowed in. I finally radioed after everyone else was in bed that it was safe to let them in. Of the four missing personnel, three were thrown in jail for leaving the checkpoint, one escaped from the checkpoint, and all their weapons were being held in the ING arms room. With all of that fixed, I went to bed for four hours of sleep. I prayed God would protect us all on our mission the next day at 4 a.m.

January 14, 2005

I had a strange feeling I might die this day, which kind of freaked me out, so I took it to the Lord. Maybe it was because it had been nine days since I was outside "the wire." It reminded me of my feelings when I first arrived at FOB Sykes in 1-24 Infantry and I had never been outside the wire before. I supposed that would always be there for as long as I was there, no matter how many times I went out. We got on a

Stryker from C Troop and readied the Iraqis who went with us. The Reconnaissance Stryker is quite different from the Anti-tank and Infantry Strykers. I forgot it didn't have a squad leader hatch next to the gunner hatch at the front of the troop area. The gunner and vehicle commander (both sergeants) rode in their hatch opening to scan for enemy and assist the driver with commands, because the vehicle belonged to them. CPT Bicks wanted to be out of the one remaining hatch, so I was inside with the rest of Team Nomad.

One team consisted of SFC Aeris (Woody) and SPC Sunburn, the next was SFC Puten and SGT Wadul, and then my team was SGT ZT and myself. It was quite different riding inside, and not out of a hatch. I had two almost opposing feelings about it: One was feeling safer, as if the mission didn't start in my mind until the ramp dropped; the other was just waiting for a car bomb or roadside bomb to hit our Stryker, and for us to go tumbling around. I felt like I had no bearing on where I was at any given moment, thus in no control of what happened to me. Ultimately, I felt safer, as was eventually evident by my ability to nap as we rolled, along with the rest of the occupants on the seats inside.

We moved north of Tal Afar, and for the first time, I had to be told when to lock and load my weapon, as I had no way to know if we were outside the wire or not, and I was too far away from the FBCB2 battle computer to see its map. After arriving in the town of Avgani, the ramp dropped, and I was the first to dismount from the Stryker. I looked around and our area looked just like our map imagery. The Iraqi soldiers quickly met up with us, about fifteen to twenty of them for each team. CPT Bicks stayed on the vehicle and we all got radio checks as we moved out. SGT ZT and I, with our team and its Iraqi officer and NCO, began to clear buildings in our assigned blocks. The town seemed small and peaceful, especially compared to Tal Afar or Mosul (a huge city, and extremely violent). I followed SGT ZT's lead, and it was just as SFC Aeris said; we were like Darth Vader walking behind all of the storm troopers from *Star Wars* as they ran around looking in doors and getting all of the people lined up for us to talk to.

We lined up all military age males in the courtyard of each house, while Iraqi soldiers asked them their names. We would then call the names up to CPT Bicks in the Stryker to see if they matched any of the names on the "blacklist," which is a list of known bad guys. We would then ask them if they had any weapons in the house, and most of them just said "*wahed boondookeya,*" which means one rifle (all Iraqis are permitted one AK47 in the home). We would ask them if they had seen any "*ali-baba*" or "*aaduu*" (thieves, or enemy), then we would thank them and move on to the next house. If they had a car in their courtyard, we would search it quickly. In the first house we came to there was one man spoke good English, and he said he worked on the medical staff at the health clinic, loved the government and the U.S. and he did not allow any terrorists in his home. "I am not a terrorist. I hate terrorists," he explained with slight pauses between each word. He even invited us for breakfast, but we told him we had several other houses to check but appreciated his kind gesture. We thanked him for his cooperation, and apologized for the inconvenience, and moved on to the next house.

At some houses, the children would cry when we came in, and we would hand them lollipops or candy, which would sometimes calm them down. We didn't shout or anything when we went in, just smoothly and calmly entered each room, but I guessed anything could scare a little kid. When the little girls cried, I thought of my unborn daughter Katelyn. After reading off many names to CPT Bicks, we got the blacklist from him to carry it ourselves. At the southwestern-most house in our area, we found a man whose name was close to one of the names on the blacklist, so we detained him. I showed SGT ZT the list, and how it was missing the third tribal name, but two of this man's three names matched what was on the paper, so ZT, along with the Iraqi soldiers, escorted him to CPT Bicks. I cleared a couple more houses with the remaining Iraqis from our team, and my shoulder ached from my assault pack, so I dropped it off at the vehicle, realizing I didn't need the weight or supplies. After cuffing and questioning the man whom we detained, we felt he was lying to us, as did Evan, our interpreter. The man claimed he had nothing to do with the "*alibaba*" and never saw any fighting in this city. I didn't feel I had done anything special, but those in Nomad congratulated me for catching someone on my first mission with them. I'd feel better if I could find out for sure he was a bad guy after all.

Most people in our area of the town were educated: nurses, police, teachers, etc, and it seemed very safe. The entire squadron found two weapons caches, and blew them up in place, which felt good to know we accomplished something. We passed out leaflets with information about the Iraqi elections, and even stormed the outer court of a mosque. A camera man came to take pictures while SGT ZT and I finished clearing it with the Iraqi National Guard (the ING actually went inside, not us), and CPT Bicks dismounted to check it out as well, after our outer cordon was in place. We teased him saying he was only coming in to get his pictures taken while dismounted, and he laughed and was a good sport about it. Soon after the caches were blown and we'd searched the last mosque, we rolled back to the FOB, and I napped most of the way back.

The rest of the day was slow except for an Iraqi soldier complaining that he felt faint and sick, but it turned out he just wanted to go "*mujas*" (leave) and was likely faking it. The docs still checked him out, but he was not getting a vacation like he seemed to want. I spent the rest of the afternoon and some of the evening moving into my new room (LT Durmsy's old one) which didn't take too long, considering it was right behind my old room, and closer to the Nomad CP. It was a doublewide, which are two trailers big instead of one. I didn't really need all the extra space, but it was nice, nonetheless. I played chess with Evan and finally beat him. After playing the violin while SGT ZT played the guitar to Garth Brooks' song "The River," I showered, and called it a night.

January 15, 2005

I spent most of the day trying to get internet hooked up at Nomad Base. After a 276th Engineers specialist helped me with the spectrum analyzer and satellite dish, we worked to connect the server to the other computers inside the command post. We finally got the PC and the laptop going, but SGT Wadul and I couldn't get our personal laptops set up. After restarting and reentering the codes and commands for an hour or more, I finally got ours done, and began work on SGT ZT's. Just before dinner, 150 Kurds showed up at the front gate. At first, they wanted to join, but soon decided someone in their hometown lied to them. They came to join under the condition they would be their own unit, would take no orders from Arabs (many Kurds and Arabs do not get along), and that they would go home in two weeks after the elections. Woody explained to them that they would not get their way under any of these conditions, because A) there wai no segregation in the ING, B) almost all of the NCOs and officers were Arabs, and C) they couldn't join only to quit two weeks later. The whole process of turning them away took hours and caused quite a ruckus with Squadron. After chow and meetings, I got CPT Bicks and SGT ZT's computers working. Then a recruit felt very dizzy, faint, and sick with a cough, so he went to the aid station. He was one of the Peshmerga Kurds from Dahuk who joined two days before. The doctors couldn't do a full test on him with the equipment they possessed, but all signs pointed to tuberculosis. The medics asked me over radio what to do with him, so I suggested we take him to the Mosul combat support hospital as soon as possible.

After that, Squadron radioed for "Nomad Five" (me) to come to the TOC. MAJ Rugrs, the Squadron XO yelled at me about several things when I arrived. The first was regarding me making any kind of recommendation over the radio as to where to send the ING soldier with tuberculosis. He said it was the surgeons' call, not mine. I acknowledged and explained the only reason I said where to send the sick Iraqi was because the medics asked what I wanted done with him. He repeated "Yeah, but it isn't your call, you don't decide those things." He yelled that Squadron and this base weren't just accepting people to join the Iraqi National Guard for medical treatment so they could quit and then go home, saying "This guy isn't even an ING soldier yet." I responded, "Actually, he is sir, I have his ID right here," as I showed him the soldier's ID card." He said, "I don't care if he has an ID, he's only been in for two days, and hasn't even been trained yet, so he shouldn't get a free hospital ride anywhere as far as I'm concerned. These terrorists know they can't get through our wire and onto this FOB, so what's the way they will get on? Join the ING for a day or so, and then try to attack us on the inside."

I said I understood his point, but this man was a Kurd in the Peschmerga. What if this man didn't know he was sick, and just came down to help fight like many of the Kurds did, who were loyal to this country, and to the US? What if he knew he was sick, and wanted to die fighting for his country instead of in bed at home? Maybe I gave people the benefit of the doubt too much, but I was shocked he assumed this man was nefarious. He began his next point. "You tell SFC Aeris and your commander that ING don't just quit and walk off this FOB! If they want to quit, or they walk anywhere outside of that ING compound, we will put them in the detention facility and YOU will personally guard them, Lieutenant! Is that understood? You better let your commander and SFC Aeris know too, because next time it happens, I'm holding you personally responsible, you got me?" I stopped explaining as I realized every time I did, he would just turn away, and keep yelling. He yelled about the 150 Kurds who tried to join (but changed their minds), then added every patrol returning to the gate would be turned away if its mission numbers didn't match.

I didn't respond and couldn't fathom his logic. If an Iraqi platoon or company left the base on a mission, and one or two soldiers ran away (desertion), the numbers would be off when they came back, so they would't be allowed in? It didn't make sense. Should they just wait outside the gate all night? MAJ Rugrs seemed tired, so I took everything with a grain of salt. Most leaders geot little sleep in the Army, which can easily cause negative attitudes. I picked up the sick soldier and took him back to the ING compound, and Evan interpreted my instructions to a sergeant major. I told them to keep him in a room separate from others, and to bring him food and water and check on him every six hours. The next day, a patrol to Sinjar would take him to a civilian hospital, but there was nothing else we could do for him. Apparently, the FOB Diamondback hospital would have turned him away regardless.

January 16, 2005

This day was great! It started with me getting help for our internet problems. After restarting the server, and checking the command prompts for the IP addresses, we got all eight of our rooms internet capable. SFC Puten's computer needed to be plugged in and SPC Sunburn didn't have a computer yet, but we ran RJ45 wire, crimped the ends with connectors and I added the remaining computers to the server system. After doing all of it, and teaching Sergeants Wadul and ZT who helped, I felt like I knew a bit about computer networks. It was odd – only God's Spirit could have led me through all of it. It may seem silly He'd care about something as tiny as internet access, but I knew He did! It did so much for the morale of the men, and I felt it was an amazing witness of the love of Jesus, as his ambassador to these men.

I reflected on how blessed I was to be at FOB Sykes. I was in Mosul – arguably the worst place in Iraq (or second worst after Fallujah), going on one or two missions a day. FOB Marez, where I had just come from, had no DFAC (since it was blown up), maybe one or two internet computers in our company command post I could use after waiting in line, and cold and crowded showers (most were broken). Mortars hit that base about every day and we had constant attacks up and down Hwy-1. I had no vehicle for easy travel on Marez. I barely got to practice my Arabic. Mosul was so loud, and one could always hear firefights or explosions. My room was nice, but kind of cramped (not that I was complaining, because I had it to myself). I was an XO instead of a platoon leader. I practiced my Arabic every day and worked with the Iraqis with two interpreters constantly available to teach me to speak and read Arabic. I had a jeep to take me where I wanted to go on Sykes, and the base was quiet, well out of range of enemy mortars. The DFAC was more than adequate, but I had a plethora of food in my room, and a microwave.

Tal Afar was so much more peaceful than Mosul. I went on a mission roughly once every two weeks, or so it seemed thus far. Our showers were so hot I turned them down to avoid burning myself and they were never broken or crowded. My room was ten feet away from our command post where I worked, and we had internet in our rooms. I reclined in my own bed as I spoke to Becky on webcam with voice chat. What an amazing number of blessings! I thanked God profusely. After I finished talking to Becky, Sunburn knocked on my door, letting me know Squadron radioed; I had Detention Center duty that night. I had thought I was assigned to the next night, but I guessed not. Anyway, it would be from midnight until noon. Twelve hours isn't too bad.

January 17, 2005

It wasn't bad at all. I was thirty minutes late and apologized to the sergeant I relieved. He explained how to conduct the checks on the detention cells, since it was my first time. I stayed in a small shed-sized shack at the road entrance to the three-cell hangar. The shack had heat in it, which was nice, but the flies drove me crazy. Every three hours, I would make rounds, checking on each cell. I made sure the detainees were treated fairly and humanely by US soldiers, confirmed detainee numbers and the names of the guards. I logged everything on an army log form. Good NCOs supervised two soldiers in each hangar cell, and they took care of any issues. Each hangar held thirty detainees, and I even saw the guy SGT ZT and I detained in Avgani the other day. Past noon, my replacement was late. I wasn't mad, because I was late arriving on my shift, so I couldn't blame him. This sergeant was two and a half hours late but had no clue he was on detainee duty that day, so I couldn't really be angry. I just prayed and waited to be relieved. The rest of the day was a nap, meetings, and fixing the internet which was down. I had plenty of time to time to read, pray, and practice my Arabic.

January 18, 2005

I got supplies for our Nomad team, and SFC Walenz, SGT Wadul, and Omar and I picked up more from the detention center facility. SGT Wadul and I wired off the satellite dishes to protect them from vehicles or people walking into them, and we also buried all the RJ45 cables connecting to our rooms-- just in time since it poured rain. I heard a 1-24 Infantry soldier had died a couple days before. An Iraqi soldier in a Stryker was clearing his weapon and apparently killed him accidentally. It was a sad thing, and I prayed for his family. It also started a new Brigade policy – Iraqi soldiers would no longer ride in Stryker's.

January 19, 2005

I went to prayer and worship in the evening, which was interesting. We sang a few songs and prayed for an hour. It was different than I expected, but still nice. The rain flooded the entire TOC area, so I had to crawl across the face of one of the bunkers to get to the chapel. SGT Wadul and I tried to get a computer game working for two hours, but finally gave up. He went back to his room, so I prayed to the Lord that even though it seemed silly to ask, if He could help us get it working so we could play. Within ten minutes, we got it working and played, using our team radio headsets to communicate between us. After our game, I talked online to Becky, doing webcam and voice chat from my bed.

January 20, 2005

Squadron required us to turn in all our trucks (except the two jeep/whaz's) for redistribution. As we passed the TOC area, MAJ Rugrs and LTC Mavis stopped us, and MAJ Rugrs told us he was confiscating our vehicle. I asked him if we were in trouble for something, and MAJ Rugrs said no, "you've done nothing wrong." It turned out they both wanted to have a Humvee, a Stryker, and a civilian truck for travel, so we would probably have only two trucks and two whaz's, but I was still grateful.

January 21, 2005

Becky woke me up on an internet chat with several 'blings' in my ear. I hooked up my web camera and microphone. She visited the hospital last night (noon yesterday her time). She said Katelyn hadn't kicked for over four hours, and from the books she'd read, and experiences of others she'd heard, this was bad. She called a friend who was also pregnant, and she told Becky to go to the hospital immediately. It turned out Katelyn was fine. Becky spoke to a neighbor in her Bible study who had a miscarriage a few weeks before, which made Becky andme realize just how much of a miracle and a blessing a baby is. It was very scary that we could lose Katelyn at any time, but we trusted the Lord, and knew that He would take care of her, of us, and of any situation we faced.

At our command post, Woody and I rerouted some cables and re-hooked up the internet and satellite dish, and I caulked the gap at the bottom of the AC/Heater unit and closed the window. Then several Iraqi soldiers showed up outside with their CSM, waiting to get new boots and ID cards. Most of their boots had holes in them. CPT Bicks came in at lunchtime to tell us we had a mission that evening in Tal Afar, and we would send just two teams into the city, with a platoon of ING on each of two objectives. My prayers were answered, because no one was injured, despite enemy contact. One of our US units caught a high value target, and the mission was successful, but before they left the gate, the gate area just inside our FOB received indirect fire. We thought it to be enemy mortars or rockets. One landed 100 meters from the gate. As SGT Wadul and I took chow out to SFC Walenz at the detention center, we learned our 155mm Howitzers positioned to fire directly into Tal Afar had fired. So, it was friendly fire which came dangerously close inside the FOB. Squadron still called it enemy fire, but several people heard our Howitzers go off and it made sense, since the enemy rarely could get close enough to mortar our FOB. Perhaps the truth would come out later. SGT Wadul and I ate dinner with CSM Weldo and had a great conversation about Christianity and Mormonism. It was enlightening, and a pleasure to "break bread" with him.

January 22, 2005

It poured rain all day. We had miniature lakes and ponds all over the base, and there was mud where there used to be dirt. CPT Bicks wanted me to go get my whaz fixed, so I drove from one end of base to the other trying to get people to look at it. I tried the logistics offices, but they couldn't help, then drove to our repair team, where Chief Anderson was, but he had two wreckers (repair trucks) down and had no time to work on a jeep. One of his wreckers was hit by a roadside bomb. I went to the civilian mechanics at the other end of the base, who said I needed permission from the FOB Mayor cell (the Liaison office on the base). I went there, got permission, and returned. They didn't finish it, so I would pick it up the next day. The rest of the day consisted of staying out of the rain as much as possible. It made things difficult having only one whaz since Squadron took away our other vehicles.

ZT asked LTC Ahmed (the Iraqi Battalion Commander who finally came back) if we could use one of his trucks, and he refused. We were shocked after all the support we had offered him and his Battalion, that he would act that way. SGM Aedo (the Iraqi Battalion Command Sergeant Major) kindly offered us his truck. He was nice, as were most of the Iraqi NCOs and officers. LTC Ahmed, however, was the one who ran away with ten soldiers and their weapons, disappearing for weeks without permission, only to come back when he realized we were looking for him. Everyone on team Nomad (except CPT Bicks), along with the interpreters, many Iraqi soldiers and officers, and many in our Squadron said LTC Ahmed was horrible, corrupt and mean. I'd heard countless stories of him stealing money, and some even said he worked for the enemy. I didn't know who else he worked for, but he surely seemed in this for himself. Several Iraqi soldiers said they would quit if he stayed there. Nomad tried to convince CPT Bicks of all this so he can convince LTC Mavis, but thus far it is to no avail. Even MAJ Sultan, the Iraqi battalion XO couldn't stand LTC Ahmed. It was very hard for any Iraqis to show him respect when he believed his soldiers existed to provide him with position, rather than himself existing to provide them with leadership (on the battlefield), love (in garrison), and life (on the battlefield). CPT Bicks spoke to LTC Ahmed, and got us another whaz jeep, so now we have three.

January 23, 2005

I woke before 7 a.m. to link our Iraqis in with B Troop. I was over in their compound area with Evan making sure they were awake and ready, and saw Major Sultan outside doing the same. The three trucks and fifteen "*jundees*" (soldiers) were ready to go, and MAJ or CPT Waad (I don't know if his demotion is still in effect) was ready to lead them on the mission. I told them to make sure they were ready to go at 8 a.m., and they were, but B Troop never showed up with a Stryker. Woody radioed to let them know the Iraqis were ready to go, and they responded with a "roger." By 9 a.m. I called again to confirm the mission was still on, and CPT Walts (B Troop Commander) answered the 8:30 linkup didn't happen with the ING, but he would meet them on the way out of FOB road. I apologized to him, explaining I thought linkup meant linkup just outside the Iraqi compound as I'd observed thus far. He said linkup meant being at his operations order briefing at 8:30 a.m., and next time the Iraqis would be left behind. When we met face to face, he explained the plans through Omar to the Iraqi Captain, and shook hands, thanking me as he got back on his Stryker. I apologized again, and he said, "Don't worry Matt, it was no problem, it's okay." He seemed in better spirits than the beginning of our conversation.

They all left, and I said a quick prayer for them. I then took KBR representatives (Kellogg, Brown, and Root civilian contractors) over to the detention facility and the ING compound to show them where to pick up and drop off the tents we saw the other day. On the way back from the detention center, I asked if the worker could take me over to "KBR land" to pick up my whaz. It was perfect timing because they were heading to the exact hanger anyway – convenient! I talked to Glenn, the head supervisor, who said my whaz had bad wiring in the windshield wipers, which they repaired. The manual choke was sticking, and he fixed that as well. The clutch hydraulics were bad, so his men repaired them, in addition to cleaning up the carburetor so the engine wouldn't stall so much. After thanking him, I told him I'd bring him a cake or something, and he said for me to bring him some rum. I told him that I didn't drink, and even if I did, I couldn't get any over here, but if there was anything else, I could do to let me know. His team needed some special tools so I said I'd see what I could find.

When I returned with the whaz, I updated others in our command post, before heading to my room for quiet time with the Lord. Just after noon I heard a knock, and it was SGT Wadul and SPC Sunburn. They both rushed in the room and started trying to tackle me. I took down SGT Wadul and started to take down Sunburn at the same time, but it was unsuccessful. The two of them had a grip on each of my limbs, and I finally rested to gain strength, but they both let up before I could strike. It was neat, because I felt like one of the guys, especially since they came to see if I wanted to go to lunch with them – which I did.

Later, SGT Wadul went to Sunday school and church with me. He enjoyed the praise and worship, but was confused about Jesus being God and the Son of God at the same time so I tried to explain by referencing the Trinity concept of one God in three persons.* Perhaps a better explanation is that the Holy Spirit impregnated Mary, and therefore Jesus (God Himself) was born into the Earth. Jesus' Father who impregnated His mother (not Joseph), was God. Thus, even though He is God himself, His Father is God, the Heavenly Father** [see note].[2]

January 24-26, 2005

Not much happened on the twenty-fourth to share, but on the twenty-fifth we had a mission which lasted from nightfall on the twenty-fifth till bedtime on the twenty-sixth. But before I get into that I want to tell about my unique experience at lunchtime on the twenty-fifth. MAJ Sultan invited me to lunch to eat some Iraqi food, so I went over to eat with him and the rest of the Iraqi officers after practicing writing phrases in Arabic on the dry erase board. The lunch was great – kooskoos with nuts, peas, and other vegetables with chunks of sheep or lamb on the bone, all served on a giant plate the size of a waiter's tray piled a foot high. Everyone had a spoon and dug into the massive pile. I made sure I stayed in my area of the giant shared plate. At first, LTC Ahmed used his hands on the food, but eventually everyone used both spoons and hands. There were a few bowls of pea soup and some other soup that all dipped spoons into to pour onto their section of food on the giant tray. I did so at first, but after others started dipping their spoons in the bowls and then into their mouths, I stopped, since it didn't seem very sanitary. After the meal I got a picture with everyone and thanked them for the food.

I learned from the medical platoon sergeant about website building, since our *"il-hagnee"* (Arabic for "follow me"; our Nomad motto) website needed to be updated. I was the computer 'guru' of Nomad, which I found funny, considering I knew so little about computers compared to friends and family back home. Computer things I normally needed help with, I now did for others because I knew more than many, though still little. While at the aid station, the medic platoon leader asked me if I could have Nomad Base send over an interpreter to speak with two Iraqi soldiers to ask what was wrong with them. A medic showed me the swollen tonsils of one Iraqi soldier, and needed to know how long it was the case. I asked the jundee, *"Ish ged youm?"* which means how many days (as I pointed to his throat). He answered, *"Arba-een,"* Arabic for forty, and began to write it on his hand. Just after translating this to the medic, Sergeant ZT arrived with Omar, who took the situation under control, so I left.

Back at our command post, I worked the website, but everyone asked me if I wanted to go on the mission for the evening. There were three Troops/Companies heading to Tal Afar, and each had about three trucks with fifteen Iraqi soldiers within. We only sent one team – SFC Puten and SGT Wadul. They asked if I wanted to go. My instincts said no, but I decided to go. This was my second mission since I had been at Nomad, and my second mission in twenty-one days. It completed my "initiation" as it were, since two missions were required before you earned your Nomad patch. We attended the B Troop mission brief in their area – their bunker was in low ground, because the three sides of it were surrounded by water at least one and a half feet deep. The brief told us we'd be with Iraqis, one platoon from B Troop and the B Troop Commander, XO, and 1SG (CPT Walts, LT Takash, and 1SG Mulany). We would cordon and search two adjacent objectives. Our Nomad/ING objective was to search a large mechanic shop. Intelligence reported the enemy would possibly rig doorways to these shops with explosives to detonate upon our entry, which increased tensions in our minds. As was always the case when I hadn't been outside the wire in a while, I was apprehensive about going out on the mission, but prayed, and was filled with strength from the Holy Spirit.

We were supposed to leave at 9 p.m., but the Commanders had to brief LTC Mavis before leaving, which pushed back the timeline. We finally left near 11 p.m. and arrived at the objective close to midnight. After dismounting and storming the building with the ING, we searched the whole place top to bottom. All we found was a bag of powder, and in a hole in the wall, a bag of ball bearings with some sharp pieces of metal. Images of the devastation at the Dining Facility at FOB Marez in Mosul formed as I looked at those ball bearings and the metal pieces. I remembered how the suicide bomber had ball bearings in a backpack with C4 explosives in it. We determined that this time the powder was just cement, and perhaps the ball bearings were for the mechanics, but it seemed suspicious for it to be in a bag located in a hole in the wall. We then found a bottle with a cap and several wicks sticking out of it which we took to LT Elmer Takash to be tested for explosive signatures.

It was neat working with Elmer because he and I had been together for so long. We went to Armor Officer Basic (AOB) Course together at Fort Knox in 2002 and were in the same platoon there. As soon as he and I found out our first duty station was Fort Lewis, Washington, we spoke more often. Upon arriving at Fort Lewis, we both went to 2-14 Cavalry the same week. He became First Platoon Leader of B Troop, and I became First PL of A Troop. After ten to twelve months, we both moved to 1-24 Infantry around the same time, to be Platoon Leaders of MGS Platoons (myself in A Company, and he of C Company). He returned to 2-14 Cav after only four months to take an XO job for CPT Bicks (who was the B Troop Commander at the time), and I stayed in 1-24 Infantry for another year or so. I'd then returned to 2-14 Cav to an XO job in the Nomad detachment. We were calling each other 'Matt' and 'Elmer' on the battlefieldt, all the way out there in Tal Afar, Iraq. As they say in the Army from time to time, "It's a small Army."

Anyway, we searched a small home just behind the shop and determined the man Yassin Al Nadharii owned the house, but not the shop. He knew who did, so after we searched his home, he showed us where the shop owner lived. We moved to the house of the shop owners which he had pointed out. We entered this "target of opportunity" house, and three males woke up and came to the main area of the house. There was no roof in what would be their "living room," and there were a couple trees growing in it. The rest of the rooms were rooved with doors but were all connected to this courtyard. After questioning the three males, we knew the largest and oldest of the three was head of the household. He made a big deal about him loving the US and said "Thank you, Bush" three times very excitedly. When we asked him about the explosive bottle we found, he explained his nephew used it as a reading lamp, but we had also found a lamp there. He either did not understand, was lying, or was unaware of the explosive bottle.

The three of them avoided speaking of their shop and kept telling us how much they loved America. The son even came forward and tried to explain he couldn't see well because of his eye, and he taught in a school in the morning. The son also spoke a little bit of decent English. When I reported to Elmer these males were the shop owners, he radioed CPT Walts for further guidance. My guidance was to detain the three males for questioning since the outside of the bottle tested positive for an explosive material like TNT. I didn't really want to detain them, because they looked so concerned, and had several children and women in the house with them. They had no weapons we could find, and I didn't really suspect them, but orders are orders, so we put the zip cuffs on them, and explained we were just going to take them away for a while to have them answer some questions. They pleaded not to be taken, but we explained we needed to take them.

After moving down the street with the detainees to the Stryker where Elmer was, the oldest man pretended to collapse, and lay on the ground, not moving. His fall looked so fake I found it hard to be sympathetic at that point. His nephew and son looked at me and told me he was sick and requested for me to just take them and not him, but I said I had no choice – he must be questioned. I said we have doctors where we are taking him, and the three of them would be taken care of. While the old man was still lying there, and the ING tried to pick him up to his feet, he started crying, and then we heard a very loud explosion nearby. Elmer told me over the radio that it was a bomb disposal team detonation of a weapons cache. We all cleared the street, and an Iraqi soldier asked me, "Mister, boom American?" I told him, "Yes," and he breathed a huge sigh of relief saying, "Good, good!" Omar translated to the old man to get up, and SFC Puten said the old man was afraid the explosion was his family, but we informed him his family was fine. He started walking again until we got to the Stryker, and then lay on the ground a second time. He kept acting decrepit and sick for the remainder of the evening, which was suspicious considering how healthy and strong he had seemed as he moved in his home.

After arriving back at the FOB, I typed up a statement explaining what happened regarding the events surrounding our capture of the detainees, and the biggest old man tested positive for detonation cord materials. No wonder his nephew and son tried to have us take them instead of the older man, whose name was Hussein. I heard Omar yell angrily for the first time around 2 a.m., when filling out tags for the detainees with their personal information. He asked Hussein, "*Shu iss mek?*" (what's your name), and the old man pretended he couldn't hear Omar. Omar sounded irritated as he shouted, "*SHU ISS MEK*," as he stood up, and Hussein answered him that time, claiming he had a hearing problem. I didn't feel as bad for the guy at this point because he seemed intentionally difficult, faking illnesses to make things more cumbersome. After talking with Elmer for a bit, we drove the detainees down to the detention center, and checked them in at the wooden hut. The old man seemed to have to pee about five times an hour, which was ridiculous. After filling out paperwork, I finally got back to my room at 4 a.m., and slept until 3 p.m.

When most everyone was at chow, the Iraqi soldiers at Avgani Checkpoint reported a masked enemy with one PKC (Russian Made Machine Gun), four RPGs, and five AK47s surrounding the police academy and gas stations just west and south of the checkpoint. I didn't know why they didn't fire if they positively identified them as enemy but told Omar to instruct them to do so. I reported the incident to Squadron, and had Omar tell the Iraqis to get a patrol ready to maneuver on the enemy, which took about an hour and a half. The patrol left the gate, and went to act against the enemy, who I was sure was gone by then. Woody was back at that point, so I went to the gym to work out with Sergeants Puten, Walenz, Wadul and Sunburn since I already was forty-five minutes late for Praise and Worship practice and Prayer Night. When we returned to Nomad Base, CPT Bicks briefed us on the next day's activities and the next few days regarding operations during the elections. We would need a lot of sleep in the next several days, since twenty-four-hour operations would commence. I was again grateful the Lord protected us on that mission, and throughout the day.

January 27, 2005

At 7 a.m. I went to the Iraqi National Guard formation at their compound with SFC Walenz and SFC Puten. It was the biggest formation they'd had in quite a while, which was likely due to pay day coming up. We told them unless they showed up to formation, we couldn't produce an accurate roster of their names, ranks, and numbers. I began to produce one later that day, and I was able to write the Arabic names and ranks beside the English names and ranks on the spreadsheet. I was slow at typing the Arabic, but I got the words right. At first, two teams were supposed to go out this morning, but neither ended up happening, because the timeline was changed. The Iraqis got two new trucks and two other trucks on the checkpoints were hit with roadside bombs, but no damage or casualties occurred, thankfully. The rest of the day we discussed plans for the elections, and SFC Puten and I taught MAJ Sultan how to read military grids on the map. Since he had a military map in his operations room, when the men at the checkpoints encountered enemy or saw a bomb, he could tell us where it was on the grid over the radio. In the evening I learned more Arabic from Omar, then attended the Squadron rehearsal for the election operations. It was a long rehearsal in one of the hangars in the civilian contractor area of our base, and we discussed where every unit (US and Iraqi) would be in the city of Tal Afar to defend polling sites. It ended late and sleep was critical since we would begin 24-hour operations at 4 a.m.

January 28, 2005

Woody and SPC Sunburn went out with A Company (of 1-5 Infantry, which is attached to 2-14 Cavalray), and SFC Puten and SGT Wadul left with B Troop. I woke with them before 3 a.m. to monitor the command post radio as they left. SGT ZT and I would replace Woody in A Company with eight Iraqi trucks and 54 Iraqi soldiers. We had a twelve-hour rotation worked out, so as 4 p.m. approached, assuming the other team could get a ride back to the FOB, we would move out to replace them, so they could have downtime. CPT Bicks could end up replacing SGT Wadul with B Troop when our team rolled out. Eventually we would get SFC Puten some relief, but he suggested that he stay longer, and told us he would be fine out there for 24 hours. Sergeant ZT didn't go after all. Wire setup around polling sites was complete, and they didn't need us to replace the other teams, because once everything was set up, the Iraqis could handle it. Woody and Sunburn came back at 4 p.m., SFC Puten at 6 p.m., and Sergeant Wadul stayed out there all night. SGT ZT and I were scheduled to leave the next day after 8 a.m. to secure the sites. Everyone would probably go out the next two days, even though everything was already set up, since those were the election days.

January 29, 30, 31st, 2005

I recorded this on January 31st, as January 29-30th were long days. I left after 8 a.m. on the twenty-ninth with B Troop, riding in the back of the Stryker with SGT ZT, SPC Sunburn and Omar. The three of them were going to A Company's polling site, and I would link up with the B Troop soldiers and CPT Bicks (who was on another Stryker). I was told we had 30 to 31 Iraqi soldiers coming with us, but that number sometimes changed at the last minute. While I sat on the Stryker for a while, CPT Walts' Stryker radioed for me to come to his location. I was driven there (up by the TOC), and hopped on the back, ready to roll. We just sat there for another twenty minutes, then finally began to roll out. CPT Walts popped his head down from the hatch and asked me how many Iraqi National Guard we had. I said, "We should have thirty-one, sir." He answered me, "You *should* have thirty-one? *How many* ING do you have?" He wanted an exact number to report for rolling out the gate, but I couldn't give it to him, because things changed so much.

Also, I had been in the back of two different Strykers for the last hour or so I didn't have good situational awareness. Rather than explain all that to him, sensing his frustration, I just answered, "I don't know, sir." He popped back up out of the hatch seemingly frustrated and explained to me when we dismounted at the polling site that being an Iraqi Liaison Officer was just like being a line Platoon Leader: you have to know exactly how many people and vehicles you have before you roll out of the gate. I agreed except for the "just like a line Platoon Leader" part. As an MGS PL, I always knew my numbers before we left the motor pool, but with Iraqis, it was hard to tell since LTC Ahmed changed them up at the last minute, throwing guys into duty from different companies, and taking soldiers off, or trying to sneak officers on leave before the mission rolled out.

The polling site was quite defensable – a two-story school with an accessible rooftop, and a walled in courtyard. It had decent high ground for its location, and there was a mosque about two hundred meters to the west of it. The whole area we defended had triple-strand concertina wire everywhere, concrete barriers on roads, spike strips, and tetrahedron metal spiked obstacles, which I believe were called 'hedgehogs' in the Second World War. In some of the inner areas of the polling site was single-strand concertina wire, and all the buildings surrounding the school had been cleared by US forces, except for the mosque to the west. Iraqis cleared the mosque on the twenty-eighth upon occupation of the polling site area. They had several battle positions around the site and one on the rooftop. Voters would enter the main road north of the school from the east, be hand searched by Iraqis, then scanned by a metal detector wand (like those at airports), before filing in ten at a time to the school's outer front court. A final search would allow entrance to the school. Ballots and voting booths were inside the school, and after voting, Iraqi citizens would move out through the outer back courtyard, west toward the mosque, and outside the wire onto the main road. January 29th, we had Strykers located at four positions, but Iraqi trucks occupied those positions on the 30th, Election Day. Prior to 6 a.m. on the 30th, US troops were all over the school polling site, but when Election Day came, U.S. military presence was set apart from the polling site, having nothing to do with the election process. It was a nationwide order, so we kept our distance on Election Day. The setup looked like this:

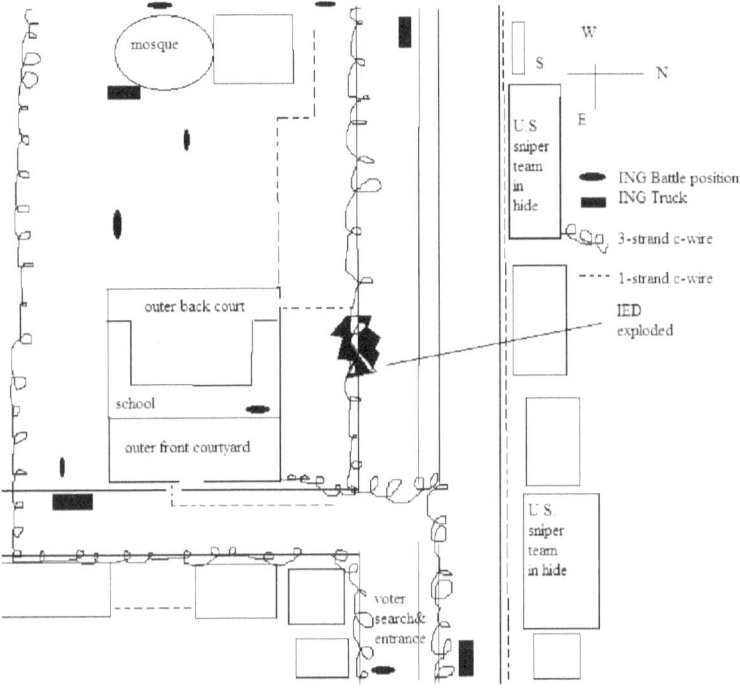

After I arrived at the site, SGT Wadul (who stayed the night of the 28th), oriented me to the polling site, explaining where everything was. There was a room inside the school, like a teacher's lounge, where he slept for a few hours prior to sunrise. He showed me where he was walking a few hours earlier when an IED exploded near him. He was on the other side of the street (the north side), but it was still close. The shrapnel flew out into the road and towards the school, as did the mud, dirt and concrete. If it hadn't been buried so deep, a piece of shrapnel would have hit him for sure. He felt blessed after that. CPT Bicks and

I walked the perimeter as a bomb-disposal team arrived to examine the crater and shrapnel, and determined that it was definitely an IED, and not a mortar, since there was some confusion as to which it was at first.

Sergeant Wadul left at noon and CPT Bicks and I linked up with CPT Kaamhl, the Iraqi officer in charge of the 30 men on site. He spoke better English than I spoke Arabic, so we talked to him very slowly and he was able to understand most of what we said. I would occasionally throw some Arabic in there when he needed it. CPT Bicks would even ask me to tell him or certain Iraqi soldiers somethingas though I were an interpreter, which I found humorous. My Arabic was probably kindergarten level – so not that good. I knew the alphabet, and could slowly read words written in Arabic, and I knew enough words to ask for certain things or tell someone certain things, but that was it. CPT Kaamhl spoke English on probably the 1st or 2nd grade level, so it was usually easier to just explain something slowly to him. He seemed like a great leader and commander, and I told him so. He didn't delegate his authority enough to the sergeants, but that was understandable, considering most of his sergeants had only been soldiers for three months.

After 2 p.m. we shots were fired between our polling site and the one to our east, so some of our Strykers returned fire. I climbed up to the roof and lay down in the prone position behind the one-foot edge of the roof, scanning for enemy. I could hear where the shots were fired from, but as usual, couldn't identify a shooter or a muzzle flash. After just a couple minutes on the roof, I realized any enemy must have seen me, because I heard several bullets whizzing just a few feet over my head and body. I wasn't sure whether to lie still (since I couldn't get any lower) or get up and run down to the second story to find a safe window to scan out of. I prayed God would protect and guide me, and ran down, but within five minutes, the firefight was over. I came all the way to the ground floor, and LTC Shaill and CSM Adams walked up to the polling site. LTC Shaill and CSM Adams used to be the Commander and Battalion CSM for 1-24 Infantry, but both moved to Brigade within a few months of each other in the spring of 2004. LTC Shaill was now the Brigade Deputy Commanding Officer and CSM Adams was Colonel Brown's Brigade CSM.

Both surveyed the area, and I asked LTC Shaill how things were in Mosul. He said, "Much quieter since the 'no roll' was put into effect." The 'no roll' was a nationwide policy – no vehicles can drive anywhere for any reason throughout the entire country for the three days surrounding the elections. There were enough polling sites in walking distance, so this order eliminated enemy use of car bombs. The US Army also put out (through the Iraqi Ministry of Defense) that any vehicles left parked in certain areas near the polling sites would be destroyed (for fear of car bombs). Before LTC Shaill moved back to his Stryker, he told me some of the 82nd Airborne guys in Mosul suffered some casualties from a roadside bomb, but otherwise, things were quite different during the election time frame in the city.

We had one more firefight in the distance, roughly 300-meters away, but again, no one on the ground could identify any enemy. When I walked around to check on things, the Iraqi soldiers at the battle position (between the school and the mosque but closer to the school) motioned for me to come to them. They tried to tell me to get down, because they saw "*Alibaba*" on one of the rooftops about 250 meters to the south. I got down behind the sandbags of their battle position and they pointed to where they saw the suspect on the rooftop. I looked through binoculars and couldn't tell if it was a large woman or an enemy, but the individual wore black. After talking to CPT Bicks about it, he told me to take some dismounts down to the house and check it out. I took about six Iraqis with me, CPT Kaamhl included, and moved south toward the house along the road in front of the school. As we got closer, I stopped and looked again, and it was clearly a woman, not enemy.

A man who lived on that street asked us if we could turn the water main back on for him, and we did so. On our way back, CPT Bicks suggested over the radio for us to go back to speak to the woman we had seen and ask her if she wouldn't mind searching the women voters for the election the next day. I didn't think it was a good idea and neither did the interpreter, but CPT Bicks said in worst case she (or her husband) would say 'no,' so off we went. We searched the house first, spoke to the owners (three males), and they brought us a pistol and an AK47. The AK47 looked like it had recently been cleaned, and even had fresh oil on it, but as CPT Bicks suggested, there was no crime in having a clean weapon. On our way out of the house, after the men said they didn't want their wives helping with the election, they offered me the pistol. Tempting as it was to take it, I turned down the offer. I found out later from SFC Puten that people are allowed one AK47 and one magazine in the home, but no pistols, so we should have confiscated it – lesson learned.

That night, CPT Bicks and I slept in the school lounge, after checking on the Iraqi soldiers one last time when things had calmed down. CPT Kaamhl spoke with us before we went to bed, and I told him in Arabic that he was a good leader. The evening was freezing cold with no heat in the room, and all I had was a poncho liner. However, I was not complaining, because I was fully aware of how so many wars were fought with men sleeping on the cold ground—or not sleeping at all-- and then having to march for miles the next day. Thinking of that made me very thankful as I tried to keep warm while sleeping.

SFC Puten arrived at the school around midnight with his crew of Iraqis, bringing the total to about 58 on site. He checked their positions and went to sleep until we all woke up around 5 a.m. to prepare to leave the school. All US forces had to leave polling sites by 6 a.m., so we left in a Stryker. We joined First Sergeant Mulany and CPL Stacy in the Medical Stryker south of the school, and the Iraqi National Guard assumed their positions. An hour later when the polls were opened, no

Iraqi voters had shown up, and we wondered if any would. Firefights broke out all over the city. We received a few mortar rounds between the school and our position, less than one hundred meters from our vehicle. Other Strykers in the area also received fire. Small arms fire broke out in our vicinity too, and CPT Walts maneuvered on it either mounted or dismounted just about every time. SFC Puten and I felt unused in the back of the Medical Stryker, because we didn't even have a hatch we could look out of, so we switched out with First Sergeant "Mo" and CPL Stacy every once in a while to give them a break, and to give us a chance to watch the action and maybe get off a shot.

We never directly observed any enemy from our position, but around 8 a.m., amidst the firefights, citizens began to show up to the polls. It was so motivating and gave us all a strong sense of hope for this country. People started at first moving a few at a time, and then came in tens and hundreds. We were all simply amazed. There were young and old men and women, some carrying their children, people of all sorts stepping quickly to the polling sites to cast votes in the first nationwide Iraqi democratic election. I was thankful to serve our country and defend Iraq. So many of them waved at us as they passed, and I greeted them in Arabic as they moved by. In just the first hour and a half, about one hundred voters had already come and voted, and I thought of how amazing this piece of history was. Occasionally fighting in surrounding neighborhoods died down, then picked back up again, yet the citizens of Tal Afar continued to pour into the booths.

Behind us (north) at the school, the lines were backed up. So many people had thought no one or only a few would show up for the election at all, but as the day rolled to a close, more than six thousand voters came to our polling site alone. A Company and C Troop had more at their polling sites, with more fighting too, which was quite amazing. SFC Puten and I practically begged over the radio to CPT Bicks and CPT Walts to come by and pick us up whenever they maneuvered on an enemy. We wanted to dismount and raid some of the buildings the enemy fired from, but they never came to get us, so we just scanned, talked to the civilians, and rested in the Medical Stryker. (I also practiced Arabic from the translation book.)

Polls closed at 6 p.m., as Iraqis counted and transported ballots. US troops occupied the school again, to remove wire, obstacles, and other reinforcements we emplaced. The Iraqi soldiers worked so hard; I was so proud of them for getting the concertina wire up so fast, especially when most of them had no gloves to handle it with. Several had cuts and chewed up hands, but just kept on working through it to get the job done. We pulled out a medical kit to patch them up, and most continued to load wire on the pallets. SFC Puten and I continued to give guidance to CPT Kaamhl and his men until we packed everything. The US Army National Guard engineers loaded the wire onto the flatbed truck after the Iraqi soldiers filled up the large truck with wire and tetrahedrons. We finally left and got back to our rooms at 2 a.m. The next day CPT Bicks and I counted the money to close out the Nomad account for the month. I began the paperwork, went to the gym and Bible study that night. I had a good conversation with Chaplain Wells after Bible study, and we compared the Army principles of leadership to Biblical principles of leadership.

---

[1] Today, I understand death is a powerful lesson and reminder of sin (Romans 5:12, 6:23), but as Proverbs 24:17 states, it is best not to rejoice when my enemy falls. Even if an attitude of Psalm 18:37-42 was acceptable in the old covenant and we can even now have a good sense to see justice done, I see it best to maintain Jesus' non-reviling attitude seen in Luke 23:34, 1 Peter 2:23; Paul also encourages those in the new covenant to not repay evil for evil, but overcome it with good, leaving place for God's wrath or His vengeance, not my own (Romans 12:17-21).

[2] * Today, I do not use such confusing language. Although Jesus can be called god (Hebrew – *elohim*, Greek *theos*) in a sense as Moses (Exodus 7:1) or Samuel (1 Samuel 28:13) were and as Hebrews 1:8 quoting Psalm 45:6 notes, he is not the only true God as he himself said in John 5:44, 17:3. He noted others who received scriptures were 'gods' in John 10:34-35 (quoting Psalm 82:6), and claimed to be the "Son of God" (John 10:36). There may be many gods and many lords, but one God, the Father, and one Lord Jesus Christ as Paul affirms (1 Corinthians 8:6-7). Peter, Paul, John, and the Hebrews author preached Jesus as a man made like us who came in the flesh, as God's Son (Acts 2:22, 1 Timothy 2:5, Hebrews 2:17, 1 John 4:2, 5:5). ** I still affirm Mary conceived Jesus by the Holy Spirit (Matthew 1:18), which is not a third person of some Trinity, but is God's power and presence, as Luke 1:35 and Acts 1:8 indicate. After Jesus poured out the spirit as Acts 2:33 shows, Jesus is now present with God in those who obey Jesus' commands, as Jesus himself said in John 14:21-23. Even now, Jesus has a God (his Father) as Jesus said in Revelation 3:12; God is one as Jesus said in the greatest commandment in Mark 12:29-30, not three.

6

February

February 1, 2005

This day was one of the longest I'd had without having ever left the base. It still wasn't over. It was 11 p.m., and I still had to inspect all Iraqi checkpoints in Tal Afar at 1 a.m., because of a new rule LTC Mavis made. He was sick of having to tell them to put on their helmets and clean up their trash at the checkpoints, so from this day on, he wanted three Nomad inspections a day: two before dark, and one after midnight. He expected someone from Nomad (with an interpreter) to leave the base every day, three times a day, and check on each the four checkpoints for thirty minutes minimum.

My actual day began at the 7 a.m. Iraqi formation. As soon as I left my whaz, I walked up to the officers who were in a heated discussion with SFC Puten and SFC Walenz. It seemed CPT Said had just slapped SFC Puten who had just told him he needed to button his jacket because it was a uniform standard. CPT Said told him, "No! I don't have to listen to you." SFC Puten reached out to show him how to button his jacket. At that time, CPT Said slapped SFC Puten's hand away rather hard, and refused to listen to him. When I arrived on the scene, I told him to do what SFC Puten said, and he replied, "I Captain, he Sergeant, no tell me. I Captain." I told him I was an officer, and I was telling him to do what SFC Puten said. He shook his head, and SFC Puten said, "That's it, I want him fired. Tell him he's fired." Evan translated this, and SFC Puten continued, "Give me your badge and go change into civilian clothes, you're fired." He said to MAJ Sultan, "I want him off the FOB." MAJ Sultan spoke to CPT Said, who still wasn't listening, so I reinforced what SFC Puten said, and after some coaxing from MAJ Sultan, CPT Said complied. He left and came back in civilian clothes and gave MAJ Sultan his badge.

While he was gone, CSM Aedo, the top NCO of the Iraqi Battalion told me CPT Said was a good man. MAJ Sultan nodded in agreement, but after he hit SFC Puten, I felt we had little choice left. We told him to get into the truck, and he wouldn't listen to us. After SFC Puten pulled out his M9 and cleared the chamber, while inserting a magazine, I got concerned for a second, wondering if I would have to stop SFC Puten, but he didn't even point the weapon at anyone, he just re-holstered it and told CPT Said again to get in the back of the truck. CPT Said answered, "No!" and I said, "What do you mean, 'No,' get in the truck!" He climbed in, and we drove him to the front gate of the FOB and told him to go home. SFC Puten told him he never wanted to see him again, and he better not attempt to come back.

SFC Walenz told CSM Aedo he wanted to meet with all sergeants at 2 p.m. He agreed, and I told MAJ Sultan I wanted to meet with all the officers at 3 p.m. in the same building after SFC Walenz was done with the sergeants. I told him I would explain to them why CPT Said got fired and explain the duties and responsibilities of an officer. I said they were getting the privileges of officers but weren't assuming the responsibilities as officers. I told MAJ Sultan he was doing a good job, but he did too much work and needed to get his other officers to do more. MAJ Sultan was a great officer and a great XO of the Iraqi Battalion, but one man couldn't run an entire battalion by himself, although he tried. At our command post before chow, I told everyone about us firing CPT Said, except CPT Bicks and Woody who weren't there. If they had been there, they would have told us we did not have the authority to fire anyone. Evan brought back a large tray of food for CPL Gharib (who they were calling Shakr now) and I brought him some ice cream. He seemed like he was used to his colostomy bag and looked healthier. I explained to him he needed to eat big meals like this every day, and in just a week or so, the doctors could fix him up permanently. He answered if we brought him big meals like that, he would do so every day.

As I did paperwork for the budget close out at the command post, CPT Bicks briefed us about the Squadron Commander's new policy regarding conducting checkpoint inspections three times a day. We all had the "this is ridiculous" look on our faces, but there was no use in arguing, because we knew CPT Bicks didn't like it any more than we. Our squadron bosses have an authoritative leadership style, often making demands of subordinates without considering how we could execute the plans. They tended to demand results without genuinely listening to the complications. I asked if it were possible for us to just make two checks, one during daylight and one at nighttime, which would be more manageable, especially since we desired our inspections to be unpredictable. This would prevent enemy ambushes against us and the Iraqis and ensure our allies at the checkpoints were not just doing the right thing only when we came around, but all the time. CPT Bicks agreed, and asked what SFC Aeris and SGT ZT thought. They both agreed, and he went off to the SCO (Squadron Commander) to sell our idea.

SFCs Puten and Walenz asked if I would come over to the Iraqi compound with them, as both said they had problems with LTC Ahmed about the firing this morning of one of his officers. I went into the ING TOC (Tactical Operations Center) and their Tal Afar checkpoints were reporting contact. SFC Puten and SFC Walenz and I listened for a bit, and then I went to talk to LTC Ahmed in his office. I said his officers should listen to us when we told them something, because we were there to help them be better. I explained why we fired CPT Said, who is lucky SFC Puten didn't hit him back. He told me it was all just a misunderstanding, but I said the insubordination was as clear as day because CPT Said refused to listen to SFC Puten and then slapped him. I explained if other officers didn't listen and behaved like that, they would be fired as well. He understood, but he still tried to explain it away as a misunderstanding. I told him that at the 3 p.m. meeting I would explain to all the officers what their duties and responsibilities were, and why things happened the way they did that morning.

I left and explained to those at our command post what I just told LTC Ahmed. CPT Bicks came in shortly after, and SFC Puten rolled out with A Company Stryker's to conduct the first checkpoint inspection with Evan to interpret. I did more budget paperwork and went to my room to have a quiet time with the Lord. I felt bad about firing CPT Said because of MAJ Sultan and CSM Aedo saying he was a good man, but as SGT Wadul reassured me later that night, an example had to made, and he did hit SFC Puten, which was completely uncalled for. In the command post, Omar and CPT Bicks tried to figure out the contact the Iraqis were currently reporting at the checkpoints. They reported two casualties at first, and so CPT Bicks went to the aid station to figure out what was going on with the wounded. Omar then told me that after the meeting with CPT Bicks and LTC Ahmed, he heard LTC Ahmed telling his officers they didn't have to listen to or do what any US soldiers said, and especially not SFC Puten. I expected something like that from LTC Ahmed, since he was a swindler, liar and a thief, but was shocked he would say it as they were leaving. He also told them if one of us told them to do something, they should say, "No!" and not do it. Now I know why CPT Said wasn't listening earlier. It was LTC Ahmed who needed to be fired and escorted off the FOB.

I went to the aid station and there were several Iraqi soldiers there – eight wounded and one dead. I couldn't believe it. The enemy crashed a car bomb into a truck carrying Iraqi troops, and then fired combined mortars, RPGs, and small arms fire all along Avgani checkpoint. I returned to the CP, and SFC Puten came back from his mission, describing the entire ambush. Two RPGs landed within ten meters of him and Evan – it was a very intense firefight, and he and Evan did a lot of crawling in their body armor to gain a better position. They both had Iraqi blood on their pants. SFC Puten also told me something disturbing about LTC Ahmed that he learned from the soldiers while visiting the checkpoints. He asked them why they didn't fire at the enemy when attacked, and they told him LTC Ahmed told them he would charge them 1000 dinar (Iraqi currency) for every round they fired. He also told them if they fired more than three rounds, he would put them in jail. An Iraqi soldier tried to tell me this the other day on the 29th of January, the day before the elections. He was explaining something in broken English about one dollar every time they shot a round. I didn't understand if he was saying he was awarded a dollar every time he shot an enemy or what, so I just nodded. The same soldier then told me that LTC Ahmed was a thief who stole money and was bad for the Iraqi battalion.

All the soldiers, sergeants, and most of the officers said it, so I didn't mention it to anyone since CPT Bicks already knew, as well as the rest of the Nomad team. Since SFC Puten had Evan with him however, he was able to hear exactly what they were telling him. I talked to SGT Wadul about it too, and he said some soldiers told him the same thing about being charged or thrown in jail for shooting their weapons. No wonder they didn't shoot back when attacked nowadays. I informed CPT Bicks about this after writing a sworn statement, and he said he couldn't believe it, and that LTC Ahmed wouldn't do that. "That's not how you run a battalion, why would he do that? It just doesn't make sense," he told us, but assured us he would talk to him about it later.

The result of the talk between LTC Ahmed and CPT Bicks was that LTC Ahmed told him he never said that, and that was the end of it.

I coordinated with Mohammed who is an Iraqi civilian on our base, a "man who can get things." He said it would take him a little longer to get the general supplies needed for the elections, but he would do so in a few days. I stopped in the Iraqi compound and told MAJ Sultan I would brief the officers the next day due to the death of their soldier and no one being available at the present time. SFC Walenz didn't end up briefing the sergeants either because most of the high-ranking NCOs were dealing with casualties and contact at the checkpoint. At the command post with CPT Bicks, we talked to some sheiks or civilian leaders from Tal Afar who came with their own interpreter. We discussed various projects we wanted to do, including dining facilities and concrete towers for the Tal Afar checkpoints. I drew a diagram and mapped out the dimensions for the towers, presenting them to CPT Bicks. He then asked me to drop off our brief slide at the TOC.

When I got up there, CPT Nerph (the battle captain) stomped his feet angrily saying, "I just printed! Man, you have got to get here earlier." I said I was just the messenger and MAJ Rugrs cut in from behind him saying, "What's the problem here?" CPT Nerph answered, "[Expletive] Nomad! I just printed and they are bringing me their brief slide now!" MAJ Rugrs looked at me and said, "No, you guys are on your [Expletive/butt], get outta here!" I left, and CPT Nerph followed me to the hallway. He said, "If you're gonna call yourself a 'five' [Nomad five], you need to take care of all coordination and do your job as an XO." He shared that I really angered him over the radio the day before when I didn't coordinate with another unit. I told him I did coordinate, and but just didn't know the status at the time I spoke to him on the radio. He lectured me about being an XO and what was involved.

It's amazing what a facial expression can communicate without saying a single word. He must have sensed my mood about his lecture by my face, because halfway through lecturing me, he stopped himself and said, "I mean, I know I'm not your commander or anything, and I don't work with you, but you've got to sound like you know what's going on when talking on the radio." It seemed he suggested one should never have a question for anyone over the radio, and only explain things, or as he put it, conduct all coordination with other Troops or Companies face to face. Most days I didn't have time to drive to every unit on the FOB to linkup with them regarding Iraqi soldiers. There are too many things for the eight of us Nomad to handle. Most people didn't know this and just expected us to do everything with Iraqi soldiers and all linkups as if it was our only mission. In a perfect world, they would be our only missions, but so much more came up during the day. He stopped talking to me, I said "Roger, sir," and left for the logistical office to print up two copies of the brief slide so CPT Bicks and the SCO would both have a copy, and he wouldn't be left hanging upon entering the brief. I briefed CPT Bicks on the way back (since we passed each other in the whazes), and he just nodded and said, "Thanks."

At Nomad Base, I typed and printed budget information and receipts, tower designs and our checkpoint inspection missions schedule that Woody had written by hand. Platoons from A Company would conduct missions with us in their Strykers, and I volunteered for the 1 a.m. and 9 a.m. shifts since SFC Puten went out during the day. When CPT Bicks returned, he and Woody and I listened as MAJ Sultan radioed that CPT Bnian refused to go on the checkpoint relief mission at 9 p.m., and his soldiers started to quit because of his refusal. Woody went over to handle the problem, and reported that CSM Aedo wanted to quit too, because he could no longer stand working for Iraqi battalion the way it was run. Woody convinced him to stay and handled the situation. I went to my room for a bit to get my things ready for the mission, and when I came back Squadron radioed for SFC Puten to come and see CSM Weldo, our Squadron Command Sergeant Major. I woke him to let him know, and then returned to the command post.

Woody opened his notes from the meeting our bosses had with LTC Ahmed regarding the firing of CPT Bnian this morning. The first thing Woody asked me was, "Did SFC Puten lock and load on CPT Said this morning?" I said he cleared his 9mm, loaded a magazine, and holstered it immediately, but didn't "lock and load" on anyone, or point his weapon at anyone. He then said, "Well, I don't think the Sergeant Major even knows about that anyway. What this is about is the meeting that CPT Bicks and the SCO had with LTC Ahmed tonight. CPT Bnian and CPT Kaamhl both resigned last night before this morning's incidents occurred." I asked why, and he summarized how LTC Ahmed said it was because Iraqi officers' men don't respect them because we (especially SFC Puten) don't respect their officers, so they didn't want to work anymore. He said SFC Puten's name came up from LTC Ahmed quite a few times, which is no surprise, considering how much he hates SFC Puten. Ever since SFC Puten started spot correcting his officers when LTC Ahmed imposed a double standard on his Battalion for the soldiers versus the officers, he had hated SFC Puten, because SFC Puten stood against it and corrected it.

As a result of this conflict, it seemed LTC Ahmed was blaming SFC Puten for his officers quitting (as well as CSM Aedo and some soldiers). One specific reason was making them do pushups for being in the improper uniform (although SFC Puten ceased telling Iraqi officers to do pushups a few weeks ago). SFC Puten walked in as they explained this, and they briefed him on it as well. He said everyone locks and loads when they get ready to go to the gate, and that he hadn't dropped any officers for pushups in weeks; he said the whole thing was LTC Ahmed trying to get him fired. It seemed that way to the rest of us too, but Woody didn't say too much after that. I told Woody if there was any question in anyone's mind, it was I who fired CPT Said this morning and kicked him off the FOB. He said we don't have the authority to do that, and I said I didn't know that this morning when we fired him. SFC Puten got in the whaz and asked if I would come up as a witness to explain it to CSM Weldo, so I did. CSM Weldo said he wanted SFC

Aeris (Woody) and SFC Walenz, so I radioed them to come up. CSM Weldo said he didn't need me there and asked me to politely shut his door. I said, "Are you sure? I witnessed everything firsthand." He answered, "Sir, I have three Sergeant First Classes here, that's all I need, they can handle this." I shut his door and walked back to Nomad Base (no one left the keys in the vehicles). I prayed on the walk back, asking God for His will in this situation, admiring the stars as I walked back.

Thirty minutes later I was updating my journal when SFC Puten knocked on my door. His first words were, "Well, they relieved me sir, I'm going to Brigade in a convoy tomorrow afternoon to Mosul. CSM Weldo told me to pack my things tonight and bring them all up to his office until my flight tomorrow." I couldn't believe my ears. I asked him what he was relieved for, and on what grounds. He said, "For doing my job as far as I can tell, I don't know. I'm so sick of this [expletive]." He had answered the Sergeant Major's question about making officers do pushups with the fact that he hadn't dropped any officers who were wearing rankin weeks. CSM Weldo assumed he was splitting hairs, and got mad at him, asking the question again. He said, "If they have rank, I don't, but I can't tell who's an officer sometimes if they aren't wearing their rank." CSM Weldo told him to shut up at that point, and asked SFC Walenz, "When was the last time he dropped an officer? Does he disrespect those officers over there? Does he ever hit any of them?" SFC Walenz's answers were all "I don't know, Sergeant Major, I'm not with him all the time." CSM Weldo asked SFC Aeris, "Why is he still punishing those soldiers over there?" SFC Aeris' answer was similar, "I don't know why, Sergeant Major." He claimed neither of them said a word to stick up for him, and he wasn't allowed to speak after that.

Every time he tried to talk, CSM Weldo told him to shush. He told SFC Puten he was relieved, and said, "Get out of my office!" SFC Puten said he went to ask SGM Collins about Funds Account money he held (roughly 15,000 dollars), and CSM Weldo walked out of the office telling him to cut out his [expletive] and get out of there. I found this one hard to believe because CSM Weldo didn't cuss (he is a brother in Christ). SFC Puten said, "Fine, I'll just keep it, I guess. I'm outta here, Sergeant Major." He said CSM Weldo then kept Woody and SFC Walenz in his office for a while after he left, and they never said a word to him the rest of the evening. After he and I talked for the initial thirty minutes upon his return to Nomad Base, CPT Bicks knocked on my door and asked me for a detailed description of what happened when CPT Said was fired.

I described the situation exactly as it happened, and he said, "SFC Puten does not have the authority to fire someone. You do not have the authority to fire someone, and I'm not sure I even have the authority to fire someone. I know none of us can just kick someone off the FOB like that, so that was completely against policy, but you didn't know, so that is okay." He shared the reason CPT Bnian and CPT Kaamhl quit was because of how disrespected they feel as officers from their men, and SFC Puten made things worse by correcting them all the time. He said, "For example, how would you feel if, when you were a platoon leader, some Russian officer came and dropped you for pushups in front of your platoon? That's what they were experiencing, and it discredited them amongst their soldiers. We've lost CPT Bnian and CPT Kaamhl, and CPT Said, and we are trying to convince CPT Kaamhl to stay, because we are screwed if he quits." I asked him, "So basically SFC Puten had to take the fall for all of this, sir?" He told me it wasn't him taking any fall but reaping the consequences of his actions. He continued, "SFC Puten knew these things, and disobeyed them, as well as direct orders for him not to push the officers or correct them. We told him to come to MAJ Sultan or me with corrections and allow us to deal with the officers. For that reason, he is being relieved."

I said I could talk to a someone to get CPT Said back if he was willing to come. He told me to "please do that" if I could, and to make sure in the future we stared treating these guys with more respect, or they would quit because their culture valued honor or "saving face." I was curious though if LTC Ahmed would attempt to get away with more because he was able to get rid of SFC Puten. I met up with Omar to prepare for our mission, as it was after midnight. He asked me if I knew about SFC Puten, so I asked, "What do you know?" Omar said, "I heard he is 'ssffft'...no more." Omar said at the meeting of CPT Bicks, LTC Mavis and LTC Ahmed, Ahmed blamed Puten for Iraqi National Guard retention problems (whichwas funny considering most of the ING had quit in the past because they hated LTC Ahmed). I told him what I knew, and he informed me that when CPT Bnian said he was quitting, he had a different story, as did CPT Kaamhl, and MAJ Sultan even had an explanation for why. He said they were all three different, but after talking to LTC Ahmed, all their stories were the same the second time.

I took this to mean LTC Ahmed tried to orchestrate the incidents to focus them on SFC Puten to get rid of him. Omar agreed with me, and told me how bad LTC Ahmed was, having stolen over fifteen thousand dollars from Iraqi soldiers in the past. He said he only cared about himself and didn't care about the Battalion. Omar said the only reason LTC Ahmed returned after being missing for over five weeks was to take more money from the Iraqi battalion. Most of the interpreters I had talked to felt the same way, as did most of the Iraqi soldiers. After our talk, we went to the Strykers waiting for us. I stopped into SFC Puten's room quickly to get his radio and said I'd pray for him. He made a snide comment about it being bound to do no good, and I just shook my head and left.

February 2, 2005

As Omar and I moved out, and I was very nervous, but turned to God in prayer, asking again for Him to surround me with His angels, and to place a hedge of protection over all of us on the mission, to include the Iraqis at the checkpoints. Hearing about how close SFC Puten and Evan came to being killed out on Hwy-47 north of Tal Afar really sank into my brain. We moved all the way to Checkpoint 301 (checkpoint Mosul as Iraqi soldiers called it) to the eastern edge of the city. An Iraqi Sergeant Major briefed me on what they had at the checkpoint. I emphasized to him I just needed to speak with him and didn't need a crowd of soldiers to surround us when I arrived at the checkpoint every time. He understood, but I had to tell him (and Omar) to get them away several times (crowds were good targets for the enemy). It was difficult to see the checkpoints in the dark, so I checked how many soldiers were at each, confirming if everyone had helmets on and was alert while scanning. I asked what problems or issues they had, tried to give them all positive reinforcement too and apologized to each checkpoint's top leader for the loss of one of their fellow soldiers in the ambush the day before.

They thanked me, and I told them I would see them in the morning. I thanked God for keeping me safe, and when I returned to Nomad Base with Omar, I told him to meet me at 8:30 a.m. for our next mission. He looked at his watch and thought I was joking. "No, we really only get four hours of sleep tonight, no joke," I said. He sighed and went to bed. SFC Puten asked if he could talk to me, so I tried to give him as much advice and support as possible, but at 5 a.m. I needed sleep, since I was waking up at 8 a.m. SGT ZT woke me at 8:30 a.m., asking if I was going on my mission. I must have turned off my alarm as I woke up, and gone back to sleep, so I thanked him for waking me up.

Omar and I rolled out again, this time with Second Platoon from A Company. The checkpoints looked much better than at night, and I better understood how they needed to look. I forgot to bring a camera but got a good picture in my mind. I made many spot corrections and adjustments but tried to affirm the officers' leadership at the same time, telling them how well they were doing with their soldiers. I reminded them to pick up trash when no cars were coming and not crowd around me when I got out of my Stryker, so we wouldn't be a huge mortar target. I watched each checkpoint run a car through to see how they searched it and gave a few pointers. After our mission, I typed up our slide for the nightly brief and went to the aid station to confirm the casualty numbers, verifying them with MAJ Sultan later. I brought back the body armor, helmets and belongings of those Iraqi soldiers. I even turned in the brief slide early to CPT Nerph, who was tickled pink. I finished more work that evening and went to bed.

February 3, 2005

At 8 a.m. CPT Bicks asked me to grab the gear from the wounded Iraqi soldiers. I gave him the bag of belongings and worked our brief slide and budget paperwork, just before the power went out (civilians had to work on our generator). CSM Aedo fired one of his soldiers today, and LTC Rugrs radioed to ask who ordered the soldier fired, and who ordered him off the FOB, because he was at the gate to be kicked off. Sunburn gave details but wasn't sure who ordered him off the base. Woody confirmed it was CSM Aedo who also wanted him off the base. Sunburn radioed again, "This is Nomad Base, it was the ING who wanted him kicked off the FOB, over." LTC Rugrs answered, "Okay, you just changed your story. First you said you didn't know who kicked him off the FOB, and now you're saying it was the ING who kicked him off the FOB. I want YOU, your SIX, and your SEVEN to come up to the TOC and see me, Five OUT!" We stared in amazement. The only change was, 'Wait one second, I'll find out,' to, 'Now I know, it was ING.' He didn't give it a second thought or let us say anything back – just an accusation, a demand, and OUT!

I took Shakr (CPL Gharib) to the aid station to get his colostomy bag checked. He had gained 5 pounds, and Neshwann, the Iraqi soldier who speaks second grade-level English went with me. I gave him some food to take to CPL Gharib and thanked him for his help. I coordinated for a few missions, and SGT ZT did the checkpoint inspections. He got in a firefight at Avgani checkpoint. He said there were about nine enemy shooting RPGs and AK47s. CPT Bicks went with him for the second mission in the afternoon to drop off the 40 Kurds who didn't want to be ING at Al Kissik (halfway to Mosul) and to meet and pay the principals of the schools which held elections. While they were out, I picked up an Iraqi soldier who was in a car accident while moving from one checkpoint to another. He had neck and back pain, but nothing serious or broken, according to the X-rays. Woody and I went to the nightly brief since CPT Bicks wasn't back yet. We leaned there that I made the Captain list, so I was promotable. My sequence number was 892 of some 4,000 lieutenants in the Army, meaning I might pin the rank around the late May/early June time frame.

I got packages from Uncle Steve and Becky and spoke with MAJ Sultan and CSM Aedo, who stopped by. I showed them my room and invited them to dinner for the next night. They decided on the spaghetti beef pasta mix. I made some beef taco mix to test the corned beef (so I would get it right the next evening). It worked well and invited Evan for dinner. He liked it and we spoke about Jesus and family. I explained to him why I believed Jesus was God on Earth (at which he innocently laughed), what his death meant for my sins, and why I loved him.* It was nice to talk about it, and I believed he understood. I prayed the Holy Spirit would speak to his heart [see note].[1]

February 4, 2005

After helping coordinate between C Troop and the Iraqis at 6:30 a.m., I slept again, until some contractors knocked on my door. They came to check the air conditioner/heater, but noticed the circuit box on the ceiling was half full of water, so they called the electrical team in. Because of the rain recently, water had leaked all over the second bed. After climbing up on top of my room, I realized there was a small space in the edges of the metal that formed a moat at the top. They drilled a hole to drain it to the outside to solve the longer a problem. I coordinated for someone to take Iraqi soldiers to the aid station and then headed off to talk to LT Cleverst about picking up the light generators CPT Bicks asked me to get. His forklift was bad, so I submitted the work request to Kellog-Brown-Root contractors who were nice enough to get it immediately. They came with the Iraqi five-ton truck and me to the repair yard. I let CW3 Anderson know I was taking six generators for the Iraqi checkpoints, and he said LTC Rugrs ordered him to not give any out until he cleared it. We called on the radio and waited for twenty minutes to reach LTC Rugrs for approval, but no luck. We told chief that we already had two loaded, and he said to take them, but not any more until LTC Rugrs approved. We joked about how restrictive it was.

We ran into SFC Puten. His flight was scheduled in three days. He got a chance to talk to LTC Rugrs and many others about his situation, and they all back him. He said the problem was CSM Weldo didn't like him, and he and LTC Mavis are the only ones who could do anything about it. Many people supported him and were writing statements. He was planning to see the Inspector General about the situation. His biggest shock was that he wasn't allowed to defend himself. Later, I taught SGT Wadul some Aikido and Jiujutsu at the gym, we played a computer game and I went to bed.

February 5, 2005

I felt like I earned my pay this day. I had a checkpoint inspection mission in the morning. I was ready with all my gear and felt nervous once again (since there had been contact at one of the last two daytime inspections). I was simultaneously excited, because I was happy to be alive and to have a great job, a wonderful wife and baby girl on the way, and an amazing God. The A Company Strykers picked up Omar and me at 10:30 a.m., and we traveled with six Iraqi trucks and about 34 Iraqi soldiers. Checkpoint-3 (Sinjar Checkpoint to the Iraqis) and 301 (or Mosul) each had eleven soldiers, while CP-201 (Avgani) had twelve. We moved to Sinjar checkpoint first and I talked to the incoming and outgoing sergeants in charge, repeating the same things as usual to them. Omar was so used to it he yelled at them before I could speak to stop crowding around us. We found the person in charge while more soldiers surrounded us to observe and complain that I didn't talk to all of them. I would love to talk to each one if I were visiting for a pleasure trip, or just making sure they were all okay, but until they could properly man a checkpoint, I couldn't afford that luxury.

My purpose at each checkpoint was to ensure they were safely positioned to best defend themselves, while simultaneously searching cars, looking for bombs, weapons, and individuals who were on the "blacklist." Before we left Sinjar Checkpoint, the incoming sergeant said he only had one truck there because the previous sergeant's whaz jeep broke down, and he needed two trucks to adequately man the checkpoint. I had Omar explain to both sergeants two trucks would stay at the checkpoint, and the eleven outgoing soldiers would ride seven in one truck with the whaz in tow, and three in another truck heading back to the FOB when we returned. I had them work together to prepare the tow, so when we returned after inspecting the other checkpoints, they could join us on the way to the base.

At Avgani Checkpoint I stressed the importance of an outgoing soldier staying at his post or battle position until the incoming soldier took his exact spot, replacing him. It was amazing how hard it was for them to understand such a simple concept, but maybe it made sense to me because I had done it for so long. It seemed they had the attitude, "Yay, my relief is here, I'm going to leave and get in the truck, I'm outta here." I made sure the incoming officer, CPT Majeef, knew this, since his guys would be relieved in twelve hours. As we left and headed south just a hundred meters to route Hwy-47, we all heard small arms fire and everyone became alert. It was a strange feeling to receive it from the inside of a Stryker without being out of a hatch. I felt thankful I wasn't out of a hatch, yet at the same time; I wished that I could be so I could help locate the enemy and kill them to protect my brothers in arms. I also feared that any second one of them would fall into the vehicle from their hatch and they would be seriously wounded or dead. The thought that I would then pop up in their hatch and replace them if this were to happen was both a relief that I could avenge them, yet also scary that I could fall just as they did.

Perhaps it felt like this for the nine dismounts in the back of Infantry Strykers. I just began to pray again that God would keep us all protected. As I prayed, there was a huge explosion. It shook the entire Stryker, and it rattled every bone in my body, especially my ribs and lungs. The gunner, LT Blade (the platoon leader) and the two air guards ducked down simultaneously as black smoke and debris poured overhead, some getting inside. My first thought as it happened was that a mortar was landing directly on top of our Stryker, and we were immobilized. The driver stopped the vehicle, and as everyone asked what happened, I looked around and asked if everyone was okay. I noticed all legs out of the hatches, and then assumed the driver was hit, because the vehicle was still stopped. LT Blade popped inside and looked forward (probably at the driver), then popped back up, peeking out to see what it was. As everyone calmed down, they assessed it as a direct hit by an RPG. I said, "Wow, I've been hit by RPGs before and that felt much bigger, as if a mortar landed directly on us, but okay." We later found out it was a roadside bomb which blew up right next to us. I knew the blast and impact were much too strong for an RPG. We poised to act on the enemy in the area, but the A Company Commander, CPT Zebald, told LT Blade to continue with inspections.

Mosul Checkpoint (301) was frustrating, but I was thankful to be alive after the firefight and roadside bomb. I briefed both incoming and outgoing sergeants on battle positions which needed to be manned. The rooftop to the left of the checkpoint needed two men on it and the wall by the gravel pit and gravel factory machine needed two men in a battle position. We returned to base, thankfully safely. The truck with whaz in tow joined us on the way back and I was proud of the Iraqis.

Between getting back and our next inspection mission before 4 p.m. I ate lunch, dropped off the brief slide and prepared more budget documents. I tried to find 'Mohammed' to sign the receipt for our internet purchase at the base market, but he wasn't there. While I waited, I ran into a sergeant who sold me some speakers when I dropped him off at his room. Back at the command post, I coordinated with SGT Wadul and SPC Sunburn for another of MAJ Sultan's cousins to be brought onto the FOB, since he wanted to join the Iraqi National Guard. CPT Said, whom we had fired, was MAJ Sultan's cousin too. The rest of Nomad was at the range with Company Three, the training company of Iraqis, practicing marksmanship. They returned before I left for my mission and crashed on the sofas at Nomad Base, looking completely exhausted.

Omar and I left for our final mission of the day, and I had much to note at each checkpoint. The sergeant at Sinjar Checkpoint lied to us this morning when he said his helmet didn't have a chinstrap, but I saw it just barely sticking out of the top and pulled the whole thing out from under his helmet. It worked fine and I said he should know better as a sergeant, and to keep the chinstrap on. Worse, after asking him if he had searched a particular car yet, he 'no,' and they didn't search too many cars that came through the checkpoint. In shock, I asked him, "You only search a *few* cars?" He told Omar he hadn't been searching *any* cars, and I rolled my eyes, shaking my head at the sky. "What's the point of being here at a checkpoint if you aren't going to search any cars?" I asked him. I continued, "The whole purpose of Iraqi soldiers being here is to search cars and people to look for bombs, bomb making materials, weapons the enemy could smuggle and checking to see if any of them are enemies! Otherwise, you are just a target out here trying not to get shot! You need to search every vehicle that comes in here!" Omar stressed this to him in Arabic and I explained what to look for as they searched the first car. After making a few more observations of the checkpoint, I told the sergeant everything else looked good because his men looked alert, but he needed to search every car that came though this checkpoint. I wondered how many bombs, mortars, RPGs and enemy personnel had rolled through that checkpoint without being found.

At Avgani Checkpoint, CPT Majeef did very well – his men searched cars, and everyone was at their post. The only correction I had was his safety. When he spoke on the radio on top of the hill to get a better signal talking to the other checkpoints and back to the battalion, he was wide out in the open, so the whole city could see him. This included the enemy snipers in the city, which I tought of every time I stepped out of a Stryker to patrol and inspect each checkpoint. The good thing about CPT Majeef searching the cars was he apprehended three detainees because the Iraqi Police at the Academy, or "Castle" as it was called, had tipped him off. They also detained three relatives who came inquiring about the three detainees the Iraqi Police Battalion called terrorists.

CPT Majeef wanted me to take all of them in, but we could only fit three in the vehicle, so I instructed his men to bring me the three suspected terrorists, and not the relatives. Each was bound with either twine or yarn, and I realized they had no flexi cuffs, nor did they have any blindfolds. The Stryker platoon gave us flexi cuffs, also giving Iraqi soldiers more to spare. We ripped first aid wraps to use as blindfolds, loaded the three suspects into the Stryker and moved out.

At Mosul Checkpoint, I was pleased to find the positions in the gravel and on the roof manned, but discovered they weren't doing searches either. However, with only eleven soldiers to do the job, it was difficult for them. The concrete barriers offered them security only to the front and no flank security from the side of the road. With two-man buddy team positions, only the sergeant in charge and one other man were available to search vehicles. I told the sergeant to search a vehicle as I watched, and he went up to the civilian after ordering him out of the car and began to search the man himself, without having anyone cover him. I told Omar to let him know he should never personally do the searching, but one of his men should cover another who searched, or he should cover one of his men while that man searched. He understood, but he still complained he only had eleven people. I admitted how ridiculous it was to try to do the job with such a small squad, and I would try my best to get more people out there. At one point during the search, he had his RPG gunner covering him, and I wondered what he would do; shoot it and blow everyone in the immediate area ten feet up if a civilian pulled a fast one?

I corrected that, and we moved back to the FOB. I thanked LT Blade and his men and told CPT Bicks and Woody how crazy it was out there, after I linked up with CPT Ishmael (the Iraqi Intelligence Officer) to give him the three detainees. They agreed how messed up it was that these men had such little training, since I compared it to the American equivalent of a new Army recruit going to basic training for one week, and after one week, leaving post and going to war, manning a checkpoint with almost no protection, new leaders and with very little manpower t. If I were an Iraqi soldier I might quit too based on such conditions, especially after getting shot at the first time. Now I knew why they got so excited when they saw the Strykers coming. My heart ached to see these men deal with such things every other day for twelve hours a day.

I asked CPT Bicks if the reason we hadn't emplaced any of the C-bunker towers I designed yet was because of lack of C-bunkers, or support to emplace them, because I saw at least eight of them throughout the FOB today and they weren't really being used, since we never got mortared on this base. I said we could take six of them as a start, load them on a large truck and transport them out to Avgani or Mosul Checkpoint while engineers set them in place as a platoon of Strykers secured the area from any enemy. He completely agreed and said he couldn't seem to get LTC Mavis to care about any of this, but only how much trash was at a checkpoint or whether Iraqis were wearing their helmets.

I drew sketches of the checkpoints and typed up the statement I promised SFC Puten. We ate chow, then confirmed Iraqi soldiers and trucks for their next mission with LT Blade. CSM Aedo was out there helping straighten things out, and as soon as I got back to Nomad, CPT Bicks was ready to talk to LTC Ahmed about my complaints, describing the solutions and suggestions we had, and also to get LTC Ahmed to sign the budget paperwork. The meeting digressed so much, because we explained how each checkpoint needed an absolute minimum of eighteen personnel and three trucks to do their jobs correctly. LTC Ahmed said "it is difficult," and he didn't have enough people, even after CPT Bicks drew on a dry erase board exactly how he could man each checkpoint, to include trucks and personnel shifts in the battalion, since LTC Ahmed did have the manpower. After CPT Bicks explained the men needed food and bathroom breaks while on the checkpoints, and every man needed a buddy while out there, LTC Ahmed described how he wanted to run each checkpoint with one company, and also wanted one company to patrol and basically interdict Hwy-47. He described battle positions and areas to patrol and over-watch Tal Afar with numerous men from each company, yet said it was too difficult to put more people at checkpoints.

THE ARMOR OF GOD | 271

It was so frustrating, especially since people's lives were at stake because of his stubbornness. Most of the soldiers in his battalion could come up with a better concept. He had never even visited a checkpoint, yet most of his soldiers had served there several times. I really hoped he would get fired and Major Sultan would take over, because MAJ Sultan listened to us and respected our experience and expertise. Below is a diagram of each checkpoint or TCP (Traffic Control Point):

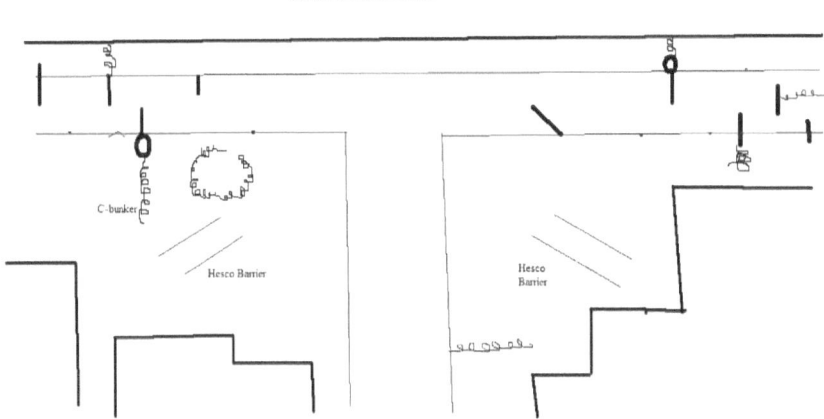

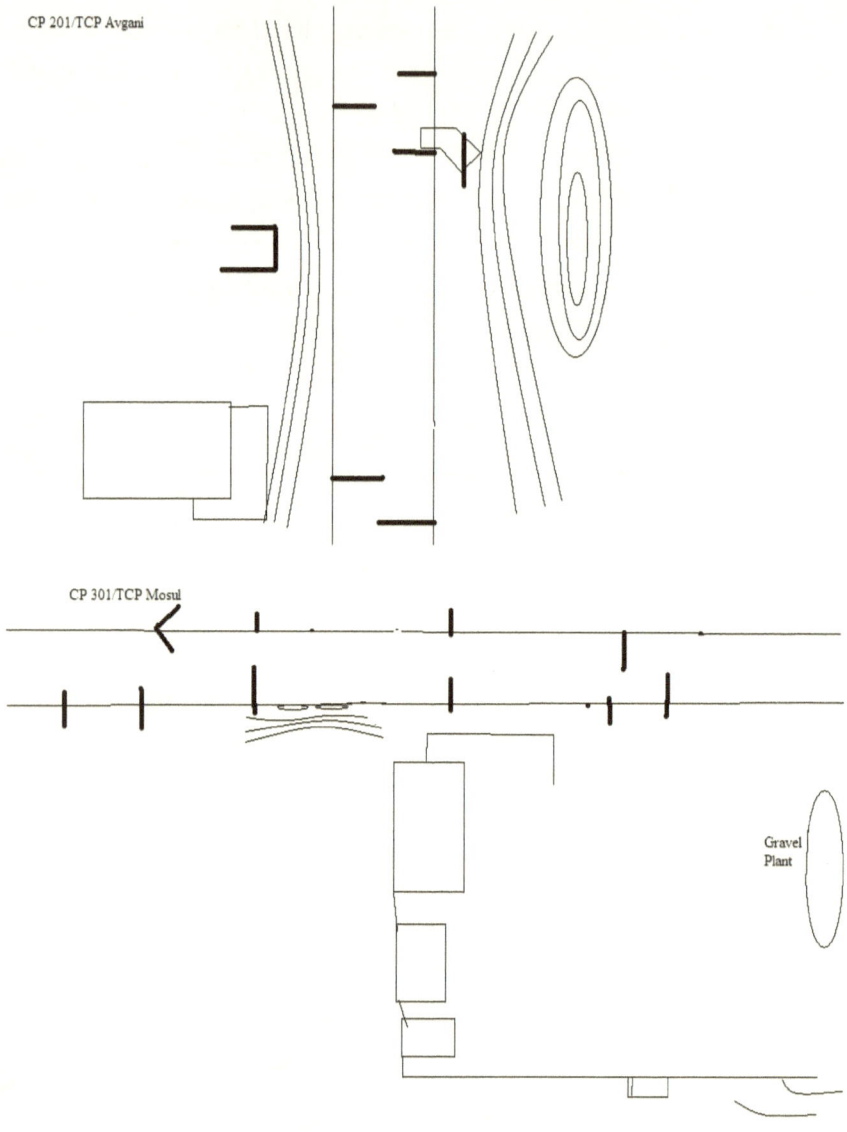

February 6, 2005

I was so frustrated about LTC Ahmed, I prayed about him a lot. I explained to Woody and the others about our meeting, and they shared my anger. I couldn't believe this man was playing with his soldiers' lives. LTC Mavis called CPT Bicks, SFC Aeris and MAJ Sultan up to the TOC and we hoped Ahmed would be fired. He wasn't, but there was some good news. In a town in the south of our sector, police got in a firefight with the enemy, killing four, capturing three, and capturing three trucks and several enemy weapons. We were happy. The Iraqi troops went down to Sinjar to pick up three detainees from Iraqi police. When CPT Bicks was on the way back in from paying the principals of the schools that hosted elections, the Strykers with him located two individuals running away and detained them. One had a cell phone linked to a detonation device, and CPT Bicks searched the other one, who had two grenades in his pockets. CPT Bicks said he was irate at the guy after realizing he had grenades intended to kill Americans or Iraqis. He wanted to buttstroke the guy with his weapon.

A day could go from great to horrible in the blink of an eye. Other than the usual routine of waking up, editing the brief slide, and running some errands, this day was good until evening. I drove to each living pad in my whaz, counting a total of 29 unused concrete bunkers. I asked Woody to verify my conclusions. "When was the last time pad one, three, or four were mortared?" I asked. "Since never," he answered. "How often are Iraqis mortared at the Tal Afar checkpoint?" I asked next. He said, "All the time." I told him what I discovered this morning and he just shook his head. We agreed our Squadron was wasting these c-bunkers here on the base, when we could build the concrete tower fortifications that we had designed a month ago. I told CPT Bicks if he could get permission for us to take them from the various pads and transport them to the checkpoints, I would do the necessary coordination to make it happen. He said it sounded like a good idea, but the problem was the engineers were short on assets to transport them and set them up.

At dinnertime, I cooked corned beef and prepared the spaghetti mix for MAJ Sultan and CSM Aedo. They liked the "American food" and both thanked me for being a good cook. SGT Wadul and SFC Walenz joined us in my room and we watched Army and Nomad videos of the war in Iraq. MAJ Sultan especially liked them and the music as well. I showed him the video of some of the Mosule Hwy-1 firefight my old platoon was in, and he was amazed. I served applesauce for dessert with some butterscotch cakes, which they seemed to enjoy. It was a decent meal and a good time, and I realized how special it was to fellowship with Iraqis. About thirty minutes later, Woody radioed telling me that Iraqi soldiers were hit with a roadside bomb, and I might want to come to the command post. I went in and listened to the radio with them.

The Stryker unit escort returned to the base and I went to the aid station to track casualties. It wasn't as bad as December 21st in the chow hall, but still devastating. On a checkpoint relief mission at 9 p.m., Iraqi soldiers hit a roadside bomb on the left side of route Hwy-47, just northeast of Checkpoint 101. One died on his way back to base, one was bleeding profusely from the femoral artery in his right leg. His name was Mohammed Ramathan, and he would be flown to Mosul when he finally became semi-stable. He was the first brought into the aid station, as blood dripped onto the floor as they worked on him. The pool of blood got larger. He moaned more until they stuck him with enough morphine. But it was too late for morphine because he had lost too much blood. I prayed for him while I watched from the corner asking God to not allow any more Iraqi soldiers to die that night; to please spare this man's life. His blood pressure dropped to zero, and he died.

They began CPR and mouth to mouth and were able to resuscitate him. He then had a very faint pulse, and they continued to squeeze the blood bag to fill him back up. He was still in critical condition but was stable enough to move to the operating room. I checked on the rest of the soldiers who came in, got names, injuries, and weapon serial numbers. A Sergeant Khudhir Jabar had pieces of glass in his head, with a large cut just above his left ear. He received three staples in his head. The surgeon amputated Ramathan's leg. He also had severe lacerations on his private and face, and his right arm was broken as well. The name of the dead soldier was Ramsi Yunis Ali. Other soldiers had minor injuries: one with a concussion, one with a hearing loss in his right ear (and a small cut on his finger), and one with some knee and shoulder pain, who also had difficulty seeing out of his left eye. When we covered his other eye, this man, named Baravan Khalat Hashm, even see me standing five feet away.

The medics and doctors thought there was glass or some type of shrapnel in his eye, so he was flown to the combat support hospital in Mosul with Ramathan. I thanked the Lord for saving their lives and thanked the docs as well. Evan and I finally left, after talking to CSM Aedo, CPT Ismail and a couple other Iraqi leaders who showed up at the aid station. I let Woody know and talked to Becky online about it. She told me that our car died and so did the computer, again – trivial compared to what these Iraqis went through that night. One great thing about talking with her was that for the first time we did our devotion together, reading the sixth chapter of Matthew.

February 8, 2005

The C Troop platoon escorting the Iraqis for checkpoint relief was hit with a bomb, but fortunately the Stryker absorbed most of the blast and only three Iraqis had minor wounds. While the Stryker's blown tires were fixed, the afternoon inspection was cancelled, so I went out at 8:30 p.m. Two Iraqis refused to go on the mission, and CSM Aedo put them in jail or "the hotel" as they call it. I was surprised CPT Ismail went out on a mission since he was the intelligence officer, but other officers refused to go, so he said he would. I admired his decision because it wasn't his job – he stood out as a good officer. We took different routes to the checkpoints because of bombs spotted in the middle of the roads. SFC Box and his mortar men turned around and took another route every time the saw them. We finally dropped everyone off, and I was scanning out of a hatch the whole time which was an interesting change. I wasn't too thrilled about it, because bombs, attacks, and mortars have increased lately, not to mention how cold, wet, and rainy it was. I had one more mission before 2 a.m. then I would get some sleep.

February 9, 2005

The last mission was quick except for having to stop and turn around due to bombs on different routes, but we made it safely to each checkpoint and the Iraqis were all right. I got in before 4 a.m. and slept until almost noon. I designed a sheet to track Iraqi casualties at Nomad Base. We were getting two new people for the Nomad team the next day, which should make things a bit easier on us. Also, Iraqis would start using their seven-ton trucks to move to the checkpoints instead of their "Nissan Battlewagon's" which should be much safer for them. We would line the seven-ton vehicles with sandbags and Kevlar blankets for extra protection if I could get some from supply. Hopefully, it would work out well.

February 10, 2005

This afternoon, the Iraqis at the checkpoints started getting a good deal of detainees. ZT got back from the morning mission reporting his firefight near Avgani Checkpoint and hitting a roadside bomb. One RPG fired at the convoy missed the Iraqi five-ton truck by about three feet. We no longer do afternoon checkpoint inspections from now on. CPT Bicks took tonight's mission since he needed to go to Avgani Checkpoint anyway to meet COL Ishmael on the ground. COL Ishmael is the Commander of the Police Academy in Tal Afar, who reported several enemy individual's names to LTC Ahmed. When the individuals arrived at the checkpoints, they were detained, since LTC Ahmed passed along the "blacklist" names to the checkpoints. We brought in a total of eight detainees from Avgani Checkpoint, and one from Sinjar Checkpoint. The one at Sinjar Checkpoint was going to Syria, but had no identification, and he drove a car not registered to him. Earlier today, civilians told Iraqi soldiers he was bad, and when he told those at the checkpoint his name, it matched what the civilians said.

Those detained at Avgani Checkpoint were an enemy leader and several enemy trying to escape to Syria. Iraqi soldiers begged for Stryker's to come because they heard the enemy planned to attack the checkpoint and escape to Syria. Later in the evening, that checkpoint detained seven more people, and when CPT Bicks and Evan went out there, it turned out all seven were old gentlemen with jobs and they were good people. Even Evan thought so, and the interpreters usually have a good sense about that. While all of this went on, I designed a detainee tracker sheet; much like the casualty one I designed the night before. It already made things easier for tonight, and should do so in the future, since I posted it in a plastic sleeve on the wall for others to add to as reports come in. Shortly after they returned, I had a long talk on webcam with Becky about our dying car, our dead computer, her going through this pregnancy and birth without me, and our friends and family. It was one of our best talks yet.

February 11, 2005

Today, I made a digital design of the Nomad coin we are trying to get made. Sergeant ZT drew the original sketch in pen, and I decided to make some digital templates. I also revised some of the checkpoint sketches. Thirty new recruits showed up at the gate today, and a roadside bomb hit the patrol I helped SGT Wadul coordinate for their gas station mission. Since it wasn't a checkpoint mission, so Iraqi soldiers were in the Nissan trucks instead of the five-ton, and we had six casualties. Two were minor, cuts on the hand. But one had a significant portion of skin and meat missing from the back of his right hand. The biggest shock at the aid station when I arrived was seeing CPT Kamhl. He was still talking and alert, so I was thankful it wasn't life threatening, but there was shrapnel in both of his ankles, and the wounds needed to be cleaned up. Other injuries were left legs, right arms, and the worst Iraqi soldier injury was severe shrapnel in the face and head. He was moaning, and it hurt my heart to see them like this. MAJ Sultan and LTC Ahmed were there with the casualties, and I even saw a few tears from MAJ Sultan, but he wiped them away and tried not to sniffle. He's a very compassionate man, and I know how much it hurt him, but he hid tears well for the most part.

It moved me to see how they tried to care for their wounded soldiers during transport from the aid station to the helicopters. After loading the injured on the chopper, MAJ Sultan and LTC Ahmed talked to them to comfort them and left as the flight took off. Of six wounded, four flew to the Mosul combat support hospital, and two returned to duty. CPT Bicks is in Mosul today at FOB Diamondback turning in the budget, so he doesn't even know. After praying for the comfort and healing of the injured and their brothers in arms, I thanked God for none dying. I pray he continues to keep them safe, and for our protection as I go out tonight. It is my "after midnight shift" turn tonight, so at 2:30 a.m. I will conduct inspections, as well as 8:30 a.m.

February 12, 2005

I'm thankful both inspections went well although the second one was delayed since the Iraqis had to change a tire on one of the seven-tons. I took pictures of each checkpoint to refine my sketch diagrams of them. The checks went quickly as Omar and I explained the usual to the leaders on the ground. They still can't seem to understand the simple concept of manning their positions or posts until properly relieved. When the incoming relief shift arrives, everyone on the outgoing shift runs to the trucks immediately; they don't understand maintaining positions until their replacement is right next to them. Hopefully, I can give them a class on it, but I doubted LTC Ahmed's officers would listen to anything I had to say while he was in charge.

LTC Ahmed lied to another group of Kurdish men from Duhok – 100 of them arrived at the gate while I was there with CSM Aedo, SGT Wadul and two interpreters. We tried to clear up any lies LTC Ahmed told them up front; CSM Aedo told them it would be cold and wet on the checkpoints and they would only have four days of leave each month at most. They were all mad and said LTC Ahmed promised them fifteen days of work and fifteen days of leave each month, which was completely ridiculous. I didn't know whether to laugh or to be angry. I set them all straight and told Omar to call LTC Ahmed on the radio and tell him he needed to come to the gate with us to process these people wanting to join. I told Omar I wanted LTC Ahmed to explain to their face that he lied to them, which he surprisingly did. They didn't care and said they wanted to sign up anyway, regardless of how much leave they got. They said they would see how it was after two months. I was shocked, but they did drive four hours, it was getting late in the day and colder outside. Maybe they just wanted to join and have comfortable, warm shelter. Not to sound too pessimistic, but I imagined they would quit after reality set in. Until we got rid of "Saddam" (our nickname for LTC Ahmed), I didn't think anything would run right in the ING.

February 13, 2005

On my way to guard the detention center, I stopped at the TOC to drop off the brief slide and was chewed out for not being aware of some van. After being told I should keep better track of things here at Nomad, I told them, "All right, but today is the first I've ever heard of this." No one liked that answer, but frankly, my tolerance had ended for this Squadron's attitude expressed as, "We only care about you/only want to talk to you if there is something we need to yell at you for." Major Diny, the Operations Officer, seemed a good enough guy, so I explained to him what was going on with LTC Ahmed. MAJ Diny was the only one not yelling at or upset with me, and seemed sympathetic, agreeing we needed to get rid of "Saddam." The battle captain still said I needed to go fix this "van" issue away, and that my noon to midnight shift as detention center guard could wait. I did the right thing and relieved the detention center guard at noon despite what they said, and then went to the command post to inform CPT Bicks about it. The tactical human intelligence team arrived when I did, checking up on the same van. Woody was back from his mission and said the van didn't exist and we never had a white van like they were mentioning. He added he was blown up and shot at that day, and Squadron's nonsense was the last thing he cared about.

Two Iraqi five-ton trucks were blown up today. One was towed to Avgani checkpoint, but the other was able to drive back to base. Surprisingly and miraculously, no one was injured. I thanked the Lord and praised Him for sparing them all. SFC Aeris and SSG Hitcher (our new NCO who worked with Woody in the past) both had a firefight just south of Avgani Checkpoint after the first roadside bomb blew up. There were at least five enemy, and a blue van with more, which got all shot up. Woody said between SSG Hitcher on the

M240, and himself on the M-4, they saw a few bodies drop. When they continued south and hit the traffic circle on a southern route, another bomb hit them. This one wasn't as bad, and I don't recall him mentioning any gunfire that time.

After this discussion, I returned to the detention center, which wasn't too bad, since I got a lot of reading done in the book of Genesis. It was quite peaceful. As midnight approached, I had a feeling the A Company NCO would be late yet again to relieve me and had the feeling he didn't even know it was his shift. Midnight came and went, and I began the search for his room, based on where some soldiers told me it was. After going back and getting more directions, searching up and down several rows in the dark, my frustration rose. I was about to give up when the Spirit convicted me, I hadn't asked for help yet. Slightly doubting, I said, "Please Lord, help me find his stupid room! Please!" Within forty-five seconds, I was shining my flashlight on a door labeled the NCOs name, and I proceeded to pound on it. He shouted "what" from inside and I knocked harder, since I wasn't about to have a conversation through his door. He opened it, and I told him he was forty minutes late relieving me, and he was very confused and walking in his sleep. I talked to him for a minute to make sure he was awake, told him I was leaving and he needed to go man the guard shack. He did a double take, asked a few questions and finally proceeded to get dressed (I assume). I went back to my whaz and thanked the Lord for helping me find his room.

February 14, 2005

I learned from different people how crazy life was in Iraq. I talked to 'Mohammed', our buyer who gets things for the Iraqi Battalion, and who also works at the base market (some call it "the Hajimall"), and he told me a lot of stuff about the way things worked in his country under the coalition forces. I asked him why the citizens of Tal Afar didn't stand up against the enemy, and he said because they didn't trust the coalition forces. He said when the citizens turned over the names of people who are enemies to coalition forces, we either released them or sent them to Abu Ghraib or some other prison instead of killing them. Sometimes they didn't have proof, but practically everyone in the city knew that certain individuals were bad. Mohammed said to me, "Do you know what the Iraqi bad people call Abu Ghraib and the other prisons? They call them education or schooling, because they learn more bad things from other prisoners in there, and how to work better. Then some of them go free after a while. Good Iraqis don't like to get the enemy sent to prison, because it doesn't do any good: they want to just cut enemy heads off, but Americans don't work that way back in the US, so they don't let us do it here." I didn't really know what to say, other than what I told Evan and Omar when they said the same thing. Proof was required to put someone away, and most people in the world like the US and other countries don't believe in executions.

After talking we finished our business – he bought 150 Iraqi uniforms and 500 hygiene kits for them. When he went to Duhok in a few days, he would email me the prices of the uniforms. CPT Bicks asked me to take his morning mission the next day since he was flying to FOB Freedom for some business. I said I would of course, and that I would also meet with LTC Ahmed for him that night, since he wouldn't be able to. He told me the issues to discuss, and to ask LTC Ahmed what issues he had. I went over there and, on the way, stopped to look at the Nissan truck Iraqi mechanics rigged this morning. It had three layers of steel added to the sides of the bed, steel plates on the floor and a giant steel plate welded to the back of the bed. One of the issues I was supposed to discuss with LTC Ahmed was that LTC Mavis wanted to replace the steel plates on the floor with a layer of sandbags, take off the inner layer of steel of the three layers for the sides and remove the back steel plate on the door of the bed. The mechanics and

I all agreed that with sandbags on the back and soldiers loaded in the back, the truck would be too heavy.

Nissan trucks were meant for driving, not for fighting missions and resisting bombs. I couldn't fathom why our Army (or the Iraqi Ministry of Defense) wouldn't allow the Iraqis to have better vehicles. BRDMs or BMPs (both Russian-made Infantry Fighting Vehicles) would work, even if they removed the main guns from them. I knew they existed, because I saw a huge number of them in Mosul on our way out to the range. How could we expect the Iraqis to defend their own country and stop the terrorists when we constantly sent them out to be blown up in Nissan pickup trucks piled with five people in the bed? The seven-ton's worked better, but they were not small enough to maneuver on sidestreets and alleyways. I also didn't understand why this Squadron didn't support the Iraqis more. LTC Ahmed and Debuse (his and LTC Mavis' interpreter) said when 5/20th Infantry was there its leaders met with Iraqi officers daily, and they supported each other. They said when 2-14 Cavalry came in, everything changed, and they didn't get any support anymore.

LTC Ahmed said he didn't even get to meet with LTC Mavis once a week, yet he had met with the LTC of 5/20th every night. Debuse and LTC Ahmed explained he sometimes goes more than two weeks without ever seeing LTC Mavis, and when he explained all of this to him, the boss said he didn't have the time to meet so frequently. Even though I didn't like or trust LTC Ahmed, he did have a point. The impression I'd gotten since I was transferred there was that Squadron didn't take the Iraqi National Guard seriously and treated them as an annoyance. The only time it seemed interested in them was when they were out of uniform or leaving trash at a checkpoint, or when they drove their vehicles unescorted on the base. Our top leaders seemed concerned with them when a problem arose, but unconcerned with our or the Iraqis' recommended suggestions for solutions. This Squadron was concerned with how many personnel the Iraqis had and how many we could use for missions and checkpoint manning. They didn't seem concerned with any Iraqi training or supplies.

It was very frustrating, and I hoped someday soon things would change, but I thought prayer was the only way that anything was going to improve. When the most powerful people on a base aren't generally interested in the opinions of their subordinates, and just make demands, it is difficult to improve that unit. One of the most important things I've tried to be as a leader is approachable by subordinates. They are the "movers and shakers" so to speak, and they see the details of what needs to be done. If I don't listen to them, or if they don't feel comfortable to tell me, "Hey Sir, this is screwed up, and this is how we can fix it," in regard to any problem, then I have failed them, my unit and myself. I knew I didn't have sixteen years or more of experience in the Army like those who ran this squadron, but I had two ears and an open mind dedicated to my country and Iraq. I also had a heart to serve the Lord and improve things. It was easy to criticize from my position, and I knew they were busy running this Squadron all day, but things were just messed up around there.

After discussing leave and pay for his soldiers with LTC Ahmed (most haven't had leave in over a month and a half), I returned to the command post. I got a chance to run up to the phones and call Becky to tell her my opinion on buying a Toyota Corolla she test drove. It sounded as though we would be buying this car, since our Ford Taurus station wagon was about to go bad.

February 15, 2005

SGT Wadul did the checkpoint missions instead of me, so I worked on requests for LTC Mavis. We still hadn't recovered the seven-ton truck the Iraqis dragged to Avgani Checkpoint and they are low on PKC (machinegun) ammunition. Six Iraqi soldiers wanted to quit out of the 150 men who joined the other day. Why? For no other reason than the fact LTC Ahmed had lied to them about what it would be like in the ING and about leave and such. The only surprise in it all was that it was only six out of the hundred-fifty, but I was sure more would turn up as time went on. On a good note, an ING was interested in becoming an interpreter. His name was Khalaf, and he was formerly in the ING back in September of 2003, when it used to be called the ICDC (Iraqi Civil Defense Corps), but then changed to Iraqi National Guard, and now from ING to IA (Iraqi Army). It technically took effect after the elections, and so I should have been referring to them as IA. They knew themselves as 'ING', and calling them 'IA' would only confuse them. We'd adjust eventually. Anyway, Khalaf used to be a CSM in the ICDC, and learned enough English to try to interpret.

Woody asked if I could talk to him to see how good he was, so I did. I inquired of his history, then had him read a few phrases in English and asked him to translate some Arabic papers. He did average at those, so I had him write down some English words and sentences and walked around the room pointing at things for him to name to test his vocabulary. I took him to the Squadron logistics center to speak to LT Von Astudillo, who is the Interpreter Manager. Before heading up, I told SFC Aeris that Khalaf's English was somewhere between Neshwan's and Evan's, but we could work on it. Woody listened to Khalaf for a bit when Khalaf interpreted for me while talking to MAJ Sultan, and said Evan was like that at first, and Khalaf just needed a few weeks to adjus. After taking him to Von, we went to the "Titan Corporation" which is responsible for testing interpreters. They had a series of tests in which they would go through some scenarios and have Khalaf interpret. He was a bit nervous and rusty but got the general point across.

Mr. "T", who is the only American citizen interpreter Squadron has, talked with him, and participated in these scenarios. Mr. "T" and I both agreed that after a couple weeks, Khalaf would improve enough to be just as good as Evan. Von suggested I tell Khalaf we would keep him for a couple weeks and if his English improved, we would keep him. He would study the dictionaries and try to immerse himself in the office to learn as much he could and improve. I took his suggestion and explained it to Khalaf. I told him that we had Arabic-English dictionaries to help him out, and that Omar would school him on how to speak better English. Evan left for *"mujas"* (vacation) and will be gone for eight days, so Khalaf came just in time. We set Khalaf a 2 p.m. appointment to be screened by the human intel team to make sure he didn't have anything to hide, and he checked out okay.

Meanwhile, my meeting with LTC Mavis was less than desirable. I was upset at his lack of concern for the Iraqis. His answers were that no one quits the ING, and they shouldn't be low on PKC ammo because they didn't shoot at anything. I went to the command post to inform Woody, then chow. When I got back, Sergeants Wadul and ZT got into an argument in the command post, but quickly moved it outside. Each thought the other didn't do his share of work There was severe screaming and shouting. SFC Walenz said SGT Wadul had a point about being tasked to do various things during the day when it seemed SGT ZT never did any unless SFC Aeris was around. SGT ZT had a point though in that he was about to give a first aid class to about eight ING, and he couldn't take the eight detainees to get processed from the Iraqi detention center to the American detention center. The two of them argued and yelled outside for about fifteen minutes, until they both went their separate ways. Both seemed quite upset afterward, and SFC Walenz said they've needed to get this off their chests for a while and he wouldn't break it up unless it got physical.

I took several Iraqi soldiers to the aid station for checkups and spoke with SFC Aeris after returning. We discussed our opinions on the "bucking of the horns" as he called it, regarding ZT and Wadul. We mostly saw the situation the same, then had some good laughs. I got a call from Von who told me the Titan guys didn't want us to have

Khalaf as an interpreter, because he didn't pass the verbal tests that day. I stood there the whole time Khalaf took the verbal tests and was under the impression the Titan guy agreed we would give him a chance. Von said the Titan guy just got a letter from his boss stating if interpreters couldn't pass verbal tests, they could not be interpreters. I said SFC Walenz already used Khalaf today and told me he turned out fine. LT Astudillo and I looked for the Titan guy, but their office was locked up for the evening. We couldn't find LTC Rugrs either.

I told SFC Aeris I would handle it, and we weren't going to lose Khalaf. We then learned Iraqi Intervention Forces were on their way along with some US Marine liaisons who were training them. I did what I could to coordinate with civilians and the base Mayor Cell to pick up some tables and chairs for the Marines' command post, and went to bed, since I had a mission scheduled for around 2 a.m.

February 16, 2005

I bled today. So did SPC Sunburn. Neither of us bled nearly as bad as our brothers-in-arms in the Iraqi Army. At least Sunburn and I were just wounded – two Iraqi soldiers lost their lives in my presence on this day. I wrote about the day, starting from early that morning, since I had plenty of time in the Combat Support Hospital (CSH) and plenty of room on my notepad to record all that happened. It kept my mind off the pain in my chin, the blood that was dripping from it as I was writing, the soreness of my body and the horror that I witnessed.

I didn't take an interpreter with me on my checkpoint inspections after midnight, and without him the entire inspection went by very quickly. I greeted each checkpoint leader in Arabic, asked if he was okay and said goodnight. I slept until 8 a.m. when SPC Sunburn, the junior enlisted member of our team knocked on my door to make sure I was awake for our mission. He was excited, because he hadn't been outside the wire in a long time, as he mentioned to me last night, so I welcomed him to come along with me that morning. By 8:30 a.m., Iraqi soldiers ('*jundees*') were ready to move out in the seven-ton trucks, except for one thing – their officer. LT Tofeeq refused to go on the mission the night before and again that morning. CPT Bicks and SFC Aeris attempted to resolve the situation by gathering all the Iraqi officers together. The three of us were furious, because the leadership should be setting the example. How could they expect their soldiers to go on missions if they were refusing to go themselves? When a '*jundee*' refused to go on a mission, he was detained, yet if an officer refused to go, nothing happened to him.

CPT Bicks shouted he wanted LT Tofeeq fired, his rank taken away, be sent to the detention center for a couple of days, and then finally be kicked off the base. LTC Ahmed showed up, and CPT Bicks told him if a company commander can't get a lieutenant to go on a mission, then the company commander must go. He continued, if LTC Ahmed couldn't get them to go, then LTC Ahmed could go out there. He scolded them all saying, "I'm ashamed of all of you. Your '*jundees*' are out there ready to go on a mission, and you can't even get your act together and send an officer. You wear that rank because you are supposed to be leaders, not just people with better privileges and more pay." Woody suggested we make all the officers man a checkpoint, but CPT Bicks wouldn't do so. LT Tofeeq's commander, CPT Kamhl was being treated for the shrapnel wounds in both ankles. The next in charge of him was LT Ali, who said he would go again to the checkpoint, even though he had just gone and it wasn't his turn. CPT Bicks told him to go, so he stood at attention, saluted and ran to get his gear. When he and his men headed back to the seven-ton trucks, I told LT Ali he was a "*jayed judan dhvabut*" (very good officer). He thanked me and we mounted the vehicles to leave. I asked Sunburn if he wanted to ride out of the hatch on the way up or on the way back, and he said,

"We could both ride out of the hatches if it's okay with them [referring to the crew of the Stryker]." They were okay with it, so we stood out of the rear hatches. I could just imagine Becky being upset with me for choosing to be out of the hatch where it was more dangerous when I didn't have to, but I was a leader, and that's what leaders (and soldiers) did.

As we left around 10 a.m., SPC Sunburn asked me if I thought we would get in a firefight that day. I answered, "It's hard to say. I'm not sure about a firefight, but we'll definitely get hit with an IED [roadside bomb] today." I didn't know if that was from the Holy Spirit or me, but it came out of my mouth. He said he and SFC Aeris practically never got hit on missions. He asked me if I liked having a battle buddy for a change, and I said it was nice. As we rolled toward the city, I tried to get comfortable while standing out of the hatch. I was too short to stand on the floor, but too tall to ride standing on the seats. I switched back and forth until I found a comfortable position on the seats, crouched down with my knees bent. I was high enough to engage any enemy in my sights, but not so high that I made for an easy target. I then tried shifting to the left and right so my bulletproof vest on my chest and back faced where I thought contact would occur, based on my position in the Stryker (back left hatch, looking to the left side of the road and to the rear).

I had the usual thoughts as I scanned the streets, buildings, and rooftops: From where would the enemy engage us? Would I see them in time? Would I get them in my sights and drop them with my return fire? Would they shoot an RPG at me? This last thought was particularly strong, because I could just imagine seeing an RPG headed straight for my head, with no hope but a prayer and a miracle from God. It may have also been a leftover thought or fear from my three-hour firefight on Veterans Day, since so many RPGs came right for us that day. Also, the last US soldier killed in Tal Afar had been hit by an RPG. We turned north in central Tal Afar and just as we were almost at route Hwy-47, near Mosul Checkpoint, I felt as if the day might be uneventful afterall. That feeling was wrong.

I heard a very quick sound, as if an RPG had been fired (although none were), and my brain saw an RPG flying right for my head, even though my eyes didn't, because there actually was no RPG. I instantly felt an extreme smack square in my chin, as though a prize fighter just slugged me. My mind thought two things: 1) The RPG hit me, and 2) Oh Lord Jesus, please save me! As I fell from the combination of the force of the shrapnel hitting my chin and the concussion of the blast, I heard the loud explosion from the roadside bomb. It was simultaneous, yet my brain processed the sound of the explosion a millisecond after my body was hit, and my nose smelled the explosion powder and debris. I fell completely inside the Stryker, and the slow motion began. My body fell from the hatch to the seat and from the seat to the floor, with my back hitting the ramp and my helmet flying off toward the front of the Stryker, since my chinstrap had been broken (cut through). Everyone inside was looking at me and asking me where I was hit. I knew my chin had been hit, but I moved my hands all over my body, especially my neck, to make sure that I wasn't bleeding seriously, yet in shock with too much adrenaline pumping to notice it. I even shouted, "Where did it hit me?" And they responded "Your chin! Your jaw is bleeding!" I nodded because I knew that already and said, "Where else?"

There seemed to be no where else, and then I noticed to my right, as I faced forward, Sunburn was falling too. I think he fell at the same time I did, but my brain processed it extremely slowly. I put my right hand to my chin to attempt to stop the bleeding and asked if SPC Sunburn was okay. He was, but thought he was hit in his right arm (which he realized later was correct). He popped back out of the hatch and I heard some gunfire, though it's hard to say if it was enemy, or if the Iraqis were shooting at nothing, as they sometimes did. I was slightly in shock but told Sunburn I'd be out of my hatch in a minute to help him cover things. I wasn't sure if we were about to start moving again. He replied, "It's all right sir, I got it." The next thing I knew, the ramp went down on the Stryker (I was on the seat by now) and everyone wanted to dismount (Sunburn was already heading out). My first thought was I shouldn't go out because I was wounded, but that thought went out the window as I went out the Stryker, after what I saw.

It was the Iraqi Army's seven-ton truck ten feet behind us, its cab in bad shape and the *'jundees'* looking at the cab. I ran out and shouted for some to follow me. The left side door of the seven-ton was completely trapped by a tree on the median just above the explosion site. The bomb had blown between our Stryker and the seven-ton right behind us, about six feet from our vehicle and two feet in front of the seven-ton. It finally started to sink in that this had been an Improvised Explosive Device. I ran straight to the right door of the seven-ton (to my left) and was surprised no one had done so yet. I looked around for a second as I was running and realized I shouldn't have done that since no dismounts had moved to secure that area yet, but as I was already there it was too late, so I shouted for two *'jundees'* as I pulled open the door.

It was a horrible sight and reminded me of the chow hall in Mosul on December 21st. There were three men in the cab. LT Ali sat in the middle, dazed and bleeding all over, the soldier in the passenger seat tried to exit the vehicle, and the driver just lay on his side on the floor of the truck. The two *jundees* began to help the soldier who had been trying to come out, and I noticed how much blood was all over his guts and legs as he was carried to the ground. His left leg seemed completely deflated in the middle, almost as if he no longer had a kneecap, which I discovered to be true after he was on the Stryker ramp for treatment. His body was still very heavy and they dragged him toward the Stryker as I attempted to get LT Ali out. I was grieved that he was so bloody and injured, especially after that morning when he had been the only good officer in the Iraqi battalion who had volunteered to go. I kept saying in my mind, "No, no, no, please help him, Lord." I wanted to cry but couldn't because the Lord gave me strength and direction instead. I shouted *"Ithnayn akthar jundees"* (two more soldiers) and had them help me get LT Ali out of the seven-ton. His ankle had cuts and shrapnel in it, including his Achilles heel. As we pulled him out, and even before that as he sat dazed in the truck, he was spitting blood, and unable to speak. I noticed a large hole in his cheek and his tongue was swollen with blood filling his mouth and all over his face. I saw a hole in his knee (he pointed to it) as we pulled him out. They carried him to the Stryker and some US and Iraqi soldiers helped me work to get the driver out.

An Iraqi soldier climbed inside to free the driver's leg, but we couldn't budge him. He wasn't moving so I asked a US soldier if he would check the driver's pulse. He checked it as I called more *'jundees'* since only one came when I last called. The driver's pulse was faint and we couldn't get him out unless we cut his leg off. I went back to the Stryker where LT Ali was and found that he was still coughing up blood. An IA soldier helped me remove his clothes to check the rest of his body. I called Omar over to the Stryker to translate what LT Ali kept trying to say, and LT Ali was apparently having trouble breathing. I had Omar tell him to open his airway by looking up with his chin forward, but to lean over so his blood wouldn't go down his throat and choke him. I went back to attempt to get the driver out once more, even though I thought he was dead, and then I saw him moving his arms and head and heard him let out a faint groan! I shouted for people to help me, "I need three guys over here, this guy just moved, he's still alive! Let's go!"

I climbed into the cab, around to the driver's seat and tried desperately to get him dislodged. It was then I saw his legs. He was lying on his right side and his right leg was blown off from his thigh down. I didn't even see the rest of it anywhere, but saw bone sticking out separate from his thigh, meat, blood and veins. It was so horrible. His left leg was twisted around the large gear stick. The left leg was not only wrapped around it, but it was also bent up between the passenger seat and his body in front of the passenger seat. Basically, his left foot was in the small of his back, and even with a US soldier helping me from the outside, after we twisted and turned and pulled, we still couldn't get his body out of the truck. After trying for a few more minuts, I gave up because my helmet kept falling off since the torn strap allowed it to fall off whenever I bent over trying to get him out. I climbed out to check on LT Ali, letting others try to get the driver out.

Sunburn and the infantrymen took care of security and cleared nearby buildings, so I continued to tend to the wounded. Since he had stepped off the Stryker, Sunburn had set up a perimeter with the Iraqis while Omar called on the handheld radio to the other Iraqi units to let them know what happened. Iraqi soldiers kept pointing at my chin to tell me I was injured, and I nodded saying *"anna arif"* (I know) as I continued to move. After a while US and Iraqi troops occupied buildings on both sides of the road. A few *'jundees'* on the perimeter fired into the distance, but I didn't know at what. I checked on the seven-ton passenger, and he was still alive and in a lot of pain, with pressure dressings on his gut and legs, and I believe I saw a tourniquet on his left leg. The medic looked up at me and said, "I don't think this guy is going to make it sir, he's lost a lot of blood, and his gut keeps trying to come out because he is bleeding internally too, see that?" I observed his gut and prayed silently to the Lord to help us save these wounded men. When I got back up to check on the driver, he was on the ground with a US soldier and some Iraqi soldiers around him. I went to check on LT Ali in the Stryker, and he was desperately trying to communicate that he could barely breathe, but there was nothing we could do for him since he had so many holes in him and we didn't have another mouthpiece breather for him (since our only one was on the other wounded guy).

The US soldier with the driver of the truck asked me to hand him a body bag, because the driver had no pulse, and he was afraid he had died. I brought him the bag and instructed the Iraqis to open it up and put him in it. It weighed heavily on my heart to picture it once again, as I was writing down these memories. It must have seemed so cold, but they pointed at his bulletproof vest and magazines and motioned for them to be taken off. I began to cut away with my dull knife and Sunburn turned around and handed me his knife. I cut the strap for the magazine holder, but someone was calling me from the Stryker, so midway through cutting off the body armor I handed the knife to a '*jundee*' and told him to continue. After I tried to help get the man with the missing kneecap onto the Stryker, I gave Sunburn his knife back, and helped load the dead driver in the body bag on top of the Stryker. CPT Zebald (the A Company, 1-5 Infantry Commander) approached me and said "LT, I got this, get on the Stryker; they're going to take you back to the aid station." I wanted to stay and continue the mission, but wasn't about to argue with him in combat, nor did I realize how split open my chin was at that point. I hopped in the Stryker and helped the medic hold the IV-bag for the wounded Iraqi soldier on the floor while LT Ali tried to sit up on the seat next to me.

I saw Sunburn get his right arm wrapped before the ramp closed and asked if he was okay. He answered, "Roger sir, my arm got hit, I'll be okay." The medic asked me if I was all right as soon as the ramp went up and I told him I would be fine, but just needed to get the shrapnel out of my chin because I could feel it embedded in my bone, as crazy as it sounds. I asked him if I could help further with the wounded guy and he asked me to just keep holding the IV-bag. I did and he checked his pulse, as I nodded to LT Ali who kept pointing into his mouth. I told him he would be okay, and we'd get him fixed up, but I didn't know if he understood. It grieved me so much to see him like that, and I was even more saddened in the next minute after the Stryker sped away. On the floor of the Stryker, our wounded Iraqi soldier's pulse was faint. As the medic lifted his eyelid, I saw his eye turn from its normal color and full of life, to a darkened glossy eyeball without life. With one hand, the medic held his eyelid, and with the other he checked his pulse, and there was no beat. I couldn't believe how his eye looked as it seemed to turn to glass, and his soul left his body.

I was so saddened and began to close my eyes and pray. I prayed also for LT Ali and tried to give him room to stretch his shrapnel filled leg. I noticed just how much blood was all over my knit glove inserts, my watch, my sleeve, my pants and my boots – some mine, but most of it was from the wounded and dead Iraqis. Near the base, I popped my head out of the hatch, because the truck driver's body bag we had placed on the roof had dripped blood into the Stryker, onto the medic's back and all over the seat. I tried to readjust what was left of his legs. They kept falling back into the hatch, so I stood out of the hatch and just held them in place, clearing my weapon with the other hand.

When we arrived at the aid station, CPT Bicks was there on the ground waiting, and as soon as the ramp dropped I ran out to the right so they could get to the more serious casualties. As someone walked me into the aid station, I told them to take care of LT Ali first. They got me a litter bed, and I said, "Where is LT Ali? He needs to get looked at first." They brought him in as I said that, and others began to ask us what time all this occurred. They had me take off my top and I dripped blood on it. CPT Bicks asked if I was okay and I told him I was good, but just had some shrapnel in my chin that needed to come out. The doctor felt all over me while asking if there were any other injuries or pains anywhere, but I told him it was just my chin. After a quick look and poke at my chin, he said he could see the shrapnel, but needed to get me into X-ray after LT Ali was done. I said that was fine, but please take care of LT Ali first.

While I was in the X-ray room, SFC Aeris showed up and was watching me. He told me it looked like I was having a rough day, and I told him it was just a little shrapnel. I bled on the X-ray table as the doc had me twist and turn to get different angles, and Woody laughed as I mentioned I didn't want to bleed on my undershirt. I told him I'd be good to get out of the wire on missions in a few days, as soon as I could wear a chinstrap for my helmet again. He just laughed and shook his head at me, saying, "I don't think you have to worry about that right now, sir." I held the gauze they gave me under my chin because the doc said not to apply pressure with it. They also stuck me with a tetanus shot. I thought he was going to take out the shrapnel after the X-rays, but they instead decided to send me to Mosul. The doc said they would be able to make the call as to whether they should take out the shrapnel and if I would need stitches. The other issue was my chipped chin bone and he felt more comfortable sending me to Mosul. They wrapped my chin, gave me another IV-bag in my arm (since the first one had dried up), and prepared me for the flight.

Sunburn was right across from me getting his arm looked at, since it had shrapnel in it too. At first, they said he was going to go with me to the hospital, but they changed their minds and decided to send LT Ali instead. I asked what things I needed to bring and they just gave me a helmet. It wasn't mine but was exactly where I left mine. I suddenly realized I must have grabbed the wrong helmet from the Stryker I rode on. The Stryker was gone, so I just took that helmet and went out the door. CSM Weldo and CPT Bicks were there, along with some Iraqi officers. CSM Weldo told me to stay safe, giving me a commemorative Squadron coin when we shook hands, and I said, "Praise the Lord, Sergeant Major, I'm blessed." He nodded saying, "Yes sir," and I ran out to the helicopter. I got in a seat and they carried in LT Ali. He had a tube in his mouth, with a breathing hand pump sticking out, that one of the medics was pumping. There was also a sucker (like dentists use) to suck the blood bubbling up from his mouth. As we took off, I asked the Lord for a safe trip and to save LT Ali. I asked

God to improve his condition, heal his body, save his life and for me to get to eat dinner with LT Ali some day. I prayed while images of the day's tragedy flashed in my head.

We landed at the Mosul Combat Support Hospital and I wondered if I would see anyone from 1-24 Infantry. After moving through the concrete barriers, I saw MAJ Beaver and called to him and waved (holding my IV-bag in my other hand). He looked as if trying to recognize who I was or perhaps wondering what I was doing there. The doctors got me a room. I saw LTC Krella talking to COL Brown and called to him without realizing I probably interrupted their conversation as the docs put me into a bed. A major came to work on me, and I asked him if he was a 'sir' or not before I saw his rank, and he told me not to worry about that now. He examined me, as PFC McKinney asked me questions for my chart. I said it happened around 10:30 that morning and I'd had about three IV-bags so far. After more questions, Chaplain Welon entered. I was happy to see him and he asked me how I was. "Blessed sir, I'm blessed to be alive." He looked at my chin and said he could see bone and meat, as I told him quickly what happened. He shook my hand and said he needed to check on some other casualties in 1-24 Infantry who were hurt more seriously from a suicide bomber at Yarmuk Traffic Circle. Minutes later, LTC Krella came in, followed by COL Brown. I told him a roadside bomb in Tal Afar tried to knock me down, but my Iraqi brothers were worse off. He shook my hand, said a few other kind words and left, as did COL Brown. The CSM for 11th ACR (Armored Cavalry Regiment) even stopped in to see me (I couldn't remember his name). He gave me a Regimental Commemorative Coin from him and the Regimental Commander, which was also nice.

The major doctor came back to look at my chin again and then had PFC McKinney take me to the X-ray room where others took more X-rays of me as I lay in different angles. After coming back, I asked for a copy of the X-rays and the sergeant in charge gave them to me on the condition that I wouldn't send them back to my wife. I told him she sent me ultrasounds of our baby, and so I should trade by sending an X-ray of my jaw. It looked peculiar, and there was the raisin-sized piece of shrapnel stuck in my chin bone showing up clear as day. I got back to my hospital bed and the doc stuck me with a couple needles to numb up my chin and jaw. He pulled the shrapnel out as I closed my eyes and prayed, and they threw it in a cup for me to see. It was made of steel from a mortar round, as well as mortar material attached to the seal. Sure enough, it was the exact size of a healthy raisin. I was so thankful it landed where it did, because for all the adjusting out of the Stryker hatch I did, God had me in just the right spot. If I had been standing an inch lower in the hatch, the shrapnel would have gone in my mouth and punctured the inside and back of my throat. If I had stood less than an inch higher, it would have gone straight through my throat, with no chin bone to stop it, and I wouldn't be writing this.

McKinney cleaned the gaping hole in my chin several times with a sterile solution, and the doc came back, debating whether he should give me stitches. I was so thankful they got the shrapnel out, since many injured people can't get it removed due to its removal causing more damage. The doc eventually decided on stitches but said I would need to come back if it got infected. After sewing me up, he said one of my minor blood vessels was cut, which was why I kept bleeding. He said the pain below my chin when I opened my mouth was the muscle and nerves which control most of the area. He stressed the importance of me continuing to stretch my mouth a lot over the next few days so it wouldn't permanently close or be extremely difficult to open in the future. I though it odd since I had five stitches or more, and didn't want to stretch them or break them, but I began to do as he ordered.

Chaplain Welon stopped in a few more times to check on me. I picked up my prescription for antibiotics and pain medicine and waited for a flight home. I discovered one wasn't coming until the next morning, but that was the least of my concerns after I found out the result of the 1-24th Infantry suicide car bomb at Yarmuk Traffic Circle. The Battalion sniper, Sergeant Plum, was killed. He died in the CSH after a couple of hours. Everyone was sad, and I prayed, after telling them all I was sorry they had lost him. A doctor allowed me to go into the ICU after they moved LT Ali there, and I was finally able to see him. I thanked the Lord he was recovering as I asked the nurse what his status was. She told me he had a piece of shrapnel lodged behind his left eye, so he would never see out of it again. He might be sent to Bayji to recover from that injury. He also had shrapnel that cut into his throat, but the tracheotomy they performed on him allowed him to breathe successfully. I asked if he would get better, and she said he was much more stable and would probably be able to move around in a month or so, but his army days were over. I inquired about his left leg, which was wrapped up. She said they hadn't even done X-rays yet because their primary concern was his head and throat/mouth injuries. I thanked the Lord again, and then thanked the nurse. The staff at the CSH was nice to me, and someone brought me a meal after allowing me to use a computer to notify Becky I was a casualty today. I wanted to get to her before the Army called her and worried her. This was what I wrote to her:

Bec [Subject Wounded-In-Action],

I just wanted to tell you, so you don't here [sic] from someone else I was WIA (wounded in action) today. Don't worry, I'm gonna be okay. I'm at the CSH (Combat Support Hospital) in Mosul now, but will be released tomorrow maybe. I was hit with an IED, and they removed a hunk of shrapnel from my chin. My bleeding has mostly stopped, and I have some stitches. I should be okay in the long run other than a nasty scar on my chin and not being able to eat corn on the cob or take big bites out of apples. Please have everyone pray for the ING wounded today as well, and then pray for my chin and any infections that could arise. Feel free to let everyone know, and I will give more details when I'm back at my room. I love you

In Christ,
Matt

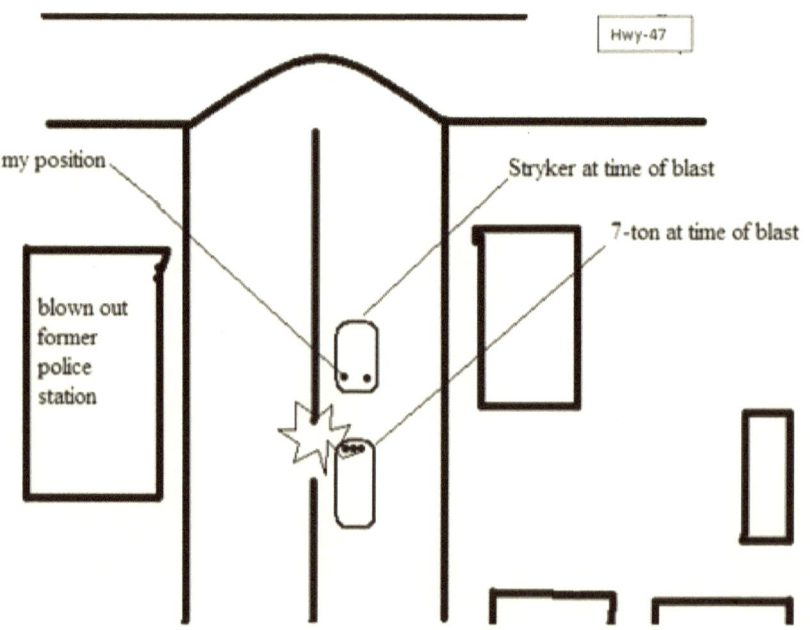

Below is a diagram of the roadside bomb site and explosion where I was hit:

February 17, 2005

I was back at FOB Sykes, writing on my computer again. I woke up in the morning still in the CSH on a bed in the triage area. I was told a flight to Tal Afar came in at 2 a.m., but even though they said they would wake me up so I could leave, no one did. I was irritated, but assumed God had a plan for me to stay longer at the hospital, so I was fine. Around noon, a helpful female major told me a flight from Tal Afar came in, but they were doing maintenance on the helicopter, so she didn't know if they were going back today or not. I linked up with the flight chief who informed me it would be about two more hours, and then they should be ready to go back.

During the two-hour delay, I waited in the open waiting room at the triage writing in my journal when I heard a familiar raspy voice. I looked over and saw someone who looked exactly like SFC E (Heath), but thought to myself it couldn't be him. Why would he be in there? He never was before, but then again neither was I, so I shouted, "SFC E!" He looked down two hallways to his right to see who was calling his name. I figured it must be him at this point, so I walked up to him and said his name again, and he turned and saw me. He looked shocked to see me, and then double-shocked after observing my chin. "What happened to you?" He inquired. I gave him a summary, and then quickly asked him why he was there, and if everyone was okay. He told me they were just hit by a roadside bomb, and Jason Gluv had some shrapnel to the temple. I noticed SGT Q (Bryce) around the corner, who suffered a hearing loss but thankfully was still able to hold a conversation. They said Gluv was in the operating room where they were removing the shrapnel in his temple, but he should be okay.

I prayed and described what happened to me since he had asked. I was simply amazed none of the Storm Troopers were in the CSH before for any combat injuries, yet there on this day Gluv and I were both in there, even though I was in a different unit. After things calmed down with Gluv, and we knew he would be okay, they assessed the damage to the Stryker. I went outside to the Strykers and ran into SGT B (Frank) and Jo and talked to them for a bit, then went back inside and talked to Jay and Randy. It was like a Storm Trooper reunion almost, although not under the best circumstances. They all seemed busy for a while, so I continued to write in my journal and eventually Heath walked over and asked me all about my situation. I gave him complete details and got the details about Gluv as well. We caught up on what had happened since he was on leave and since I've been gone – it was nice. I showed them all my shrapnel and X-rays and they nodded and joked.

After they left, I checked on Gluv in the ICU. He was awake. He had the same reaction as everyone else. He was shocked to see me coming to visit him, then even more shocked after noticing my huge bloody scab, stitches and swollen chin. They had gotten the shrapnel out and his head was patched up. He described when he was hit on Hwy-1 and told me it was squirting out for a while and he felt dizzy. I explained what happened to me, and we caught up. I joked with him and said, "Yeah, you heard I was getting a Purple Heart, so you decided to come and get one too I see, huh?" He just laughed and returned a joke of his own. I ended the conversation to head off to Tal Afar and thanked God for a safe flight back.

When I landed, I saw a smoking Stryker and hoped it was smoking because of engine problems and not because of an explosion or mortar. My hopes were squashed as I ran from the landing pad at Sykes to the aid station parking lot. The Stryker was smoking black from the top, seven out of eight tires were popped, and two of them on the right side were ripped open, burned white and smoking from the inside. I asked the LT as he came out of the Stryker if it was a mortar (before I saw the right side of the vehicle) and he answered angrily it was a roadside bomb. I saw US soldiers walking around carrying IV-bags, with burns all over their faces and hands. I asked a medic if everyone was going to be okay, and she said SGT Hernandez had died. They explained it was a fuel bomb engulfing the entire Stryker in a fireball, and everyone was burned. SGT Hernandez caught shrapnel in his neck and side; the two spots that no body armor covered.

My heart sank, and I wondered when this madness would end. It seemed injury and death surrounded us every day and there was nothing we could do about it. Nothing seemed to get better. More names were added to the casualty list. This enemy we fought continued to pour in from Syria and Iran and other surrounding countries. They continued to spring up in the cities of Iraq after being paid or otherwise motivated to fight American and Iraqi forces. They seemed to have a never-ending supply of people and weapons; regardless of how many we detained and how many caches we found and destroyed every day. When would it end? President Bush claimed we would leave this country when the Iraqis could defend themselves. When would that be? We were still in Afghanistan and Bosnia, and there was little enemy activity in those countries compared to there in Iraq. What was the real end state?

I discussed this with SSG Hitcher after he picked me up in my whaz from the aid station. We headed back to Nomad. He agreed with me that we really had no answers. I also wondered why they hadn't improved the protection on the Strykers in this Squadron. In 1-24 Infantry, it was standard – each Stryker had a minimum of two sandbags in all possible locations around the top perimeter and at least two Kevlar blankets if feasible. At Nomad, I've ridden on Strykers with no sandbags on them, or others with only one or two here or there, and nothing else providing any protection from car bombs.

At Nomad Base, everyone greeted me with smiles. I got hugs and handshakes from all. I showed them the shrapnel. Sunburn's arm was in a cast and sling. The shrapnel apparently tore right through the muscle that allows him to move his wrist up and down. He would be in the cast for ten days. Everyone was so surprised to see me, but they had a meal ready for me since it was still close to lunchtime (they usually get an extra one for somebody). I ate and updated them on what happened in Mosul. They informed me that the times when the Iraqis did checkpoint rotations had changed. They occurred only during the night and early morning before sunrise to avoid further contact and remote detonated bomb. CPT Bicks told me I was back just in time to do the brief slide, which was funny considering I was thinking about doing it as I flew back on the helicopter. Then he laughed and told me it was already done and welcomed me back. I let Sunburn read what I wrote in my journal about the events of the day before, and he agreed with everything I wrote. I sadly informed everyone about SGT Hernandez's death and the mood changed quickly. SGT ZT and SPC Sunburn both knew him and said this was his second tour in Iraq. He left behind a one-year-old child, and everyone just shook their heads in sadness. I imagined what Becky and Katelyn would do if I got killed, and couldn't bear the thought, so I tried to talk of other things.

The rest of the day I tried to stretch my mouth more than an inch wide. I also found out online that my friends' mom who has cancerous tumors was doing better. I had prayed for her daily and he said the chemo is working. Thank God. I'd been in need of some good news. I talked to Becky's sister Suzy, who told me she bawled when she found out I was wounded. I asked why, since it was just wounded, not killed, but she said it just hurt her so badly. I managed to talk to some other friends too, and Becky came on describing that she shared the email I sent to her with others in the family, and she thanked God I was still alive. She said she even cried when she called my dad at work to tell him, after just blankly staring for fifteen minutes at the email I had sent her. I also talked to my brother Chris. Everyone seemed relieved I was safe. After I recounted to Becky all that had happened, I slept.

February 18, 2005

Today was a crazy day, but I was thankful there were no more deaths, at least to my knowledge. Iraqi pay finally arrived. We watched the officers closely to guard against theft. CSM Aedo also came over to the command post with about a hundred soldiers trying to quit. The pay chart listed him as a staff sergeant, and he became upset. In short, he caused a riot. The soldiers said if he went home or to jail, they would go with him. Woody screamed at them to go away and yelled at CSM Aedo that it was completely unacceptable to start a riot like that, and that it didn't solve anything. We told him he would be paid properly no matter what rank was listed on the sheet. CPT Bicks drove up after returning from Squadron, and we let him jump right into the situation. Woody said we needed to get rid of MAJ Farhan and LTC Ahmed or this problem would only get worse. CPT Bicks just flipped out and said he didn't even have the authority to fire a LT for refusing to go on mission. He said LTC Mavis didn't even have the authority to do that, which was ridiculous.

Apparently, LT Tofeeq is still there, with no consequences for his refusal to go on a mission twice in a row. The only ones who could fire an officer seemed to be the general in charge of the Iraqi Army and maybe LTC Ahmed. I couldn't believe that double standard. We could kick an enlisted Iraqi soldier off the FOB and fire him in a heartbeat, but we weren't allowed to touch the officers. We all just threw our hands up and stormed off in different directions. I decided to go over to the Iraqi compound and monitor the pay, since CPT Bicks ordered them to go pay their soldiers to get everyone calmed down over there. I watched and added up how many Dinar each of them was paid for the day. Interestingly, there were no more *'jundees'* (common soldiers), according to the Iraqi Ministry of Defense. All normal soldiers were promoted to either staff sergeant or sergeant. In the US Army, sergeant is E-5 (fifth enlisted rank) and staff sergeant is one rank higher, but in the Iraqi Army, SSG (or S-SGT as they write it) is just below sergeant. The only other enlisted rank in the Iraqi Army is first sergeant. The Ministry of Defense did away with the rank of Sergeant Major. It was confusing, but at least they were making their own decisions.

I learned of some misconceptions everyone had about how my wound would be treated. I ate dinner with SGT Wadul, who confirmed what I had heard. The medics at Nomad (or at least some of them) told CPT Bicks and some others I would be gone for a long time and I would be sent back to the states for reconstructive surgery. It was amazing how quickly it spread, because CPT Nerph in the TOC thought the same thing, as did most of the Nomad team. SGT Wadul said they didn't expect to see me again for a while and were completely surprised I was back. I talked to SFC Aeris about it and he said that the medics told him that my jaw was fractured and I needed to have it reconstructed back in the states. He and ZT didn't expect not to see me for months. The rest of the evening involved capturing three enemies from Sinjar Checkpoint, one of whom was on the Brigade blacklist.

February 19, 2005

I worked on the designs for our Nomad Coin as well as the Iraqi Battalion Coin, which came out well. Woody helped me with them. It took a while, but I thought we perfected the design. We had two thousand dollars in the 'recruiting' portion of the budget to purchase about three hundred Iraqi Army coins and about one hundred Nomad coins. We didn't need one hundred Nomad coins, but they could only be bought in quantities of one hundred, so we would have extra. When SGT Wadul returned from checkpoint inspections, he informed us that five Iraqi soldiers quit and walked off Sinjar Checkpoint.

It wasn't while SGT Wadul was there, but the sergeant at the checkpoint told him five soldiers threatened to shoot him if he didn't let them leave, so they stacked their weapons and body armor and magazines in a pile and left. I wondered why it didn't occur to the Iraqi sergeant to detain them after they deposited their weapons and armor. This reduced the checkpoint manning from eleven to six individuals. We knew this would happen, since the soldiers had all got paid and now wanted to quit and go home to their families. The leave rotation was just starting, but they couldn't wait. Woody and I told CSM Aedo and MAJ Sultan that in the US Army, if someone deserted in a time of war, they would get shot. Perhaps the IA needed to do so as well. It was the responsibility of the Ministry's of Defense since the Iraqis were now running their own country.

The Iraqi Intervention Forces and US Marines working with them under CPT Fenelly were good from what I heard and had found several weapons caches all over Tal Afar. They weren't supposed to stay long, but I hoped they would, because they seemed to be good at storming houses and capturing the enemy. I felt bad for the Marines though, because they drove around the city in up-armored Humvees, which are not effective against roadside bombs. I supposed if the Iraqis could do it in Nissans, the Marines weren't so bad off compared to them. I still wouldn't want to be out there in anything less than a Stryker or an Abrams tank, but that was the nature of an armor officer. Below are pictures of the coins we designed and were planning to give out.

February 20, 2005

LTCs Mavis and Ahmed met to discuss the Iraqi *'mujas'* (leave) situation, agreeing they would send many at a time to the Sinjar Iraqi Police Battalion. MAJ Farhan and CSM Aedo swung by looking to leave the FOB. CSM Aedo had arranged for himself and five other IA soldiers to go to Sinjar for leave, and MAJ Farhan and six others were to go to Baghdad to get the pay for the Battalion for the month of February. LTC Rugrs stopped us because these individuals weren't on the brief slide yesterday to go on leave, so therefore they could not go. I told MAJ Sultan and CSM Aedo that Squadron said no, but hopefully they could go *'mujas'* the next day. CPT Ishmail and SGM Mohammed complained about the five soldiers who had left the checkpoint that day. I said they needed to get a standard from their higher headquarters as to what the punishment should be. We told them there must be some punishment. In Saddam Hussein's old army, people were hanged for deserting. I suggested they get the names of the deserters, give them to LTC Ahmed, and conduct a raid on their homes in Sinjar to snatch them back and throw them in the detention facility.

At the very least, I thought they should be put on a list for the future if they ever tried to join the Iraqi Army again or pass through any checkpoints. I practiced some Arabic with Khalaf, who we were now calling 'Oakley' since he wore an inscribed Oakley brand black beanie all the time. We got another new interpreter named Faisil, who had been an interpreter in Baghdad. He was even better than Oakley, so he would be SFC Walenz's training interpreter.

February 21, 2005

Today I worked with some Civil Affairs soldiers near the Squadron TOC to get the bonus pay for wounded Iraqi soldiers. I worked the paperwork and we paid them in the evening. We also put together a graduation ceremony for the new Iraqi medics for their Combat Lifesaver Certification Class at 11 a.m. SGT ZT returned from inspections saying three '*jundees*' ran away from Mosul Checkpoint. None ran from the other two because Major Abid and the sergeant at Avgani and Sinjar checkpoints told their men if they ran away, the leader would shoot them. The threat seemed to work well, which is what we were beginning to notice. Sadly, many Iraqi soldiers didn't respond well to kindness. Many didn't appreciate it, but instead complained, made excuses, and tried to get favors and advantages because of our kindness. They misttook kindness for weakness and ignored us or walked all over us if we tried to motivate them with negative or positive reinforcement. It was a shame some only responded to fear and threats, but it seemed to be part of their culture.

I worked on the website for a bit and we sent about 79 Iraqi soldiers to Sinjar, 25 of which were escorts to drop the remainder off for their long-awaited leave. After lunchtime, I sorted out some budget details with CPT Bicks, since he was changing command on March 9th, and we needed to prepare to close the accounts again. Tedious, but neat to count over $20,000 in my hands – but it was just paper with numbers, meaningless when I took a second to think about it. After dinner, Omar and I spoke with LTC Ahmed. I informed him about my ideas about what to do if someone deserted a checkpoint, in addition to reminding him the good MAJ Abid did that day at his checkpoint. I discussed with him the importance of him purchasing a new truck, since we have twenty-thousand dollars or more in the vehicle account to close out. I got him to sign a document receipt for some things back in November that CPT Bicks had me type up. We sorted out some issues with the casualty and detainee tracker system because we found that we still had not paid about ten Iraqi soldiers who had been wounded prior to that day's date.

I talked with Becky on webcam before going to bed – it was great to see her beautiful smile and pretty face. It would be only two and a half more months until I would get to see her and our baby, Lord willing – or as they say in Arabic; *'Inshaallah.'*

February 22, 2005

I worked on the *'ilhagnee'* (follow me) Nomad website and studied Arabic while most of the team went to SGT Hernandez' memorial service. I held down the fort with SFC Walenz, who went to train Iraqis, then came by and said he had a successful conversation with LTC Ahmed who said he wanted to conduct more training, even with his officers. He agreed to a class I would teach on the duties, roles and responsibilities of officers, so I ended up doing some last-minute preparation and teaching. I picked up Iraqi soldiers who had appointments at the aid station. Most of them were routine checkups for prior wounds, and I got my stitches taken out. The doctors only saw three, so all three were removed, but I thought the doc at the CSH had put in five. They said some of them may be underneath my large scab and I should come back if I discover any more. I was healing fine, but the bone would take at least another four weeks to heal.

MAJ Jenkins (the lead surgeon) said until the scab falls off over the next couple weeks, I shouldn't wear a helmet and consequently a helmet strap, because it could cause further damage. He said after it fell off and the skin could handle it, I could go on missions according to my own comfort level. This was good and bad. Good because Becky and the family would be much happier that I wasn't going on any missions for the next couple weeks. Bad because I felt like I was letting the team down, and I wanted to support them by sharing the load and conducting checkpoint inspections and going on missions with them. Sunburn still had at least another ten days before he could hold a weapon with his right arm, so I supposed we were both in the same boat: "on the bench," as SFC Aeris (Woody) put it. Speaking of wearing a helmet, I finally got my own helmet back when a soldier from A Company knocked on my door to change out my helmet for the helmet I accidentally grabbed the day I was wounded. The clip portion of the chinstrap was ripped and gone, like I suspected, from the shrapnel that cut through it and into my chin.

After dinner, I went over to LTC Ahmed's office to teach the class with SFC Walenz, and surprisingly, about fifteen officers showed up. We weren't even sure LTC Ahmed would still allow the class, but he did. I explained each slide about the responsibilities of his officers and Omar interpreted. I noted names of each officer in his battalion. Just before starting the class, I asked him if he wanted to give the class to his own officers since he seemed to understand it all after I went over it with him, but he declined. As I started briefing the first slide, he changed his mind and began to brief them himself. I sat down happy, because it was quicker that way, and that was our endstate goal anyway – the Iraqis being able to train their own men. I stayed and had Omar whisper in my ear everything LTC Ahmed said, and he was good at briefing. After the hour-long briefing I told LTC Ahmed what the next class would address, and if he wished, I could brief him ahead of time. He agreed and I left, just as CPT Bicks arrived for his evening meeting.

February 23, 2005

What a busy day! I started working on the Nomad website for a bit, then LTC Ahmed came by. I created a book in which to sort and keep budget paperwork. It worked so well LTC Ahmed asked me if I could make one for him, so I started another for him and got Evan to translate it into Arabic (Evan also gave me a neat alarm clock/reading light.) We had a patrol of Iraqis ready to go to Sinjar to grab up the soldiers who deserted, but we had to cancel it because LTC Mavis wasn't present to allow a patrol to go out. Patrols would leave the FOB all the time without Strykers before the elections, but after the elections, none can leave without Stryker escort, nor without LTC Mavis' direct approval, which made things cumbersome. It took away power from the Iraqi Army rather than giving them more authority. We felt that subordinate officers and senior NCOs in our squadron had little decision authority as well – as if we were a squadron with two lieutenant colonels and 500 privates for all the decision-making power we had.

At chow, I ran into LTC Rugrs and MAJ Diny, so I asked them when it would be clear to leave. Both told me not until LTC Mavis directly approved it. LTC Rugrs then said the Iraqis weren't going to Sinjar to do a mission anyway. I corrected him stating they were going to pick up runaway soldiers to bring back to the detainee center. He told me they were really going to Sinjar to get drunk, have sex, party and vacation, and it didn't do any good to keep the runaways in the Iraqi Army, because he didn't want quitters. One week we were told no quitters allowed, and to detain people who wanted to quit, and the next week we were told to let them go. On a good note, I did get about five packages from my brother, my uncle and my parents. My parents sent food, food, and more food, my brother sent me a cool Arabic program to help me learn the language better and my uncle sent some funny videos.

February 24, 2005

At the start of the day, I received two important email messages from SFC Puten, who had been fired. In summary, his first email mentioned that his new assignment was to evaluate all the Iraqi Army units in northern Iraq, and if I could collect sworn statements from Major Sultan and CSM Aedo, along with others in the 109th Iraqi Army "Wolf Battalion" (those we trained on our base), we could have LTC Ahmed removed (possibly imprisoned) and replaced with a good leader. His second email mentioned that some in Abu Gharib prison knew about LTC Ahmed and his working with the enemy. SFC Puten also shared that he was enjoying his new job working with special Iraqi units and was working to get a platoon of Iraqi T55 and T72 tanks to come help the 109th Iraqi Battalion in Tal Afar. SFC Puten wrote these emails to LT Durmsy, the former Nomad XO before me, who shared them with me at the start of the day. We spent some time 'whispering in corners' today and the process has started.

When MAJ Sultan and CSM Aedo got back from leave, we would get their statements and get rid of LTC Ahmed for good, hopefully sending him to jail. The most amazing thing about all of this was that as I prayed for SFC Puten before he was fired, I had asked for God's will, and had a feeling He was going to turn the firing into good (as God often does with bad things). Sure enough, SFC Puten had become more effective than ever. SFC Aeris said that happened a lot in the Army. It was kinda like Obi Wan Kenobi in *Star Wars,* "If you strike me down, I shall become more powerful than you could possibly imagine." SFC Puten seemed to be in the perfect place to make a huge difference in the Iraqi Army outside of our squadron's control. It would be great if we could remove LTC Ahmed. There had been too many suspicions and facts floating around about of his thievery, and we had thought for a while that he was connected to the enemy.

I practiced a bit of Arabic and taught a class to LTC Ahmed and the rest of his officers on the Army's troop leading procedures. I drew examples of what to do and how to do it when they received missions, issued warning orders, made tentative plans, started necessary movements, reconnoitered, completed the plan, issued the final order, then supervised and refined. Half of them seemed to be learning and taking notes, and when I was done (Faisil interpreted for me), Ahmed told me his officers already knew everything I had covered the last 45 minutes. But, CPT Ishmail and MAJ Khalid, the Intelligence Officer and Operations Officer respectively, were both very interested in doing some type of ground reconnaissance before missions, so I talked to them afterward about it while we drank chai.

February 25, 2005

An interesting day –it started with Omar going on leave and the chow hall burning down. No terrorist activity involved, just a grease fire in the kitchen, but there wouldn't be any meals in there for a week. No one was injured, thank God, and shortly after hearing this news, CPT Bicks said we had a secret mission to Al Baaj, where a haven of enemy was said to be located. We were to look for anyone out of the ordinary, especially people with a Syrian or Yemen dialect, Sudanese, or anything else unusual. The mission was scheduled for the next morning, but it looked like it wouldn't happen. LTC Ahmed came by this morning to tell me Mosul Checkpoint was engaged by enemy around 5 a.m., leaving a disabled blue pickup truck there. The remaining vehicles escaped, leaving the dead enemy in the driver's seat. They were scared to approach the vehicle for fear it was rigged with explosives. (I'll explain more about this later.)

LT Ali came back from the hospital, and we shook hands and took pictures together. He couldn't talk very well, but it seemed he could see out of his left eye, despite what the doctors said. He still had a hole in his throat from the tracheotomy. His left leg was still wrapped up, but he hopped out of his truck and walked around with his crutches, happy to see me. I told Evan to tell him I was glad he was back, and that I had prayed for him on our helicopter flight to Mosul together. He thanked me, and then I got back to fixing the entire Nomad team some food. I had gotten so much food from my uncle and parents that I could probably feed the entire team for a week. Now that LT Ali was back, it looked like God had answered my prayer about being able to have dinner with him. As soon as he could eat food more comfortably, I would have him over for dinner. Anyway, I finished fixing several noodle dishes, chicken and rice, and other assorted foods for the team, thanking God for being able to bless everyone with meals during this time.

We were distributing as many posters and flyers and pamphlets as we could, because Zarqawee himself was suspected to be coming through our area to escape back to Syria. He was the top Al Queda leader of the entire terrorist network in Iraq, and intelligence was reporting he was on his way. We were making sure each checkpoint was extra secure, and no bypasses could be taken, so we could catch this guy. I prayed we would. Well, we didn't catch Zarqawee himself, but we caught his top aide, and news about it was on BBC News. I thanked the Lord and still prayed we'd get Zarqawee, although his aide was sixty kilometers from the Syrian border, so he could have already escaped a different way. Many interpreters and others told me that most terrorists here come from Syria, Sudan and Yemen, and it made me so mad that they could just come to Iraq and attack us.

Later in the afternoon at the TOC LTC Rugrs suspected the Iraqis had made up the Mosul Checkpoint attack to cover up killing (or almost killing) a civilian, so I typed up a report for him explaining the "who, what, when, where, why" with a narrative which included the story of how four to seven individuals drove past the first several barriers, firing on Iraqi soldiers, attempting to run the Mosul Checkpoint. Six Iraqi soldiers (five with AK47s, one with a PKC machine gun) shouted for the vehicle to stop, returned fire while taking cover behind barriers and ditches, each firing 17-20 rounds while the PKC soldier immobilized the vehicle with 70-75 rounds. They had shot the driver in the head, as the remaining enemy retreated southwest into Tal Afar, while Iraqi soldiers wounded two more enemy as they retreated behind buildings. It also included the Iraqi First Sergeant's fear of approaching the vehicle due to possible explosives and that CPT Bicks and a US Army sergeant investigated at noon and didn't find a single shell casing of rounds fired (the vehicle driver was alive and unconscious). Finally, the report included that a US medic applied first aid to the driver's head and leg wounds evacuated the individual to the Tal Afar hospital.

LTC Rugrs said it looked much better, but still sounded fishy. I quoted his own words back to him since the report looked totally different from what LTC Ahmed told me: "The first report is always wrong, sir." He didn't say anything to that, so I went back to the command post. SGT ZT went over to talk to LTC Ahmed to get his cell phone number so we could start tracing his calls and others above us could listen to him possibly contacting the enemy. Sergeant ZT started off talking about Civil Affairs stuff and gradually worked into how much easier it would be if LTC Ahmed could talk to the Civil Affairs team or the buyer directly for purchases, so he popped the question, and LTC Ahmed, unsuspicious and happy, handed over his cell phone number. Genius – hopefully, we would catch him in the act.

February 26, 2005

The chow hall was surprisingly up and running ahead of schedule, and I ate lunch and dinner there. I guessed my team Nomad cooking days were over then. I had horrible headaches today, but I worked extensively on the budget. In the evening, after we paid several wounded Iraqi soldiers, including LT Ali, I checked my email. My parents sent me a collection of emails from various friends and families that touched me deeply. It was filled with responses to prayer from back in December after the chow hall exploded and this month after I was wounded. Everyone seemed so grateful and thankful God was answering prayers, and they all seemed to be growing so much closer to God through prayer. In response, I shared that I thanked God for all those who were praying, all He'd taken me through and asked Him to bless others with an even closer relationship with Him – and I also thanked my Mom and Dad for sharing the emails with me.

February 27, 2005

CPT Bicks told us that from this date on, Iraqi soldiers would permanently man Avgani and Mosul Checkpoints twenty-four-seven in three-day shifts. This came as a surprise, especially from LTC Ahmed, since he didn't even like the idea of them staying out there twenty-four hours at a time. I suppose he felt the risks were getting too great. It was dangerous for so many men in mostly unarmored vehicles to drive up and down the roads all the time. It would certainly change things, but maybe now they would speed up the process to get fortifications up there. The other news was that Saddam Hussein's half-brother was captured. He was a pretty dangerous and evil man back in the old regime and, apparently even after US forces occupied Iraq, he led the insurgents and organized the resistance against us (separate from Zarqawee, who led a different group of terrorists). Thank God, and I prayed He continued to help us catch Zarqawee, since he could still be in the area. Still hoping and praying.

February 28, 2005

The morning showed showed pictures of dead bodies, fire, and wounded men in Hillah, Iraq, just south of Baghdad, where up to 125 people were killed and another 130 wounded when a car bomb exploded in a crowded area. All were civilians, many of whom were outside a hospital (where the explosion occurred) preparing for physicals to join the Iraqi Army or perhaps the Iraqi Police Battalion. I watched the death toll in disbelief. These people were all innocent civilians, belonging to this country, and killed by terrorists. They weren't soldiers, nor were they armed. The cowardice and evil of this enemy filled me with a rage I almost couldn't describe. I was in shock watching the screen and wondering how people could be so evil. My only solace, and this again will sound bad, was that the evil cowardly suicide bomber who did this was right that moment in hell forever – experiencing the "weeping and gnashing of teeth" Jesus mentioned so many times * [see note].[2]

Avgani Checkpoint had a firefight, but thankfully, no casualties. In the evening, I taught a class to the Iraqi officers on reporting in a format which sends a clear picture of any enemy situation. They all seemed to have a general idea of it already, but all of them said afterwards that they still benefited from my class. It was fun teaching them, and I even drew Avgani Checkpoint on butcher paper and went through an example so they could understand better. They seemed to like it, which felt good. CPT Ishmael asked some questions, as did a few other officers, and I helped explain to them how the intelligence gathered from reports was used to prepare future operations. One of them mentioned a few houses where some citizens lived who always placed roadside bombs and fired on Avgani Checkpoint. I told them they could put this information together to conduct a raid or cordon and search those houses, and they agreed. The Iraqi Army was going to conduct a cordon and search of the neighborhood south of the mosque and school near the checkpoint, but LTC Mavis cancelled it and I was extremely disappointed. Otherwise, my chin hurt more in the evening (for the second evening in a row), for some reason.

When US forces captured the half-brother of Saddam, they caught 15-25 other "henchmen" as well. Syria evidently handed them over to the United States for fear we were going to invade them with the other coalition forces. It made me laugh, and at the same time, angry. I laughed because of their fear we would invade them because of what we did to Saddam Hussein, and because of their status as part of the "Axis of Evil" that President Bush so named. It angered me because they were knowingly holding these terrorists and just gave them up only to avoid a war with us. I knew, as did everyone else in Iraq, that Syria was a breeding ground as well as a safe haven for terrorism and its radical followers. I had thoughts about destroying their military with missiles, bombs and artillery to teach them a lesson.

[1] As previously noted in footnotes 12 (December 25) and 16 (January 23), and as scripture confirms, Jesus is the Son of God, not God himself. The fact that I spoke of his death here should have been evident that Jesus died, and God cannot die, therefore Jesus is not the one true God. Jesus had the power to "take up" his life again from the command he "received" from his Father as he said in John 10:18 ("take up" should be rendered "receive" as both are the same exact Greek word – *lambano*). Yet disciples constantly preached God raised Jesus from the dead (see Acts 3:26, 4:10, 5:30, 10:40, 13:30, Romans 4:24, 1 Corinthians 15:15, Galatians 1:1, Ephesians 1:20, and numerous other scriptures). Jesus himself claimed to be dead but is now alive forevermore (Revelation 1:18).

[2] As noted on November 22 and December 25 footnotes, the dead know nothing, and there is no knowledge or wisdom in the grave (Ecclesiastes 9:5, 10). Today I take no solace in others' suffering, but I do find encouragement that God will execute righteous judgment upon all – indignation and wrath to those who follow unrighteousness and do evil, but eternal life to those who patiently continue to do good, seeking glory, honor, peace, and immortality (Romans 2:5-10). I do not believe

this judgment to have already occurred but expect it to happen on the day in which God has appointed – by the man whom He chose – Jesus the Messiah (John 5:27, Acts 17:31).

7

March

March 1, 2005

Sergeant ZT got promoted to Staff Sergeant. A decent crowd showed up for the ceremony, including a few former acquaintances with whom I had never seemed to get along (I supposed my outspoken witness for Christ was the reason. (Personality clashes defined it as well, because I didn't cuss, smoke, drink, or talk about women, sports, motorcycles or weightlifting). I could feel intense spiritual warfare but tried to get along. It was a brief ceremony, I read off the promotions orders and then we placed the new rank on him and shook hands. Afterwards, we had dinner and an evening reminiscing about college days.

I heard a familiar voice, and suddenly, SFC Burtl from Third Platoon A Company, 1-24 Infantry was standing outside my door, with SSG Lingo, one of his squad leaders. I was shocked to see them and asked them what they were doing at Nomad. SFC Burtl told me they were here supporting an Airborne Unit that came to the base that night. I let him know where I would be if he needed anything. It was good to see familiar faces. They asked me what happened to my face and I explained about the bomb. SSG Lingo began to explain about Gluv, but I told him I was at the hospital that day, so I already knew.

I then overheard SSG ZT talking to Faisil (Face is his nickname), explaining that he lived in Virginia. I asked ZT where and he told me he had attended Old Dominion University for a semester, which is where I earned my degree. After talking for a bit about ODU, it turned out that he knew a few people that I knew, including one that I was commissioned with in 2001: Christopher Sig. They grew up together, and I knew Chris for four years at ODU in ROTC (Reserve Officer Training Corps – a college program that trains cadets to be officers) in the Monarch Battalion. We shared stories, and familiar faces, and he informed me he had been in the Marine ROTC for a semester, and they used to run past the Army guys on the nine floors of the tallest building on campus, BAL (Batten Arts and Letters building). We may have even run past each other once or twice during physical training back then, who knows? His mom taught Spanish there, and after describing my Spanish teacher, it turned out that she was his mom! His mother taught me some Spanish at ODU – small world!

March 2, 2005

SSG ZT and I went to get the supplies Mohammed returned with yesterday. He had about fifty washtubs (one was broken), ten brand new boots, some squeegee wipes and giant bags of detergent with brushes. I then attended a mission briefing on our operation for the next day. CPT Bicks was on a mission, so I went in his stead. I returned to the command post with the info after getting enlarged graphics of the area in which the Iraqis would operate. When I got back, SSG ZT and SFC Aeris asked me if I was going to go on the mission. Immediately a conflict arose in my mind, especially after the conversation that I had with Becky the other night. It wasn't so much conflict about going outside the wire, but the possibility of further risk and injury I could do to my chinbone and surrounding flesh. Earlier, we had talked about doing what the doctor said about my chinstrap, but as others kept pressuring me to go outside the wire, and combined with my own desire to contribute to the team and to be part of something big, I wanted to go.

Instead of waiting for everything to heal fully and properly, I hated to miss out. I prayed about it all day, asking God to allow me to go if it was His will, but to keep me away if it wasn't. He must have wanted me to stay here for some reason, because I never got a chance to even ask CPT Bicks if I could go because I was so busy. I took those with appointments to the aid station. When I returned, SSG Hitcher was furious with the Squadron XO. An informant tipped the Avgani Checkpoint Iraqis that a certain truck coming from Mosul was carrying explosives. They described the truck and Nomad base sent the report up to Squadron. The Squadron XO wanted to know every microscopic detail about the situation, but there was simply no more information to report. The informant had driven through the checkpoint, passed his information on to the Iraqi soldiers and left, not wanting to leave his name. LTC Rugrs said our reporting was horrible and Nomad was a "hindrance to this Squadron!" I couldn't believe he said that over the radio. I could understand why SSG Hitcher was so furious, but just shook my head at how bad morale was in this squadron.

CPT Bicks wanted me to get more large maps of Baaj with building numbers. I did so when assets became available close to midnight. I didn't mind staying up late while they slept since I wasn't able to go with them.

March 3, 2005

I woke before 6 a.m. to monitor the radio in the command post. I listened to the mission, and things sounded slow. No huge terrorist strike force was hiding out as intelligence predicted, but it sounded like each company found a few detainees with illegal items, so I suppose it wasn't a waste. When everyone got back around 1 p.m, they said the IA seemed excited to be on a mission clearing houses once again, as opposed to "rotting on the checkpoints all day long." It was mostly a quiet day for me. SGM Collins stopped by to request a detail of 30 Iraqi soldiers to erect some tents and LT Durmsy stopped by to confirm the request. He asked me where everyone was and I told him they were on a mission, but I wasn't because of my still healing wound. We talked about all the gore we had seen thus far in this war, in only five months. It was a good conversation and ended with us talking about the Mosul chow hall suicide bombing December 21st of the last year. Rich was SSG Vankomen's boss in A Troop before coming over here, and they were close.

Shortly after everyone got back from the mission, 88 Iraqis tried to go on leave. I signed the leave slips, and then CPT Bicks tried to coordinate with LTCs Rugrs or Mavis to give permission for them to leave, since this leave mission "wasn't on the brief slide." Once again, I was awed by the lack of decision-making power in this squadron. No one could find either Rugrs or Mavis, so just as Rommel and his fellow field marshalls in WWII wouldn't wake up Hitler to inform him of the Allied invasion, all progress and activity ceased. SFC Walenz said we thought the military was supposed to work off a chain of command, because two people should not make all the decisions in a unit this size. But that was what was happening.

At chow I had an interesting discussion with SGT Wadul about ghosts and how they relate to scripture. I worked on the budget since it was high on the priority list. We figured out how to spend the rest of the money, and I would surely be running around for signatures. I explained to SSG Roy, our new medic from the same reserve unit as SFC Walenz, that we always told the Iraqis to be ready at least forty-five minutes before we needed them. I described "Insha Allah" (literally, God willing), since so many times, after asking Omar or Evan or another interpreter when the Iraqi soldiers would be ready, they'd answer, "Fifteen minutes, Insha Allah." This normally meant they wouldn't be ready in fifteen minutes. I wrote a silly math formula for it on one of the marker boards, and it got a quite a few laughs.

March 4, 2005

After my business with Mohammed at the mall for budget paperwork and some items, I returned to the office where CPT Bicks and I went over all the paperwork (it seemed to grow every time we talked). He showed me what we needed to fix, and we counted some money to make sure everything worked out right.

While driving around the base, I stopped to talk to SFC Burtl, who was still on base, along with SPC Kramer and others on his Stryker. They then asked if I knew about Gertson. Immediately my mind shifted to the conversation I had with LT Durmsy the other day. He said something about three people from A Company, 1-24 Infantry having died since I have been at Nomad, and I did a double take. I told him I only knew of two: CPT Jacobsen, and SSG Johnson. Lt Durmsy had told me that he talked to someone who told him there were three. This couldn't be what they were about to confirm, I thought. Not Specialist Gertson. He had already been wounded by ball bearings in his back in the chow hall on the 21st of December. He was a big guy and was a Sniper. He was a Storm Trooper. He knew Jesus. It couldn't be him. But, sure enough, it was. "What about him?" I asked SFC Burtl, as if I couldn't see what was coming. "He was killed, sir."

My heart sank, yet at the same time, I didn't believe it. I couldn't picture it. He lived right across from me in our "Red Square" living pad area in Mosul in 1-24. I saw him just about every day. Even though he was a Sniper, he was one of my men. He was one of the Storm Troopers I looked after, along with the Mortars and Mobile Gun

System men. I remember talking about CPT Jacobsen with him as his wound closed over the ball bearing in his back in the days following the DFAC bombing. I remember him telling me Captain Jacobsen's last words: "I'm all right, check on my men." Gertson was going to write Rikka Jacobsen and tell her this, as well as how much respect he had for CPT J. I wondered if he ever got the chance to write. They said Gertson was killed in a drive by shooting a few weeks ago. It didn't sound like something that happened in combat, but they elaborated. He was standing near the commander, CPT WanTarp, in Mosul, when a car drove by and an enemy shot an AK47 at them as the car sped away. They described that the bullet went through his left ribs, through his upper abdomen and came out his right arm. They laid him on the ramp of the Medical Evacuation Vehicle (MEV) and he died within a minute or so. Just picturing it made me feel horrible that something like that could happen to him, so I stopped attempting to imagine it.

SFC Burtl then told me the terrorists had been doing a lot of drive-by's and they were about to shoot CPT WanTarp one day. They said an Arab walked up toward them with an AK47 tucked along his side, with his right arm straight in line with his body. Some guys from 2nd Platoon saw him and fired on him. They filled his chest and head with holes and 5.56mm and 7.62mm. They said he dropped to the ground, but the man came very close to shooting CPT WanTarp.

I hated the evil in Iraq. People say Christians should not hate, but this is untrue. We should not hate people or good, but evil and sin are supposed to be hated. Even God hates them. My memories of the killed Iraqis on the sixteenth of February when I was wounded filled my head, and I thought of SPC Gertson. He was such a big, strong and good guy, always finding something to smile about. I would get filled with such an intense anger at these terrorists sometimes. I, like many of us, constantly had my head filled with thoughts of killing them all and blowing up a city, but then I would realize no city is entirely bad. There are way more good people in the cities of Mosul, Tal Afar, and

Baghdad than evil people, and it was the small percentage of evil people who made it horrible there. If a city were completely evil, I trust the Lord would perform His miracle of destruction as he did in the book of Genesis, to the cities of Sodom and Gomorrah. I thought it would be nice if He would turn these terrorists into pillars of salt like He did Lot's wife, but I knew it was His plan and timing that count, not mine.

Gertson was killed on the nineteenth of February, three days after I was wounded. This was the first I'd heard of it. I asked SFC Burtl and his guys how SGT Pena was doing, since he was close to Gertson and was his Sniper section leader. They said badly, and I can't imagine how much this war has hurt him. SGT Pena was with CPT Jacobsen when he was dying and took it badly in the days following. Now with him losing SPC Gertson, he was more than ready to go home and get out of the Army. After hearing this news, I said my 'goodbyes', and told them to have a safe trip, as I would be praying for them.

When I returned to the command post, we learned an enemy sniper at Avgani Checkpoint shot an Iraqi soldier in the gut from the buildings to the south, and they rushed soldier to the FOB. CPT Bicks wanted me to go to the aid station for the arrival of the casualty, and SSG ZT asked why SSG Roy (our medic) couldn't go, or why SSG ZT himself couldn't go. I told him I didn't understand either and he suggested I just finish my paperwork and meet him at the aid station. He took care of that while I finished paperwork, tracked down Mohammed in his room and then met SSG ZT and CPT Bicks at the aid station. The wounded Iraqi soldier was in surgery and the docs said he was going to make it. I was relieved and thanked the Lord.

I stopped at LTC Ahmed's office on the way back to get his signatures for the documents and he complained about the lack of support he got from this squadron. He stressed the importance of creating a dirt wall around the checkpoints so snipers couldn't fire on his men, but told me he never got any help when he needed it. After CPT

Bicks reviewed all the work I did on the budget and its supporting documents, he signed them, and I took them to Squadron. I continued to pray for an end to this conflict and terrorism.

March 5, 2005

While SGT Wadul cleaned the command post, we pulled the chairs out onto the gravel and I read the Bible out in the fresh air on the nice morning. I didn't even feel like I was in Iraq for a little while. While Sgt Wadul cleaned, I showed Omar the amazing prophecies I was reading in the book of Isaiah. He thought it was neat, and I talked to SGT Wadul a bit about them. We both agreed it was just insane that some people think everything in the Bible is made up when there are so many accurate predictions hundreds or thousands of years before they occurred. Sunburn came up while we were talking and remarked, "I must admit, there are a lot of good stories in the Bible, but that's all they are – stories." SGT Wadul and I began to question Sunburn as to how he would explain the fulfilled prophecies in the Bible. I asked him how to explain the prophecy of Tyre and Sidon, two cities both destroyed hundreds of years after it was recorded in Isaiah 23, among other books of the prophets of the Old Testament.

I asked him how to explain Cyrus, the ruler of Persia whom Isaiah predicted by name over one hundred years before he was even born. Isaiah predicted Cyrus would allow the Israelites to return to Jerusalem, protect them, and rebuild their temple. I asked him to explain Psalm 22, written almost a thousand years before Jesus was crucified, yet it describes his death as a "piercing of the hands and feet," before crucifixion was even a method of execution (let alone before the Romans became a world power). It says the Messiah would be "poured out like water," just as he was when the spear was thrust through his side and water sprayed out, signifying he was dead. It even told of his clothing being divided and Roman soldiers "casting lots" for them. The passage even predicts some would mock him and shake their heads as they surrounded him. Sunburn couldn't explain any of it, and ironically just shook his own head.

He attempted to argue that we've come from chimpanzees. SGT Wadul and I laid waste to that theory mainly by explaining severe differences between man and chimpanzee, how the "missing link" between species is still "missing", and people still have people and apes still have apes. We agreed peppered moths of Dover, England prove micro-evolution, but not macro-evolution. We said scientists have only been able to create SOME amino acids in a controlled environment, and NOT "create life in a Petri dish" as so many seem to believe.

At some point, SFC Aeris walked up and joined the conversation, and soon he and I were having great fellowship about the Lord. It was simply amazing, and I thanked God we had the wonderful opportunity to do so. He asked me several questions about how it felt to be so "devout," as he put it, and to be in the military surrounded by "all of the bad stuff." I asked if bad stuff meant combat, evil, terrorism and death, or the drinking, cussing, taking the Lord's name in vain and talking about having sex with females all the time the way American soldiers do. Woody wanted both, including my whole philosophy or Biblical perspective on each. So, I told him how immensely it bothered me being surrounded by people who were obsessed with drinking, cussing and pornography, yet how, at the same time, it caused my faith to increase, since the Lord helped me to shine as a light in a dark place, making me stronger. I said that at the same time, it helped me to remember the bad things I'd done in the past, and how I didn't always put the Lord first myself, so I was just as bad as others sometimes, and knowing that kept me grounded and humbled * [see note].[1]

Woody understood and could relate to everything I told him, and so I moved on to the combat aspects, after elaborating just a little further on that first subject. For the fighting and combat portion,

I tremendously enjoyed sharing with him the example where soldiers in the gospel of Luke asked John the Baptist what they should do, and he mentioned among other things for them to be satisfied with their wages. He didn't tell them to stop soldiering, or to throw down their arms and refuse to fight any longer. I also mentioned the Roman centurion who demonstrated so much faith in Matthew 8:5-13, who Jesus marveled at to his disciples "Truly I tell you, not even in Israel have I found such faith." I said if John the Baptist and even Jesus himself didn't have a problem with these being soldiers, then he approved the profession. *

I then gave Old Testament examples of Saul as soldier and king killing Amalekites, after God commanded all of them to be destroyed, to include women and children, oxen and sheep. I said the Bible portrayed Amalekites as evil guerilla terrorists who had harassed the Israelites since their arrival in the Promised Land. I shared that I felt that I was eradicating evil in the world, and at the same time loving my neighbor as myself, by fighting to protect Iraqis from terrorism, giving them their freedom **[see note].[2]

He said I had changed a lot since he knew me two years earlier when I was last in the squadron. I inquired how, and he said I wasn't as "in-your-face" about my relationship with the Lord as I used to be. I told him one of the things I'd learned about Christianity was that some people like to only be a good example for others, and hope people will catch on to Christ that way, whereas others only like to preach, talk and teach about it and about Jesus, and not lead by example or serve. "It's so extremely important to do both, because if I am a wonderful person, doing great things with my life and for others, but never tell someone about Jesus, then who am I glorifying? I am glorifying myself, because no one will know why I am good, or why I do the good things I do. Yet on the other hand, if I only talk to people and try to talk all the time about how to 'get saved,' then people will be turned off and wonder why I talk the talk, but don't walk the walk." I said I loved to talk about Jesus, but in the military environment, I tried to talk about him only if asked questions (and then boy do I talk!) or if someone attacked God, His Word or Christianity. This was a great discussion I loved, and from which we both benefited. I prayed afterward that God would use it to continue to inspire both of us to draw closer to Him. I knew He was answering that prayer right then.

Martinez from the Tactical Human Intelligence Team came by to talk to MAJ Sultan, who had just returned from leave-- a return for which I was personally very thankful. Coincidentally, LTC Ahmed went to Mosul with some of his officers and men to talk to his brigade commander. It was perfect timing since Martinez was preparing the packet to get LTC Ahmed thrown in jail. I printed a picture of him we had on the computer for the packet, and Lord willing, we would be able to get rid of him after he returned from Mosul.

March 6, 2005

CPT Bicks flew to Diamondback to turn in the budget. I went to church, which was always a blessing, especially since they read Psalm 61, which ironically Becky read to me the other night (God must be trying to tell me something). When I got back, MAJ Sultan and CSM Aedo were in the office talking to SFC Aeris and handed us their statements to get rid of LTC Ahmed. They said the police and customs building fire that occurred the night before (which I forgot to mention) was connected to LTC Ahmed. CPT Bicks and LTC Mavis had ordered Iraqi soldiers to occupy this police station, but Ahmed didn't like the idea. He ordered his men not to occupy it and to stay away from it at all costs. "Mysteriously," that same night, the station burned down when enemy attacked it, which shows strong links to him contacting the enemy. I prayed we could lock him up.

March 7, 2005

In the evening two of the checkpoints had contact. Avgani Checkpoint received indirect fire and a mortar round exploded, injuring one of Iraqi who got some shrapnel in his knee and a cut on his leg, but will be okay. He didn't even lose much blood, thank the Lord. Mosul Checkpoint received some small arms fire and some PKC machine gun fire, but no injuries, and it ended quickly. Near 10 p.m. CPT Bicks got a mission for the next morning, which he and Sunburn would go on. It was a flash Traffic Control Point south near Al Kissik, with the aim to catch some incoming enemy, possibly 28 of them, in seven trucks.

March 8, 2005

When Evan came into the command post at around 11:30 a.m., I wrestled with him a bit. He got away, and put up a fight, until I went in to deliberately take him down. I pinned him down while Omar grabbed the flexi cuffs to put on his hands. I kept asking him if he was okay because I didn't want to hurt him. SGT Wadul put some flexi cuffs on his feet and then we hogtied them together with some engineering tape. Omar put a black watch cap on his head and we carried him outside, putting him on the back of the four-wheeler to take pictures. It was pretty funny, so we took it a step further by putting him on SFC Aeris' porch (who was napping) and SGT Wadul or SSG ZT wrote up something like, "I won't be late to work anymore." We put a small rock on the paper to hold it down to Evan's chest and then knocked on SFC Aeris' door and ran back to watch from the command post window as Woody opened his door. He saw Evan, shook his head, and we roared with laughter. SGT Wadul and I went outside to release Evan. It was all in good fun, and after we released Evan, he wanted to see the pictures, so he was a good sport about it.

Midday, enemy fired on Avgani Checkpoint, from just south of the mosque. The power station (where we had troops stationed permanently) returned fire, killing three enemy, and the rest of the ten to twenty enemy ran away. We congratulated the Iraqis and sent the report up to Squadron. A few hours later, there were reports of a large crowd of fifty armed people near the checkpoint. This was CPT Bicks' last day as our commander since CPT Reagle would assume command the next day. The last of the scab from my wound on my chin finally fell off, so there was just a nasty and vulnerable looking scar there. I planned on going out of the wire on the tenth, in just two days. I would just wear my helmet strap below my chin, but I thought I should be good to go. Even though it was safer inside the base, I knew I needed to get back out on missions once again. Praise Jesus!

March 9, 2005

We had the change of command ceremony for CPT Bicks and CPT Reagle. CPT Reagle became our new commander for Headquarters Troop and Nomad Detachment. Evan left for a couple weeks leave to take one of his brothers (who has been paralyzed since youth) to Germany for treatment; another of his brothers was a doctor there. Evan said he would try to be back soon, crying as he left, saying we were like a second family to him. I signed my evaluation report that arrived from LTC Krella. It was my first evaluation with only one man as my rater and senior rater. On the back it said, "Serving as rater and senior rater in accordance with AR 623-105, para 2-20." (That paragraph deals with the loss or death or incapacitation of your rater rendering him unable to successfully complete an evaluation report.) I prayed I never receive one again for circumstances such as with CPT Jacobsen. LTC Krella was a great Battalion Commander though, and he gave me a wonderfully outstanding rating, of which I felt unworthy. After he checked "Outstanding Performance, Must Promote" and "Best Qualified" he wrote:

>LT Matthew Sacra's performance as an MGS platoon leader in combat has been brilliant. He has flawlessly executed countless missions fighting counter-insurgency in the heaviest fighting in Mosul, Iraq. He has executed over 31 Battalion level combat operations that resulted in over 175 enemy KIA, 96 detainees, and capturing numerous High Value Targets. LT Sacra is calm under fire and is ready to be a company commander upon completion of the Captains Career course. A must select for promotion to Captain and attendance at the Captains Career Course. Truly unlimited potential by an incredibly talented platoon leader.

Like I said, I felt unworthy of it. I was already being promoted to Captain, so the evaluation didn't affect much, but it warmed my heart that a man whom I hold a great amount of respect for would say this about me.

March 10, 2005

I finally went back into action outside the wire in the evening. Much of the day was consumed by the usual coordination that took place in the CP. We had a grand feast with MAJ Sultan and the rest of his officers. It was rice and lamb with soup and pita bread, and all of it was delicious. Woody, CPTs Reagle and Bicks, SSG ZT and Omar all joined us for the meal. When evening came, I went out on a checkpoint inspection mission, which turned out to be the longest one yet, from 7-10 p.m. After dropping off the men at Sinjar Checkpoint, we proceeded to Avgani Checkpoint to drop off supplies for them (since they lived there now). We did the same thing at the power station between Avgani and Mosul Checkpoints, and dropped off supplies at Mosul Checkpoint. Afterwards, our Stryker escort platoon went to escort a logistics convoy near Al Kissik (halfway to Mosul). I waited at Mosul Checkpoint until they returned, and then rode back.

Just as the convoy entered the city, the action occurred. We saw several people in alleys sneaking around but could never tell if they had weapons. We also observed some individuals on a rooftop. We fired warning shots above their heads, but they remained on the roof. Just then, they fired an RPG at one of the Strykers at Avgani Checkpoint (we saw from Mosul Checkpoint). It hit directly into the side of the Stryker as they reported it, although Iraqi soldiers reported it as a mortar round. We fired Mark-19 grenades at the guy on the roof, but the weapon malfunctioned after the first round missed. Someone else may have gotten him though. On our way back, the air guards of the Stryker I was in fired at a man with an AK47 in an alleyway. I stayed inside the Stryker on the ride.

March 11, 2005

This day was mixed with sorrow and blessings. Early in the morning, in addition to the other things going on, Squadron received intelligence that Mohammed Younis Ahmed was coming to Tal Afar. He was third on the list of most wanted terrorist leaders in all of Iraq, so I briefed Omar to call to inform all checkpoints. In the afternoon Woody and I checked all the Iraqi Army vehicles for serviceability. I discovered how many were being repaired, how many were broken just sitting there, how many worked and which ones needed armor plating for missions. We met with CPT Abdullah (the Iraqi Maintenance Officer) to discuss the priorities we needed him to work on. Later, Mosul Checkpoint called us reporting they captured two of his sons. We ran the names up to Squadron, and sure enough, they were his children. We congratulated the Iraqi soldiers at the checkpoint where they detained the enemy. An added blessing to this was that Mohammed Younis Ahmed himself, who had already sneaked into Tal Afar, drove up to the checkpoint from inside the city. He demanded the release of his sons, threatening the Iraqi Army saying, "Do you know who I am?!" It reminded me of some mobster threatening cops at a police station or something. Hilariously, the soldiers at the checkpoint said, "we sure do," then cuffed and detained him. We all laughed and were so proud of them and happy at such a huge success. They brought all three back to the base. Praise the Lord!

The success seemed small though in comparison to the life we lost today in the Squadron. SSG Griffith from B Troop was killed in action this evening. Tthey rushed him back to base and through the gate, but by the time he got to the Squadron Aid Station, he was dead. Reports from others said he had been dismounted, running after some terrorists, and chased one down an alleyway, right into an ambush. He was shot through the side of his chest, and even though the rest of his team members killed the guy that shot him, it was still a sad day and a loss of a great warrior.

March 12, 2005

God miraculously spared many lives thisday, and for that I thanked Him. I went to bed just before midnight and woke before 5 a.m. to see if our raid mission was still on for the morning. It wasn't my turn for checkpoint checks, but I went anyway. SGT Wadul was supposed to do them, but Woody and I had been trying to coordinate to raid a house where a suspected weapons cache was located. The Iraqi supervisor at Mosul Checkpoint told SFC Aeris on numerous occasions he wanted to go raid a house from where the enemy fires mortars at him. The Iraqi Army didn't want to hit it on their own but wanted Stryker support and a Nomad element with them. I decided I would go with Sunburn as my battle buddy, and since it was SGT Wadul's turn, it would have been the three of us. When we got to the checkpoint, I asked the supervisor, but he had no clue where this house was, despite reports from Woody that he could lead us to the exact house. After some discussion, we realized he might not have been the same guy SFC Aeris talked to.

At daybreak, I realized this was the first time I had seen the checkpoints in daylight in almost a month. I was amazed at the improvements made but was disappointed in the leaders' complacency at each one. The leader at Mosul Checkpoint didn't have nearly enough people at each position. There were wonderful new fighting positions all over the checkpoint and he had forty men permanently assigned to stay at that checkpoint to cover the area. At any one time he had two men on perimeter security and two men on the road to stop cars. So out of forty men, he was using only four of them. SGT Wadul, like a good NCO, threw a fit, and yelled at him to use his men properly and get them out there immediately. I walked the perimeter and saw where he could have used about ten people to man battle positions and ten people on the roads stopping, searching and covering traffic from both ways. That way, twenty people could rest and twenty could work. Such concepts were basic to leaders in the US Army but didn't come easily to those in the Iraqi Army because they hadn't done it correctly long enough. Most sergeants and officers in our army could take any position and any number of men and come up with a way to safely defend it and work in a rest plan for the people at the same time.

We moved on to the power station, where the Iraqis used a decoy with a helmet on top of it to draw sniper fire; discipline and positioning there were great. The LT there said he knew the house from which motars were fired at Mosul Checkpoint. We told him to get ten men together, and suddenly he wasn't so sure he knew the exact house, then was unsure of the right vicinity, so it looked as if we'd do the mission another day. We checked Avgani and Mosul Checkpoints, and things looked better at both, but the latter still didn't have enough men out – apparently fifteen guys quit the checkpoint, leaving weapons and body armor behind as they walked off. When we arrived back at the FOB, SFC Aeris confirmed as we described the leader of Mosul Checkpoint, that it was the same man we talked to. Woody said the same man who insisted he didn't know the target house was the one who told Woody that he did know. Maybe the LT was scared for some reason.

We hired a new interpreter: Omar's brother, who may not last since his English is poor. As the evening ended, my anger came to a head at the evil source of this war, mixed with my thankfulness at God's miraculous deliverance of our soldiers. We heard reports on the radio of five casualties at Avgani Checkpoint. I had Omar's uncle Ali (another new interpreter) ask the Iraqi Army if they had any casualties at any checkpoints and they reported none. I realized they must be American casualties – our men heading for our base.

As they approached the gate the Squadron XO radioed for Humvee ambulances to stand by to transfer the casualties upon entry at the gate. The head surgeon at the aid station radioed that the Medical Stryker should take the casualties directly to the Squadron Aid Station since it was only another minute and a half from the gate to the aid station. This seemed common sense to all of us listening, yet LTC Rugrs quickly snapped back at MAJ Jensen, "It isn't your call; it's the call of the guy who is with the casualties and is working on them on the way." It sounded dangerous for a Stryker to stop, drop ramp and transfer casualties, which would take at least forty-five seconds. It would be so much faster to just head straight through the gate to the aid station and only move casualties once upon final arrival. Fortunately, the medics in the Stryker had sense to push full speed to the aid station. I prayed for God to keep them all alive and to begin healing them immediately. He answered my prayers.

The 1-5 Infanrty LT I went out with this morning stopped by and told me it was the biggest destruction of a Stryker ever, and he didn't know how the crew even survived. He said their 1SG lost both legs. After they told me the name of their first sergeant, 1SG Roach, I realized who it was. Becky had volunteered at the thrift shop at Fort Lewis for a while, later accepting a job there. Kim Roach was one of her fellow employees, the wife of 1SG Roach. I couldn't imagine the shock she had in store, to find out her husband just lost both of his legs and would never walk again (except for the ingenuity of modern prosthetics). The injuries of the other five casualties weren't as bad, but one had a severely damaged ankle. The LT described the inside of the Stryker. Each metal layer was peeled up on the inside from the explosive force of the 155mm howitzer round. Each peel of metal of the Stryker floor was a couple feet high, and he just shook his head in amazement, eyes popping out, saying, "I just don't know how no one was killed; I don't know how they all survived." I answered him, "It's a miracle, man. Thank God. There's no other way." He told me the Stryker was rendered destroyed, unsalvageable, and it was being recovered as we spoke.

I imagined how different the result would have been if a Humvee were the vehicle hit by that 155mm round that exploded at the Avgani Checkpoint intersection with route Hwy-47. CPT Reagle was trying to get us Humvees so our Nomad unit wouldn't be dependent on Strykers, but had that been a Humvee, there would be nothing left of it nor anything left of the passengers. I hoped this would settle the case for the Humvees, at least in the city of Tal Afar, if a Stryker could get messed up that badly. An hour later, CPT Reagle returned from his checks and recounted the details of what he witnessed out there. He was with the platoon reacting to this situation. He said the back ramp of the Stryker was completely blown off, and I couldn't even imagine it. He described the inside of the Stryker the same as the LT did, with a few other details including how three or four tires were blown completely off the hub and road. The inside was completely black around the explosion and the hole in the bottom of the Stryker was five feet long and three feet wide. It must have been quite an awful thing to look at.

CPT Reagle shared details of their search near the mosque south of Avgani Checkpoint. The escort platoon secured the dried-up ditch or wadi system around the mosque and he searched there for a while with Major Diny and LTC Mavis. MAJ Diny dug and found a lid to a giant oil drum, about a foot underneath the sand. He opened the lid and there was a cache of one brand new mortar tube, some mortar rounds at least 60mm size and several RPG fuses. They combed the sand further and CPT Reagle found another cache with twenty mortar rounds in it, and RPG rounds as well. While they continued to search the wadi, fire came from the mosque and a few surrounding buildings. PKC machine gun fire hit the dirt right next to LTC Mavis where he sat on the edge. CPT Reagle described it just as it would look in a movie – a handful of bullets hit the dirt in a row less than eight inches from LTC Mavis' right side, and he quickly slid down safely to the bottom of the wadi.

The firefight continued, with Strykers shooting into the buildings and mosque, until Apache helicopters arrived. After months of enemy fire from that mosque south of Avgani Checkpoint, hellfire missiles fired into it, and it burned, flames coming from almost every window. Hours later, as CPT Reagle explained all of this too me, it was still burning. That mosque was not only the daily battle position for the enemy, but was also the site of an Imam who preached Jihad against the US and Iraqi Armies in Tal Afar. This resolved most of the contact, and then they evacuated the blown-up Stryker.

First Sergeant Roach was at the Mosul combat hospital doing fine. I was so thankful God spared their lives, on what seemed impossible odds. I was also thankful the mosque burned and that we found two large weapons caches which would then not be used to kill my brothers-in-arms in both armies. I was in awe LTC Mavis that came so close to certain death and survived – his wife and son would be happy. I was also thankful that the two times that morning when I drove over that exact spot, the bomb did not blow up in the Stryker I rode in. It was amazing the daily danger we faced; although we had lost people, God still delivered us from so much.

My rage at this intense evil grew stronger when things like this happened. I could only imagine seeing some terrorist with his weapon, or his hand on a remote or wired explosive device. I imagined chasing him down and strangling him or stabbing him to death for his hatred. Perhaps this sounds like a paradox, which war can be for a Christian, but it reminded me of my favorite Psalm, which relateed so closely to my life. One set of verses in particular:

"I pursued my enemies and overtook them; and did not turn back until they were consumed. I struck them down, so that they were not able to rise; they fell under my feet. For you girded me with strength for the battle; you made my assailants sink under my feet. You made my enemies turn their backs to me, and those who hated me I destroyed. They cried for help, but there was no one to save them; they cried to the LORD, but he did not answer them. I beat them fine, like dust before the wind; I cast them out like the mire of the streets." Psalm 18:37-42 (NRSV) [see foonotes on November 11, December 5, and second footnote on March 5].

March 13, 2005

I had a wonderful blessing around noon. I arrived at the detention center for my guard shift from noon to midnight and a Sergeant First Class there explained detention center guard was now a platoon mission – platoon leaders and platoon sergeants supervise it. He told me the platoon relieving his was already on its way and I didn't need to be there. What a blessing, since there was so much paperwork for the new budget to do, in the way of request forms and such. I thanked the Lord, and the day flew by after that. I have a mission at 1 a.m. to do the usual post-midnight checkpoint checks. I would check on them, deliver flashlights to the power station and Avgani Checkpoint, and then return.

I made it back, safe and sound at 3 a.m. I prayed just about the entire time. Since my chin was still healing, I buckled my chinstrap underneath my neck and put a cloth pad under my neck to protect the healing scar and give the bone some padding. I also ride inside the Stryker, hoping my chin won't re-break or chip while it was so close to healing completely. Oddly, it used to feel unsafe to ride out of a hatch (although more fun), and now it seemed much safer than sitting inside the middle of the Stryker. After the last night's explosion, the middle of the inside of a Stryker seemed like the last place one would want to be. I noticed how "on edge" I was, especially when we hit a couple bumps in the road. I jumped and braced myself, then felt foolish when it was only a rock. The feeling went away when I realized no one could see me, since the others were out of a hatch, and I could tell from their legs they were jumpy too, since they had just lost their first sergeant last night to that bomb. Speaking of 1SG Roach, he was doing better. One of his legs was fused, so perhaps he would only lose one.

I dropped off about thirty flashlights we had bought for the Iraqi soldiers at the power station and Avgani Checkpoint, and we headed in. It was creepy at Avgani Checkpoint at first, because we didn't see a soul there after driving through twice. We wondered if the soldiers were killed by the enemy, or if they just abandoned the checkpoint, or perhaps were all asleep. Instead, I was so proud of them – not only were they manning all their positions, but they were wide awake, expertly camouflaged, and very still as they scanned for enemy. I chose to not take an interpreter with me because there wasn't much discussion in the late-night shift, but I wish I had, to properly tell them what a good job they did. I would get the chance that afternoon. They seemed happy to get their flashlights anyway, and I was extremely thankful the Lord once again spared us all out there that night. Jesus rocks!

March 14, 2005

I wrote a statement to nail Major Farhan, the corrupt pay officer of our Iraqi Battalion, which summed up my morning and evening. I had previously left a note for the front gate to alert me if he entered the base, since several Iraqi soldiers, NCOs, and a few officers (including the Battalion XO and CSM) told me he could not be trusted and had stolen money in the past. I personally escorted him to our command post, inquiring of the amount of money the Baghdad Ministry of Defense gave him. Here are some trimmed snippets from my statement:

He informed me through our interpreter Omar he had 470,000,000 Iraqi dinars. I asked if he had paperwork to back that up, and he claimed he didn't. He then showed me a 56-page list of how many soldiers were in the Battalion, and what they were paid. I, SSG ZT, and SGT Wadul noticed of the 3 bags of money, one had been opened and poorly resealed. It was obvious more money should exist, and we asked him where it was. MAJ Farhan said 470,000,000 dinars was the total, for all the soldiers in the Battalion. After looking through his paperwork, we noticed on page 56, an amount of 508 million dinar was stamped by the Ministry of Defense. I asked him what happened to the other 38 million dinar that was not in the back of his truck, and he insisted the Ministry of Defense didn't give him the amount they signed, stamped, and confirmed in several places on the last page. We asked him for evidence of this, and he told us there was none, but they only gave him 470 million dinars, and not 508 million.

I again informed him the Ministry of Defense would have noted this on the paperwork, and he had absolutely no receipt of it in his presence. He told us he could go to Baghdad and get it, but the Ministry of Defense took the rest of the 38 million. He repeated the same story, after we asked him several other unrelated questions. We noticed his hands severely shook, and he kept avoiding eye contact. He then told me 470 million was enough for all the soldiers in the Battalion. This, I did not doubt, because the number of soldiers listed was 827, which is completely inaccurate. There were 574 people listed in the Battalion from our most recent personnel report from yesterday. At the time of MAJ Farhan's departure to Baghdad, there were even less soldiers than this. Even though this is the case, MAJ Farhan still drew money for 827 soldiers. We asked him again why the bag was opened, and where the extra money was, and he again told us the Ministry of Defense took it.

When Captain Reagle began to talk to him and tell him he was going to call the Ministry of Defense and ask them if this was true, MAJ Farhan began to shake even more. Captain Reagle also noticed the last page said 56 of 57 pages. CPT Reagle asked where the last page was, and MAJ Farhan said the Ministry of Defense took it, and it was a duplicate of the 56th page. CPT Reagle again stated he would confirm all of this with the Ministry of Defense when he called Baghdad and MAJ Farhan then changed his story. He next stated the Ministry of Defense gave him all of the money, but the remaining 38 million dinar was in a bank account in Baghdad belonging to LTC Ahmed, MAJ Farhan, and LT Raafa (who is no longer in the Battalion). He explained he put the money in this "Battalion account" because he knew they didn't need this much money, since he knew the Ministry of Defense gave them more than enough money. He then stated he had no receipt for depositing this money in the bank account, and that all Iraqi army Battalions do this.

CPT Reagle stated again that he would inquire about this to the Ministry of Defense. After this, he attempted to tell our interpreter Omar, who is the best interpreter our unit has ever had, he was translating badly to us. Omar told Major Farhan his own paper was translating badly, because the numbers didn't match up with what he told us.

When I supervised the payment of the Iraqi soldiers, we discovered many of Major Farhan's friends who had quit months ago were still on the pay roster from the *Ministry of Defense*. Although some were Omars cousins, he still informed me of this, proving he was unbiased, also showing MAJ Farhan failed in his duty to update records for a fourth month in a row. Major Farhan later changed his story again, telling me the reason he didn't have all 508 million dinars was taxes. I asked him to repeat what he was saying once more, and he did so. The last page with totals and subtotals showed 517-million dinars with 9 million in taxes leaving 508, demonstrating again his vain efforts to explain the missing money. Omar, Major Sultan, Captain Ismail, and Command Sergeant Major Aedo confirmed this has occurred before, and said Major Farhan, Lieutenant Colonel Ahmed, and the interpreter Debuse typically divided the extra money.

My 1 p.m. checkpoint missions took two hours, longer than normal, but it was worth it except for the sickening "off-roading" north of route Hwy-47 to avoid a roadside bomb site. I felt ready to vomit riding in the back of our mortar Stryker with no hatches, no air and all that bumpiness. I ran into C Company of 1-24 Infantry and spoke to LT Stanley and CPT Hossfeld about their mission. They would occupy some buildings just south of the mosque near Avgani Checkpoint, with eyes on that intersection, the mosque and the entire wadi system and bad neighborhood there. It wasgood to see 1-24 in action, and I know they would help us against the evil of this city. I stopped first at Mosul Checkpoint, dropping off thirty new boots to the leader, thoroughly inspecting as I walked around the posts. All were properly manned and in good discipline. I was so impressed at one of them because of a soldier continuing to scan for enemy on the horizon (usually they turn around and stare at me as I inspect), I attempted to pull a dollar to reward him out of my empty pocket. It turned out I didn't have a dollar (US dollars are worth a good deal to them), but I told Omar to translate how proud I was of him.

I oversaw vehicle searches at the checkpoint and explained to LT Dan Burkhart and CPT Zebald (A Company, 1-5 Infantry) exactly what I did during these checks. Dan wanted to come along for the ride to get out of the FOB, and CPT Zebald was on some other mission with the platoon leader of those vehicles. Little did I know that he would report my inspection later at the brief, according to what SFC Aeris and CPT Reagle told me. They said he brought up to LTC Mavis and the rest of the officers and senior enlisted, "Man, that Nomad 5 was awesome on those inspections. He was all up in the IA's grill, making sure they were doing the right thing, on the ground checking everything." I couldn't believe a compliment came from someone in this Squadron, but then again, CPT Zebald is an Infantry Captain, so he was unbiased towards me. Perhaps he also just had the love of Christ in him too; Chaplain Wells told me that when CPT Zebald took command, his first words were "I'd first like to thank my personal Lord and Savior Jesus Christ for giving me this opportunity to command, because without him, I wouldn't be here." That was always an awesome thing to hear.

Anyway, I made some on the spot corrections to how they searched vehicles and helped them take better cover on the road. At the power station, the Iraqi Army was in good shape, except for one wall that wasn't covered by a battle position. After giving the leader about seven pairs of new boots for his men, I told him to get some more security on his right flank, and then left. At Avgani Checkpoint, I was impressed by the security there, and by an Iraqi soldier who was digging a fighting position next to the road in the cliff side with a pickaxe. I was so proud he was fortifying himself and doing such an outstanding job at it. Omar congratulated him for me and I let Woody and CPT Reagle know how good these guys were doing later that evening. Sinjar Checkpoint was our last stop, and they needed work on searching vehicles because the leader there was kind of clueless as to how his men should search a vehicle, so I had to explain it to him. Three of four good inspections were great, especially for the Iraqis. I thanked God for another safe trip out and back, and for giving me the opportunity to see the progress of the Iraqi Army out there. I also thanked him for the wisdom and instruction He gave me with the pay situation today.

March 15, 2005

On some budget errands, I stopped by LT Durmsy to talk to him, and LT Astudillo was calling me "Captain Sacra." I told him Rich Durmsy would be a CPT before me, and they asked me what my sequence number was. I said 892 or something like that, and they said I would be promoted on the first of April then, since all of the sequence numbers from about 300 or so to 1,000 would promote on the first of April, so it looked like I would be a Captain in just over two weeks. I was a bit excited, but at the same time, I would be praying I didn't lose my job here at Nomad (God willing), because I did love it there, even though I still felt like I just got there. In the afternoon, when I returned from the above errands, including dropping off the brief slide, the memorial service for SSG Griffith was held. I didn't go since someone needed to stay and man the command post.

As the evening approached, we got about 80 new Kurdish soldiers, and SGT Wadul, Sunburn, and SSG ZT went to process them into the Battalion. Today Squadron halted all Tal Afar traffic at the checkpoints except for mission essential and emergency vehicles. From what I could figure, it was just a test exercise by Squadron. After dinner I went over to the Iraqi compound with Omar, and we continued paying the Iraqi Army. I was dreading it, but it was fun, just practicing my Arabic, laughing and joking with Omar and CSM Aedo.

One amazing discovery I made was when I was telling CSM Aedo things I liked, and he was telling me the same. I told him *"anee eheba Isa"* which means "I love Jesus." He nodded his head and smiled and pointed to his chest saying "*anee eheba Isa*" as if to say that he loved Jesus too. I asked if this was true, and Omar told me it was. I didn't realize he was a Christian, so I asked Omar to tell him I didn't know he was my brother in Christ. CSM Aedo told Omar to tell me he knew himself that I was his brother, even though I didn't know. I was so happy and shocked, and full of smiles for the rest of the evening. CSM Aedo also told me the cross represents Christ and he wanted one to wear around his neck. I told him that I had a large silver cross at home I always wore while in civilian clothes, and I would get him a cross to wear. He thanked me. We paid the soldiers until 11 p.m., and then I told them we would continue in the morning.

March 16, 2005

The day was another blessed day serving the Lord. I got up nice and early and Omar and I set off to pay all the 89 people going on leave. When all were paid, LT Mohammed came into the room, complaining to MAJ Sultan. He seemed quite upset. I asked Omar what he was saying, and he said LT Mohammed claimed LTC Ahmed just fired him (after Ahmed was back for just one day). I asked for what reason, and he said LTC Ahmed found out about LT Mohammed writing a statement against him for his corruption in the Battalion. He was terribly upset, and I told him he wasn't fired. He insisted he was, and that LTC Ahmed took his pistol, his badge and the key to his room, and told him to leave the base. I assured him as we learned from our inability to fire LT Tofiq when he refused to go on missions, only the Ministry of Defense has the authority to fire officers. I had Omar explain to him he was not fired, regardless of what LTC Ahmed said, and I would get his things back for him.

We finished paying everyone, and the last twelve men requesting pay were deserters. MAJ Sultan said some were gone for fifteen days when only given five days of vacation, and some were gone for two months. They only came back because they heard the Battalion was getting paid. I said we could just refuse to pay them and keep them in the Battalion so they would learn a lesson, but MAJ Sultan said he didn't want them because they only came for money. I told him to collect their badges and uniforms and sit them in a truck ready to be dropped off at the gate and kicked off base. MAJ Farhan seemed too excited about this and said he would take their pay back with the extra money to the Ministry of Defense. Omar laughed, because we both found it funny that MAJ Farhan still thought he was going to the Ministry of Defense. If we had our way in Nomad, he would never handle money again, and preferably never leave this base again, except in flexi cuffs on his way to Abu Ghraib prison.

As far as LT Mohammed was concerned, I asked him if he got paid yet and if he was going on "*mujas*" today. He said he was paid already but was not going on leave. I asked if he would like to go on "*mujas*" for a few days to cool off, while we handled LTC Ahmed. He said even though he hadn't been on leave for a while, he didn't want to go. He wanted his job back and was upset LTC Ahmed fired him because he didn't like him. I led him over to our command post and explained the deal to SFC Aeris. Woody said it was garbage that 'Saddam' fired LT Mohammed, and we needed to get his things back. I went over to talk to LTC Ahmed with Omar and inquired as to what he bought while he was in Dahuk first, before discussing the firing. He didn't purchase the big truck that he was supposed to, nor did he bring back a truck we'd been expecting for months now, that he claimed was being fixed. He did buy some sniper rifles to give to each of the checkpoints and the power station, and supplies for the vehicles, and showed me some pictures of the trucks he wanted to purchase from Dahuk.

After discussing that, I brought up the issue of LT Mohammed. He said he fired the LT because of "personal differences." When I asked for specificity, he claimed LT Mohammed and he didn't get along, and that LT Mohammed complained about him. I told him I needed LT Mohammed's keys and badge because he didn't have the authority to fire him, only the Ministry of Defense could do that to officers. LTC Ahmed told me he received permission from the Ministry of Defense to fire LT Mohammed, which was a bold-faced lie. He then explained that this was his Battalion, and he could fire anybody and do whatever he wants. He said LT Mohammed shouldn't still be on the base right now because he was fired and told to leave. I explained to him that not only did he not have the authority, but also LTC Mavis would not allow him to just send an officer off the base like that. He said it wasn't LTC Mavis' Battalion but was his, and he could do whatever he liked. I told him no one leaves or enters this FOB without LTC Mavis' say so, and therefore the firing had to go through him. I again asked for the keys and badge from LTC Ahmed. He told me he would give me the keys, but not the badge.

I was about to escalate our conversation when Woody radioed that he needed to discuss something, so I went back to the command post. Perfect timing since CPT Reagle was there. I explained the entire story to him, and how we needed to get rid of 'Saddam' fast or he would "clean house" of everyone who opposed him or wrote a statement on him. I said if we lost the battle for LT Mohammed no one would ever stand up and witness against LTC Ahmed again, nor would they write any statements. CPT Reagle and SFC Aeris went to talk to LTC Mavis after the three of us discussed the matter further. SFC Aeris said, "He's got to go. But you know what, it isn't going to happen. All this stuff SPC Martinez [from tactical human-intel] is doing isn't going to help. We'll just keep trying to square away the checkpoints and avoid LTC Ahmed, but he'll stay, because nobody can get rid of that guy. No one will."

Although I preferred optimism, I felt like SFC Aeris was right. It did seem like a lost cause sometimes, especially since he was still there after all we've heard about him. Omar told me 'Saddam' was close to MAJ Gazwan, a former Iraqi officer whose father is the leader of the Anti-Iraqi Forces (AIF) in Mosul. This connection was apparently realized months ago, and further alluded to LTC Ahmed's collaboration with the enemy, but nothing was done about it. I told them how absolutely ridiculous it was that we were spending all of these resources to gather intelligence and hunt down third-rate terrorists in the city of Tal Afar and Mosul, yet we had a leader of the AIF right there on our own base and couldn't do a thing about it. I got so mad at one point, I pondered us dressing up in Iraqi uniforms with ski masks at night and injuring him to the point that he would be unfit to command this Battalion. He was evil, but there must be another way, and the Holy Spirit also convicted me against such thoughts, however tempting it might have been to take matters into our own hands.

Fortunately, the battle for LT Mohammed was won. The talk with LTC Mavis proved successful. CPT Reagle took my suggestion and told the Squadron Commander exactly what LTC Ahmed said about it being "his" Battalion and not LTC Mavis'. Apparently, LTC Mavis said to SFC Aeris and CPT Reagle, "When is he going to realize I own this place." He agreed LT Mohammed was not fired, and that Saddam had no power to fire any of his officers. I was finally pleased with my own chain of command after this. CPT Reagle even said the Squadron Commander would like to see a slideshow of all crimes LTC Ahmed had committed, which I was working on. Hopefully, I would have completed it by the next day.

I went to lunch with Omar and had a good talk with him. Eventually, our conversation shifted to the Yazidi religion, and what they believe about Jesus. It sounded like he basically believed the same thing I did about Jesus, but just to make sure, I broke it down for him. I explained about Jesus being a perfect sacrifice for our sin, and that he was God himself [again, see footnotes on December 26, January 23, and February 3]. He seemed to understand and affirmed he believed the same thing about Jesus, including his death and resurrection. Omar even said he would come to church with me to learn more about Jesus, which is exciting. I wrote down several names of God on a napkin for examples, and Omar wanted to keep it, so he did seem genuinely interested. I praised the LORD I was given that opportunity.

When I dropped off the brief slide, Rich Durmsy said LTC Rugrs appointed me the Squadron UMO (Unit Movement Officer). At first, I was upset, because I mentioned that I just got here and now they were going to move me. He told me this was just an extra duty, since the Squadron XO thought I wouldn't be busy with the Iraqi Army when our Squadron redeployed to go home. I would likely be one of the last people in the Squadron to leave Iraq at the end of our twelve months, but that was okay, if it was God's will. As badly as I wanted to be home with Becky, I know God may have plans for me to serve Him there a bit longer. As UMO, I would oversee staging all the vehicles in the Squadron, organizing them into convoys to Kuwait and finally the plan to ship them home. I would track all the movement when we initially begin to ship supplies and equipment back home to Fort Lewis. The paperwork would probably begin in the next month or so, and I would be doing a full-time job as Nomad Detachment XO and Squadron UMO at the same time by June or July. That was a long way off, so I would cross that bridge when I came to it.

SFC Walenz and I, along with SGT Wadul, SPC Sunburn and "Face," the interpreter, all ate dinner with MAJ Sultan and a few other officers. MAJ Khalid gave me an outstanding Arabic-English and English-Arabic dictionary. It not only had extensive vocabulary and pronunciations but was also filled with a great deal of verbs, tenses, and pronouns. It was a wonderful gift, and I thanked him for it. Our dinner ended with drinking some chai tea (a spicy beverage steeped in boiling water which often serves as an excuse to sit and extend time together after dinner), and then we were interrupted by our presence being requested at the gate.

Four new recruits came to join the Iraqi Army on the return leave escort patrol from Sinjar this morning. A mechanic who had been fired also returned to fix the Iraqi bus which was having problems. SFC Walenz and SGT Wadul handled that, and I returned Nomad base to man the radio. LTC Mavis radioed an intelligence update suggesting a car bomb would attack somewhere in either Mosul or Tal Afar the next day. He briefed the precautionary measures we would emplace, and about an hour later intelligence reported separately that a car bomb was on a base somewhere in Iraq. It could have been ours or any other FOB, but somewhere in Iraq on a US FOB there was a car bomb. I guessed it was on FOB Marez, but hopefully we wouldn't hear about its success. I had checkpoint checks to do the next day, which included paying the soldiers at the checkpoints and power station.

March 17, 2005

Around 10 a.m., I did my checks with CPT Reagle and LT Burkhart. The two of them ended up inspecting checkpoints, since I was paying soldiers. Since the soldiers stayed out there permanently for many weeks at a time, we had to take their pay to them. Omar helped me carry the bag of *"floose"* (Arabic for money), and we paid them all with Majors Farhan and Sultan. I thanked the Lord there were no explosions or injuries. So often we took it for granted.

Sunburn and I were invited to the nightly brief, since we were receiving our purple hearts. The orders were read and LTC Mavis pinned them on us, presented us our certificates and orders, and moved on to the next person. Five soldiers in the Squadron received them. One lieutenant received his second one: one for a roadside bomb and the other from an RPG. As the evening ended, SFC Aeris had great news about his dad – the night before he had heard his that father had a heart attack and managed to call his sister, who told him that things were not looking good. I prayed immediately and told him I would pray throughout the night as well. Well, he talked directly to the doctor treating his father. She told him had they spoken last night, she would have said to come home immediately, since his father wasn't going to make it. "Tonight" she said, "it's a different story. He's looking a lot better, and things are healing." I praised the Lord and thanked Him for answering that prayer. God is awesome!

Woody also mentioned a source was willing to point to several enemy in his neighborhood near the mosque (which was not completely burned down but quite damaged and charred). SGT Wadul volunteered to go with me tonight to participate in this possible Cordon and Search, but the source decided not to come with us tonight preferring the next morning. Hopefully, he would work on our schedule in the future, but I supposed it may have been God's will for us not to conduct the Cordon and Search mission tonight. Without the raid, the night's inspections went very quickly.

As we prepared to head out of the base, LT Mohammed oversaw the 33 men going out to occupy Combat Outpost Wolf. It was located just south of Checkpoint Avgani and had great observation of the mosque, intersection and surrounding wadi. Since the occupationa couple days ago after C Company of 1-24 Infantry left, enemy activity had cut back dramatically, thank God. I talked to LT Mohammed before leaving and said to him, "I told you that you weren't fired." He smiled and nodded, and we moved out. One of the things that impressed SGT Wadul and me was that LT Mohammed and CPT Ahmed (there are many Ahmed's) conducted a shift change brief, identifying what occurred the past 24 hours, including observations from the outpost and friendly and possible enemy locations. After returning from our check, an Iraqi soldier faked sickness (malingering) and was rushed back to the FOB. He would be sent back out the next day.

March 18, 2005

I paid the Iraqi Army their money, mainly the officers since they still had not been paid. Here are trimmed snippets of what occurred from my sworn statement:

SFC Walenz entered the room just as I was instructing the Iraqi Army officers present that they were not to pay soldiers who just joined the IA within the last week. The pay drawn from the Ministry of Defense was slated for February, and soldiers arriving in March are not entitled to this pay. The officers present agreed and complied. Minutes later, LTC Ahmed, the Battalion Commander, entered the room insisting I pay those soldiers who arrived a week ago, because they had trained in Dahuk, Iraq for the past month, and were on the pay roster from the Ministry of Defense. I told him they were not authorized pay for February, since they joined in March. He explained through Omar the new soldiers were training in Dahuk with every right to February's pay, then demanded the rest of the money be brought to him.

I explained to him and all his officers present the reason we had problems paying his soldiers was because there is no organization – the leaders of his Battalion could not even produce a list we requested of how many soldiers they have in their companies, and when their soldiers joined. LTC Ahmed then told me this was none of my business, and it was his Battalion. He told me I needed to bring all the Iraqi dinar to him, and he would oversee paying his men along with his other officers. He said coalition forces and LTC Mavis had nothing to do with his Battalion and its pay, and I should turn all the money over to him at once. I asked Omar to confirm what LTC Ahmed just stated, and LTC Ahmed said it again. I asked, "It is none of my business?" His answer was the same – LTC Mavis and American forces have nothing to do with Iraqi pay, and he (LTC Ahmed) supervises it.

I also added that prior to January, LTC Ahmed had complete autonomy in paying his men, but that his XO, Major Sultan, CPT Ismail, the intel officer, and Command Sergeant Major Aedo, among others, testified he withheld soldier pay for no reason, took extra money for himself and Major Farhan and failed to return remaining battalion funds. I told LTC Ahmed he received funds for 827 men when his battalion had not had more than 700 men since November 2004, yet he stated they were training in Dahuk to join the Iraqi Army (though none had badges nor had they ever stepped foot into his battalion: the 2-11th Iraqi Army Battalion).

I was so mad when he said that "none of your business" garbage and that I needed to get him the money, I wanted to knock him out. I just wanted to punch him in the face, knocking him out cold. The Holy Spirit let me know I needed to leave before I did something that got me into trouble. I am always slow to anger, but my rage toward terrorism and the obvious fact that this man was an enemy leader put me over the top after he said that. He looked so arrogant as if he was trying to challenge me in front of his officers. I yelled back to him sarcastically, looking at him and Omar, "Oh YEAH, sure, okay fine, I'll go get his money right now. Perfect! No problem! Yeah, great, I'll just go get it all, and he can have all the money for HIS Battalion." As sarcastic as I was, even so Omar could understand, 'Saddam' still thought I was going to get the money for him and didn't sense my sarcasm at all. We left, and as I prepared to drive off, MAJ Sultan came up to the whaz and I told him, "I came this close to punching LTC Ahmed out."

I drove back and explained it all to CPT Reagle, and SSG ZT was stunned I was so angry. I told them I had no intention of giving him any money. CPT Reagle talked to LTC's Mavis and Rugrs, who both supported me. LTC Rugrs even said it was great of me to do that, and those soldiers who just joined have no right to receive pay for February. I typed a lot of statements on 'Saddam' for the packet we are building on him to put him away for good. I longed for that day so much. I also did some budget paperwork for the further requests we have to send up to Brigade. I was thankful the Lord gave me much-needed wisdom for the situation in addition to the much-needed peace and strength I needed for the rest of the day.

March 19, 2005

I mostly worked on compiling the packet to get rid of LTC Ahmed. I helped Omar revise his sworn statement, proofread several others and organized the packet to submit a copy to LTC Mavis. LTC Ahmed demanded over the radio for CPT Reagle and me to come see him, saying he "must" meet with us or LTC Mavis. We ignored his request. CPT Reagle flew to FOBs Freedom and Diamondback for meetings and to pick up funds. He told me that LTC Mavis was so angry after hearing Brigade ordered an investigation that he didn't know about, as well as the information on LTC Ahmed being a possible terrorist leader, he called the Brigade Commander, COL Brown, and requested to have LTC Ahmed removed immediately. Prayers would be answered, and he would be gone very soon, but I didn't just want him fired, but thrown in prison, so if I must wait longer and be patient to have that happen, so be it. It was just so unjust that we detained people outside the wire based on just where they lived or because we found a pistol in their house or they seemed slightly suspicious, when an obvious criminal and enemy leader was on this base running an Iraqi Battalion, stealing government money and moving about free to do as he pleased. I couldn't wait to detain that evil man.

After an hour of sleep, I woke at 2 a.m. and went out with Jimmy to the city. Jimmy used to be an interpreter before I arrived, but quit, and just came, so we re-hired him. Since there was a free hatch available, I rode out of a hatch for the first time since February 16th. There were supposed to be fifteen people going to the power station and thirty going to Mosul Checkpoint. Only forty-four showed up - one guy's name was on the list twice. The second two-and-a-half-ton truck in our convoy drove way too slowly – between fifteen and twenty-five miles an hour, when we were trying to maintain at least forty. When we got to Avgani Checkpoint, the two Iraqi Army trucks passed it and went to the power station. I told Jimmy to call them on the radio to get them back, which he did about ten times. It was irritating, and after twenty minutes, they finally moved the 300 meters from the power station back to Avgani Checkpoint, then acted like they didn't know they were supposed to drop off a supply of water bottles there (we'd discussed it earlier in the day and I had reminded the leader before we left). We had to scream at them to start taking water off the trucks when they got there, because everyone was just sitting there, most of them without helmets on. Some said they didn't even own a helmet. After dropping off the water, the truck drivers started driving up the hill in the wrong direction and off the road.

At Checkpoint Mosul, the leader and nine men were awake, checking the perimeter and doing a good job. The incoming leader had no idea how to do his job, in my opinion. His men slowly got off the trucks and lit cigarettes; some pulled their own belongings off the truck and just stood there. I yelled until my voice went hoarse. Jimmy then told me that the truck that stopped at the power station only dropped off one guy instead of four. It was so messed up at that point I just said, "Forget it! If they need more guys at the power station, they can drive there without Stryker escort. I'm not fooling around with their garbage anymore!" I yelled at them to quit smoking and to get everything off the truck immediately. They did, and the two leaders (incoming and outgoing) told me both they and their men were going to stay at the checkpoint for a day to do a proper shift changeover to show the new leader and his men what to do. That made the most sense out of everything that had happened thus far.

When they were ready to go, I instructed the drivers to turn off their lights every time they stopped the truck and only turn them back on when driving again, since they kept sitting there with lights on, making us a big bright target every time they stopped. They understood and then got in the trucks to leave while I finished talking to Jimmy. Before I could turn around, one of the drivers drove off when the bed door was down. The supervisor told him to stop, but he just kept going. I went up to the door shouting for him to stop and ripped open the door. He hopped out and I pulled him to the rear of his truck and hit the bed door shouting, "What's this? What are you doing?" He started to fix it, and when finished, I had Jimmy tell him he was never to drive anywhere with it down. I couldn't believe we had to educate on such simple things. I guess common sense wasn't that common. We headed back after that, and thankfully everyone was safe. Now I just needed to do the gas station change out at 7 a.m. and conduct some checks. As irritating as it all was with my voice so hoarse from shouting so much, I was thankful that we were all alive, and that God again surrounded us with His angels.

March 20, 2005

That mission was a quick one. We left early and zoomed past the gas station while the Iraqi platoon occupied it. 1SG Thamer was in charge, and he was the best enlisted soldier they had. He was a great leader and always out front leading his troops, doing the right thing all the time, and his men loved him too. He occupied it with four vehicles and twenty men, and then we proceeded to Combat Outpost Wolf. Everything looked in order except for them needing more food and water. They did a great job of piling sandbags up in front of the outer court of the house and doorway, and just needed a few more on the roof, which I told LT Mohammed. He still doesn't have his badge and pistol back, but we would get them for him. Meanwhile, he was carrying the sniper rifle, so I didn't think he minded too much, though I doubted he was the best marksman out there. I tried to explain that the best marksmen should carry the sniper rifle, but Oakley was my translator, and he didn't understand at all. I returned after being out only an hour and was thankful nothing happened, because for some reason I was more nervous that time - maybe because it was daytime, and I was out of a hatch.

After a nap, I completed mechanic fund paperwork. Woody and CPT Reagle both had a meeting with a group of Liaison reservists who would be coming here with about one thousand Iraqi troops permanently. They discussed some changes, such as us possibly shifting around the 2-11 Iraqi Army Battalion, and what would become of our Nomad team. It mostly sounded hopeful. The only part I didn't like was about us having to possibly be out on our own away from Squadron, as we moved with the 2-11th. CPT Reagle and SFC Aeris had an hour-long meeting with 'Saddam', and figured out a new plan for Iraqi pay – we will send another officer with MAJ Farhan to return the funds and draw the soldiers' pay for March.

March 21, 2005

After a gym workout with SSG ZT (my first in a while), I sorted out the pay issues for sending MAJ Farhan with MAJ Abid (the new pay officer) to the Ministry of Defense. We counted the remaining money that needed to be paid to the wounded and the deceased soldiers' families and set it aside in separate bags with amounts written inside each bag. I also counted the rest of the money to be returned to the Ministry of Defense, which was about 113,917,000 Iraqi Dinar. Combined with the 38,000,000 in the bank in Baghdad (which MAJ Farhan deposited illegally), the amount should have been 151,917,000 Dinar. CPT Reagle's idea was to write a letter to the Ministry of Defense (on the full amount of money enclosed) and seal it in an envelope with my signature over the envelope to prevent breaking the seal. He then suggested hiding it in the bottom of the bag that Farhan and Abid would take back to Baghdad and the Ministry.

Major Farhan had sealed the bag and was ready to leave, so we didn't have a chance to hide our letter within the bag. We didn't want him to find it and somehow deceive the Ministry of Defense while stealing the money. We didn't exactly trust MAJ Abid either, but hopefully he would be a bit more honest than 'Saddam' and MAJ Farhan. I realized we needed to create a diversion to get MAJ Farhan and MAJ Abid out of the room so SSG ZT and Omar could finish the letter, put it in the envelope I pre-signed, seal it with tape, untie the money bag and slip it into the bottom of the bag. I told them to come into my room because I had something for them (having told SSG ZT to handle things while I created a distraction). Oakley came in to interpret for me. I explained I wanted them to take some of my snacks and candy with them for their trip. They were amazed at the amount of food I had and thanked me as they took some snacks. They began to walk to the door, but I called them back for more.

I was glad I had Oakley because he interpreted slowly, which stalled us (they didn't notice). I told Oakley to tell them one box I pointed to was full of sweet candies and the other was chocolate. They nodded, took some more and moved on. I called them back again; this time it was close because MAJ Abid had his hand on the door handle. They were only in my room for about a minute at this point, and I knew SSG ZT wouldn't be done yet. I walked to my food table and began to pull out some mandarin oranges. I told Oakley to tell them that they would need to wash down all the sweets I gave them with some fruit, and they took it. MAJ Abid said he didn't eat fruit, so MAJ Farhan took it. They began to walk out, even opening the door this time, and I panicked. "*Daqeeqa!*" I shouted, which means "just a minute" in Arabic. I turned to scan my table and room for something else to stall them with and grabbed some paper plates, quickly realizing I had given them nothing for which they would need to use paper plates. Thankfully, the Holy Spirit directed my mind to a box. It quickly dawned on me – I had given them a lot of things to carry. They halted, and I asked them to shut the door so flies wouldn't come in. Oakley translated, and I pulled out a box for them to store some things in, and they nodded and smiled as if it was the perfect idea. Praise God!

They again thanked me and asked if I needed anything from Baghdad while they were there. As nice as the offer was, I turned it down, not only because I couldn't think of anything I needed, but I didn't feel right taking anything from a criminal and thief like MAJ Farhan. They started to leave, and I had Oakley ask them, "Are you sure there is nothing else you need?" I pointed to a box, held up some pens (feeling foolish), and then my eyes drifted to a deck of cards. I was thankful for having seen them. I picked them up and asked them if they knew what they were. MAJ Farhan nodded, and said, "yes, yes" in English. "I'll show you a trick" I said, "watch." I shuffled the deck while holding it in my hand, thumbing through the cards in a single stack. I told Oakley to have them tell me when they wanted me to stop, and I would tell them what card it was. I thumbed, until he said stop, and I said "*Sit-a*" ('six' in Arabic), and then flipped the card up, showing him the six of hearts. They were impressed, and Oakley asked me to do it again. I said, "Okay, one more time" and did the trick again, this time looking at MAJ Farhan, so he could see my eyes, that I wasn't looking at the cards. This time, when I got the number right, he was even more shocked, as if to say, 'I was watching the whole time, how did he do it?'

This time all four of them (MAJ Sultan was there too, observing) asked me to do it one more time, and I did so. After doing the trick, I gave the deck of cards to MAJ Farhan and told him that when they made stops, they could play cards on the way to Baghdad. There was nothing left to stall them with, so I said a final silent prayer as we went out the door, praying that SSG ZT and Omar would be done. MAJ Farhan and Abid went to their truck next to stow all the items I gave them, then opened the door to the office to get the bag of money. I almost wanted to squint my eyes, thinking they would catch SSG ZT tying up the bag or something, but he was standing behind the desk away from the bag, and they walked over and grabbed it, putting it in the truck. I breathed a huge sigh of relief, waved them off and went back in to talk to SSG ZT. He said Omar was typing so slowly and as I explained how I stalled them, he told me it was just in time too. He just finished tying the bag after putting the envelope all the way at the bottom of the bag when they opened the door. I thanked the Lord and laughed.

Shaker Abrahim then came by asking for his pay, so I paid him after checking his name off the list. We briefed Woody and CPT Reagle on what had happened with the bag and I typed up the brief slide, in addition to the second slide LTC Mavis wanted me to add: one displaying Iraqi equipment, based upon what the Brigade Iraqi Security Forces website said their MTOE was. MTOE meant Mission Task Organization Equipment, which basically states how many rifles, vehicles, radios, binoculars and everything else a particular unit needed to be equipped with. I then began to scan individual sworn statements and documents relating to the target packet we had been building on LTC Ahmed, which took the rest of the evening. I had the entire packet on digits, the originals which I would return to the tactical human intelligence team and the copy to send to LTC Mavis to review, so he would know the deal on Ahmed's crookedness.

March 22, 2005

I picked up CPT Kamhl from the gate. He returned on crutches from his February 11th injuries and was happy to see me. I was happy to see him also, and we had a good talk on the way back to the Iraqi compound. I dropped him off and returned to the command post, where now PFC Sunburn was. He'd been demoted night after Article 15 proceedings. The sergeants had noticed his tardiness off and on, and he had even made CPT Bicks late for a mission one day. They said the warnings and counselings weren't working. The Iraqis radioed a message from the Tal Afar Iraqi Police Battalion – the hospital was under attack! We were irritated no one sent the Quick Reaction Force from Squadron, especially since they were out there already. We received reports from Iraqi police, soldiers and commandos (who now occupy an outpost with A/1-5 Infnatry) of rifle, sniper and RPG fire. Squadron wanted us to coordinate with the Iraqis and A/1-5 Infantry inside the base to prepare to send a patrol out to react. CPT Reagle and SSG ZT went, but the contact had ended by the time they arrived.

SFC Aeris, CPT Reagle and I showed LTC Mavis the packet on LTC Ahmed. He was excited to look through it, but insisted we add a few more statements to the twenty we currently had. He smiled and asked us about several crimes he knew of and wondered if they were written down in a statement. It was nice to see him so eager to get rid of 'Saddam' as well.

I did my checkpoint inspections around 1 a.m., which where okay except for how slow and inacurrate Omar's uncle Ali was in his translating. On the way out and back an infantryman out of the other hatch with me reminded me to stay lower becasue of roadside bombs. Usually, I reminded myself to remain a bit higher out of my hatch to see better, but he kept saying "You might want to get lower in case we hit an IED, sir," and, "Sir, you should get down a bit." They had sandbags up too, but I guessed it was always better to protect from bombs than err on the side of seeing better down alleyways.

Iraqi soldiers detained a man who lived in the house next to the power station they. He had four AK47 magazines on him and a radio like those soldiers use. He claimed it was for his brother who is in the Iraqi Police, but we took him just to be on the safe side. If he checked out okay, he would be released within a few weeks or less. Another two detainees are a different story. They passed through Checkpoint Avgani in a purple car with passports to Syria (which the checkpoint leader claims are a forgery), a large sum of money and a large gasoline container in the trunk. The Iraqis guessed it was meant either for smuggling gasoline or possibly to make a large bomb. Either way, it was better to be safe and take them in than to let them go, so I brought them in too. I dropped them off at 3 a.m., and Major Sultan ran outside in his civilian clothes to meet me and coordinate for some enlisted soldiers to come take the detainees to the detention center.

March 23, 2005

I got three hours sleep before going on my 7 a.m. mission. Omar was feeling better (he had a tooth pulled the day before) so he wanted to come with me. I had him bring the flexi cuffs, since the power station and Avgani Checkpoint leaders were completely out of them. At Mosul Checkpoint, the leader and his men were doing an excellent job of searching vehicles and personnel passing through, but he didn't have enough of his men on security. Out of thirty men, he should have most of them awake during the day, since that is when most action occurred. I told him every fighting position on the perimeter needed two men in it, while six handled traffic, while he and one soldier roamed (meaning sixteen awake and manning at a time, minimum).

The power station had a broken PKC (Russian-made Machine Gun), so I took that back. I gave flexi cuffs to Mosul and Avgani Checkpoints, as well as the power station, but LT Mohammed at Combat Ouptost Wolf was out of them, and I had forgotten to ask at Sinjar Checkpoint. LT Mohammed was happy to see me once again and gave me a mini grandfather clock. I laughed and thanked him. It was funny because just the other day he gave SFC Aeris a cockoo clock. I didn't know where he was getting these (probably from the house they occupied, or a neighboring one), but it sure was funny; I wondered how many more we would get from "Father Time" over there. I corrected Sinjar Checkpoint because they were improperly searching vehicles and personnel.

We returned safely, and I paid a few individuals from a fund to take to surviving families. General Bergen came to the Iraqi Army compound, and CPT Reagle and SFC Aeris walked in there with him. The rest of the evening wound to a close after I learned more Arabic verbs from Oakley.

March 24, 2005

Another day serving in the Kingdom of God in this wilderness [see note November 26th]. I couldn't thank Him enough for all He showed me daily. CPT Reagle whispered that he and LTC Mavis spoke with General Bergen, who also talked to the Iraqi general that visited, and LTC Ahmed would be fired. I was thankful, but wished it were "imprisoned." The Iraqi Battalion and I would take what blessings we could get. LTC Ahmed also gave us a receipt for some purchases that he made while in Dahuk, and I filled out the necessary budget paperwork for it. I also did one for Jimmy, who is no longer an interpreter for us, but a "civilian contractor." He still lived in the same room and hung out in the office, running errands for us much like Mohammed who acquired and purchased as a contractor for us. Jimmy showed us the cost for the six-cylinder Toyota Land Cruiser. Funny, it was $28,900.00 as advertised, and not $33,500.00 like LTC Ahmed told us. Not a big surprise though, coming from him. I would be so happy the day he was gone. Since we were firing him instead of throwing him in jail, maybe we should just have released him with cuffs and in uniform in downtown Tal Afar. Knowing him though, I was sure the enemy would welcome him, especially since he obviously had some type of contact with them.

CPT Reagle returned from his checks and showed us a disk LT Mohammed gave him. A random civilian gave it to the Iraqis. It was a disturbing video with a masked enemy in a police uniform firing mortars from east of Checkpoint Mosul. Arabic chanting of the Koran was in the background, just like in some Mosul attacks. Omar said the terrorists recited the verses in the Koran mentioning killing non-believers wherever found, as well as those allied with them. Someone in the office asked Omar what the Koran was, and inquired if it was the Bible. Omar told them the Koran was stupid and trash (or words to that effect). I answered it was not the Bible for sure.

Looking through my Koran (Islamic Foundation of America interpreted by Dr. Muhammad Muhsin Khan), Surah 9, verses 3 and 4 state, "And give tidings of a painful torment to those who disbelieve. Except those of the Mushrikun (polytheists, disbelievers in Allah) with whom you have a treaty, and who have not subsequently failed you in aught, nor have supported anyone against you." Also verse 5, which states, "Then when the Sacred Months (the first, seventh, eleventh, and twelfth months of the Islamic calendar) have passed, then kill the Mushrikun wherever you find them, and capture them and besiege them, and lie in wait for them in every ambush." Terrorists use these Koran verses for violence, not peace.

The video was from 2003, but still disturbing – it showed three terrorists standing behind a bound (hands and feet) Iraqi who was on his knees. The terrorists wore masks, and the two standing on the left and right of the middle one held AK47s. The prisoner said (Omar interpreted for us) he was an Iraqi government official who worked with US and coalition forces. After he said that, the terrorists grabbed him by the head and he struggled to get away as one of them reached for a pocketknife. His efforts were futile, and with his arms and feet bound, his squirming only brought him to the floor, lying on his left side. The terrorist on the right grabbed the man by his hair, while the one in the middle moved the pocketknife toward the government official's throat. The bound man tried one last time to tilt his head away, and the terrorist just began cutting in a saw-like manner while blood poured out all over the floor. The man was still alive during the ordeal and his eyes began to twitch. The terrorist continued to saw and cut, and within five seconds he had severed the man's head and held it in his hand. The terrorist then tried to place the head, with eyes wide open, right on top of the body and then the film stopped. How sick. I got so mad after seeing the video and told Omar even if we didn't find and kill those men, God would judge them and send them to Hell. Eternal suffering sounded like perfect justice for evil such as that [see December 25th and February 28th footnotes].

SFC Aeris just shook his head and said, "Isn't it crazy a human being could do that to another?" "It's absolutely sick." I answered. We took the video to the intelligence officer and it was on my mind most of the day. It made me want to go outside the wire and just find one terrorist to kill with ruthless efficiency. If only I could have superpowers and invulnerability for just one day. I would walk down the streets of Tal Afar with no weapon and no armor, and just wait for the terrorists to come out and shoot at me, trying to capture me. I'd break every one of them in half at the hip or spine and lay them all in the streets while they were still alive. * I could probably clear almost the whole city that way. After that, I thought I'd leave them there to the citizens of Tal Afar. I must trust God would deal with them though. It's crazy how many prophecies are currently fulfilled now that Israel is a country again, and that we were there in Iraq after crushing Saddam Hussein's regime. I remembered Jeremiah 51:47-48 about Babylon being destroyed from the invader from the north. ** I felt like the end times were close, so perhaps God would fight this battle for us very soon. Only He could know [see note].[3]

Lunchtime was another meal with the Wolf Battalion – more lamb and rice, with tomato/potato soup to mix with everything. It was delicious, and we stayed a while after for tea and business talk. Later in the evening I went to a rehearsal with the chaplain, CPT Vingen (the Squadron personnel officer) and a Sergant Stuckey from B

Troop. They played guitar while I played violin and the chaplain led the singing.

March 25, 2005

SSG ZT, PFC Sunburn and CPT Reagle went on a raid at 5 a.m of a house where an old man tried to drop a grenade on CPT Reagle a few days earlier. They caught him and detained him as he tried to insist, "I hate terrorists, and I'm not a terrorist." No surprise there; I was sure he was telling the truth, especially since he probably considered US soldiers to be the terrorists. SSG ZT dropped some plans on the floor on purpose as he walked through the old man's house. They were for the raid itself, and he dropped them because the name of our "source" was included on them. An interpreter who used to work on the FOB quit and joined the enemy, so we put his name and picture on the "plans" as the "source" for the raid. The hope was that the enemy would turn on him and think he was a spy, which he was as far as we were concerned. As they left the courtyard of the old man's house, a large bomb exploded. They all described the shockwave they felt, but thankfully no one was injured. SGT Wadul returned from his pass in Qatar and SSG Hitcher returned from his two weeks of leave in the US. More personnel could stretch the checks out, so we could each be going two days a week or so. Things would improve with so many more people there.

For my 4 p.m. mission, the Iraqi Army was ready, but A Company of 1-5 Infantry was not. I'd previously let them know of a change to our time, but perhaps their radio operator either failed to write it down or failed to pass it on to the next shift. They were an hour late, but we went out to drop off ammo at Combat Outpost Wolf, along with a PKC machine gun. Our next stop was at the Tal Afar hospital to check if everything was okay, see if any enemy had given them problems or if any "citizens" with gunshot wounds had come for threatment in the past few days. All was okay there, so we proceeded to the gas station to pick up the platoon of Iraqis manning it there. As I ran across the road, the Iraqi soldiers told me two snipers were in the area.

I had a bad feeling, but it turned out to be nothing. Other than frustration with Ali's poor translations and the broken hatch on the back of the Stryker in which I rode, it was a blessed time outside the wire.

March 26, 2005

My 3 a.m. checks were nice and quick. I went without an interpreter and was back in forty-five minutes. I found out from our escorts that the March 12th roadside bomb which destroyed a Stryker was an anti-tank mine rather than a 155mm artillery round. After a nap, I printed up a newspaper article my parents sent me from the Baltimore Sun March 23, 2005 on a couple incidents in Mosul. It showed a picture of a blown-up car with a disgusted civilian. I recognized the background as the giant mosque in east Mosul I had driven past so many times as a platoon leader. The article read as follows:

"Ordinarily Iraqis rarely strike back at the insurgents who terrorize their country. But just before noon yesterday, a carpenter named Dhia saw a group of masked gunmen with grenades coming towards his shop and decided he had had enough. As the gunmen emerged from their cars, Dhia, 35, and his young relatives shouldered their own AK47's and opened fire, police and witnesses said. In the fierce gun battle that followed, three of the insurgents were killed and the rest fled just after the police arrived. Two of Dhia's nephews and a bystander were injured, police said. 'We attacked them before they attacked us,' Dhia, who did not give his last name, said at his shop a few hours after the battle, his face still contorted with rage and excitement. 'We killed three of those who call themselves mujahedeen. I am waiting for the rest of them to come, and we will show them.' It was the first time private citizens are known to have retaliated successfully against insurgents."

The article went into further detail, but just reading this was enough to give us all hope this country may make it on its own some day after all. What a blessing. I prayed others in this country would continue to stand and triumph against these evil men who only bring destruction to this war-torn country.

Enemies mortared Avgani Checkpoint today, and I thanked God that no one was injured. "Face" got back today, sharing how he watches the trials of terrorists on TV. He said many terrorists captured were Syrian (which I knew), but some were Syrian officers. The US even captured a colonel in the Syrian intelligence agency. Faisil explained how Syrians come in and fund and teach tactics to terrorists and insurgents in Iraq. He said the Iraqi way to execute someone was to shoot them in the head with a pistol. Cutting heads off didn't come into play until Syrian military trainers sneaked in and trained Iraqis. I shared the article my parents sent, and he told me of large groups of people in neighborhoods in Tal Afar who fought terrorism in the city and stopped the insurgents. He said it had been going on for a couple months but there were still a few neighborhoods in the city completely ruled by the enemy.

March 27, 2005

Omar came to Sunday Bible Study with me and stayed for worship afterwards. I thought he seemed confused at first, but after it was over, he said he understood everything. The chaplain gave a personal testimony and related it to the resurrection of Jesus, using scripture from Luke. A Turkish man walked in at the beginning of the service and told us he was a Muslim, but he would stay and watch. I prayed for both him and Omar to open their hearts, that the Holy Spirit would draw them to the Father and to a relationship with Jesus. Omar told me he really enjoyed it and would tell me his questions and comments after he had time to think. We returned to the command post and he immediately told Face about it (Face is a non-practicing Muslim). Face said he would like to come next Sunday to see how I worshipped. Omar expressed that he had never been to a worship service like that, and that he really liked the singing and the message from the chaplain.

I didn't know if Omar ever went to any Yazidi services, or even if they had worship services, but he said with a smile it was nothing like he had ever been to. [As for the Yazidi religion, what the internet describes and what Omar described are two different things. He described it basically as Christianity except with a greater focus on angels and what angels do in our lives. I'm not exactly sure where reality lies between the two]. It felt great to be possibly planting a seed. I prayed God would continue to draw them to Him, and who knew, maybe Face would enjoy it too. Omar and I had missed dinner, so I cooked spaghetti in my room. He enjoyed the soft meal, as his tooth was hurting. I showed him pictures of Becky and Katelyn (in her tummy) and some general pictures of America from my travels across the country. I prayed he could get to America for good some day. I had helped him fill out his visa application, so he was making steps in the right direction. I loved how Jesus worked every day!

March 28, 2005

Other than Major Sultan reporting a roadside bomb and us eating dinner with the Iraqis, the day was uneventful. While we ate dinner, MAJ Sultan jokingly said we needed to make a badge for the new Iraqi who joined today. He spoke of the lamb that got into one of the bunkers, and he laughed. He wanted us to take a picture of it before they killed it. Just before we went to look at it, CSM Aedo came into the room. He had returned from leave with one hundred Iraqi soldiers. He gave me a wooden snake and a bayonet as gifts. I thanked him, and he went with us to the bunker to see the lamb. It snorted at SGT Wadul who jokingly pulled his 9mm and hid in the corner. The lamb was cute, and even walked up next to the toilet to pee. It was sad that they were going to kill it, but such is the life of a lamb supper I suppose. CSM Aedo jokingly pulled his knife out, claiming the lamb was a terrorist. We all laughed, then went to bed.

March 29, 2005

Praise the Lord! I survived another mission, but not the usual checks. I cleared some buildings. I prepared in the afternoon for my 7 p.m. checks, learning we needed to switch the soldiers out at Combat Outpost Wolf. CPT Reagle showed me on the map two different buildings that needed to be cleared and assessed as possible Combat Outposts. One was in the north section of Tal Afar on Hwy-47, between the power station and Checkpoint Mosul on the south side of Hwy-47. The other was a house located halfway between Sinjar and Avgani Checkpoints, just beyond a field. Coincidentally and very thankfully, after hearing this news I learned that a bomb disposal team found and detonated another antitank mine that same hour, at that very intersection. I invited SGT Wadul to come along for the ride, since he loved to go on raids and house clearings, even though it was my turn to do checks. He looked at me as if to say, "Are you kidding, of course I want to come!" It was nice having a battle buddy. We gathered the Iraqis and planned.

The Iraqis occupying the gas station had to be picked up as well, in addition to the usual swap out at Sinjar Checkpoint, so we had our work cut out for us. My plan was this: Drop off soldiers at Sinjar Checkpoint to swap out, as we headed straight up Hwy-47 to Combat Outpost Wolf. CPT Ahmed and his men would swap out with LT Mohammed's men, and we would continue with the Strykers to clear the first building. After clearing it, we would return to COP Wolf, pick up LT Mohammed and his men and head south on Hwy-47 to the western building to be cleared. While exiting that building, we would call the gas station platoon and have them meet us on Hwy-47 as we rode to Sinjar Checkpoint, and then back to the FOB. It worked mostly as planned. As I exited the base, I felt particularly more nervous than usual. Perhaps it was because my leave was less than a month away – I didn't know. I prayed the whole way out of the gate as I rode in the back hatch of the Stryker. I told God of my fears, asked for safety and that He would slow and hinder the enemy in every way possible. I also asked that He would help me trust Him so I wouldn't fear.

    I thanked God immensely for allowing us to find and destroy that antitank mine earlier – the same kind which destroyed the Stryker with 1SG Roach in it. So far, antitank mines and 155mm rounds were the only things that put a dent in Strykers. I could just imagine what would have happened to us had they not found it. I thanked the Lord repeatedly. Within a few minutes, my fears were gone, and I was ready to get down to business. As we passed Combat Outpost Wolf, the Iraqis supposed to stop there followed us to the northern potential outpost we had cleared. We yelled at them to go to Wolf, but they didn't. Either Ali translated horribly (a strong possibility), or they were scared and wouldn't go. I cleared the house with the dismounts from A/1-5 Infantry. We busted into the house, clearing every room. I made it to the roof and SGT Wadul cleared the ground floor and some of the basement. There wasn't a soul in the house, but there was food stockpiled and the house was perfect.

    I surveyed the roof for a few minutes and noticed the excellent angles of fire and observation points along the rooftop. I could see about twenty blocks south of that building into the city of Tal Afar and could see every inch of Hwy-47 from the power station to Mosul Checkpoint. It was a perfect place to observe enemy activity in the city as well as the main route in case the enemy tried to place bombs there. By the time we left, the Iraqi soldiers designated for Wolf finally got the message to roll out (after SGT Wadul screamed at them). We got to Combat Outpost Wolf and ran inside and checked it out while soldiers swapped out. We discovered several soldiers were missing Kevlar helmets and many had no ammunition in their four magazines apiece. They said Major Sultan told them to get ammo from Wolf when they arrived there and to switch helmets with the guys out there. This didn't sound like MAJ Sultan, but I gave them the benefit of the doubt, planning to talk to him when I returned. SGT Wadul yelled, and they got the message to not go anywhere out of the FOB without a helmet and ammunition. The leadership understood, and we moved out.

The next house was horrible. We entered it after busting the door open and discovered a family with kids. They came out into the inner courtyard and we told them to get down and move to the middle. We cleared room by room, and they said they had no weapons. There were little girls crying as we did so, which burned my heart, but I had a job to do, so I numbed myself to it. I could only imagine how scary it must have been for them. CPT Reagle had given me a directive: regardless of the occupants of any house I searched, if it was a good tactical potential outpost, we would compensate the family for it and occupy it. Fortunately, this particular house was not only in a horrible spot to observe the city and Hwy-47, but its walls were too low to provide cover from enemy gunfire. On our way out, we talked to one of the kids who spoke English and was a student in Tal Afar. I congratulated him and apologized to the family.

After telling them good night, we left, and of course the gas station platoon still had not moved out as planned. Ali called them from our position all the way back to Checkpoint Sinjar, and they still hadn't moved out. We waited for about five minutes and they finally came rolling in. Upon returning to the FOB, I briefed CPT Reagle on how things went, and how good the potential outpost in the north was, versus how bad the one with the family in the west was. SGT Wadul and I also discussed the helmets and ammunition with Major Sultan, and he said they didn't have any 7.62mm for the AK47s. I told him we had just given them some and soldiers must have ammo before leaving base. He nodded and agreed, and then provided us with a receipt from 1SG Thamer for oil they purchased from the gas station. The mayor had accused them of stealing oil, but they had been purchasing it, not stealing it. I sat down with MAJ Sultan and had a small conversation with him speaking broken English and me speaking broken Arabic. It was quite comical, but we both learned more. After signing the mission rosters for the next morning's raid. We would be raiding two mosques (only Iraqi Army personnel w go inside) in south Tal Afar, so I went to bed to get some rest so I could be awake by 4 a.m.

March 30, 2005

Thankfully, the Lord kept us all safe and alive during the mission. I had no fear in me whatsoever this time as I rolled out. I prayed on our way out, but even before that, God blessed me with a strength and extra confidence for the morning. It was a bit of a drive to the two mosques, and we organized into two teams. My team included SFC Aeris, SGT Wadul and Oakley at the main mosque on the five-way intersection. CPT Reagle's team included SSG Hitcher, PFC Sunburn and Omar at the secondary mosque about five hundred meters to our south. LT Haadi led the Iraqi soldiers with CPT Reagle's team and 1SG Thamer led those with my team. We dismounted, and the Iraqis entered the outer courtyard of the mosque while we secured the outside with a few others. I noticed a couple small holes that a person could fit through underneath a shack to the right of the mosque. They looked like they led into a few big underground rooms, so I decided to check it out as soon as we could spare a couple Iraqis to support me. At this point, CPT Reagle called and reported that his team found a few AK47s in the mosque, with about four magazines. The Iraqi soldiers took them and searched another nearby mosque.

I noticed no one from the A Company Stryker was out of the hatch scanning. They were all inside sleeping. I walked over to yell at them, but SFC Aeris asked me to let him handle it, so I did, since he could probably fix the squad leader better than I. I walked back over to the mosque, and 1SG Thamer came out and headed down the little cave hole with me. I turned my M-4 tactical light on and slipped down the hole, about six feet or so below the road level. There were about four rooms down there, and a lot of rubble and trash. We sifted through some until I came into a room with discolored dirt. It was lighter than the rest on the ground, looking recently dug up. We began digging at first with rocks and knives, then someone finally got us a shovel, but it turned out to be nothing. I was kind of hoping we would find something, but there was nothing there, and the mosque itself was a dry hole too. After taking some pictures of 1SG Thamer in the underground cave, I noticed a long since dead cat, no fur and stiff as wood. I climbed out and we loaded back onto the Stryker, heading back.

The only shots fired were warning shots by SFC Aeris at some old pickup truck with an old guy in it heading toward him. He turned around and drove off. Surprisingly, that was the only time anyone on the squad leader's Stryker stuck a head out of the hatches while sitting there. When we were almost at the FOB, one of Thamer's trucks got a flat, so SFC Aeris helped them fix it and said he would ride back with them at that point, since he was already on "FOB road." After getting off the Stryker back at Nomad base, the squad leader asked SGT Wadul if he had laughed after finding out about 1SG Roach getting blown up and wounded. SGT Wadul said, "of course not," but the squad leader insisted some E-5 sergeant in Nomad said so to his platoon sergeant who told him to wipe the smirk off his face. We both had no clue what he was talking about. SSG ZT was already an E-6 by then, and we recalled that CPT Reagle was the only one out that day. He had helped them gather the pieces of the Stryker, so it wasn't any of us. Most of us were pretty upset with the performance of the A Company guys, but it didn't matter because B Troop would be taking over as escort for the next couple weeks.

I practiced some difficult Arabic, learning rules of verbs with Omar. It seemed Evan was not coming back – he was due the twenty-eighth, but we would adjust as usual. The Iraqi Army had a truck accident in the afternoon and six of them were injured. Three were at the Combat Support Hospital, two of them had head trauma and one had elbow problems. The other three returned to duty. I was thankful that they were okay, and that no one died.

March 31, 2005

I woke up sick with a cold or the flu. I took a long nap after noon and then went to the command post. Woody told me to go to the aid station, SGT Wadul hooked me up with some medicine and CPT Reagle told me that I didn't need to be in their getting everyone else sick. He added, "I think we've got the radio covered" which was hilarious, because there were about seven people in the office at the time, and SFC Aeris started cracking up. I quarantined myself in my room and began to pray and read scripture. Ever since Chaplain Wells brought up the subject of "Can you lose your salvation?" last Sunday, I felt a burning in my heart to study with a concordance and figure out what the original Greek writing says on the topic. I asked the Lord to reveal the truth, and then I went through John 15, Romans 10, and Romans 11, and found it fascinating to read the original Greek words and meanings. After four hours, I determined I'd done enough for the day.

---

[1] Had I not been "just as bad as others sometimes," I could have shared the true expectation God and Jesus have for us. As God said to Abram and the Israelites, He expected them to be blameless and holy, meaning set apart from others and without moral fault, seen in Genesis

17:1, and Leviticus 19:2 Jesus expected no less in John 5:14, 8:34-36, and his disciples reinforced sinning no more, or ceasing from sin – 1 Corinthians 15:34, 1 Peter 1:16. Sin never keeps one humble, but just makes one a child of the Devil, and not a child of God as 1 John 3:7-10 makes clear.

[2] *Today, I'm not convinced John the Baptist's and Jesus' words equate to approval of the profession of arms which may likely involve killing for many. Like the November 11 and December 5 footnotes state, the new covenant does not seem to allow for this. Security may be a different issue. **God-approved Old Testament killings (by His commands) to physically conquer a promised land to His kingdom of Israelites, does not mean a child of God in the new covenant, whose citizenship is in heaven (Philippians 3:20), whose kingdom is not of this current world or age may fight for national borders (Luke 17:20-21, John 18:36). It does not require physical fights or conquest.

[3] * I do not hold such harmful sentiments today. Again, see December 25 and February 28 footnotes. ** Regarding the supposed fulfillment of prophecy of Babylon and Jeremiah 51, I am uncertain today. Regarding the role today's political nation of Israel plays compared to the Biblical Israel of God, there is room for much debate. See Pauls notes on "circumcision of the heart", "they are not all Israel who are of Israel", and the "Israel of God" in Romans 2:28-29, 9:6-8, and Galatians 6:16. I understand this to be Jews and Gentiles (non-Jews) joined together as one in Christ Jesus (in Hebrew, *Yeshua ha Maschiach*), even if the political nation of Israel has a role to play.

8

April

April 1, 2005

I completely "spring forward" for Daylight Savings Time, so I was an hour behind most of the day. CPT Reagle was on mission, so I went to listen to LTC Mavis' plan for Iraqis to occupy an A Company fort, and to explain to him about our lack of Iraqi helmets – the numbers didn't add up, so I told him we'd count all helmets in the compound to figure it out. I got back just in time to shower and change for my promotion 'ceremony.' I didn't even realize the hour time difference when LTC Mavis, LTC Rugrs, MAJ Diny, CPT Durmsy and LT Berry showed up for my promotion. I looked at my watch and wondered why they were there an hour early. MAJ Sultan was on a mission with Jimmy making purchases (he left two days ago), so he wasn't there to pin me, but LTC Mavis and CPT Reagle did it, which was fine. LTC Mavis talked briefly about how I came to A Troop of 2-14 Cavalry as a lieutenant, did well, went on the twenty-five mile rucksack march with sore feet afterward, moved to A Company of 1-24 Infantry, and then came back here to Nomad. He and CPT Reagle pinned my Captain rank on my collar and hat respectively, and then told me to make a speech.

I'm not one for speeches, so I just said, "First and foremost I want to thank my personal Lord and Savior Jesus Christ for keeping me alive to get this promotion, because you've gotta be alive to get it, and we all know I had a close call." I also thanked my former peers from A Troop, Rich and Garrett, for coming out, as well as the others. After saying, "I've enjoyed working with everyone and pray that we all get home safely," that was it, and they all came and shook my hand. After they left, we got on with the rest of the day. Woody and I went over to the Iraqi compound and inspected the remaining helmets they had, since they claimed there were none. Apparently, our Iraqi Battalion's name is now the 109th Iraqi National Guard Battalion and not the 2-11th Iraqi Army Battalion. LTC Mavis said Brigade never completely made the change and now all orders say the 109th, so they are back to that once again. Regardless, we discovered about a hundred helmets, so we now knew it was possible for them to occupy the fort with seventy men, as LTC Mavis desired. Several people noticed I made Captain today, the most surprising were the contractors and chow hall workers whom I didn't even think noticed such stuff.

Later, SGT Wadul said the Stryker he had ridden on had been hit by a bomb in the exact spot where I was hit over a month earlier. The force knocked him down inside the Stryker, but thankfully neither he nor anyone else was injured. They also shot someone who ran from the scene but didn't know if he was wounded or killed. SFC Aeris also told us an enlisted man with the last name of Todd stole a Humvee and drove it to one of the towers in the northern section of the base. He breached the wire from the inside, drove out of the FOB about a kilometer, parked the Humvee, dismounted, and walked by himself ten kilometers into the city of Tal Afar. He was already under field grade Article 15 proceedings for falling asleep on guard, and this just made matters much worse for him. According to SSG ZT, Todd was in all his gear, knocking on doors of people in the city and going to their roofs looking for terrorists. There was a rumor he killed someone while there, possibly enemy, but who could say? His intentions were supposedly to kill as many terrorists as he could before being killed himself (or so he thought), rather than face punishment. It sounded plain crazy, and now his charges would be worse. It was incredible he walked the streets of Tal Afar by himself for a day and wasn't killed.

April 2, 2005

SFC Aeris and SSG ZT started the morning early with Omar and Ali on a change of responsibility mission. With enough helmets, seventy Iraqis went to "Fort Apache" in two trucks and very meticulously occupied it. SFC Aeris was impressed with how the mission went. In the evening, a couple platoons from A/1-5 Infantry would clear and occupy Fort or Combat Outpost Defiance in another area of the city. I was sure after several more weeks, Iraqis would take over that until eventually they would occupy outposts and forts all over the city. It sure denied the enemy freedom of movement and maneuver when we could observe and cover half of the city. In fact, there was now little contact on Hwy-47, except for the one kilometer stretch of road where there was no outpost or unit to maintain eyes on it. Soon, the enemy would be out of room in the city and would be forced to leave. I prayed for that day, and for the day they were forced to leave all the cities in Iraq.

Shortly after lunch I worked on all the reports to send up to the Brigade Liaison team. The logistical report was the most crucial because it displayed how short on ammunition, soldiers' equipment and other supplies the unit is. I also sent up the personnel and tactical updates and bi-monthly full reports. I dropped off the updated casualty roster that I had finished in the morning. I gave it to the Civil Affairs sergeant since they were the ones who paid injured soldiers and the families of killed soldiers.

When I came out of the Squadron bunkers, my whaz was gone. I couldn't believe someone would have stolen it but wondered if possibly somebody from Nomad came up and took it because they needed it badly for some reason. I resolved not to get mad until I found out what happened. When I got back to Nomad Base, I told everyone my whaz was stolen. They were shocked, and then SGT Wadul told me Sunburn had it and was loading it with sandbags. I asked how he got it and SGT Wadul told me that it was here at Nomad. "When I came out from the Squadron bunkers, it was gone, so I walked back," I told him. He laughed and apologized, saying he came out of the TOC and didn't realize he had parked in the larger parking lot, and when he saw my whaz there, he thought he must have parked there, so he took it. He left the whaz he originally took at the Squadron parking lot. I told him I was glad it was just an accident, but, "go get it," so he did.

Squadron radioed an intelligence report requesting all units to send up a 100% percent accountability report and for all Commanders to come to the TOC. We got accountability of all our Nomad team and the Iraqis too. When CPT Reagle returned from the TOC, he read a report that an Iraqi Police Battalion officer in Tal Afar heard from a source that the enemy had a "soldier" captured in the neighborhood east of the police headquarters. Since no one was missing, and it was coming from the untrustworthy police, it was hard to believe, but we got ready anyway. The plan was for CPT Reagle, SFC Aeris and SSG Hitcher to go out with A Company 1-5 Infantry to pick up the Iraqis from the gas station on the way (1SG Thamer's men). That part went okay.

The horrible part soon after that. From what they described to me, the police at "the castle" (police HQ) had the source mount on the lead Stryker, occasionally popping his head out of the hatch to positively identify the location of the house in question. As they approached it, he pointed to a house down an alleyway, which the Strykers were too wide to negotiate. They dismounted to check out the building. As they approached it, they took fire from what SSG Hitcher or "Hit man" described to me as "all directions." SFC Aeris directed Iraqi soldiers to bring one of their trucks down the alleyway, since it could fit. It was a good thing he did. Enemy from the roof tossed a grenade as the A Company infantrymen tried to take the high ground. One infantryman was hit in the lower back and the other in the nose, cheek and back of his neck with shrapnel from the grenade. The A Company men and Nomad team returned fire along with the Iraqis and evacuated the casualties as fast as they could – onto the pickup truck and then to a Stryker.

When the rest of the unit returned to the Castle, some A/1-5 Infantry soldiers noticed a man wandering around who matched the complete description of one of the enemy fighters. It was not too surprising since several Iraqi police tended to be terrorists at night, after taking off their uniform (or sometimes not even bothering to take it off). In the case of this guy, he didn't even bother to change outfits. They were sure he was one of the people firing at them, judging by the shape of his hood and his outfit. The infantrymen tackled and zip cuffed him.

Meanwhile, back at Nomad base, I was in the middle of a conversation with SGT Wadul about the effectiveness of a Stryker verses a tank in an open field versus any urban environment. We argued and then agreed, and changed the subject, until hearing a report on the radio of the Stryker on its way back to the gate with casualties. We became dead silent and listened more closely. After looking at each other and agreeing with SSG ZT that Third Platoon of A/1-5 Infantry were those out with SFC Aeris and the others, our eyes got significantly larger. Someone radioed for the gate to be ready to open for the casualties and I threw on my hat and said, "I'm going to the aid station." SGT Wadul said he would come too and would stop at chow afterwards. SSG Roy walked in and asked if I wanted him to come too, but I wasn't sure if it was our guys (Nomad or Iraqis) or A Company who had been wounded, so I said I'd radio him if it was ours.

We drove to the aid station and waited with hearts beating fast next to LTC Mavis, MAJ Diny and CSM Weldo who came up too. My bad feeling was incorrect because I kept imagining it was SFC Aeris who was injured. The helicopters were already starting to spin up for takeoff to the Mosul Combat Support Hospital, so we knew the injuries were serious. We saw the Stryker dust trail as it screamed across the desert shortcut around the Squadron Headquarters and Iraqi compound which we took the day I was injured. A sewage truck of some sort was on the road, so SGT Wadul and MAJ Diny quickly ran out to wave it out of the way, so the Stryker could have a fast and unimpeded approach to the aid station. It pulled in and dropped ramp quickly, as dismounts poured out of the back, carefully placing the two bodies onto the litters which medics from the aid station brought onto the ramp the second it came down.

I had prayed earlier but prayed again that they would be okay. For some reason, my fear that it was SFC Aeris came back again, and as they put the first injured soldier onto the litter, I imagined it being him and I kept thinking 'not the big guy.' I don't know why it kept entering my head, but I quickly realized it wasn't him when it was a much smaller body was brought onto the stretcher (Woody isn't fat, but they don't call him "beast" for nothing). I couldn't recognize the man on the litter because his face was covered with blood and a large chunk of his nose seemed to be missing, or at least mangled and covered with darker blood. I thought for a second it might be CPT Reagle, but my heart quickly told me it wasn't. I heard from someone there that SSG Cassidy and SSG Ioasa Tava'e (a Samoan) were the two were the two who were injured. One doc said the guy with shrapnel in his nose was gasping for air – supposedly a good sign since he was still able to breathe on his own. I recalled that LT Ali was in similar shape when he and I were injured and he survived. I didn't know about the back of his neck bleeding at the time, but still prayed again for them both as SGT Wadul and I went to chow. Since it wasn't Iraqis or Nomads injured, we didn't need to be at the aid station getting in the way.

We ate quickly and grabbed some food for SSG ZT who was panicky at first, because he hadn't heard anything, since the rest of the team still wasn't back yet. At chow, I ran into MAJ Jenkins and asked him how the casualties were doing. He told me one guy was going to be fine, but the other wasn't looking like he was going to make it. "The guy with the nose shrapnel sir?" I asked. He nodded 'yes' and walked away. I was shocked. I prayed again, hoping things improved, asking the Lord to save his life, and if it was already too late, to bring him back. I knew I prayed had that for CPT Jacobsen when he was killed, but for some reason I thought God might grant it this time.

Back at the Nomad office, an Iraqi soldier was in a lot of pain, and his leg or foot was clearly injured. SFC Aeris and "Hit Man" put him on the floor and SSG Roy began to take off his boot. His foot had been run over on departure from the objective. We called the aid station, put him on a litter and carried him to the Iraqi ambulance. SSG Roy and SGT Wadul took him there, with 1SG Thamer in the back with his injured soldier. I was thankful no one died, but just before 10 p.m. Squadron radioed that all Internet and communications devices needed to be shut down on the FOB. That's never a good sign, because it meant there had been a death in the Brigade somewhere. Woody nodded; he was sure it was the guy from A/1-5 Infantry and we all were silent for a few seconds.

The midnight mission for checkpoint checks was cancelled, and word came down that no one would be leaving the FOB morning. All bad signs, as they point to the death of SSG Ioasa Tava'e in A Company. According to 'Hit Man' and SFC Aeris, he was shot in the nose and it came out through his neck. The internet is shut off now, and I still have a mission at 7 a.m. I hoped I would find out that the dead soldier was not SSG Ioasa Tava'e. It sounded bad I supposed, to hope it would be someone else rather than him, but we were all exhausted from the deaths that seemed to occur at least once a month (either US or Iraqi). It was all so horrible. I prayed once more this war would end quickly in our favor, and I would get to go home at the end of this month, fully intact, to see my beautiful wife and healthy baby girl – God willing.

April 3, 2005

At 3 a.m. I heard a knock at my door – it was LT Dan Burkhart, who had gone to bed early last night for his 3 a.m. mission and never got the word it was cancelled. I told him it was scratched completely, and he left. I slept three hours then hopped on the Stryker with Oakley and B Troop. After passing Sinjar Checkpoint and the gas station (for 1SG Thamer and his men), we headed to Combat Outpost Wolf. I got on the ground with CPT Ahmed and had him pick eleven of his men with the worst boots. Some were ripped from the soles completely. After replacing their boots and inspecting Wolf, we moved to Avgani Checkpoint, where I distributed the remaining two pairs. The man in charge didn't quite know what was going on, because only eight people were awake, four were on security and four were running traffic. One man was searching vehicles by himself at the northern approach, while the two men at the southern approach were just waving vehicles through, not even searching them.

As much as I loved to teach people tactics and procedures, it was getting ridiculous. I instructed him that if he had 27 people at this checkpoint, then at least twelve needed to be awake during the day, six on security and six running the traffic control point. I had Oakley explain to him the importance of searching every vehicle, since terrorists continued to smuggle weapons and explosives through the city. I showed him how only one man searching a car without a battle buddy to cover him is as good as dead. He understood, and I also told Oakley to explain that drivers and passengers should be searched outside the vehicle before the vehicle was searched. Before I explained that procedure, they were merely looking in the car with the people still inside it. I even gave the leader at Mosul Checkpoint a demonstration in one of his ING trucks parked inside the checkpoint. I also told him how important it was to have two men at each battle position, and he adjusted things accordingly.

After two hours we returned from our checks, without inspecting the power station or Fort Apache. Checkpoint Avgani had a cute "Peschmerga puppy" (Peschmerga are Kurdish soldiers, and the puppy seemed to be theirs) waddling around, harmlessly nipping at heals and pant legs; he was furry and seemed well fed. At the FOB gate, there were about 400 civilians just outside: 300 attempting join the Iraqi Battalion, the other 100 seeking other jobs. In his usual fashion, LTC Ahmed refused to hire any, telling CPT Reagle he had another 200 men or so coming soon from Dahuk where they have been training. I wasn't comfortable having to turn away so many people who wanted to join, but we told them, "Sorry, it's full, so you must leave." It took several hours to get the crowd of 300 to leave. Some wouldn't leave unless threatened, so I told the driver of the M93 Fox vehicle present to drive back and forth on the road to herd them away from the gate. It seemed to be working, so we left, and shortly after returning to Nomad, base radioed for us to summon a platoon to force them off the main road. It was unfortunate because we had told people to come between 9 a.m. and noon on Sundays for recruiting, many volunteers came, and we were forced to send them away. It wasn't my call, so there was nothing I could do.

MAJ Farhan and MAJ Abid finally arrived with the money, over a week late once again. I inquired why they were so late, and they said it was because of some "Iraqi holiday" or something. I counted the money from the Ministry of Defense, and it matched the sheet this time but oddly, the last page with the total number on it had signatures but no official stamp. Funny that the Ministry would put an official stamp on fifty-one other pages of the financial record, yet not stamp the last page with the totals. I would have to do more checking later, since I had a mission at 2 a.m. and didn't feel like messing with it right then.

Around 3 p.m. we received a report from Sinjar Checkpoint of a civilian requesting help for his friend because terrorists were surrounding his friend's house. This informant's friend apparently had just killed an insurgent, and now several insurgents had begun to gather around this man's house. It could be another attempted ambush like the night before, but we couldn't be sure so we would probably respond.

At 6 p.m. SSG Hitcher and I passed out boots to the mechanics who had cracks and complete rips in the soles of their boots. SGT Wadul prepped for his mission and MAJ Sultan and Jimmy came back truckloads of refrigerators, stoves, and other cooking supplies so they could support themselvesand not be dependent on the US for food any longer. Within a week or so, they would be all set up. CPT Abdullah, the Iraqi maintenance officer, also brought over a huge number of receipts for the giant truckload of oils, parts and tools he had purchased for his maintenance bay. It was great to see things finally coming together when people other than LTC Ahmed handled the money. When 'Saddam' was given money, he would come back with no receipts, no bids on prices and mostly overpriced items that frankly stank. He would occasionally bring back something good, but we knew he stole money every time. When MAJ Sultan and CPT Abdullah got items, they returned with everything they needed, a receipt to match, and change left over for us. It wouldn't be long though, until we could fire him. It was so hard to be patient because we had been patient for months. The paperwork was on the way though.

The best part of my day was in the evening, after chapel services. The chaplain's message related to a story about his eight-year-old daughter, and it made me think of how much fun Becky and I will have raising Katelyn. The best part was after the service. SGT Walker, a medic from A/1-5 Infantry came up to speak to me. As soon as he said his first sentence, I recognized him, but didn't remember from where. He started with, "Sir, you don't know me, but I've actually seen you before." He looked down, as if searching for the next sentence, and I pondered why I recognized him. He started again, "You were in charge at the EFMB (Expert Field Medical Badge) Land Navigation Lane of 2003, and you said something that really blessed me." I smiled, because I thought I knew where he was going with it, as I reminisced about the event. "It was the month of December, and I can't remember what you said leading up to it, but I remember you said in front of everybody something about, 'This is the month my Lord and Savior was born', and I was like,'Yeah, praise the Lord, he's a man of Christ!' I want you to know that really blessed me, and I never forgot it."

He almost brought tears to my eyes. The most important thing in the world to me above anything else is to spread the love of Jesus to others. It's so hard to see the fruits of our labors most of the time in this life, and although I know "in the Lord your labor is not in vain" (1 Cor 15:58), I still feel sometimes people aren't seeing Him in me enough, or they aren't getting the message of His love. SGT Walker saying what he just did really touched my heart and left me smiling for the rest of the evening. I recalled to SGT Walker the circumstances surrounding what I said that day in December, since I ha a photographic memory most of the time. It was about my fourth month of being the Mobile Gun System Platoon Leader in A/1-24 Infantry. The Expert Field Medial Badge testing would begin in December 2003 at Fort Lewis, and medics would come from posts all over the west coast to compete for the badge. They wanted a first lieutenant in charge of land navigation, and although I was an Armor Officer and not Infantry,

I received the task, and was given about fifteen infantrymen to work with from 1-24 Infantry.

I would give the candidates (thirty to sixty of them a day) a site orientation brief and a safety brief with my top sergeant at the time, SSG Jones from B Company. Badge Land Navigation standards were numerous and had to be read aloud. To save my voice, I would have soldiers from the crowd read the tasks, conditions and standards. Most days, and that December day in particular, I got volunteers to read in a slightly comical way. That day I asked, "Who here was born in December?" A few people raised their hands, and I pointed saying "you, you, and you, read the task, conditions, and standards." Everyone laughed, but I then stated what SGT Walker remembered. "Hey, it's nothing personal or anything, but my Lord and Savior was born this month too, so no hard feelings" * [see note].[1] With that, half of the crowd gave a loud "Hooah" and one or two shouted an "Amen." After recalling the story, SGT Walker nodded, and then while I gave him a ride back to his pad, we talked about how God had blessed us.

April 4, 2005

I didn't sleep since I figured I'd just be more tired by the time my mission came, so I talked to Becky and my friend Dane and his wife Suzy, who is Becky's sister, on webcam. I went on my mission with Omar and checked out Fort Apache, the power station, and Sinjar Checkpoint. Fort Apache was amazing. CPT Said was in charge there and gave me a tour as I arrived. The battle positions were awesome and about 21 men out of 70 were awake, which was a good number. CPT Said back; he turned out to be a good officer, even though he had taken some bad advice from LTC Ahmed way back when he hit SFC Puten. Anyway, the leader at the power station had all twenty of his men up, with no one sleeping. I kindly told him this was not good leadership unless he was doing some sort of "all men to your battle stations" type of drill. Omar and I discussed with him for thirty minutes about how even though SGT Wadul yelled at him earlier for not having anyone on the roof pulling security, he needed to find a balance.

He said ten on and ten off was what he wanted, so I told him that was fine, but he shouldn't have all twenty of his guys awake just because we came by to inspect. I explained the importance of finding the balance between security for the power station and battle buddies, yet health (sleep, food, breaks) for his men. He understood, and we left. At Sinjar Checkpoint, the leader didn't seem to have a good rest plan, so I educated him. Three of his men at one end of the checkpoint slept, which was fine, but the three who were supposed to be awake on security were half asleep under a concrete bunker. I asked them and the leader if he was trying to get his men killed while they slept. He said no and tried to argue. I told Omar to tell him that the next day was payday, and that if he wanted all his pay, he'd better do his job right. We returned after 4 a.m. and got a few hours of sleep before Omar and I paid the 600 Iraqi soldiers on the base.

April 5, 2005

Days like this only seemed to get harder. It was slow and fine at first. Aside from CPT Bicks returning from leave and packing for his move to Brigade, the only thing worthy of mention inside the wire was paying the Iraqi soldiers at the gate. At 5 p.m. LTC Rugrs even radioed to all, "There've been no IED's, and virtually no contact at all today; everything is quiet, which is very unusual, so be cautious." Just as he said this, three mortars impacted near Combat Outpost Wolf with thankfully no damage. At 6 p.m. I was ready to go pay soldiers out in Tal Afar, and my goal was to pay all of them that night. For several reasons, I missed that goal. SSG Bidwell, the Headquarters Troop supply sergeant, volunteered to take a turn, as did SGT Rodriguez from supply. We also had a staff sergeant medic with us, who came out to conduct a sick call at Wolf for the Iraqi soldiers. SGT Wadul came along too, since he loved going out all the time anyway, just for the fun of it. The Iraqis brought four trucks with them, and among them were MAJ Farhan, MAJ Sultan and CPT Majeed. It was good that they came out to pay their soldiers, and I was pleased to see MAJ Sultan happy and outside the wire.

We made it to Wolf without incident and brought the money inside for pay operations just as the Strykers drove south to the hospital to drop off deceased Iraqi civilians whose bodies were in the freezer for a while at the Squadron aid station. As they drove away and disappeared from our sight, Iraqi soldiers at Wolf (unbeknownst to me at the time) captured a detainee. A source claimed this man worked with the terrorists and may have been one himself, so they captured him. SGT Wadul did checks with SSG Bidwell and I observed the pay with Omar. At that time, the Iraqis opened fire at something outside. Had it been just a couple bullets fired, I would have most likely continued pay operations, since a few rounds popped off was normal for them. However, a large volume of fire ocurred, including from Fort Apache across the street to the east. I left those in the room to continue paying while I walked briskly to the door of the building, outside and behind the sandbags they had set up there (which seemed to be improved upon every day). The soldiers outside pointed south down the street to a red house about two hundred meters south of Fort Apache.

We took fire from a truck way down the road at least 500 kilometers away. I observed from the second story, then from the third story and finally found a good area on the third from which to observe. The Iraqis surprisingly exercised controlled fires from Fort Apache and Wolf and as I looked down the road once more, I noticed them across the street at Fort Apache firing PKC along the wall of a red building. Just after the PKC fire stopped, I saw a puff of smoke from the building just to the right of where their PKC fire impacted. There was enemy firing from that building, but they shot the weapon above their heads in our direction, without aiming or exposing themselves. I took an aimed shot at where the fire had just come from, to hit the weapon or to suppress them. Just after firing one round, the Iraqi soldiers fired a few more, and then they all stopped because we received no more enemy fire over our heads or around us. I was impressed at how controlled the Iraqis were during the shooting, especially when they stopped together. Usually, their fire was sporadic and un-aimed, and we needed to pound them on the head with a "cease-fire" stick. They did it all themselves this time, which made all of us proud of them. Thankfully, no one was injured.

They explained to me about the detainee, and I presumed he was a friend of terrorists, if they shot at us within minutes of his capture. The Strykers began to approach again from the hospital (where they also received fire and returned it with their .50 cal). When they returned, SGT Wadul briefed them on what had happened, and they informed him their half shaft was broken and the Stryker was on the verge of needing a wrecker. I continued pay operations and had the Fort Apache guys run the ten meters across the street (ten at a time) to get their pay. Sometime during the pay, MAJ Sultan briefed me on the location of two roadside bombs on route Hwy-47 between the power station and Checkpoint Mosul. I let LT Ngante know so he could report it to Squadron. We finished paying all 73 of the Fort Apache guys, after completing the 31 at Wolf where we were. SGT Wadul, SSG Bidwell and SGT Rodriguez completed their checks of Fort Apache while the SSG medic completed sick call. We loaded the moneybag on the Stryker and prepared to move out.

As we were loading onto the Strykers, we heard of a tragedy from the Iraqi radios. The "*mujas*" bus and patrol returning from vacation in Sinjar was hit with a roadside bomb. As we boarded the Stryker, we heard the massive casualties report. LT Ngante was our escort and since his Stryker was on its last legs, he took us back as Squadron radioed for all available medics and interpreters on the FOB to go to the aid station immediately. At Sinjar Checkpoint, we realized we hadn't picked up 1SG Thamer and his men from the gas station, so we called them. They had already left and responded to the bus situation, securing the area and evacuating casualties to the FOB. It turned out the bomb was placed just one kilometer west of Sinjar Checkpoint.

   I prayed for the casualties a lot on the way back and Omar said he didn't want to go to the aid station. I asked him, "Why, because you don't want to see the wounded and dying guys?" He nodded yes, but I said, "I know Omar, nobody does, but it is important. You and he [pointing to the medic] might be able to save somebody's life." He nodded, and I asked him if he prayed, to which he also nodded again. Just after passing Sinjar Checkpoint, the half shaft fell off the Stryker, so one of the sergeants on the Stryker ran out to get it with us. We finally limped back to base in the Stryker at fifteen miles per hour and headed straight to the aid station. The medic and Omar went inside while SGT Wadul and I carried the giant bag of money to a truck we waved down. LT Elmer Takash happened to be driving and he gladly gave us a ride. I hadn't seen him in a while. As soon as I arrived at the Nomad CP, I thanked Elmer and we dropped off the money.

   The team was gone but CPT Bicks was there with Ali, monitoring the radio. After we talked for a bit, he went to bed and I heard on the radio that CPT Zebald and the engineers were returning with two casualties. They were hit, I believed, with a roadside bomb somewhere as well. I prayed for them and took a vehicle (as soon as one was available) to the aid station to get the report of what happened to the Iraqi bus, since COL Brown had inquired. I talked to SSG ZT, SFC Aeris and CPT Reagle. CPT Ismail was there, and he told me SGM Mohammed and MAJ Khalid were okay, but CPT Ismail himself was not doing well at all. The bus was hit with a huge bomb, resulting in 57 casualties: 54 wounded, and three dead. Of the wounded, 23 of them had shrapnel wounds that would allow them to return to duty and 31 were serious enough to be flown to the CSH. SSG ZT carried the three KIA into the freezer. He recognized the faces but didn't know who they were. One had his head caved in on top and the other had his neck mostly cut off by shrapnel. Most of the wounded had shrapnel to their faces, necks, shoulders and heads. I headed back after we sent the report and just continued to pray throughout the evening for those still alive and hanging on. Hopefully, the Lord would spare those seriously wounded and no more would die of wounds at the CSH.

SGT Wadul checked on the detainees brought back from the bus incident. One was seriously beaten and cut and the Iraqi soldiers had hanged him by his arms inside the Iraqi detainee cell. The beaten man was apparently the one who signaled his buddies to set off the bomb at the bus and the other was an accomplice they captured in a neighboring house. The soldiers in the Iraqi detainee cell had 2x4's with nails through them and a shovel on a table, ready to perpetrate further beatings on the murderers who just killed their brothers. SGT Wadul put a stop to it, as did CSM Aedo, but I heard he had already executed two terrorists on the spot at the site of the explosion. The Iraqis rounded up the terrorists almost immediately after the explosion. CSM Aedo was with the security detachment that went to Sinjar. He told us they captured two enemies immediately, and he fired a "controlled pair" from his 9mm at point blank into the head of the terrorists. I was glad they caught the guys, but this tragedy ripped my heart – it was the largest single incident of casualties since the 109th Iraqi National Guard was formed. I thought, "When will this war and hatred end?" My guess was it wouldn't until Jesus returned to establish his Kingdom here on Earth. It was nearly 2 a.m. – I went to bed.

April 6, 2005

Today began with me walking over to the Iraqi compound and walking through the bus from last night. CPT Reagle, Woody, SSG ZT, 'Hitman' and I all saw it briefly in the dark last night after we returned from eating midnight chow together, but I decided to get a good look today. It was horrible. I took pictures outside and in, and there was blood everywhere inside, on nearly every seat. Some seats were completely covered and stained in it, or still soaked from blood which hadn't dried. Shattered glass filled the seats too, but mostly the floor. Giant holes in the metal sides of the bus existed next to several seats, which formerly held the dead soldiers from last night, and a few who are in intensive care right now. Some shrapnel went completely through the right side, through people, and completely through the roof of the bus. Two Iraqi soldiers came in the bus as I got to the back of it, and they surveyed the damages too. There were still many bags and clothes inside from the returning soldiers on vacation. I stepped in a large mixture of blood, glass, and other matter on the floor, and as I made my way back to the front of the bus, I noticed a couple more disturbing sites.

One of the most disturbing was a piece of scalp about the circumference of the top of a can of soup, complete with skin, hair, and burned edges. I think it was from someone's temple area because it was the edge of the hair, and the skin had a forehead look to it. I don't know if it was from one of the dead soldiers, or one seriously wounded, but it seemed so surreal – a piece of one's head just sitting there in the seat. A couple seats forward from that was about a handful worth of brain – slightly blood-stained brain matter just sitting there in the seat. Just awful. As I continued to walk, I could imagine the panic during this event. Iraqi soldiers returning from a good vacation with their families, about two minutes away from Sinjar Checkpoint, when a giant explosion occurs, and 54 of them on the bus are instantly wounded, with three instantly killed. I could almost hear shouts in Arabic and Kurdish as they grabbed their own wounds, cried, moaned, attempting to render first aid, and get their buddies off the bus. The placement of the bomb was on the side of the road, not underneath the bus. Had it been underneath the bus, there would be very few casualties, but from the side of the road, it penetrated the weak sides and shattered nearly every window. The enemy must have planned this days ago.

On my way out of the bus, Omar came on to look at the bus in the daylight. We slowly walked toward the Iraqi soldier living quarters as he said they were about to start pay operations for the "*mujaseen*" (vacationers) who returned. I inquired further about last night and discovered that 1SG Thamer hadn't been told to go to help the "*mujas*" patrol. He simply heard it on the radio, contacted "*sifer wahid*," (the Iraqi TOC) and said he was going to help from the gas station. It was a good thing, because there were no vehicles to transportall the wounded since the bus was towed back later in the evening. Thamer was just an amazing soldier for this country.

Omar also told me a story about one of the soldiers killed whose name was Mamo Musso Ali. Mamo had a few brothers who used to be in the ING. Back when the police force was very weak in Tal Afar, as it was in all of Iraq, the Iraqi National Guard occupied the police academy building inside the city. Some of Mamo's brothers went on vacation and after changing into civilian clothes they walked to the traffic circle near the gas station to hail a taxi. Several terrorists with guns observed this and shot and captured them, knowing they were ING. He said the terrorists cut off their heads at that point. Mamo's parents pleaded with him (as the only surviving members of his family back in Sinjar) not to go back to the ING. Mamo told his parents "No, I must fight for my country, and I must stop the evil terrorists who killed my brothers." There are so many soldiers and men like this in Iraq, and I don't think the media or even most American soldiers know about it. Too many U.S. soldiers just thought the ING were responsible for the chow hall bombing in December, or all Iraqis were bad soldiers or terrorists in disguise. I was positive a few out of the thousands who joined were, but only a few.

When we began pay operations, I saw CSM Aedo and asked him about killing the enemy last night. First, I inquired if he was okay, because he was in a car accident outside Sinjar as they escorted the vacationers back to the FOB. He had some back and neck pain, but said he was fine otherwise. It turned out the initial report of him killing someone was wrong. He said he and other soldiers shot their weapons over the head of someone who ran away (the enemy who signaled the explosion) to get him to stop, and they captured him. MAJ Khalid, now promoted to LTC Khalid, confirmed CSM Aedo didn't shoot and kill anyone. He said Americans didn't like it when they killed the enemy instead of capturing them, so they didn't kill them. If they had their way, they would torture and kill every enemy they captured, but the American justice system was in place at that time, thank goodness.

LT Burkhart conducted checks at Forts Apache and Wolf as I paid Iraqis at Mosul Checkpoint. SFC Box and SSG Stone (the C Troop Mortars) looked at me as if I were crazy for volunteering to stay at Mosul Checkpoint by myself without them or Strykers but told them I'd be fine. I trusted most of the ING with my life and, "besides," I told them, "you'll be just down the road, if I need you badly for some reason, I can call on the ING radio from here to there. It'll only be for an hour or less." They still looked at me as though I was crazy but agreed. The pay went fine, and I even had time to conduct checks of the checkpoint when I finished observing pay. A few kinks in the security, but overall, it was decent. The Strykers picked me up, and we moved to the power station. Many soldiers from there and from Avgani Checkpoint, our final stop, were from the "Doosky" tribe. They kept saying "Doosky," so I asked Oakley what it meant, and he said it was their tribe. I kept repeating it and most of them laughed. I would ask them, "*Aante Doosky* (you are Doosky)?" Most of the answers were "*naam* (yes)" so I would say, "*Anna Doosky* (I am Doosky)." They'd laugh even more then, especially when I said, "*Anna Doosky awal,*" which means I am the first "Doosky."

We all returned safely without any serious incident (thank God), after linking up with 1SG Thamer along with his guys at Sinjar Checkpoint from the gas station. Normally, we would rely on the interpreter's word of how many personnel and how many trucks for Iraqis returning to the FOB (for reporting purposes), but this time I felt led to get out of the Stryker to count for myself. I thought it odd God would want me to get out, because in the big picture, why would the numbers matter? I counted and what Oakley told us was off. On the way back to the Stryker, I realized why the Lord wanted me out there. I didn't understand completely, but I knew He wanted me to see what I saw. A civilian stood near the vehicles and 1SG Thamer went to talk to him. Normally, we would impatiently yell at them to get away and tell the leader to get in the truck and leave. Patience and compassion overcame me as Thamer talked to this man. The man began to beat his own face with an open palm as he wept. I asked Oakley what was wrong, and he said 1SG Thamer had told the man about the bus explosion. Apparently, one of the soldiers who was killed was his brother. I felt horrible for him; he looked so devastated and continued to cry on Thamers' shoulder, still hitting himself. I gave them a few minutes and as I walked to the Stryker, I told him with sorrow etched on my face, "*Ah-sif*" (I'm sorry). We loaded the Strykers and entered the FOB.

I read an article on *StrykerNews* about LTC Krella's response to some reporter from *The News Tribune (TNT)*, article dated March 31st, who claimed the Stryker was a horrible design, and put soldiers in Iraq at risk. His response from the website:

Strykers perform well, save soldiers' lives
Last updated: April 5th, 2005 02:35 AM

I read the article (TNT, 3-31) about the Stryker's substandard performance in Mosul with interest. I offer readers the following facts based on six months of fighting a counterinsurgency with Strykers in Mosul, Iraq, and ask them to make their own conclusion.

These facts are purely as they apply to one Stryker infantry battalion – 1st Battalion, 24th Infantry Regiment – which has operated in Mosul since October 2004 with 75 Strykers.

The article specifically faulted the Stryker's substandard survivability and maintenance to the point of stating it places soldiers' lives at risk. I would argue that nothing could be further from the truth.

Since October 2004, our battalion's Strykers have been engaged with 122 improvised explosive devices (IEDs), 186 rocket-propelled grenades (RPGs), 33 car bombs (of which 10 were suicide car bombs) and countless mortar and small-arms engagements.

In November and December, we were fighting an enemy that massed up to 70 insurgents during attacks. As a result, the battalion has had seven soldiers killed in action and 102 wounded in action (81 of whom were able to return to duty within 21 days).

Most casualties have come from doing what the nation expects us to do – dismounted infantry operations closing with and destroying the enemy.

The insurgents' most dangerous and powerful weapon is the suicide car bomb. I have watched four of 10 suicide car bombs slam into Strykers, creating explosions that are equivalent to 500-pound bombs. One was a suicide truck carrying 52-by-155 mm rounds (a net explosive weight 10 percent greater than a 2,000-pound U.S. guided bomb) that detonated within 25 meters of a Stryker.

In all 10 suicide car bomb attacks, not a single soldier riding on the Stryker lost life, limb or eyesight.

One example: Over the last six months, one Stryker, has been hit by a suicide car bomb, nine IEDs, eight RPG direct hits and countless small arms. The infantry squad has had six wounded, but every soldier is still in Iraq and still fighting on a daily basis.

After each attack, the Stryker continued to stay in the fight or was repaired in less than 48 hours.

Not only is the Stryker survivable, it is incredibly reliable. Our 75 Strykers each have at least 20,000 miles on them. We average more than 1,000 miles a month on each Stryker, and amazingly we average greater than a 96 percent operational readiness rate. That is three or four Strykers down at any given time.

This is the highest operational readiness rate of any armored vehicle in the Army inventory. We average less than 24 hours to refit a vehicle after it has received battle damage. The electronic computers, monitors, mapping software, weapons cameras and radios that give us incredible situational awareness average greater than a 94 percent operational readiness rate.

Much like every other weapon system the Army has fielded, it will continue to get modified and better with time. Remember, we are on the fifth major modification of the M1 tank.

These are the irrefutable facts without emotion. Now let me share with you some emotion.

I have watched this vehicle save my soldiers' lives and enable them to kill our nation's enemies. In urban combat, there is no better vehicle for delivering a squad of infantryman to close with and destroy the enemy. It is fast, quiet, incredibly survivable, reliable, lethal and capable of providing amazing situational awareness.

These qualities distinguish it from every other platform in the Army inventory, but most importantly it delivers the most valuable weapon on the battlefield – a soldier.

Do not just take my word on the Stryker; ask one of the 700 soldiers in this battalion which vehicle they want to go to combat in.

That was LTC Krella's response – if anyone could write an awesome response to the article attacking the Stryker, it would be him. I thanked God I had the privilege of serving under him for a time, and for being in Mosul to experience so much of what was in his response. I felt blessed to have been a part of it, and especially blessed to still be alive.

April 7, 2005

I typed a list of upcoming events and errands for Squadron. We needed to get living containers cleared out in the Iraqi compound so they could make room for another Iraqi Battalion under the same Brigade as the 109th or 2-11th Wolf Battalion. The fourth (or eleventh) Brigade Headquarters was coming to operate from this FOB. Even if we couldn't get rid of LTC Ahmed, at least his boss would be there to manage him, that is, if his boss was honest. LTC Mavis directed today that no Iraqi vehicles could leave the FOB until they had at least one layer of sandbags on all floors of the trucks with steel or kevlar blankets protecting the doors. When I inspected the Sinjar patrol, none of the five trucks were to standard. The patrol of trucks was on its way to Sinjar to take the three dead soldiers' bodies to their families, along with the condolence payments. Sadly, aid station medics reported that two more Iraqi soldiers died of wounds at the hospital today.

After inspecting the trucks, I showed LT Haadi (the leader of the patrol) a truck the mechanics had upgraded, pointing to it as the standard. I explained all trucks needed to look like it, including five-ton trucks heading to Checkpoint Mosul that night. LTC Ahmed tried to tell me they didn't have enough time and that it would make the trucks too heavy. I mostly ignored him after telling Faisal it wasn't negotiable. "The trucks aren't going to leave the FOB unless they all have this stuff on them," I explained, pointing to the standard with one layer of sandbags and steel plating and kevlar blankets on the floors and doors. It was essential and would undoubtedly save lives, so I let them know how serious I was, so MAJ Sultan and others made it happen.

SFC Walenz and I inspected the two big trucks to be used in that night's transfer of Iraqi soldiers from Checkpoint Mosul to Fort Union. After we showed them the requirements, we showed SGM Mohammed where some sandbags were and where to put the steel plates. Fort Union was going to be the newest COP, at an intersection with Hwy-47, but because the Engineers had not yet installed barriers, the occupation was postponed. Instead, SSGs ZT and Hitcher would drop the Iraqi soldiers at Fort Defiance where they would join A Company 1-5 Infantry soldiers until material was made available from the Engineers.

April 8, 2005

My 7 a.m. check lasted until 10:30 a.m., which was probably the longest time it had taken me to do normal checks. We picked up two big trucks from Fort Defiance (now called Fort Tava'e to honor him). I checked Wolf and the power station out first, then Fort Apache and Avgani Checkpoint, checking supplies at all of them. The 10th Iraqi Army unit had officially relieved us of Checkpoint Mosul, so we would never have to inspect it again. Fort Tava'e looked good. They had a well fortified position to share with a platoon from Apache. The only weakness was that one of the walls was damaged so badly from its previous occupation by 5-20 Infantry over a year earlier that one or two enemy mortars could collapse it. I made sure no soldiers were near that wall.

On our way back to the FOB, we stopped at the power station to pick up about 37 new Kurdish soldiers from Dahuk, loading them into an armored five-ton truck. I could just imagine what would happen if an explosion occurred at the rear of it though, with them so tightly packed in there. I prayed continuously on the way back that God would protect us from any enemy fire or bombs. Thankfully, my prayers were answered. When I got back to the Nomad area, I typed up the supply report, including the five places we checked, with a list of personnel, ammunition, food, water, sandbags and other combat supplies. I then tried to get information about our two Iraqi soldiers who died of wounds in the hospital. I also needed to find out how to coordinate for Sunburn's return from the hospital. He had been there the last couple days to guard a wounded detainee whom the Iraqis had beaten senseless. Finally, the latest talk was that 3rd ACR (Armored Cavalry Regiment) from Fort Carson, Colorado, would be coming there, and that our Squadron would move elsewhere – or we (2-14th Cavalry) might share the FOB with them.

I returned to the Nomad office and learned 1SG Thamer and his men were under fire from the mosque near the gas station, from an enemy sniper nearby. LTC Ahmed instructed them to take cover behind the concrete wall but ordered them not to return fire into the mosque. I got so mad when I found out that I told them to call LTC Ahmed and order him to tell his men to return fire into the mosque. US soldiers were not authorized to enter a mosque, only Iraqi soldiers, but there had never been a policy forbidding return-fire into a mosque. Since LTC Ahmed had a history of ordering his soldiers not to shoot the enemy, and was suspected of collaborating with them, none of this surprised me. Our interpreter Jimmy told him four times, but he still ordered 1SG Thamer to not return fire at all. My response was if 'Saddam' didn't order Thamer to return fire on the mosque we would send a Stryker over to fire a missile into it. By the time Jimmy sent the message however, LTC Mavis arrived with his three command Strykers to settle the situation. They also escorted Thamer's men back to base, which meant one less stop for me when I did my next checks at 5 p.m.

For the 5 p.m. checks, I dropped off 10th Iraqi Army Battalion lisasons at Checkpoint Mosul since it was their territory. It was kind of scary since Squadron had just reported a roadside bomb one kilometer to the west and we drove right over it. I just silently asked the Lord that it not to detonate under us. Once again, He answered prayers. I breathed a sigh of relief after driving over the spot two times with no explosion. Had we seen it we could have destroyed it, but it must have been buried in the dirt or cemented under the road. Our next stop was Checkpoint Avgani where I almost shot a man on a bicycle. The enemy was using the tactic of placing bombs on bikes and the man wouldn't stop at my repeated shouts while I was inspecting the checkpoint. I aimed and instantly switched my selector switch on my M-4 from 'safe' to 'semi'. Ceasar, the sergeant in charge out there, shouted, "Sir, it is okay, I know this man, and he is not a terrorist!" The man stopped at that time and I put my weapon back on safe.

I told Ceasar to tell his friend to stop when told or someone might shoot him in the future. He said "okay" and continued to direct his men to search vehicles. They weren't searching the vehicles in front of the concrete barriers in the road, so I made the correction. I explained if a car bomb exploded, his men would be much safer behind concrete and sandbags than if they were right next to the car. Overall, the checkpoint looked much better with sandbags emplaced and less trash. I remembered back when it was badly defended with just twelve to eighteen men and trash was everywhere. It looked much better, and they are much safer. Having them permanently occupy the checkpoints was one of the best tactical decisions we made. Not only were they safer out there, but they no longer had to chance getting blown up by roadside bombs while traveling to and from the base so often.

CPT Reagle was the acting Operations Officer since MAJ Diny was on leave. It looked like I would be commanding Nomad for the next three weeks until I went home on leave to see Becky and Katelyn, who was due to be born in about three weeks. My evening took a horrible turn for the worse when I talked to Becky on webcam. She had spoken to Tamara Minnock (SGT Jason Minnock's wife) and had some bad news. SGT Minnock was fine, but my former Stryker in 1-24 Infantry was traveling in a convoy that had been hit by a car bomb. While Jay was on leave, SGT Youn filled in as LT Kim's gunner for the last mission before SGT Minnock returned. Before even telling me the rest, Becky came right out and said, "Matt, you need to pray for Youn. He is in a coma and probably isn't going to live."

I suddenly became dizzy and my whole head started to tingle. Every single time I heard news like this, I seemed to feel worse than the previous time. It never got easier, and I never got used to it. It only got worse. I prayed right then, asking the Lord to heal Youn and not to let him die. Even as I prayed, I felt he would die for some unfathomable reason. I didn't want to believe that, so I just continued to ask God to help Joseph Youn. Becky continued, "To show you how serious it is, they flew him straight to Germany and also flew his parents straight to Germany to see him, because they don't expect him to live, and his parents may have to make the decision to pull him off of life support." I shook my head in shock, almost denying it was true, as if it was just a "what if" scenario. "Even if he recovers, from a medical standpoint, they think he will either be a vegetable or have the mentality of a five-year old for the rest of his life. He'll never be the same even if he survives, but they don't expect him to live." "Did he take shrapnel to the head?" I asked her. "Yes, but they aren't sure if it was that or his head banging when he fell inside the Stryker. Do you know Williams?" She asked me. "Of course, he was my driver."

Instantly, I thought about him, and she would go on to tell me he was like SGT Youn or worse. "He has second- and third-degree burns and he will be recovering for probably two or three months. He's not as bad as Youn, but he was burned pretty badly." I was thankful, but still obviously concerned for Youn. I also wondered how Will was burned if he was the driver and the hatch was closed. It didn't make much sense, but I'm sure I'd find out. "What about LT Kim, the LT who replaced me?" I asked her. "He's injured too, but he's like you when you were injured, he'll be able to return to duty. He caught some shrapnel in the head or neck somewhere or something." I couldn't believe all I was hearing. Other than the chow hall explosion, A Company 1-24 Infantry was fine when I was there. After I left the unit in January, just over a month passed, and within three days of each other, I was wounded, Gluv was wounded and Gertson was killed. Now this. I was sure everyone would make it from the Storm Troopers and even after Gertson was killed I thought at least the MGS and Mortars would be okay. I guessed you never expect it to happen to you. You never think that one of your own would die, or fall. The list just got longer and longer.

DeArthur was okay apparently, and Jay was feeling very guilty since it should have been him in the hatch where Youn was. Of course, it wasn't his fault, but I would pray that he'd find peace with it, as the same goes for all of us. Becky and I talked about me dying, but I didn't really have much to say on the subject since I was more upset about those that I'd lost already. She said all of this with SGT Youn and the rest of the crew on my old Stryker occurred a few days ago, but she had just heard about it the night before, which was more like early in the morning for me. Maybe it was good Youn had survived this long, and with more prayer and modern medicine, he would be okay. I prayed God would answer this one.

April 9, 2005

Aside from the horrible news of the night before, this was a great day, filled with the Holy Spirit. I needed to brief LTC Mavis on my plan for executing a couple Cordon and Searches early the next morning. We had a couple target terrorists in some houses just east of

Fort Apache and just south of the infamous mosque. When I arrived at Nomad base, I discussed the target packet with SFC Aeris, and we modified the plan he had suggested earlier and solidified liaison teams. I completed the plan and was ready to brief the boss when about 300 Iraqi soldiers came to the front gate from Dahuk. Despite our telling LTC Ahmed to have them come one hundred men at a time, he informed them to come all in one day. What a task it was. SGT Wadul and a few others went to the gate and began to in-process them. I had Omar interpret the casualty list first thing this morning, and once it was finished, we had the name of the other individual who died of wounds at the hospital.

A "red hat" (training) Iraqi sergeant came over because 'Saddam' fired him. We informed him he wasn't fired and to ignore LTC Ahmed. He wrote a statement describing the events surrounding his firing. He had known about some terrorists near Sinjar, so Squadron Intelligence guys took him on a mission for US forces, so he was gone twenty days. When he returned, 'Saddam' took his money and badge and told him he was fired for working with coalition forces as an Iraqi and being gone for too long. Fortunately, we had all of this in a statement in addition to his testimony (in semi-decent English), "He also tell us if there is a road bomb or car explosion if you see any terrorist don't fire or shoot at them because if you do, I will punish you and cut your pay also." You would think this combined with the other twenty statements I had would be enough to put someone in jail, but right now 'Saddam' was still not even fired. Hopefully, this wouldbe one of the final nails in this guy's proverbial coffin. Each day I got more and more irritated with LTC Ahmed.

At lunch the chow hall had mint chocolate chip ice cream and it was the first time in over six months I'd had my favorite ice cream. What a great treat. At 3 p.m. LTC Rugrs met us, along with CSM Ido and MAJ Sultan to speak to the Iraqis in the compound. Woody and I walked around with them. It was kind of funny watching LTC Rugrs discuss with them the importance of and methods for keeping their living quarters clean, and even funnier watching him treat LTC Ahmed so respectfully when he showed up in the middle of the inspection. LTC Rugrs had answers for everything and explained how easy it was. SFC Aeris and I sort of hung back, laughing at how the Squadron XO and SGM Collins (our Operations SGM) thought everything would be fixed if they just told the 109th leaders what to do. We'd tried this for monthsand it didn't sink in. SFC Aeris even got into it afterward because SGM Collins tried to blame us for the Iraqi bathrooms being broken and their rooms being a mess. He didn't take any of that garbage though and told the Sergeant Major how it was (all this was discussed in private between the two of them). On a random side note, it still feltweird to be referred to as "Captain Sacra," but I had about six years to get used to it I supposed.

At the end of the inspection, LTC Rugrs told me he would come back in two days with a giant crane, and if things didn't improve, he would just start taking out living containers and all Iraqis would live in tents. I smiled at him and said, "Yes sir; please do, because we've been telling them and they never listen. If they can't take care of what they have, they shouldn't be given the right to have it." He affirmed he would take them out from the compound with a crane and that would be the end of it. He left and I went to brief LTC Mavis on my plan for the next day. Somewhere in between the inspection and dinner, Fort Apache observed four mortars exploding near the buildings, but no one was hurt and the fort was undamaged.

As I was about to brief LTC Mavis on my plan, he asked me why I didn't just wait until the 8:30 p.m. meeting (I missed the radio call regarding this meeting). Looking at my watch, I saw it was 8:26 – thank the Lord on that one! All the commanders gathered together and I felt out my of league with about eight Captains in the room and two Lieutenant Colonels. It seemed so weird to be the same rank as all the Captains. Anyway, the meeting was informative and it was good to be there with other commanders, getting information directly from the boss. We discussed the warning order from the morning, and the implementation of two plans: 1) the integration of the Iraqi Army Brigade into the city of Tal Afar (all three Battalions), and 2) the arrival of the 3rd Armored Cavalry Regiment. It all sounded like great news. The 109th Battalion would hold most of the city of Tal Afar (central, north, and west), 12th Battalion would hold the southeast portion of the city and the 10th Battalion would hold the northeast corner.

The 3rd ACR was as follows: three Heavy Cavalry Squadrons (Abrams Tanks and Bradley's), an Aviation Squadron, a Support Squadron, the Regimental Headquarters Troop and a Military Intelligence Company. The Aviation Squadron consisted of two Air Cavalry Troops (Kiowa reconnaissance helicopters), one Air Attack Troop (Apache helicopters and the like), a Maintenance Troop and a Lift Troop (their own planes for troop transport). This compared to our SBCT (Stryker Brigade Combat Team) in the following way:

1-25 Infantry Division (SBCT) (commonly referred to as first Brigade) had three Heavy Stryker Infantry Battalions (1-24, 3-21 and 1-5 Infantry). It also had the 2-14 Cavalry RSTA Squadron (Reconnaissance Surveillance Target Acquisition), 2-8 Field Artillery Battalion, 25th Brigade Support Battalion and a Brigade Headquarters Troop. Integrated into the Brigade were several Brigade-owned assets attached to various Battalions or Squadrons. These were a Company from the 73rd Engineer Battalion, an Antitank Company and a Military Intelligence Company. We also had some air units attached to us for this deployment and various Medical Companies, but they were not integral to the Brigade.

Third ACR was bigger and heavier (in a combat sense). It would be amazing to see the results of their serving in our Brigade sector. They were due to begin deploying on the thirteenth of April, in just four days. By the twentieth of this month, their first arrivals would be able to begin operations, and by the fifteenth of May they would have the entire Regiment in the northern Iraq area. The current brief from LTC Mavis was that two Heavy Squadrons (including their Regimental Headquarters) would be on base with either the whole Air Squadron or just one Air Troop. Either way, with those units on the FOB, and pushed out into the city, the enemy wouldn't stand a chance. Most of us would have to double up on sleeping and living quarters, but it would be beyond worth it.

A Company, 1-5 Infantry would be liaisons for the 12th Iraqi Battalion, B Troop would be liaisons for the 109th and C Troop would be responsible for the 10th Battalion. Since each Troop would liaison with its own respective Iraqi Army Battalions, our job at Nomad would be to coordinate mainly with the Iraqi Army Brigade as a whole. Liaison teams already existed for this, but we would most likely be reorganized somehow as a Squadron point of contact for them. On or around April 19th, Iraqi Battalions would be fully employed in the city of Tal Afar with more Combat Outposts than we could count on two hands. This combined with 3rd ACR moving in would crush the terrorist presence. I was sure they would either leave the city or cut back tremendously on their attacks and bombs, since they wouldn't have so many corners and streets to safely operate on.

It amazed me when I looked at the progress of the war from the beginning. After the defeat of the Iraqi Army under Saddam Hussein's regime and President Bush declared an end to the "major combat operations," the war switched to occupation operations against an insurgency. The Iraqi Army was rebuilt at first as the Iraqi Civil Defense Corps, to the Iraqi National Guard, and finally, the Iraqi Army. With the change of the names, they were not only reorganized, but given greater responsibility, and in some cases, greater firepower, and capabilities. During these transitions, US. and Coalition Forces attacked insurgents from Tactical Assembly Areas outside cities to Forward Operating Bases (FOBs) inside and, in some cases, still outside of cities.

Soldiers occupied homes, buildings and other areas inside all cities, conducting dismounted patrols to stop insurgents.

As bases improved, soldiers moved from cities to bases while insurgents became re-supplied and funded and joined in arms with terrorists from Syria, the PLO, Yemen, Saudi Arabia, Sudan, Iran and other nearby countries. This was probably the biggest setback since the end of major combat operations. After the elections, it continued, but with forces reacting from FOBs, and increasing the existence of COPs (Combat Outposts) inside the cities. We were able to maintain control once again since Iraqi police couldn't. Now, we transitioned to Iraqis again, except it was the Iraqi Army, and not a "turn-and-run" weak police force. Once they occupied outposts all over the city, US forces would maintain a few COPs in addition, but would mostly react when needed if the Iraqi Army couldn't handle a situation. Iraqis would conduct regular operations from inside the city and our operations would cut back severely, especially as things quieted down.

The terrorists would be forced to occupy surrounding smaller cities like Sinjar (who had great police), Avgani, Biaj, Ramadi and a few others. These cities were not even one-fifth the size of Tal Afar, so they would be very easy to search, occupy or manage with occasional Cordon and Searches, Raids and other operations from maybe a Cavalry Troop or an Iraqi Company once in a while. I could see this war slowly coming to an end, provided the Iraqi Army gave us the "warm and fuzzy" that we could leave. When I say leave, I mean, "pull back" out of most of the cities in Iraq. I thought the US would always maintain a presence there, at the very minimum a giant FOB near Baghdad with an Air Force Base, both able to quickly react to anything in the rest of the country within hours. Examples are South Korea, Bosnia and Kuwait, to name a few.

The big question on everyone's mind was: what would happen to 2-14 Cavalry when 3rd ACR arived? We still didn't know.

There were so many options at this point, and it was either COL Brown's or COL McMaster's decision (Commanders of 1-25th SBCT and 3rd ACR respectively), or perhaps even above them. Other than staying there and occasionally running missions in Tal Afar or the outskirt cities and towns, other options were FOB Endurance or perhaps even Syrian border patrolling. That would be fun because that was what a Squadron like ours was designed to do. It would also provide the desperately needed surveying of the border to stop terrorists from coming in through Syria and other countries.

I enjoyed the meeting (surprising for a guy who hates meetings). Our 4:30 a.m. Cordon and Search mission was cancelled because of too many damaged Strykers at the present time, as well as a "juicier" target to be executed tonight. After I got back to the office and explained our future plans, CPT Reagle came in and told us about a chart he saw as the acting Operations Officer. It depicted areas in Iraq based on how many US Troops were in each sector per amount of enemy contact in each. Most charts depicted troop numbers a little lower than the amounts of enemy contact, but this northern sector for Mosul and Tal Afar was extremely low compared to the rest of Iraq. Because of this, 3rd ACR was deploying to this sector with 1st Brigade and we all welcomed them. This wasn't official, but I imagined his chart looked like this (although probably much more complex):

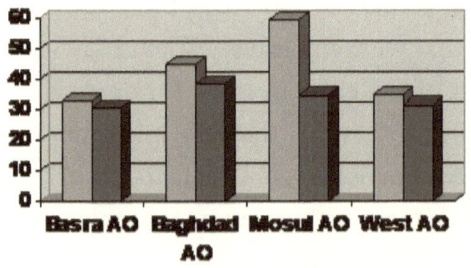

April 10, 2005

I paid Mohammed the 3,580 bucks we owed him for Iraqi Army boots and sunglasses, then picked up some batons for the Nomad team, since everyone wanted them. After returning from that, I emailed folks at the hospital to arrange for the return of our men who were injured in the bus explosion. I also had to figure out how to use a secure program on the secret internet computer that allowed multiple people in the Brigade to talk, like a chat room on the normal internet. The next morning, I had a meeting to discuss any issues we had in Nomad and to discuss the report I was sending – a report which required me to fill out a "commander's assessment" of Iraqi training, resources, operations, and even the Iraqi Battalion Commander. In the past, CPTs Reagle or Bicks would have filled it out, but since I was the acting Commander, I got to fill it out. Hopefully, the assessment would result in improvement. I was extremely honest. I didn't want to complain too much, but I explained that formations didn't occur anymore, discipline was poor, uniforms were not to standard and organization was practically non-existent under LTC Ahmed's command, since he refused to allow us to make any corrections or do anything with his Battalion.

SFC Walenz was barely teaching any classes since he couldn't get any of them to show up. He didn't even make spot corrections on uniforms anymore because the soldiers didn't listen since 'Saddam' didn't enforce standards on his officers nor allow his senior NCOs to enforce them on the soldiers. He ordered his men not to return fire on the enemy and had no leadership or command abilities. I stated all of this in the report on the section requiring my assessment of him. Hopefully, it would facilitate getting him detained or fired, which I also mentioned in the report. I included SFC Walenz's input on the training aspects and the overall assessment, and he was glad an officer was not telling him to "stay in [his] lane."

The best news of the day occurred in the evening when Becky emailed to let me know that Youn was still alive and doing better! I praised and thanked the Lord, asking for continued healing. Unfortunately, she also mentioned that LT Scotty Riley was severely injured. I had no idea how badly until a bit later in the evening when I talked online to my friend Mike. These were his words as I read them on the screen: "LT Riley was hit by a roadside bomb; he took shrapnel to the chest and brain. This happened two days before the other Stryker accident. He was flown to Germany and all Becky knew was he lost vision in one eye (possible removal of the eye) and the other eye can only distinguish between light and dark." Once again, I found myself staring in shock. I couldn't imagine what Scotty must look like now, and that he would never see the same again. Tiffany, his wife, must be devastated too – both know the Lord, and I was sure they were praying (as I just had), but his life would be severely changed. I was thankful he was alive though. Other sad news tonight was that Omar had decided to quit. He said he didn't like working there anymore because he was overworked and very tired. SSG Hithrick and I had a long talk with him until after midnight – maybe he would change his mind.

April 11, 2005

I had my online conference with MAJ Oskey and other advisors in the Brigade after 7 a.m. It was surprisingly short, and I only brought up two issues: 'Saddam' and our supply needs. The rest was a work in progress, but these needed immediate action. MAJ Oskey said both our Iraqi Battalion Commander and the one who worked with 1-5 Infantry needed firing. Theirs was due to incompetence, whereas ours was based due to both incompetence and corruption. I told him our preferred course of action was for LTC Ahmed not to be fired or moved to another position, but to be detained. However, I would take what I could get. He wasn't aware we wanted to pursue this as a course of action and so I filled him in on it briefly, but also followed up with an email. It was great to be in a meeting like that. It was amazing that as soon as I was promoted to CPT, my position had changed due to MAJ Diny going on leave and CPT Reagle moving to his job. It was like a mini-command immediately after making captain – a small taste of what it was like to be on the level of a commander of a unit. I got information directly from the mouth of not only the Squadron Commander of the unit, but also the Iraqi Security Forces Coordinator in our Brigade.

I practiced my Arabic alphabet and writing out the colors in Arabic with Omar. He seemed motivated to teach me, and it looked like our talk last night was effective, because he said, "I will stay for you." 'Hitman' and I explained how hard this team worked each day, including some of the other interpreters. We reminded him how much more difficult the conditions were for the soldiers out in the city of Tal Afar. "How can you or I complain about working hard, when the soldiers out there are sleeping on worn mattresses, in a dangerous place, with little electricity or heat? How can we complain when we get to watch movies, go to the chow hall and stay on the FOB most of the day? We go out on missions maybe two hours at a time and then come back; yet the Iraqi soldiers are out there for two weeks at a time and scan the perimeter of their [checkpoint or outpost] for eight hours or more each shift, hoping not to get shot. When we go out on missions, we are safe in a Stryker and when we get to [key locations] *'jundies'* and walls that keep us safe surround us. I would feel horrible to take for granted all I have and complain about it compared to what they are dealing with." 'Hitman' and I had said this among other things to him night before. He didn't have much to say, and I guessed he thought, maybe even prayed, about it overnight.

Captain Kaine Walts, B Troop Commander, came by as a forklift arrived with about 500 hygiene kits for the 109th. I talked with him, 1SG Molloph, Elmer Takash and two others about the transition of B Troop taking over operations with the 109th Iraqi Army. We scheduled a recon of the 109th Tal Afar sector so he could see their locations and we could scout out the granary which the 109th headquarters would occupy in a few days. He was well informed on 'Saddam', so we mentioned he might want to work with LTC Ahmed. I also suggested if he happened to talk to LTC Ahmed, he should not mention the occupation of the granary because it could end up being 'mysteriously' burnt down by enemies. He laughed, remembering hearing about the police and customs building, and suggested we tell 'Saddam' we'd occupy some fruit stand or market area a few clicks north of the granary, then wait and see what happened. I did so when I talked to 'Saddam' with SSG ZT. SSG Hitrcick was the senior NCO since SFC Aeris left for the US for his two weeks of leave. It was just over two weeks until I would head off for mine. It seemed far away still, so I was trying not to think about it.

I came up with a plan for the checks tonight and for sending some Iraqi soldiers on leave at 3 a.m. We had a couple more Iraqis arrive from the hospital as planned and they were able to return to light duty. I began to print out and prepare a continuity book for CPT Walts so he and Elmer could track all we had done with the Iraqi Army, picking up where we left off. The weird thing was they would almost completely take over as liaisons, yet in less than a month's time, 3rd ACR would be there in full force and would take it over from them. As the day went on, I refined my plan for the evening and 'Hitman' did great filling in for Woody advising me and helping get missions tracked and accomplished on and off the FOB. We even sent a truck out with A Company to retrieve the 37 Iraqi soldiers from Fort Tava'e. Now that they were back at the FOB from Company Four, they could refit for either the occupation of the granary or of the next outpost: Fort Union on Hwy-47.

At the evening briefing LTC Mavis rejected my Iraqi leave mission without explanation, so I talked to CPT Reagle afterwards for advice. I also dropped off the "corruption packet" on a thumb drive to the operations and intelligence office computers (as requested by MAJ Oskey this morning). On my way out, LTCs Mavis and Rugrs were talking to CPT Layes (C Troop Commander). At a good time, I brought up the Cordon and Search mission, requesting to action some targets at 4:30 a.m. since he'd cancelled the 3 a.m. leave and re-supply missions. He then touched on the leave mission, asking why I chose such times. I looked at him confused, and told him "No sir, the eight vehicles were going to go out at [3 a.m.] together, seven vehicles going to Sinjar to drop off and pick up leave guys (three big trucks, four escorts) and one truck would go into Tal Afar with the Strykers to drop off the hygiene kits." LTC Rugrs jumped in and said, "But then you have to have two units of Strykers that go with each group..." He started to crescendo with his voice getting louder, as LTC Mavis kept trying to speak.

Finally, LTC Mavis put up his hand with a very annoyed face at the Squadron XO, almost telling him to shut up. The Squadron XO closed his mouth, bowing his head like a hushed puppy (it was comical, and hard not to laugh). LTC Mavis asked why we created a resupply mission to the city, and I explained 3 a.m. was our time for checks anyway and we would drop off the kits then. He then said we weren't doing the Iraqi checks anymore because B Troop took those over as of the last night. "Weren't you at the meeting last night when we discussed this?" He asked me, annoyed. "Yes sir, I was, but I thought we were transitioning now, since Charger is still escorting our checks right now." CPT Layes quickly cut in and I realized he was trying to cover for something, so I admitted to the boss that I wasn't completely certain the transition had taken place yet. CPT Layes privately told me afterward that he and CPT Walts worked out a deal that he would finish up inspection escort duties while several of Kaine Walts' Strykers were in maintenance. I apologized and said, "Oh, sorry. You guys gotta fill me in on that stuff." "I thought Kevin [Reagle] told you earlier when he talked to you," CPT Layes said. "No, he talked to me, but not about that stuff," I answered. After this I had a quick meeting with LTC Ahmed, then bed.

April 12, 2005

PRAISE THE LORD! I should not even have been alive right then, were it not for His protection and angels surrounding me. I'll get into that momentarily. 1SG Thamer wasn't with his men that day because he was getting ready to go on vacation, so I double-checked his trucks. None were to standard, so I made them all put more steel and sandbags in the trucks. I said kevlar blankets would not be enough to protect them from a bomb – they needed either steel or sandbags underneath. They fixed the trucks and then I noticed an extra truck out there with no sandbags. I asked where they thought they were going and Omar interpreted, "They are going to Sinjar to get cigarettes and some other supply things." I shook my head and said, "No, no, they are not, nobody approved that." Omar told me the Battalion Commander said they could go, and their names were on the sheet. He said LTC Ahmed told them to put their names on the sheet as though they were heading to the gas station, and they could turn off and go to Sinjar.

I shook my head and went back to confirm with 'Hitman' and ZT if they had approved this, which they had not. Even after kicking that truck out of the line and telling them not to go, they tried to sneak back in line while we waited for the B Troop Strykers. SSG Hitcher went out this time and told them to get lost. CPT Kaine Walts arrived, and we left, after I told him about 'Saddam's' nonsense. At the gate Squadron radioed that all units leaving base must have their protective gas masks and gloves. The Nuclear-Biological-Chemical threat in the area had increased because intelligence had reported finding a car bomb with dangerous chemicals somewhere in Mosul or northern Iraq. We came back and got them, but MAJ Sultan and Omar had none, nor did any Iraqis. I told them what I learned from a history lesson about soldiers in World War I who were gassed. Pee naturally filters some gasses and chemicals, so I educated Omar, MAJ Sultan and 1SG Thamer (who wanted to go on the mission even though he was supposed to go on leave). I told them every ING soldier outside the FOB needed some type of ski mask, sock, rag, bandanna or something to urinate on and then to breathe through. I said it may sound gross but could save their lives by breathing through a pee-soaked rag long enough to get away from any chemical attack or explosion.

They relayed the message to all their soldiers and by then B Troop Strykers had returned. We left and I kept having a feeling we were going to get hit with a roadside bomb. It was not the first time I'd had that feeling, so I just scanned and stayed low. I prayed once again for the Lord to hinder the plans of the enemy and for His hedge of protection over us. I prayed once again for angels, wisdom, and safety. While passing the granary to the gas station I saw a huge blast out of the corner of my right eye and heard the explosion. A bomb had exploded next to one of the Iraqi trucks and the explosion was about the size of a shed. Omar was with CPT Walts on his Stryker, and they dismounted. Kaine took charge, so I continued to scan and secure as the Iraqi soldiers fired several warning shots. I asked the driver of the lead truck if everyone was okay, and he said *"kool zain"* (all good). It turned out someone had attached a small explosive device to a full metal fuel can. The explosion was smaller than I'd seen in the past, but I was grateful no one was injured. I thanked Jesus and we continued past the granary. Strangely, a few minutes after the explosion my right leg started bouncing uncontrollably, but I managed to stop it. Odd.

That explosion was nothing compared to the next one we faced, dismounted. I noticed the granary would be a great place to occupy with a company of the IA and their headquarters. We continued north, stopping near the hospital and school there. The Strykers set up a coil formation (like circling the wagons) and we dismounted to survey the area on foot. I looked around and took some pictures while CPT Kaine Walts talked to MAJ Sultan. We discussed which buildings looked best as a future outpost. Kaine liked one across the street with a flag and satellite dish. I agreed, since it had the best field of view and was the tallest building in that vicinity. There was another building with good observation on the surroundings to include the route, and MAJ Sultan liked that one better. CPT Walts said, "Okay, well let's go check it out then." Kaine Walts, his interpreter, MAJ Sultan and I, along with LT Shay and a few sergeants behind us, started walking toward the corner of the building from the open field. As we approached the corner, there was a huge explosion not more than five feet from us..

It seemed to happen in slow motion, because I remember having so many thoughts as it occurred. The first three I remember were these: "Oh my goodness, not again, and not so close while we are on the ground; this thing is right next to us." Also, "We are dead, a giant IED with a huge fireball just exploded next to us and we are dismounted." The last of the three was, "Here comes the shrapnel, it's about to hit my face." All these thoughts seemed to occur simultaneously as shrapnel, dirt, cement, rubble and other debris came flying towards us with the fireball. As it hit us, we were engulfed in a huge black cloud of smoke and soot. It was hot out already, so I don't really recall feeling the heat from the explosion of fire I saw to my left. I took only about three steps to "run for cover" before I realized the explosion had already occurred, shrapnel had flown, I was still alive and I needed to carry out the casualties.

The next three split second thoughts were: "I'm still alive, I can't believe it; how was I not killed? God protected me; there is no other way to explain it. He doesn't want me to die." And then, "CPT Walts and MAJ Sultan were a couple feet to my left, they are still in that cloud of debris, smoke and soot; they're injured for sure. I've got to carry them out of here." My last was, "Oh my word, they've got to be injured badly or missing limbs if they are even still alive." Kaine Walts emerged from the smoke and I saw his bloody nose as he began walking slowly toward the Stryker. I looked back into the blast site at MAJ Sultan and he was hunched over, running behind CPT Walts toward the Stryker. Omar, LT Shay and the other interpreter asked if everyone was okay, as I believe we were all shouting to know. I pulled Kaine to get him to the Stryker faster and snapped a picture as the ramp dropped. He sat on the ramp dripping blood and tried to lie down.

Thoughts of CPT Jacobsen flashed through my head and I was almost certain Kaine had a concussion, as did the rest of us. His was much worse, so I stopped him from lying on the ramp. "You're gonna be okay, it's just a bloody nose," I told him. "You gotta sit up, you can't lie down right now." He tried a second time, obviously dazed, and then stood up off the ramp. I thought it was a good thing, thinking he would step up into the Stryker, but he held his M-4 up and looked angrily in the direction of the blast as he started to walk in that direction. "No no no! You can't go back over there Kaine, we've got to go back, you need to get checked out," I shouted. It was slightly comical, especially since no one was injured beyond that and some hurt eardrums. He reminded me of 'Robocop' the way he moved back toward the blast before we grabbed him. I don't know if he wanted revenge or just wanted to continue the mission by checking out that building, but he was dazed and in need of the aid station. As I told those standing around to get him back on the Stryker, SFC Kirby started shouting he was mad and told everyone to get CPT Walts on the Stryker and said, "Let's go!" As the men did so, that Stryker's .50 cal fired on something, as did several other troopers in the other Stryker with their M-4s. I didn't know if there was a firefight or if they were just shooting at people running away. It turned out that they were all well aimed warning shots near people in the area. They tried to send the message to everyone to clear the area.

After we hopped on the Strykers, I popped out of my hatch (although I was on a different one than I came on). I noticed as soon as I popped up that there was a helmet up top, and I was in someone's spot. As the ramp rolled up, SSG Hasby said, "You want the hatch sir? I'll take it." "No, I got it, I'm good," I answered him. He asked me again "Are you sure sir? I can take it. are you hit?" I looked down at him and said, "Okay, I guess that is your helmet, right?" "Yes sir," he answered. "Okay, go ahead, you got it," I said, as I switched with him. The interpreter on board asked me who was hit and I told him CPT Walts, but he would be fine. He replied, "CPT Walter? He is good man! Oh no!" "He's going to be okay," I told him. "God saved us all; He protected us…it was a complete miracle. We should all be dead right now, but we are all fine." He then asked me if I was injured, but I had never bothered to check myself. I felt around and no blood came off onto my gloves, so I figured I was good, but the adrenaline was slowly wearing off and I felt a slight stinging on my face and some pain in my left arm and leg.

As I continued to thank Jesus aloud repeatedly, I looked all over myself and noticed some small welts on my arm and felt some on my face. We quickly headed back to the FOB and I prayed for us all continuously. LT Shay updated Squadron when we got back, and I stopped and talked to Chaplain Wells and CPT Durmsy. Rich Durmsy pointed out that I had a bunch of small cuts on my face, and as the day went on, I began to feel them more and more as all the adrenaline wore off. I waved down CPT Layes who was on a 4-wheeler on the way out and asked him if he was going to the aid station to see Kaine Walts. He said "No, why, is he hit?" I answered, and he sighed as I explained it was just a bloody nose and a concussion. I hopped on the 4-wheeler with him and yelled over the wind to him as he drove, explaining what happened. When we got to the aid station, Kaine was getting the last of the blood cleaned from his nose while another doc checked his ears.

They sent me in to get checked out too, but I was fine. The only wounds I really had were some cuts on my nose, cheeks and face near my ear. They were just deep enough to draw blood, but not deep enough to do any lasting damage. Compared to the first time I was injured, I didn't really feel wounded, even though as the day went on my face became swollen a bit and I had several signs of a minor concussion (headache, nausea, dizziness, loss of equilibrium, etc.). I was very tired and sore all over (especially my head, face, and left limbs), but knew I shouldn't lie down or sleep. I called up MAJ Sultan to ask how he was doing and explained to him that he shouldn't sleep because he could go into a coma. I told Omar the same and we all stayed awake the whole day.

Sergeant Wadul and Sunburn picked me up from the aid station and were very worried at first, but I told them it was just a few cuts, nothing like last time. SGT Wadul said, "You know sir, if you keep getting wounded like this, we aren't going to let you go outside the wire anymore." I answered him back, "Well, I figure the third time is the charm, so maybe just once more and then I'll be good." The rest of the day was slow until the evening. I felt so blessed and sent out a mass email to everyone praising the Lord for saving me. I still couldn't believe we were protected from certain death. That IED could have destroyed a Stryker. It was designed to explode up and facing the road, so at first I wondered if we had just caught the back blast of it, but we were so close (three to five feet) it wouldn't have mattered. SSG ZT and 'Hitman' said they could see the smoke from the explosion from FOB, over three miles away. The magnitude of the blast and how close we were blew my mind. With no exaggeration, I was literally no more than five feet away and CPT Walts no more than three feet away. I had debris in my goggles and noticed my sunglasses had several dings and a crack in them. Had I not been wearing them at the time, I would be short an eye at a minimum. Praise Jesus! This is what the scene looked like:

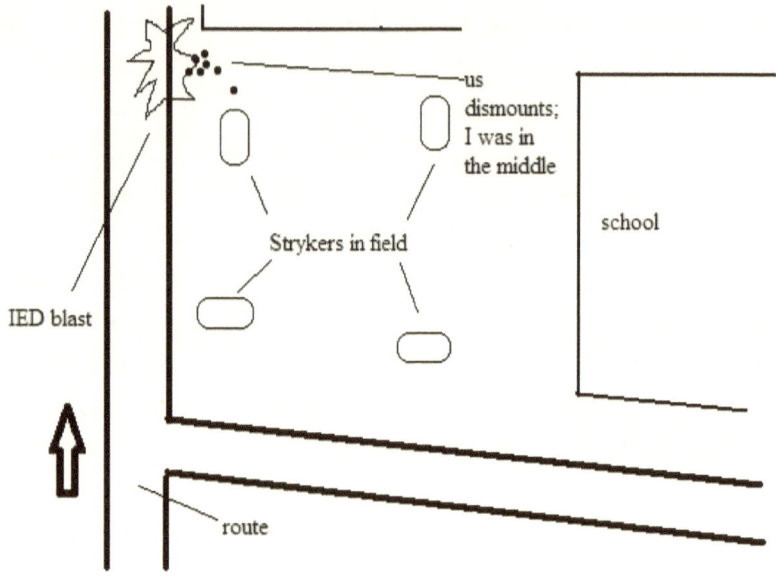

Evening events darkened after 7 p.m. as we heard a radio call about casualties and a car bomb from Mosul Checkpoint. We knew it wasn't our Iraqi soldiers, but the 10th Iraqi Army, still it concerned us. The Squadron XO radioed he wanted all available interpreters at the aid station immediately to receive the mass casualties. I grabbed interpreters and left. Then I discovered what had happened. Even though I had heard on the radio something about children being wounded, it still didn't prepare me for what I saw. The Strykers came screaming up to the aid station minutes after I arrived and the ramps dropped with medics standing by with litters.

The Stryker occupants gently placed a little boy on the first litter. He looked not more than nine years old and had blood on his chest and head. He moaned and tossed and turned as one arm lay limp; he almost fell off the litter, but a soldier steadied him. I watched and prayed as they brought out more children. I believe the total was eight people: seven children and one adult. Another adult was there but didn't look injured. He had blood on him but was walking around talking and trying to help the children. I thought he was the father of some of them. I learned a father of a few of the little girls and one of the boys had died at the checkpoint. They brought more children out of the Strykers. Some little girls were able to walk, thankfully, but it broke my heart to see their dresses and hair covered in blood. Some had shrapnel in their heads. I couldn't help but picture each as though she were my own daughter. I was disgusted someone would do this to innocent little children.

One little girl, approximately eight years old, lay barely moving on a litter as she was carried into the aid station, and her face was completely wrapped in gauze except for her mouth so she could breathe. The side of her mouth stuck out, as though it had been torn from her cheek. More were brought in, each with horrible wounds that pained all of us to see. "I hate that," said CSM Weldo, as the last child was taken out. One boy, who must have been about ten, was put on the ground as others were carried in; his head was covered in blood and gauze, and his arm was also wrapped in gauze and lay limp in a sling. They checked his pulse and declared him dead. The medics shook their heads sadly and asked someone to cover him with a blanket.

I organized the interpreters, sending Fasil in when they needed someone who spoke Turkish. One little girl with wounds on her head and arm but able to walk and sit up was in tears. She cried as she told 'Face' she hoped they could get revenge on the bad people, but she was "afraid from the Americans." He explained we were there to help and make her better. I stood next to her while a medic cleaned her up and 'Face' put his hand on her shoulder to comfort her as they spoke. She was about eleven years old and said she forgot to say her prayers today, as she started slapping herself in the face ('Face' told her to stop). We asked her if she wanted to pray right then, but she said she would do it when she returned to her house. It reminded me of when 1SG Thamer told a man his brother was killed in the bus incident. I told her, "I am praying for you right now and God will make it okay."

'Face' translated, and she just stared at me with such big upset eyes in need of comfort. I wanted so badly to just reach down and hug her, but the medic was cleaning up the blood and I also didn't want to scare her. The helicopters began to spin up. Medics took several litters to them, while others remained in the main section and operating room of the aid station. Most of the families went together by air and some we later transported to the Tal Afar hospital.

The soldiers in the Strykers told me what had happened. They said the enemy vehicle pulled off to the side of the road as Iraqi soldiers were about to search it. The driver wouldn't get out, and then he just blew himself up in the car, devastating the soldiers who searching him, as well as surrounding families inside and outside of their cars. One of the sergeants said he checked the pulse of several Iraqi soldiers at the checkpoint, and they had none – there were five dead. They told me the father of several of the children was dead. I prayed again as I headed back, as helicopters took off and our interpreters were no longer needed. I got back, and after filling everyone in on what happened, I went to my room. I talked to Becky on webcam and she said, "No offense, but your face looks horrible." "That's because I got blown up again today, honey," I answered her. "No, I don't mean that; I mean your eyes and your soul. You like you are completely exhausted mentally and emotionally." I nodded after she said that and explained how everything just seemed to keep building up and hurt more and more, but fortunately God gave me strength to carry on and not let those things keep me down. There was no way I could go on without Him.

April 13, 2005

At 9:30 a.m. I went with Iraqis to Checkpoint Sinjar to occupy the gas station and to do a couple recons of our future Fort Union, the granary. We also dropped off a PKC machinegun with ammunition at Combat Outpost Wolf. I got on the back of LT Shay's Stryker and felt a dreaded fear. It reminded me of other Strykers I've ridden upon without enough protection. It was crazy that we enforced proper force protection with sandbags and kevlar blankets with Iraqis, yet some of our own Strykers roledl out with absolutely none. The sides were sandbagged well but there was nothing on the back at all, absolutely nothing. I realized they had an M240 mounted there and wanted it to flow freely, but I'd been on other Strykers with M240s which were sandbagged very well and also had kevlar blankets. As nice as it was to have a machine gun on the back of the Stryker, I'd rather have my neck and head intact. A soldier with bomb shrapnel in his neck can't fire an M240 anyway. It began to seriously bother me because of all the threats in Tal Afar and of all the injuries we'd had out there. Roadside bombs were the biggest threat and the largest casualty-producing encounter.

Counting Iraqis, over 300 soldiers had been wounded by roadside bombs with over 25 deaths. We'd had less than 50 injuries and 10 deaths from small arms fire, so the larger of the two threats should be dealt with first and foremost, meaning lots of sandbags and kevlar blankets all over every Stryker, especially parts where a bomb could easily send hot shrapnel at high rates of speed at one's head, face, and arms. I told the lieutenant it bothered me and even turned the M240 sideways so it protected my face. I could see everything out on the horizon and next to the Stryker fine. I was most concerned with surviving a roadside bomb first so I would be able to engage enemy in a firefight.

It reminded me of a disagreement I had with SFC E (Heath) back in our Mobile Gun System platoon. Enemy were rarely right next to our vehicles. They were off to the side of the road, down alleyways, in wadi's, on second and third stories and on rooftops. I'd never heard of an enemy within five feet of the vehicle unless he was in a car about to ram us and explode. You only needed to be out of your hatch far enough to cover the above-mentioned threat areas and our larger concern was roadside bomb protection anyway. It didn't matter how much of the battlefield you could see or where you scanned if a bomb exploded right next to you. So, a soldier should travel high enough to counter the largest threat areas but low enough for the surrounding sandbags, Kevlar blankets and other protection measures to do their job: absorb the shrapnel before it gets to the soldier. I was quite aggravated, mostly by the constant smacking of the M240 into my arm and head since I couldn't secure it in a position to provide me much protection.

We took a different route to the gas station and for some reason, as we turned off Hwy-47 and down the dirt road, fear overwhelmed me. I quickly admitted it to the Lord and asked Him to fill me with strength and to help me trust Him. Almost immediately, He did so and for the rest of the mission I felt much better. We dropped off the gas station patrol and headed into the granary. After surveying the entire compound from inside, LT Shay and I dismounted with MAJ Sultan and Ali. We checked out a couple buildings inside the granary compound and it looked as though there would be a lot of space for the battalion to occupy its headquarters there. The entire compound was probably half a mile wide by one mile long and long with walls all around it, buildings inside and of course, the gigantic silos.

We went to the office building and spoke with the manager who suspected we would be occupying it. I pointed to LT Shay and me and said, "We won't occupy it" (which was true, since it would be the Iraqi Army and not the US). We asked him who lived in the three houses inside the compound and how often people and workers come in and out. Other than the supply vehicles and management, about twenty workers come in and out every three days. It sounded perfect. We took a further look around while I took some pictures, and soon headed to Wolf to drop off the PKC. En route to COP (Combat Outpost) Wolf, we stopped at a couple of large unoccupiedbuildings just north of Fort Union. It bugged me to clear it with only four of us (MAJ

Sultan, Ali, the lieutenant, and I), because you couldn't effectively clear a building with just four people. We knew it wasn't occupied in the past, but you never knew if the enemy had moved in or booby-trapped the place. We checked out both buildings, entering the second one from the roof of both, and they were clear. We decided they wouldn't be useful to us. I took some pictures and we continued mission. We didn't dismount at Fort Union, but I got some perfect photos from the sides and rear of the building. Despite some concerns, I was sure we would defend it well against car bombs.

We returned to the FOB, and after eating lunch with Rich Durmsy and LT Berry, SSG ZT, Hitman and I learned that COL Brown definitely wanted 2-14 Cavalry back in the Brigade, so we would end up moving east to either FOB Marez or Endurance. This should occur the end of May, so I would only have a job in Nomad for another month and a half. After we moved, there would be no Iraqis for us to advise, since both other bases already had advisor teams. I would probably take on Unit Movement Officer (UMO) for the Squadron as a full-time job and the rest of the team would be sent elsewhere. It didn't make any of us happy to hear that, but that was life in Iraq and in the Army.

At the brief, LT Cookran gave an amazing brief on how he and his engineer platoon fill in holes with concrete and spray paint them afterwards with an engineer symbol. It was an amazing brief about a process that would help deny the enemy the ability to place more bombs in holes. After he finished his brief, the entire roomful of people applauded. I complimented him personally afterwards because I never knew he was that good. He had done a lot of research and a lot of work and it was impressive. Also, at the briefing, LTC Mavis scolded me for presenting an information slide on the Iraqi Army. He stressed the 109th IA fell under B Troop and they would brief movements. He didn't state it nicely, but I was happy because never again did I need to do a brief slide (at least this deployment).

More of our duties were being phased out and absorbed by B Troop. We didn't do checkpoint inspections anymore, so no one really went outside the wire except for me to help LT Shay and CPT Walts enough to get them rolling on how to take care of the 109th. I coordinated with the Engineers, the 109th and B Troop to have a meeting at 8 p.m., and we discussed the plans for Fort Union with MAJ Sultan. It was good seeing them have the same plan I had in mind. We were on the same page, so I let B Troop and MAJ Sultan do most of the talking with 'Face' interpreting. I explained the plans and movements for the next day (rather excitedly) to SSG Hitcher and he smiled at me and said, "You really enjoy this don't you sir...look at this guy, he's all into some coordination and planning." I laughed and admitted I did love it. "I love being a 'Six' [semi-command position]; XO is okay but being a Platoon Leader or Commander is better for me. I love planning and tactical stuff."

April 14, 2005

The blessings continued. I gave LT Shay and SSG Hasby a tour of the IA compound and we observed several soldiers who had recently been added to Company Two were training hard. It was awesome and I wished I had my camera. I smiled seeing them disciplining soldiers and training them for combat. It saddened my heart slightly, though, to think that some of them may die. Trying not to think further of that, I just smiled at the good job they were doing and moved on. We stopped by the Iraqi TOC and they offered us chai, and MAJ Sultan also gave me a chai set. CPT Walts, 1SG Mulany and LT Shay also ate lunch with Face and MAJ Sultan and discussed a few other matters. An Iraqi officer came in and gave us information on eleven bad guys believed to be terrorists who had just come into a village just outside of Sinjar. We planned to hit it sometime this week. We had a few laughs before our talk became serious. Kaine Walts told me he read an email stating LTC Ahmed was fired effective immediately and the order was just awaiting General Kali's signature. He read this on Monday, so 'hopefully it will happen soon,' I thought. Then the blessings flowed.

The first was that a C Troop Stryker hit a roadside bomb on Hwy-47 (where I just was the day before) that was so big it blew one of the tires over two hundred meters off the road. The entire Stryker was blown up in the air and continued to roll forward after it landed with no wheels. Miraculously, not a person on board was injured – no one had a scratch! The size of the crater in the road was a few feet deep and the size of two Strykers wide. The Stryker was rendered completely totaled.

Shortly after hearing this, I was called to the TOC to send the reports off to Brigade. On my way out, LTC Mavis, CPT Reagle and COL Lueck were all standing outside the TOC, and LTC Mavis said, "There he is." "Did you need me sir?" I asked. He told me LTC Ahmed was fired and needed to get his things packed and leave immediately! I was in shock and said, "Praise the Lord!" He told me to get the interpreter "Suzie" and either SSG Hitcher or ZT and have them stand by with LTC Ahmed. B Troop would transport him to Al Kissik or somewhere else afterward. I sped back to the command post and told them about it. Everyone was excited. SSG ZT was there with Hitman, Suzie, LTC Mavis, COL Lueck and CPT Reagle. They apparently told LTC Ahmed that he was being transferred to a staff position or something.

When I brought Oakley over there for SSG ZT while 'Saddam' packed his belongings, MAJ Sultan and CPT Ismail were outside along with SGM Svouk and a few others. I asked if they knew, and MAJ Sultan showed me a letter (in Arabic) and was happy. I didn't have time to read it, but I guess it said LTC Ahmed was relieved and being moved, or perhaps that MAJ Sultan was the new Battalion Commander, or both. Hitman and ZT said other than trying to delete a number from his cell phone (which they didn't allow) and trying to tell the Brigade IA Commander he was moving, Ahmed left quietly. Hitman almost drew his 9mm when LTC Ahmed prayed and then grabbed for his pistol afterwards, but he placed it on the desk and stood up. They noticed several pistols and rifles in his room, but other than that everything seemed normal. B Troop transported him out of there and he was officially gone. Praise God! The prayers worked…but it took some persistent praying and some patience and perseverance (a lot of P's). I was very thankful and I knew we would see a drastic improvement in the Iraqi Battalion.

'Face' and 'Jimmy' were talking about getting the Iraqis to send a detail or squad of men to pick up some trash, but when Jimmy called them no one came. Finally, 'Face' radioed them to come pick up some supplies and some other presents. I heard 'Face' and Jimmy laughing after calling this up and they filled me in. When a squad arrived within five minutes, Face had tricked them into coming with an empty truck to load supplies, and instead they had to pick up their trash. It gave us a good laugh.

April 15, 2005

The morning started with LT Shay and me having a meeting with Major Sultan. When we arrived in his new office (Ahmed's old one), I gave him a laminated map and marked in permanent marker where the outposts, checkpoints and forts were. He liked the map, and after discussing the occupation of Fort Union that night, I briefed him on a general concept for future operations. I had to leave halfway through the meeting because my Unit Movement Officer course started at noon, so SFC Walenz and LT Shay discussed future training and leave for the 109th. My suggestion (which was exactly what SFC Walenz was thinking) was to have three Companies out of the FOB on duty and one company (or two platoons of a company) that temporarily returned to base to prepare for "*mujas*."

They would then go on vacation and after returning, that company would undergo a week of training under SFC Walenz and LT Shay's platoon. After the week of training, that unit would go back out to switch out with another one outside the FOB. I thought it would work well because not only will each company have a set rotation for leave, but they would also get a good week's worth of good training in before heading back out of the wire. They all seemed to love being outside the wire at the COP's, so after a good week of hard training on the FOB, they'd be ready to get back out there. MAJ Sultan liked the idea and the three of them-- and 'Face'-- continued to discuss things as I left for my course.

When I returned, SSG ZT briefed me on some sad news. The lieutenant at the power station tried to take some initiative and sent one of his Iraqi trucks over to get some fuel from Mosul Checkpoint. Three of his men were killed when a bomb destroyed the truck. Two died instantly and the third soldier burned inside the truck, unable to be evacuated. I hadn't gotten their names yet. It was so sad this had to happen when they were trying to take some initiative. I prayed for their families and for the soldiers who grieve their loss. It angered me that people just sat in their homes in this city and waited for US or Iraqi forces to drive past their house so they could blow them up. It was such a tragic war.

On a brighter note, I got two emails – the first from a friend saying he read my email about being wounded on a link on my church's website (I didn't know they had one). It was a surprise to see my email on there. The pastor shared, dated April 14, 2005:

This week I read an email from Matt Sacra. He and his wife, Rebecca, regularly attend our Saturday night "conneXion" service. She is due with their first child on April 30th, the same day he is expected home to see his family. Pastor Peter says Matt emails him often, but this one everyone needs to read!

Subject: Wounded again; Praise Jesus!

All:

I was wounded again today, so I just wanted you to hear it from me. Please get on your knees and thank Jesus immensely though! I wasn't wounded as badly as last time, but the explosion was worse, and I should be dead!

I was dismounted from the Stryker with another Captain and some others, and we were about to round the corner of a building. No exaggeration, we were all 3 to 5 feet on the ground away from a fireball producing IED (The explosion was seen miles away). It was at the curb on the road right next to us. I prayed for Jesus' hedge of protection and angels to allow no harm to come to us, and He delivered! Thank you all for your prayers.

The only way we survived was God's protection. Make no mistake. Rock and shrapnel hit my face, but none penetrated past the first layer or two of my skin. Rocks, concrete, and debris hit my eyes, but my Oakley sunglasses cracked and absorbed the hits. Other than a few minor cuts on my face, and welts on my left arm and leg, I am fine, and should be ready for action again tomorrow.

I say again, PRAISE THE LORD! The other Captain got a nosebleed and a couple scratches, but that's about it. Keep praying, it's working! It's a miracle that the 6 of us are not missing limbs, eyes, or worse!

In Christ,
Matt (Love you Bec!! See you in a few weeks!)

"For He will command His angels concerning you to guard you in all your ways. On their hands they will bear you up, so that you will not dash your foot against a stone." Psalm 91:11-12

It smiled to think others will be blessed by an awesome miracle from our Creator and Savior. As I was writing, over fifty Iraqi soldiers, a platoon of US soldiers, engineers, bomb experts and helicopters went out to prepare to occupy the new fort. I got the second email from my friend Shelton's mom. It was extremely encouraging and brought wonderful praise to our Lord. 'Sac' is my nickname. Here it is:

Sac, I pray all is well with you. Shelton's email about your injury was a bit rattling – at first. But I had to remember What a Mighty God We Serve. I had to remember that the Lord is our light and our salvation, whom shall we fear? I had to remember that the Lord is the strength of our lives; of whom shall we be afraid? I had to remember that when the wicked, even our enemies and our foes, come upon us to eat up our flesh, they will stumble and fall. I had to remember that though a host should encamp against us, our hearts shall not fear; though war should rise against us, in this will we be confident. For in our time of trouble (God) He shall hide us in His pavilion. I had to remember that now shall our heads be lifted up above our enemies round about us: therefore will we offer in His tabernacle sacrifices of joy: We will sing, yea, We will sing praises unto the Lord. While Shonti was in Iraq I reminded him constantly that God will never leave or forsake you and I know you know that. Sac, you are a true warrior for Christ who is putting on the whole armour of God. I am so proud of you because I know you stay in His presence and you are under His anointing. My prayer is for you to walk out of Iraq – I always hold God to His promises because I know His promises are true for He is not a man, so He does not lie. I speak life for you for I know you shall live and not die because God said it in His Word. The word of your testimony has already and will lead many to Christ. PRAISE GOD! Be encouraged – like the song says Don't wait until the battle's over, shout now – I'm shouting now. Hallelujah. Love Ya, Ms. G

I shouted for joy and praised God after reading that, and it greatly encouraged me and gave me strength from the Lord. Then one more amazing thing happened. While SSG Hitcher was out with B Troop on LT Shay's Stryker, a car bomb hit. Both ducked and saw and felt the fireball as it billowed across the Stryker. Those watching in the Stryker behind thought the entire Stryker was destroyed, since it was entirely engulfed in flames. Other than some singed hairs on 'Hitman''s neck, no one was even injured. Our God and that Stryker are both amazing. Soldiers searched nearby houses afterwards and apprehended a man with a video camera, a cell phone and some grenades. 'Hitman' said when they grabbed this guy, he tried to kiss LT Shay, who punched him as a result. The terrorist fell from the punch just as the Stryker ramp dropped, and it landed on the guy's head. It didn't hit the ground as hard as normal and the terrorist surprisingly survived, likely with a severe concussion. 'Hitman' then grabbed him and threw him in the Stryker.

April 16, 2005

Sergeant Wadul returned with B Troop from the Fort Union occupation around 5 a.m. and said it went great. Helicopters circled above, traffic stopped on the roads while Strykers scanned and bomb teams went in with sniffing dogs to ensure the place was not rigged with explosives. Engineers emplaced barriers and wire outside while the Iraqis cleared rooms and built positions with sandbags. It turned out the terrorists were not pleased with the Iraqi Army's occupation of yet another fort, so they attacked it that afternoon, firing light and heavy machine guns, rifles, sniper rifles and even RPGs. I heard later that there were about six RPG fins on the ground in various places. The IA fought well and only one of them was wounded, in the leg.

Fortunately, LT Shay had just set out to do checks and so two minutes after the firefight began, Strykers showed up. When the sixty some IA soldiers continued to engage the enemy, followed by .50 cal and Mark 19 from Strykers, the enemy retreated into the maze of houses. LT Shay took the casualty back to the FOB and I thanked God it was only a gunshot to the leg, nothing worse. I also found out that the report from the day before was incorrect; two Iraqis were killed. One was killed immediately and the other burned in the truck. There was no third death. CPT Reagle also got hit with a huge roadside bomb just north of Tal Afar. Other than a ringing in the ears (later checked at the aid station), he was fine.

Our status officially changed as a Nomad Team. We were then a section attached to B Troop and didn't fall directly under Squadron anymore. B Troop would handle reports and issues with Squadron. On my final radio transmission to Squadron, CPT Nerph tried to argue with me. I simply told B Troop on the Squadron channel that the Iraqi Army had a source at Combat Outpost Wolf who was willing to lead Strykers to a terrorists' house – those responsible for blowing up the leave bus. He tried to tell me I wasn't to task units to do that, and the information had to go to Squadron first. I corrected him and explained that B Troop worked with the 109th IA and I was just letting them know, not tasking anyone. He got all mad and responded with more of an explanation and wanted me to acknowledge. I had already told him that I understood, so I answered, "Roger, I already said that. I understand." After that, I determined that the conversation was over, so I started to walk away. He angrily said something else about me responding with "acknowledged" or something, but I ignored him and switched radio channels.

April 17, 2005

Another day in paradise. When 'Hitman' and ZT returned from a mission, 'Hitman' admitted what many of us felt (except maybe SGT Wadul) "I'll be honest man, I don't like going out the wire anymore, not after getting hit by that [car bomb] the other day, that junk was crazy." I completely agreed with him, as did SSG ZT. I paid Mohammed who returned from purchasing generators and sunglasses. I checked the budget, and we were almost completely out of money. That was exciting since the Ministry of Defense was now going to be responsible for funding the Iraqi Army Divisions and Brigades who would send supplies and funds down to Battalions. Thatwas opposed to what we used to do, which was to send funds from MNSTC-I (Multi-National Security Transition Command – Iraq) to the Iraqi Security Forces Coordinators at Brigade, to Battalion liasions (us here in Nomad) and finally to the Iraqi Battalions. Not only was it going to be a huge load off us, but it also symbolizeed the increase of responsibility of the Iraqi forces and the decrease in responsibility of US forces.

Sergeant Wadul, Major Sultan and I went with Lieutenant Shay and B Troop to the granary. I prayed as we went out again as always, and we soon arrived at the granary compound without incident. While LT Shay, an engineer LT and MAJ Sultan discussed ground operations through Oakley, SGT Wadul and I made our way to the top of the granary silos and up to the top of the huge tower in the middle of it, which I'm guessing was over 1,000 feet. I found a great number of battle positions up there and took some good photos to share. We climbed up a a small ladder with a metal cage around it onto the top of the roof, and we were so high. My fear of heights kicked in, and even worse, a fear some terrorist watching might snipe us, shoot an RPG or mortar and we would fall or be seriously injured up there. I prayed for strength and once again, God granted it. I made it to the top with SGT Wadul and SSG Hasby and took some pictures from up there. The city of Tal Afar looked beautiful from up there and it was a shame it was such a violent and dangerous place to live at that time .

The granary would make an amazing fort or outpost and the wonderful tactical positions there were endless. The only problem was the noise of the machines running up there, so the men would require earplugs and radio-talk would be more difficult in some places. We made our way back down and into the Strykers and found out Combat Outpost Wolf had received enemy fire from a building just down the street. They returned fire, raided the building and captured two detainees. The men captured were supposedly the owners of the house/ blacksmith shop and claimed to know nothing about the terrorists with masks who fired upon Iraqi forces from their building. After finishing an inspection of COP Wolf and grabbing the detainees on our Stryker, we headed south to check out a possible bomb and checked on the gas station. Thank God we all got back safely.

I ate lunch with MAJ Sultan and later discussed discipline and punishments in the Battalion with CSM Mohammed. He listened intently as I explained how things could work better in the 109th. I asked him a question to see if he would get it right, and he did. "What are the three most important things to the soldiers in your Battalion; what do they care about the most?" 'Face' interpreted and CSM Mohammed answered in Arabic, "*Mujas, floose, wow ukul* (vacation, money, and food)." I laughed after he said exactly what I expected. I said although we didn't want to affect the vacation of the soldiers since it was the only means of getting money to their families, we could strongly influence their decisions by adjusting their pay and food. I suggested every time a soldier was insubordinate, his sergeant or first sergeant should write it down. On payday, each company could come one at a time, with its first sergeant and his list taking money away from those who had been insubordinate or undisciplined. They could give the money to the battalion or return it to the Ministry of Defense. I gave other examples, like feeding a soldier Halal meals instead of well-cooked hot chow. He got excited and started writing down what I said. Hopefully they would implement that plan and discipline would improve drastically.

Later, I wrote down Iraqi Army issues to speak with B Troop about. I shared the biggest issues we currently had with the IA with LT Shay and he had begun to work on them already. CPT Ismail, the Iraqi Battalion Intelligence Officer, came by our office with detainee paperwork. We typed it up after interpreters translated it. I took them over to the detention facility with CPT Ismail and showed him and 'Face' some Bradleys and Abrams tanks from 3rd ACR which had just arrived. They were impressed.

Toward the end of the evening, I met with Major Sultan, taking 'Face' again as well as LT Shay. I brought my laptop with each granary picture and showed them to MAJ Sultan and the officers from Company Two (the new ones from Dahuk). They all seemed eager to occupy it and do a good job helping their brothers outside the wire. For the first time I was impressed with every officer in a company. They showed the same interest and vigor for planning as they did for training the other day when I gave LT Shay and SSG Hasby a tour of the IA compound. I explained frame by frame everything about each position and location and its respective view. 'Face' interpreted, and MAJ Sultan even briefed them on several of the pictures. The Company Commander and other officers asked several questions and assured me they were ready to take charge and occupy it.

They also said whenever they heard their brothers outside the wire were in contact, they wanted to go and help, but American forces on the FOB would't let them. I said I could relate but said once their battalion occupied the granary as its headquarters, all missions would be based out of there and no US forces would occupy the granary. I told them it would be MAJ Sultan's call as to what came and went in the Battalion, and Iraqi Army forces would do most of the fighting, only calling on the US forces for support as needed. I concluded by saying that over the next few months the fight in Iraq would transition so Iraqi Army soldiers did 70% of the missions with US doing 30%. LT Shay talked to MAJ Sultan about the re-supply mission the next night and the exact date of the granary occupation. Assuming they all had helmets and body armor, MAJ Sultan's men would be ready.

Before I went to bed, Becky and I spoke on webcam – a disturbing discussion about me possibly dying. I said I thought it was because I had been wounded again and we had less than two weeks until I came home for leave. She agreed and we shared scriptures with each other, like Matthew 6:34 and 1 Peter 5:7, dealing with our worries and fears. I prayed God would bring me home safely to my ladies and continue to allow me to glorify Him and build His kingdom.

April 18, 2005

Little happened today until evening. I met with MAJ Sultan about a few issues like his amount of body armor and helmets (or lack thereof) and the future occupation of yet another outpost on Hwy-47. I was surprised when I went over there because the 109th IA had a new Battalion Commander. MAJ Sultan would be the XO once again and COL Hajji was the new boss. He was a Kurdish Muslim man and on first impression seemed very well educated and respectable. He and MAJ Sultan were apparently good friends from long ago in the army. I didn't know Kurds were even allowed in Saddam Hussein's army, let alone to be officers, but I guess he was. Aside from COL Hajji and MAJ Sultan stressing the importance of getting helmets, body armor and occupying the granary silo first before any other outposts, I learned a great deal about the future of the 109th.

COL Hajji explained how the Iraqi Army was supposed to work and he mapped out the terms for soldiers joining and staying in.

He said a team from the recruiting station in Arbil would come to the Wolf Battalion soon to examine all its soldiers and officers. This team, supported by the Ministry of Defense, would cut the size of the Battalion down to its authorized numbers in addition to making sure all soldiers adhere to Iraqi Army rules. All soldiers had to be between the ages of 18 and 40, able to read and write, pass a health and complete medical examination, to include surgeries, hearing loss, and other disqualifications, and both their mother and father had to be Iraqi citizens. If any soldier did not meet these requirements, he would be released. I inquired about those who'd already been wounded in action and he said they would be compensated for the rest of their lives, which was good. Each soldier meeting all requirements would contract for two years in the Iraqi Army and receive a social security number tracked in the pay and equipment systems. The new system of punishments would apply to him and he would be detained for any absences.

I was shocked to hear all of this – things were finally getting organized. COL Hajji explained (through Face) that the 109th IA (formerly ING) was like a rogue outfit, one of the last units to change to an actual Iraqi Army Battalion. He said many officers would be cleared out of this battalion because of them not being qualified to be officers in the Iraqi Army. When the Wolf Battalion initially hired individuals off the street, it just assigned them rank and positions. The Iraqi Army did this entirely differently, with contracts and registration numbers and military education for officers. The requirements for Iraqi officers were the same as for soldiers with the addition of these: graduation from high school (not as common in this country), completion of at least two years in an officer training academy or military college and passing grades in lectures and on tests for completion of their training. Many officers in the Battalion did not meet the requirements and would be given the chance to attend the academy, become a sergeant or regular soldier or be told to leave. Some would possibly not even meet the requirements to become a soldier, so they would not even be given any of the above chances.

During this discussion I learned from Oakley (who popped in) that one Wolf Battalion captain (who had promoted himself to major) was a sergeant in the Iraqi Civil Defense Corps, where Oakley was a sergeant major. It was amazing to learn all of this and exciting to see that the 109th, or whatever it will be called, would be reformed. I learned all Iraqi Army soldiers were required by the Ministry of Defense to work two weeks and then have one week of vacation, which might have been wonderful for them, but it was bad for training purposes. Maybe it would work, who knows? At the end of our conversation, we discussed the occupation of the city and it seemed COL Hajji was on the same page as MAJ Sultan and me. He seemed very cooperative and willing to give his best to this Battalion, the Iraqi Army and his country.

When I returned to the Nomad office, CPT Reagle was there discussing the future of Nomad and the Squadron. FOB Marez (my last base in Mosul) would be our destination and Nomad would dissolve before we left. The original plan was for everyone to go to the Troop they came from in Nomad and for SFC Aeris and me to remain the only liasons to the Iraqi Army Brigade which was in charge of the 10th, 12th and 109th IA. Since we were going away, I would likely become the assistant S4 (Supply and Logistics) in the Squadron, my primary job being Squadron UMO (Unit Movement Officer), and Woody might return to B Troop. Regardless, Nomad would be gone for good in two weeks to a month. After we finished teaching B Troop and 3rd ACR how to be liaisons to Iraqi Battalions, they would be responsible. After all of this was completed, we would move to FOB Marez and continue life in Iraq from there. 3rd ACR would assume responsibility for Tal Afar and the surrounding area, backing the 4th Iraqi Army Brigade, which would consist of the 109th in west Tal Afar, the 12th in east Tal Afar and Al Kissik, and the 10th in northeast Tal Afar, Fort Tal Afar and Abu Mariyah.

April 19, 2005

This day was very windy. After we completed a quick mission to Checkpoint Sinjar, the wind picked up more and more and a sandstorm blew into the entire city, FOB and surrounding areas. It wasn't nearly as big or as bad as the one back in October when I first got to Iraq but was nonetheless cumbersome. It provided excellent concealment for Sergeant Wadul and about 40 Iraqi soldiers and one officer who occupied Fort Tejon on Hwy-47 halfway between COP Wolf and Checkpoint Sinjar. I spoke to some of them the dire need of the 109th for helmets and body armor.

An odd thing happened in the morning when a Major Bennet from the Brigade Advisor Support Team group came by to use the internet (there are two Major Bennets here). I was talking to him and he asked me where I was from originally. I told him I was born and raised in Maryland. He said he had spent time at Fort Meade, and I related we lived close to Ft. Meade when my dad worked the for National Security Agency. He said his brother-in-law worked there and asked if I knew the name Marion Brown. I said the name sounded familiar. My next question was, "Does he have a son named Tim or Timmy?" "Yeah, that's my nephew!" He answered. What a small world! It turned out MAJ Bennet is the uncle of an old friend of mine from elementary, middle school, and high school. Here I was in Iraq, living in the same area as his uncle. I sent Tim an email and continued with my day after reminiscing with MAJ Bennet for a while. I would be going with a B Troop platoon to Dahuk the next day – a four-hour drive. It would be nice though, because Dahuk is in Kurdistan, and I heard US troops there could leave body armor and weapons in the Strykers because it was so peaceful and terrorism-free in that city.

April 20, 2005

This day was both an amazing blessing yet also a humbling experience. We tried to get the Iraqis ready after 5:30 a.m. for our trip to Dahuk. When they were finally ready, about twenty of them loaded into the back of a truck in civilian clothes, with only about two in uniform. I shook my head in disbelief and told them all to get out. They had leave passes signed by the Battalion Commander – the Iraqi Brigade Commander gave them permission to go on leave today. I explained to them once more that LTC Mavis wasn't allowing any leave. I hated for them to be all ready and tell them they weren't going on '*mujas*' when someone told them they could go, but it wasn't my rule. Anyway, it took too long for them to get ready so the four Strykers, two modified Humvees and the FMTV (a big army truck – CPT Durmsy was in this one) headed off without them. LT Burkhart was in one of the Humvees. As soon as I realized we were taking out Humvees I was concerned about roadside bombs. On the way up I rode in a Stryker, but my huge concern was for Rich Durmsy and Dan Burkhart, so I prayed a lot for them on the way out and as we rode on Hwy-47.

As we passed COP Union, I felt imminent doom. I prayed harder and as I prayed, I saw smoke from the explosion (even from inside the hatch) and heard the huge blast of the roadside bomb. I sat up straight immediately, asked if everyone was okay and who was hit. Our Stryker pulled over and LT Shay said one of the Humvees was hit and injuries were minor. I was certain it was Dan Burkhart's Humvee. The ramp on our Stryker dropped and I imagined having to evacuate casualties right there on route Hwy-47 where there could be more bombs buried and most definitely enemies watching. I was partly right bout the Hwy-47 part, but fortunately wrong about everything else. We dismounted right off route Hwy-47 and needed to search a vehicle. Since we weren't reacting to casualties, I assumed everyone must be okay. I found out later it had in fact Dan's Humvee and it blew up on his side, but only cracked the thick glass on the outside and nothing more; this was simply amazing considering SSG Stringfellow saw the rest that failed to explode: 122mm mortars.

I guarded the vehicle owner with my M-4 while Oakley searched him, and LT Shay searched the vehicle. He didn't have anything on him, so we let him go, and on my way back into the Stryker I heard over the radio that we were going to secure the area while we waited for the bomb-disposal team to come and blow it. I also heard several bombs were daisy-chained, but obviously unfinished since they hadn't blown up yet. We kept an eye on the area while waiting for the bomb-disposal team so the enemy didn't have an opportunity to finish it. When the bomb-disposal folks arrived with another security element, we took off for Dahuk as I thanked the Lord for everyone being okay.

The borders of Kurdistan, the republic or province of Iraq full of mainly Kurds, was amazing. There were checkpoints out in the middle of nowhere on roads with walls surrounding them and walls lining the countryside. Where walls weren't practical there were chain-link barbed-wire fences. Every so often was a hill almost like a large manmade mound with a battle position at the top and two or three Kurdish Peschmerga manning the weapons. White rocks spelled out the English letters 'ING" on the green grass of the hillsides. It was like we were in a completely different country. I was out of the hatch at this point to see the giant lake in the area which stretches for miles. I gave PFC Parsons a break (and a nap). I took several pictures and was in awe at the beauty of the giant blue lake, flowing fields of green, brown, and yellow vegetation and lush trees.

The houses looked European or even American. It didn't look anything like the rest of Iraq. You could tell they took genuine care of their land – barely any trash on the ground at all – I had to search for it instead of having to scan for a clean spot of ground in the rest of

Iraq. Speaking of searching and scanning, we mostly set our weapons on the top of the Strykers and manned cameras instead. Oakley popped up from LT Shay's hatch briefly and recognized it from his trip there 15 years ago. He was Kurdish too, from the Yzidee religion. He immediately said, "Oh, very very safe here, no problems. You come here Kurdistan you have no problems – very nice, very beautiful." I smiled and praised God, and he popped back inside. I took so many pictures because it reminded me of the beautiful parts of Seattle or Tacoma, Washington near where I was stationed at Fort Lewis.

  We finally arrived in Dahuk. It was "off da-hook" as some say, and I was again stunned. It was like being on a vacation. I was so glad for this opportunity and we parked our Strykers on the hills at the edge of the city near some houses and dropped ramp. Everyone took their gear off and put their M-4's in the Strykers. Other than my M9 under my Desert Combat Uniform top and a small knife, I was in the same uniform I wore in the US before deploying – no body armor, no helmet (or even a hat) and no M-4. It was great. At first it felt awkward, but when children from surrounding houses came up to us and shook our hands and tried their best to speak to us, it was very warming. No snide looks from adults giving us the "I want to cut off your head" stare like in Tal Afar, Mosul or other cities. I even walked over to a school after playing a soccer game with some of the kids.

  SSG Holmes and SSG Stringfellow joined me and we accidentally ruined every teacher's class. The kids couldn't be controlled, and they poured out of the classrooms to shake our hands, wave at us, or say "Mister, mister, what's your name? How are you?" It was so funny, and the teachers just shook their heads or told the kids to get back inside. The principal invited us in for chai and it felt so weird to be in a school in Iraq with no gear on or anything. The school was nice and clean and way better than any school in Tal Afar or Mosul I'd been in. We sat and talked (through Oakley) to them for a bit and then left. Twenty minutes later, the teachers and principal decided to let the children off with a half day in celebration of our visit. The kids ran, flocked and swarmed us, and it was wonderful. They showed us artwork, tried to talk to us, and many shook our hands. If one of us began to cheer, all the children began to cheer in a big crowd around each US soldier on the ground. If we clapped our hands, they did it, and chanted or cheered as well.

If they understood perfect English, it would have been a perfect opportunity to share Christ with them, but I just enjoyed the children, as he would have. I felt like the President of the United States since I had literally hundreds of children shaking my hand. Some came back and shook it a second time. After playing and running with them, I climbed on top of a Stryker and they came up to me about fifteen at a time with pens and paper, handing them to me for autographs. It was hilarious. I printed my name in all caps and then followed it up with the Arabic/Kurdish spelling of 'Matt' with Arabic/Kurdish letters (which are mostly the same as ours, with a few exceptions).

The Humvee came back from inside the city center and I decided to take a trip in too. A few of us piled in there and headed into the center with our gear, although we really didn't need it. As we drove through the streets, completely clean and well-paved (to include the medians), I noticed almost every block had a traffic cop and every three or four blocks had a police officer with a 9mm pistol. It showed the difference for this country was in its people. Like any true democracy, the people had the power to make the difference. There was zero terrorism in Kurdistan and its cities like Dahuk because the people didn't tolerate it. They had excellent physical security with walls, wire and checkpoints, and their cities were so clean it would be hard for anyone to hide a bomb in the road. Government officials were everywhere. If a terrorist somehow managed to sneak in and attempted to make a bomb, at least five people would see it and report it immediately to a policeman or other government official less than one hundred meters away. The people cared so much they'd probably be willing to risk their lives assaulting a terrorist, much like Todd Beamer did with others on his September 11, 2001 flight.

If only the people of Tal Afar, Mosul, Ramadi, Baghdad, Fallujah and other cities cared about getting rid of terrorists, what a change there would be. All Multi-National Forces were doing our best to increase security by better equipping the Iraqi Army and occupying outposts and forts in cities, but the people in each city would have to step up to the plate and refuse to tolerate terrorism in their neighborhoods. All it would take is for a citizen to call our hotline when they saw a bomb, or discreetly walk over to an outpost to inform the IA when a terrorist placed it. If a neighbor noticed another neighbor with an RPG launcher, he could contact the police, Iraqi or US forces, and we could respond immediately to confiscate it. I knew we were a long way off, but we had also come such a long way. I remembered reading about an operation the last summer when the city of Tal Afar was under siege by US forces. Now half the city was more stable since Iraqi Army forces had occupied it, cutting off the terrorists' options.

We drove downtown in the Humvee – just four of us plus Oakley. Three stayed at the Humvee, while Oakley and I walked around to buy some things in the market, including three movies on one disk. Then I watched the Humvee with SGT Lee while the other two guys left. Shortly after they left, some kids came up to try to talk to us and sell us gum and necklaces. I talked to them, but after getting my food, movies and three waters, I had only one dollar left, so I didn't buy anything from them. They kept telling me I needed to get a Pepsi, but I had three waters (bought for a dollar) and had no desire for a Pepsi. They insisted off and on for five minutes, so finally I said, "Okay, bring me Pepsi." They brought two of them and handed me one, putting the other on top of the Humvee for SGT Lee, who also insisted he didn't want the Pepsi. He didn't drink it at first, but after ten minutes or so, he finally decided to open it. I started mine right away, even though I preferred to drink my water. It was a gift, so I drank most of it.

I bartered for a bead necklace for Becky, but the kid wouldn't take my dollar and phone card. We got ready to go and right before I got in the Humvee, the kids started saying, "Mister, you give me dollar, give me dollar. Dollar for Pepsi." I was shocked, because I had thought it was a gift, so I handed back the rest of it and just got into the Humvee. I could barely move (it was very cramped). The kids kept yelling for me to give them a dollar as we drove away and I told them, "You gave me Pepsi!" We drove off and stopped at a supermarket on our way back to the Strykers. It was as nice and as clean as an American one, if not cleaner. The only difference was the bathroom (like all bathrooms in this country) was a hole in the stall with a weird water flushing system inside. Othewise it was like a US supermarket. When I came outside, there were those kids again, asking for money from SGT Lee; they had followed us across the city somehow to get their dollar. I finally decided to give them my last dollar as we drove off, but I couldn't get it out of my pocket, so I threw them a 250 dinar bill, which is just less than a quarter. We got back to the Strykers and waited for CPT Durmsy to return with the big truck full of supplies. Several children still swarmed the Strykers and there were a few little girls I imagined Katelyn might look like when she is five years old.

We threw candy to the kids as we drove off and headed back to "war-country." As we left Kurdistan, I marveled again at the Peschmerga security outposts everywhere. A soldier had a bloody nose, so I rode out of his hatch. We soon made it back to Tal Afar and as we entered the city I feared for my life more than both times I was wounded. I felt such an impending doom as we reentered the city and drove down route Hwy-47. I was irritated, with a mix of anger and fear, and couldn't understand the logic behind having the M240 able to swivel without sandbags when firefights were so rare, yet bombs were so common. I prayed persistently the entire way back and told the Lord my every thought. I popped my head down occasionally, checking on the FBCB2 battle computer screen at extreme danger areas. Surprisingly, there were no explosions on Hwy-47, and we all made it back to the FOB safe and sound, Praise Jesus!

When I got back in, I shared the experience with team Nomad and they briefed me on what happened while I was gone. One of the new advisor teams working with the 10th Battalion reported a roadside bomb by talking to us face to face since they didn't have radios up and running. Its location was the same spot where Sunburn and I were wounded. Just as SGT Wadul was about to call it up, he heard on the radio it had already blown up when some soldiers passed it, killing one Iraqi 10th Battalion soldier. I couldn't believe the stupidity of what had happened. The three cardinal necessities in any military organization are this: shoot, move, and communicate. Because the internet had been a higher priority to these new advisor support teams than radio communication with other units, it cost the life of one of their IA soldiers. By the time they found out about the bomb, walked down to our Nomad office and we called it up, they could have just called it up immediately themselves (if they had a working radio) and directed the soldiers to take a different route. Because of incompetence another soldier was dead. Some may not have cared as it was an Iraqi soldier, but to me, and many of us, they were just as important as US soldiers on the battlefield.

Becky and I talked on webcam for a bit, and she mentioned the lovely baby shower the wives of my old platoon held for her. I vented to her about the sandbag issue, and she mentioned it reminded her of the discussions some of us had back in my old unit about riding high out of the hatch. I recalled disagreements in the platoon about it, and that I always told everyone we didn't need to see positions right beside our Strykers as badly as we needed to see down alleyways and the second or third stories of buildings. Some insisted on being so high out of the hatch when the largest threat in Mosul was car bombs and the largest threat in Tal Afar was roadside bombs. You couldn't spot most of them, and even if you could, it would be too late at that point because they would blow and seriously wound or kill you. So, it always made more sense to me to ride low in the hatch so I could see out and engage any enemy in the alleyways or buildings, but not so high that I was more likely to catch shrapnel.

Becky said one of the topics at her baby shower was Sergeant Youn and how if it were someone else in his position, they would have been fine. She said the other wives described how Jo Youn liked to ride high out of his hatch saying, "I like to be higher so I can see." I was thankful he was still alive, but I knew his life would never be the same. He may never be of the same mind. I explained to Becky that it bothered me intensely that due to poor tactical opinions, people were killed or seriously injured. I always tried to tell everyone to get lower when I noticed they were riding too high, but perhaps it was a hard lesson for some to learn. Becky also told me Will and LT Kim were still recovering from third-degree burns. They were still in the hospital because of doctors' fears of infection. I didn't realize LT Kim's wound was so bad, but I was once again glad they were all still alive.

April 21, 2005

Staff Sergeants ZT and Hitrick did the gas station mission and re-supply and said there were two roadside bombs there near the entrance. They secured the area while bomb disposal folks came, but it just drove home the point that we needed to rethink the way B Troop and the Iraqis conducted these gas station missions. Back when we occupied checkpoints and rotated them every day, we lost many Iraqi soldiers to roadside bombs. We eventually learned it was best to permanently occupy them. We were now making the same mistake with the gas station. Men occupied it almost every day and it was always in the morning during daylight hours. Bombs had been placed on just about every route into the traffic circle at the gas station, to include the gas station itself (that morning). I brought it up to LT Shay and CPT Reagle, but neither seemed concerned. CPT Reagle's answer was, "It'll be okay; they just take different routes." I told him different routes didn't matter if it was in daylight and bombs were located just outside the gas station, which had only two entrances, and both had bombs there.

SSG ZT said the one near him and the Stryker he was on was built from three 155mm rounds wired together with det cord, ready to blow from inside a garbage bag. We either needed to occupy the gas station permanently or occupy it when no one was awake in the city. For some reason, the enemy rarely seemed to detonate bombs between midnight and 5 a.m. This was my biggest concern, but no one wanted to really listen except for our small Nomad team. I supposed more people would care if someone died out there on the way to the gas station or several people were seriously wounded. Then they would wake up and relearn the same lesson as before saying, "Oh, we shouldn't send Iraqis out in the daytime to the gas station every morning since enemies blow up roadside bombs there all the time."

Sergeant Wadul and Sunburn did the Cordon and Search and raid tonight with Oakley, who was all too excited to raid a mosque and capture an Imam. I didn't know how it went because it was after midnight and they came back after I was already in bed.

April 22, 2005

First Sergeant Thamer and his men were going out in the morning for the gas station mission and eleven others were on their way to Checkpoint Sinjar. I had a horrible feeling about the gas station mission and was still mad about it from the previous day. I'd also never seen Thamer so scared. He was usually full of energy and excitement for missions, but that day, I saw dread in his eyes and knew without speaking to him as we shook hands that he was thinking and feeling the same thing I was. I pictured in my mind rolling out to the gas station in the two Strykers with his four trucks in the middle of the convoy. I saw a vision of an explosion near the entrance and the second Iraqi truck being totaled, two IA killed and the rest in that truck wounded. I saw myself and others running out of the Strykers to evacuate casualties and could feel the horrible feeling I'd had before when soldiers were killed. The vision seemed too vivid and too real to be just a daydream. I had it this in the morning as I prepared for the mission, again as I shook Thamer's hand and yet again after what he told me.

Oakley interpreted as Thamer asked why we were still going to the gas station. He asked me why we were going there when the pumps were broken from an explosion. He never once said he was scared or concerned for his life and the lives of his men, but I could see it in his eyes. He told me the gas station owner had told him the day before that the pump was broken and wouldn't be fixed for another two weeks. I told Oakley to tell him this concerned me too and I had suggested to CPT Reagle we that should either occupy it permanently or go in darkness; I had explained my concern that he and his men could get ambushed. I didn't tell him of my vision, but after he told me this about the place being closed for business anyway, I shook my head sadly and said I'd talk to CPT Walts about his men not occupying it and having that mission cancelled.

He thanked me, and I inspected his trucks, having my vision again. I was so disturbed by it I stopped halfway through the inspection and went to radio B Troop. I felt strongly led at this point and felt God's Spirit was showing me what would happen if they went. I radioed LT Shay and told himwhat Thamer had told me. I waited while he asked CPT Walts and I prayed a quick silent prayer for the situation. A minute later, he called back and said the gas station mission would be cancelled until further notice, but he still wanted us to swing by with just the Strykers after dropping off the Sinjar Checkpoint men to confirm the gas station's closure. He mentioned that I should have Thamer and his men stand down, and I praised the Lord.

I walked out quickly to 1SG Thamer, finding it hard to hide my excitement. I thanked God repeatedly as I walked out to the IA trucks and decided to have some fun with this. I changed my face to sadness and disappointment as I approached Thamer and shook my head from side to side. His eyes sank, as did his head. I put my right arm gently on his left shoulder, and after bowing my head down, looked up at him and said *"maku benzene khana mahooma* (there is no gas station mission)." I began to smile as I said it and he repeated it right back at me inquisitively. I motioned my hands and said it again with a big smile. He shouted happily in Arabic and gave me a huge hug.

It felt so good and I felt in my heart God had His hand in this completely. Thamer continued to shout happily and turned to tell his men, who shouted with joy and began to turn their trucks around to head back into the compound. He hugged some of his men who jumped out of the trucks and several of them shook my hand thanking me. I looked up and said, "Thank God," to which Thamer and others nodded. I still wasn't comfortable with me having to go out there past the gas station but was incredibly happy the IA weren't going. I felt I could handle myself getting wounded again, but not Thamer and his men possibly dying. I also had the feeling the enemy weren't trying to blow up Strykers there, but the Iraqi Army trucks instead, which weren't going out now.

I put on my gear as I walked toward the Strykers, and Sunburn told me the TOC wanted me up there for a meeting. I said I was going on mission. LT Shay walked up to me and told me the same thing, so I figured I should go to the meeting. SSG Hitrick decided to go on the mission for me and I went to the TOC. Other than handing off the corruption packet on LTC Ahmed to CPT Gaddy, there was a target packet for me to pick up from the intel officer. The meeting was more like a few sentences about the target packet and that was it. I read it over, and when I got back to Nomad the Strykers had left. I prayed 'Hitman' would be okay and he got back soon, having confirmed the gas station was open for walk-in business, but no cars were at the pumps, so the manager must been telling the truth when he spoke to 1SG Thamer.

I briefed COL Hajji and MAJ Sultan on the target packet, slowly explaining that two enemy leaders from Tal Afar were in Syria, expected to cross the border through Rubiyah that day or the next. I described both types of cars they would travel in (one with a taxi sign on it and no hubcaps) and the weapon and two mortar rounds they were suspected to be carrying into the country. Reports said the gray taxi-sign car would be used as a car bomb against one of the outposts or forts in Tal Afar. The interpreter repeated in Arabic and they aggressively took notes. I explained we didn't know from which checkpoint they would enter the city, but all his men must take extra precaution if they saw either of these cars and protect themselves from an explosion.

After the briefing, we all prepared to go to the range to shoot some weapons and did so after we returned from lunch. Hitman, SFC Walenz, Sunburn and I ended up going to shoot. Although we invited MAJ Sultan and COL Hajji, they were busy equipping their soldiers with the new arrival of helmets and body armor from Al Kissik. I was so thankful those came for their men. After confirming our shot groups and sights, the four of us left the range just as an M2A3 Bradley platoon from 3rd ACR arrived to shoot. Back at the office, Omar sat at the computer desk. I couldn't believe he was back because I thought he might quit permanently. He seemed in good spirits and happy to be back with us, so we filled him in on all the latest since he'd been gone.

In the evening MAJ Sultan came by to tell us COL Hajji would be leaving for his home because his uncle died. We paid our respects and he briefed us on the next day's plans. He said he'd have the men in formation for inspection at 8 p.m. in their new helmets and body armor. As the hour approached, tanks rolled out intermixed with Strykers and it was an awesome sight to see. Omar and I went to inspect the troops. I brought some Swiss Cake Rolls and handed them out to the most squared away looking soldiers. They stood at attention, dressed right at close interval and opened the ranks for the inspection. It was very impressive and made me smile. COL Hajji, MAJ Sultan and all 2nd Company officers were present to participate in the inspection. It was very professional and I made sure to tell them all, especially the leaders. I was so glad these soldiers from Dahuk came and so thankful that COL Hajji wasn't at all like LTC Ahmed. He was very cooperative with us and cared about his men, wanting to be a part of what they did in the unit, which I knew was in good hands.

We told them the news that Nomad would be dissolved in a few weeks and they were sad, but I assured them their battalion was doing great, which they knew. I thanked them again and congratulated them on how well the soldiers looked. Other than some of the soldiers having body armor a size too big (I shared how to fix it), we didn't really have any issues. After talking about some tactics and solutions during and after the inspection, I went back to the CP and we all ate at 9 p.m. when Neshwan brought us some chicken, bread, and vegetables. That pretty much concluded the evening, and I thanked the Lord we all survived another day.

I read a *StrykerNews* article reporting that another Iraqi battalion partnered with a US unit near Al Hatr, Iraqi (southwest of Qayyarah) received a tip from an Iraqi citizen who reported a weapons cache to the Iraqi police. Coalition forces confiscated several hundred to a few thousand weapons, including grenades and several types of ammunition such as mortar and artillery rounds. The greatest find (in my opinion) were the 307 anti-tank mines and 150 rockets! I was amazed, thinking of such large numbers of weapons and mines – lives to be saved from this find will be numerous! Anti-tank mines had destroyed Strykers in the past, so this would seriously help our cause in this country, not to mention hinder the enemy immensely. The last paragraph of the article also mentioned 2-14 Cavalry's successful raid of the mosque the night before, of which Oakley was proud to tell me he grabbed the "jihad-preaching" Imam and escorted him out in cuffs. Praise God!

April 23, 2005

Sunburn and I, Omar, and 80 soldiers with two officers from Company Two of the Wolf Battalion, occupied the granary around noon. 1SG Thamer and his 23 men in the security platoon joined us and eleven guys to switch out at Sinjar Checkpoint the following morning (since it was so close to the granary). LT Shay's platoon escorted them, as did the engineers to finish emplacing barriers, wire and other obstacles and protection for the granary. I prayed before leaving, and on our way out of the FOB. I asked God to not only protect us as usual, but also to convict enemies to lay down their arms and not interfere with us at all that day at the granary. I asked if they or any bombs lay in wait for us in any rooms or tunnel systems of the granary, that they would not harm us. I asked if enemies planted bombs on our routes, that they would either explode at inopportune times, not detonate at all or explode in the enemies' faces. I asked for our enemies to fight amongst themselves and not against us. We had no contact period. Not a single round fired or a single bomb detonated.

We took a southern route to the granary, rather than the typical one we always take.

After arriving, Sunburn and I led *'jundies'* through the tunnel system below, leading with our tactical flashlights on our weapons. We checked every nook and cranny down each tunnel and room, eventually searching the silos, and finally the big tower itself. While we did this, LT Shay and half his platoon secured the ground while the other half helped the Iraqi Army set up wire. After clearing the tower and identifying key positions the IA needed to occupy high above, I told Omar to have at least ten of them bring their sleeping mats and gear up to the top so they wouldn't have to run up and down the tower all day. It was once again an amazing view and I loved looking at the city from above. I also enjoyed seeing Strykers and Bradley's rolling through the city. With two Squadrons in this area and the IA occupying the granary, enemies would feel a tight squeeze in this city. I could imagine their anger watching the IA occupy and fortify the granary, the biggest, tallest and safest building in the entire city. With sniper rifles and PKC machine guns the IA will be able to cover from the Hwy-47 intersection all the way to the gas station.

Enemy freedom of movement areas got smaller and smaller. Eventually, there would be only a couple neighborhoods for them to hide in and operate from until forced to leave Tal Afar completely. It was exciting to be a part of this and I thanked the Lord again for our safe occupation of the granary without any incident. After the engineers completed setting up their wire and cleaning out the new future headquarters building, we headed back. It sounds quick, but the whole endeavor took us about six hours. I thanked God again for an awesome day of safety and prayed He would continue to help the IA at the granary and the other outposts to be safe and fight off any enemy, stopping them from emplacing any roadside bombs.

April 24, 2005

Strong winds blew dust and sand throughout the base and for several hours throughout the day we couldn't see a thing. 1SG Swett stopped to confirm the time I was leaving the next day. I was kind of shocked because I hadn't expected to leave until the 27th. Apparently that was the day I should arrive from Kuwait into the US My helicopter flight was at 11 a.m., but I needed to check in at 8 a.m. I packed for my trip, spoke to Becky on webcam and slept for two hours. A specialist from B Troop or Squadron knocked on my door at 2 a.m., asking me if any of the checkpoints reported contact. We didn't have enough people (or interpreters) to monitor the radio at all hours. I woke Omar, who radioed – no contact outside the wire. I asked the specialist why he came to my door and he said the last several nights he came to SSG ZT's door, who had pointed to my door as the place to come with any IA issues…fabulous. I would be flying in six hours, so it couldn't bother me now.

From left to right: Woody in front of our Nomad sign (above Omar and Major Sultan); Our Cavalry unit insignia painted on the side of a bunker (above the Iraqi National Guard insignia); Nomad on a mission

REST & RELAXATION (April 25-May 15, 2005)

I'm back in Iraq after an amazing time at home. My helicopter ride and plane rides were quick on the way home and even faster on the way back. I was in Kuwait for less than a day both ways – much better than the three- or five-days others have had. I was able to call Becky from Ireland on April 27th and after Dallas-Fort Worth I caught a flight arriving before 2 p.m. It was great to see her and May 13th she dropped me off at Seattle-Tacoma airport.

Rebecca was still pregnant and on April 30th, Katelyn still hadn't arrived. Becky and I were worried at first but prayed and trusted the Lord's timing for Katelyn's birth. At first, I wanted her to be born the day I got there. When her due date came and still no Katelyn, we realized God was allowing us to get to church on Saturday night and Bible study on Sunday night before Katelyn came. Late Monday night, Becky began contractions and called her mom after waking me up at 1 a.m. Tuesday morning. The contractions increased and her mom said to go to the hospital. Becky was concerned because we'd gone Friday when she thought it might be happening and it was nothing; she didn't want to waste another trip. I took her in and the doctors said this was it! Contractions and pain increased, so they gave Becky an epidural which helped. Hours later we pushed together since she was seven centimeters dilated. She quickly rose to nine and soon every doctor in the room tried to turn the baby. Her head was coming first but she was turned on her side and the doctor discussed the options of using the vacuum, forceps, or a c-section.

Becky began to cry because we had prayed for a natural birth and she didn't want to harm the baby. She asked the doctor if she could continue to push, and he approved. It was 12:40 p.m. – just a few minutes later—and I could see the baby's head with some hair. At 12:49, Katelyn Tambry Sacra was born (8 lbs even, 19.7 inches). It was scary just before she came out because a bunch of the doctors jumped on the bed and started pushing on Becky's belly. They explained afterward that Katelyn had 'shoulder dysplasia'and it could have been extremely dangerous if they didn't get her out right then. As soon as she was cleaned, I got a good look at Katelyn and she was beautiful. Becky and I thanked God for such an amazing miracle and so many other miracles surrounding Katelyn. We were in the hospital for the mandatory 48 hours (for first baby) and checked out on Thursday.

All three of us managed to make it to church Saturday night and Pastor Peter Deagon asked me to show the slideshow I had prepared. I shared countless miracles to everyone from the stage with Pastor Peter while the slides were on the screen. A young man named Derrick was about to leave for Basic Training, and after more training, to Iraq. I prayed over him with many others and introduced the assembly to Katelyn. She was such a good baby. She only cried once when she was hungry during the service and otherwise just looked around. As the swelling of her head went down the rest of the week, she became even more beautiful. I never thought babies were cute until I saw her. People asked what her names meant, so I shared: Katelyn is Celtic/Gaelic for 'pure beauty,' and Tambry is of unknown origin, meaning 'immortal.' Before we knew it, Katelyn was a week old and I had only a couple days left with her and Becky. It was sad to leave her. Despite the many hours awake at night, I treasured every second with them both.

I also heard sad news while home and even sadder news on my trip back to Iraq. A couple days after I left an anti-tank Stryker (like my old ones) in Tal Afar hit a roadside bomb. The four manning vehicle hatches had died: LT Edens from A Company of 1-5 Infantry, one of his sergeants and two soldiers transitioning aboard from 3rd ACR. A car bomb killed over 25 people at a funeral for a Kurdish leader in Tal Afar. Additionally, LT Bublis from B Company of 1-24 Infantry was hit by a car bomb in Mosul and was at Walter Reed because he had sustained a serious head injury from shrapnel.

At the Dallas-Fort Worth airport on my way back to Iraq the other day I ran into SPC Darrell Bez (one of my soldiers from the Storm Troopers) and a 1-24 Infantry staff sergeant. Both were sad to tell me that 1SG Bordelin, B Company 1-24 Infantry First Sergeant died. When the car bomb hit, it killed a sergeant instantly when the silver nitrate entered his lungs, sent shrapnel into LT Bublis and burned 80% of 1SG Bordelin's body. CPT Shaw, the new B Company Commander, had severe knee and leg damage. 1SG Bordelin even helped evacuate the other casualties with his burns before he and the rest were evacuated back to the states. 1SG Bordelin died in the States from his wounds just a couple days ago. I remember passing him on the FOB and he always had a joke or something nice and jovial to say. His men thought he was the best First Sergeant-- and almost too nice to be one.

SPC Bez also updated me on the Storm Troopers. Sergeant Youn, whom he visited at Walter Reed during his leave, was off life support, thank God, doing much better. He still couldn't talk, but recognized Bez when he entered the room, and his eyes got big. He grasped Bez's hand tightly when handed a keepsake and seemed to understand what he was told. I couldn't wait to see the improvement when I plan to visit him at the end of the year. Bez said the explosion was far north on Hwy-1 but not quite up to Yarmuk traffic circle. He said the car bomb didn't even contact Youn's Stryker. It exploded off to the side and blew the Stryker onto the median. He described the ramp being broken in the down position and all eight tires blown. While other Strykers secured the area and a wrecker headed out, they evacuated the casualties.

Will got burned when the side panels inside the vehicle blew off into his face, and LT Kim had burns from the outside explosion. Bez said everyone's helmets had been blown off and SFC Nubear helped take charge and get them out, as did others in the platoon. Since the Stryker was totaled, the platoon stripped it of everything of value before it was hauled away. Bez filled me in on LT Riley, but most of it I already knew from Becky. His condition seemed to be the same, but Bez said Scotty hadn't been wearing eye protection, which I couldn't believe. Even assuming he was wearing eye protection, it wouldn't have kept the shrapnel from hitting his frontal lobe and might have only saved one eye. The one he has left could still only see light and dark. Regardless, I would continue to pray for him.

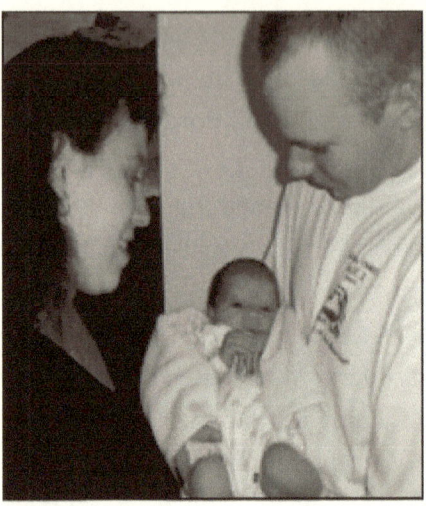

Becky, Baby Katelyn, and Matt in May of 2005

---

[1] Today, I understand Jesus was not born in December. Through scripture and other research, I've concluded his conception was likely in December, causing his birth to be in September or October, during the scriptural Feast of Tabernacles (Hebrew *Sukkot* or booths). Although I am not required to keep this feast in the New Covenant, my family and I have enjoyed celebrating it with God and Jesus since 2012, along with other feasts. Like other feasts, it is extremely rich in Biblical history, symbolism of God and Christ in us, as well as the Kingdom of God in the age to come.

III

Fobbit in the "Four" Shop

9

May

FOBBIT: *Funny name for someone who rarely leaves the FOB to go on missions; normally an officer, NCO, or enlisted soldier who works on staff or in a headquarters.*

May 16, 2005

As Toby Heath passed us and flew off on his helicopter after his concert for the troops, our choppers arrived. I stood there with SGT Bowman, waiting to get the two of us on a flight. A bunch of people showed up and I kind of put myself in the face of the crew chief with my ticket so he would see me. It felt pushy, so I backed off a bit and told the Lord I was willing to wait on His timing. If He didn't want me to get that flight and had another one for me, I was okay with that. Well, right after I prayed, the crew chief looked at me and said, "How many for this ticket, just you?" "Just me and him" I said, pointing to SGT Bowman. "Get on" he said, pointing to the chopper. "Yes! Praise God!" I shouted, and we ran to the Blackhawk helicopter.

We flew all over Mosul on the way back, stopped at Al Kissik halfway to Tal Afar, then landed safely – no incidents, thank God. I ran into SFC Aeris after walking off the helipad and after a brief time chatting with him and then CPT Reagle, he drove me back to my room. SSG ZT was back at Charger Troop as a section leader, which was good for him. SGT Wadul was back at his old platoon, which I believed was the same as Sunburn. SSG Hitrick was a training NCO for B Troop I think, and SFC Aeris was trying to involve himself with the command group Strykers, since he'd already finished platoon sergeant time at the Troop level and there weren't staff positions for his rank at Squadron. I was the "Assistant S4 (Supplies and Logistics)" officially and "primary UMO (Unit Movement Officer)" for the Squadron, my subtitle as additional duty. All I did that first day was return to my room and sleep for sixteen hours.

May 17, 2005

Since Nomad was officially dissolved, the only ones living in our old area were Woody, CPT Reagle and myself. Our old Nomad office was locked and the Internet was gone, belonging to the advisor teams now. The 109th Iraqi Army was entirely off the base, occupying the granary or "grain silo" as they called it. Our interpreters were sent to the various Troops and I heard Major Sultan got himself transferred to Mosul to be closer to his home south of there. Since the 109th Battalion Headquarters occupation of the granary, they'd established one more outpost on Hwy-47, covering more dead space. There were just two spots on Hwy-47 not covered 24/7 by friendly forces, so roadside bombs on that road should have been almost non-existent in the coming weeks.

When 2-14 Cavalry moved, my biggest concern about my new job was the convoy to FOB Marez, since 3rd ACR owned this sector, and we weren't really needed anymore. What was scary was I'd ride in an armored Humvee all the way from FOB Sykes to FOB Marez in Mosul, and so much could happen between them. I had to trust God to take care of me though, but I'd had bad dreams about it. My first real day as Assistant S4 (assistant logistics officer) was good-- just learning the job and getting acquainted with SFC Grimm, who is the S4 NCO, and the few other members of the S-4 'shop'/team. CPT Durmsy (the S4 or logistics officer) was at a conference in Kuwait getting information on our redeployment to Fort Lewis in late September. CPT Cleverst was the LST (Logistical Support Team) Platoon Leader, just like Liz was back in Mosul for 1-24 Infantry. At meetings, I learned 3rd ACR wanted to send all our Troops off the FOB down south near Baaj to work on some abandoned base site until June when they would lose control of 2-14 Cavalry (us) and we would go to Mosul.

May 18, 2005

I learned more about our upcoming Squadron reconnaissance mission ordered by 3rd ACR. I moved from my double-wide room near the IA compound to a single-wide room near the Squadron area by the TOC (Tactical Operations Center) and ALOC (Administrative Logistical Operations Center). Although it was a single-wide, I didn't need much room and was thankful I wouldn't have to share a room just yet, although it may be just around the corner. Ed Wells (the Chaplain) helped me move the heavy stuff and I carted the rest in our truck. I walked through a dust devil walking back from lunch. I saw a huge one forming and it got so big – about five feet in diameter at the bottom, and about 50 feet high. I hesitated at first, wondering if it would pick me up, but decided to squint my eyes under my sunglasses and go for it. It was a neat experience. I got very dusty when sand hit my face and body, but it didn't really hurt. When I looked at the ground, I noticed a perfectly symmetrical shadow like a spiked circle, and it was spinning. It amazed me how exact it was while it spun.

May 19, 2005

I learned so much about logistical operations and vehicles and surprisingly found it all interesting, especially since we had an operation south of Bi'aj scheduled for May 26th. I learned more of unit re-supply for various tactical missions and larger operations. I made myself a chart of the weights of different tactical vehicles and HET (Heavy Equipment Transport) classifications. It would probably sound boring compared to the combat operations I'd been on in the past, but it was essential for me to understand. I'd never liked the idea of being on staff, but it was an important role because the support logistics provided to a unit (as well as other staff sections) was vital to its survival on the battlefield. I learned more about the MDMP (Military Decision-Making Process) for planning a large operation and how to prepare it for briefing. The more planning and adjusting we did behind the scenes the easier it would be for the Squadron (or Battalion) Commander to make informed decisions and employ his unit more strategically on the battlefield in our Area of Operations.

May 20, 2005

We watched a video of the area south of Baaj in preparation for the operation. So far, the plan was for our Squadron to do a full reconnaisance of this area almost as far south as the Euphrates River. The purpose was to figure out who was in the area and if there was enough terrorist activity to warrant a presence of another 3rd ACR unit. After viewing the recon video, it seemed unnecessary, but we didn't know what we'd find in the small villages. There were many border forts out there and a whole lot of sand, that was about it. Baaj was already scheduled to have a unit from 3rd ACR and a company from the Iraqi Army to build a base in the town.

May 21, 2005

After an extremely slow day of more planning, I was just thankful to be alive.

May 22, 2005

Large staff-planning meetings from 9 a.m. to 5:30 p.m. for our upcoming zone reconnaissance mission in the south were tiring, but I learned a lot and it was neat to see the makings of a large-scale operation affecting hundreds of soldiers. MAJ Diny was in charge while LTC Mavis was on leave and he fostered a laid back and humorous atmosphere. As I prepared to put together the logistical slides and graphics with CPT Cleverst, CPT Durmsy returned. We were happy to see Rich back from Kuwait and he was glad to be back. He filled some of us in on the process involved with redeployment. He was glad I would be working with him and said how much of a load it would take off him.

At chow he told me of the huge explosion that shook him out of his temporary bed in Mosul while waiting to get a flight back to Tal Afar. It was an M1114 Humvee from 73rd Engineers and a lieutenant was among the three casualties. I hoped it wasn't LT Cookran. I'd likely know whoever it was because I got acquainted with most of them since 73rd Engineers was attached to 1-24 Infantry. It was sad to hear and very scary. In the upcoming convoy to Mosul, I would likely ride on an M1114 Humvee, which had been bothering me for days. I especially didn't like the idea of riding during the daytime when roadside bombs were more common in Tal Afar, Mosul and the route in between.

Anti-tank mines were more prevalent these days and even though they can destroy Strykers too, your chances of survival were much greater than if you were in a Humvee. It scared me to think of going to FOB Marez in a Humvee in the middle of the day. Any suicide car bombs could crash into us during the daytime, devastating a Humvee. I trusted the Lord to protect me but often wondered, "What if it is His will for me to be killed?" My concerns were not dying and being with my Savior but leaving behind Becky and Katelyn to go on living without their husband and daddy, respectively. I prayed God would continue to grant us all safety, especially when we began to move to Mosul in mid-June. Rich also told me about a raid conducted by a unit in Mosul where a soldier was killed on the second floor of the target building, shot by a terrorist twice in the gut. My heart sank. Even though he didn't know the unit, I had a feeling it was 1-24 Infantry.

After Aaron Cleverst completed the graphics for the upcoming operation, I completed the written logistics portion of the order. I later confirmed it was a soldier from the 1-24 Infantry Scout Platoon who died in the raid. I felt the usual pain in my heart and soul and couldn't imagine how LT Bourque (the Scout Platoon Leader) must be feeling. This was the second person in his small platoon who had died. I was so sick of war, but knew we are here for a reason. I just prayed the country would become stable enough for the Iraqi government and military to completely control the terrorism so we could all live in peace, safety and freedom.

The lieutenant from the 73rd Engineers who died was a new officer who had joined recently while our unit was deployed. His death, and that of his gunner, was still tragic even though I didn't know him. I was thankful it wasn't LT Cookran. Two soldiers from 3rd ACR were injured out in Sinjar. One-- by fratricide (friendly fire)-- was shot in the buttocks and the other was shot in the head and may die. My job seemed small in comparison to these events. Rich taught me ammunition reports, since I'm the 2-14 Cavalry Ammo Officer as I then had an additional duty to track all ammo for the Squadron.

May 23, 2005

We briefed the order for Operation Erandus ("The River"), which went well. I briefed one third of the logistical portion of it while CPT Cleverst and LT Collins (the Medical Officer) briefed other portions. COL McMaster was in there, so I got to see him face to face. He was apparently famous for his history in 3rd ACR during Operation Desert Storm. He was in the Battle of 73 Easting and now was the Regimental Commander of 3rd Armored Cavalry Regiment. This was the second time this unit had been to Iraq in the past few years. They were in Operation Iraqi Freedom I, crossing the border from Kuwait into Iraq.

May 24, 2005

I saw *Star Wars, Episode III-- Revenge of the Sith* and not much occurred on the battlefront or in the office. Becky emailed about how things were going at home. She and Katelyn were fine, but my brother-in-law Nick (who lives at our house) was not. Just like Anakin Skywalker, Nick was on the brink of choosing which side he would be on for his life, God's or the worlds. I could look back and see myself choosing between light and darkness. He has a gentle and kind heart, but at the same time, seemed extremely interested in the ways of the world and not interested in the Lord. It could have been only my impression, but seemed things were at a crossroads for him. He had been through a lot since his dad left his mom a couple years ago. Hopefully, with prayer, he'd draw closer to the Lord. I felt helpless, being so far away, to have any influence on him or his situation other than prayer. Perhaps God meant for me to feel this way so I would lean on him as my only support for such things.

May 25, 2005

Late at night, everyone moved to starting positions for the mission and the only small incident was a roadside bomb in Tal Afar between Fort Union and Avgani Checkpoint. Perhaps the enemies emplaced it recently, or before we had all the extra security in the area, but the Iraqi Army couldn't see anyone placing it because the IA still had no Night Vision Devices. There were no casualties and no damage to the Combat Observation Lasing Team M1114 Striker Humvee (Striker with an "I" is a variant Hummer). Shortly after the explosion of that roadside bomb, enemy from on unknown location fired a few rounds of rifle fire. Thankfully, the Lord spared another Humvee, but it tightened my nerves, especially since the day was soon approaching in a couple weeks when I would ride in an M1114 Humvee to FOB Marez in our convoy. I hoped we would go as close to midnight as possible when we convoy to Marez, although the destruction of the Engineer Humvee in Mosul occurred late night or early morning, so no time was safe.

Throughout the day I worked on the Deployment Equipment List for our redeployment to Fort Lewis, Washington. The list consisted of all the vehicles and MILVANs (large metal military shipping containers) that would go back to the States. I entered serial numbers, put vehicle names and bumper numbers and coordinated the information before turning it in the next day. Working on this, and just working on staff in general, involved so much work, yet it didn't show much. In other words, fixing, collecting information and editing for this one document consumed my entire day and it seemed I had nothing to show for it since it was just a digital chart or list. I was thankful to be inside the wire and not being shot at or blown up on a regular basis, so I was not complaining. How ironic that one list I worked on could save time and heartache for nearly 500 soldiers in this Squadron when we arrived in Kuwait to clean the vehicles, load them and other equipment on ships and leave this continent.

I learned about the enemy planting a second explosive beneath a landmine in northern Iraq. This was particularly scary because I'd wondered lately why the enemy hadn't done something like this before. I'd even told others that if our enemies were smart they would place two large bombs in the same location. After blowing the first one and causing casualties, they could detonate the second when soldiers were on the ground evacuating casualties, which would be extremely devastating. I feared this concept when I was wounded the first time. I remembered dreading getting off the Stryker in case there was a second bomb emplaced. When the ramp dropped and I saw the injured and dying Iraqis, there was no way I could stay on that Stryker. I was sure others have the same feeling when evacuating casualties across this country. Your love for those injured surpassed your fear of becoming injured, and so you helped them. It happened all the time and reminded me that the opposite of fear is love.

Lieutenant Colonel Krella had all 1-24 Infantry officers read *Gates of Fire* by Steven Pressfield before we deployed as part of an Officer Professional Development meeting on this fear and love concept. Most said fear's opposite is courage, but courage is more like a way of dealing with fear rather than its opposite. I understood the concept as the author explained it but was able to put it into practice in Iraq. It also reminded me of Jesus, who died for all of humanity. Though he feared and agonized about the cross in the garden of Gethsemane, he completed his mission through the love he had for God and us, the opposite of his fears. LTC Krella even quoted Jesus in that meeting, comparing love in John 15:13 to what we do as soldiers: "Greater love has no one than this, that he lay down his life for his friends." It had a deeper meaning in Iraq than it did even when we prepared to deploy [1 John 4:18 relates too].

In other good news for northern Iraq, coalition forces found another massive enemy weapons and ammunition stockpile. I imagined this would save many lives. Hopefully more caches would turn up and the enemy would run out of supplies, although I thought they continued to be re-supplied by terrorists in Syria, Jordan, Saudi Arabia and other countries far away. Maybe some day we would be able to cut off every avenue of entry to stop the inflow of weapons and explosives. That was part of the purpose of the mission our Squadron was on– to approach near the Euphrates River and the Syrian border – nearly one thousand square kilometers. It was like the US Marines in the recent Operation Matador when Marines went all the way to the Euphrates. Part of our plan was to link up with those Marines when the Squadron arrived at the Euphrates River in a few days. Meanwhile, we should find promising results in the various towns and villages on the way to the Syrian border. There was even rumor of a terrorist training camp somewhere out there between the starting line and the border. Hopefully, they'd discover it and grab up or destroy all enemies in the entire area.

May 26, 2005

I had a good conversation with Rich about roadside bombs and our uneasiness about this convoy in relation to Marez. I showed him my video of our November 11th firefight (a shortened video clip of it). I also explained the countless miracles we had that day and how good God is. We spoke of those we knew who've been killed or seriously wounded. He said his biggest fear was to be severely burned or to lose a limb. Mine was the same, plus losing a piece of my brain, or particularly a leg. I even told him the scary dreams I've had over the past several nights. I continued to have this dream about tying a tourniquet around my left leg while sitting in the left side behind the driver of a Humvee. I didn't know if it was just a fear produced by the sum of several thoughts and concerns, if it was the devil trying to cause me to doubt or a premonition from the Lord. I prayed it wasn't the latter, but if I survived, I knew I'd be thankful. It was better to lose a leg than my life. I trusted God would take care of me and allow me to help Becky raise our daughter, but I didn't know His will. The strange thing was that this dream began even before I was told I'd be riding in a Humvee. When I discovered I would be riding in one, the fears magnified, especially after learning about the explosion the 73rd Engineers experienced.

C Troop cleared some areas of interest and detained a man at his house with a Dragonov sniper rifle and 600 rounds. A Troop had problems because two Strykers lost wheels and drive shafts due to wear and tear. Rich came up with a cool plan of relaying information between Squadron and A Troop (for their logistical concerns) and 2-8 Field Artillery on FOB Endurance, which would likely save some troopers a day's worth of driving. That was great news for this crucial reconnaissance mission.

May 27, 2005

I spent another day plugging away at the computer working on charts and figures. I attempted to contact CPT Cleverst down at the FARP (Forward Arming and Refueling Point, an area designated in a combat zone closer to objective area that allowed for forward positioned vehicles, usually aircraft, to get fuel and ammunition) at Sahl Sinjar Airfield and was unsuccessful. In fact, everyone in the Troops was so far away from the FOB we could barely reach anyone. I needed to confirm the times for the CH47 (Chinook helicopter) drop of Class I and Class III (food/water and fuel/oil) scheduled for May 29th and 30th.

During the operation that day, A, B and C Troops stopped pickup trucks, searched buildings and found RPG launchers and several hundred rounds of different types of ammunition, including a few mortars, rockets, rifles and explosive materials. One unit even found Saddam Hussein paraphernalia. Another discovered rifles, binoculars and several thousand rounds of more ammunition. With finds like these,

3rd ACR would strongly consider maintaining a presence in those areas. Since practically no one had been in that area since the beginning of the war, at least in force like we are now, our presence should be seriously disrupting the terrorists. Hopefully, we'sd find more weapons and enemy to completely stop the flow of terrorists and munitions from this side of the border.

May 28, 2005

C Troop, in a cordon and search, found four brothers with a satellite phone. The number was associated with known terrorists, so three of them were detained. In other news, I saw LTC Krella's memorial service speech from May 26th for the two 73rd Engineers and SGT Morton, the sniper from 1-24 Infantry. Someone posted his speech on the *StrykerNews* website. After opening comments, he shared some history and then honored the three who had died. He went into extreme detail, so I've removed a few pages of specifics. I left his conclusion after he listed those who'd died in 1-24 Infantry, or "Deuce Four" as it is known:

"Forgive me if I go long but these were extraordinary men. Again we are drawn together as a band of brothers to mourn the loss of three Deuce Four warriors and sappers. We are truly a band of brothers. The bonds of camaraderie and friendship that we share from fire team to battalion are as strong as the very bonds of marriage. These bonds are forged and bound under the stress and fire of daily combat. We are bound together in shared friendship, shared hardship, shared loss and a desire over any other to ensure you care for the man on your left and right flank.

William Shakespeare in **Henry V** *describes the bond that we all share. At the battle of Agincourt in 1415 AD, the English were outnumbered 5 to 1 and* faced a formidable French foe that blocked their return route to England. The English were certain that no one would make it out alive. Henry V turned to his men to tell them about the uncommon bond that is shared in combat. He states:

From this day to the ending of the world. But we in it shall be remembered; We few, we happy few, we band of brothers; For he today that sheds his blood with me today shall be my brother."

Today we mourn the loss of three brothers in arms – LT Aaron Sessan, SPC Tyler Creamean and SGT Ben Morton...

...These three warriors joined the rest of the Deuce Four Advance Party. CPT Bill Jacobsen is in charge of the formation while 1SG Bordelon calls out the names to make sure all are present. SPC Tommy Doerflinger, CPT Bill Jacobsen, SGT Robert Johnson, CPL Jonathan Castro, SPC Lionel Ayro, PFC Oscar Sanchez, SGT Nathanial Swindell, SGT Adam Plumondore, SPC Clint Gertson, SGT Anthony Davis. 1SG Mike Bordelon, SPC Tyler Creamean, LT Aaron Sessan and SGT Ben "Rat" Morton. These 14 warriors now stand high above us overwatching us, providing guidance and direction in the most difficult times. Never was so much owed by so many to so few.

On this day, we ask almighty God to grant us patience and steadfast resolve in all that is to come. We ask the Master Physician to reach down and use his healing hand to heal our wounded brothers. May God Bless Deuce Four, 1st Brigade, and may God Bless America."

[His "Advanced Party" analogy was his way of saying the dead were preparing "heaven" for others – in military terms, an advanced party is a uniquely formed small team from within a larger unit which deploys ahead to a location to prepare for the arrival of the rest of the unit.] Many folks replied to his speech on the site, and I felt led to as well. I talked to Becky briefly online for the first time since I'd been back from leave, and it was wonderful. I conveyed to her most of my fears and she encouraged me by reminded me of God's plan for me.

May 29, 2005

That day was a big eye opener for me concerning my job. As Rich and I briefed our mission analysis slides for the convoy of the entire Squadron to Mosul, we were interrupted with an issue. We were expecting to receive repair parts for three Strykers by helicopter, but the choppers left without them. It turned out the maintenance guys responsible for getting the parts on the 'birds' tried to find Rich instead of linking up with the helicopters. I left the meeting to take care of the issue, which ended up being exceedingly difficult. All we needed was for a helicopter to take three parts to the Sahl Sinjar Airfield so the Chinook helicopters could pick them up and take them to the Troops at the Euphrates. The 3rd ACR air operations officer didn't feel we were priority enough. I explained that our Squadron was the main combat effort of the Regimen and we required all the assets available to contribute to our operation. If these three replacement parts didn't get to the Troops in charge of maintaining the Strykers, three of them would be unable to assist in any combat, as well as requiring more vehicles to protect and tow them to a safe maintenance location. After running back and forth to different tents and the Regimental TOC, I talked to enough people to get those parts to their destination.

About eight terrorists in a house out in the middle of nowhere just north of the Euphrates River opened fire on C Troop with RPGs and rifles. Unlike in downtown Tal Afar or Mosul, the terrorists had nowhere to run. It was fight and be destroyed, or surrender, with no third option. C Troop fired over a thousand rounds of .50 cal, a couple cases of M203 heat rounds and three or four AT-4's (anti-tank weapons) into the house, killing four enemies and capturing four, three of whom were wounded. One was thankful to be alive and he shared information regarding who he was, who the others were and for and with whom they all worked – amazing! He said of the four killed two were Syrians one was Algerian and one from another country, perhaps Jordan. Of the four captured, I thought one was Moroccan, two were Saudi's and the other perhaps from Yemen. Nearby locals claimed that every few days a brand-new car with masked men would come across the border and pass through the town, storing weapons or moving on into a main city in Iraq. We would be able to shut off their supply of people and equipment from Syria and Saudi Arabia.

I stayed with the men at the helipad with the repair parts and ammo until the helicopters came. I helped them load them onto the UH60 Blackhawks before 2 a.m. – a late night but it felt great to finish the day having tremendously helped the guys outside the wire by getting the supplies out to them.

May 30, 2005

I coordinated more air missions for supplies Troops needed. I went to the Squadron TOC and contacted CW3 ("Chief") Anderson (the maintenance officer) and CPT Cleverst on the tactical satellite radio and wrote down what supplies they needed. They requested one thousand bottles of water, twenty-eight cases of Gatorade, ten five-gallon cans of antifreeze, twenty-five-gallon cans of oil, three Humvee tires and two trailer tires for themselves and the Troops (both about one hundred miles from FOB Sykes). I spoke with SFC Cunningham, the mechanic sergeant in charge, who got the repair parts and vehicle fluids, while SGT Murman, the Logistical Support Team sergeant, got the water and Gatorade. I coordinated pickup and dropoff locations and times. At noon the next day the Troops would conduct stationary reconnaissance screen missions to the north, looking into the vicinity of the town of Baaj. This would be a perfect time since they would be stationary for the day, so I confirmed coordinates with the 3rd ACR air coordination officer who grumbled about all the time in the air which increased the maintenance needed for the helicopters.

Later, CPT Nerph told me the Troops needed tactical satellite radio batteries and then one of C Troops's Strykers needed a new engine. I had to coordinate how to get another engine, which we didn't have at FOB Sykes. After figuring out the problem, I went back and told Rich (who was working on other things) and we determined a solution by calling and talking to Brigade. It turned out the 17th Corps Support Battalion (who supplied 3rd ACR) was carrying a logistics package to our location. After pulling some strings, we got two Stryker engines loaded onto their convoy and it should arrive at Sykes the next day. We'd have the one we needed plus an extra in case another Stryker went down. I'd link up with the Regimental Support Squadron to get those engines shipped down to Sahl Sinjar Airfield. The engine and other parts would bring three Strykers back into the fight, which was great for the upcoming siege and occupation of Baaj.

May 31, 2005

I got everything on the Blackhawks that morning to linkup with our forward logistical unit. It felt good to help the Troops with all they needed. Ironically, hours after the 'birds' flew away, a TOC sergeant told me they desperately needed ice out there. If only they had said something sooner, I could have put them on the choppers. Fortunately, a ground logistics convoy was scheduled to take the Stryker engine out that night. I coordinated for both, but then received word they no longer needed the engine, and the Regimental Support Squadron already had over a hundred bags of ice on tonight's convoy to Sahl Sinjar Airfield.

As the evening approached, Rich prepared to leave for Mosul so he could prepare a place to receive Squadron on FOB Marez while I prepared to eventually send Squadron convoys from FOB Sykes for our big move. He called me before he left the gate because he had forgotten to give up his room key, so I rode over on an all-terrain vehicle or "four-wheeler", and I loved it. I rode all over back and forth driving kind of crazy off the roads since no one was around. When I returned from the gate, I got word the Troops needed two five-gallon cans of hydraulic fluid, a case of one-quart tubs of hydraulic fluid and six cases of meals, so I drove further in the four-wheeler to link up with SFC Cunningham and we found what meals we could and the hydraulic fluid. We got what we could and then I headed to MAJ Bennet of the advisor team to get some 'Hallal' meals (Iraqi box meals).

His sergeant, SSG White, led me over to an old 109th Iraqi Army bunker where I discovered Neshwan, CSM Aedo, CPT Kamel and several other Wolf Battalion folks still hanging out there. I couldn't believe it! I was certain they were gone, so it was wonderful to see them again. Neshwan and CSM Aedo wanted to talk, but I was in a hurry. Before heading to the advisor team, I had stopped by the 17th Corps Support Battalion convoy heading to Sahl Sinjar Airfield to first confirm they could transport these supplies. They were happy to help, but I only had an hour before they left and time was running out. I got the meals with Neshwan's help and promised him and CSM Aedo I'd be back the next evening for dinner around five or six. They were so excited, as were several other *"jundies"* I recognized. I loaded everything on the convoy and let everyone in the TOC that our supplies were on the convoy.

SSG White told me a vigilante group had been fighting the terrorists east of the granary in Tal Afar. After two car bombs exploded in their neighborhood, the citizens had enough. They get into huge firefights with the terrorists. Our advisor teams linked up with the vigilantes and supplied them with ammunition and other supplies. It was exciting to hear, because it could mean the difference between victory and defeat in Tal Afar. SSG White and I shared how blessed we'd been throughout our time in Iraq. I told him of the close calls I'd had in firefights and from bombs. He told me about an ambush on Hwy-1 (where I was ambushed November 10th) in which an RPG hit the back of his Humvee. He said it was a miracle no one was injured. He felt an incredible peace from the Lord as they were under enemy fire. We both praised God for our protection thus far and prayed to safely make it home to our families. You just never knew when you were going to run into a brother in the Lord. It was a great conversation.

I got back to the office and managed to do webcam with Becky (and Katelyn), which was amazing. I could hear and see Katelyn cooing and crying and talk to her through the voice chat option. I didn't know if she recognized me yet because she was not quite a month old, but it was special. I loved seeing both of my lovely ladies and Katelyn seemed to get cuter every time I saw her. It was just four more months till I'd be with them again for good and I couldn't wait.

Finally, I learned about terrorists attempting to give poisoned watermelons to some Iraqi soldiers manning a checkpoint in our Brigade sector. They had paid the delivery guy over a thousand dollars to drop off the fruit. I'd always wondered if the terrorists would resort to poisoning, and now they had. I was frankly surprised this was the first time they'd used this tactic. I would have thought they would have used poisoning before they brought a bomb into the chow hall. Hopefully, they could find out who paid this guy, and where they were.

10

June

June 1, 2005

Six more days till I'd have the scariest ride of my life in a Humvee to Mosul. Rich made it successfully, so it couldn't be that bad...just very scary. I had to remember that I had put on the Armor of God, and all would be okay. I mostly worked on the transportation mission request and attempted to get vehicles lined up to go to FOB Marez on the fourth of June. If the 3rd ACR transportation officer could get it approved, we'd be more than 85% complete with our move off FOB Sykes. While working this I heard wonderful news from the front. Around 3 a.m., B Troop detainined their target, Abu Anwar, and another male with him on our Brigade target list (both armed). Anwar was said to be the leader of the terrorist training cell responsible for recruiting and training terrorists and foreign fighters in the area who came in to kill Americans and fight the new government of Iraq. C Troop also stopped a vehicle speeding away from Baaj as 2-14 Cavalry surrounded the city, detaining three male occupants. One of the males in the car, and one in the house they later returned to, was on the target list as well, so all four were held and would be processed.

After learning all of this, I saw a *StrykerNews* article which included C Troop's firefight from the other day. I found valid a point this 3rd ACR Major made-- and they have way more troops in their Regiment than we have in our Squadron. Several areas in our sector were neglected due to lack of manpower, which was why he had such a good point:

U.S. Army officers in northwest Iraq say they don't have enough troops

Officers from the 3d ACR comment on the situation in Tal Afar. According to the article the 3rd ACR has taken operational control of the region from elements of the 1/25 SBCT [Stryker Brigade Combat Team]. BY TOM LASSETER, Knight Ridder Newspapers

TAL AFAR, Iraq - (KRT) - US Army officers in the badland deserts of northwest Iraq near the Syrian border say they don't have enough troops to hold the ground they take from insurgents in this transit point for weapons, money and foreign fighters. From last October to the end of April, there were about 400 soldiers from the 25th Infantry Division patrolling the northwest region, which covers about 10,000 square miles.

"Resources are everything in combat ... there's no way 400 people can cover that much ground," said Maj. John Wilwerding, of the 3rd Armored Cavalry Regiment, which is responsible for the northwest tract that includes Tal Afar. "Because there weren't enough troops on the ground to do what you needed to do, the (insurgency) was able to get a toehold," said Wilwerding, 37, of Chaska, Minn. During the past two months, Army commanders, trying to pacify the area, have had to move in some 4,000 Iraqi soldiers; about 2,000 more are on the way. About 3,500 troops from the 3rd ACR took control of the area this month, but officers said they were still understaffed for the mission. [...]

When an attachment of 25th Infantry soldiers, doing a sweep in tandem with the 3rd ACR, came across a house near Rawah last week, they were expecting to sit down and talk with the locals about water quality. In June 2003, American troops had destroyed an insurgent training camp in the area, killing more than 70 suspected fighters with helicopter strikes and a large ground offensive. It was one of the biggest camps discovered in postwar Iraq.

Last week, when the ramp of an armored vehicle began to open outside the house near Rawah, an insurgent shot a rocket-propelled grenade at it and other insurgents let loose with machine-gun fire.

The 25th Infantry soldiers responded first with .50-caliber machine-gun fire and then two shoulder-launched rockets. Four insurgents - three from Saudi Arabia and one from Morocco - were killed, Maj. Diny said. After the house caught fire, four more insurgents surrendered. They were from Syria, Jordan and Algeria. "They'd come to Iraq to kill Americans; they were looking for jihad" - or holy war - Diny said."

I ate dinner with CSM Aedo, MAJ Abid and 1SG Raul. I gave CSM Aedo the cross I had brought back for him from the States, and he put it around his neck immediately. He really seemed to love Jesus judging by the way he acts and talks. I didn't have an interpreter, so I "winged it" with the little Arabic I knew and the little English they knew. I noticed MAJ Abid spoke and looked different. He then told me he was injured in the chin by a suicide carbomb, and his eardrums were blown out. This happened near the granary; surprisingly, no one was killed, although several were injured. We had a great evening and I got to talk to Becky on webcam again too.

June 2, 2005

We had a meeting to synch MAJ Diny on everything. He was back to being the Squadron XO once again, LTC Mavis was back from leave, and MAJ Gauthier was the S3 (LTC Rugrs was gone). MAJ Diny decided we'd have one of these meetings every day until we reached Marez so we could hammer out any issues still pending or that we need help on. As much as I didn't like meetings, I thought it was a good idea because a lot could happen in a 24-hour period, especially with convoys. So many little questions and tasks came up, and with computer and internet issues, I couldn't relay them all to Rich. Our logistical slides and portions of the operation order were due to reach CPT McGarry ("Mac") by 6 p.m., but I still had multiple issues to work out and questions to be answered before turning them in.

I also planned and coordinated our Sinjar Mountain recovery mission. We have various vehicles and communications equipment up there to retreive. There were other many things I was unaware we needed to retrieve for the move to FOB Marez. I worked with the Logistical Support Team for hauling assets, talked to LT Burkhart to assess the Heaquarters assets needed and spoke with 3rd ACRs 1st "Tiger" Squadron to complete the signover of the installation property up there (things that stay on the mountain because they belong to the Army but not our specific unit). We all met at 4 a.m. with big army trucks and flatbeds, hauling assests. 3rd ACR was ready too, and the only element missing was the platoon from our (2-14 Cavalry) A Troop. I drove up to the TOC with Dan because A Troop had just told him they thought the mission was cancelled "since we aren't going to Mosul anymore." What!?! Why would we not go to Mosul and FOB Marez anymore? When I reached the TOC, they said LTC Mavis put out at 8 p.m. that we had new mission orders from Brigade and were no longer going to Mosul but would remain on base. I couldn't imagine why, but perhaps it would be explained later. By 5 a.m. the matter was corrected, and they went to Sinjar Mountain. After all this mess I attempted to get an hour of sleep but was unsuccessful.

June 3, 2005

Well, I was very tired of course because of that craziness the night before (or rather, the morning), but we briefed LTC Mavis at 9 a.m. on our operations order. Our plan for the Marez move was good, save a few errors, and the boss had a couple suggestions and questions about why we weren't shipping more of our assets sooner. We explained we just didn't have the trucks and resources to do it, and he just made a face. Afterwards we fixed errors to get hard copies of the plan to the Troop Commanders by 4 p.m. for the full briefing to all top leaders. Thirty minutes prior, MAJ Diny and Mac (CPT McGarry) called me to the TOC to explain the new plan the boss had drawn up and wanted executed.

Mac and I flipped our lids later about it, because the previous plan had been good, and now we had just over an hour to completely reconfigure everything. LTC Mavis wanted all assets to leave sooner, so I had to completely change the shipment of all vehicles, military storage containers and logistics. Mac had to rework the entire planning piece of all the rest. We couldn't believe it happened, but this was the life of a staff officer. You could work and plan for five days only to have it completely scrapped for one man's opinion, urge (or wisdom) to do it another way. Then you were stuck having to rework the entire plan in just a day, causing you four times the work and headache. It was nuts, but I learned a lot. On a side note, while I was working on all this, SFC Grimm noticed a big spider. I looked around the corner expecting to see just a decent-sized spider and saw what looked to be a baby camel spider or tarantula. It was very nasty looking, so I squished it.

The brief to the Commanders went okay, but there was a lot of "You'll get a finished product after I make the changes by tomorrow," going on. The boss surprised me when he said gunners in Humvees didn't have to ride out of the hatches, since there was no need to expose them unnecessarily. I learned a ton about planning and staff life and a great deal from Mac about the Army, staff, command and branch choices. One of the biggest personal blessings came out of all these changes. It turned out that with the new plan LTC Mavis made it made more sense for me to stay behind and push equipment and vehicles until the last minute, then fly to Marez. So, I have a helicopter flight set for June 8th – praise the LORD!

June 4, 2005

We had an early morning sandstorm so strong you could barely see ten feet in front of you. The wind was very powerful and everything was left dirty after this one. Many folks scrambled to get things loaded into the military shipping container for administrive personnel and logistics staff. All of us were leaving except for SSG Johnson, SGT Murman and myself, so everything was simple. By the end of the day, I had moved all my things into the planner room in the TOC, since Mac was flying out that day and MAJ Gauthier was already in Mosul. I updated and finalized the Transportation Movement Request for those vehicles and equipment leaving the next day. I'd come to realize it changed slightly each day, due to various circumstances like not enough flatbed hauling trucks arriving, or a new priority coming up, etc. I could adjust and adapt to one or two changes, but if the entire plan changed again, it'd be another nightmare.

On the tactical side of the house, I heard from CPT Nerph that 3rd ACR had absolutely no enemy contact whatsoever in Tal Afar, which was amazing. Maybe things were finally improving with additional US and Iraqi troops in the city. As the evening ended, I prayed for the convoy and inspected it (around midnight) and went to bed.

June 5, 2005

Eight flatbeds came instead of the eleven slated for the convoy, but civilian contractors sent five trucks, making up the difference. It was nice being in the TOC, since I was in one of the back rooms and I got to just sit in relative peace. It was also nice hearing things immediately if any changes occurred rather than talking on the radio or having to go over there and check. I made necessary updates to the Transportation Movement Request matrix and coordinated with SGT Murman to get all the shipping containers and mission essential vehicles loaded. B Troop should head out tonight, leaving only C Troop, the TOC and just a couple other items. We'd be more than 50% complete for the Squadron in regard to Troops and over 80% complete in regard to equipment. At the other end, Rich must have been busy (or having connection issues) since he hadn't answered my messages in almost two days.

I cleaned the plans room in the TOC as CW2 "Chief" Dunn packed his things. I noticed how hot the room was, so I covered some windows to block out some sun and heat. I tidied up the room, sweeping and moving things out of the way, and cleaned off the desk for a decent setup for the remaining days I'd be there (until June 8th). It felt good to take a dirty unorganized remnant of an old office and turn it into a workspace. It was for only for a few days, but it was still nice. I received an email from Elmer Takash, who was now the 2-14 Cavalry Liaison Officer to Brigade at FOB Courage. A neat upcoming operation for a "March Against Terrorism," (not to be confused with a "March For Peace") would take the entire Brigade in Mosul working together to allow the citizens of Mosul to demonstrate against terrorism.

Iraqi soldiers and police would secure the inner cordon of the marching area while our Brigade units secured the outer cordon perimeter of the entire city, making sure no enemy could come in. It was planned for June 13th, and there would be a "no roll" in effect, just like during the elections. No vehicles would be allowed to drive in or around the city, which meant no car bombs. We'd have snipers and marksmen in positions all around the city to kill any enemy attempting to plant any bombs or fire RPGs, rifles or indirect. This should also show the terrorists they couldn't stand against us and they didn't own the city. With almost the entire Brigade deployed throughout the city and the "no roll" in effect, the enemy would be severely hindered. The only risk would be if a terrorist could somehow get into the march with bombs strapped to him, but I was sure the Iraqi Army and Iraqi Police would search all participants.

After reading about that operation, I coordinated and confirmed some convoys, while a 3rd ACR logistics Major fussed about our all-terrain vehicles. I told him I would fix the situation tomorrow, and he proceeded to insult CPT Durmsy and our Squadron saying how bad it looked, but that he wasn't mad at me. I defended them both, explaining these all-terrain vehicles were not our highest priority compared to movement from here to Mosul and future operations. He continued complaining, so I wrapped up the conversation (I was sick of hearing it --especially all the curse words) and left for chow.

When I returned from chow I went into my "new office" and LTC Mavis, MAJ Diny and CW2 Dunn were all in there smoking cigars, getting ash on the desk I had just cleaned off for my computer and filling the room with smoke. I looked around and my disgust must have shown on my face because LTC Mavis looked at me and said, "We designated this as the smoking room, so it is okay to smoke now in here." MAJ Diny and he both said something about me in there, and I said, "That's okay sir, I don't want to get an allergic reaction, so I'll just get my computer and move rooms or something." I was angry I had done so much work and now the room was wasted. It'd likely still be nasty and smoke-filled for a while, considering the filtration system in there. I grabbed my things and headed back to my living quarters to relax for the evening. It was upsetting seeing that, but in the "big picture" it mattered little. A huge rainstorm just came in which was kind of nice, so I'd just enjoy the rest of my evening.

June 6, 2005

My frustrations with the planner room office were in vain. When I went into the TOC the room was completely cleaned out, swept and ready to be shut up. Within hours, other rooms of the Tactical Operations Center were packed into three Humvees or military shipping containers. Nearly everything in the Squadron was down at the logistics yard ready to load and convoy. Throughout the day I corralled the all-terrain vehicles into one area to sign them over to 3rd ACR. It was hard tracking down the last two of nine we would sign over to them. One was in Mosul with D Troop and they are awaiting haul assets to ship it tous. The other was broken and unaccounted for.

SSG Johnson and I searched for it and learned the 445th Transportation Corps convoy dropped off some equipment and left the FOB. This was called a "turn and burn" in the logistical world, meaning all their driving was done during the night and early morning hours. Normally drivers would arrive around midnight, sleep until midday when they would drop off their things, and then prepare for their next drive. That was what the 445th was supposed to do. Since the second of June I had them scheduled to drop off equipment and then haul twenty shipping containers and Humvees back to FOB Marez in Mosul. Now it could not happen since they left, and according to some civilian contractors, 445th didn't even come with very many haul assets anyway. They came with two trucks with platforms, which would have only hauled four pieces of our equipment anyway. SGT Murman learned this after lunch, but thankfully, the civilian contractors had five trucks heading out that night, so we could put pieces on them. It wouldn't be nearly as many as we thought we'd ship, but it was better than having absolutely nothing going out.

I told Major Diny and other senior NCOs about the new problem. CPT Layes (C Troop) gave his convoy briefing at about 5 p.m. and I informed him he would have five civilian trucks going with him and we were now short on haul assets. It was amazing the amount of logistical support it took to get just one Squadron off one base and onto another. I never realized exactly what went into it at the Troop or Company level as a Platoon Leader, but I did now.

I couldn't find every all-terrain vehicle, but I did sign over six of nine to SFC Colon in addition to the five Humvees we had. SFC Colon was cool about it and he let SSG Johnson and me keep one until we leave the FOB, which was nice. When I thanked him, he just said, "No problem, sir. It's common sense. You can't do what you need to do to get out of here unless you can get around the FOB, so it makes perfect sense to me." He noted that his 3rd ACR Major wasn't happy about it, but said, "It's the right thing to do anyway, you know?" He was easy to get along with, so I thought I'd rely on his help until we got out of there. He cared about us and seemd to know his job well. By the time the day ended I had been operating completely out of my room, which I supposed was my new office. C Troop (minus one Platoon) and the TOC would roll to Marez that night.

June 7, 2005

My search for the all-terrain vehicle landed me at the civilian contractor carpentry shop where I talked to the guy in charge of fixing them. He said about three weeks ago this Thursday (May 19th or 20th) some soldiers came with a forklift and told him they needed to take it away because they were leaving FOB Sykes for Mosul and they would get it fixed there. They'd described it the same as I: broken transmission, broken wheel or tire, etc. SGT Murman said none of his men had used their forklift for that, but he would check further when he arrived at Marez. That led me to email MAJ Diny (who is now in Mosul), CPT

Durmsy and the Troop XOs and commanders. I told them my investigation led me to three possibilities.

The first was that 3rd ACR came in with a forklift and a fake story about going to Mosul, they took it and it was now in one of their 1,000 shipping containers on this FOB – unlikely, but a possibility nonetheless. The second possibility was that one of the Troops took it, deciding to get it fixed and then keeping it with the justification that they had fixed it, so they would get to use it (even though it belonged to HHT). The third possibility was that one of the Troops took it to Mosul with the intent of getting it fixed and returning it to Squadron but forgot about it and additionally forgot to inform us or the leadership at Headquarters and Headquarters Troop. If I didn't get an answer in the next day or so, we'd likely declare it lost or missing and initiate a detailed official investigation.

At chow I talked with SSG White from one of the advisor teams and he asked me if I knew a LTC Crowe. I thought he said LTC Krella at first and immediately wondered why he was asking me this. He said LTC Crowe was killed today, and they just brought his body back to the FOB. It didn't make sense that LTC Krella would be killed in Tal Afar, so I confirmed the name, and it was then I more clearly heard "Crowe" instead of "Krella." I still was in shock, because the other night when SSG White helped me get meals from the Iraqi Army I had just talked to LTC Crowe. He was also the head 109th IA advisor after Nomad left. I remember explaining to him all that Nomad was responsible for while filling him in on the 109th. He just returned from leave the night I saw him a few days ago, and according to SSG White, LTC Crowe had a nine or ten-year-old son. SSG White said LTC Crowe knew his job very well and was very smart, but also dangerous. He said sergeants dreaded going out of the wire with him because he took unnecessary risks and endangered his life and others.

I never observed this, but as we sat pondering if that was how he was killed, SFC Lywellan came over and sat down. When SSG White asked if he knew about LTC Crowe, SFC Lywellan said, "Of course, I was there; I carried his gear that was soaked in blood." He described how the team was in support of a 3rd ACR operation when a roadside bomb exploded five feet from LTC Crowe while they were all dismounted. He dropped to the ground immediately as 3rd ACR men pulled him into the M113 Armored Personnel Carrier and shut the ramp, pulling forward to the advisor team position. In those thirty seconds, after the ramp then dropped, SFC L noticed LTC Crowe was as white as a ghost. His femoral artery was completely severed and by the time the soldiers in the M113 realized it, it was too late. They performed CPR on him as they cut off his clothes – shrapnel had gone straight through the artery and come out his behind. There was blood everywhere in the vehicle and he died within two minutes total from the time he was hit. I didn't know why 3rd ACR men would perform CPR on him without first locating and stopping the bleeding of his femoral artery.

In the sadness of this tragedy, I was again grateful God saved us all the second time I was wounded. I was five feet from the bomb that day and could easily have been killed as LTC Crowe was. I won't begin to assume the reasoning behind the Lord's will in my surviving and the Lieutenant Colonel dying, but perhaps this would save lives in the long run. I didn't know. I did know I am so sick of death and war and wouldn't mind if I didn't have to come back here ever again.

With no haul assets to take anything to Mosul, we would have a break, especially for the C Troop platoon. I hung out with them for a bit, watching some videos they had of roadside bombs or car bombs hitting Strykers and other vehicles. After talking to SSG Julio Oquendo for a bit, I headed off to check email in the 3rd ACR tents one more time. Julio is a friend from my old church, and Becky and I would usually see him and his wife on Sunday evenings for Bible Study, so it was nice talking to him again.

June 8, 2005

I slept in a bit, predicting there was still no answer to my emails and request for more assets. I was correct. I drove around base to see if any trucks bound for Mosul could possibly take some of our equipment. I ran into a captain (first name Mark) from the Transportation Company out of Balad who lost a soldier on April 22nd up here. I asked him if it was the soldier who was quartered by shrapnel and what was left of him landed on the female in the seat to his right. He affirmed it was and said she was very emotionally scarred. The shrapnel had come up through the seat and the soldier's butt, splitting him in half and knocking off his helmet. The other piece came through the door, cutting through his waist area and covering the female soldier in the passenger seat with his remains. I apologized for his loss and he explained that after the incident his Commanding General finally listened to them and allowed them to get upgraded armor modification kits for their Humvees. Before this incident, Mark said it was like pulling teeth to get any upgraded armor for his company.

SGT Murman located nine civilian contractor trucks heading to Mosul, so we could send our equipment escorted by the remaining platoon from C Troop. Simultaneously, I received an email from CPT Johnston from Brigade telling me ten more civilian contractor trucks were inbound. With this news, we decided to keep SGT Murman there until the next night to load the remaining equipment onto those ten trucks. After I told LT Raymond the information, he needed to head back with his platoon and those trucks, so I checked who flew today from our Squadron. SSG Johnson and several others from the Troops made it out. It looked like just two enlisted men from the crew of a broken Mortar Stryker, SGT Murman and PFC Cox, from 176th Signal Company were here, and lastly, me.

While I was at the 3rd ACR flight tent, a sergeant said they had a new system for tracking flights since a Chinook from their unit went down in 2003. I remembered hearing about it on the news. He said it was a mass casualty incident – the CH47 was hit with three surface-to-air missiles. Everyone aboard was leaving for his or her mid-tour leave. The saddest case was one of the fourteen or so soldiers killed was going home for his mother's funeral. The sergeant said the father was then forced to bury the mother and the son. I couldn't imagine the pain going into that, but hopefully the rest of the family could find strength in the Lord. Even two years later, I was sure the pain was still very real.

June 9, 2005

Lieutenants Raymond and Shay and a communications guy woke me at 2 a.m. telling me Squadron was trying to get a hold of me and wanted information. He set up the tactical satellite radio in my room and then we took it outside to talk to Squadron at FOB Marez. I was surprised at how small and compact it was. The transmission was slow and since I was extremely tired, I was very annoyed at this whole concept. I felt it was ridiculous that they needed me to communicate with them this way when I'd been sending so many emails each day and checking with them at least four times a day. After the conversation with the "Battle Captain" at Marez, they wanted me to email a list of what was left here and what was leaving that night in the convoy. I had already emailed this list and was irritated I had to do it again at 2 a.m. I went to the 3rd ACR tents and couldn't send it from any of the secret computers there because they were all locked except one, and it had severe dysfunction in its email program.

I had success at a different tent and then slept from 3 a.m. to just before 8 a.m. Squadron requested that I call at 8 a.m. so I went outside and tried for 25 minutes. I received one transmission from them after all my calling, asking me to repeat myself. After another fifteen minutes, I gave up and went back to sleep until 10 a.m. when Sergeant Murman came by saying the ten civilian contractor trucks weren't in. I couldn't believe it. I went to the Regimental headquarters and logistics tents. The secret internet was down across the entire Regiment. I went back to my room and tried the tactical satellite again for about forty-five minutes, getting no response whatsoever. At lunchtime I talked to a major from Fort Knox who oversees the Armor Captains Career Course. He informed me that the Armor School w have moved to Fort Benning, Georgia by 2008, and answered several questions I asked. After lunch I checked to see if any internet (secret or otherwise) communications worked but they did not. Why did I have the feeling that all of this would somehow be my fault? I kept thinking I'd be blamed for not communicating with Squadron.

I was correct – when I finally spoke to Captains Nerph and Durmsy, 'Nerph' was panicked they hadn't heard from me in many hours, but Rich was calm about things. 'Nerph' said MAJ Diny wanted me to contact them every two hours. I said, "What!?!" and then he stressed the importance of communicating. I explained to him how I'd been trying all morning and he said it was what MAJ Diny wanted. I found it hard to believe Major Diny came up with this one because it didn't sound like him. It reeked of a spastic monkey behind the whole concept; I mean, if a convoy didn't show up, or we were sending one out that evening, I should just call them once or twice to keep them informed, not this every-two- hours nonsense. Rich told me kind of quietly on the phone that the whole "every two hours" thing was just because someone panicked when they couldn't get a hold of me. He suggested I just do it for a while until they got sick of it.

Ironically, I'd just started to appreciate the tactical satellite radio, due to the luxury of calling from just outside my room, when CPT Nerph told me while I was talking to him on it that our connection was poor and to contact him via phone (from a 3rd ACR tent). I kept up with the calling every two hours or so and there was little change. We managed to get out a few vehicles on the civilian contractor trucks headed for Mosul. I didn't get to bed until after midnight though, because I got to talk to Becky at the internet café. It was great because this was the first time in about a week that I'd talked to her. The bad part was it seemed as though my brother-in-law was getting worse and choosing sin. All I could do from here was pray and write a letter. So, I wrote one as led by the Lord – hopefully, it would help him.

June 10, 2005

The day went by very slowly, which was a good thing since I had free time after verifying all over the base that there were no assets to haul. I guess that was the only bad part about it, but it was a relaxing day.

June 11, 2005

What an interesting turn of events and perfect timing for early morning (or perhaps late night). I stayed up past 1 a.m. to link up with a SGT Wilkinson from D Troop who was expected to come in on the convoy. I was just about to give up looking for him when I ran into some guys on a convoy who said they were about to leave in twenty minutes and were supposed to take a Stryker with them. Shocked, I asked if they notified the crew of the Stryker. They weren't sure but said the HET (Heavy Equipment Transport – big army hauling truck with flatbed) was attempting to lift the Stryker at that moment on the other side of the FOB. I sped from the gate to the repair yard area, and sure enough, some transportation guys and the flatbed truck operator were trying to get the Stryker on the flatbed by themselves. They told me they only had twenty minutes, so I quickly drove over to a living pad, and knocked on Specialists Perry and Hall's door. I told them the situation and they both jumped up, packed their remaining stuff and loaded it onto my four-wheeler (which I noticed had a flat right rear tire).

We rushed to the Stryker and I told them not to worry about their room because I would clean it and turn in the keys. Aside from the broken Stryker almost flipping when they pulled it onto the flatbed, all went okay at the loading. We stuffed their gear in the Stryker and the HET cab had two seats for Perry and Hall, so they rode back with that convoy before 4 a.m. I contacted our 2-14 Cavalry TOC in Mosul to update them and grabbed a few hours of sleep until Sergeant Wilkinson woke me up. He let me know his plan for searching for the missing D Troop generator he thought was on this base. I called Squadron again at 10 a.m., then tried to get my four-wheeler fixed by the civilian contractors. They had no spares and my flat had too many holes to repair, so they took it off and suspended that axel. I'd been driving it around all day like that. Once the axel was tied up, I went to pad three and fixed up SPC Hall and Perry's room. After some confusion about a convoy later that evening (which we thought was going to Mosul but wasn't), Sergeant Murman and I learned the 536th Transportation Company would arrive at 1 a.m. for a "turn and burn." If he and I linked up with them, I could see if they had room for any more personnel.

June 12, 2005

Praise God! My prayers were answered, everything got off okay and arrived at the destination. I linked up with the 536th Transportation convoy commander and he had just enough room for Staff

Sergeants Lad and Gomez and Specialist M. A sandstorm rolled in at that time. I wore my goggles, but sand and dust still came through and scratched my eyes. I updated Squadron around 2 a.m. and confirmed the convoy was on its way. I headed to my room, after cleaning and sweeping SSG Lad and SPC M's room. I nearly forgot to get their keys, but was thankful God reminded me and I turned them in to the Mayor's Cell (those who manage facilities and everyday functions on the base, such as laundry, traffic, building ownership, maintenance, etc.).

June 13, 2005

Other than checking on a trailer that Rich wanted me to confirm was still there, I did almost nothing work related. I enjoyed the cool air conditioning in my room, watched some good movies and read. It was nice to have a complete day off. I was lacking many things I would have had if I were on FOB Marez, but all in all, it was very relaxing.

June 14, 2005

The plan for was for SGT Murman and Cox to roll out at night with me flying out the next day, but it didn't happen. When it came time to link up with the incoming convoy there were two miscommunications. Confusion on the time meant the convoy was ready to leave when we thought it was just arriving. Additionally, they had no room for SGT Murman's truck. I confirmed with a sergeant in the Mayor's Cell who gave me a guarantee we would get our things out the next night.

June 15, 2005

A huge sandstorm rolled in, blanketing the entire base and countryside with dust and sand – you couldn't see past 25 meters. It wasn't the worst I'd ever seen, but still bad. I turned in the top portion of the tactical satellite which belonged to 3rd ACR, then things started to get hilarious. I should have said we were going that night "God willing" because we then weren't. Captain Al from 3rd ACR told us no convoys were heading anywhere as previously scheduled due to lack of air coverage. The lingering sandstorm meant no flights could take off to support the convoys, so it looked like once again we were stuck.

June 16, 2005

After chow two sergeants major stopped and asked me about my Nomad patch. I explained to them it was my combat patch and they asked me if the Army approved it. I just said I didn't know, took it back (they had pulled the velcro patch off to look at it) and walked away. As I took it back, they suggested I go talk to Major General Rodriquez and ask him if he authorized the Nomad patch. I just said, "All right," and left. In a combat zone with so many people wearing things normally unauthorized in the US, it should hardly matter if I wore a combat patch for Nomad. People had their blood types velcroed to their uniforms, their vehicle number and all kinds of other things. I didn't bother MG Rodriquez – he probably had better things to do with his time than talk to a captain about a patch – and I had better things to do with my time too.

June 17, 2005

Sergeant Murman, Private First-Class Cox and I waited three hours from midnight t to 3 a.m. for the 17th Corps Support Battalion convoy to come to Sykes and escort him and Cox to Marez. Of the five roadside bombs engineers found, I believe we saw three explode from the base. During those hours we noticed three huge flashes all the way out in the city which lit up the sky, all at separate times, the largest being the last one close to 3 a.m. The 17th Corps Support Battalion unit finally left 30 minutes later with SGT M and PFC Cox. I contacted Squadron to let them know before I went to bed.

Sergeant Murman told me later when we were both in Mosul it was the worst convoy he'd ever been on. When they left the FOB Sykes gate and the convoy reached Sinjar Checkpoint, someone radioed that another convoy was inbound, and they would have to "squeeze" past it. Squeezing past was a bad idea, especially between Sinjar and Avgani Checkpoints where the roads were extremely narrow. SGT Murman described that his convoy drove so slowly that he told PFC Cox to come down from the .50 cal. and get inside the vehicle completely. He couldn't believe they were going only two miles-per-hour and was certain someone would get hit. After the slow roll through Tal Afar, they made it to Mosul virtually without incident, but the air support flying with them warned the convoy commander of a roadside bomb upon their entry to Mosul. The convoy commander decided to drive past it and the air support suggested they at least move to another lane or another side of the road.

Next, they passed a confirmed car bomb on the side of the road. SGT M radioed, "Are you kidding me? That car on the side of the road is a confirmed [car bomb]? I'm going to engage it then." They radioed him not to engage it because Strykers were on the way to deal with it. He was stunned. The entire convoy drove past a confirmed car bomb while told Strykers would be there soon. He said they approached an area where 1-24 Infantry were conducting a cordon and search and they didn't want his convoy to pass them. They suggested they find another route into FOB Marez and the convoy commander agreed. Fortunately for SGT Murman and the others, the air support asked 1-24 Infantry to just allow them to pass because it was already past sunrise, and the convoy was so long. They allowed the convoy to pass, and SGT Murman peeled off into FOB Marez while the rest of the convoy went left into FOB Diamondback. As they parted, he breathed a sigh of relief to be finally at our new home.

    I found out about all of this shortly after arriving in Mosul myself. After signing over the last all-terrain vechicle to 3rd Armored Cavalry Regiment, I turned in my keys to the Mayor Cell and waited for my helicopter ride after 1 p.m. I prayed for an uneventful and safe flight, with which (other than a few strong winds) the Lord blessed us. I hobbled off the chopper with my heavy bags, and before I even made it out of the flight area on FOB Diamondback, I saw SFC Grimm sitting at a table waiting for me. I was so thankful he was there waiting with our Humvee. We drove around Mosul Airfield and across the street to FOB Marez. He showed me the office and it is wonderful. CPT Cleverst came in soon and had the second key to our room, which we will be sharing for many days. Our office was almost twice the size of the former one, very well air-conditioned and in the same building as most other Squadron staff offices. It seemed like a modern building, as if it were recently a motel.

    I ate dinner at the new dining facility with SFC Grimm, who showed me where everything was. They'd named it Mosul Memorial Dining Facility and it is a wonderful memorial. There were weapons clearing barrels at the entrances with twelve-foot concrete barriers surrounding the entire building. There were two search lanes with about four soldiers standing by to search people on their way in. In addition to the sandbag filled (and highly decorated) walls inside to protect from any possible explosions, there was a six-foot thick concrete ceiling. No mortar could get through that. In the center of the chow hall, and noticeably at the exits, was a giant glass encased plaque with the names of all the individuals killedlast December. I was impressed. It was a "Good use of our tax dollars," as SFC Grimm repeatedly stated.

LTC Mavis put the final notice on me for wearing my Nomad patch. He said I had to take it off due to a new rule from Major General Rodriguez. MG Rodriguez also ordered that all Desert Combat Uniforms must be returned to normal and any modifications to them must be undone. He also never wanted to hear, "I just came back from mission," or, "I just came out of the wire," as an excuse for being unshaved or being out of the full and proper uniform. I briefly talked to Lieutenants Dale Koughan, Dave Vebb and Kyle Cewald and CPT Gary Rickens Who were sitting at a table near mine. It was great to see them and others from 1-24 Infantry again.

During the entire long and bumpy trip back to the living quarters, Rich and I discovered that one of our tires had a leak which continued to get worse. Eventually, the right front tire ripped and slammed into the underside of the truck with every turn of the tube. It became more and more hilarious to us as we limped down the road in the dark back to the living containers behind the gym. At one point I stuck my head out of the window to view the tire, and it flung a giant rock toward my eye. I felt the rock hit the edge of one of the eyelashes of my right eye just before it slammed hard into the top of the cab. That shocked Rich-- and especially me. I thanked the Lord it wasn't any closer because I could have lost my right eye. We dropped off the truck at the repair facility, which was not far from our rooms.

While helping Rich carry a desk to Major Diny's room, we got into a comical situation. At first, he tried to get inside it somehow to carry it more easily. The result was a complete flipping and dropping of the desk. We both laughed, and he said, "How do you want to carry this thing?" I answered him, "Well, first of all, not with you inside it." He laughed so hard he couldn't pick it up for a few seconds. We eventually got it into the room, and he headed off to bed. I told him that I'd get the truck fixed while he was gone the next day. He was leaving first thing in the morning for Dahuk to purchase a bunch of supplies before our funds were due to close out. SGT Murman had to go with him and be the gunner. I felt bad for him because he just got in this morning and was already going to be in Dahuk all for a whole day. I thanked God I was safe at Marez and there should be no more big convoys or moves for menow until we leave Iraq for Kuwait. I must just have to survive any mortar attacks on the FOB (which were rare nowadays) and pray all our boys made it home.

June 18, 2005

It was about 106 degrees. The repair team had many Strykers to fix, so I got a ride to the office with medics since it would be a three-mile walk or more. SFC Grimm took me to the Mayor Cell so civilian contractors could fix the tire on our truck. In less than an hour I was mobile again. I decided to visit some 1-24 Infantry friends before heading back to the office. Gumfi was excited to see me. I haven't heard SFC E's side yet, but "G" told me Heath took off his shirt one day and wanted to fight Gumfi because he was so mad at him, which sounded silly. Gumfi was working in the 1-24 Infantry Battalion Headquarters and said he was happy there. I swung by the Storm Trooper area and after no one answered at Heath or Randy's doors, I knocked on Jay's. He was glad to see me, and we caught up on things, including the pictures of Katelyn. I ran into DeArthur, Will and Bryce. It felt great seeing them all again and they were pleased to talk. I checked on Gluv too, who was quite possibly the most excited to see me. Everyone asked about me being injured twice and about Katelyn and Becky. It was mid-afternoon so I left, briefly saying "hi" to SFC Nubear. He seemed fine and I told him I'd stop by later when I got more time.

That night I learned one of the Troops in the Squadron almost had a friendly fire incident early this morning. LTC Mavis mentioned the various factors involved, including that the soldier who shot at a Stryker wasn't wearing a communications helmet. The more LTC Mavis talked, the madder he became until he was yelling. He asked me if the S-4 shop had checked on our January order of communications helmets. This was the first I'd heard of it and Rich was in Dahuk, so there was only so much SFC Grimm and I could do after I found out about it, especially when the people who had the information were either on mission or on leave. LTC Mavis yelled about how we had all day to do it, he wanted me to find out now and it should have been my priority.

I left the brief early and SSG Johnson updated me on the paper trail he had followed to track down and determine exactly what happened to our order of 71 helmets. I later explained it to LTC Mavis after he calmed down, so he knew we were trying. He seemed semi-satisfied with what I shared. Aaron Cleverst was back from Dahuk with Rich, so we rearranged the room together. I was thankful everyone made it safely back from Dahuk.

June 19, 2005

I was determined to get all the information from Rich that I could. His leave would begin in two days, so this was the last chance to learn from him before I have to run Squadron logistics while he was gone. We spent much of the day driving around to various places while he showed me and explained to me what they were, how they operated and what tasks needed to be completed. I saw the new 2-14 Detention Facility and talked to some of the prisoners in Arabic. They seemed well behaved and from what I heard, they hadn't committed any serious crimes, but had just broken curfew.

In the evening I drove to dinner in one of the Humvees, and when I went back out after diiner, it wouldn't work. I prayed and tried to get it started, but it wasn't working, so I walked down to the 1-24 Infantry chapel. I had about five minutes to get there and about fifteen minutes of walking to do. I didn't want to miss any of it, so I prayed again that God would somehow get me there faster. I kept looking back as I walked, but no one seemed to slow down to offer a ride, so I just walked faster. The next thing I knew, SGT Murman came driving behind me in his all-terrain vehicle and I hopped on with a smile. He asked me where I was headed and after I told him, "To the Deuce Four chapel," I let him know he was an answer to prayer. He laughed and quickly dropped me off. It was nice.

During the service, SSG Lytle had the opportunity to deliver the message. It was from the book of Malachi, and the Lord spoke through him. It was a great message about being obedient to God's word and not living in sin, which was not preached enough in today's churches. After the service, I talked briefly to SGT Pena, SSG Lytle, LT Chandler (Liz) and Chaplain Welon. Everyone was excited to see me, as I was to see them. SGT George had vehicle maintenance to do, so he couldn't be there tonight, but I heard he'd been expecting me ever since he heard 2-14 Cavalry was scheduled to return to FOB Marez.

I walked back to the room with Chaplain Ed Wells, and he seemed to be excited to participate in services with Tim Welon. This will be an exciting time these next four months. On the tactical side of things, I read the article on *StrykerNews* today by MiShayl Gilbert from the News Tribune about us capturing the top planner for Zarqawi. I didn't hear about it while at FOB Sykes, but apparently it occurred on the sixteenth. What shocked me was Zarqawi's planner didn't blow himself up or shoot himself. Despite his ravings to get suicide bombers to blow themselves up, he must either not have believed any of the nonsense he filled their heads with or was too scared to do it. Either way, I was thankful because numerous lives were likely saved because of the capture of that evil man. Local civilians turned him in – it was great they were turning over leaders like this. It shouldn't be long before Zarqawi himself was turned over to US forces. I could only pray…and pray I would.

June 20, 2005

The Lord really showed me just how much He could help me mentally on a day like that day. With Rich leaving at noon, I tried to pull info out of him, but it was also hard for him to remember everything. As I stated, "There are so many things that I don't know, but I don't even know of what I don't know." He agreed and said there were probably several things he didn't even know that he knows. People would ask him random questions, and he'd pull the answer from somewhere, and it was usually something I had no clue about. I finally got about an hour to talk to him about several things I had questions about, but he couldn't get too deep on the answers. I mostly got just the quick answers to who, what, when, where and why for the biggest handful of issues.

I drove over to FOB Diamondback to drop him off, and we ended up eating lunch in the chow hall there. Kevin Richardson (a Department of Defense civilian) wasn't in his office, so Rich couldn't wait for his flight there as he had hoped. As we ate at the dining facility, I became frustrated. There were no inner barriers from explosions. I couldn't believe a small chow hall like the one out at FOB Sykes learned the sad and painful lesson of December 21, 2004, yet FOB Diamondback hadn't. What was worse was that the Dining Facility on Diamondback served more non-Americans than any other DFAC in the northern sector.

I dropped off Rich, got into the office and immediately tried to read and gain a grasp of issues I'd face that week. I answered several emails from others in the Squadron and Brigade and got interrupted before starting on any of my issues. It was like running a huge corporation and a customer service desk from the same small office with the same three people. Just when you started taking care of big coordination issues, answering emails, phone calls and working on a spreadsheet or plan, a customer came to the desk. As the logistics officer, there are many questions only I could answer since they required decisions on my part. CSM Weldo came in with an issue that he needed help with, as did a representative from D and A Troops. Major Diny came in with the D Troop commander later and asked me to figure out how to resolve a handheld radio issue. D Troop didn't get any radios, so I somehow had to find out which Troops got what and how we could redistribute more to D Troop. I examined Detention Facility issues, ordered communications helmets and prepared for moving ammo to the brigade area. In the middle of those, CPT Nerph asked if I could get civilian contractors to move the fuel container for the power generator at the detention facility, because it was huge and in the way.

Troop XO's and others came in asking questions to which I had no answers because I didn't know what Rich had decided prior to handing over this responsibility to me. After attempting to figure out where to acquire bottled water to supply headquarters and the Troops, I finally (and far too late) prayed. As I sat at my desk, I asked the Lord for help to sort all this stuff out mentally and to make the required decisions based on the little information I had. He sure answered. As my mind cleared and I organized thoughts and plans in my head, answers came walking in. The first was SGT Murman, who fixed the bottled water issue. He picked up pallets with a forklift a few times a week and brought them all from the supply area to our repair and logistics support team areas. With SGT Murman, SFC Grimm and SSG Johnson in the office at the same time, it was almost like a meeting. I asked questions, bounced ideas off them and made some huge decisions. I also organized files and folders on the computers and in the office. I wrote down several issues on sticky pads and as the day progressed, I got rid of several "stickies" worth of notes and 'missions' to get done.

I finally got to a point where I decided to check my personal email instead of going to dinner. It was a sacrifice well worth it. Becky needed serious prayer about an issue with my brother-in-law and needed my advice. I prayed about it first, and just let God guide me in a quick internet chat conversation with the two of them. This was cut short by a 9 p.m. meeting I was unaware of. I had to plan an operation brief for the next morning, so I took many notes. Around 11 p.m. I made it back to my room for the evening, listened to praise music, made myself some dinner and prepared for bed.

June 21, 2005

After the 9 a.m. operation order I had a Brigade meeting, ate lunch and worked many tasks in preparation for the big Squadron mission the next day. The operation was a cordon and search in a small town south of Mosul, but north of Hamam Al Alil just north of a bend in the Tigris river on the east side. That afternoon I felt led to mention something to LTC Mavis I'd heard from men about the Squadron. Instead of being more concerned about the real issue, he was mad at me for telling him so late. I thought he would be able to open or close with remarks on the topic at the rehearsal at 4 p.m. In fact, I had told CSM Weldo about it prior to telling the LTC and the sergeant major thought it was a good idea so the boss could announce it to the Squadron. I guess he and I were both disappointed.

June 22, 2005

I woke before 4 a.m., since all primary staff members were required to be at the office while the mission kicked off. Thankfully, everyone made it back safely and there were about fourteen hundred machine gun rounds found in a cache inside the small town along with a roll of detonation cord, a container of black powder and one 122mm rocket. I believed a suspect or two were detained in the process as well. 1-24 Infantry also conducted an operation – a massive surge of Strykers and troops combined with Iraqi Army troops in their sector. They set up traffic control zones, but sadly a suicide car bomb hit a C Company vehicle, seriously injuring nine civilians and killing three.

June 23, 2005

I thought I'd get something accomplished on my never-ending task list, but I thought wrong. LTC Mavis decided at last night's brief that the staff wasn't showing enough information in our slides. He gave MAJ Diny a list of things he wanted to know from all the staff, which in turn caused us to have to create more slides. Just because he wanted to see certain items in stock broken down by which Troop had how many of each item, it took me half of the day. We all briefed MAJ Diny and he showed us what we needed to change on our slides before we briefed the boss at the staff update. I worked on an ammo breakdown by unit and Squadron totals until after 2 a.m. My slides still weren't complete because I seriously lacked vital information from all the Troops.

June 24, 2005

I got to the office before 8 a.m., just in time to get the rest of the info from the Troop Commanders and put it in the slides. The brief went well, but the boss still wanted to see even more info on my slides. I worked on that and completed the plans for Dahuk. As the day rolled on, so did the issues, emails and tasks. It was funny how the decisions of one man, or the receipt of one email, could create hours if not days of extra work – work often useen, seldom appreciated and possibly even unnecessary. I was still thankful I was not being shot at, but this staff life was quickly draining me. I thanked God that He gave me strength to not flip out.

June 25, 2005

Praise God for one of the biggest miracles that I've heard in a while! In the afternoon, the Mobile Gun System platoon of C Company of 1-24 IN, led by LT Roy, hit a roadside bomb which failed to explode properly. Bomb experts determined it was two anti-tank mines. Had both exploded properly, they would have torn that Stryker apart. I thanked God they didn't – this is the second time I knew of when LT Ray was saved from certain death. The other time was before I arrived at Marez back in October when a mortar round impacted at his living quarters, ripping a hole in his roof and destroying most of the belongings in his room while he was out on a mission. SFC Grimm, CPT Meyer and the rest of the team made it back safely from Dahuk. I prayed for no incidents and God was good! SFC Grimm said there wasn't even a shot fired through Mosul when they drove down Hwy-1. I was amazed!

I wondered if God had opened a door for my career and life. I received an email about what was called a Functional Area – something I could do instead of staying in Armor Branch. If I stayed in Armor Branch (Tankers, Scouts, and Cavalrymen) after the Armor Captains Career Course, I would serve as a staff officer in a tank, Stryker or cavalry unit. This could be a few years as an S3 Assistant (planning operations), S1 (personnel), Battle Captain (running the fight and TOC when the XO wasn't present) or some other position before I would command a company. After serving as a Company Commander for a year, I would either move back to staff, take a second Company Command or move to some training or recruiting job. Once making major on this path, I would have to wait some time to become an S3 (Operations Officer) for a Battalion or Squadron, then a Battalion or Squadron Executive Officer. At the Lieutenant Colonel level, officers served as a Squadron Commander or Battalion Commander, among other jobs.

The Functional Area path was more simplistic and focused. It put a captain into a specific area of expertise where he or she would remain, never to return to the basic branch of Armor (or any other branch). Functional Areas included psychological operations, civil affairs, information systems engineering, information operations, strategic intelligence, space operations, public affairs, information systems management and simulation operations. Other functional areas included foreign area officer, acquisition, human resource management, comptroller, operations research / systems analysis, force management, nuclear research and operations and finally strategic plans and policy.

If I followed the path email mentioned, I could go immediately after the Captains Career Course and be trained in Civil Affairs or Psychological Operations. I would be practically permanently stationed at Fort Bragg, North Carolina, and would deploy every six months or so, for about four to six months overseas and then come back again. There would be no training center rotations and it would set me up for success if I got out of the Army after eight years. Regardless, I had to pray and seek the Lord's guidance for this, since my life was not my own. He'd continue to open doors for me if thhat was His will. In all honesty, the most interesting sounding Functional Areas to me personally were Strategic Plans and Policy, Simulations Operations and Civil Affairs, in that order. I didn't know if there was any possibility of switching to another Functional Area later, but it seemed like God had opened this door for me. I'd emailed Becky about the issue and hopefully with the whole family praying, God would show us the way.

We continued to plan for our operation to move down to the Euphrates River. We had just moved to Mosul and a General decided he wanted us to maintain a presence near the Syrian border and the Euphrates. The current plan was for 2-14 Cavalry to set up a FOB (Forward Operating Base) there until the third heavy Squadron from 3rd ACR could replace us there. One Troop would stay behind at FOB Marez and the other two would go along with all the staff and headquarters. I supposed the General was concerned with quickly establishing a presence in the area and stopping the flow of foreign fighters into Iraq. We could just be the best choice for it, even though none of us wanted to go.

June 26, 2005

I woke just after 6 a.m. to a loud explosion in Mosul. The evil suicide driver of the car bomb knew exactly what he was doing because he parked at the portion of a police station to inflict the maximum number of casualties. There was also a mortar attack on the station in the same time frame with four rounds of 82mm mortars. The casualty count was sadly high: ten police and two civilians killed, and eight police wounded. The police building and three surrounding buildings were damaged. Civil Affairs and Information Operations personnel headed out to assess the damage and investigate after the casualties were evacuated. I guessed I'd still experience the horrors even if I chose to go Civil Affairs. I prayed most of the terrorism and evil in this country would be extremely rare by then.

Other than the above tragedy, the day was a long one of learning and of work until the evening. Since it was a Sunday, I made it to chapel, but my violin playing quickly came to an end during the first song when a loud pop occurred. I saw it out of the corner of my left eye, as well as the dust that went with it, and felt something hit my face. For a split second I thought, "Oh my goodness, I'm being shot in church!" Thankfully, I wasn't shot, but unfortunately, my bow broke. On the upstroke during the song, the horsehairs completely popped out of the end, still glued together and hit my face, leaving rosin dust in the air. Chaplain Welon didn't notice until later and Chaplain Wells almost laughed when he saw the face I made. I had great fellowship with the praise team (including SGT George) and with the chaplains afterwards. I made dinner in my room and went to bed as midnight approached.

I think 9 p.m. was the earliest I'd made it back to my room at night. It just showed me how staff life was – and some staff officers worked later than I. I looked at my future if I stayed in Armor branch (even though I love Armor) and just got tired thinking about it. I could work for seventy-two hours straight and not sleep and would still be behind. I remembered CPT Jacobsen used to tell me that when he worked on Brigade Staff, he didn't get home most nights until 9 p.m. or later. He recalled one day before we deployed that he had explained to his then new 1-24 Infantry boss that one of his goals was to eat dinner with his family once or twice a week. I found it sad (as did Captain J) that staff life kept him from having dinner with his family so many nights. That was why he didn't seem to mind working as our Commander until 6 p.m. or so, since it seemed early to him. As honorable as it was to go through all of that, I had a huge desire to spend time with Becky, Katelyn and any other kids we may have. Staying Armor and trying to get a Command that way wasn't worth it to me.

June 27, 2005

I continued work on several projects, leaving the office just after 9:30 p.m. – a new record for going to bed early. We'd see what happens next.

June 28, 2005

It got me nowhere. I must have been psychic. I came in for the staff update meeting at 9 a.m. and got ridiculed by every other captain I ran into. "What is this, you work banker hours?" I learned the staff meeting was cancelled and most of them said, "You'd know that if you worked late here all night like the rest of us." I couldn't believe it. The one night I decided to leave early (if 9:30 p.m. could be called early) and I got teased for it. Then SFC Grimm told me Major Diny wanted to see me. I inquired what it was about, and he said MAJ Diny came in and asked sarcastically, "Is he pacing himself?" I talked to Major Diny and he reminded me I needed to be working later at night and earlier in the morning. I guessed I was supposed to go to sleep at 11 p.m. and be back in the office between 7 and 8 a.m. That was craziness, but it sealed the deal for me.

  Major Diny had a sense of humor and didn't yell, but he helped me realize something: staff life was expected to be longer and harder. I now knew that even with a good boss you were expected to work such ridiculous hours. I knew it probably wouldn't be as bad when I was in the States and not in a combat zone, but what if it was? It sounded that bad when Captain Jacobsen working in this very same Brigade. I'd rather spend that time with family, so it was not worth it to stay in Armor, even if it was the branch I've come to know and love. All of this coincided with an email from a Lieutenant Colonel I'd contacted about Function Areas. He let me know he could help me get into Arabic language for Civil Affairs since my Defense Language Aptitude Test score was a 98; he wanted to know if I was interested. I read an email from Becky who preferred a branch transfer over me staying Armor. She'd been praying, and I prayed again, and answered the LTC that I was interested. The process would begin right away, and the Lord would show me if I was to back out, since that was what I asked Him for in my prayer.

  The rest of my day was spent determining what equipment should stay behind in Iraq when we redeployed to Fort Lewis, Washington. MAJ Diny helped me, and we learned a lot by visiting the property office over on Diamondback. I worked issues and planned for the upcoming operation in the south near the Euphrates River. It defied common sense that our Squadron would conduct this mission when we had deadlines to load shipping containers and prepare to transition with 4-14 Cavalry in just over a month (mid-August). No one could even tell us what the duration of this mission was. Well, since it was midnight, and the rest of the staff had left, I supposed I should go to bed.

June 29, 2005

I attempted to turn the scales in my favor regarding work tasks. It appeared that each day five tasks got added to my list, and each task was accompanied by about five to fifteen implied subtasks. This was in addition to whatever remains from the the previous day's tasks. Some days I'd get all five done and think I could take care of something else the following day for the future redeployment to Fort Lewis, but within the first thirty-five minutes of the morning, I'd be bombarded with more tasks. It never ended – one had to re-prioritize every task received, every day, to do what was most important, and put off what was somewhat (but still very) important. Then came the favors people ask of you and the questions they needed answered, sometimes in phone calls, but usually in emails or walk-ins. Most questions required contacting several people or doing several things to find the answers.

The evening of tiresome staff work ended with me finishing slides while I checked a secret computer for the upcoming operation – eight emails, each with at least one attachment or two, and all were filled with information on the important operation. Some slideshows were twenty-two slides long. I was sure we were expected to know it all by morning. The biggest disappointment that day was that I finally got time to type a memorandum for Omar (which he'd asked for four months) but the boss wouldn't sign it so I guess I'd have to. He handed it back to Major Diny saying he just, "Didn't feel he knews Omar that well." Minutes until midnight LTC Mavis and Major Diny left, as did I. Things could always be worse. These were the times when it was easiest to feel bad and forget about the things God does for us and has done for us in the past. Perhaps I needed to reflect on that and thank Him.

June 30, 2005

I got so bogged down with planning and ammunition procedures that I got dizzy. So many things were happening at once and my brain was so tired from sleep deprivation and data overload that I couldn't process it all. I read several orders about our mission down south near Rawah. We would support the main effort, which was led by a Special Forces unit. The most aggravating thing yet again was there was no mention of a withdrawal plan for 2-14 Cavalry and the Brigade. We were preparing for redeployment in a month and a half and needed answers. The mission did sound exciting, not that I'd be roaming around the battlefield in a Stryker. The entire Task Force and supporting elements would move in all at once on July 15th, surprising the enemy in sector. We should end up catching several training camps, foreign fighters and terror cell leaders.

One tactic the enemy used down in that area was the quick setup of tents for the training of foreign fighters. They did quick training on roadside bombs, combat and car bombs, before rapidly tearing down the tents as the terrorists evacuated the area. They were literally mobile training camps, so if we moved in right, we should be able to disrupt their operations and catch several terrorists in the area. Depending on how well equipped they were out there, and how strong their resolve was, there might be several firefights. I prayed the entire operation would go smoothly and quickly, as well as the establishment of an outpost within an hour of Rawah. Once this was all established, the Iraqi Army should be able to move into the area to continue operations.

11

July

July 3, 2005

I'd been so busy that I didn't even get to write for the past few days. I couldnn't believe how much work was involved in this logistics staff job – just insane. I didn't even remember all the details of the staff work I'd done. It was probably not exciting anyway. I made it to church though, although I came close to considering staying in the office because of the amount of work I had to get done. Church was at 8 p.m., and I returned to the office and worked until 3 a.m.

July 4, 2005

Extremely tired, I woke at 6 a.m. after little sleep to attend the "Prayer Breakfast" in the new chow hall. COL Brown was the guest speaker, and he talked about Jesus' sacrifice and compared sacrifice to Oscar Sanchez. Oscar Sanchez was the soldier at the Hwy-1 combat outpost on December 29th last year when a suicide bomber drove a pickup truck loaded with a 2,000-pound bomb into the barriers surrounding the building. COL Brown mentioned that Sanchez could have just hidden behind a wall and saved his life, but the truck would have hit the building past the barriers had he done that. Instead, the truck exploded he shot at it from his Stryker in vicinity of the barriers, saving the occupants inside, but sacrificing his own life. It was sad that heroes die like that, but he laid down his life for his friends, as Jesus taught.

After the prayer breakfast, I began my grueling day of staff work and contemplated if it was worth it to be safe inside the wire while working those unbelievable hours. Life could always be worse though and I was so thankful for my Savior, my wife and daughter, and my friends and family who prayed for my safety. When I thought about it, life could still end at any second, because a mortar round could hit my truck or room when I was driving or sleeping, and life would be over without me ever leaving the wire again. I sometimes pictured that on my way back to my room and wondered if I'd be wounded trying to drive to an aid station or the combat support hospital. It was better not to think such things, I supposed.

July 5, 2005

I started the day tired, mentally exhausted and drained; yet my time with the Lord lifted me up and gave me strength for the rest of the day. I realized I was taking too much of the burden of this job on myself while SFC Grimm and SSG Johnson went to their rooms around 6 or 7 p.m. most nights. They'd always ask me if there was anything they could do, but I felt I had to do everything. I felt this way for two reasons: one, because I was still learning this job, and felt I must immerse myself in everything about it; and two, because I was ultimately responsible for everything in the shop while Rich was gone. I didn't want to let him down or disappoint Major Diny by not knowing answers to questions or turning in non-standard work (my NCOs would turn in good work, but I knew exactly what Major Diny wanted).

I read a Bible verse in Exodus about Moses delegating! What a day for the Lord to put this one on me. In Exodus 18, after Moses attempted to solve every problem and dispute between his people, his father-in-law, Jethro, told him in verse 17, "What you are doing is not good. You will surely wear yourself out, both you and these people with you. For the task is too heavy for you; you cannot do it alone." It was amazing how God seemed to guide me to where I needed to be in scripture to read and hear what I needed to grow. As Jethro gave Moses advice, he mentioned to Moses, "You should also look for able men among all the people, men who fear God, are trustworthy, and hate dishonest gain; set such men over them as officers over thousands, hundreds, fifties, and tens. Let them sit as judges for the people at all times; *let them bring every important case to you but decide every minor case themselves.* So, it will be easier for you, and they will bear the burden with you. *If you do this*, and God so commands you, then *you will be able to endure*, and all these people will go to their home in peace" (Exodus 18:21-23 NRSV, emphasis added).

God was obviously trying to tell me something, and it was a big something. I really needed to include SFC Grimm and SSG Johnson in more of the load around the office. I started right away by reevaluating my tasks to accomplish for the day in terms of major and minor. I gave them minor tasks and left the major ones to me. If I gave a major task to one of them, I just made sure I looked it over before they executed it, or sent it via email to someone, or whatever it needed. The day got even better when CPT Roger Turble came back from leave. I tried not to "attack" him all at once with tasks, but he was more than willing, so I had him help me to make a manifest of vehicles by the dates of July 11th, 12th, and 13th for movement to Rawah.

We had a huge briefing and soon time was running out. LT DeFabbs also showed up, ready to help organize the Logistical Support Team. He would be our new LST Platoon Leader, and hopefully would replace CPT Aaron Cleverst, who was on leave. LT DeFabbs was a workhorse, ready to help constantly and willing to learn a lot from all of us. He also helped me with slides for the briefing, and together, the whole team helped me get accomplished what needed to be done. Praise God! I delivered the briefing to the boss and the Commanders tonight with confidence, and it went well. The boss liked the slides, and I finally felt like I understood the whole plan. Bedtime came at midnight once again, but midnight was much better than 3 a.m. Thankfully, God stepped in with open arms as He always did and carried me through the day. What a blessing!

July 6, 2005

We had another busy day of staff work and preparation for the upcoming Brigade rehearsal. LT DeFabbs reorganized the LST a bit better for his leadership style of "delegation." It was amazing. We had a few good discussions throughout the day, and I found out he is a Christian. He got excited when I told him my biggest mission in life was to serve and bring glory to Jesus Christ and follow Him. After I mentioned that, he energetically engaged in a discussion with me about the Bible and religions. It was more interesting than the work we did that day.

July 7, 2005

This was the day of the Brigade rehearsal. I had fun making printouts that LT DeFabbs contributed of all kinds of transportation and tactical vehicles. We all made cutouts and stapled them to folded index cards so they could stand on their own for all to see during the rehearsal if needed. It turned out they weren't needed for the rehearsal, but it was informative. Major Diny told me the cards were "above and beyond" what he expected. The remainder of the day, I took time to email family and friends (for the first time in five days). It was desperately needed. I enjoyed talking to LT DeFabbs about the miracles I'd experienced here in combat. We both shared stories, and I could tell we'd learn a lot from each other. I was sure we'd have many great and interesting conversations.

Unfortunately, this day was another day that would be remembered in history for the worse. As I drove to chow with SSG Johnson, we heard on the Armed Forces Radio that six explosions occurred in London, England, due to terrorism. The initial report I heard was two double-decker buses and four subway trains were targeted. Later, as reports were refined, it turned out to be four explosions total, with one occurring on a double-decker bus and three in the subway trains. At least thirty-seven people were killed and another 700 wounded. I couldn't believe it. It reminded me of September 11, 2001, and I'm sure it felt the same way to the British. I couldn't imagine the number of little children killed or wounded.

We were fighting terrorism on the battlefield in Iraq and these monsters were attacking innocent civilians back in cities. It was uncertain whether the bombs were left on the vehicles or worn by suicide bombers. No one could tell if the subway bombs were placed on the actual "carriages" (as the British call them) or inside the tunnels. I could only imagine the panic after the explosions, as trapped civilians tried to escape the smoke-filled areas. I was sure there were several people completely blown away and many more with missing limbs. It must have looked like the chow hall back in December of last year.

Horrible! The only solace I found in all of this was that those responsible would be dealt with by a just God, and our world would adapt its security measures to prevent attacks like this in the future. Terrorists have attacked the United States with airplanes and bomb-filled vans, attacked Spain with bomb-filled trains and Britain's famous underground and double-decker bus systems with bombs. I was wondering what was next--car suicide bombings back home? I prayed this would not be the case.

July 8, 2005

I realized I was spending too much time in the office, so I left in this afternoon to pack some bags and turn in my NBC (Nuclear, Biological, and Chemical) suit and other gear. It was nice to get out of the office so as not to burn out. The plan and manifest kept changing, causing me to refine my manifest matrix. At least I didn't have to recreate the entire thing. I supposed I should expect this until we executed the plan.

July 9, 2005

There just wasn't enough time to get everything done with so many people coming in and out needing something all the time. Whenever I would sit down to get something done, people would walk in and ask questions which had nothing to do with us. It seemed everyone came into our office if their question had anything to do with items, supplies, movement of things, etc., so practically everything was related. I found myself divided between customer service and mission accomplishment. The good news was we coordinated with a bunch of other units in the Brigade and picked up hundreds of cots, dozens of tents, nets and other necessities for going to Rawah. That should help the soldiers out down there immensely. CPT McGarry and I had a meeting with the Brigade Support Battalion to plan how many assets could haul our shipping containers and vehicles. The cut-outs we made the other day proved most useful in simplifying this entire operation.

July 10, 2005

I tried to update transportation mission requests for the next two days, but people interrupted me all day with last minute changes they hadn't previously told me about. Sometimes I would lose perspective. Why was I there in that country, and in that war, when all I did was sit behind a computer and edit changes or come up with slides and matrices? I was so busy I missed church that day. I felt bad for my impatience and frustration, but the visits just wouldn't stop. The job made me feel like I was changing into a person I didn't want to be. I wanted to be filled with joy from the Lord, not with frustration from being overworked. I felt like I needed a vacation again, but I had only been back a month and a half. I needed more sleep, more prayer and more reading of scripture.

July 11, 2005

Praise God...Rich came back. Thankfully, he was able to grasp the changes regarding redeployment to Fort Lewis that occurred during his absence rather quickly, so I was able to focus on the convoys, which was easier since the first convoy left this morning. It was divided into two serials (separate mini convoys) and the slide I created paid off. Seven different people came in asking for a hard copy of it. It was exciting also to work on the shipping container situation with Rich and

Major Diny since it dealt with redeployment. Someone said the other day that we have less than one hundred days...I hoped they would go by quickly. SGT Murman did an awesome job with everything. It was sure hot today and he loaded a great number of vehicles and was the key to the entire moving and loading operation on the ground.

July 13, 2005

Three serials (mini-convoys) from our July 12th convoy went south, arriving safely. I ran errands and updated our Deployment Equipment List (DEL) – a tracker of vehicles and containers for large movements, in this case for our redeployment to the US We pushed off more serials and a Stryker from 2nd Platoon B Troop rolled over a sand drift in the road and caught fire. The crew all miraculously escaped, but the Stryker burned to the ground since the fire couldn't be put out. once the tires caught fire. The recovery plan was currently in the works for that. I was just thankful everyone was okay.

July 14, 2005

Well, I found out further clarification on the Stryker rollover from the last night, and even saw some pictures when CPT Vince Maykovich (B Troop Commander who switched with Kaine Walts) arrived at Marez with a Stryker convoy security element. It was such a tremendous miracle those men made it out alive from that accident. After talking to SSG Hitcher (who was also part of the security element) and Vince, I found out the guys in the Stryker had to literally dig their way out of the Stryker. It flipped upside down, and the ramp would not open, so the men were forced to dig through the sand out of the air guard hatches, and tunnel to safety while the Stryker burned. All their weapons, night vision devices and gear burned with the Stryker. I was amazed looking at the pictures, and thanked God everyone was safe – truly another miracle in this wilderness.

We also had someone injured that day. It was reported as a broken leg, but later turned out to be a sprained ankle. The casualty evacuation took far too long, and Major Diny was on the phone telling Brigade how unsatisfactory it was that hours had gone by and this soldier was still waiting on helicopters to pick him up. There were no "brown-outs" (or sandstorms) to prevent aircraft. The wounded soldier was finally evacuated, and he should be released for minimal duty within ten days.

Colonel Brown and Major General Rodriquez had an interesting conversation on the Task Force Freedom tactical satellite radio. COL Brown was with a Brigade element in Rawah with the Squadron Task Force, and it was amazing how he explained the situation down there to MG Rodgriguez. COL Brown shared how horrible the weather was, and they couldn't even see hands in front of faces. Colonel Brown and Lieutenant Colonel Mavis both did a reconnaissance to look for a new base location closer to Rawah and off the Al Jazeera desert plateau. They thought they might find a better spot to build the base, since the sandstorms were just too bad down there. We all listened to the radio as COL Brown described the safety risk and the difficulty of getting logistical support. He also cited if it was difficult for US forces to build and sustain a base, it would be ten times more difficult for the Iraqi forces.

He said the limited visibility environment only allowed for a few hour windows of each day to see clearly and conduct missions; the risk was too great. He also mentioned the low morale of the troops (which wasn't usually a planning factor for Generals). Colonel Brown's recommendation was for MG Rodriguez to fly out to see for himself, also suggesting they move the entire base of operations to FOB Summerall and not build one out there in the middle of the desert. I got so excited, possibly prematurely, because it sounded like someone was finally talking some common sense. I felt COL Brown was bold in saying how bad the conditions were out there for a base. Sadly, LTC Mavis stressed how badly he wanted CPT Durmsy (the main logistical supply officer – who could coordinate for supplies better from Mosul) down there with him primarily because LTC Mavis himself and the troops at Rawah with him didn't have ice. Major Diny discussed it with LTC Mavis over tactical satellite radio, and basically won the "argument." However, the next transmission from LTC Mavis was, "I want him down here."

It didn't make sense. Even redeployment preparations aside, Rich could get supplies just as fast (if not faster) down to Squadron from here in Mosul than he could from down in Rawah. I was praying that God would move this 'mountain' and either scrap the whole mission or at least let the Squadron Task Force stage from Rawah. Another sad point of my day was learning that my brother-in-law received my letter, dismissed my concerns conveyed within, and promptly balled it up. I supposed it was a reflection of how much I mattered to him. Things could always be worse. It was amazing how problems in a relationship with a family member or friend could be just as painful as war sometimes. I'd bet God feels this way – poor relationships with Him hurt Him just as much as what goes on over here at times. Perhaps it was all tied in together for Him, I didn't know. I was just praying He continued to make a difference over there and at home and would help me to fulfill His purpose for me in this life.

July 15, 2005

Many prayers were answered that day. Most of the Squadron Task Force pulled back to FOB Summerall near Bayji along Hwy-1. I also prepared two duffle bags and my rucksack to be placed in the shipping container for the next morning. Customs inspectors would arrive and inspect the staff personal bags, looking for any illegal items such as ammunition, war trophies and pornography. Once all bags were cleared, inspectors would seal the container for shipment home. Since most of our men were down south at Summerall and Rawah, it was difficult to get any containers sealed. Our current deadline for getting all 36 out of 41 sealed was August 23rd, and there was currently no end in sight for the Rawah mission. Five remaining containers will go at the last minute, to put any 'last minute' items in. As I sat there typing this after 11 p.m., the plan changed and there was a new site for a base located about three kilometers north of the city of Rawah.

July 16, 2005

Large moves shrink in insignificance compared to life and death. Many bad things happened. In the past couple weeks, a few mortars had hit FOB Courage (formerly known as Freedom) and FOB Diamondback. I had a meeting on Diamondback, and as I drove in the SUV with SFC Grimm I kept thinking a mortar round would hit in front of me, next to me or on top of our vehicle. I imagined my neck being cut up or my chin hit in the same spot except gaping open. I tried to focus on other things, but my mind seemed to keep drifting in that direction until we were inside the concrete tower having our meeting. It wasn't as bad on the way back, and after lunch I went about my day.

An hour after lunch I heard loud pops and explosions on the FOB. Normally, it was difficult for me to tell the difference between incoming and outgoing mortars, but this time I was certain it was incoming. I was on my way to the bathroom and contemplated climbing onto the roof to get a better view but decided against it since I didn't know how close the impacting rounds were. I talked to SGT Murman an hour later and he explained that he saw them impacting an area near our living quarters. They hit the parking lot I had been in that morning.

I had been loading a shipping container which was fun since officers rarely do stuff like that. It beat being behind a desk for a change and was a good workout. I was in the spot where the mortars hit when I drove up to help transfer some fuel from SFC Grimm, and I kept anticipating mortars. None had hit our FOB for a month until that day, but I had had strong feelings they were coming. SGT Murman said if the same enemy mortar team set up again that night and elevated their mortar tube just a bit, they would get direct hits on the living containers in our area – a scary thought. I thanked God everyone was safe; only one Humvee had a shattered windshield and a tire punctured. Iraqi police were not so blessed. A suicide bomber wearing explosives walked up to a police station in Hamam Al Alil (just south of Mosul) and blew himself up, killing six police and wounding another eleven. I wished there were a way of stopping these terrorists, but if the US forces had a hard time doing it, it must be even harder for minimally trained police officers.

July 17, 2005

I got a lot of work done and had a better attitude about it. The command group had contact in Rawah, hitting two roadside bombs and received RPG and rifle fire. LTC Mavis even did a few cordon and search missions, discovering a building on the north side of the city that was rigged to blow up upon entry. He called in the Air Force 'fast movers' to drop a 500-pound laser-guided missile, which showed we meant business.

Our COP (Combat Outpost) at Rawah was officially emplaced two kilometers north of the city, well within mortar range. The enemy tested that range by firing three mortar rounds at the newly emplaced COP. There were no damage or casualties, but our forces were unable to locate the mortar team. I worked on the logistics status report to get several necessities sent to our Rawah forces. Major Diny and the rest of the crew at "rear-TOC" (Tactical Operations Center) were all scheduled to fly down to FOB Summerall by the nineteenth, in just two days. At that time, SFC Grimm, two maintenance sergeants, the supply sergeants and I would be located at Marez. Major Diny said I would be the liaison to push supplies down to FOB Endurance where CPT Roger Turble would push them further to FOB Summerall and Major Diny and Rich Durmsy would push them all the way out to COP Rawah. It was an incredible distance and number of moving pieces. Rawah was one-fourth the size of Tal Afar and located on a peninsula, which should make it easier to cordon and search the entire city.

I moved the belongings from my room into a concrete building (the CSMs old office) so mortars wouldn't be an issue. Everything would be close and there are great showers just around the corner from the office. I was excited to be the liaison for 2-14 Cavalry and being in Mosul also helped me accomplish my Unit Movement Officer duties for redeployment, at least regarding shipping containers, equipment list and property book issues. I also made it to chapel to worship. Chaplain Welon delivered a message about the book of Acts and the Holy Spirit giving the disciples power. He delivered it (as always) with such an amazing passion.

July 18, 2005

I became completely burned out – way too many tasks and questions came at me, and I just had to get up and leave to vent to someone. It was insane. I was thankful I was not on staff the entire time of my deployment. I did learn of A Company 1-24 Infantry finding a weapons stockpile in northern Mosul which included thousands of rounds of ammunition, hundreds of missiles, rockets, mortars, dozens of weapons and mines. It was a huge miracle which allowed me to imagine peace in this city. It was also a huge setback to the enemy, but I couldn't help but wonder how many more caches like these were out there in this city?

July 19, 2005

The slow, painful, pounding and honing millstone of redeployment, convoys, property books and meetings pertaining to such things was driving me slowly insane in this "Fobbit" life.

At Rawah, a B Company of 3-21 Infantry Regiment Stryker hit two roadside bombs, which caused no casualties, but blew out three tires and caused a fuel leak. Hours later, at 9 a.m., a car bomb hit their MGS Platoon parked at a median in Rawah. Thirty minutes later, a suicide car bomb hit the same platoon, producing neither damage nor casualties, thank the Lord. The same company then encountered a car filled with five enemy pointing a machine gun at them, and the US soldiers fired .50 caliber machine guns, killing two enemy while three fled on foot to a shack where they were captured. There were two vehicles at the shack full of dozens of RPG and mortar rounds, hundreds of machine gun rounds, and a few weapons including a sniper rifle, hand grenades and many bomb-making materials along with enemy propaganda.

We'd uncovered a key entry point for terrorists and weapons. I was guessing most enemy in Rawah were foreign fighters, many from Syria, and I was willing to bet most of the weapons came from Syria too. Although Rawah was a quarter the size of Tal Afar, it seemed just as hostile (if not worse). The intelligence before we went down there suggested the Rawah police were friendly to terrorist cells. Our B Troop also located two anti-tank mines stacked together along one of the routes to Rawah. I could only imagine the damage those would've caused. A bomb-disposal team reduced them, and I prayed we could stop people from placing any in the future. The route was a ten-hour drive, but God worked miracles every day, and I prayed He would protect all the Troops who traveled that route.

In the afternoon, 2-14 Cavalry found an enemy safehouse (tipped off by a friendly civilian). Two vehicles there near a trench had stockpiles of weapons and ammo inside. The safe house was made to withstand a huge blast, so LTC Mavis requested to have a JDAM bomb dropped on it. General Rodriquez was there and approved the request. Air Force planes flew in, and the bomb destroyed all the targets. That was about it for the Cavalry down in Rawah, but up in Mosul, B Company of 1-24 Infantry two soldiers found several weapons in two cars which were in a traffic accident. One of the terrorists who fled the scene was detained when Strykers arrived. He admitted to being a foreign fighter from Tunisia during the questioning. I still couldn't believe how far these people come to fight us.

July 20, 2005

Major Diny left for FOB Summerall (near Bayji). I was able to get on webcam and talk to Becky and Katelyn. They both looked so adorable, and Katelyn cooed and smiled as I sang to her through the microphone. It lifted my spirits since I hadn't talked to them in weeks. Major Diny relayed that everyone at Marez would move to FOB Summerall except for SFC Grimm and our mail clerk. When I talked to Rich at 11 p.m., he had no clue about any of it, and called it a "knee-jerk reaction" on the Squadron Commander's part. I was not even stressing over it, because we were eight weeks away from flying to Kuwait. Besides, I was sure it'd change by the next evening. Such was life in the Cavalry.

July 21, 2005

Well, I was right – it changed – from crazy to totally insane. Now everyone was going to Rawah and not to Summerall. I would fly July 23rd and land at Rawah. I really didn't understand the purpose of having the Squadron Unit Movement Officer (me) all the way out there when there were so many deadlines to meet on Marez for redeployment, but perhaps that wasn't considered. At least I'd get to see someplace new, including the Euphrates River. I finished work at 6 p.m. for the first time. I packed in the morning before lunch so I should be all set to leave for Saturday. I placed the ammunition request for additional rounds needed in Rawah and prayed.

July 23, 2005

I picked up my laundry, hoping and praying our flight would be cancelled. LT Von Astudillo and others were all prepped and ready on the airfield with me. Helicopters came in, but they weren't ours. I checked on flights and it turned out that because of brownouts (sandstorms), no one was going anywhere south that day. We went back to Marez from Diamondback. God was good! After eating, I swung by the chapel and SGT George was surprised to see me, asking, "Aren't you supposed to be gone already?" I said I was supposed to fly at 4 p.m., "But we had a little Divine Intervention!" He laughed and just said, "See? We prayed! I wasn't worried...you came in the other day saying, 'Oh, I'm gonna be gone for a month,' but God's got it!" I joined in with Guzman, SGT Fees and SGT George in song, and we praised the Lord for a couple hours. It was great, and for that time I forgot I was in Iraq. I hoped we wouldn't get on a flight until Monday July 25th, so I could sing with the praise team at Sunday's service.

July 24, 2005

It was a relaxing Sunday, probably one of the best days of rest I'd had since I'd been back from leave. I spent the afternoon with SGT Kevin George. It was nice to have a great day of rest and one filled with worship. I felt rejuvenated throughout the day and had fellowship with MAJ Brown (the 1-24 Infantry Surgeon) after the service. We spoke of the amazing miracles the Lord had performed for us all over there. I learned more about LT Riley's injury, discovering he was wearing eye protection, but his sunglasses were either blown off his face or disintegrated.

I learned from SGT George that 'JFK' (Jeff the Fighting Kurd), LTC Krella's former interpreter, was thrown in jail some time ago because they discovered he'd been working with Anti-Iraqi Forces. He always seemed so strong willed against them and it was hard to believe. SGT George said LTC Krella was irate when he found out and SGT George recalled they found a document on him with various names of terrorists, where they could be reached and backup numbers. It was still unbelievable, but I was sure that the more I hear about it, the more it would sink in. It really made you wonder whom you can trust. LTC Krella probably knew 'JFK' just as well if not better, than I knew Evan and Omar. It was just more craziness.

July 25, 2005

After my morning meeting, I coordinated for our redeployment. I thought, in just four weeks I should be this FOB consolidating shipping containers for redeployment. In ten weeks, I should be arriving at Fort Lewis, to Becky and Katelyn. I wrote the beginnings of a song based on Psalm 91. One more day in this wilderness and one day closer to heading home to my ladies – excellent.

A lot happened down in Rawah and along the routes in and out. A suicide car bomb hit a 3rd Platoon of B Company 3-21 Infantry Stryker, blowing all hatches open, including engine compartments. The Stryker had six tires flattened, and soldiers on board suffered lacerations and burns to the face and hands. The same platoon, hours later, found a massive weapons stockpile which included dozens of rockets, mortars, ammunition, bomb-making materials and even a Russian DShK anti-aircraft and heavy machine gun along with brown military uniforms and ski masks. B Troop 2-14 Cavalry detained three males in a suspicious vehicle with a shovel, who tested positive for explosive handling. They had dug three holes nearby, likely to emplace roadside bombs. At the detention facility during further questioning, none of their stories matched as to why they were there that morning.

In the afternoon, 3rd Platoon of B Company 3-21 Infantry observed wires coming from the six gas cans on the back of a blue pickup truck and fired a TOW missle at it. The vehicle blew up with little surrounding collateral damage to the area – one less car bomb to be used against US or Iraqi troops. B Troop hit a roadside bomb on Hwy-1 but thankfully had no damage or casualties.

July 26, 2005

I woke up at 4 a.m. to an extremely loud explosion and was stunned at the sound and feeling of everything shaking. It sounded like a 120mm mortar had landed in the parking lot about five meters from my room. I froze and waited for more, but there were no more. Later, I learned it was a 73rd Engineers Buffalo armored vehicle which had hit a roadside bomb in Mosul. The crew was all okay, thankfully.

July 27, 2005

I took a CH-47 (Chinook) helicopter ride to COP Rawah. The flight wasn't too bad; the CH-47 Chinook helicpopters picked us up from Diamondback around 10 p.m. last night. It was hot, and we slept on the ride. The moon was out and very bright, although not full, but the illumination and visibility didn't matter since all I could see for miles and miles was sand anyway. We all landed at Rawah at 1 a.m. and trudged up toward our sleeping area. As I walked up the hill of sand, my legs sank into the moondust. The sand was so finely ground that you literally sank a foot or so into it, and every Humvee or other vehicle driving on the outpost creates a giant dust cloud. Hopefully, engineers working on the COP would continue to scrape the moon dust and sand away to rock beneath, as they had for the helipad area. After climbing to the top of a hill, and being covered in dust, I put my gear down just on the inside of a giant open tent, and slept on the ground, since there were no cots left. I woke up covered in dust and dirt at 6 a.m. to mortar rounds being fired. Others must have had the same startled face as I because MAJ Diny said, "That's H and I fires; it's us."

'H & I fires' stands for harassment and interdiction fires; we used this method of firing our mortars to deter the enemy from firing mortars at us (it kind of let them know that we can hit them back if they try anything), as well as to prevent them from trying to creep up near our COP. I couldn't get back to sleep after that, especially since my back and legs hurt from the hard rock I slept on. I then pulled a beetle from my lower back trying to make its way into my rear-end. A few minutes later, I closed my eyes again and felt something on my nose. I opened my eyes, and it was CPT Greg Rouson, my old friend and college buddy, touching my nose to tease me awake. I hadn't seen him since I passed through FOB Endurance (with my old MGS Platoon) last November. We ate breakfast and spent the morning talking. It was neat to catch up on old times and new. Greg no longer worked for the 2-8 Field Artillery but is on the Brigade starff. I took a good look around the outpost, and even got some pictures later in the evening. It was beautiful in its own God-given way, since He did make it, even though it was desert. I enjoyed seeing the Euphrates River by moonlight and catching a glimpse of the city of Rawah.

We focused on the mission and the arrival of the IIF (Iraqi Intervention Forces). Unfortunately, when the IIF made their way out here, they had two mishaps that cost them dearly. The first was a negligent discharge of an AK-47, killing one Iraqi soldier and wounding another. The second died of wounds later at the hospital. It'was so sad that one of their own soldiers accidentally killed two of his friends, just because his weapon wasn't on safe. The second mishap was a vehicle accident in which their ammunition truck burned down, with most of their ammo inside. Thankfully, no one was hurt but they now had very little ammo for their upcoming operations in Rawah. For an Iraqi force that was supposed to be trained better than the regular Iraqi Army, they weren't looking too good.

The next day's mission should be exciting. We now had two Cavalry Troops, one 3-21 Infantry Company and another from 1-5 Infantry, as well as the Iraqi forces. The entire Task Force would surge in the city starting at 4 a.m., searching the entire city. We'd also got approval for any troops who were in contact to fire the Multiple Launch Rocket System artillery, which was the largest artillery rocket in the entire theater, with twice the kill radius of 120mm mortars and much more accuracy. I hoped they would capture more terrorists.

I worked in a tent and right across from me was an agent from some government agency who spoke English and Arabic. He listened to phone calls all day through headphones on a computer, noting any key words in conversations from locals. It was cool seeing all the agencies and units at work in Rawah. I was thankful I had come down there, and it seemed almost no one from our Squadron was at FOB Summerall anymore. Rich Durmsy was there too, and he, Major Diny, SSG Johnson and even the boss and I worked on redeployment. It was great to see LTC Mavis concerned about it, and exciting to plan.

July 28, 2005

The operation began with no huge caches found, but there were also no major incidents, or any casualties. We detained some individuals for having a phone set to detonate bombs, and others for having anti-coalition force material or propaganda. The few caches found were in empty buildings. It was about 127 degrees the day before and down to 119 this day. Just going to the bathroom was a huge chore, and the giant trench dug for waste was only twenty meters from where I worked in the plans tent. Since Greg had left to close some accounts, I enjoyed his cot that night.

I heard from an intelligence guy that the IRA (Irish Republican Army) laid down their weapons in response to the second terrorist attacks last week in London, as well as the terrorist attacks at resorts and markets in Egypt. I was still amazed no one was killed in the second London attacks. God works miracles constantly. It was tragic that 59 were killed in Egypt with over 116 wounded. I would've thought this giant magnet we'd created in Iraq for terrorists to come fight Americans would minimize terrorism elsewhere in the world, but it goes to show how big this world war on terror really was.

July 29, 2005

An operation this afternoon resulted in the capture of a couple enemy. The 2-101st Aviation Air Weapons Team observed a vehicle turning and fleeing from US forces on the ground. C Troop chased the car down, detaining the individual and vehicle, finding multiple weapons, grenades, ammunition, body armor, Iraqi uniforms, a couple computer thumb drives and a cell phone with three battery chargers. We'd analyze those digital devices quickly to reveal phone numbers, names and other information that should prove useful. The Iraqi Intervention Forces managed to occupy the Rawah town water station. They'd stay until the next elections in December, which should curb much of the violence in the town, just like when we set up combat outposts (COPs) in Tal Afar with Iraqi forces.

July 30, 2005

God's Spirit helped me to have a great attitude despite the place I was in. I felt blessed to be in that hot and nasty 'moon dusty' environment, especially since we had so many blessings people in former centuries didn't. I was still trying to verify if the Romans came here during their reign on much of the world. I was sure the Greeks came this far east, or even farther, but it was difficult to verify. It motivated me to think that warriors (soldiers) fought on these grounds wearing leather and bronze or iron armor, carrying heavy shields, spears and swords. They had no cold water, no air conditioning and meals were certainly primitive, as were the unsanitary living conditions. I doubted most of them even had tents to sleep in, so they probably slept on bedrolls on the ground at night and moved and fought during the daytime. It helped me to focus on what I was doing out there, and be thankful for the life and century God had placed me in. Little today regarding combat operations was worth mentioning.

July 31, 2005

The media came to visit and LT Elmer Takash flew in. We promoted him to Captain. It was good to see him. After his promotion at the brief, I went to Chaplain Wells' tent for chapel services at 8 p.m. There were seven others there, and he'd had about fourteen at his 10 a.m. service. We sang, then talked about the rich man following Jesus in Luke 18. Afterwards, SPC Roberts Jr. came in and talked to Ed and me about miracles from the Lord. His most recent miracle was in the chow hall last December 21st in Mosul. He described the fireball in front of him, and how he stared in shock as nothing touched him from the explosion. He had been a premature baby at two pounds, one ounce, and wasn't expected to live. God must have had good plans for him in this life. After he left, I gave Ed my testimony. He enjoyed hearing how I went through several religions in my teenage years, thinking I knew best back then.

A suspicious Serka employee was found on top of one of our radar devices on FOB Marez and an Indian cook working for Kellogg, Brown and Root was found with a digital thumb drive with pictures of the FOB, to include the ammo area, the airfield on Diamondback, convoys and other military facilities and activities. You never knew whom you could trust in that place. I hoped we continued to screen people for this type of stuff and could get rid of all the moles and leaks on our bases.

12

August

August 1, 2005

In the morning, engineers completed the Intelligence "fusion cell" building, so the plans shop and Intelligence personnel left the work tent and moved into it. The engineers did a great job. It had at least three air conditioners built into the wall, several 220v power outlets and doors and stairs leading into it. There was plenty of operating room in there for planning and meetings. Now that they were gone from our tent, we had admin, logistics and Civil Affairs personnel working there. It was a bit dusty, but I wasn't not complaining because we had one Environmental Control Unit – a military version of an air conditioner. We sealed up one end of the tent to keep the cool air in and the dust out, and we spread out our tables, so I now had a workstation for my personal computer. The climate was much more relaxed and it was an enjoyable day.

The night was less enjoyable. Our enemies must have finished planning and gone into ambush and attack mode. The enemy could really get a lot done behind our backs. Iraqi Intervention Forces discovered a big weapons cache with multiple explosives and bomb-making materials (including five gallons of acid), some rockets, lots of ammunition and several weapons. Praise God Iraqi forces found all of this, but you would think after two full days of searching the city with all our forces surging in Rawah we would've found these days ago. The enemy either had stealthy methods of transporting these weapons and munitions, or they had always had great hiding places. B Company of 3-21 Infantry also found two completely assembled car bombs in Rawah. Bomb disposal folks destroyed the two, and thirty minutes later a third car bomb hit B Company, wounding three soldiers. None of the soldiers had to be evacuated because the wounds were minor, and I was again thankful for that.

Before all this, LTC Mavis decided to drive to Al Qaim on the Syrian border with a few Strykers since things were too slow in Rawah. On their way back, a suicide car bomb hit them, wounding five US soldiers. CPT Harrelson (a.k.a. 'Huggiebear') was the worst of the wounded, with damage to his face and a broken arm. The other four suffered some burns and concussions, and I believed one of them, along with Eric Harrelson, would most likely not return to duty anytime soon. We'd see them again when we arrived back in the States in just a couple months. The soldiers were taken to the Combat Support Hospital (CSH) in Balad, and the damaged Stryker still wasn't back to Rawah yet for repairs.

The worst news was a six-man team of Marine Corps snipers southeast of Rawah along Lake Buhayrat Al Qadisiyah were compromised. They were in a hide position in a building. They were shot and their bodies were found in the building. A lance corporal was missing, and the other five were killed. I couldn't fathom how an entire Marine sniper squad could be killed like that, with the amount of training and firepower they had. Locals reported terrorists carrying the wounded missing soldier into a white taxi with yellow markings. Soldiers and marines were setting up checkpoints all over the area to search for him. Now I understood why CPT Jacobsen was always so paranoid about protecting our snipers when they went out on a 'hide.'

August 2, 2005

Fortunately, the last of the snipers was found, but sadly, he died of his wounds before he was found.

August 4, 2005

A busy day, tactically. The enemy tried to shoot at the Rawah Bridge Checkpoint, and B Troop also found a weapons cache consisting of about 200 inert 60mm mortar training rounds. I learned sad news about C Company 1-24 Infantry which had a casualty from a sniper round – PFC Thompson died of wounds this afternoon – our first death in the Brigade in nine weeks. It was always sad when someone died, but especially when we were getting so close to redeployment. 1-14 Cavalry (our sister Squadron) lost a soldier two days before they redeployed, which must have been extremely hard (he was on his very last mission). My prayers were for us making it these last nine weeks until we were in Kuwait and heading home to Fort Lewis with no more deaths. It was a big prayer, but God works miracles every day.

August 5, 2005

What a beautiful day! We had a 'rock drill' rehearsal at FOB Marez for Brigade, so MAJ Diny, Rich, Scott Vingen and I flew from Rawah to Mosul. However, our Blackhawk helicopter flight was not direct. We went southeast, crossing the giant lake in the center of the country of Iraq just north of the Euphrates River. It amazed me how beautiful the water was. The lake was so huge that when we got to the middle of it, you could see no land at all from the aircraft, which was great because it made me feel like we were flying over the ocean. The waves were so peaceful and it looked like a great place to go swimming. Strangely, there were no boats on the lake at all. Most of us wondered why, and just guessed that perhaps the lake was too salty for much fishing, so it wasn't used very much. It was really baffling though because I would love that lake if I had to live in that part of the country.

When we got to the other side of the lake, I noticed two small boats, a couple houses just off the shore, and a small town of probably less than one hundred people just a mile away. Shortly after flying over the lake, I noticed the increase in the density of palm trees on the ground. I realized we were not going to Mosul, and soon we were over entire forests of palm trees. Before I knew it, a giant city was underneath us, and I thought it might be Baghdad. As we flew further into the city, I checked out the vast expanse of all the houses, buildings and a few mini-skyscrapers, and realized it had to be Baghdad, which we confirmed upon landing. We dropped some passengers off, and picked some up, and then took off heading north. It was a great treat to see Baghdad, since I'd never seen it before and it is the capital of Iraq. I couldn't help but keep thinking an RPG or rocket would be shot at us every minute as we flew over the city, but it just turned me to pray more and trust God.

SFC Grimm picked us up when we arrived at Mosul Airfield and told us about mortar fire on Diamondback and that they just received ten to twenty rounds of incoming enemy mortar fire on Marez. In the evening we contacted the TOC by phone out to Rawah and discovered a suicide car bomb had hit 3rd Platoon, 73rd Engineers. The Stryker was damaged, but absolutely no casualties...a huge blessing. It was especially great everyone was okay because they also received RPG and rifle fire during the explosion, so it seemed the enemy tried to mount a coordinated attack, but by the grace of God failed miserably. Praise God!

After riding around with Major Diny, Rich, Scott and SFC Grimm, they dropped me off at the Marez chapel, where I talked with Chaplain Gazaway. I discovered he felt the same way I did regarding biblical conditional security versus eternal security. I talked to SGT Kevin George and SPC Guzeman (aka 'Goose') and another SGT George and we "got our praise on." It was an awesome time, and we developed notes to the lyrics of some songs I had written. I sang them with SGT George, while 'Goose' played the keyboard and came up with the chords. The other SGT George played drums, and it was great to hear my songs sung and played like that. We first worked on the song I wrote at Airborne School in 1999 called "Everlasting," to which I already had a tune, but they added a great deal of good stuff to the beat. We then worked on "My Refuge, My Fortress, My God (Psalm 91)" which was my newest song, which has more of a gospel beat to it. After a few hours of praise and fellowship, I took a shower (my first real one without bottled water in 10 days). I got to call my parents. Sleeping without having dust all over everything was a bonus too.

August 6, 2005

The rehearsal went well in the afternoon, after we briefed COL Brown in the morning. Once on the Diamondback airstrip, we waited as helicopters came, and we loaded everything. The birds took off, and halfway (or more) to Rawah, a giant sandstorm rolled in. The pilots tried going south and then tried flying low, then high at a thousand feet or more, but nothing was working. I remembered praying that God would just clear our path and guide our path, and He sure did – right back to Mosul! Praise the Lord! It looked like I'd have to "suffer" through one more day of air conditioning, showers, real bathrooms and a great chow hall. SFC Grimm just happened to be there at the airfield waiting for others, but he ended up picking us up instead. After putting my things down in my room, I went straight to the chapel, and SGT George and more of the gang were singing and praising. I joined in, and during a quick break I said to SGT George, "You must have prayed again, didn't you?" "Of course," he answered, and I shared with him and the other brothers what had happened. I felt like God blessed me with another night there to praise and worship Him, so that was exactly how I spent the evening. How awesome!

August 7, 2005

I managed to make it to the morning and evening worship services! It was great and we had a wonderful time praising the Lord. There were still no flights to Rawah, and I was thankful.

August 8, 2005

There was talk of a ground convoy if we didn't get a helicopter ride soon. I found it ironic there were no sandstorms for the ten days I was in Rawah, and then when I came back to Marez a sandstorm lasting several days stopped me from returning!

August 9, 2005

I finally reached Rawah and didn't mind. I thanked the Lord that we had a safe helicopter ride, since I heard some choppers had been shot at lately. It was good to rejoin the unit, even if I'd miss the praise team the next couple weeks. It seemed like home for some reason. Maybe that was just the Army life…wherever you went seemed like home after a couple days.

August 12, 2005

It was slow the last few days. Tactically, we had another suicide car bomb hit B Company of 3-21 Infantry in Rawah and several men were evacuated. Thankfully, all would be okay, but the Stryker wasn't. I started a book on the differences between biblical Christianity and all other religions, sects and cults in the world. After discussing it with some who noticed it on my desk, I presented a challenge to Rich Durmsy and Major Marz (42nd Infantry Division Liasison). When the three of us worked out together, I challenged them to stop cussing for twenty-four hours, to see if they could do it. Since I didn't cuss, they challenged me to eat no sweets or candy for twenty-four hours (I normally eat them all day). For each cussword spoken, or each sweet or candy I'd eaten, there was a penalty of ten pushups.

August 13, 2005

Rich and Major Marz both did sixty and ten pushups respectively and we unloaded the entire mail shipping container. The manual labor was a welcome change. We had some cool God and Scripture-focused conversations in the tent 'office.' It started when LT DeFabbs shared his earlier conversation with his fellow logisticians and I shared some related scriptures. He got excited and before I knew it, Major Marz joined our discussion about Scripture. He said he wasn't just about working out the body, but also the mind and the spirit. I laughed, and he mentioned Psalm 91. I thought it was funny since I had just memorized Psalm 91 over the last couple weeks. He wanted me to recite it so I did, and then we moved on to the other part of the discussion.

Mike DeFabbs said he felt like a 'half-baked' Christian, and I asked him if that meant he was 'lukewarm.' He said, "Yeah, that's what I feel like." I asked him, "Did you know Jesus talked about lukewarm

Christians?" "No, did He?" "Yeah," I said, "I'll show you what He said." He became excited and I had to show him the verses in Revelation on the internet since I didn't have my Bible with me. I showed him about Jesus saying, "Because you are neither hot nor cold, I am about to spit you out of my mouth." The funniest part was when Rich read the commentary below the verse in which the writer mentioned a statistic of 80% of Americans claiming to be Christians, followed up with a "Need I say more?" He immediately felt the author was judging and claiming to be a true Christian and that 80% of Americans were possibly lukewarm. I defended the page since he seemed to be reading in between the lines, and he got angry until I told him he was putting words into the author's mouth. We just laughed about it in the end, but it was nice to be talking about Scripture.

August 14, 2005

Greg left for Al Asad with a few other staff members for a meeting, and the LTC Mavis and team went to the Syrian border north of Al Qaim, so it was relatively quiet. I attended chapel and brought Major Marz with me. After the service, we talked for a while, and then ate lunch in the chaplains' tent. Chris Mayr, Ed Wells, Major Marz and I spoke of the war, reminisced about home, etc. That night at the Field Feeding Tent we were having steaks for the first time. Instead of calling it chow though, we'd all been calling it "DeFabbs's restaurant" since LT DeFabbs supervised the Field Feeding Team. The steak was great. We continued the challenge from the day before and everyone agreed that between the hours of 7 a.m. and 7 p.m. they wouldn't cuss and I wouldn't eat sweets. CPT Durmsy and MAJ Marz slipped a few times, but were getting better, and I was getting better at refraining from candy. Another day was done.

August 16, 2005

I flew from Rawah that night. The Lord blessed me with perfect weather and a nice full moon for visibility. The trip on the helicopter was a bit windy toward the end, but we made it safely to Mosul Airfield, thankfully, and I got a ride to FOB Marez from FOB Diamondback. By the time I got to bed, it was after midnight.

August 17, 2005

My first day back at Marez from Rawah and I felt so blessed. I took a shower, did a lot of coordinating, ate in the chow hall and visited with folks while practicing the violin at the chapel.

August 18, 2005

We completed our last Squadron combat operation simultaneously with the last Brigade surge in Mosul. I hadn't heard of anything bad in the last few days, so everyone should be doing okay. I worked on the billeting plan to figure out where everyone would stay in the first couple weeks of September. We basically had the rest of 2-14 Cavalry returning from Rawah, 4-14 Cavalry coming from Kuwait and a couple infantry units too. I met with Major Brennam from the Mayor Cell to discuss where we could put everyone. To discuss the plan, I linked up in the evening with CPT Jason Gentile from 3-21 Infantry. So far it sounded great to everyone, which I was grateful for since God gave me the plan. I was getting too bogged down with room assignments and prayed (which I don't often remember to do for menial work tasks). After my meeting tonight, I practiced at the chapel and taught a civilian named Danny how to play the violin. He was a fast learner and caught on quickly. After about forty-five minutes, I dropped him off at his sleeping pad and headed off to shower and bed.

August 19, 2005

It seemed like something was going on everywhere on this full-moon Friday. Enemies fired mortars at COP Rawah and fired two rockets at Iraqi forces in the water treatment facility in the city of Rawah. Fortunately, no one was injured. In Mosul a 1st Platoon A Company, 1-24 Infantry soldier was shot in the back of the neck by a sniper but was in stable condition at the hospital. Around noon the 1-24 Infantry TAC (Tactical Command Post with a few headquarters Strykers including LTC Krella's) chased a vehicle at high speeds (with Apache helicopters following from the air). The vehicle's two occupants then fled on foot. The Battalion TAC pursued dismounted, and a firefight took place. One enemy was wounded, and one US soldier was wounded, with gunshot wounds to both legs and his right bicep. Both went to the hospital.

Not knowing their names, I first thought it was LTC Krella, but I told myself just because the TAC was hit didn't mean that it was Lieutenant Colonel K. I then had this feeling it really was him this time, and as I left the office, I prayed for him and for whoever was injured in First Platoon.

There was no dining in the chow hall allowed. We had to get trays to go and eat elsewhere due to an alleged imminent threat of attack while the base tightened security. In the afternoon in Rawah, our Brigade's Anti-Tank Company lost a Stryker to two artillery rounds made into one roadside bomb. It had hull and multiple wheel damage, but incredibly no casualties, even though the hull was breached. "God is good, all the time." C Troop in Rawah detained vehicle occupants who tried to flee a checkpoint, finding explosive detonators and other bomb materials. In Mosul 2nd Platoon of A Troop hit a roadside bomb with two wounded who were able to return to duty.

Our 'Praise Team' had 8 p.m. practice at the Brigade Support Battalion chapel for Sunday's service. A big event was planned because it was going to be at the Morale Welfare and Recreation Center and people from all over the FOB were coming, as every chapel and chaplain from the Brigade would be participating. It should be a great event, but security would be tight since terrorists on the FOB were bound to take advantage. After practice, SGT George mentioned that LTC Krella was shot that day, and they would have a new commander just to finish out the deployment. I was stunned. Sergeant George was the medic who worked on him and carried him on the stretcher. He said as they stepped off the Stryker, LTC K pushed out ahead and was shot from behind. One round hit his legs and the other hit his bicep as he fell to the ground and rolled, returning fire. The team loaded him onto the stretcher and carried him into the Stryker, as he mentioned his leg was not to be moved while SGT George worked on him. SGT George said the wounded enemy was the one who shot the colonel.

He wasn't certain but heard that CSM Prosser turned to shoot the enemy whose weapon jammed and prepared to fire. CSM Prosser threw his weapon down after it jammed too (or ran out of ammo) and then charged the terrorist, tackling him and beating the tar out of him (the terrorist was a repeat offender and had already been at Abu Gharib once). SGT George wasn't sure if all of that was true but said CSM Prosser's uniform was covered with LTC Krella's blood, the terrorists' blood and the terrorists' pee. This was apparently not the first time LTC K was injured. SGT George mentioned the time back in November when his thumb caught a ricochet which I remembered hearing about, but when I asked LTC K back then, he just made a joke about it. There was a second time when shrapnel or something grazed his shoulder, but SGT George wasn't certain. LTC Krella would get the Battalion back in a few months after his fractured femur healed, but he wouldn't see any more action with them in Iraq. I thanked God he was okay. It could have been a lot worse, especially so close to the femoral artery. Praise God!

August 20, 2005

This was such an awesome day. I got a lot of work done but also had time to praise God and fellowship with other believers. At 3 p.m. we held our rehearsal for the 'praise team' music ministry in the morale tent. We set up on the stage and each of us took our positions as we rehearsed together. I ended up getting my own microphone for the violin which everyone was excited to hear (although I'd not practiced as much as others). In the evening after chow and more work I met with SGT George at the Marez Chapel and we went through the songs one by one to make sure I had the right key and notes for each.

Next, we started talking about salvation and walking in Christ versus backsliding. We openly discussed our common viewpoints about blaspheming the Holy Spirit and losing salvation, which led to further discussions and wonderful testimonies about trials we'd been through. I showed him one of the books I was reading entitled *The Believers Conditional Security* by Daniel Corner, which he seemed highly interested in (all 801 pages of it). We prayed before he left and thanked God for our wonderful fellowship and for the service the next day.

August 21, 2005

It was an amazing night! The day flew by as I tracked shipping container information, and by the evening the choir and team lifted up our praise to the Lord at the 8 p.m. service. The songs were great and after SFC Hicklin gave a testimony we played more and then Chaplain Welon preached about Paul and Jesus and their examples for our lives. It was truly a celebration. Colonel Brown was there as well, and he talked briefly in the beginning. During the last song everyone stood and shouted and praised God and I wanted to throw down my violin and jump up in the air and shout but kept playing. I forgot I was in Iraq and just focused on singing and playing praises to God. Afterwards, Chaplain Welon said there had beenover 300 people at the service. Hopefully, several came to know Jesus that night and many others deepened there relationships with him.

August 24, 2005

Not much transpired the last three days, or even this day, other than a funny email exchange. LT DeFabbs decided to write to me in a goofy "olde English" manner as follows:

"*Enlightened and regal Captain of Armored Knights of the realm of Duke Mavis, Knowest thou quantities thereof? The Mortar rounds, that is. Oh, or also thine tents. Most respectfully in full anticipation of an adaquate response to satisfy any inquiry from the Duke, Leftenant DeFabbs.*"

I couldn't help but crack up laughing. Here is a snippet of my reply:

"Leftenant DeFabbs...Thine mortar rounds shall dain the numeral of Two hundred and one hot smote rounds of 120mm, and twenty sheckles of granduer illumination of thine same tube size...Forthwith, a quantity of tents I shant give, haven'tst the knowledge of them. Alas, I jest...haha...betwixt yesterday and yon morrow; thou shouldst receiveth twenty of four tents, with a poole of thirty of six to arrive on Septembre twentieth and eighth, togethereth with thine ammo. Fare thee well, brave leftenant, soon thou shalt be knighted a first leftenant under yon Duke of Mavis, who wilt surely be pleased with thee.

Captain of Armored Knights,
Enlightened and Regal
Duke Mavis Realm."

August 28, 2005

I heard an explosion around 1 a.m., and learned it was incoming, but fortunately no one was injured. Five mortar rounds landed at FOB Blickenstaff too, but no Iraqi Commandos were injured. There was another impact of rounds on FOB Diamondback, but again no casualties. At chapel we prayed for the families of those killed in action because sadly, SGT Morton's ("Rat's") wife was having such a hard time with her husband's death in May that she killed herself. That was so horrible. I couldn't imagine how hard it was for families, but I did know how much it hurt to lose a brother-in-arms. I prayed God would give them strength and comfort in Him to make it through the rest of their lives.

13

September

September 2, 2005

It had been quiet in our sector, although I heard that back in the US New Orleans was suffering from Hurricane Katrina and so many were still dying there in our own country. I prayed the National Guard could do something about the starvation and death there. The videos of it looked just like things in Iraq sometimes.

September 4, 2005

We had an awesome sermon at 10 a.m. by the 130th Engineers Chaplain Assistant SPC Tyler Egli who preached on worrying. He did a great job, had a funny story and included scriptures from Matthew 6:25-34. It helped me focus on alleviating my worry and trusting God with each task or mission-related event in my day. I was concerned about two work related things: getting ammunition to Rawah and conducting a 15-6 investigation for a missing M14 rifle from C Troop (missing paperwork really). After coordinating for the loading of all the mortar rounds into the shipping container scheduled to leave for Rawah the next morning with the 172nd Stryker Brigade units, I returned to the office. At chow I had a wonderful conversation with Chief Oakley and his counterpart from the 172nd. We mostly talked about church, scripture, devotions and the amazing miracles since we'd been in Iraq.

He shared that he had been hit in the left side of his head with a ball bearing in the chow hall on December 21st of the last year. He said his entire left side, especially his ear, was numb, and he couldn't hear very well, so he thought he'd lost his ear. He said he crawled for the door and remembered seeing Colonel Brown standing over him, asking him if he could walk. He described the doctors' fear of him having a hemorrhage in his head and being flown to different places, even to Balad, but he was spared. The ball bearing eventually came out of his head, but he expressed just how much God had blessed him. If it had been an inch to the right, entering the back of his head, he could have been killed. I shared with him the similar miracle of my shrapnel the first time I was wounded; how God had me in just the right spot so the steel and mortar stopped at my chinbone and didn't hit my throat or anywhere more dangerous.

September 5-6, 2005

Both days were filled with good manual labor. We organized the logistical support team yard to create an area where the troops could put extra supplies, then had a nice wood and cardboard bonfire. B Troop arrived from Rawah, as did Chaplain Ed Wells, so we were now roommates. Chaplain Gazaway from the 113th Engineers led a Bible study on sin that night and I sure learned a lot. It was an awesome time.

September 11, 2004

I was supposed to fly to Kuwait the day before, but due to Hurricane Katrina, there was a huge shortage of flights since the 256th Brigade Combat Team now had priority for redeployment from the war theater to tend to their families in Louisiana. I didn't mind waiting for that cause and I enjoyed the praise and worship of the last chapel service I would in Iraq. I played the violin for the morning service when Chaplain James Gazaway preached, but for the evening service I just sang. My favorite was "Down, Down, Down," written by Sergeant Kevin George. My flight was scheduled for around 4 a.m. the next day. I was finally leaving Iraq.

September 12, 2005

I took my (hopefully) last C130 ride for a couple years. A crewmember said they had loading difficulties in Balad when they were shot at while taking off, so the plane was late. We had a short and questionable takeoff at 5 p.m. because there was a broken Cessnaon on the runway that we didn't want to clip during liftoff – not comforting. As usual, it felt like we were going to crash once we got into the air because the pilot practically did barrel rolls as we elevated out of Mosul to avoid any possible surface-to-air missiles. We turned left and right, and it felt like the plane was heading back to the ground a couple times, but we finally elevated to the cruising altitude.

Landing in Kuwait was smooth and when I got off the plane, I realized I was no longer in enemy mortar range, so the worst was over. I had to stay hydrated and avoid any hazardous situations around the vehicles and I should be home free.

September 13, 2005

I was extremely busy from 6 a.m. to 8 p.m. We got the final group of Strykers on the heavy flatbeds from Iraq in the morning, prepared them for shipping and then fueled and staged to drive to Kuwaiti Naval Base. Once there, they began washing them at the wash racks. After a couple days all our Strykers will be clean and moved to the sterile yard at the port ahead of schedule. I briefed drivers and vehicle commanders of the 7 p.m. convoy and put shipping labels on all vehicles. I had a great conversation afterwards with LT Snyder from Blackjack. He was new to the Squadron and the Army, so we spoke about the Army, career options and eventually turned to Christianity and our service to the Lord.

September 14 –24th, 2005

The past ten days were slow, but we made progress, nonetheless. As if the tragedy of Hurricane Katrina wasn't enough for the people of New Orleans, I saw on the news at the chow hall that Hurricane Rita was now in the Gulf of Mexico and was recorded as the third largest hurricane in history with 185 mile an hour winds; that was unbelievable. President Bush had declared a state of emergency along the gulf coast as people evacuated. Between the Tsunami in Indonesia and these two hurricanes, it seemed as though the year was the worst year of water in human history since the great flood. I had a flight scheduled for the twenty-fifth, but it had been bumped to the twenty-eighth. No matter how many delays, when I finally made it back to Becky and Katelyn, I'd be happy.

14

Epilogue

I arrived home safely in October, and from my second Iraq deployment (Operation Iraqi Freedom 09-11) from August 2009 until July of 2010, during which I commanded the Headquarters Company of 4th Brigade, 1st Infantry Division, and then Bravo Troop, 1st Squadron, 4th Cavalry Regiment. I thank God and Jesus for their love, the life and opportunities I've had, and my amazing wife Rebecca and our five daughters: Katelyn, Ashley, Alyssa, Hannah, and Rachel.

15

Author's Biography

LTC Matt Sacra is currently retiring from a 20-year active-duty career. In addition to the 25th Infantry and 1st Infantry Divisions, he also served at the Joint Readiness Training Center, the 11th Armored Cavalry Regiment at the National Training Center, the 1st Security Force Assistance Brigade, and the Maneuver Center of Excellence.

He was blessed to teach at the Army Logistics University and the United States Military Academy at West Point. Since his first deployment, Matt not only has taught leadership, culture, decision making, and tactics, but also history, strategy, policy, and innovation, incorporating his deployment experiences.

He also continues to pursue and teach Judeo-Christian history, scripture, and theology to those he serves in the Church, including his wife Rebecca and their five daughters.

"You who live in the shelter of the Most High, who abide in the shadow of the Almighty, will say to the LORD, "My refuge and my fortress; my God, in whom I trust." For He will deliver you from the snare of the fowler, and from the deadly pestilence; He will cover you with His pinions, and under His wings you will find refuge; His faithfulness is a shield and buckler. You will not fear the terror of the night, or the arrow that flies by day, or the deadly pestilence that stalks in darkness, or the destruction that wastes at noonday. A thousand may fall at your side, ten thousand at your right hand, but it will not come near you. You will only look with your eyes and see the punishment of the wicked. Because you have made the Lord your refuge, the Most High your dwelling place, no evil shall befall you, no scourge come near your tent. For He will command His angels concerning you, to guard you in all your ways. On their hands they will bear you up, so that you will not dash your foot against a stone. You will tread on the lion and the adder, the young lion and the serpent you will trample under foot. Those who love me, I will deliver; I will protect those who know my name. When they call to me, I will answer them; I will be with them in trouble, I will rescue them and honor them. With long life I will satisfy them, and show them my salvation."

PSALM 91 (NRSV)

Acronyms and Terms

1-24 IN (First Battalion, 24th Infantry Regiment pronounced "One-Two-Four" or "Deuce Four")
1SG (First Sergeant, top NCO of company)
ACR (Armored Cavalry Regiment)
COL (Colonel)
COP (Combat Outpost)
Counter-Manpad (a patrol designed to counter terrorists attempting to shoot down a plane)
CPT (Captain)
CSH (Combat Support Hospital – pronounced "cash")
CSM (Command Sergeant Major, top NCO of battalion, or written as "battalion SGM")
DFAC (Dining Facility)
FBCB2 (Digital display and radio link with Force Battlefield Command Brigade and Below)
FOB (Forward Operating Base)
Humvee (High Mobility Multi-Wheeled Vehicle - "Humvee")
ING, ICDC, IA (Iraqi National Guard, Iraqi Coalition Defense Corps, Iraqi Army)
Jundee = Arabic for "soldier"
LT (Lieutenant – either "first" or "second" lieutenant)
LTC (Lieutenant Colonel)
MAJ (Major)
Mayor Cell (the establishment, building, and group, that manage facilities and everyday functions on the FOB, such as laundry, traffic, building ownership, maintenance, etc.)
MGS (Mobile Gun System – usually referring to my platoon of anti-tank Strykers)
M240 (Machine Gun that fires 7.62 mm rounds)
Mortars ("Mortar Section")
PFC (Private First Class)
PKC (Russian-made Machine Gun)
PL (Platoon Leader)
PVT (Private)
RPG (Rocket Propelled Grenades)
S4/S-4 (Logistical Officer/workstation or staff office)
SFC (Sergeant First Class)
SGT (Sergeant)
SGM (Sergeant Major; Highest ranking NCO

SPC (Specialist)
SSG (Staff Sergeant)
TOC (Tactical Operations Center - where the Battalion command and control operates)
TOW (Tube-launched Optically tracked Wire-guided missile)
"whaz" (Russian version of a Jeep)
XO (Executive Officer)

Reference Map

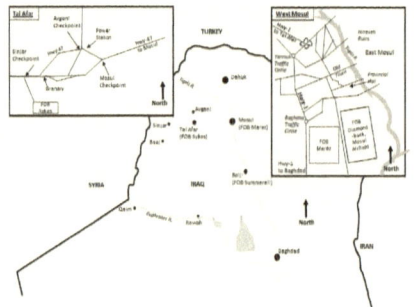

Reference Map (not to scale – designed by Matt Sacra)

www.ingramcontent.com/pod-product-compliance
Lightning Source LLC
Chambersburg PA
CBHW030900080526
44589CB00010B/84